Children's Illustrated Dictionary

John McIlwain

DORLING KINDERSLEY

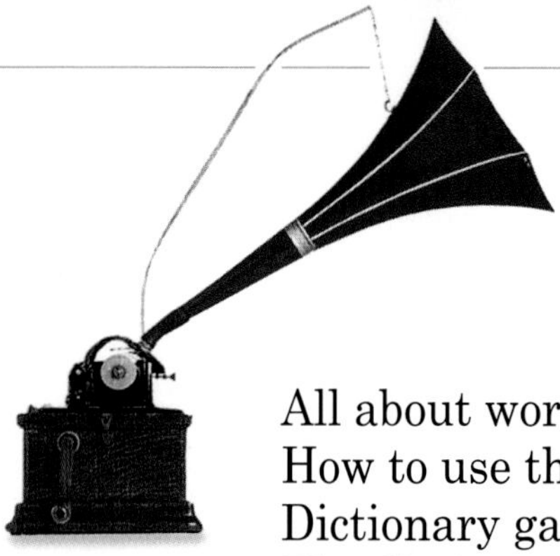

Contents

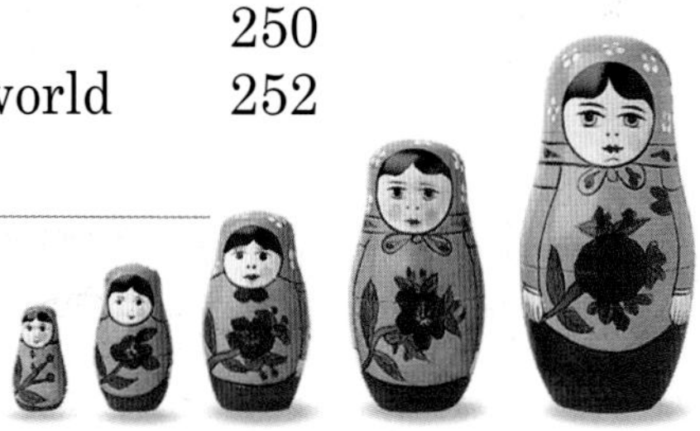

LONDON, NEW YORK, MELBOURNE, MUNICH, AND DELHI

Senior Editors Nicola Tuxworth, Susan Peach
Senior Art Editor Rowena Alsey
Project Editor Lee Simmons
Art Editor Marcus James
Editor Claire Watts
Designers Cheryl Telfer, Diane Clouting

Managing Editor Jane Yorke
Managing Art Editor Chris Scollen
Production Jayne Wood

Photography by Andy Crawford, Steve Gorton, Susanna Price, and Tim Ridley

Illustrated by Grahame Corbett, Peter Dennis, Bill Le Fever, Nicholas Hewetson, Louis Mackay, Roger Stewart, and Jolyon Webb
Language Consultants The Centre for Literacy in Primary Education, London, England
Pronunciation Consultant Sheila Dignen

2009 Edition:
Project Editor Niki Foreman
Senior Art Editor Sheila Collins
Managing Editor Linda Esposito
Managing Art Editor Diane Thistlethwaite
Publishing Manager Andrew Macintyre
Category Publisher Laura Buller
Production Editors Maria Elia, Vivianne Ridgeway
Jacket Editor Mariza O'Keeffe
Jacket Designer Akiko Kato
Geography Consultant Simon Mumford
US Editor Margaret Parrish

DK India
Head of Publishing Aparna Sharma
Design Manager Arunesh Talapatra
Editorial Manager Glenda Fernandes
Assistant Editor Samira Sood
Designers Malavika Talukder, Govind Mittal
DTP Coordinator Sunil Sharma
DTP Designers Dheeraj Arora, Preetam Singh

First published in the United States in 1994
This revised edition published in 2009 by
DK Publishing
375 Hudson Street, New York, New York 10014

10 11 12 13 10 9 8 7 6 5 4 3 2
CD207—05/09

A catalog record for this book is available from the Library of Congress.
ISBN 978-0-7566-5196-1

Color reproduction by Colourscan, Singapore
Printed and bound by Toppan Printing Co. Ltd., China

Introduction

The Dorling Kindersley Children's Illustrated Dictionary is specifically aimed at children of seven years and up, an age when children are becoming increasingly independent readers and writers and when a dictionary can be a valuable companion.

In addition, this book will help children develop their awareness of words and the relationships between them. An introductory section explains the concept of parts of speech, such as nouns and verbs, that are also listed under each entry in the dictionary. The final section looks at word beginnings and endings, spelling patterns, and common abbreviations.

Words and pictures

Unlike many other dictionaries, *The Children's Illustrated Dictionary* is not just about words—it also contains pictures. Children today are used to information being presented in a visual form through television, movies, and computers, and are skilled readers of images. As a result, they require books to be increasingly visually sophisticated.

The colorful photographs and illustrations in this dictionary are fresh, exciting, and highly relevant to children's interests and concerns. These images will help to draw young readers into the book; they also work with the text to give clear and concise definitions.

Vital skills for readers and writers

Using a dictionary can teach children many useful skills. One of the most important is the ability to locate information that is organized in alphabetical order. Once acquired, this skill will enable them to use many other reference books, from telephone directories to encyclopedias, that are organized along the same principle. The clear design and layout of this dictionary make it easy for children to learn how to look things up.

The Children's Illustrated Dictionary can also help to widen vocabulary and improve spelling. Young readers and writers can find out for themselves what an unfamiliar word means or check any spellings about which they are unsure.

A dictionary with a difference

A unique feature of this dictionary is the 26 full-page entries, where words and pictures are grouped by theme.

Browsing through these word collections, on subjects as diverse as costumes and time, children will enjoy recognizing known words and concepts and discovering new vocabulary and information. These pages offer many opportunities for discussion and provide the basis for further exploration of a wide range of topics and themes.

A lasting work of reference

The Children's Illustrated Dictionary combines a core of common vocabulary with words that have a high interest level for children of this age group. It provides them with both a rich source of information about the world and an important resource for developing their reading and writing skills.

All about words

In every sentence that we speak or write, there are several types of word. They are called "parts of speech." Each of them has its own name and its own job to do in the sentence. In this dictionary, each word entry has its part of speech printed below it in *italic* type. The parts of speech that are labeled in the dictionary (verbs, adverbs, adjectives, interjections, prepositions, and nouns) are explained on these two pages.

*She **runs** to school every morning.*

Verbs

Verbs are sometimes called "action words" because they are words that describe what a person or a thing is doing. **Sit**, **think**, **sleep**, **sing**, and **climb** are all verbs. A sentence must contain a verb to make sense. There are a few special kinds of verb, such as "being" and "helping" verbs, that do slightly different jobs in a sentence.

*The dog often **lies** on the floor.*

*They **were** both very angry.*

Being verbs

Being words, such as **am**, **is**, **are**, **was**, and **were**, all come from the verb **to be**. They link someone or something with the words that describe them.

Helping verbs

Verbs such as **have**, **be**, **will**, **must**, **may**, and **do**, are sometimes used with other verbs in a sentence. They show how possible or necessary it is that an action takes place. Helping verbs can also be used to show a verb's tense.

*It **may rain** tomorrow.*

***I do like** sandwiches!*

Verb tenses

The form of a verb shows whether the action it describes takes place in the present, the past, or the future. This is called the verb's tense. When a verb, such as **hang**, appears in this dictionary, the entry looks like this:

hang
hangs hanging hung
verb

The second line of the entry shows how the verb is written in three different tenses—the present, the continuous present, and the past tense. These tenses are used like this:

Present tense:
*She **hangs** up her T-shirt.*

Continuous present tense:
*She **is hanging** up her T-shirt.*

Past tense:
*She **hung** up her T-shirt.*

Adverbs

An adverb is a word that gives more information about a verb, an adjective, or another adverb. Adverbs can tell us how, when, where, how often, or how much. **Slowly**, **yesterday**, **upward**, and **very** are all adverbs. Many adverbs end with the letters "ly."

*These newspapers are all published **daily**.*

*They played **happily** with the balloon.*

Nouns

A noun is a word that names a thing, a person, or a place. **Cat**, **teacher**, **spoon**, and **city** are all nouns. Nouns do not have to be things that you can see—words like **truth** and **geography** are also nouns.

*They often went to the **café** for a **snack**.*

*The **present** came in a round **box** tied with **ribbon**.*

Adjectives

An adjective is a word that is used to describe a noun. **Fat**, **yellow**, **sticky**, **dark**, and **hairy** are all adjectives.

*The car was **big**, **red**, and **shiny**.*

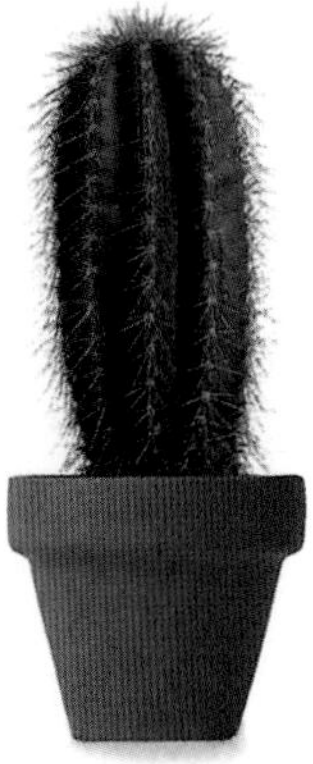

*A **tall**, **green**, **prickly** cactus.*

Comparatives and superlatives

If you want to compare a person or thing with another, you often use an adjective in the comparative or superlative form. **Taller**, **easier**, **better**, and **quicker** are comparatives. **Tallest**, **easiest**, **best**, and **quickest** are superlatives. Comparatives either end with the letters "-er," or include the word "more." Superlatives either end with the letters "-est" or include the word "most."

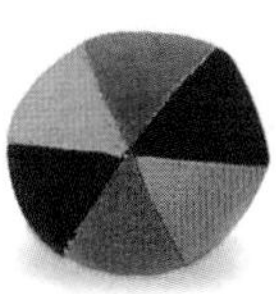

Adjective:
*This ball is **big**.*

Comparative:
*This ball is **bigger**.*

Superlative:
*This ball is the **biggest**.*

Interjections

Interjections are words such as **hello** and **good-bye** that can be used on their own, without being part of a full sentence. Exclamations, such as **Oh**! and **Ouch**!, are also interjections.

Conjunctions

Conjunctions are words such as **and**, **but**, and **of**, that are used to join parts of sentences together.

Prepositions

Prepositions, such as **in**, **with**, **behind**, and **on**, show how one person or thing relates to another.

*She held the ball **above** her head.*

How to use this dictionary

Read the information on these two pages to find out how to get the most from your dictionary. Most pages in the book look like the double page from the letter **R** section shown below. There are also 26 full-page entries in the dictionary that provide a whole page of pictures and vocabulary on a theme. The page shown here is about cars.

What's on a page

Guide word

Use the guide word at the top of the page to help you find the page a word is on. The left-hand guide word, **rabbi**, tells you that this is the first word on the page.

Headword

This is the word you are looking up. The headword is printed in heavy, black letters at the start of the entry. The definition underneath explains what the headword means.

Guide word

The right-hand guide word, **rate**, tells you that this is the last word on this page.

New letter section

Each new letter section starts with a big letter, like this **R**.

Alphabet

Use the alphabet running down the side of the page to help you find your place in the dictionary. The highlighted letter tells you that you are in the **R** section.

rabbi

A B C D E F G H I J K L M N O P Q R S T U V W X Y Z

Rr

rabbi
rabbis *noun*
a teacher of the Jewish religion and law.
■ say **rab**-eye

rabbit
rabbits *noun*
a small mammal with long front teeth that lives underground in burrows. Rabbits are normally active in the evening or at night. They eat grass, roots, and leaves.

race
races *noun*
1 a competition of speed.
*A swimming **race**.*
race *verb*
2 a group of people who share the same ancestors and may share some physical characteristics.
racial *adjective*

racket
rackets *noun*
1 a bat with strings used for playing sports such as tennis and badminton (see **sport** on page 197).
*badminton **racket***
2 a loud, annoying noise.
*He was making a **racket** with his drums.*

radar
noun
a device that tells you the position and speed of ships, cars, and aircraft by sending out radio waves.
*An airport **radar** screen.*
■ say **ray**-dar

radiator
radiators *noun*
1 a thin, metal tank with hot water flowing through it that heats a room.
2 a metal tank that allows air to cool the hot water in the engine of a vehicle.
■ say **ray**-dee-ay-tor

radio
radios *noun*
a device that sends or receives electrical signals and changes them into sound.

radioactivity
noun
the energy released by the center of atoms breaking up in some substances. High amounts of radioactivity can be harmful to living things.
*They tested for **radioactivity** outside the nuclear power plant.*
■ say ray-dee-oh-ak-**tiv**-i-tee
radioactive *adjective*

radius
radii or radiuses *noun*
a straight line drawn from the center of a circle to its outer edge.
radius

raft
rafts *noun*
1 a floating platform made of logs that have been tied tightly together.
2 a hollow mat made of rubber or plastic and filled with air that can be used as a boat.
*life **raft***

rag
rags *noun*
a small, torn piece of cloth.

rage
rages *noun*
anger or uncontrolled temper.
*In her **rage**, she slammed the door shut.*

raid
raids *noun*
a sudden surprise attack by a group of people.
*The police made a **raid** on the house, arresting two women.*
raid *verb*

rail
rails *noun*
1 a long bar for holding on to, or for hanging clothes on.
*Use the **rail** to help you climb the stairs.*
2 a long line of metal track that trains run along.
3 the railroad.
*We traveled by **rail** around Europe.*

162

railroad
railroads *noun*
1 a network of tracks that trains run on.
2 a transportation system that uses rail tracks, together with trains, stations, and land.

rain
rains *noun*
water that falls from the clouds in drops.
rain *verb*
rainy *adjective*

rainbow
rainbows *noun*
an arch of colors that appears in the sky when the sun shines while it's raining.

raindrop
raindrops *noun*
a single drop of rain.

rainfall
noun
the amount of rain that falls over a particular area.
*The chart shows the annual **rainfall** in South America.*

rain forest
rain forests *noun*
a dense, hot, wet jungle that grows in tropical areas.

rake
rakes raking raked *verb*
to gather up leaves into a pile or to smooth over soil.
rake

rally
rallies *noun*
1 a large, public meeting held to discuss something that is important or worrying to people.
*The party held a political **rally** in the park.*
2 a long-distance car race that tests drivers' skills.

ram
rams *noun*
1 a male sheep.

ran
*from the verb **to run***
1 *Last week, he **ran** a 400-meter race.*
2 *She **ran** a bookstore.*

ranch
ranches *noun*
a huge farm where cattle or other animals are reared.

rang
*from the verb **to ring***
*He **rang** the doorbell.*

ranger
rangers *noun*
a person who looks after a forest or a wildlife park.
■ say **rain**-jer

rascal
rascals *noun*
a mischievous person.

rash
rashes *noun*
a patch of red, itchy spots on your skin.

raspberry
raspberries *noun*
a juicy, red fruit that grows on a bush with thorns.
■ say **raz**-bair-ee

rat
rats *noun*
a common rodent that looks like a large mouse. Some kinds of rat eat plants, while others eat small animals. They can gnaw through stone, wood, and even metal with their strong front teeth.

rate
rates *noun*
1 a speed.

rate

a b c d e f g h i j k l m n o p q r s t

Pictures

The photos and illustrations show you exactly what things look like and help to define the headwords.

car

car
cars *noun*
a vehicle with wheels that is moved by an engine and used to carry people from place to place.

a b c d e f g h i j k l m n o p q r s t u v w x y z

39

Word box

Families of linked words are enclosed in a box. All the words in this box start with the same word, **rain**.

Full-page entries

All the pictures and labels on a full-page entry are linked to the main headword. This page shows different car types, with their various parts labeled.

Alphabetical order

The headwords in this dictionary are listed in alphabetical order—the same order as the letters of the alphabet. Words that begin with **A** are grouped at the start of the dictionary, followed by **B** words, and so on up to **Z**. Where several words start with the same letter, the second letters of the words are used to decide which comes first. So **cat** comes before **cot**, because **A** comes before **O** in the alphabet. If words start with the same two letters, then the third letter decides the order. So **radius** comes before **raft**, because **D** comes before **F**.

How the entries work

Headword
The headword is printed at the start of the entry. This shows you how to spell the word.

Plural
This tells you how to write a noun when there is more than one of the thing it is referring to. Here, **rams** is the plural of the headword **ram**.

Definition
This part of the entry explains what the headword means. If a word has more than one meaning, the first meaning given is normally the one that is most common. Other meanings are listed below.

ram
rams *noun*
1 a male sheep.

2 a device for pushing against something with force.

They used the log as a ***ram*** *to break down the door.*
ram *verb*

Part of speech
This shows whether the word is a noun, verb, adjective, interjection, adverb, or preposition. Find out more about parts of speech on pages 4–5.

Tenses of verbs
These three forms of the verb **share** show how it is written in the present, continuous present, and past tenses. These tenses are explained on page 4.

share
shares sharing shared
verb
1 to have or use together.
2 to divide something into parts to give to others.

They ***shared*** *the melon.*

Sample sentence
The sentence that follows the definition gives you an example of how the headword is used. In the sample sentence the headword is always written in heavy, black type like this: ***shared***.

Comparisons
The two forms of an adjective that are shown here are called the comparative and superlative. They are explained on page 5. **Rarer** means "more rare" and **rarest** means "the most rare."

rare
adjective
unusual or not common.

A ***rare*** *blue morpho butterfly.*
■ comparisons **rarer rarest**
■ opposite **common**

Opposite
This tells you the word that is the opposite of the headword. For example, **common** is the opposite of the headword **rare**.

Pronunciation guide
This guide helps you to pronounce difficult words. It respells the word so that you can sound out the letters. Part of the guide is in heavy, black type. This shows you which part of the word to stress, or say more loudly.

radioactivity
noun
the energy released by the center of atoms breaking up in some substances. High amounts of radioactivity can be harmful to living things.

They tested for ***radioactivity*** *outside the nuclear power plant.*
■ say **ray**-dee-oh-**ak**-tiv-i-tee
radioactive *adjective*

Related words
Other words that are related to the headword are listed here. This related word, **radioactive**, is the adjective that comes from the headword **radioactivity**.

Dictionary games

See if you can solve these word puzzles, using your dictionary to help you. The games will help you learn how to use the dictionary quickly and easily. You can play all of the games on your own, but you can also play with a friend. Try giving a point for each correct answer and then see which of you gets the highest score. The answers to all the puzzles are somewhere in this dictionary. Have fun!

Alphabetical birds

How quickly can you arrange these 12 bird names in alphabetical order? You could use the alphabet at the side of the page to help you sort them out. For more help, turn to page 6, where alphabetical order is explained in detail.

pelican

parrot

flamingo

peacock

stork

eagle

owl

ostrich

duck

budgerigar

crane

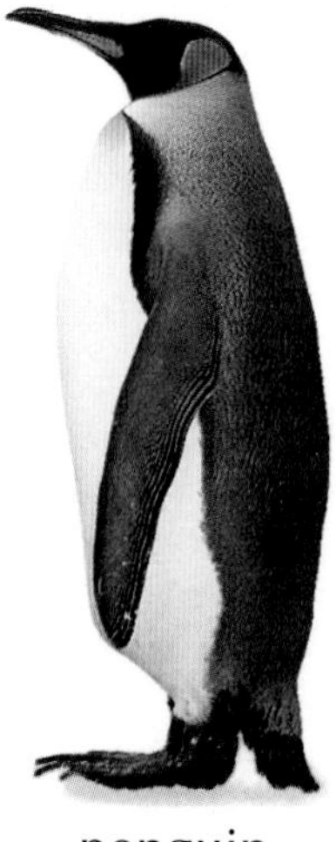
penguin

True or false?

Here are some word definitions for you to read. Can you tell which are true and which are false? Remember to check every part of the definition before you decide whether it is true. You can find out whether you were right by looking up the words in the dictionary.

An **elephant** is a huge mammal that lives in Europe and North America.

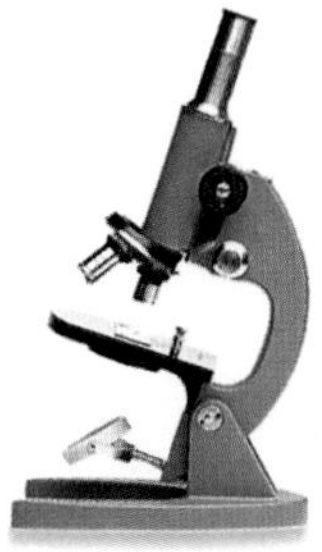

A **microscope** is an instrument that magnifies very tiny things so that they can be seen in detail.

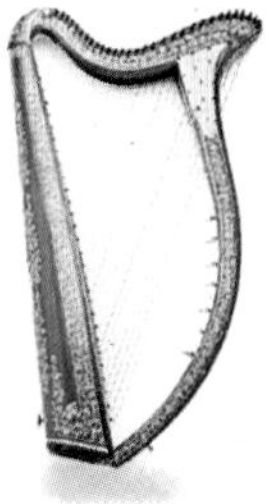

A **harp** is a musical instrument that you hit with sticks or your hands to make a noise.

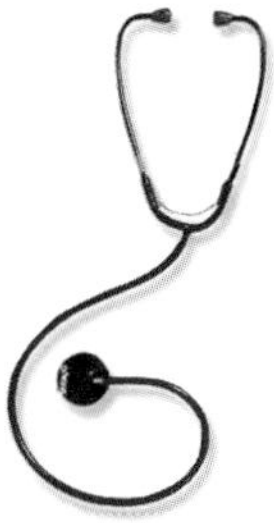

A **stethoscope** is an instrument that is used by doctors for looking in your ears.

An **iguana** is a large lizard found mainly in Central and South America.

A **mosaic** is a picture or pattern made of small squares of colored stone.

A **plumber** is a person who repairs the glass in broken windows.

An **amphibian** is an animal that can live in water and on land.

Sound-alikes

Below are some pairs of pictures. The two words that go with each pair sound the same but are spelled differently. Can you figure out what they are? The first letter of each answer is shown as a clue.

Here's an example to help you:

h

hare hair

s

f

p

s

Sound-unlikes

This is the opposite of the game above. The two words that go with these pairs of pictures are spelled the same, but sound different. Can you figure out what the words are? The first letter of each answer is given as a clue.

b

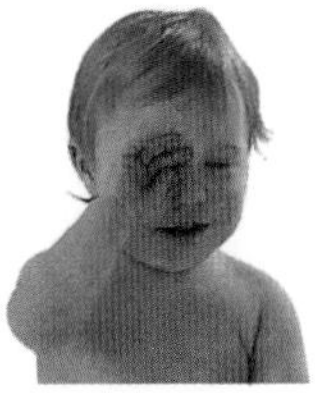

t

w

Odd word out

If you look carefully at these pictures of animals and objects, you will see that in each group there is an "odd word out." Which is it and why? If you get stuck, the special full-page entries in the dictionary will help you.

angelfish

gray whale

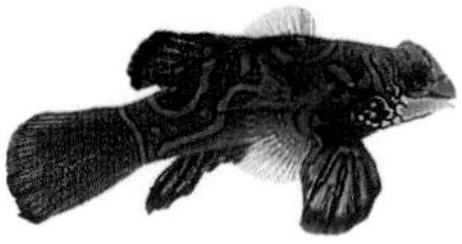
mandarin fish

great white shark

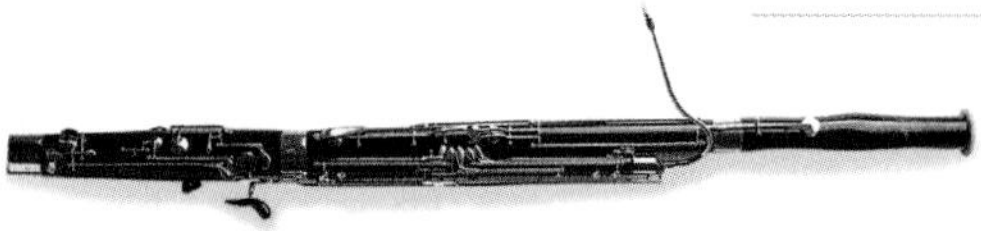
bassoon

fiddle

balalaika

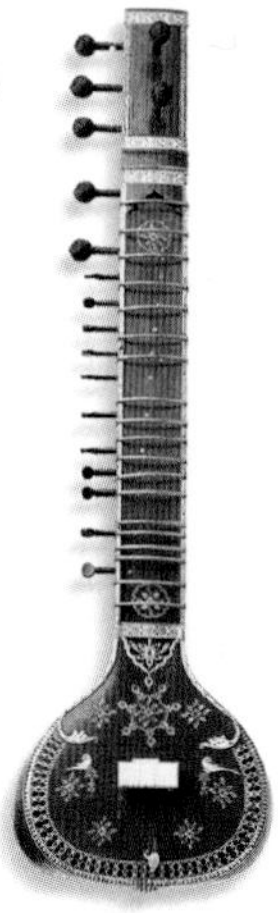
sitar

Triceratops

Stegosaurus

Tyrannosaurus rex

crested water dragon

Action words

The people in these pictures are all doing something. The words in the list are all "action words," or verbs. Can you match the right verb to each of the pictures? There are more verbs than pictures, so choose carefully. Check your answers by looking up the words in the dictionary.

juggle
kneel
climb
throw
hit
crouch
bend
stretch
drum
explore

Word detective

Be a detective and follow the clues to answer these questions. The answers are all in the dictionary.

- Which mammal gnaws down trees to build dams in rivers?
Look for a word beginning with b.

- What are emeralds, sapphires, and rubies?
Look for a page of sparkly things.

- Which word connects an egg, a nut, and a crab?
Look on page 183.

- What is the opposite of few?
Check on page 125.

- What is the name of a planet and also the name of the silver-colored metal used in thermometers?
Look for a word beginning with m on page 229.

- Which animal has withers, hocks, and a forelock?
Look for a page of large, plant-eating mammals.

- Where would you find a sprit, a main sheet, and a daggerboard?
Look for a page of vessels that travel on water.

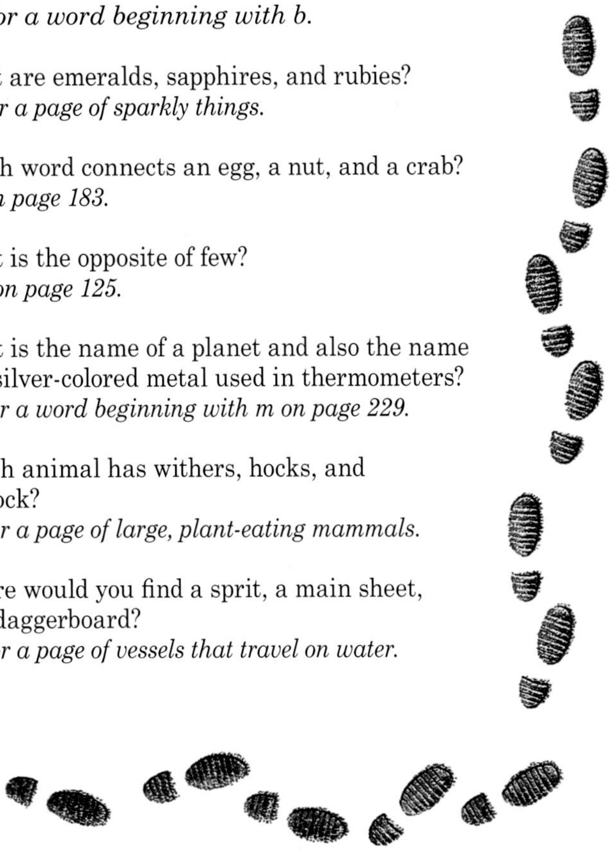

Guess the word

Some words have more than one meaning. Each of these groups of pictures illustrates three different meanings of the same word. Can you figure out what it is? Check in the dictionary to see if you are right.

Here's an example to help you:

A drink of **punch...**	*...throwing a* **punch...**	*...and a hole* **punch.**

Rhyming words

This is a game where you have to spot the "odd word out." The words that go with each of these groups of pictures all rhyme except one. Which one is it?

The first letter of each word is there to give you a clue. Remember that there can be lots of different ways of spelling the same sound.

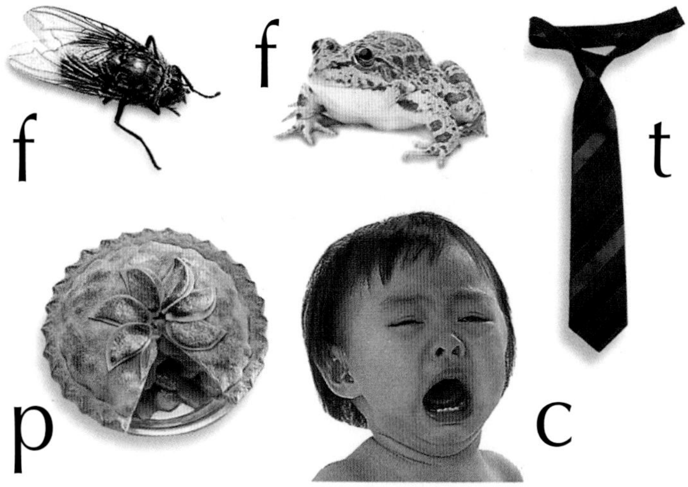

A B C D E F G H I J K L M N O P Q R S T U V W X Y Z

A a

abacus
abacuses *noun*
a frame with sliding beads, used for counting.

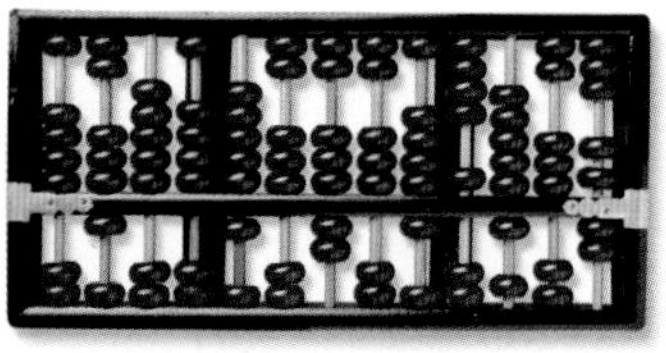

abbreviation
abbreviations *noun*
a short way of writing a word or a group of words.
*"Ave." is an **abbreviation** of "avenue."*
■ say a-bree-vee-**ay**-shun

abdomen
abdomens *noun*
the part of an animal's or a person's body that contains the intestines and stomach (see **insect** on page 108 and **sea life** on page 178).
■ say **ab**-do-men

ability
abilities *noun*
a talent for doing something.

*He had the **ability** to play many instruments at once.*

about
preposition
1 on the subject of.
*We talked **about** the play.*
2 on the point of doing something.
***About** to leave.*

about
adverb
more or less.
*There were **about** 300 people at the circus.*

above
preposition
over, or higher than something.

***Above** her head.*
■ opposite **below**

abroad
adverb
in or to another country.
*She went **abroad** for her vacation.*

absent
adjective
not there, or away.
*He was **absent** from school because he had a cold.*
■ opposite **present**

absorb
absorbs absorbing absorbed *verb*
to soak up.

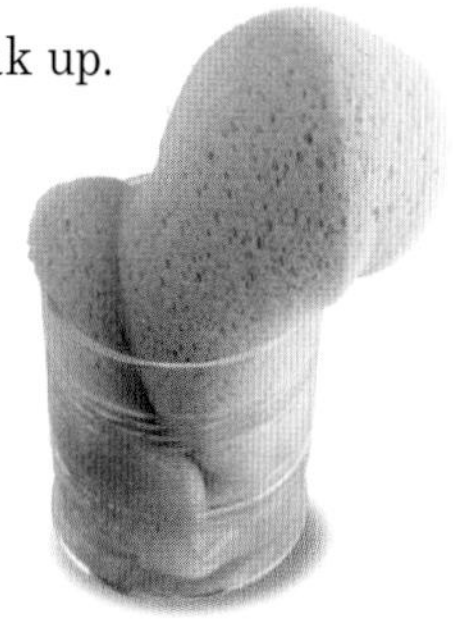

*A sponge **absorbs** liquid.*
absorbent *adjective*

absurd
adjective
silly or ridiculous.

*She looked **absurd** leaving for school in her pajamas.*

accent
accents *noun*
1 the way people say words.
*She had a foreign **accent**.*
2 a mark on a letter showing you how to pronounce it.
***"Café"** is pronounced "kafay."*

accept
accepts accepting accepted *verb*
to take something that is offered to you.

accident
accidents *noun*
something that goes wrong by chance.

*He spilled the juice, but it was an **accident**.*

accordion
accordions *noun*
a musical instrument that you squeeze to make a sound.

accurate
adjective
exactly right.
*A stop watch gives **accurate** time.*
■ say **ak**-yur-rut

accuse
accuses accusing accused *verb*
to say someone has done something wrong.
*She **accused** him of lying.*
■ say a-**kyooz**

ace
aces *noun*
a playing card that has one main symbol in the center.

ache
aches aching ached *verb*
to feel a steady pain.

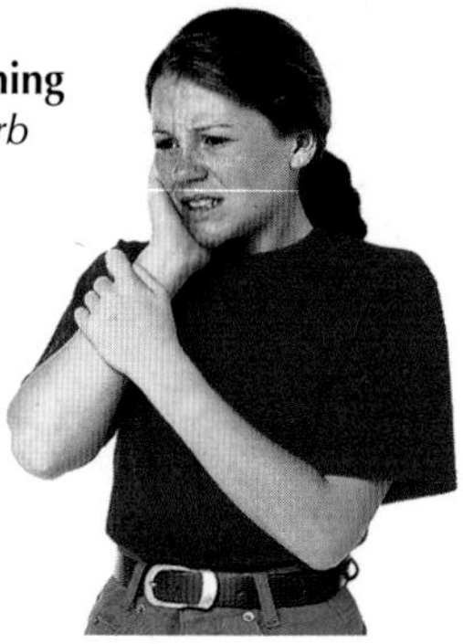

*Her tooth **ached**.*
■ rhymes with **cake**

acid
acids *noun*
a sharp-tasting, sour liquid.
*Some **acids** can burn you.*

acorn
acorns *noun*
the seed of an oak tree.

acrobat
acrobats *noun*
a person who performs gymnastics on a stage or in a circus.

across
preposition
from one side to the other.

***Across** the bridge.*

act
acts acting acted *verb*
1 to behave in a certain way.
*He was **acting** very strangely.*
2 to take part in a play, a film, or a television program.

action
actions *noun*
anything that somebody does.
*His quick **action** put out the fire.*

activity
noun
1 energetic movement.
active *adjective*
2 something that has been planned for you to do.

adapt
adapts adapting adapted *verb*
to change something to suit a special purpose.

*This mug has been **adapted** so that a baby can drink from it.*

add
adds adding added *verb*
1 to put one thing with another.

***Add** cherries to the mixture.*
2 to find the sum of two or more numbers.

21+54=75

*Twenty-one **added** to fifty-four equals seventy-five.*
addition *noun*

addict
addicts *noun*
someone who cannot give up a habit that they have.

address
addresses *noun*
the building and area where someone lives or works.

adjective
adjectives *noun*
a word that is used to describe a noun.

adjust
adjusts adjusting adjusted *verb*
to make a small change to something.

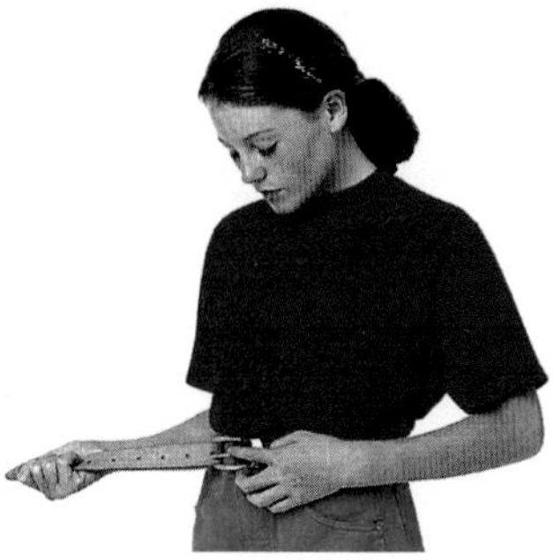

*She **adjusted** her belt.*

admire
admires admiring admired *verb*
to think that something is nice or good.

*She **admired** her new hair style.*

admit
admits admitting admitted *verb*
1 to say reluctantly that something is true.
2 to allow someone to enter.
*A ticket **admits** you to the movie theater.*

adopt
adopts adopting adopted *verb*
to take a child into your home as part of your family.

adult
adults *noun*
a grown-up person.
■ opposite **child**

advantage
advantages *noun*
something that is useful to have.
*Her long legs gave her an **advantage**.*
■ opposite **disadvantage**

adventure
adventures *noun*
something you do that is exciting and new.
*Exploring the river was a real **adventure**.*
adventurous *adjective*

adverb
adverbs *noun*
a word that describes a verb, adjective, or another adverb.
*The tortoise moved **slowly**.*

advertisement
advertisements *noun*
words or pictures that try to persuade you to buy or to do something. Advertisement can be shortened to "ad."

■ say **ad**-ver-tiz-ment

advice
noun
suggestions to help you decide what you should do.
*Follow your dentist's **advice** on brushing your teeth.*
advise *verb*

A B C D E F G H I J K L M N O P Q R S T U V W X Y Z

adviser
advisers *noun*
someone who gives advice or makes suggestions.
*He was made student **adviser**.*

aerial
adjective
in the air.
*An **aerial** photograph.*
■ say **air**-ee-al

aerobics
noun
energetic physical exercises that are done in time to music.

■ say air-**roh**-biks

aerosol
aerosols *noun*
a can that forces out liquid in a fine spray.
■ say air-**ro**-sol

affect
affects affecting affected *verb*
to make something or someone different.
*The drought badly **affected** the harvest.*

affection
noun
the feeling that you like someone very much.
affectionate *adjective*

afford
affords affording afforded *verb*
to have enough money to buy something.
*We can **afford** to go away on vacation this year.*

afraid
adjective
scared.

*He was **afraid** of mice.*

after
preposition
1 later than.

*It is **after** 8 o'clock.*
2 behind.
*He was **after** me in the line.*
3 following.
*The cat ran **after** the mouse.*

afternoon
afternoons *noun*
the period of time between noon and evening.

again
adverb
once more.
*The fans cheered when their team scored **again**.*

against
preposition
1 next to something, touching it.

***Against** the fence.*
2 opposed to, or not on the same side.
*She was **against** the decision.*

age
noun
1 how old someone or something is.

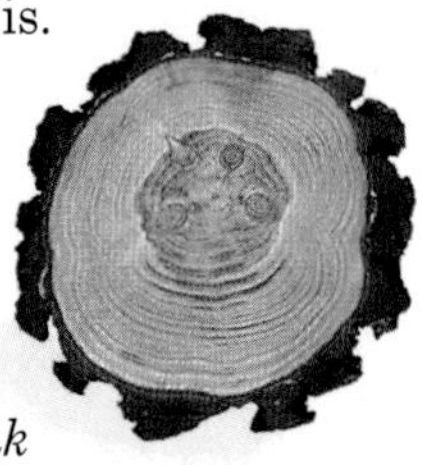

*The number of rings in a tree's trunk show its **age**.*
2 a period in history.
*The Iron **Age**.*

aggressive
adjective
ready to attack.

*Cats can be **aggressive** if they are frightened.*
aggressively *adverb*

agony
agonies *noun*
extreme pain.
*The runner was in **agony** when he broke his leg.*

agree
agrees agreeing agreed *verb*
to think the same as someone else.
■ opposite **disagree**

agriculture
noun
farming.

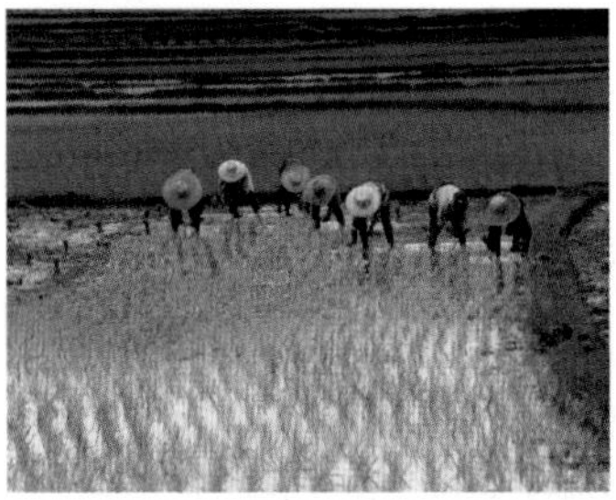

*One form of **agriculture** in Thailand is rice growing.*
agricultural *adjective*

aground
adverb
stranded on rocks or sand, or in shallow water.
*The ship ran **aground** in the storm.*

ahead
adverb
in front.

*He walked on **ahead** of the others.*

aid
noun
1 help.
*The helicopter came to the **aid** of the stranded walkers.*
2 a machine or a device that helps you do something.

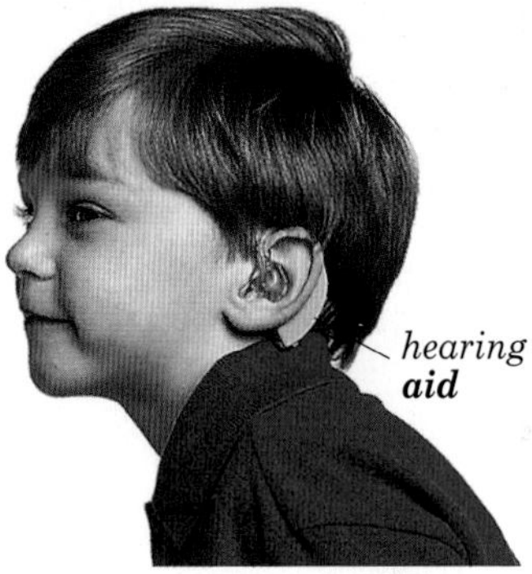

*hearing **aid***

aim
aims aiming aimed *verb*
1 to point an object at someone or something.

***Aiming** at the target.*
2 to try to do something.
*We **aim** to please.*
aim *noun*

air
noun
the mixture of gases that plants and animals breathe.
*A layer of **air** surrounds Earth.*

aircraft
noun
any vehicle that can fly.

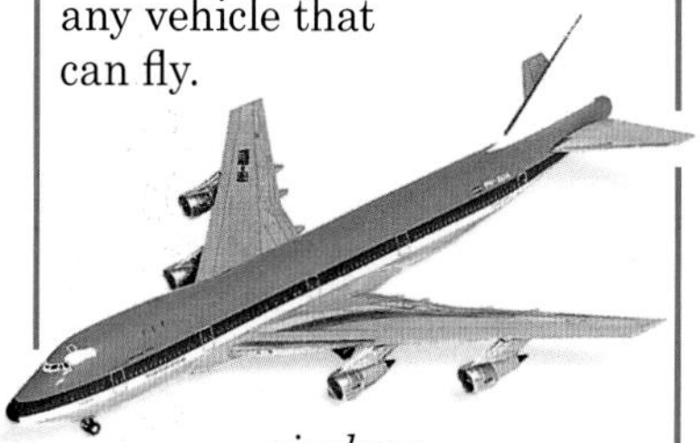

airplane

aircraft-carrier
aircraft-carriers *noun*
a ship for aircraft to take off from and land on.

airline
airlines *noun*
a company that owns and flies aircraft.

airmail
noun
mail that is carried by airplane.

airport
airports *noun*
a place where people go to travel by airplane.

ajar
adjective
slightly open.

*The door is **ajar**.*

alarm
noun
1 a loud noise that warns you of something.

*burglar **alarm***

2 a feeling of fear.

album
albums *noun*
a blank book for displaying pictures and other items.
*A photograph **album**.*

alcohol
noun
a strong drink, such as wine or beer.
■ say **al**-ka-hol

alert
adjective
watching and listening very carefully.

*The dog looked very **alert**.*

alien
aliens *noun*
something that seems strange or foreign.
■ say **ay**-lee-en
alien *adjective*

alike
adjective
very similar.

*These brothers look **alike**.*

alive
adjective
living.

*Flowers need water to stay **alive**.*
■ opposite **dead**

all
adjective
every part of, or everyone.
*He ate **all** the cake himself.*

allergy
allergies *noun*
an unpleasant reaction to something that doesn't affect most people.

*He has an **allergy** to cats.*
allergic *adjective*

alligator
alligators *noun*
a large reptile that lives in swamps and rivers. Alligators eat fish and other animals that come close to the water's edge.

allow
allows allowing allowed *verb*
to let someone do something.

*Her parents **allowed** her to stay up and watch the program.*
■ opposite **forbid**

almost
adverb
nearly.

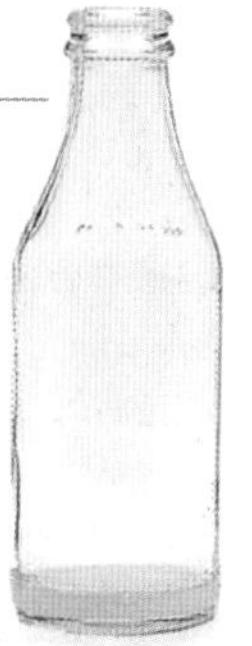

*The bottle is **almost** empty.*

alone
adjective
by yourself, without anyone else.

*He was **alone** on the island.*

along
preposition
from one end to another.
*We walked **along** the beach.*

aloud
adverb
so that it can be heard.
*He read the letter **aloud**.*

alphabet
alphabets *noun*
a series of letters or symbols, written in a particular order, that people use to write words.
alphabetical *adjective*

ABCDEFGHIJKLMNOPQRSTUVWXYZ
abcdefghijklmnopqrstuvwxyz

Roman ***alphabet***

aeiou — *letters* — bcdfghjklmnpqrstvwxyz

vowels *consonants*

Α Β Γ Δ Ε Ζ Η Θ Ι Κ Λ Μ Ν Ξ Ο Π Ρ Σ Τ Υ Φ Χ Ψ Ω
α β γ δ ε ζ η θ ι κ λ μ ν ξ ο π ρ σ τ υ φ χ ψ ω

Greek ***alphabet***

А Б В Г Д Е Ё Ж З И Й К Л М Н О П Р С Т У Ф Х Ц Ч Ш Щ Ъ Ы Ь Э Ю Я
а б в г д е ё ж з и й к л м н о п р с т у ф х ц ч ш щ ъ ы ь э ю я

Cyrillic ***alphabet***

א ב ג ד ה ו ז ח ט י כ ל מ נ ס ע פ צ ק ר ש ת

Hebrew ***alphabet***

أ ب ت ث ج ح خ د ذ ر ز س ش ص ض ط ظ ع غ ف ق ك ل م ن هـ و

Arabic ***alphabet***

ક ખ ગ ઘ ઙ ચ છ જ ઝ ઞ ટ ઠ ડ ઢ ણ ત થ દ
ધ ન પ ફ બ ભ મ ય ર લ વ શ ષ સ હ ળ ક્ષ જ્ઞ

Gujarati ***alphabet***

あいうえおかきくけこさしすせそたちつてとなにぬ
ねのはひふへほまみむめもやゆよらりるれろわをん

Japanese ***alphabet***

All of these messages say "Happy Birthday" in different alphabets.

Happy Birthday
Roman

Χρόνια πολλά
Greek

с днем рождения
Cyrillic

יום הולדת שמח
Hebrew

عيد ميلاد سعيد
Arabic

જન્મ દિન મુબારક
Gujarati

お誕生日おめでとうございます。
Japanese

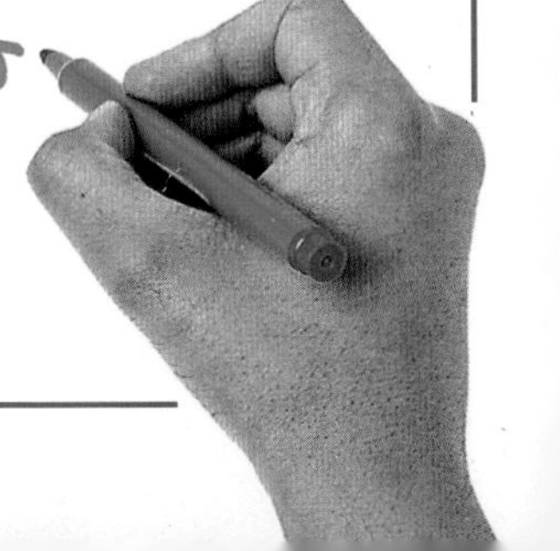

already
adverb
by this time.
*She was **already** eating breakfast when he woke up.*

also
adverb
as well.
*Sue is **also** coming with us.*

alter
alters altering altered *verb*
to change something.
*I have **altered** my story to give it a happy ending.*

altogether
adverb
including everyone or everything.

*There are eight apples **altogether**.*

aluminum
noun
a silvery-white metal that is light but strong.

***aluminum** container*

■ say al-**loo**-mi-num

always
adverb
1 very often.
*He is **always** playing loud music.*
2 forever.
*I will **always** remember our vacation.*
■ opposite **never**

amazing
adjective
very surprising or out of the ordinary.

*An **amazing** hat.*
amaze *verb*

ambition
ambitions *noun*
what you want to be or do.
*Her **ambition** is to travel to the Moon.*

ambulance
ambulances *noun*
a vehicle for taking sick or injured people to and from the hospital.

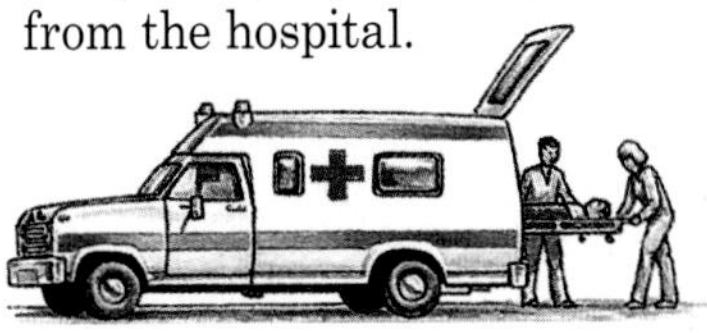

ambush
ambushes ambushing ambushed *verb*
to hide and wait for someone, then attack them by surprise when they come along.

among
preposition
in the middle of.

*There are poppies growing **among** the corn.*

amount
amounts *noun*
how much there is of something.

*Twice the **amount** of flour as brown sugar.*

amphibian
amphibians *noun*
an animal that can live in water and on land.

tree frog

■ say am-**fib**-ee-an
amphibious *adjective*

amplifier
amplifiers *noun*
a piece of equipment to make music sound louder.

amuse
amuses amusing amused *verb*
to make someone smile or laugh.
*The cartoon **amused** them.*

anagram
noun
a word or phrase made by changing the order of letters in another word or phrase.
*"Team" is an **anagram** of "meat."*

ancestor
ancestors *noun*
a relative from a previous generation.

Archaeopteryx

hoatzin

Archaeopteryx *is an **ancestor** of birds like the hoatzin.*
■ say **an**-ses-tur

anchor
anchors *noun*
a large, heavy, metal hook that digs into the seabed to stop a ship from drifting away.

■ say **ang**-ker

ancient
adjective
very old.

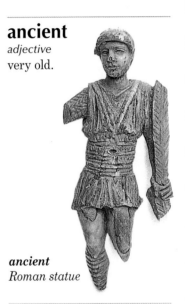

***ancient** Roman statue*

angel
angels *noun*
a messenger from a god or God.

anger
noun
a strong feeling of annoyance.
angry *adjective*

angle
angles *noun*

a corner where two lines or surfaces meet.

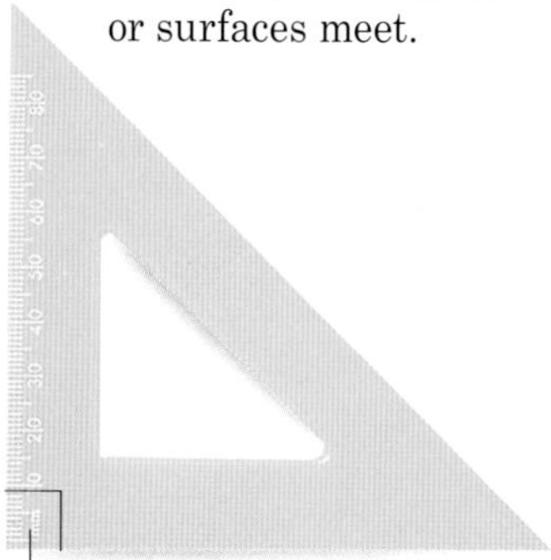

right ***angle*** *(90°)*

animal
animals *noun*

any living thing that breathes and moves around. Insects, fish, birds, mammals, and reptiles are all types of animal.

bird

fish

insect

mammal

reptile

animation
animation *noun*

still pictures, often in cartoon form, that appear to move.

ankle
ankles *noun*

the joint between your leg and your foot.

anniversary
anniversaries *noun*

a special event that is remembered every year on the same date.
Wedding ***anniversary****.*

announce
announces announcing announced *verb*

to say something for everyone to hear.
"I'm going," he ***announced****.*

annoy
annoys annoying annoyed *verb*

to make someone irritated.

The flies ***annoyed*** *her.*
annoyance *noun*

annual
adjective

happening every year.
Independence Day is an ***annual*** *holiday.*
annually *adverb*

anonymous
adjective

by an unknown author.
An ***anonymous*** *letter.*
■ say a-**non**-uh-mus

another
adjective

1 different.
Do you have ***another*** *pen? I think this one is broken.*
2 one more.
Do you want ***another*** *cookie?*

answer
answers answering answered *verb*

to reply to a question.
answer *noun*

ant
ants *noun*

an insect that lives in large, organized groups. The males and egg-laying females have wings.

wood ***ant***

antelope
antelopes *noun*

a mammal that is found on dry plains in Africa and Asia. Antelopes eat grass and other plants.

nyala

antenna
antennae or **antennas** *noun*

1 a part on certain animals' heads that is used for feeling (see **insect** on page 108).
2 a device for receiving radio and TV signals for broadcast (see **universe** on page 229).

antibiotic
antibiotics *noun*

a medicine that kills bacteria.

antiseptic
antiseptics *noun*

a substance put on cuts and grazes to prevent infection.

anxious
adjective

worried or nervous.
■ say **ank**-shus

any
adjective

some or every.
- ***Any****body can do that, it's easy!*
- *She didn't tell* ***any****one what she had seen.*
- *I'm going out, and you can't do* ***any****thing to stop me!*
- *It might be cloudy, but we could go for a picnic* ***any****way.*
- *Have you seen my pet mouse* ***any****where?*

apart
adverb

away from each other, or separate.

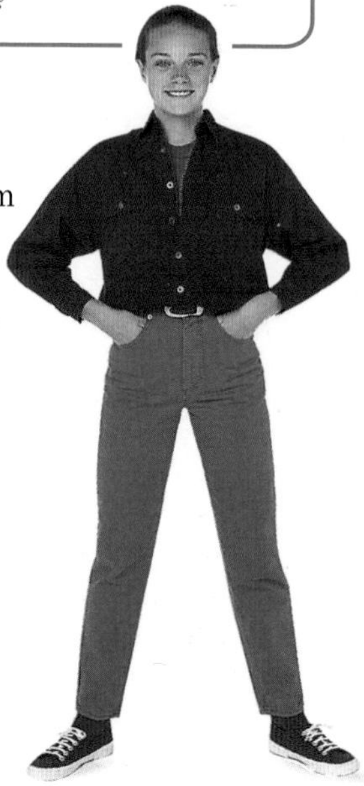

Standing with feet ***apart****.*

apartment
apartments *noun*

a home that is made up of a set of rooms inside a larger building.

ape
apes *noun*

a mammal that lives in forests in warm regions and feeds on insects and fruit. Apes have no tails and can walk on two legs.

gibbon

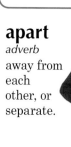

apologize
apologizes apologizing apologized *verb*

to say you are sorry.

apparatus
noun
the equipment you need for a particular task.

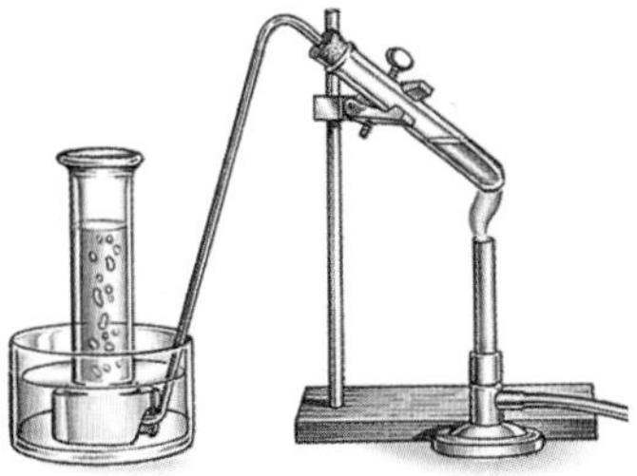

scientific ***apparatus***

appear
appears appearing appeared
verb
to come into view.
The Sun ***appeared*** *from behind the clouds.*
■ opposite **disappear**

appendix
appendices or **appendixes** *noun*
a very small part of your lower intestine.

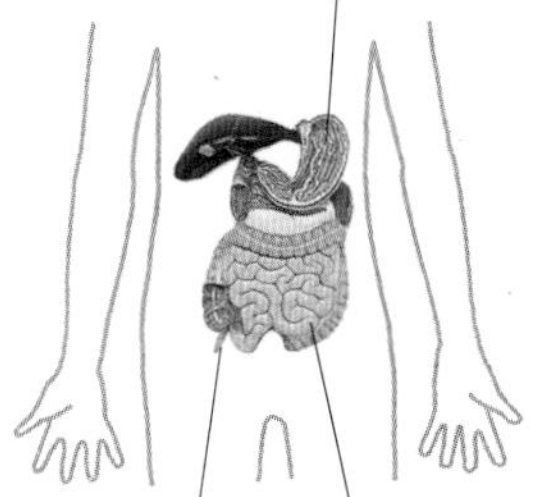

appetite
appetites *noun*
a desire for food.

He has a huge ***appetite.***

applause
noun
clapping and cheering.
The ***applause*** *rang out as the team ran onto the field.*

apple
apples *noun*
an edible fruit with a smooth skin and crisp flesh.

appointment
appointments *noun*
a meeting at a certain time.
A dental ***appointment.***

appreciate
appreciates appreciating appreciated *verb*
to be grateful for something.
She ***appreciated*** *the flowers that her daughter sent her.*
■ say a-**pree**-shee-ate

approach
approaches approaching approached *verb*
to come near to something.
The train slowed down as it ***approached*** *the station.*

approve
approves approving approved
verb
to think that something is right or good.
Does your mom ***approve*** *of your new shoes?*

approximate
adjective
almost accurate, or not exact.

The ***approximate*** *number of marbles in the jar is 50.*
approximately *adverb*

apricot
apricots *noun*
an edible fruit with soft flesh and a pit in its center.

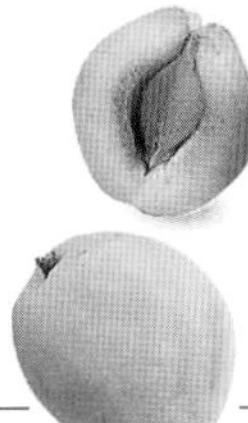

aquarium
aquariums or **aquaria** *noun*
a glass tank to keep fish and other water animals and plants in.

arch
arches *noun*
a curved part of a building or bridge.

architect
architects *noun*
a person who designs buildings.
■ say **ar**-ki-tekt

area
areas *noun*
1 a certain piece of ground or space, or part of a surface.
This is a play ***area.***
2 the amount of space something covers.
The wood covers a large ***area.***

argue
argues arguing argued *verb*
to talk angrily with someone because you disagree with them.
argument *noun*

arithmetic
noun
the adding, subtracting, multiplying, and dividing of numbers.

25+17=42
adding

36−25=11
subtracting

14x7=98
multiplying

28÷2=14
dividing

arm
arms *noun*
the part of your body between your shoulder and your hand.

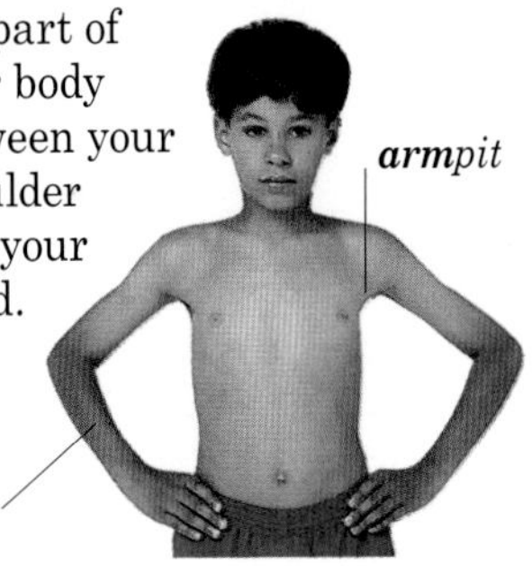

armadillo
armadillos *noun*
a nocturnal mammal that lives in North and South America and eats insects, snakes, and frogs. The armadillo's body is protected by hard, bony plates.

armchair
armchairs *noun*
a soft, padded chair with arms.

armor
noun
a suit of thick, metal plates worn long ago to protect knights in battle.

army
armies *noun*
a group of people and machines that fight on land.

around
adverb
1 nearby.
I left my bag ***around*** *here.*
2 in every direction.
For miles ***around****.*

around
preposition
1 from place to place.
We walked ***around*** *the city.*
2 on all sides.
We sat ***around*** *the table.*

arrange
arranges arranging arranged *verb*
1 to plan something.
She ***arranged*** *to meet me at 10 o'clock.*
2 to place something in a special order.

arrest
arrests arresting arrested *verb*
to catch hold of someone and officially accuse them of breaking the law.

arrive
arrives arriving arrived *verb*
to come to a place.
The plane ***arrived*** *at the airport.*
arrival *noun*

arrow
arrows *noun*
1 a pointed piece of metal that is shot from a bow.

2 a pointed shape that shows you which way to go or look.

art
noun
the creation of something, often through drawing, painting, sculpture, or design.

artery
arteries *noun*
one of the tubes that carries blood from the heart to the rest of the body.

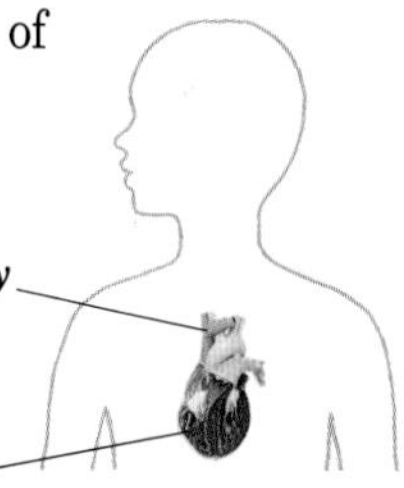

artificial
adjective
something false that is made to look like the real thing.

an ***artificial*** *flower*
■ ar-tuh-**fish**-ul

artist
artists *noun*
someone who creates pictures, sculptures, music, or other creative things.

artistic *adjective*

ash
ashes *noun*
1 the gray powder that is left behind after something has been burned.

wood ***ash***

2 a deciduous, broad-leaved tree, with spreading branches that grow in pairs.
The female ash produces winged seeds.
The wood is hard and strong.

ash *leaves*

ashamed
adjective
feeling guilty about something you have done.
She felt ***ashamed*** *about teasing her little brother.*

ask
asks asking asked *verb*
to try to find something out from someone.
Ask *your dad if you can come with us.*

asleep
adjective
resting the whole body and mind with the eyes closed.

sleep *verb*

aspirin
aspirins *noun*
a type of medicine taken as a pill, used for relieving pain and fever.

assemble
assembles assembling assembled *verb*
1 to put something together.
I ***assembled*** *a model boat.*
2 to meet together.
They ***assembled*** *in the hall.*
assembly *noun*

assist
assists assisting assisted *verb*
to help somebody.

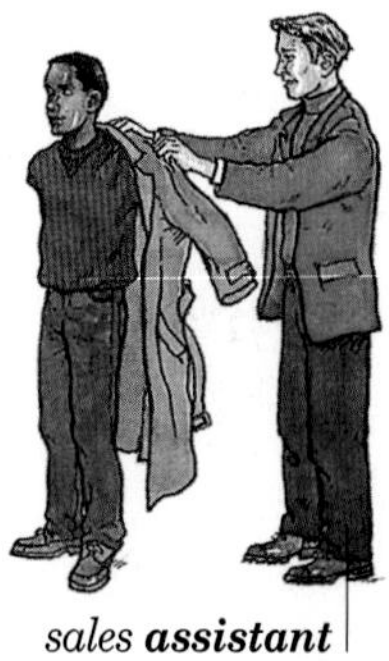

He ***assisted*** *the customer with his coat.*
assistance *noun*
sales ***assistant***

assortment
assortments *noun*
a collection of different types of the same thing.

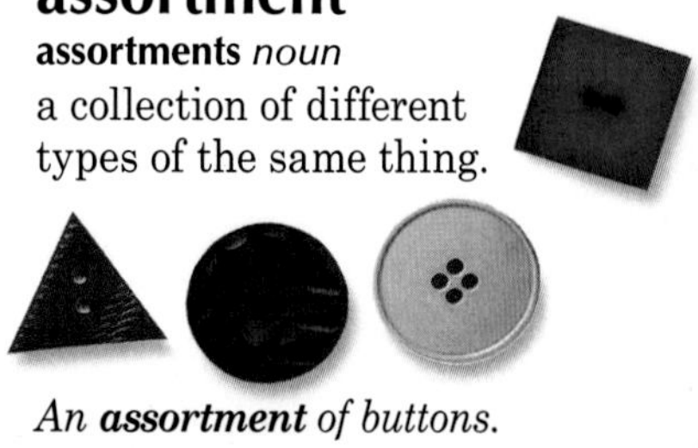

An ***assortment*** *of buttons.*

A B C D E F G H I J K L M N O P Q R S T U V W X Y Z

asthma
noun
an illness or allergy that can make breathing difficult.
■ say **az**-ma
asthmatic *adjective*

astonish
astonishes astonishing astonished *verb*
to amaze someone very much.
She ***astonished*** *the crowd by winning the race.*

astronaut
astronauts *noun*
a person who is trained to travel into space.

astronomy
noun
the scientific study of stars and planets.

ate
from the verb ***to eat***
I ***ate*** *a whole loaf of bread yesterday.*

athlete
athletes *noun*
a person who takes part in races or sports competitions.

athletics *noun*

atlas
atlases *noun*
a book of maps.

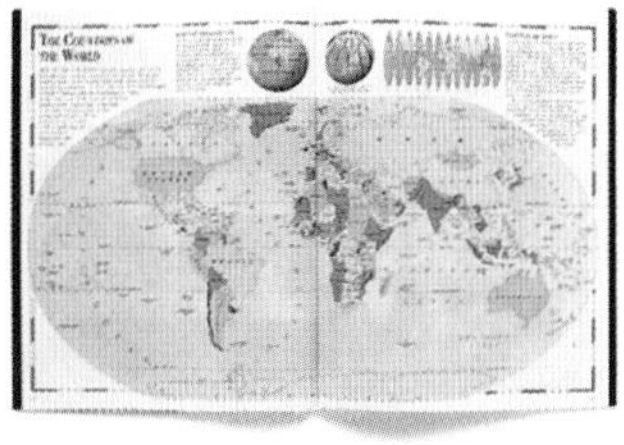

atmosphere
noun
1 the layer of air that surrounds the Earth.
2 the feeling in a room or a place.
The dark room had a gloomy ***atmosphere****.*

atom
atoms *noun*
a very tiny part of any substance.

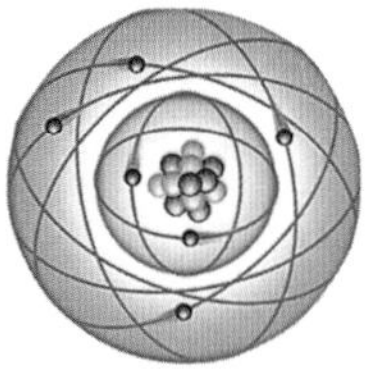

magnified ***atom***

attach
attaches attaching attached *verb*
to fasten.

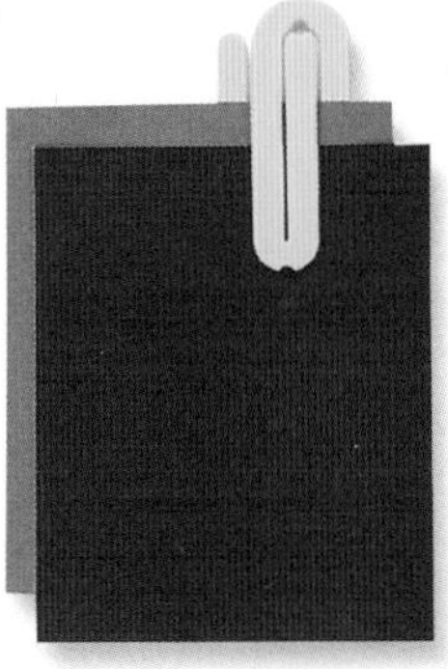

Attached *with a paper clip.*

attack
attacks attacking attacked *verb*
to try to hurt a person or an animal.
The wild dog ***attacked*** *the flock of geese.*

attempt
attempts attempting attempted *verb*
to try to do something.
They ***attempted*** *to climb the wall, but had to give up.*

attend
attends attending attended *verb*
to go to an event, or to go somewhere regularly.
I ***attended*** *school for 11 years.*

attention
noun
1 listening carefully.
Pay ***attention*** *in class!*
2 standing stiff and straight.
Stand at ***attention****.*

attic
attics *noun*
a room at the top of a house, usually in the space under the roof.

attract
attracts attracting attracted *verb*
1 to interest.
The museum ***attracts*** *many visitors.*
2 to make something come closer.

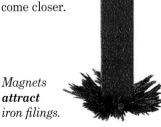

Magnets ***attract*** *iron filings.*

attractive
adjective
pleasing to the eye, mind, and senses.

audience
audiences *noun*
the people who come to watch a show or concert.

aunt
aunts *noun*
the sister of someone's parent, or their uncle's wife.

author
authors *noun*
a person who writes books, poems, or plays.

autograph
autographs *noun*
a signature, usually of a famous person.
■ say **au**-toe-graf

automatic
adjective
1 without thinking.
Blinking is ***automatic****.*
2 working by itself, without any assistance.
Automatic *doors.*

automobile
automobiles *noun*
another name for a car.

vintage ***automobile***

autumn
autumns *noun*
one of the four seasons. Autumn follows summer and comes before winter. It is the time when the leaves on some trees change color and fall to the ground.

A B C D E F G H I J K L M N O P Q R S T U V W X Y Z

avalanche
avalanches *noun*
a large amount of snow, rocks, and ice that suddenly slides down a mountain.

avenue
avenues *noun*
a type of street. It is often wide and sometimes has a line of trees down each side.

average
adjective
ordinary.
*He was of **average** height for his age.*

average
averages *noun*
1 a usual amount.
*My grades were above **average**.*
2 a number of things spread out equally.
*He eats 14 apples a week, an **average** of 2 a day.*

avocado
avocados *noun*
a green, pear-shaped tree fruit with a leathery skin and smooth, creamy flesh.

avoid
avoids avoiding avoided *verb*
to keep away from something.

*The car swerved to **avoid** the dog.*

awake
adjective
not asleep.
*I stayed **awake** all night.*

award
awards *noun*
a prize.
*A rosette is an **award**.*
award *verb*

aware
adjective
knowing something.
*He became **aware** that someone was watching him.*

away
adverb
1 not here.
*The teacher was **away** today.*
2 to another place.
*I put all my games **away**.*

awful
adjective
very bad.

awkward
adjective
1 difficult to use or inconvenient.
2 clumsy.

*A newborn foal looks **awkward** on its feet.*
awkwardly *adverb*

ax
axes *noun*
a tool that is used to chop wood.

Bb

baboon
baboons *noun*
a large monkey that is found all over Africa. Baboons live on the ground and eat plants and small animals.

baby
babies *noun*
a very young child (see **growth** on page 94).

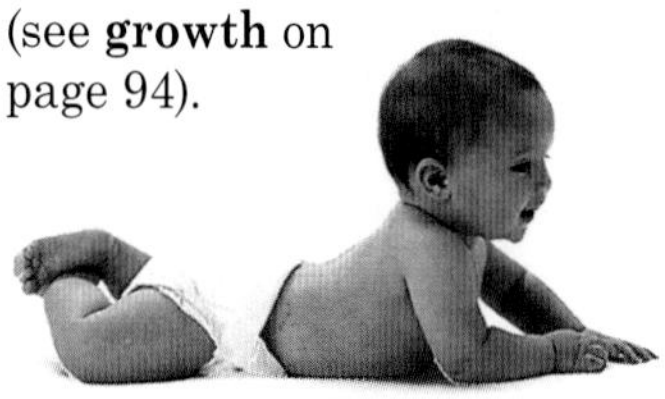

back
adverb
returning.
*I am going to the store. I'll be **back** later.*

backpack
backpacks *noun*
a large bag with shoulder straps, often worn by walkers to hold clothes and equipment.

backward
adverb
moving toward the back.
*I fell **backward** into a prickly bush.*

bacon
noun
salted meat from the back or side of a pig.

back
backs *noun*
1 the part of your body that is opposite your chest and between your neck and your bottom.

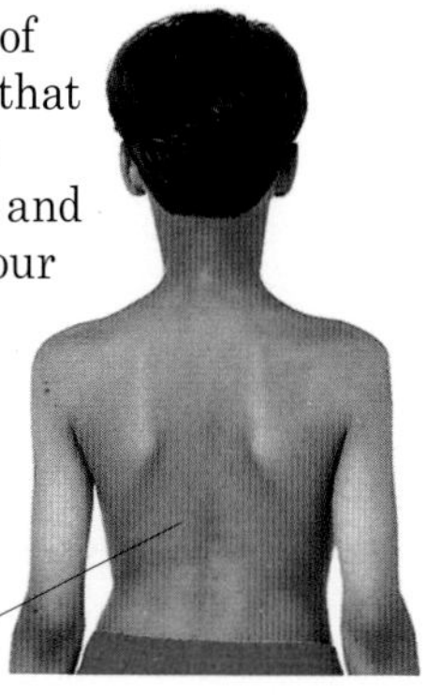

back

2 the part opposite the front.
back *adjective*

***back** of a clock*

bacteria
noun
very small organisms. Some cause disease, while others help your body.
*Some **bacteria** help break down food in your stomach.*
■ say bak-**teer**-ee-uh

bad
adjective
1 wrong.
*Stealing is very **bad**.*
2 serious.
*I have a **bad** earache.*
3 rotten, or faulty.
*The food had gone **bad**.*
■ comparisons **worse worst**

badge
badges *noun*
a decoration that can be pinned or sewn onto clothes.

sheriff's ***badge***

badminton
noun
an indoor game played by two or four people on a court. Each player uses a racket to hit a shuttlecock over a net (see **sport** on page 197).

baffle
baffles baffling baffled *verb*
to confuse someone or make a person puzzled.
*The quiz completely **baffled** him.*

bag
bags *noun*
a container that you can carry things in, usually made of material, plastic, or paper.

baggy
adjective
fitting loosely.

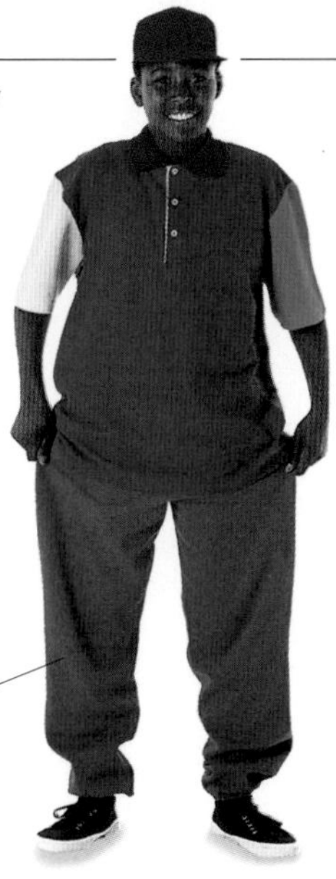
baggy *pants*

bake
bakes baking baked *verb*
to cook in an oven or fire. Pies, cakes, and bread are baked.

*A baker **bakes** bread.*

balance
balances balancing balanced *verb*
to keep steady so you do not fall over.
*The tightrope walker **balanced** on the high wire.*

balcony
balconies *noun*
a platform for standing on that is attached to the wall of a building above the ground.

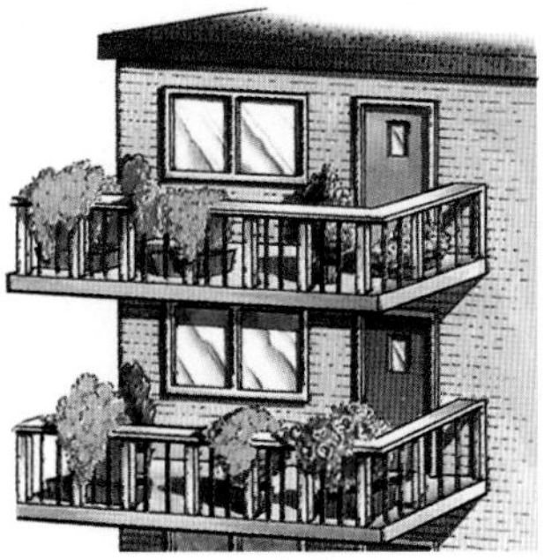

bald
adjective
without any hair.
*A **bald** head.*

ball
balls *noun*
1 a rounded object used to play many games and sports.

beach ***ball***

2 a big, grand party where there is dancing.
*A summer **ball**.*

ballet
ballets *noun*
a performance on stage that tells a story in music and dance.
■ say bal-**lay** or **bal**-lay

ballet *dancers*

balloon
balloons *noun*
a bag of rubber or other material filled with air or another gas.

hot-air ***balloon***

bamboo
noun
a tall, tropical grass with hard, hollow stems. Bamboo can be used to make garden poles and furniture.

bamboo *poles*

ban
bans banning banned *verb*
to forbid people to do something.
*Smoking is **banned** on public transportation.*

banana
bananas *noun*
a tree fruit with a smooth, thick outer peel and a soft, edible center. Bananas grow in hot, damp regions.

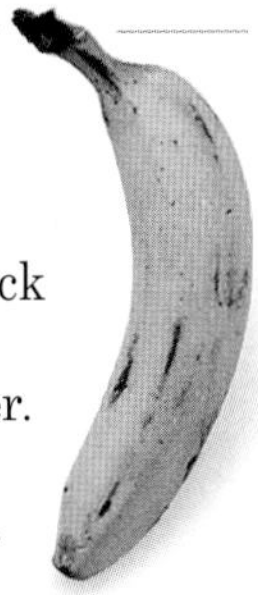

band
bands *noun*
1 a group of people who play music together.

2 a strip of material such as fabric, elastic, or metal that holds things together.

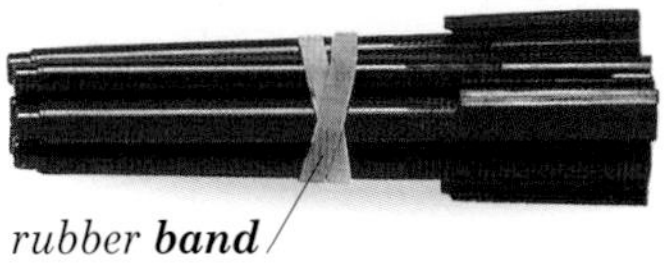
rubber ***band***

bandage
bandages *noun*
a strip of material that is used to wrap around a wound to keep it clean.

bang
bangs *noun*
a sudden, loud noise.
*The firework went off with a loud **bang**.*

bank
banks *noun*
1 a steep, sloping piece of ground, often on the side of a river.

2 a company that looks after people's money and also lends money.

banner
banners *noun*
a large flag or piece of cloth that has a picture or a message on it.

bar
bars *noun*
1 a long, narrow piece of metal.

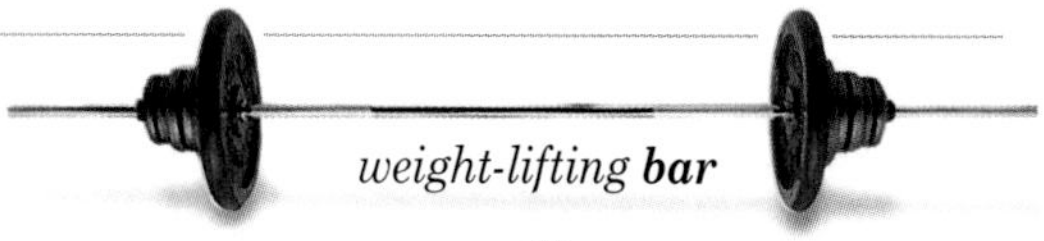

*weight-lifting **bar***

2 a counter or a room where drinks or snacks are sold.

barbecue
barbecues *noun*
1 a grill over an open fire that is lit outdoors and used for cooking meat, fish, or vegetables.

2 a party or special meal where food is cooked on a barbecue.
■ say **bar**-bi-kyoo

bare
adjective
without any covering.

***bare** feet*

bargain
bargains *noun*
something bought cheaply.
*My shoes were a real **bargain** in the sale.*

bark
noun
the rough wood on the outside of a tree trunk.

bark
barks barking barked *verb*
to make a rough, loud noise like a dog.
bark *noun*

barley
noun
a type of cereal grown on farms to make food and beer.

barn
barns *noun*
a large farm building used for storage or for keeping animals in.

barrel
barrels *noun*
a large, rounded, wooden or metal container for storing beer and other liquids.

barrier
barriers *noun*
a structure built to stop someone or something from passing through.
*The police placed a **barrier** across the road.*

base
bases *noun*
the bottom of something.

*lamp **base***

baseball
noun
a game for two teams of nine players, which started in the United States. The winning team is the one that scores the most runs (see **sport** on page 197).

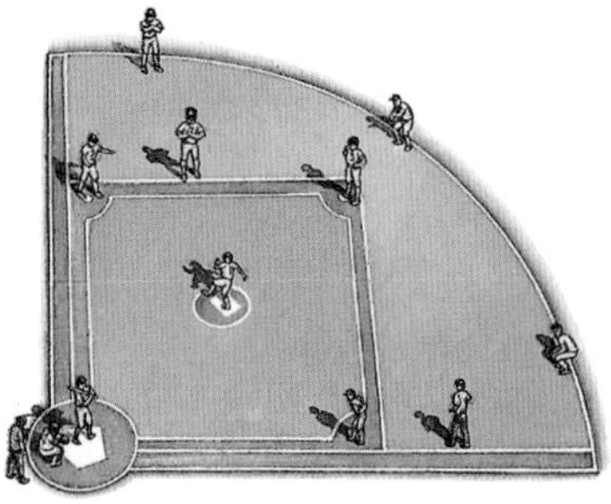

basement
basements *noun*
a floor in a building that is partly or completely below ground level.

basin
basins *noun*
a large, bowl-shaped container used for holding water. Basins are often used for washing.

basket
baskets *noun*
a container for carrying things in, usually made of cane, twigs, or straw.

basketball
noun
a team game with five players on each side. Points are scored by throwing a ball through a raised hoop called the "basket" (see **sport** on page 197).

bat
bats *noun*
1 a stick, often made of wood or metal that is used to hit a ball (see **sport** on page 197).

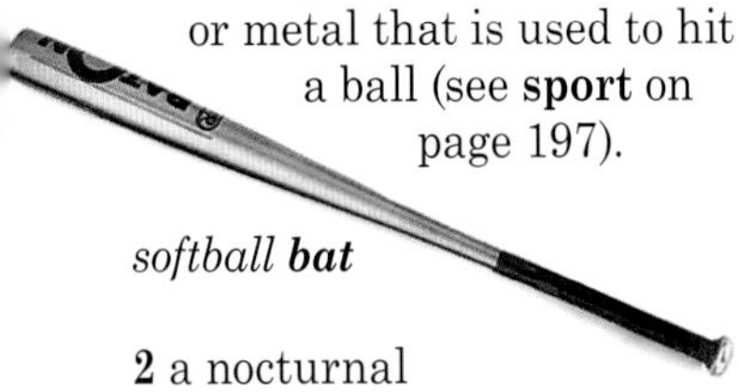

softball ***bat***

2 a nocturnal mammal with wings. Bats live in caves and dark places and eat insects, fruit, or small animals. They rest hanging upside down (see **mammal** on page 124).

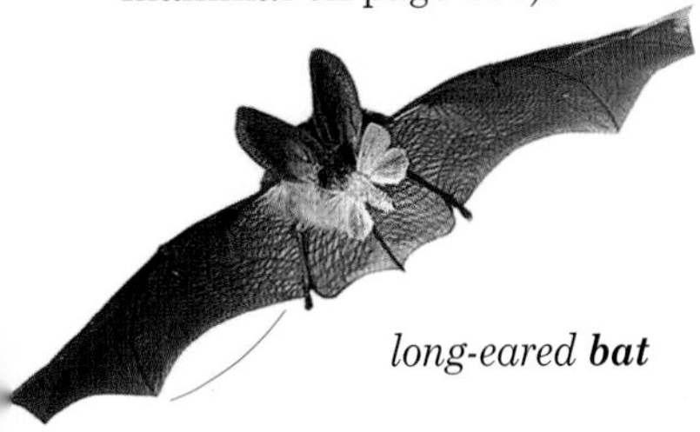

long-eared ***bat***

bathtub
bathtubs *noun*
a large tub for washing the whole of your body.

baton
batons *noun*
a thin piece of wood or metal. Conductors of orchestras and band leaders use different types of batons to keep time.

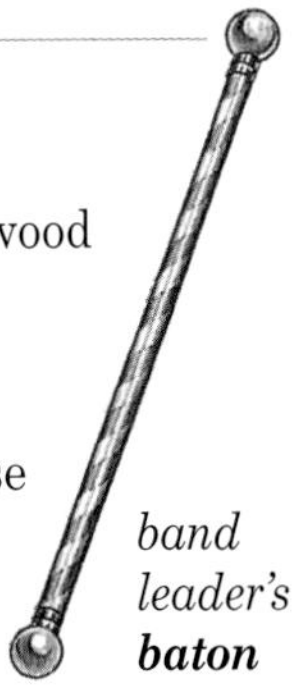

band leader's ***baton***

battery
batteries *noun*
a closed container of chemicals that makes and stores small amounts of electricity.

watch ***battery***

battle
battles *noun*
a fight between two armies that are at war.

bawl
bawls bawling bawled *verb*
to cry very loudly.

bay
bays *noun*
a deep, inward curve in a coastline or the edge of a lake.

beach
beaches *noun*
land at the edge of a sea or lake, usually covered in pebbles or sand.

bead
beads *noun*
a small piece of wood, stone, or glass that can be threaded onto string.

beak
beaks *noun*
the hard, bony mouth of a bird or dinosaur (see **dinosaur** on page 61).

toucan's ***beak***

beam
beams *noun*

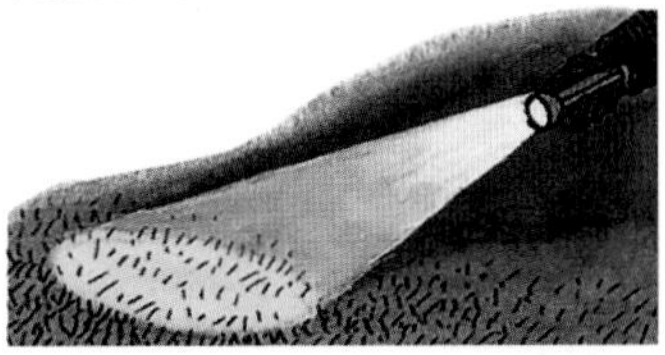

1 a long, narrow ray of light.

2 a long, strong piece of wood or metal, often used in buildings to hold up the roof.

bean
beans *noun*
a seed or pod that is eaten as a vegetable.

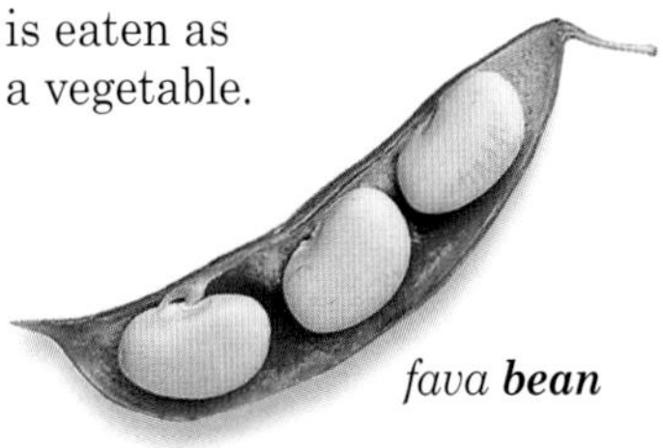

fava ***bean***

bear
bears *noun*
a large mammal with thick fur that usually lives in forests. All bears eat meat, but some also eat honey, roots, plant buds, berries, and fruit.

Canadian black ***bear***

bear
bears bearing bore born or borne *verb*
1 to produce or give birth to.
This plant ***bears*** *red berries.*
2 to carry or support.
Can that branch ***bear*** *your weight?*
3 to put up with.
I can't ***bear*** *to think about it.*

beard
beards *noun*
the hair that grows on the lower part of a man's face if he does not shave.

beat
beats beating beat beaten *verb*
1 to defeat someone.
My friend ***beat*** *me at chess.*
2 to hit or stir repeatedly.
She ***beat*** *the eggs.*
3 to make a repeated movement, or noise.
My heart is ***beating*** *loudly.*

beat
beats *noun*
a steady stroke or sound.
A metronome ticks with a steady ***beat***.

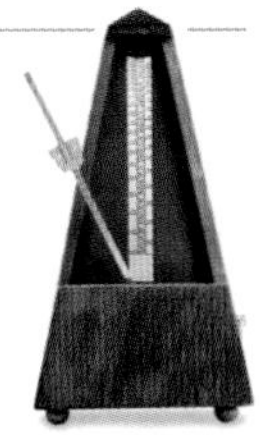

beautiful
adjective
very pleasant to look at.
What a ***beautiful*** *view!*
■ say **byoo**-tuh-ful

beaver
beavers *noun*
a large rodent that gnaws down trees to build dams and island homes, called lodges, in rivers. Beavers eat bark, roots, and twigs.

a b c d e f g h i j k l m n o p q r s t u v w x y z

beckon
beckons beckoning beckoned
verb
to make a sign that tells someone to come to you.

become
becomes becoming became
verb
to change or grow into.
*A tadpole **becomes** a frog.*

bed
beds *noun*
1 a piece of furniture that you sleep on.
2 the bottom of a river, lake, or the sea.

bee
bees *noun*
a flying insect that usually lives in large, well-organized groups. Bees feed on pollen, nectar, and the honey they make from nectar.

beech
beeches *noun*
a deciduous forest tree with smooth, gray bark and spreading branches (see **tree** on page 223).

***beech** leaf*

beef
noun
the meat from a cow or bull.

beehive
beehives *noun*
a type of box that people keep bees in. They collect the honey that the bees make.

beer
beers *noun*
an alcoholic drink made from cereal grains.

beetle
beetles *noun*
an insect with hard, often brightly colored wing cases. Some beetles eat small insects; others eat wood and plants.

*jewel **beetle***

beetroot / beet
beetroots / beets *noun*
a hard, red root plant with leaves that is eaten as a vegetable (see **vegetable** on page 233).

before
preposition
earlier.

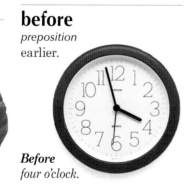

***Before** four o'clock.*

before
adverb
in the past.
*I've heard that story **before**.*

beg
begs begging begged *verb*
to ask for something very strongly.

*The dog **begged** for a piece of meat.*

begin
begins beginning began begun
verb
to start something.
*The story **begins** in a castle.*
beginning *noun*

behave
behaves behaving behaved *verb*
to act in a particular way in front of other people.
*Our class **behaved** well at the zoo.*
behavior *noun*

behind
preposition
at the back of.

*She stood **behind** her friend.*
behind *adverb*

being
beings *noun*
someone or something that exists.

believe
believes believing believed *verb*
to feel strongly that something is true.

bell
bells *noun*
a cup-shaped piece of metal that makes a ringing sound when it is struck.

belong
belongs belonging belonged
verb
to be someone's possession or property.
*That book **belongs** to me.*

below
preposition
lower than.

***Below** her waist.*
■ opposite **above**

belt
belts *noun*
a narrow strip of fabric or leather that you wear around your waist.

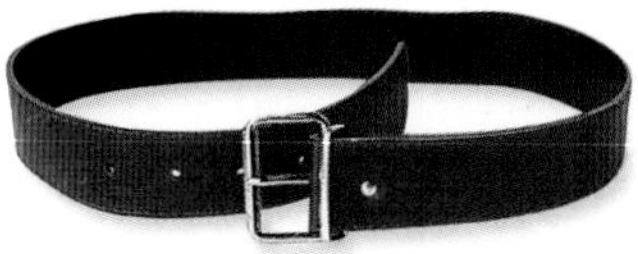

bench
benches *noun*
1 a long, wooden seat.

*park **bench***

2 a worktable.

bend
bends bending bent *verb*
to change something straight into a curved shape.

*She **bent** over to touch her toes.*

bend
bends *noun*
a curve.

***Bends** in the road.*

benefit
benefits benefiting benefited *verb*
to receive help from someone or something.
*The school would **benefit** from having new computers.*
benefit *noun*

beret
berets *noun*
a soft, flat hat.

■ say buh-**ray**

berry
berries *noun*
a small, round juicy fruit with seeds inside.

*blue**berries***

beside
preposition
at the side of.

*The ball is **beside** her.*

best
*from the adjective **good***
better than any other.

bet
bets betting bet *verb*
to believe that something is going to happen.
*I **bet** it's going to rain later.*

better
*from the adjective **good***
1 more able.
*You are good at science but he is **better**.*
2 well again.
*I'm feeling **better**, thanks.*

between
preposition
in the middle of.

***Between** her knees.*

beware
verb
to be careful of something.
***Beware** of the dog.*

beyond
preposition
farther away than.
*The hills lay **beyond** the river.*

bicycle
bicycles *noun*
a vehicle with two wheels that you ride by turning the pedals with your feet. Bicycle can be shortened to bike.

big
adjective
large in width or size.

*The jacket is too **big** for him.*
■ comparisons **bigger biggest**

bikini
bikinis *noun*
a swimming outfit with two pieces, worn by girls and women.

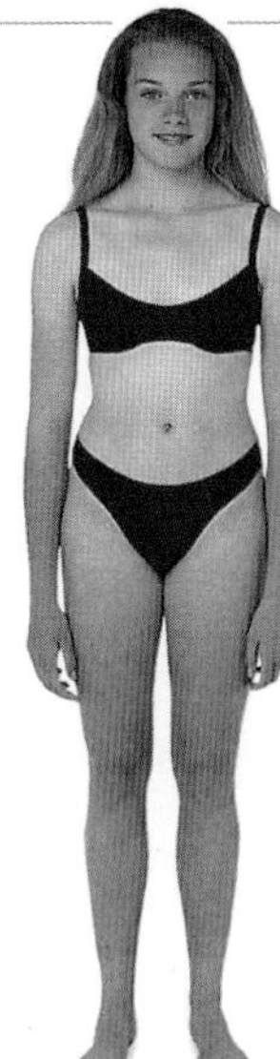

bill
bills *noun*
1 the hard, bony mouth of a bird.

2 a piece of paper that shows you how much you have to pay for something.
*The waiter brought us the **bill** at the end of our meal.*
3 a plan for a new law that must be voted on by a country's government.
*The new education **bill** will be discussed in Congress today.*

billow
billows billowing billowed *verb*
to spread out and be blown about in the wind.
*Smoke **billowed** out from the chimneys.*

bin
bins *noun*
a box or container used for storage.

binoculars
noun
two small telescopes joined together that make things that are far away look closer.

biodegradable
adjective
able to be broken down by bacteria.
*Most paper is **biodegradable**.*
■ say by-oh-dee-**gray**-duh-bul

A B C D E F G H I J K L M N O P Q R S T U V W X Y Z

bird

birds *noun*

an animal that has warm blood, feathers on its body, and wings (see **skeleton** on page 188).

birthday
birthdays *noun*
the anniversary of the day you were born.

birthday cake
birthday cakes *noun*
a special cake with candles on top that is baked for your birthday.

birthday card
birthday cards *noun*
a card that people send to you on your birthday, to congratulate you on being a year older.

birthday party
birthday parties *noun*
a party to celebrate someone's birthday.

birthday present
birthday presents *noun*
a gift that you give to someone on their birthday.

biscuit
biscuits *noun*
a type of bread made in small, soft cakes.
■ say **bis**-kit

bit
bits *noun*
a small piece of something.
*The mouse nibbled a **bit** of cheese.*

bite
bites biting bit bitten *verb*
to use your teeth in a cutting action, usually with food.

bite *noun*

bitter
adjective
having a sour, sharp taste.
*Strong coffee can taste **bitter**.*

black
noun
1 a color.

2 very dark.
*A **black** night.*

blackberry
blackberries *noun*
a black or dark purple fruit that grows on prickly stems called brambles.

blackbird
blackbirds *noun*
a bird that lives in gardens and fields, and eats insects and seeds. The male has black feathers and the female has brown feathers.

blackboard
blackboards *noun*
a hard, dark smooth surface for writing on with chalk in classrooms.

blade
blades *noun*
1 the flat, sharp, metal part of a knife or a sword.

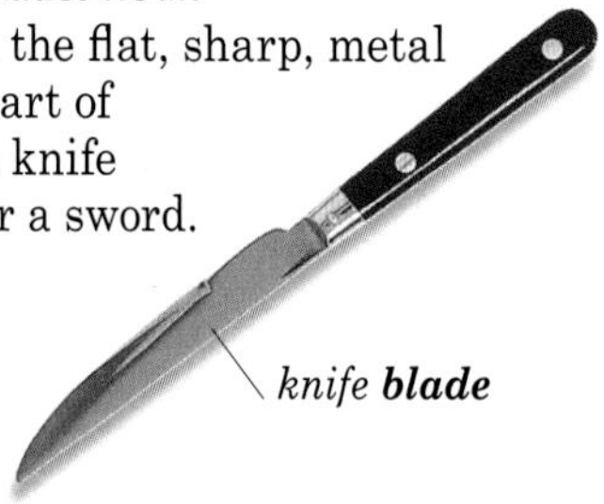

2 a stem of grass.

blame
blames blaming blamed *verb*
to think or say that someone has done something wrong.
*She always **blames** me for letting the toast burn.*

blank
blanks *noun*
An empty space.

A hen lays ___.

*The last word has been left **blank**.*
blank *adjective*

blanket
blankets *noun*
a soft covering, usually made of wool that is used to keep people or animals warm.

blast
blasts *noun*
a powerful explosion or gust of wind.
*A **blast** of cold air came in through the window.*

blaze
blazes blazing blazed *verb*
to burn very brightly.

*The fire **blazed** through the old building.*
blaze *noun*

blazer
blazers *noun*
a jacket that is often worn as part of a uniform.

bleach
noun
a very powerful chemical that removes color. Bleach can burn your skin.

bleed
bleeds bleeding bled *verb*
to lose blood.
My nose started to ***bleed*** *when I fell over.*

blind
adjective
unable to see.

Some ***blind*** *people have guide dogs.*

blink
blinks blinking blinked *verb*
to open and shut your eyes quickly.
The bright light made me ***blink****.*

blister
blisters *noun*
a bubble of watery liquid that forms under your skin when it has been burnt or rubbed.
Tight shoes give me ***blisters****.*

blizzard
blizzards *noun*
a very heavy snowstorm.

blob
blobs *noun*
a small lump of something with no shape.

a ***blob*** *of face cream*

block
blocks *noun*

1 a solid shape, such as a block of wood.
2 a rectangular area surrounded by four streets.

block
blocks blocking blocked *verb*
to be in the way.
The road was ***blocked*** *by the fallen tree.*

blond / blonde
adjective
having light-colored hair. Blond is used for boys and men, and blonde is used for girls and women.

blond *boy*

blonde *girl*

blood
noun
the red liquid that flows around our body through veins and arteries. Blood carries nutrients and oxygen to our skin and muscles.

bloom
blooms blooming bloomed *verb*
to produce flowers.
Fruit trees ***bloom*** *in the spring.*

blossom
blossoms *noun*
the flowers on a tree that appear before the fruit.

hawthorn ***blossom***

blot
blots *noun*
a stain on paper, usually made by ink or paint that has been spilled.

blouse
blouses *noun*
a type of shirt, usually worn by girls or women.

blow
blows blowing blew blown *verb*
1 to move in air, or be moved in air.
2 to force air out of your nose or mouth.

He ***blew*** *up the balloon.*

blue
noun
a color.

bluff
bluffs bluffing bluffed *verb*
to trick someone into believing something.
She pretended to be brave, but she was ***bluffing****.*

blunt
adjective
having a rounded end or edge.

■ opposite **sharp**

blur
blurs blurring blurred *verb*
to make something unclear and difficult to see.
The view through the window was ***blurred*** *by rain.*

blush
blushes blushing blushed *verb*
to turn red because you are embarrassed or shy.

board
boards *noun*
a flat piece of wood, or very stiff paper.

boast
boasts boasting boasted *verb*
to tell people about something in a proud and annoying way.
He ***boasted*** *about his money.*

boat

boats *noun*

a small open vessel that carries goods and people across water.

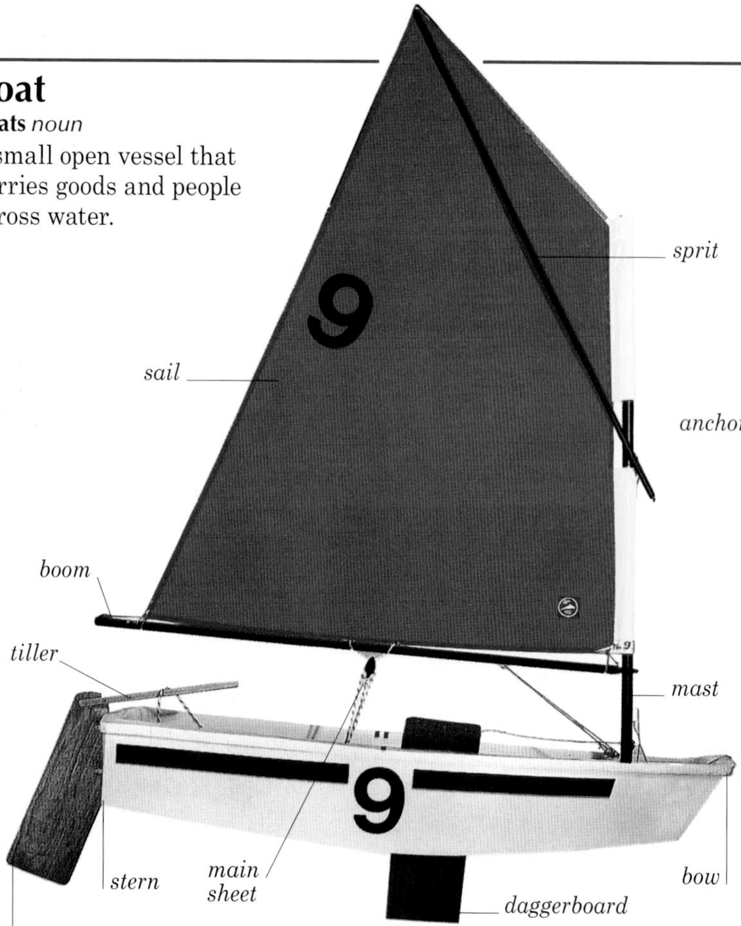

dinghy

junk

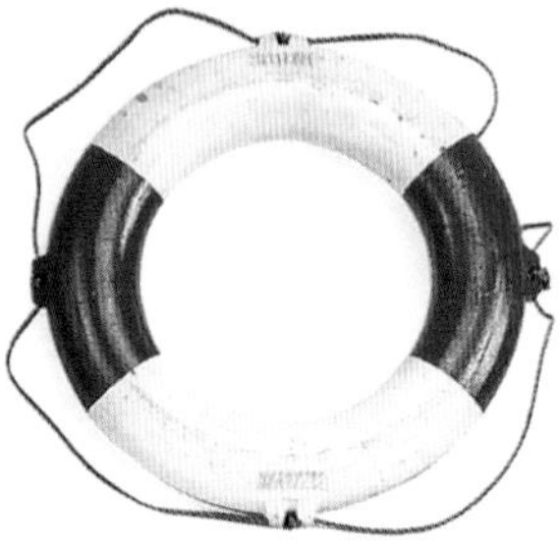

life buoy

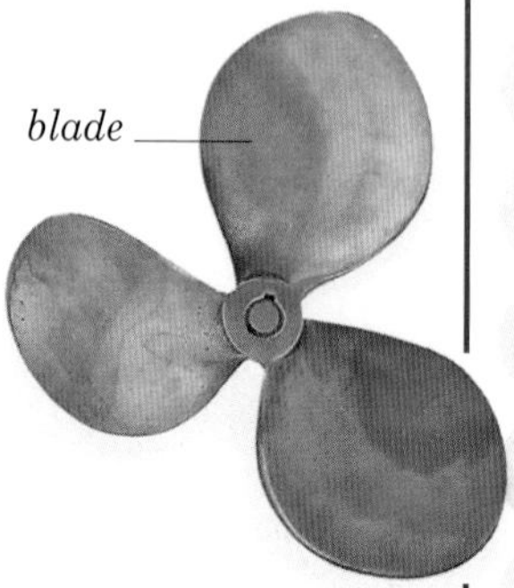

propeller

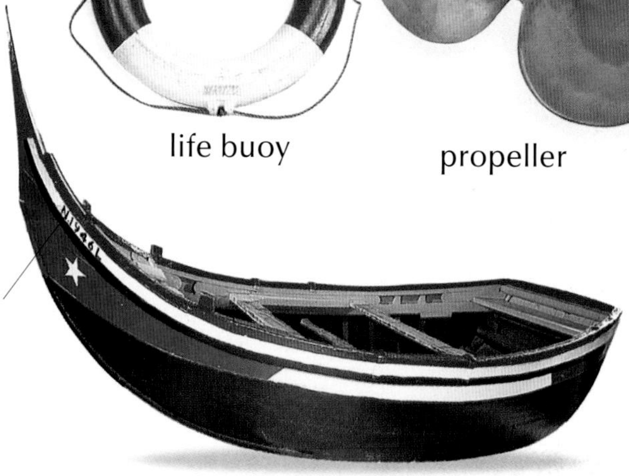

fishing **boat**

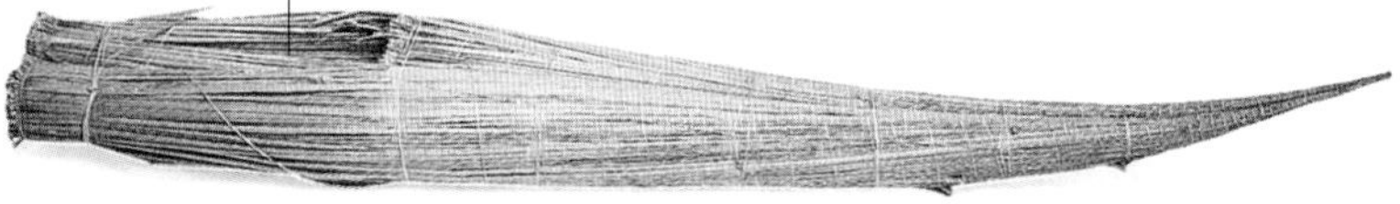

reed **boat**

paddle

coble (fishing **boat**)

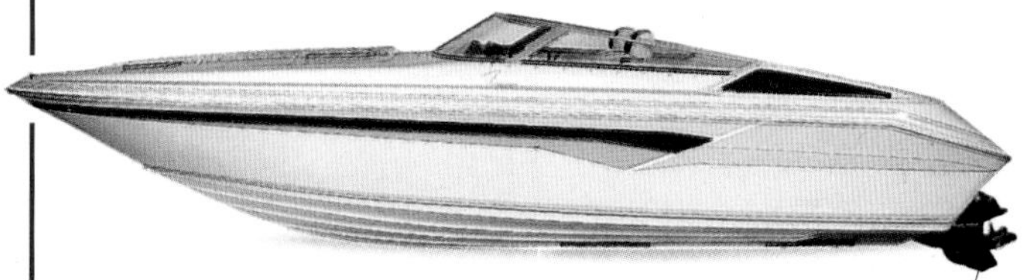

power**boat**

narrow**boat**

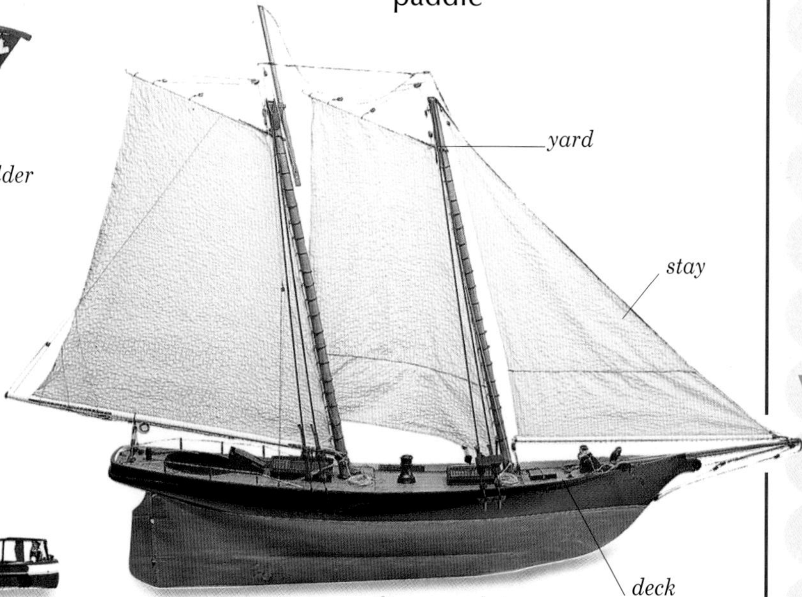

sailing yacht

body
bodies *noun*
all the physical parts that make up an animal or person.

boil
boils boiling boiled *verb*
to heat a liquid until it starts to bubble and steam rises from it.

bold
adjective
brave and fearless.
*The **bold** knight marched up to the dragon's cave.*

bolt
bolts *noun*
1 a metal rod that is used to fasten things together.

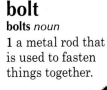

2 a sliding metal bar that is used for fastening a door.

bomb
bombs *noun*
an exploding weapon that can cause damage to anything around it.
■ say **bom**

bone
bones *noun*
the hard parts of an animal's or person's body that make up the skeleton.

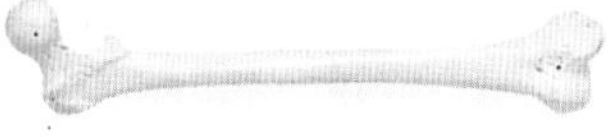

*femur (upper leg **bone**)*
bony *adjective*

bonfire
bonfires *noun*
a large outdoor fire.

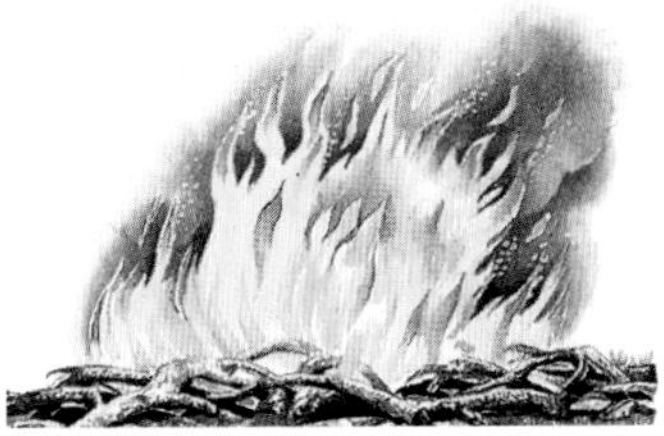

book
books *noun*
printed pieces of paper, joined together inside a cover.

boom
booms booming boomed *verb*
to make a deep, loud sound.
*His voice **boomed** out through the loudspeaker.*

boomerang
boomerangs *noun*
a curved piece of wood that comes back to you when you throw it. Boomerangs were used in the past as a weapon by Australian Aboriginals.

boot
boots *noun*
a type of shoe that covers your foot and part of your leg.

*rain **boot***

border
borders *noun*
1 the boundary between two countries.

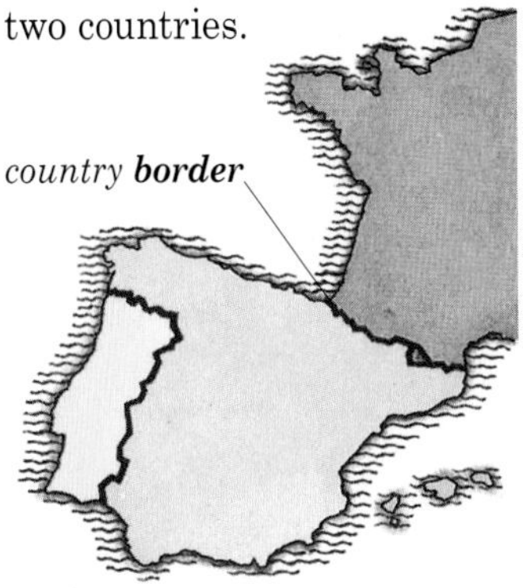

*country **border***

2 a strip around the edge of something.

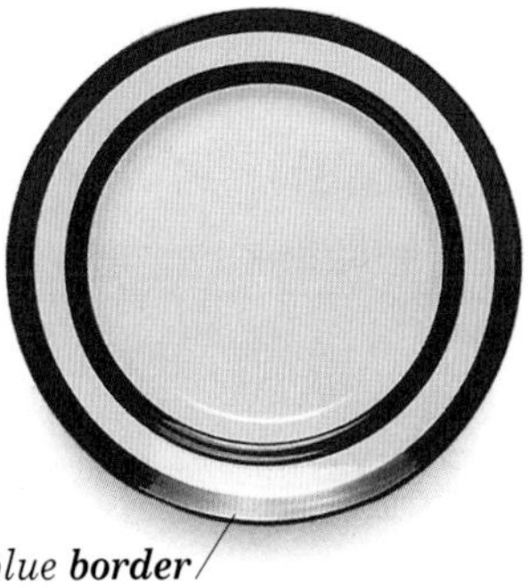

*blue **border***

bore
bores boring bored *verb*
1 to be very uninteresting.
*She **bored** us for weeks by telling the same joke.*
2 to make a round hole in something.
*They **bored** a hole in the ground in search of oil.*

bore
from the verb **to bear**
1 *She **bore** 10 children.*
2 *Luckily, the bridge **bore** the truck's weight.*

born
from the verb **to bear**
*I was **born** 10 years ago, so I am 10 years old.*

borrow
borrows borrowing borrowed *verb*
to take something for a while and then return it.
*I **borrowed** my friend's pen.*
■ opposite **lend**

boss
bosses *noun*
the person who is in charge at work.

both
adjective
not just one thing, but two.

***Both** bowls contain rice.*

bother
bothers bothering bothered *verb*
to worry or annoy someone.

bottle
bottles *noun*
a container for liquids, usually made of glass or plastic.

bottom
bottoms *noun*
1 the lowest part of something.

*The **bottom** of the sea.*
■ opposite **top**

2 the part of your body that you sit on.

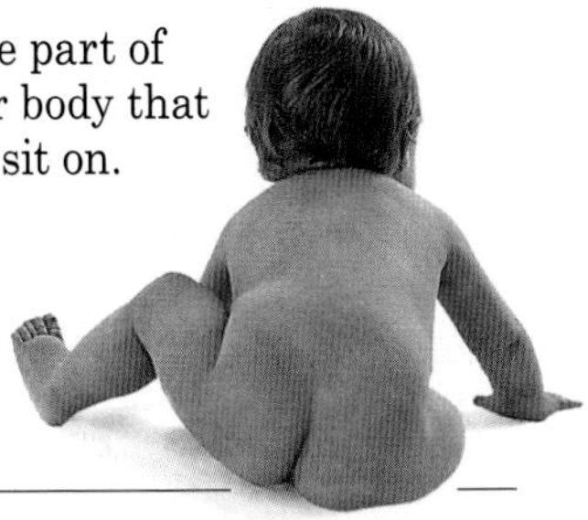

bought
from the verb **to buy**
I ***bought*** *a present for my friend yesterday.*
■ say **bawt**

bounce
bounces bouncing bounced *verb*
to spring up and down.

bounce *noun*

boundary
boundaries *noun*
the edge of a piece of land.

bouquet
bouquets *noun*
a bunch of flowers that has been specially arranged and wrapped.

■ say bo-**kay**

bow
bows bowing bowed *verb*
to bend from the waist as a greeting or a sign of respect.

■ rhymes with **now**

bow
bows *noun*
the front of a ship.
■ rhymes with **now**

bow
bows *noun*
1 a knot with two loops.

2 a curved piece of wood with a string attached at each end, used for shooting arrows.

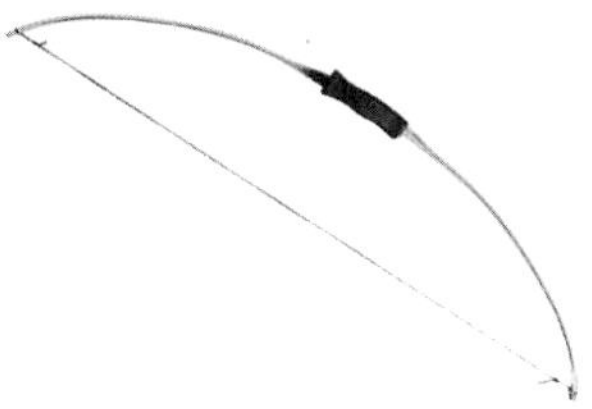

3 a wooden stick with horse hair attached at each end, used for playing musical instruments.

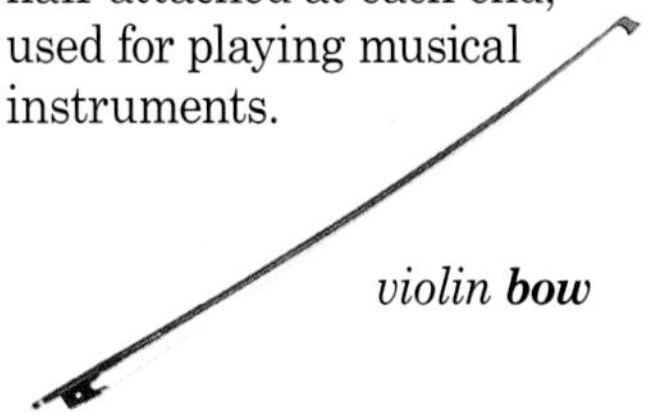

violin ***bow***

■ rhymes with **go**

bowl
bowls *noun*
a curved, open container, usually used for food.

bowl
bowls bowling bowled *verb*
to roll a ball in ten-pin bowling.

box
boxes *noun*
a container to store things in.

cardboard ***box***

boy
boys *noun*
a young male person.

brace
braces *noun*
a piece of wire that is fitted around your teeth to help straighten them.

bracelet
bracelets *noun*
a decorative band or chain that is worn around your wrist. Bracelets are usually made of metal or beads.

braille
noun
a type of writing where letters are represented by raised dots. People who are blind read the dots by feeling them with their fingertips.

■ say **brayl**

brain
brains *noun*
the part of your body inside your head that controls how you think and move.

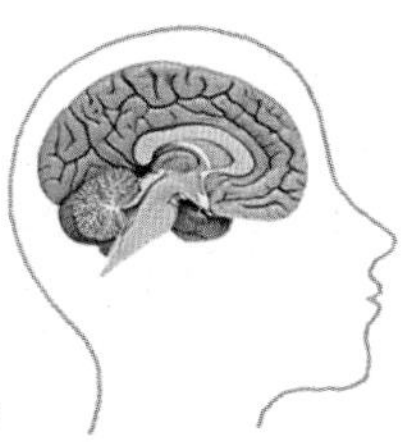

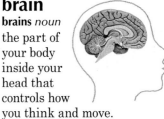

brake
brakes *noun*
a part of a vehicle that slows it down or stops it.

brake
brakes braking braked *verb*
to slow down or stop a vehicle by using the brakes.

branch
branches *noun*
the part of a tree that grows out of the trunk.

brass
noun
a hard, yellow-colored metal made from a mixture of copper and zinc.

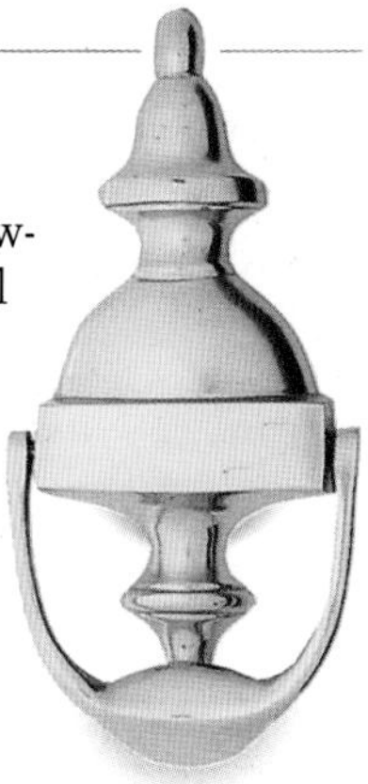

brass *door knocker*

brave
adjective
willing to do something even though you are afraid.
The ***brave*** *girl dived into the lake to rescue her brother.*
■ comparisons **braver bravest**
bravery *noun*

bread
noun
a food made from flour and baked in an oven.

break
breaks breaking broke broken *verb*
to damage something so that it cannot be used.

*The cat is always **breaking** things.*

break
breaks *noun*
a period of rest.

breakfast
breakfasts *noun*
the first meal of the day, eaten in the morning.

breathe
breathes breathing breathed *verb*
to take air in and out of your lungs, through your nose or mouth.
breath *noun*

breathless
adjective
having difficulty in breathing.
*Running for the bus made the old man **breathless**.*

breed
breeds breeding bred *verb*
to keep animals so that they produce young.
*She **breeds** racehorses.*

breed
breeds *noun*
a particular type of animal.

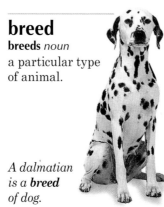

*A dalmatian is a **breed** of dog.*

breeze
breezes *noun*
a gentle wind.

bribe
bribes bribing bribed *verb*
to pay someone secretly to do something that they shouldn't do.
*The prisoner **bribed** the guard to set him free.*

brick
bricks *noun*
a block made out of baked clay, used for building things.

bride
brides *noun*
a woman on the day she gets married.

bride

bridge
bridges *noun*
a structure that is built over an obstacle such as a railroad or a river.

brief
adjective
short in time.
*He made a **brief** speech, lasting only five minutes.*

bright
adjective
1 giving off a lot of light.
*A car has **bright** headlights.*
2 clever.
*The **bright** pupil knew all the answers.*
■ comparisons **brighter brightest**
brightly *adverb*

brilliant
adjective
1 very smart or clever.
*The inventor had a **brilliant** idea.*
2 very bright.
*Diamonds are **brilliant**.*

brim
brims *noun*
1 the edge of a hat.

brim

2 the top of a container, such as a glass or a cup.

*Full to the **brim**.*

bring
brings bringing brought *verb*
to take something or someone with you when you go somewhere.
*May I **bring** my friend along?*

bristle
bristles *noun*
stiff hairs, usually on an animal or a brush.

nail-brush

brittle
adjective
easily broken.
*Icicles are very **brittle**.*

broad
adjective
very wide.

*The river was **broad** at its mouth.*
■ comparisons **broader broadest**

broadcast
broadcasts broadcasting broadcast *verb*
to send sound or pictures by radio or television.
*The Olympic games are **broadcast** all over the world.*

broccoli
noun
a vegetable with edible green or purple buds. Broccoli is related to the cauliflower.

brochure
brochures *noun*
a small book that contains information.
■ say bro-**shur**

broke
from the verb ***to break***
I ***broke*** *my pencil in half.*

bronze
noun
a brown-colored metal made from a mixture of copper and tin.

An ornament made of ***bronze****.*

brooch
brooches *noun*
a piece of jewelry that is usually pinned onto clothes.
■ say **broach**

broom
brooms *noun*
a stiff, long-handled brush that is used for sweeping.

brother
brothers *noun*
a male person who has the same mother and father as someone else.

brought
from the verb ***to bring***
I ***brought*** *my dog with me.*
■ say **brawt**

brown
noun
a color.

brush
brushes brushing brushed *verb*
1 to sweep.
2 to touch something lightly as you pass by it.
The woman ***brushed*** *past me in the street.*

brush
brushes *noun*
a tool with a handle and bristles.

animal ***brush***

bubble
bubbles *noun*
a light ball of liquid with air inside.

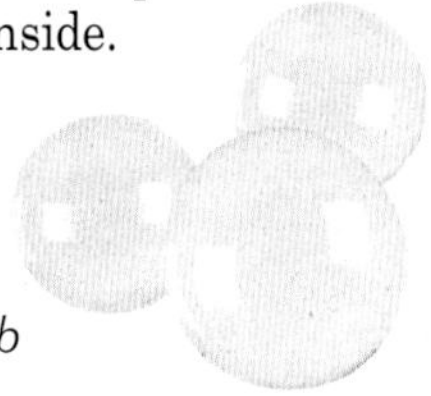

bubble *verb*

bucket
buckets *noun*
a large container with a handle, usually used for carrying liquids.

buckle
buckles *noun*
an object for fastening two ends of a belt or strap.

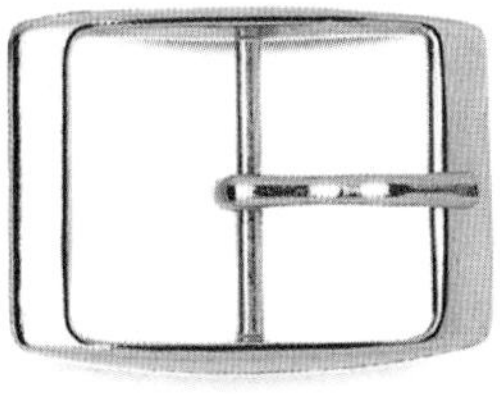

bud
buds *noun*
a small swelling on a plant, containing young leaves or flowers (see **tree** on page 223).

tree ***bud***

Buddhist
Buddhists *noun*
a person who follows the teachings of Buddha, a religious teacher who lived about 2,500 years ago.
■ say **boo**-dist

buffalo
buffalo *noun*
a large mammal that lives on open plains and eats grass.

bugle
bugles *noun*
a brass musical instrument that you blow through to produce sound.

build
builds building built *verb*
to join things together to make a structure.
The bird ***built*** *a nest out of twigs.*

building
buildings *noun*
a structure, usually with walls and a roof, for sheltering people or objects.

bulb
bulbs *noun*
1 the rounded glass part of an electric light.

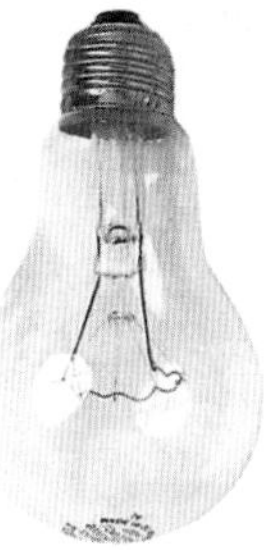

light ***bulb***

2 the rounded part of some plants that grows underground.

daffodil ***bulb***

bulge
bulges bulging bulged *verb*
to swell or be lumpy.
Her pockets ***bulged*** *with food.*

bull
bulls *noun*
1 a male mammal of the cattle family.
2 the male of some large animals, such as elephants, whales, and seals.

bulldozer
bulldozers *noun*
a machine with a large, metal blade at the front for moving earth and rocks.

bullet
bullets *noun*
a pointed metal object fired from a gun.

bully
bullies *noun*
an unpleasant person who frightens others.
bully *verb*

bump
bumps bumping bumped *verb*
to knock into something.

bump
bumps *noun*
a rounded shape on a smooth surface.
*Toads have **bumps** on their skin.*
bumpy *adjective*

bunch
bunches *noun*
a group of things together.

***bunch** of carrots*

bundle
bundles *noun*
a group of things that are loosely joined together.

***bundle** of twigs*

bungalow
bungalows *noun*
a small house with all its rooms on one level.

bunk bed
bunk beds *noun*
one of a pair of beds that are placed one on top of the other.

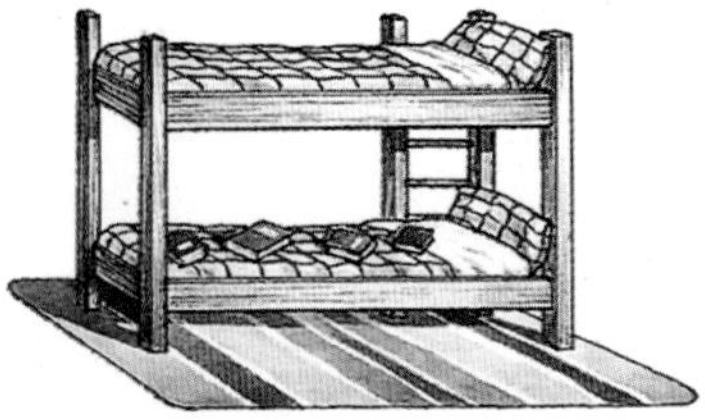

buoy
buoys *noun*
an object that is tied to an anchor and floats on water. Buoys are used as a warning or guide for ships and boats.
■ say **boo**-ee

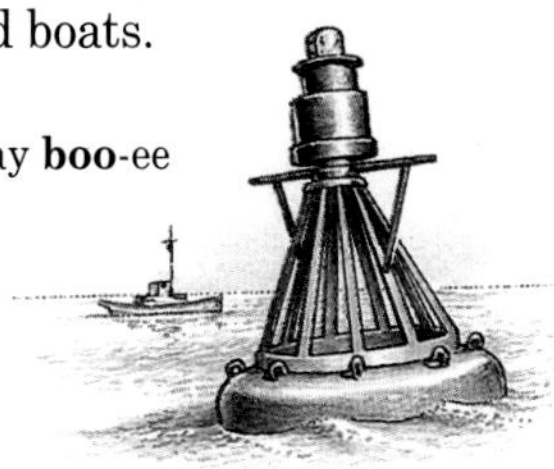

burglar
burglars *noun*
a person who steals things from people's houses.

burn
burns burning burned or **burnt** *verb*
to damage or destroy by fire.

burrow
burrows *noun*
an animal's underground home.

*rabbit **burrow***

burst
bursts bursting burst *verb*
to split open.
*The water pipe **burst** and flooded the kitchen.*

bury
buries burying buried *verb*
to put something in the ground and cover it over.
*The dog **buried** its bone.*
■ say **bare**-ee

bus
buses *noun*
a road vehicle for carrying a large number of passengers.

bush
noun
1 a large round-shaped plant. Bushes are smaller than trees and have many branches low to the ground.

2 the wilderness in Australia, New Zealand, and Africa.

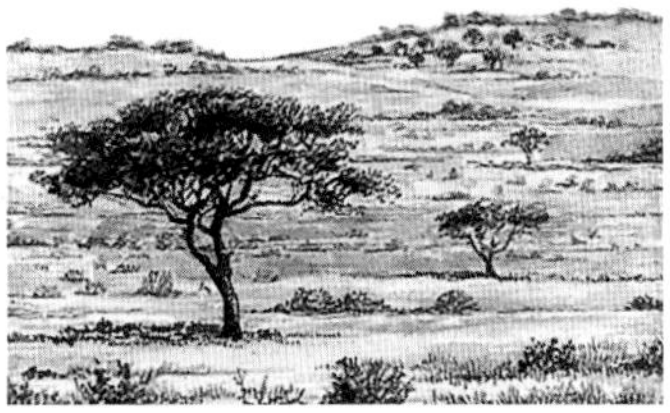

business
businesses *noun*
1 an organization that sells products or services.
2 the things that only you should know about and look after.
*Mind your own **business**.*
■ say **biz**-nis

busy
adjective
doing lots of things.
■ say **biz**-ee

butcher
butchers *noun*
a person who prepares and sells meat.

butter
noun
a soft, yellow food made from cream.

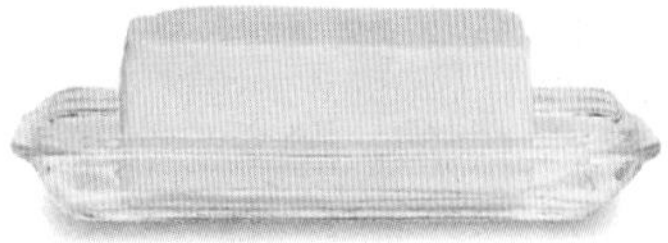

buttercup
buttercups *noun*
a small wildflower with yellow petals.

butterfly
butterflies *noun*
an insect with wings covered in very fine, colored scales. Butterflies begin life as caterpillars. Most butterflies eat plants (see **growth** on page 94).

*birdwing **butterfly***

button
buttons *noun*
1 a small object used to fasten two parts of a piece of clothing together.

2 a switch to activate an electronic device.

buy
buys buying bought *verb*
to pay for something.
*I'm going to **buy** a book with my allowance.*

buzz
buzzes buzzing buzzed *verb*
to make a low, humming noise.
*The bees **buzzed** in the hive.*

byte
bytes *noun*
a piece of information that a computer stores in its memory.

Cc

cabbage
cabbages *noun*
a vegetable with a short stem and tightly wrapped layers of broad leaves.

cabin
cabins *noun*
1 a small, simple house.

2 a room for passengers or crew on an airplane or ship.

cable
cables *noun*
1 a very strong rope or chain.

2 a bundle of wires for carrying electrical power or signals, often laid underground.

*electric **cable***

cactus
cacti or **cactuses** *noun*
a plant that grows in hot deserts. Cacti store water in their stems and have prickly spines that protect them from animals.

café
cafés *noun*
a place where people buy and eat meals, snacks, and drinks.
■ say ka-**fay**

cage
cages *noun*
a container with metal bars for keeping animals or birds in.

cake
cakes *noun*
a sweet food that is made from flour, sugar, eggs, and butter and baked in an oven.

calculator
calculators *noun*
a small electronic machine for doing math quickly.

■ say **kal**-kyuh-lay-tor

calendar
calendars *noun*
a chart of all the days, weeks, and months of the year.

calf
calves *noun*
1 a young cow or bull.
2 the young of some mammals, such as elephants or whales.

3 the back of your leg below the knee.

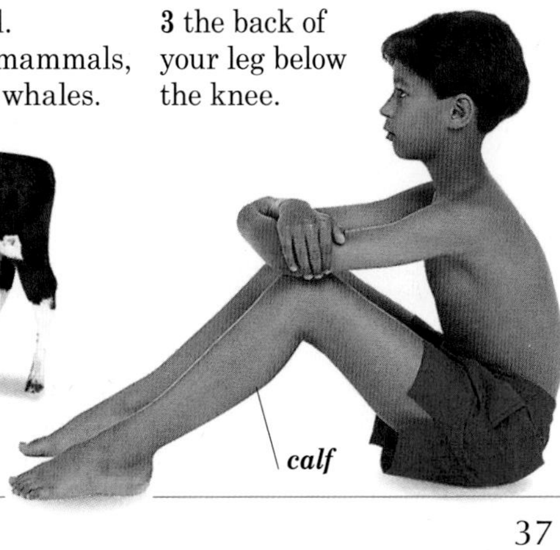

calf

call
calls calling called *verb*
1 to shout out.
*They **called** for help.*
2 to give something a name.
*I **called** my dog Spot.*
3 to phone or visit somebody.
*My cousin **called** to see me.*

calligraphy
noun
beautiful handwriting, using ink or paint.

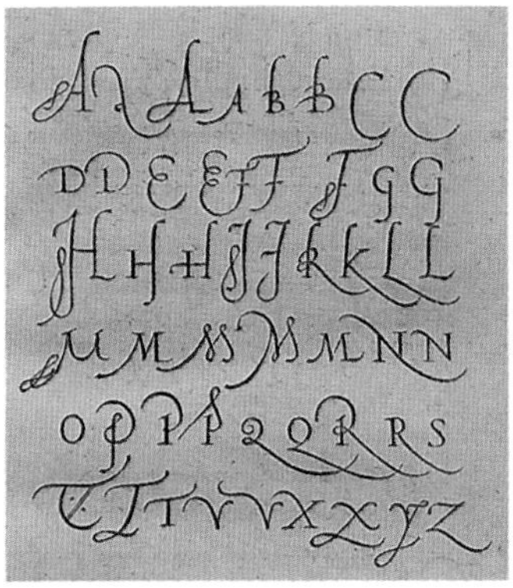

■ say ka-**lig**-ruh-fee

calm
adjective
1 still and quiet.
*The sea was **calm** after the storm had passed.*
2 peaceful.
*Yoga makes her feel **calm**.*
■ say **kahm**
■ comparisons **calmer calmest**

came
*from the verb **to come***
*He **came** with us yesterday.*

camel
camels *noun*
a mammal with one or two humps on its back that lives in hot deserts. Camels store fat in their humps to help them go without water or food for long periods of time.

*dromedary **camel** with one hump*

camera
cameras *noun*
a piece of equipment used for taking photographs or for making videos or films.

*digital **camera***

camouflage
camouflages *noun*
a disguise that helps to hide an animal or person.

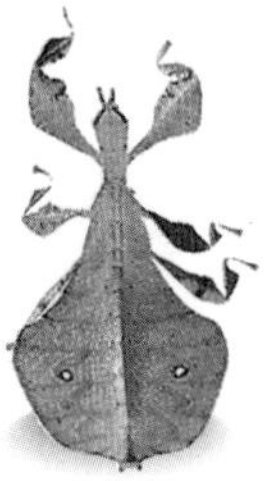
leaf insect

■ say **kam**-uh-flazh
camouflage *verb*

camp
camps camping camped *verb*
to stay in a tent outdoors.

camping *noun*

campaign
campaigns *noun*
a series of events organized to bring about a goal.
*She led a **campaign** to stop the new highway.*
■ say kam-**pain**

can
can could *verb*
to be able to or to know how to do something.
*She **can** touch her toes.*
■ opposite **cannot** or **can't**
■ always used with another verb

can
cans *noun*
a metal container used for preserving food or drink.

canal
canals *noun*
a water channel that has been built across land for boats and ships to travel on.

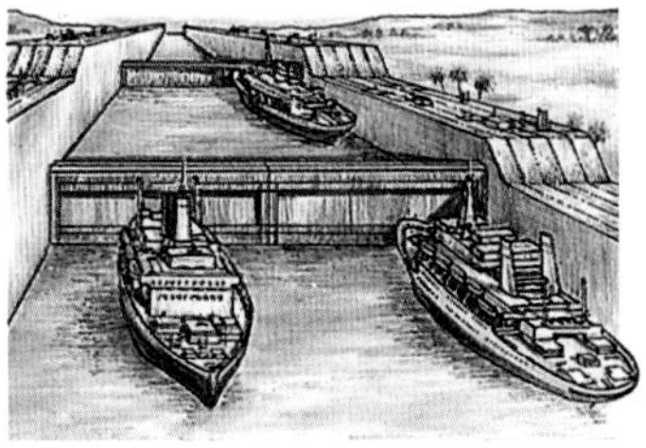

canary
canaries *noun*
a yellow bird that is often kept as a pet because it sings. Wild canaries are green.

cancel
cancels canceling canceled *verb*
to stop something that has been planned.
*We **canceled** our trip.*
■ say **kan**-sul
cancelation *noun*

cancer
cancers *noun*
a serious disease in which harmful cells spread through the body.
■ say **kan**-ser

candidate
candidates *noun*
someone who seeks or is put forward for a job or honor.
*Presidential **candidate**.*

candle
candles *noun*
a stick of wax with a string called a wick running through it. Candles are burned to give off light.

candy
candies *noun*
food usually made of sugar.

cane
canes *noun*
1 a walking stick.
2 the thick, hollow stem of some plants.

*sugar **cane***

canoe
canoes *noun*
a light, narrow boat. A paddle is used to move the canoe along.

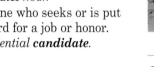

canyon
canyons *noun*
a steep-sided, rocky valley.

capable
adjective
having ability or skill at something.
*They are both **capable** cooks.*

capacity
capacities *noun*
the amount that something will hold.

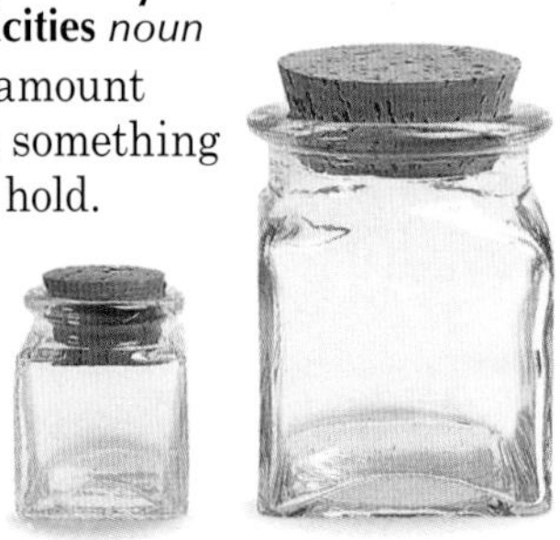
*These jars have different **capacities**.*

capital
capitals *noun*
1 a city where a country has its government offices.
*Moscow is the **capital** of Russia.*
2 a large letter of the alphabet used to start a sentence or a special name.

capture
captures capturing captured *verb*
to catch and hold on to someone or something.

car

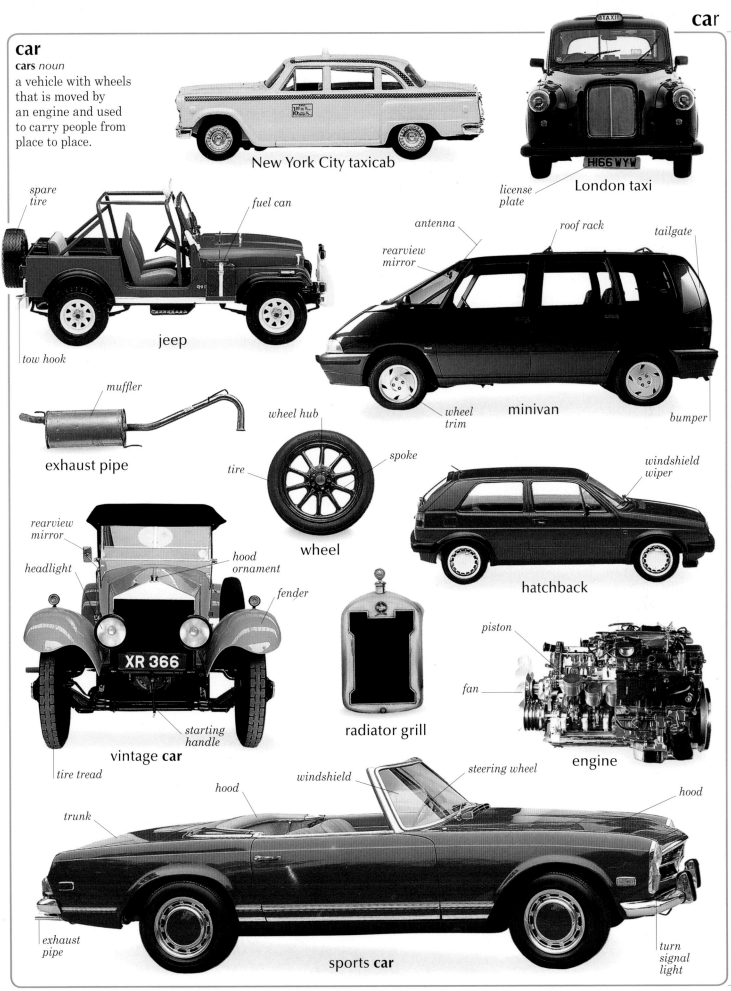

cars *noun*
a vehicle with wheels that is moved by an engine and used to carry people from place to place.

New York City taxicab

London taxi

jeep

minivan

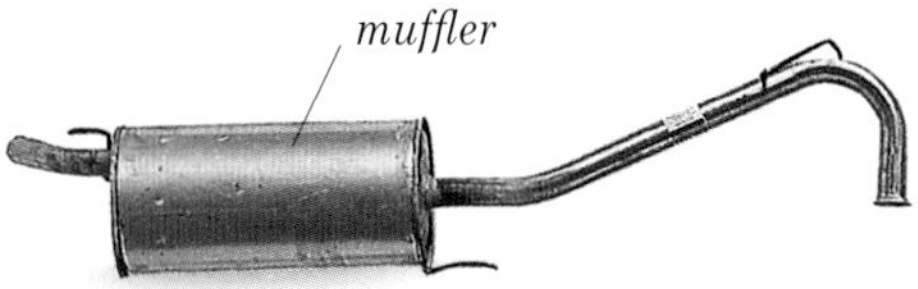

exhaust pipe

wheel

hatchback

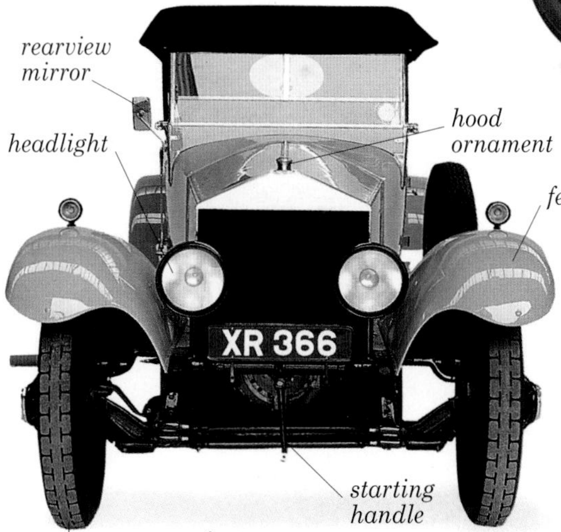

vintage **car**

radiator grill

engine

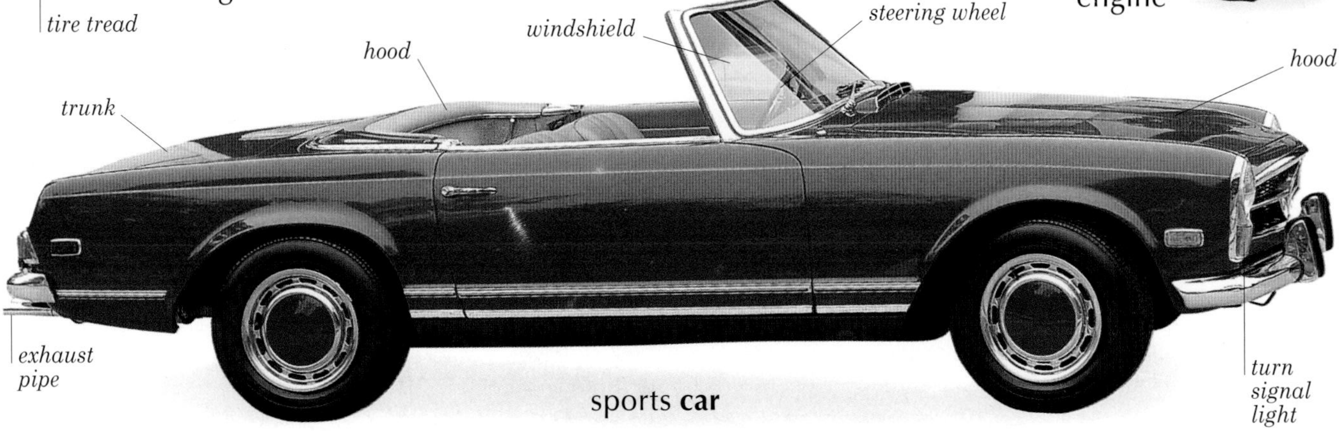

sports **car**

caravan
caravans *noun*
a group of people or vehicles traveling together, often for safety when traveling across difficult or dangerous land.

cardboard
noun
a very strong, stiff type of paper used to make boxes.

care
cares caring cared *verb*
1 to be interested.
*I **care** about what you do.*
2 to look after someone.
*I **care** for my sick mother.*
3 to feel affection for someone.
*He **cares** for his girlfriend.*

career
careers *noun*
the jobs someone has during their working life, usually in the same occupation.
*She taught in three schools during her **career**.*

careful
adjective
being aware of dangers or problems.

*Be **careful** when you cross the river.*
■ opposite **careless**

cargo
cargoes *noun*
all the different goods that a ship or aircraft carries.
*A **cargo** of bananas.*

carnival
carnivals *noun*
1 a special event with a street procession, music, and dancing.

2 a traveling fair with rides, games, and shows.

carrot
carrots *noun*
a hard, sweet-tasting root vegetable.

carry
carries carrying carried *verb*
to hold something while you move it somewhere.

carton
cartons *noun*
a small cardboard container for holding liquid, food, or objects.

cartoon
cartoons *noun*
1 a funny drawing that makes people laugh.
2 a moving film made by photographing thousands of drawings one by one.

cartridge
cartridges *noun*
a container of ink for use in a pen or computer printer.

carve
carves carving carved *verb*
to cut something into a shape.

case
cases *noun*
1 a container.
2 a particular event or example.
*There have been several **cases** of the flu at school.*

cast
casts casting cast *verb*
1 to choose someone for a part in a play or film.
*He was **cast** as the king.*
2 to shape something in a mold.
*A statue **cast** in bronze.*

castle
castles *noun*
a large house with high stone walls and strong defenses against attacking armies.

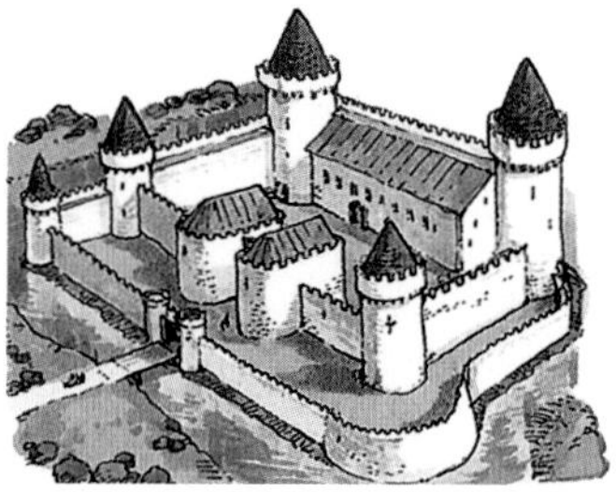

cat
cats *noun*
a mammal that is often kept as a pet. Cats eat small animals and are fierce hunters (see **pet** on page 148).

catalog
catalogs *noun*
a book that shows you the things you can buy from a shop or a company.
■ say **kat**-a-log

catch
catches catching caught *verb*
1 to get hold of something that is thrown to you.

2 to get on a vehicle.
*I **catch** the bus to work.*
3 to get an infection.
*I **caught** the measles from my sister.*

caterpillar
caterpillars *noun*
the larva of a butterfly or moth.

cattle
noun
cows, bulls, or oxen.

cauliflower
cauliflowers *noun*
a vegetable with a short stem and a hard center, made of small flowers.

caution
noun
attention to possible danger.
*Drive with **caution**.*
■ say **kaw**-shun
cautious *adjective*

ceiling
ceilings *noun*
the surface of a room that is above your head.
■ say **see**-ling

celebrate
celebrates celebrating celebrated *verb*
to do something enjoyable for a special reason.
*We had a party to **celebrate** my birthday.*
■ say **sell**-uh-brate
celebration *noun*

cell
cells *noun*
1 a small room in a prison.

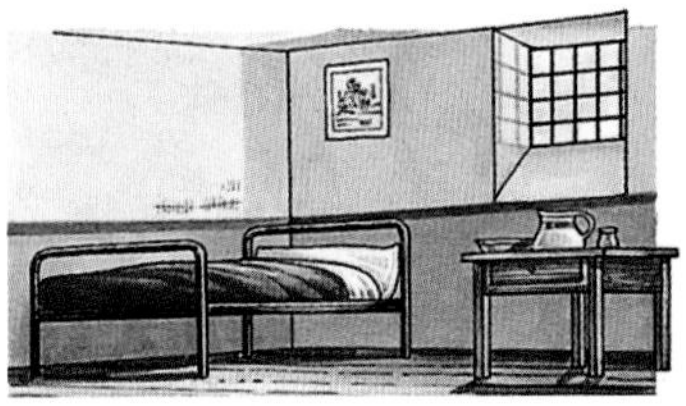

2 the smallest living part of an animal or plant.

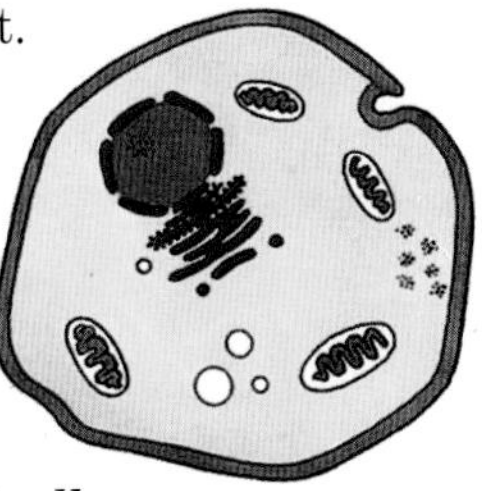

*animal **cell***

cellar
cellars *noun*
an underground room.

cell phone
noun
a handheld mobile telephone that connects to other telephones by radio waves.

*She is speaking on her **cell phone**.*

cement
noun
a clay powder that becomes hard when mixed with water.

centipede
centipedes *noun*
a tiny, blind animal with many pairs of legs that lives in dark places. They paralyze their prey with a poisonous bite.
■ say **sen**-tuh-peed

central
adjective
1 in the middle.

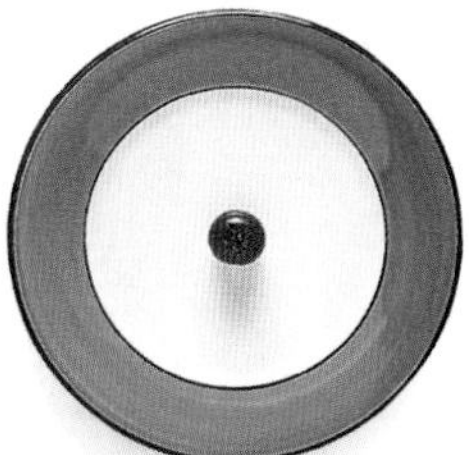

*The tomato is in a **central** position.*
2 of most importance.
*The heroine is the **central** character in the story.*

century
centuries *noun*
a period of a hundred years.
*The building is several **centuries** old.*
■ **sen**-choo-ree

cereal
cereals *noun*
1 a grain crop grown on farms. Wheat, rye, barley, and oats are cereals.

2 a breakfast food made from the grains of a cereal crop.
■ say **sear**-ee-ul

*breakfast **cereal***

certain
adjective
sure, or definite.
*Are you **certain** this is the right train?*
■ opposite **uncertain**

certificate
certificates *noun*
a piece of paper that proves certain facts.
*She received a **certificate** for passing her math exam.*

chain
chains *noun*
metal loops joined together to make a strong cable.

chair
chairs *noun*
a piece of furniture for sitting on.

chalk
chalks *noun*
a soft, white rock made from the fossils of tiny seashells.

challenge
challenges challenging challenged *verb*
to ask someone to try to do something better than you.
*He **challenged** her to a race.*

chameleon
chameleons *noun*
a type of lizard that lives in trees in hot regions and eats insects, rodents, and small birds. Chameleons can change color to match their surroundings.

■ say kuh-**mee**-lee-on

A B C D E F G H I J K L M N O P Q R S T U V W X Y Z

champion
champions *noun*
someone who is the best at a sport.

chance
chances *noun*
an opportunity, or possibility.
*He was given the **chance** to study abroad.*

change
changes changing changed *verb*
1 to become different or to make something different.

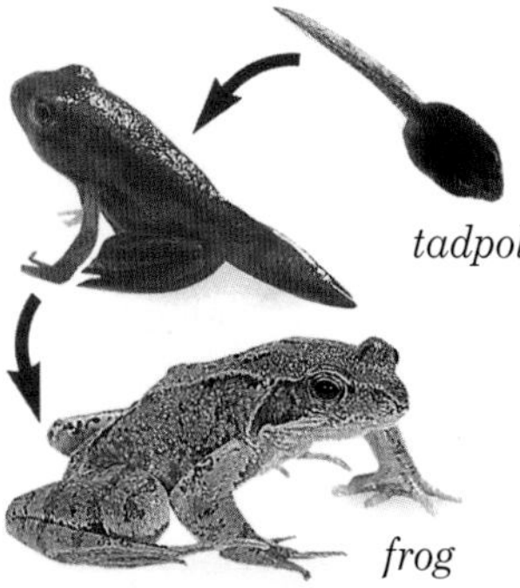

*Tadpoles **change** into frogs.*
2 to give up something in return for something else.
*He **changed** seats.*
change *noun*

change
noun
small amounts of money.

channel
channels *noun*
1 a passage or track for water to flow along.
2 a television or radio station.
*What's on the other **channel**?*

chaos
noun
complete confusion.
■ say **kay**-os

chapter
chapters *noun*
a section of a book.

character
characters *noun*
1 what a person is like.
*A miserable **character**.*
2 a person in a play or film.
*He played the **character** of the young king.*

charity
charities *noun*
an organization that gives aid to those who need it.
*The Red Cross is a **charity**.*

chart
charts *noun*
a map or diagram that provides information.

*A pie **chart** showing popular forms of transportation.*

chase
chases chasing chased *verb*
to run after something or somebody.

cheap
adjective
not costing much money.
■ opposite **expensive**

an expensive ring

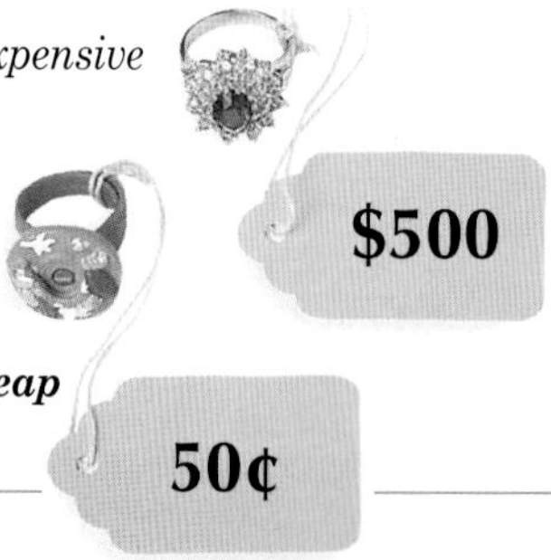

*a **cheap** ring*

cheat
cheats cheating cheated *verb*
to trick someone, or to be dishonest so that you have an advantage over them.

check
checks checking checked *verb*
to look at something to make sure it is all right.
check *noun*

check
checks *noun*
a pattern of regular squares in different colors, often on cloth or paper.

cheek
cheeks *noun*
the side of your face below your eye.

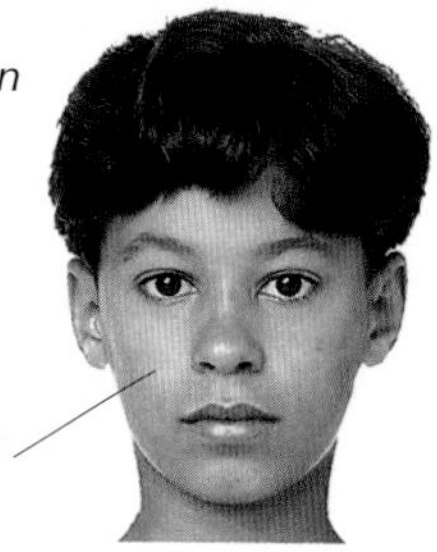

cheer
cheers cheering cheered *verb*
to shout out loudly and happily.

cheer *noun*

cheese
cheeses *noun*
a food made from the thickened parts of milk.

cheetah
cheetahs *noun*
a spotted mammal that belongs to the cat family. Cheetahs live on the dry plains of Africa and prey on other animals. They are extremely fast runners.

chef
chefs *noun*
a person whose job it is to cook and prepare food.
■ say **shef**

chemical
chemicals *noun*
any substance that can change when joined or mixed with another. Chemicals can be natural or manufactured.
■ say **kem**-i-kul

cherish
cherishes cherishing cherished *verb*
to love or value someone or something highly.
*She **cherished** her pet rabbit.*

cherry
cherries *noun*
a round, soft fruit with a small pit in its center.

chess
noun
a board game for two people. The winner is the person who takes the other player's king.

chest
chests *noun*
1 the front of your body below your shoulders and above your stomach.

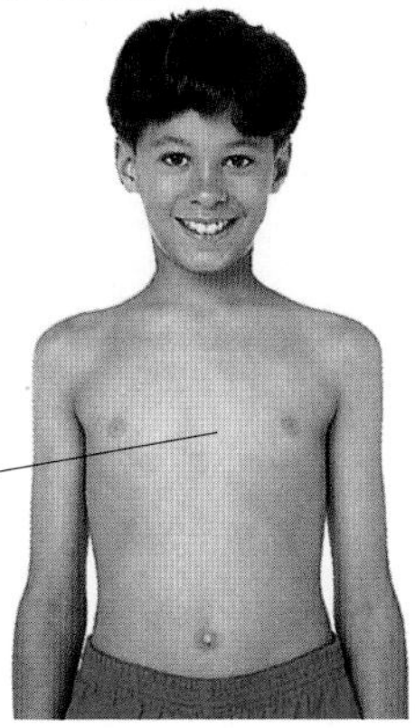

chest

2 a wooden box with a lid for keeping things in.

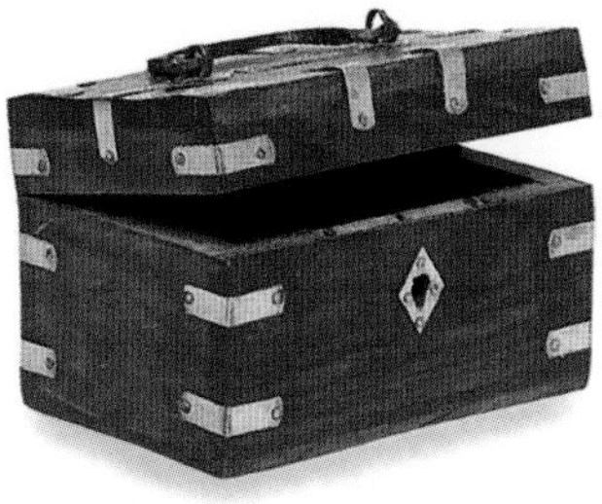

chew
chews chewing chewed *verb*
to use your teeth to break up food.
■ say **choo**

chick
chicks *noun*
a young bird.

child
children *noun*
a young person. A child legally becomes an adult at the age of 18.
■ opposite **adult**

chimney
chimneys *noun*
a pipe above a fire that takes smoke out of a building.

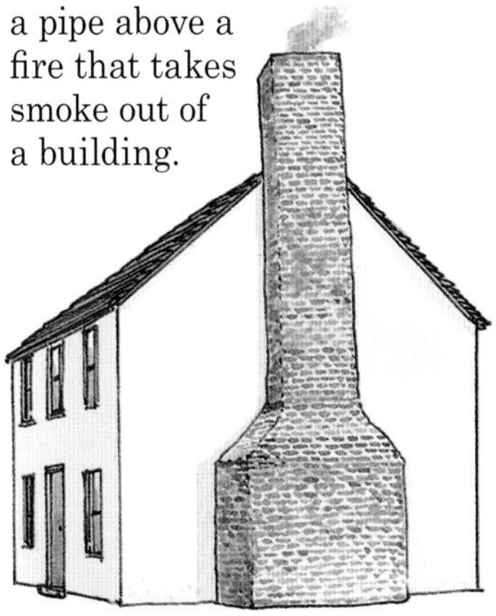

chimpanzee
chimpanzees *noun*
a mammal that lives in groups in forests in central Africa. Chimpanzees are related to the ape family. Their main diet is fruit and nuts, though sometimes they eat small animals.

chin
chins *noun*
the part of your face between your mouth and your neck.

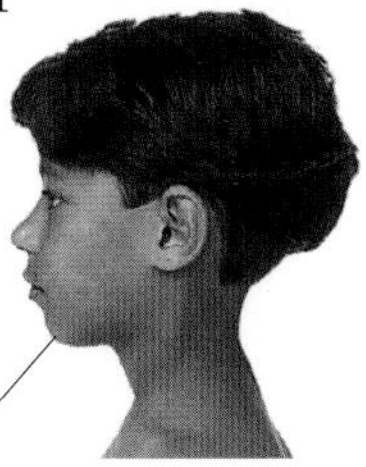

chin

china
noun
a type of delicate pottery made from fine, white clay.

chip
chips *noun*
1 a small piece of something that has broken off something larger.

*wood **chips***

2 a gap or mark on something, showing the place where a small part has broken off.

chip

3 a small piece of material with many tiny electronic circuits printed on it. Chips are used in electronic devices for storing information.

silicon
chip

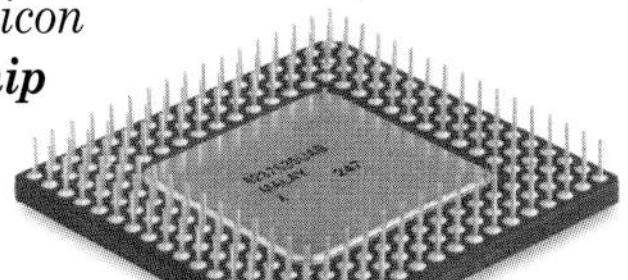

chocolate
chocolates *noun*
a sweet food made from crushed and roasted cocoa beans, milk, and sugar.

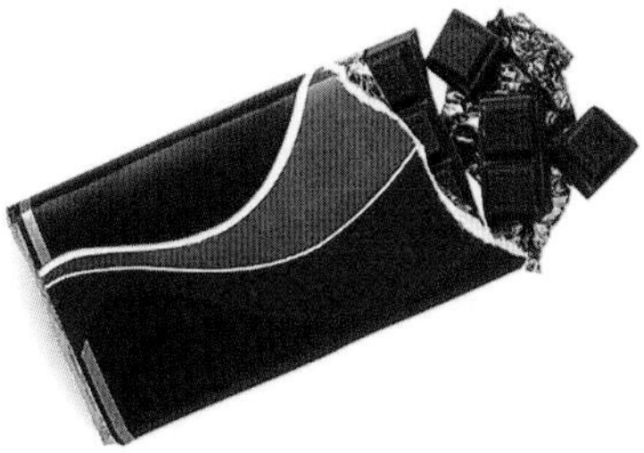

choir
choirs *noun*
a group of singers.
■ say **kwire**

choke
chokes choking choked *verb*
to stop or almost stop breathing.
*The firefighters almost **choked** in the dense smoke.*

choose
chooses choosing chose chosen *verb*
to decide that you want one thing and not another.
*I **chose** the blue pants, instead of the red ones.*
choice *noun*

chop
chops chopping chopped *verb*
to cut up something with a sharp tool.

a b c d e f g h i j k l m n o p q r s t u v w x y z

chopstick
chopsticks *noun*
a thin piece of wood or plastic used in pairs for eating food.

chorus
choruses *noun*
lines in a song that are repeated at the end of each verse.
■ say **kor**-us

Christian
Christians *noun*
a person who believes in and follows the teachings of Jesus Christ and believes that Jesus is the son of God.

church
churches *noun*
a building where Christians hold religious services.

chute
chutes *noun*
a sloping channel for sliding things down.
*Water **chute.***
■ say **shoot**

cigarette
cigarettes *noun*
a rolled-up piece of paper filled with tobacco that can be lit and smoked. Cigarettes can harm your heart and lungs.

cinder
cinders *noun*
a small piece of partly burned wood or coal.

circle
circles *noun*
a flat, exactly round shape.
circular *adjective*

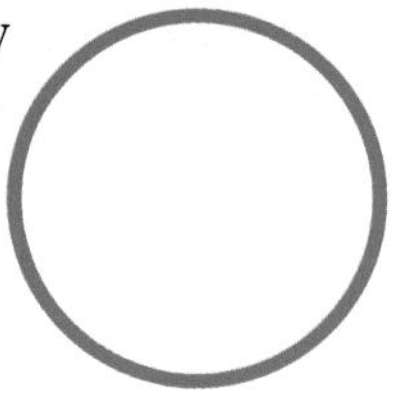

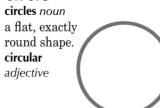

circuit
circuits *noun*
1 any completed path or track.
2 the completed path of an electric current.

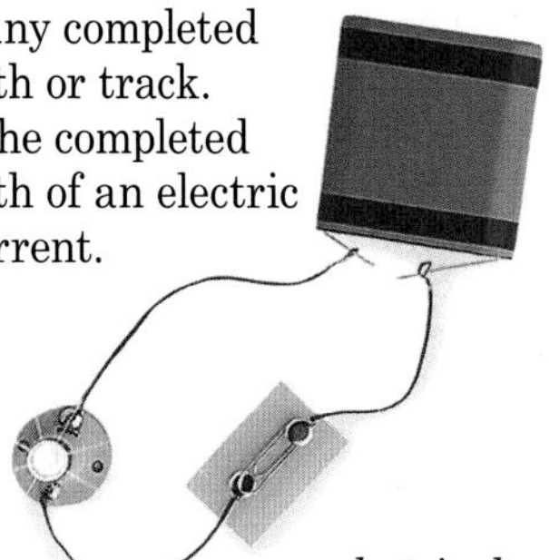

*electrical **circuit***

■ say **sir**-kit

circus
circuses *noun*
a show with clowns, jugglers, and acrobats that travels around the country.

citizen
citizens *noun*
a person who lives in, and belongs to, a particular place.
*An American **citizen**.*

city
cities *noun*
a very large, important town.
*New York, San Francisco, and Chicago are US **cities**.*

civilization
civilizations *noun*
a large group of people living in a well-organized way.
*The Aztec **civilization**.*
■ say siv-uh-li-**zay**-shun

claim
claims claiming claimed *verb*
to say that something is yours.
*She **claimed** first prize in the competition.*

clang
clangs clanging clanged *verb*
to make a deep, loud, ringing sound.
*Bells **clang.***

clank
clanks clanking clanked *verb*
to make a short, metallic sound.

*Chains **clank.***

clap
claps clapping clapped *verb*
to make a short, sharp sound with your hands.

Clap your hands.
clap *noun*

clash
clashes *noun*
a loud, metallic sound.
*Cymbals **clash.***

class
classes *noun*
1 a group of pupils who are taught together.
*My **class** is learning French.*
2 a group of people, animals, or things that are similar to each other in some way.
*Butterflies belong to the **class** of insects.*

classify
classifies classifying classified *verb*
to sort things out into groups of different types.
*Books can be **classified** as fiction or nonfiction.*

clatter
clatters clattering clattered *verb*
to make a repeated rattling sound.

*The plates **clattered** to the floor.*

claw
claws *noun*
one of the long, curved, pointed nails that many animals and birds have on their feet.

*owl's **claw***

clay
noun
a soft, fine earth that is soft and sticky when wet and hard when dried or heated. Clay is used to make pots and bricks.

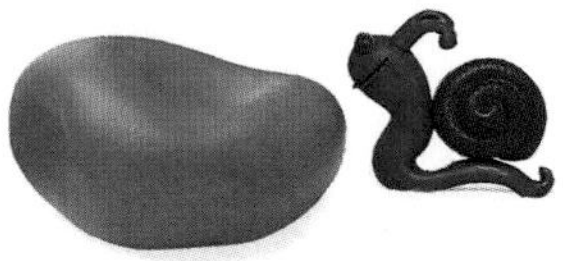

*modeling **clay***

clean
cleans cleaning cleaned *verb*
to remove dirt or stains.

clean
adjective
without any dirt or stains.
***Clean** silver.*
■ comparisons **cleaner cleanest**

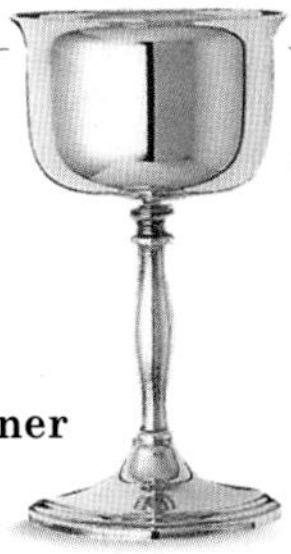

clear
clears clearing cleared *verb*
to move things that are in the way.
*The walkers **cleared** a path through the bushes.*

clear
adjective
1 easy to see through.
*The water was so **clear** that I could see the fish.*

2 easy to understand.
*A **clear** explanation.*
■ comparisons **clearer clearest**

clench
clenches clenching clenched *verb*
to curl up your hand or hands tightly.

*She **clenched** her fists.*

clever
adjective
able to learn and understand things easily.
■ comparisons **cleverer cleverest**

click
clicks clicking clicked *verb*
to make a short, sharp sound with your fingers.
***Clicking** your fingers.*

cliff
cliffs *noun*
the high, steep side of a mountain or rock.

climate
climates *noun*
the type of weather that a place has over a long time.
*The **climate** in southern Africa is hot and dry.*

climb
climbs climbing climbed *verb*
to move upward, using your hands and feet.

climb *noun*

cling
clings clinging clung *verb*
to hold onto something very tightly.

***Clinging** upside down.*

clink
clinks clinking clinked *verb*
to make a soft, ringing sound.
*The ice **clinked** in the glass.*

clip
noun
1 a small metal or plastic object to fasten something together.
*A paper **clip**.*
2 a short section of film.

clock
clocks *noun*
an instrument that shows the time.

clockwise
adverb
moving in the same direction as the hands on a clock.
■ opposite **counterclockwise**

close
closes closing closed *verb*
to shut something.
■ say **kloze**

close
adjective
near to something.
***Close** to the house.*
■ say **klos**
■ comparisons **closer closest**

clot
clots *noun*
a soft lump in a liquid.
*A blood **clot**.*

cloth
noun
woven material that is used to make clothes and other things.

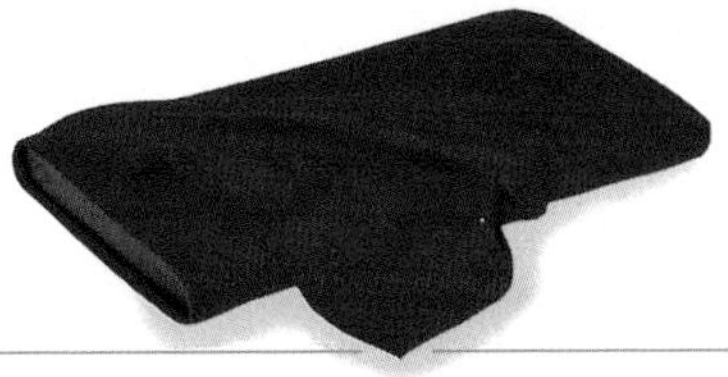

clothes
noun
the things that we wear.
clothing *noun*

cloud
clouds *noun*
a mass of tiny drops of water, or pieces of ice, floating high in the air. The water falls as rain, and the ice falls as hail or snow.

cloudy *adjective*

clown
clowns *noun*
a circus performer who wears funny clothes and makes people laugh.

club
clubs *noun*
1 a group of people who meet together for a purpose, and the place where they meet.
*A drama **club**.*
2 a thick, heavy stick that is used as a weapon.
3 a stick with a shaped head that is used to hit balls in golf (see **sport** on page 197).

clue
clues *noun*
a piece of information that helps to solve a mystery.

a b c d e f g h i j k l m n o p q r s t u v w x y z

clumsy
adjective
moving awkwardly, or without skill.

*The big shoes made her walk in a **clumsy** way.*
■ comparisons **clumsier clumsiest**

coach
coaches *noun*
1 a bus or railroad car.

2 a person who teaches people a special skill.
*A baseball **coach**.*

coach
coaches coaching coached *verb*
to teach somebody how to do something.
*She **coaches** the hockey team every Saturday.*

coal
noun
a hard, brittle, brown or black rock that is burned as a fuel. Coal is made from fossilized plants that died millions of years ago.

coast
coasts *noun*
the seashore.
coastal *adjective*

coat
coats *noun*
1 an item of clothing you wear over your clothes to keep warm outside.

2 an animal's fur.
3 a layer of paint.

cobra
cobras *noun*
a large, poisonous snake that lives in hot regions. Cobras can flatten the bones of their necks into a hood shape when threatened. They kill their prey with a bite that paralyzes them.

cobweb
cobwebs *noun*
a very fine, sticky net made by spiders to trap flies.

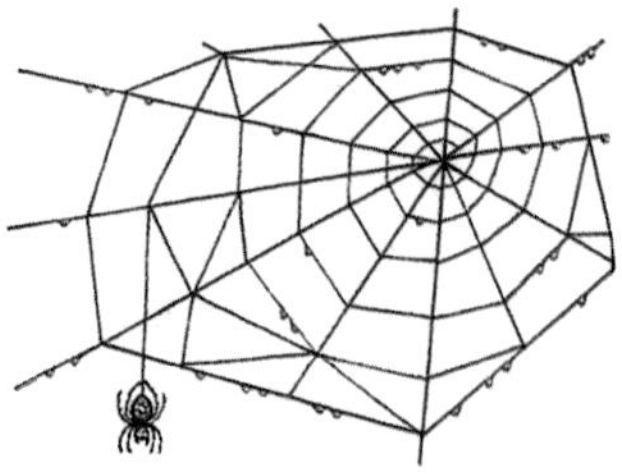

cockatoo
cockatoos *noun*
a parrot with head feathers that it can lift up or flatten. Cockatoos eat fruit, nuts, and plant roots (see **bird** on page 28).

cockpit
cockpits *noun*
the place where a pilot sits in an airplane.

cocoa
noun
a powder made from cocoa beans, the dried seeds of the cacao tree. Cocoa is used to make chocolate and as a flavor in food and drink.

cocoa beans *cocoa drink*
■ say **koe**-koe

coconut
coconuts *noun*
the fruit of the coconut palm tree. The hard, outer shell has a layer of sweet, white, edible flesh inside and contains a thin liquid known as coconut milk.

cod
noun
a large sea fish that lives in shoals close to the ocean floor. Cod use their sharp teeth to eat smaller fish, shellfish, and worms.

code
codes *noun*
1 a set of rules.
*The safety **code**.*
2 a series of signs, symbols, or letters for sending messages secretly or quickly.

*SOS message in Morse **code***

coffee
noun
a drink made from the roasted and crushed seeds of the coffee plant. When roasted, the seeds are called beans.

coffee

*roasted **coffee** beans*

cog
cogs *noun*
1 a wheel with shapes cut out around its edge. Cogs are used together in machines to turn other things around.

2 the tooth-shaped, metal parts around such a wheel.

coil
coils *noun*
something that is twisted around into circles.

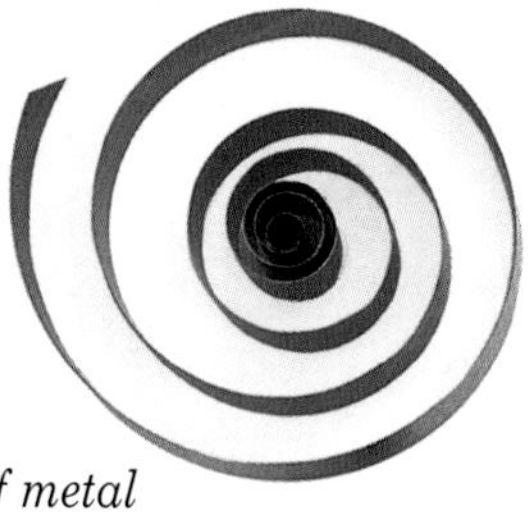

***coil** of metal*

coin
coins *noun*
a piece of money made of metal.

cold
adjective
having a low temperature.
*A **cold** day.*
■ opposite **hot**

cold
colds *noun*
an infection that often makes you sneeze and cough and may give you a sore throat.

collapse
collapses collapsing collapsed *verb*
1 to fall down suddenly.
*The tent **collapsed.***
2 to fold up.
*My umbrella **collapses** so I can put it in my bag.*
collapsible *adjective*

collect
collects collecting collected *verb*
to bring together.
*I **collect** autographs.*
collection *noun*

collide
collides colliding collided *verb*
to crash into something.

*Our cars **collided.***
collision *noun*

color
colors *noun*
what something looks like when light is shining on it. Yellow, green, red, and blue are the names of some colors.

*fruits of different **colors***
colorful *adjective*

column
columns *noun*
1 a tall, vertical, round post that is used as a support or to decorate buildings.

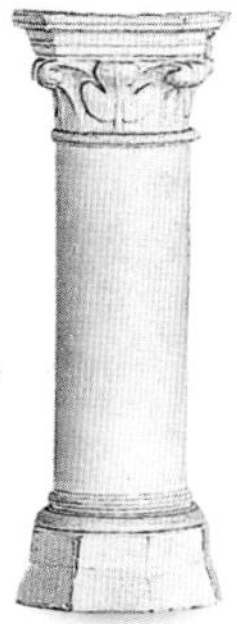

2 a list where things are written underneath each other.

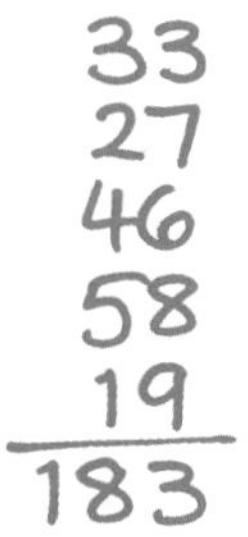

*Adding up a **column** of figures.*

comb
combs *noun*
a piece of wood, metal, or plastic with teeth. A comb is used to arrange hair.

combine
combines combining combined *verb*
to bring things together to make something else.

*Blue and yellow paint **combine** to make green.*
combination *noun*

come
comes coming came *verb*
to move toward, or arrive at, one place from another.
*Hurry up! The train is **coming.***

comedy
comedies *noun*
a movie, play, or radio or television program that makes you laugh.

comet
comets *noun*
a huge ball of dust, ice, and gases that travels around the Sun, often followed by a luminous trail of gases.

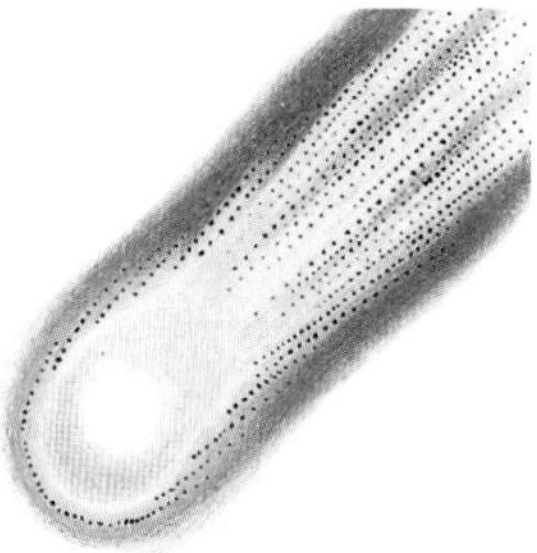

comfortable
adjective
pleasant and easy to sit in or wear.
*A **comfortable** chair.*
■ opposite **uncomfortable**

comic
comics *noun*
a magazine that contains stories told in pictures.

command
commands commanding commanded *verb*
to order someone to do what you want.
*The teacher **commanded** them to sit down.*
command *noun*

common
adjective
often seen, or normal.
*Seagulls are a **common** sight along the coast.*

common sense
noun
the ability to act sensibly in different situations.
***Common sense** stopped us from driving in the fog.*

communicate
communicates communicating communicated *verb*
to talk, write, or send a message to someone else.

***Communicating** by telephone.*
■ say kuh-**myoo**-ni-kate
communication *noun*

community
communities *noun*
a group of people who live together in the same place.
■ say kuh-**myoo**-ni-tee

commuter
commuters *noun*
a person who travels a long distance to and from work every day.
commute *verb*

compact disc
compact discs *noun*
a small, flat circle of plastic that can have sound, or sound, words, and pictures, recorded on it. Compact disc is shortened to CD.

A B C D E F G H I J K L M N O P Q R S T U V W X Y Z

company
noun
1 a group of people who work together to make or sell something.
A computer ***company****.*
2 people or animals with whom you spend time.
My cat is good ***company****.*

compare
compares comparing compared *verb*
to look at several things to see how they are the same and how they are different.
My teacher ***compares*** *me with my sister all the time.*
comparison *noun*

compass
compasses *noun*
1 an instrument that shows the direction you are facing. The magnetic compass needle always points north.

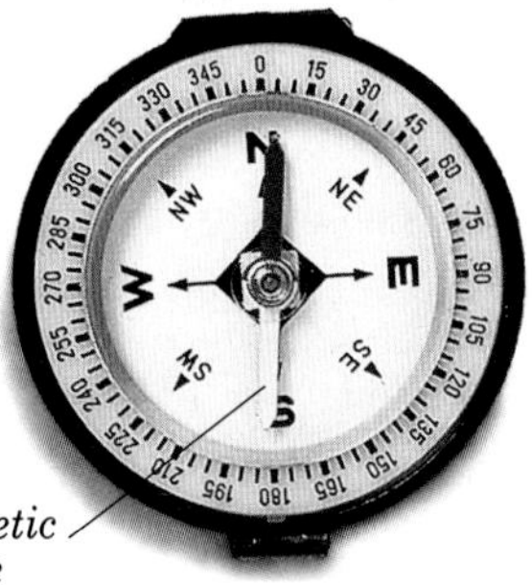

magnetic needle

2 a tool with one fixed leg and one movable leg that is used for drawing circles.

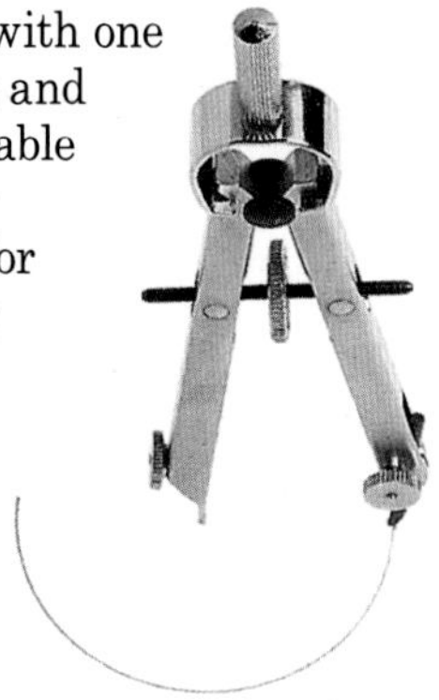

competition
competitions *noun*
an event where one person or a team of people try to do better than their opponents.
Our team came second in the swimming ***competition****.*
compete *verb*

complain
complains complaining complained *verb*
to say that you are not happy about something.
The passengers ***complained*** *about the late train.*

complete
completes completing completed *verb*
to finish something.

Completing *the jigsaw puzzle.*
complete *adjective*

complicated
adjective
hard to understand, or difficult.

a ***complicated*** *knot*
■ opposite **simple**

composer
composers *noun*
a person who writes music.
compose *verb*

compromise
compromises compromising compromised *verb*
to end an argument by both sides deciding to give up part of what they want.
They both wanted to ride the bike, but had to ***compromise*** *by taking turns.*
■ say **kom**-pro-mize
compromise *noun*

compulsory
adjective
that which must be done.
Math is a ***compulsory*** *subject at school.*

computer
computers *noun*
an electronic machine that arranges and stores information digitally, using a set of instructions called a program. Used for communication.

laptop ***computer***

concentrate
concentrates concentrating concentrated *verb*
to think carefully about something.

Concentrating *on a puzzle.*
■ say **kon**-sen-trate
concentration *noun*

concert
concerts *noun*
an event where people sing or play music for an audience to listen to.

conclusion
conclusions *noun*
1 the end of something.
The story's ***conclusion*** *was a happy one.*
2 a decision that is based on all the things you know.
She came to the ***conclusion*** *that it was a sensible idea.*
conclude *verb*

concrete
noun
a mixture of sand, cement, stones, and water, which is used for building.

concrete *paving stones*

condition
noun
1 the state that something is in.

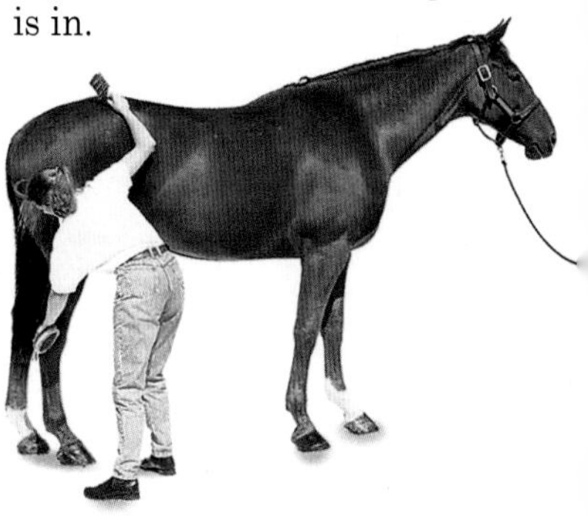

Grooming helps to keep a horse in good ***condition****.*
2 a rule.
He went out on the ***condition*** *that he was back before dark.*

confident
adjective
believing you can do something, or being sure something will happen.
I'm ***confident*** *I'll win.*
confidence *noun*

confiscate
confiscates confiscating confiscated *verb*
to punish by taking something away from someone.
I had my football ***confiscated****.*

confuse
confuses confusing confused
verb
1 to make someone puzzled because of some difficulty in understanding.
*The instructions **confused** me.*
2 to find it difficult to tell one thing from another.
*I always **confuse** the twins.*

congratulate
congratulates congratulating congratulated *verb*
to say to someone that they have done well.

***Congratulating** the winner.*
congratulations *noun*

conifer
conifers *noun*
a tree that has needles instead of leaves. Conifers stay green all year round and have cones instead of flowers.

Scotch pine

connect
connects connecting connected
verb
to link up two things.

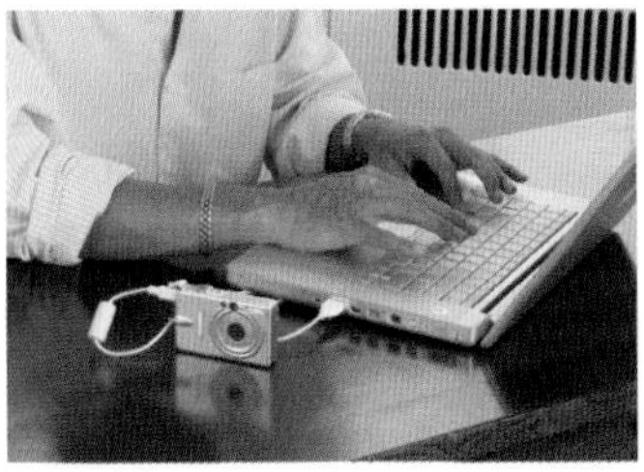

***Connecting** the digital camera to the computer.*
connection *noun*

conscience
consciences *noun*
a feeling inside you that tells you what is right and wrong.
*A guilty **conscience**.*
■ say **kon**-shuns

conscious
adjective
awake and aware of what is happening.
*The man was still **conscious** after the accident.*
■ say **kon**-shus
■ opposite **unconscious**

conservation
noun
the protection and careful use of something. Conservation groups try to protect animals, plants, and the environment.

consider
considers considering considered *verb*
to think about something carefully.
*She **considered** going out, but decided not to.*

considerate
adjective
thoughtful toward other people.

*He is very **considerate**.*

consonant
consonants *noun*
any letter of the alphabet that is not a vowel (see **alphabet** on page 16).

constant
adjective
going on without stopping.
*A **constant** problem.*
constantly *adverb*

constellation
constellations *noun*
a group of stars.

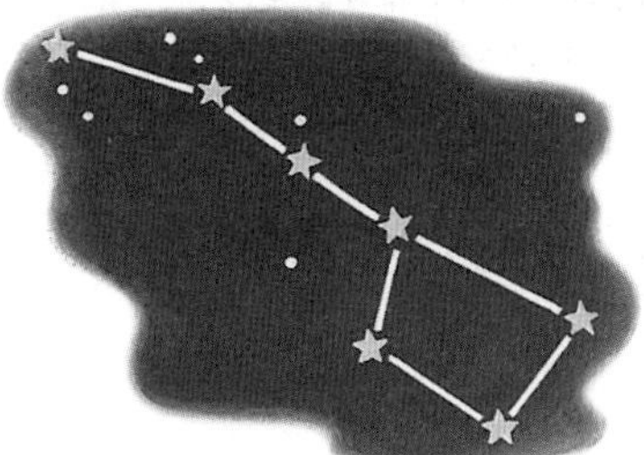

The Big Dipper

construct
constructs constructing constructed *verb*
to build.

***Constructing** a model.*
construction *noun*

contact
contacts contacting contacted
verb
to communicate with someone.
*You can **contact** me by phone while I'm away.*
contact *noun*

contain
contains containing contained
verb
to have something inside.

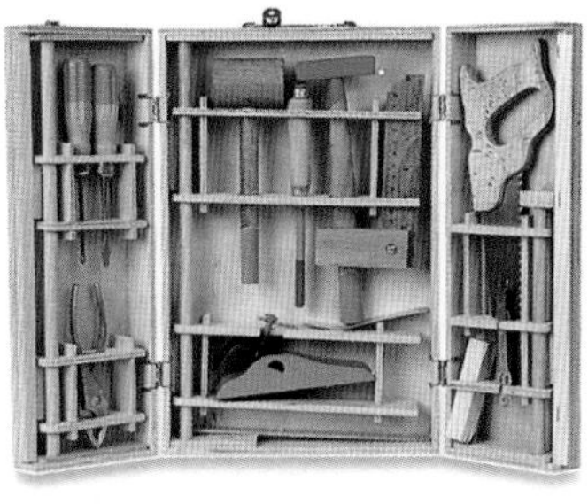

*The box **contains** tools.*
container *noun*

content
contents *noun*
an object inside something, such as a box, bag, or book.
■ say **kon**-tent

*lunch box **contents***

content
adjective
happy and satisfied.
■ say kon-**tent**
contented *adjective*

contest
contests *noun*
a match or competition between people.
*A juggling **contest**.*

continent
continents *noun*
one of seven very large areas of land that usually includes several countries.

*the **continent** of Africa*

continual
adjective
happening often, or without stopping.
***Continual** noise.*
continually *adverb*

continue
continues continuing continued
verb
to carry on.
*The match **continued** after the rain had stopped.*
continuous *adjective*

contract
contracts contracting contracted
verb
to shrink or make smaller.
*Your eye pupils **contract** when light is shone on them.*

contradict
contradicts contradicting contradicted *verb*
to say the opposite of what someone else has said.
*The politicians **contradicted** each other.*
contradiction *noun*

contribute
contributes contributing contributed *verb*
to give a part of something.
*We all **contributed** to the meal.*
contribution *noun*

control
controls controlling controlled
verb
to have the power to make something or someone do what you want.

*These toy planes are **controlled** from the ground.*

convenient
adjective
useful, or easy for you.
*A **convenient** time.*
■ say kuhn-**veen**-nyent
■ opposite **inconvenient**

conversation
conversations *noun*
talk between two or more people.

*A friendly **conversation**.*

convince
convinces convincing convinced
verb
to persuade someone to believe something.
■ say kuhn-**vins**

cook
cooks cooking cooked *verb*
to prepare and heat food so that it can be eaten.
cookery *noun*

cook
cooks *noun*
someone who prepares food.

cool
adjective
slightly cold.

*This box keeps drinks **cool**.*
■ opposite **warm**

cooperate
cooperates cooperating cooperated *verb*
to work with someone in a helpful way.
*We **cooperated** on a project.*
cooperation *noun*

copper
noun
a red-brown colored metal that turns green when it comes into contact with moist air.

***copper** ore*

***copper** pipe*

copy
copies copying copied *verb*
to do the same thing as someone else.
***Copy** me! I'll show you how to do it.*
copy *noun*

coral
corals *noun*
a hard substance that is made of the skeletons of small sea animals. Coral is found in warm seas.

core
cores *noun*
the middle part of something.
*An apple **core**.*

cork
noun
the soft, springy bark of the cork oak tree, which is used to make mats, tiles, and seals for bottles.

***cork** oak bark*

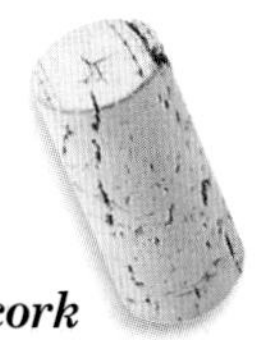

*wine **cork***

corn
noun
a tall plant that grows seeds on large ears. Corn is used as food for people and animals.

corner
corners *noun*
the place where two lines or surfaces meet at an angle.
*A street **corner**.*

correct
adjective
right, with no mistakes.
■ opposite **incorrect**
correction *noun*

corridor
corridors *noun*
a long indoor passage with doors leading off it into rooms.

cosmetics
noun
the things that people use to change the way their skin or hair looks.

lipstick

eye pencil

cost
costs costing cost *verb*
to have a price.
*A computer **costs** hundreds of dollars.*
cost *noun*

costume

costumes *noun*

1 an outfit worn in a particular period of time. *Historical **costume.***

2 an outfit worn for a special reason. *Theatrical **costume.***

gauntlets

silk stockings

16th-century **costume**

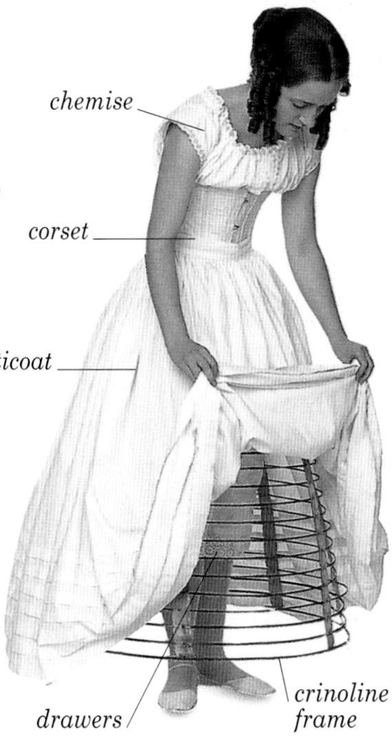

19th-century lingerie

Ancient Greek **costume**

18th-century **costume**

handbag

mules

cloche hat

14th-century **costume**

19th-century **costume**

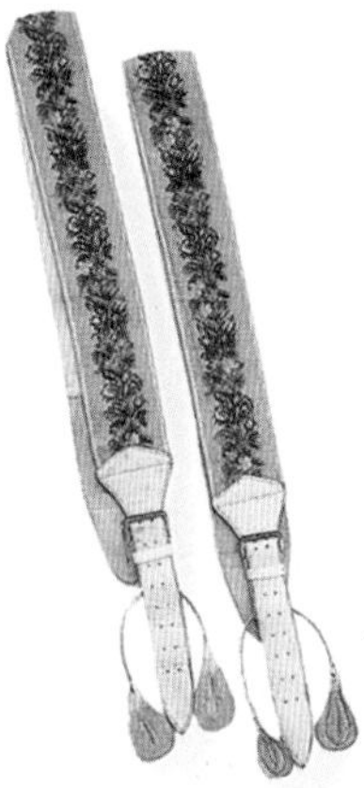

suspenders

cotton
noun
1 soft, white hairs that surround the seeds on a cotton plant.

2 thread or cloth woven from cotton plants.

cotton *thread*

cough
coughs coughing coughed *verb*
to force air out of your lungs with a sharp noise.
■ say **kawf**

council
councils *noun*
a group of people who are chosen to make decisions for an organization or community.

counter
counters *noun*
a flat surface in a store or bank where you are served.
The cheese ***counter****.*

country
countries *noun*
1 an area of land with its own borders, people, and laws.

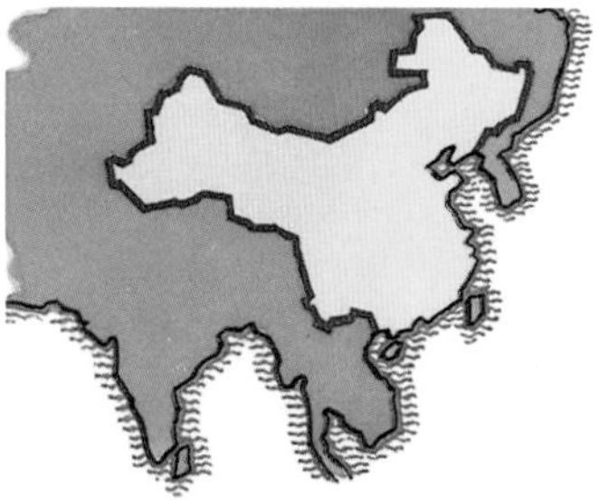

China is one of the biggest ***countries*** *in the world.*
2 land outside towns and cities.

courage
noun
being brave when you are in danger or difficulty.
It takes ***courage*** *to admit that you are wrong.*
■ say **kur**-ij
courageous *adjective*

course
courses *noun*
1 the plan of lessons that students must follow in a school or college subject.
Our history ***course*** *starts on Monday.*
2 the ground where many outdoor sports, such as golf and horse-racing, take place.

horse-racing ***course***

court
courts *noun*
1 the place where it is decided whether people have broken the law and what punishment they should receive.
2 a piece of ground, marked with lines, on which some sports are played.
A badminton ***court****.*

cousin
cousins *noun*
a child of the sister or brother of someone's parent.

cover
covers covering covered *verb*
to put something over or on something else.

Cover *your mouth.*
cover *noun*

cow
cows *noun*
1 a female mammal that eats grass and is reared on farms to produce milk and beef.

2 the female of some large animals, such as elephants and whales.

coward
coward *noun*
a person who is easily scared.

crab
crabs *noun*
a shellfish with 10 legs and a soft body protected by a hard covering. The front pair of legs end in claws, which the crab uses to catch its prey.

coral ***crab***

crack
cracks cracking cracked *verb*
to become damaged so that it splits, but does not break.
The mirror ***cracked*** *when he dropped it.*
crack *noun*

cracker
crackers *noun*
a thin, dry biscuit often eaten with cheese.

crackle
crackles crackling crackled *verb*
to make sharp, snapping noises.

craft
crafts *noun*
1 an activity that requires skill.

paper ***craft***

2 a boat, airplane, or spaceship.

crane
cranes *noun*
1 a machine that lifts and moves heavy objects.

2 a large bird that lives near marshes and lakes and feeds on plants, small insects, and animals. Cranes have a loud, echoing cry.

crowned ***crane***

crash
crashes crashing crashed *verb*
to fall or collide with a loud noise.
The tray of china ***crashed*** *to the floor.*
crash *noun*

crate
crates *noun*
an open container for storing and carrying things, usually bottles.

crawl
crawls crawling crawled *verb*
to move along on your hands and knees.

*Most babies **crawl** before they learn to walk.*

crayfish
noun
a spiny shellfish that looks like a small lobster. Crayfish live under stones during the day and hunt for small fish and insects at night.

crazy
adjective
foolish or strange.
■ comparisons **crazier craziest**

creak
creaks creaking creaked *verb*
to make a low, squeaking sound.
*The door **creaked** open.*

cream
noun
1 the oily part of milk that rises to the top. Cream is often used to make sweets and desserts.

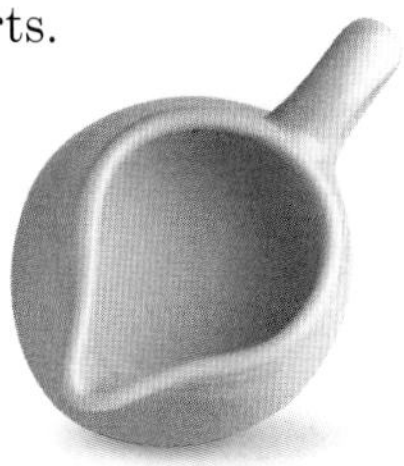

*a pitcher of **cream***

2 a yellow-white color.

crease
creases *noun*
a line or fold, usually made in cloth or paper.

crease *verb*

create
creates creating created *verb*
to design and make something.
*She **created** a beautiful painting.*
■ say kree-**ate**

creature
creatures *noun*
any living thing.

creek
creeks *noun*
a small, narrow inlet or bay in the coast.

creep
creeps creeping crept *verb*
to walk forward very slowly and quietly.

*The cat **crept** up on the birds.*

crew
crews *noun*
1 the people who work on a ship or airplane.
2 a team of people who work together in a job.
*The film **crew** was ready to begin shooting.*

cricket
crickets *noun*
1 a jumping insect that eats plants. Crickets rub their wings together to make a singing sound. They have long back legs for jumping.

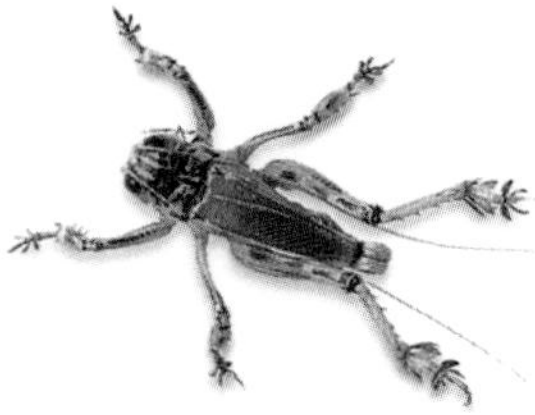

2 a team game played with 11 players in each team. The winning team is the one with the most points, called runs. Runs are scored by the person batting (see **sport** on page 197).

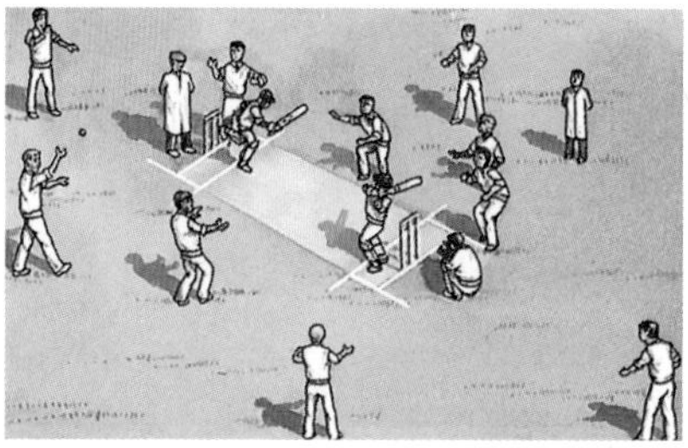

cried
*from the verb **to cry***
*The baby **cried** all last night.*

crime
crimes *noun*
an activity that is against the law.
*Murder is a very serious **crime**.*

criminal
criminals *noun*
a person who takes part in a crime.

crisp
adjective
dry and easily broken into pieces.

***crisp** cookies*

■ comparisons **crisper crispest**

criticize
criticizes criticizing criticized *verb*
to say what you think is wrong with something.
*He was upset when I **criticized** his painting.*
■ say **krit**-i-size
criticism *noun*

crocodile
crocodiles *noun*
a reptile that lives on land and in water. Crocodiles are fierce hunters and hunt at night for fish, mammals, and frogs (see **skeleton** on page 188).

crop
crops *noun*
a vegetable or plant that is grown on a farm for food.
*The potato **crop**.*

cross
crosses crossing crossed *verb*
1 to go over something, from one side to another.
***Crossing** the street.*
2 to put one thing across another.

*He **crossed** his fingers.*

cross
crosses *noun*
an object or sign made by two lines crossing each other.

cross
adjective
angry.

*I get **cross** when people litter.*
crossly *adverb*

crossword
crosswords *noun*
a word puzzle with clues. You write down the answers by putting each letter of the answer into a separate square.

crouch
crouches crouching crouched *verb*
to bend down low, with your legs curled underneath you.

crowd
crowds *noun*
a large number of people gathered close together.

crown
crowns *noun*
a circle of precious metals and jewels. Kings and queens wear crowns on their heads on special occasions.

cruel
adjective
unkind and hurtful.

crumb
crumbs *noun*
a very small piece of food, such as bread, cake, or crackers.

crunch
crunches crunching crunched *verb*
to crush or chew something noisily.
*She **crunched** a juicy apple.*

crush
crushes crushing crushed *verb*
to damage something by squeezing it very hard.

***Crushing** a can.*

crust
crusts *noun*
1 a hard covering.

*pie **crust***

2 the thick, hard outer covering of Earth.

crutch
crutches *noun*
a support for someone who has difficulty walking.

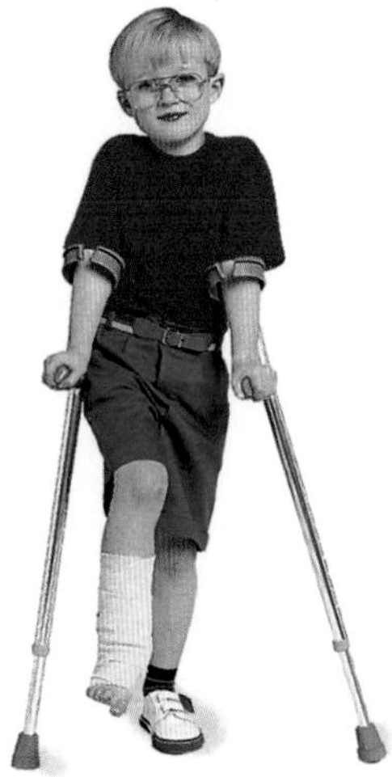

cry
cries crying cried *verb*
to have tears falling from your eyes because you are upset or sad.

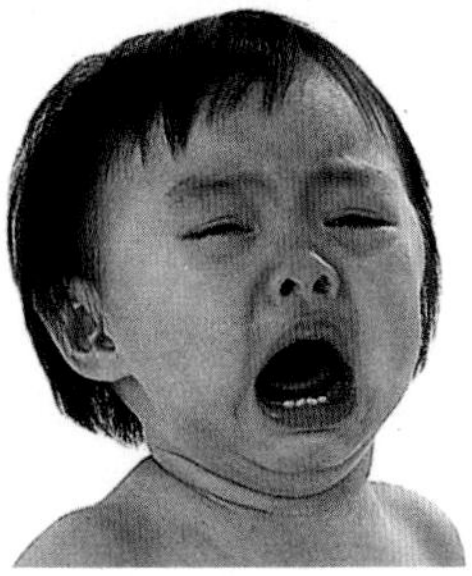

crystal
crystals *noun*
a piece of clear quartz with flat sides that has been formed naturally.

■ say **kris**-tuhl

cub
cubs *noun*
a young mammal, such as a fox, lion, or bear.

*fox **cub***

cube
cubes *noun*
a solid shape with six square sides.

cucumber
cucumbers *noun*
a green vegetable with a crisp, white flesh that grows on vines. Cucumbers are a popular vegetable to use in salads.

cuddle
cuddles cuddling cuddled *verb*
to hug someone in a loving way.

*A mother **cuddling** her daughter.*

culprit
culprits *noun*
a person who has done something wrong.
*The **culprit** had the stolen money in his pocket.*

cunning
adjective
able to trick people.

cup
cups *noun*
a container used for drinking liquids.

cure
cures curing cured *verb*
to make somebody well again after they have been ill.

curious
adjective
1 eager to find out about things.
*She was **curious** to see what was behind the door.*
2 strange but interesting.
*I saw a very **curious** animal the other day.*
■ say **kyoor**-ee-us

curl
curls *noun*
a small, curved piece of hair.
*Her hair is a mass of **curls**.*
curly *adjective*

currency
currencies *noun*
the money of a country.
*The **currency** of France is the euro.*

current
currents noun
1 a flow of water or air moving in a certain direction.
*The **current** carried the boat out to sea.*
2 the flow of electricity through a wire.
*Switch off the **current** when you change a lightbulb.*

curry
curries *noun*
1 a hot, spicy dish made of meat, fish, or vegetables, usually served with rice.

*vegetable **curry***

2 a mixture of hot spices used to flavor food.

***curry** powder*

curtain
curtains *noun*
pieces of material that are hung from a bar and can be pulled across a window or space.

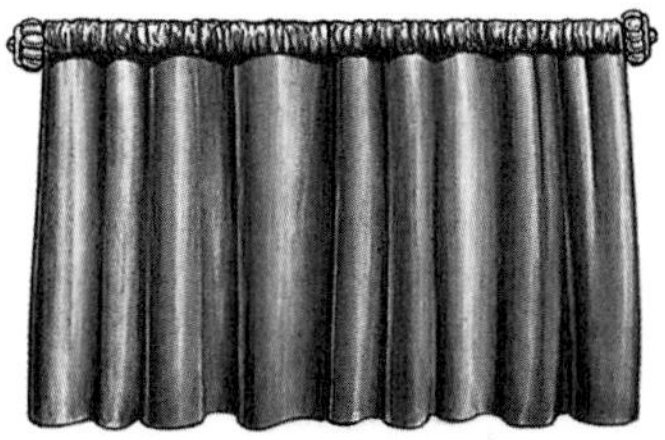

curtsy
curtsies *noun*
a formal way for women to greet someone.

■ also spelled **curtsey**

curve
curves *noun*
a line that bends smoothly.

curve *verb*

cushion
cushions *noun*
a type of pillow used for sitting or leaning on.

customer
customers *noun*
a person who buys something from a store or a company.

cut
cuts cutting cut *verb*
to divide something into parts, using a sharp tool.

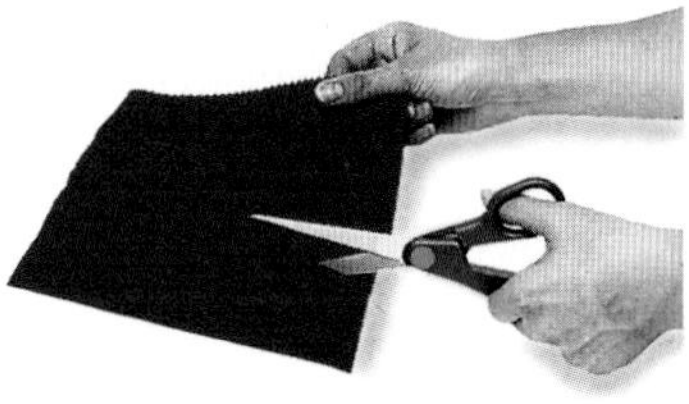

***Cutting** with scissors.*

cut
cuts *noun*
a wound, often made by something sharp.

cutlery
noun
knives, forks, and spoons.

cycle
cycles cycling cycled *verb*
to ride a bicycle.

cycle
cycles *noun*
changes that happen regularly in a particular order.
*The life **cycle** of a butterfly.*

cyclone
cyclones *noun*
a tropical storm with very strong winds.
■ say **sye**-klone

cylinder
cylinders *noun*
a solid or hollow object with circular ends and straight sides (see **shape** on page 182).
■ say **sil**-in-der

cymbal
cymbals *noun*
a round, hollow, brass musical instrument that makes a loud, clashing sound when hit.

Dd

daffodil
daffodils *noun*
a plant that grows from a bulb and has a large, trumpet-shaped flower at the end of each stem.

dagger
daggers *noun*
a knife with a short, sharp, pointed blade, that is used as a weapon.

daily
adverb
every day.
Letters are delivered ***daily****.*
daily *adjective*

dairy
dairies *noun*
a place where milk and cream are stored and butter and cheese are made.

daisy
daisies *noun*
a common plant with white or pink flowers. Daisies close their petals when it is dark. Some kinds of daisy are wild, while others are grown as garden plants.

dam
dams *noun*
a wall built across a river or stream to hold back the flow of water.

damage
damages damaging damaged *verb*
to harm something.

The collision ***damaged*** *the front of the boat.*
■ say **dam**-ij
damage *noun*

damp
adjective
slightly wet or moist.
A ***damp*** *towel.*
■ comparisons **damper dampest**
damp *noun*

dance
dances dancing danced *verb*
to move around to music.

dance *noun*

dandelion
dandelions *noun*
a common, wild plant with a thick root and a single yellow flower on each stem. Fine hairs attached to the seeds mean that the seeds are easily blown away by the wind.

seeds

danger
dangers *noun*
a situation that might be harmful to you.

Danger*—falling rocks.*
dangerous *adjective*

dare
dares daring dared *verb*
1 to challenge someone to do something frightening to show they are not afraid.
2 to be bold or foolish enough to do something frightening or dangerous.

dark
adjective
1 with little or no light.

The street was ***dark*** *away from the streetlights.*
dark *noun*
2 with a lot of black in it.
Dark *blue.*
■ comparisons **darker darkest**
■ opposite **light**

dash
dashes dashing dashed *verb*
to run very quickly for a short distance.
I ***dashed*** *onto the platform, but the train had just left.*

data
noun
facts and figures about something.
■ say **day**-ta

database
databases *noun*
a large amount of information stored in a computer.

date
dates *noun*
1 the day, month, and year.
2 a sweet, sticky fruit with a pit in the middle.

daughter
daughters *noun*
a person's female child.
■ say **daw**-ter

dawdle
dawdles dawdling dawdled *verb*
to move or do things slowly.

*Stop **dawdling**!*

dawn
dawns *noun*
the early part of the day when it starts to become light.

■ opposite **dusk**

day
days *noun*
1 the part of the day when it is light.
■ opposite **night**
2 a period of 24 hours, starting and ending at midnight.

dazed
adjective
not able to think clearly.

*He has a **dazed** look in his eyes.*
■ say **day**-zd

dazzle
dazzles dazzling dazzled *verb*
to shine a bright light into someone's eyes so that they find it difficult to see.
dazzling *adjective*

dead
adjective
no longer living.

***dead** leaves*
■ opposite **alive**

dead
noun
a time when everything is still and quiet.
*The **dead** of night.*

deadly
adjective
able to kill.

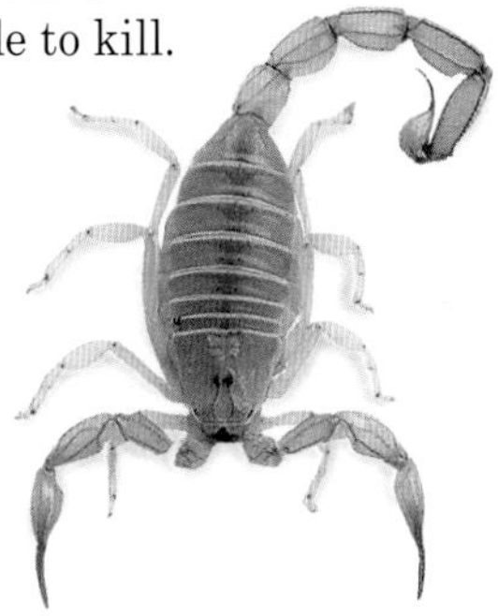

*A scorpion's sting is **deadly**.*

deaf
adjective
not able to hear well or not able to hear at all.
deafness *noun*

dear
adjective
1 loved very much.
*A **dear** friend.*
2 highly respected.
***Dear** Sir.*
■ comparisons **dearer dearest**

debt
debts *noun*
money or a favor that you owe to someone.
■ say **det**

decade
decades *noun*
a period of 10 years.
*The **decade** of 1920 to 1929.*

decay
decays decaying decayed *verb*
to rot away.
*Your teeth will **decay** if you don't take care of them.*
decay *noun*

deceive
deceives deceiving deceived *verb*
to trick a person into thinking something is true when it isn't.
deceit *noun*

decibel
decibels *noun*
a unit of measurement that shows how loud a sound is.
■ say **des**-si-bell

decide
decides deciding decided *verb*
to make up your mind.

*He couldn't **decide** what to eat.*
decision *noun*

deciduous
adjective
losing leaves every year.

■ opposite **evergreen**
■ say de-**sid**-yoo-us

decimal
adjective
counting numbers and parts of numbers in tens.

3.752

*A **decimal** number.*
decimal *noun*

deck
decks *noun*
one of the floors of a ship.

declare
declares declaring declared *verb*
to say something to everyone.
*The judges **declared** the winner at the end of the competition.*

decline
declines declining declined *verb*
to decrease or get worse.
*His health **declined** steadily.*
decline *noun*

decorate
decorates decorating decorated *verb*
to make something look better by painting it or by adding extra things to it.

***Decorating** a room for a party.*
decoration *noun*

decrease
decreases decreasing decreased *verb*
to become smaller.
*The number of whales in the world is **decreasing**.*
■ opposite **increase**

deep
adjective
going down a long way from the surface.

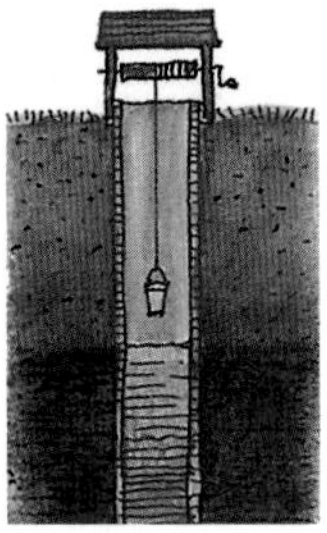

*A **deep** well.*
■ comparisons **deeper deepest**

deer
noun
a mammal with hooves that eats grass and leaves. A male deer is called a stag and has large, branching horns called antlers. A female deer is called a doe.

stag

defeat
defeats defeating defeated *verb*
to win a game or a battle against someone.
*She **defeated** her brother at chess.*

defend
defends defending defended *verb*
to protect or guard.
*Birds stay with their eggs to **defend** them from attackers.*
defense *noun*

define
defines defining defined *verb*
to describe accurately what something means.
definition *noun*

definite
adjective
certain and clear.
*Are you **definite** about that?*
definitely *adverb*

degree
degrees *noun*
1 a unit used to measure temperature and angles. The symbol for a degree is °.
2 a certificate awarded by a college or university.

delay
delays delaying delayed *verb*
to take place later than expected.
*The airplane's departure was **delayed** for seven hours.*
delay *noun*

delete
deletes deleting deleted *verb*
to remove something.

*word **deleted***

deliberately
adverb
on purpose.
*He **deliberately** pushed me.*
deliberate *adjective*

delicate
adjective
easily broken or damaged.

***Delicate** butterfly wings.*

delicious
adjective
tasting very nice.
*The ice cream was **delicious**.*

delighted
adjective
very pleased.

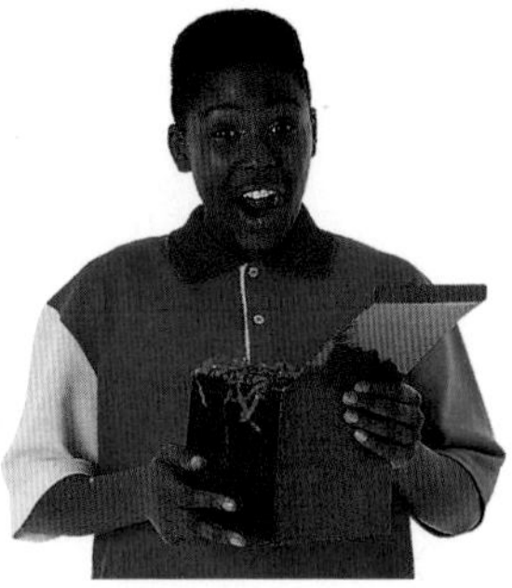

*He was **delighted** with his birthday present.*

deliver
delivers delivering delivered *verb*
to bring something to someone.

*They **delivered** the new sofa this morning.*
delivery *noun*

demand
demands demanding demanded *verb*
to ask someone for something firmly, not expecting them to refuse.
*She **demanded** to know the truth.*
demand *noun*

demolish
demolishes demolishing demolished *verb*
to destroy something.

*They started **demolishing** the house yesterday.*

demonstrate
demonstrates demonstrating demonstrated *verb*
1 to show someone how to do something.
*He **demonstrated** the new food mixer.*
2 to take part in a public rally or meeting to show that you feel very strongly about something.
*The marchers **demonstrated** against the new highway.*
demonstration *noun*

denim
noun
a type of strong, cotton cloth that is often dyed blue.

dense
adjective
thick.
*A **dense** fog.*

dent
dents *noun*
a hollow left in the surface of something after it has been hit or pressed.
*The car had a **dent** in its hood.*
dent *verb*

dentist
dentists *noun*
a person who examines and repairs your teeth.

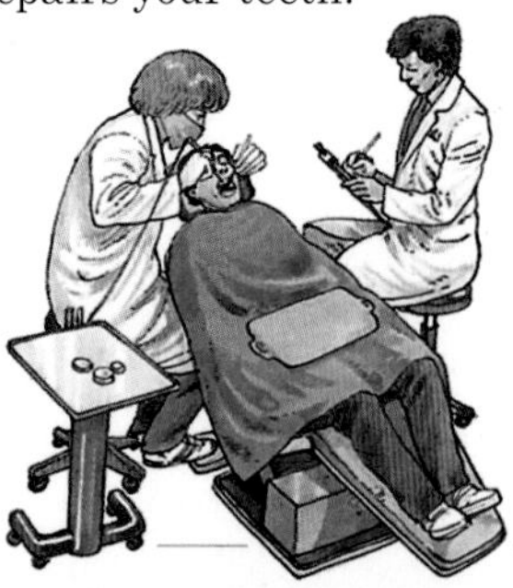

depart
departs departing departed *verb*
to leave.

*The boat **departs** for the island every hour.*
departure *noun*

depend
depends depending depended *verb*
to need or rely on someone or something.
*I'm **depending** on you to be there on time.*

describe
describes describing described *verb*
to say or write what something or someone is like.
***Describe** your house to me.*
description *noun*

desert
deserts deserting deserted *verb*
to leave without permission, not planning to return.
*He **deserted** the army.*
■ say de-**zert**

desert
deserts *noun*
a large, dry, sandy or stony area of land, with few plants.
■ say **dez**-ert

deserve
deserves deserving deserved *verb*
to have earned some reward because of something you have done.
*He **deserved** a rest after working so hard.*

design
designs designing designed *verb*
to plan what something is going to look like.

***Designing** a book.*
design *noun*

desire
desires *noun*
a strong wish.
desire *verb*

desk
desks *noun*
a table that you use for working on, often with drawers in it.

desperate
adjective
1 ready to do anything without thinking of the risks.
*A **desperate** escape plan.*
2 very serious or hopeless.
*A **desperate** situation.*

dessert
desserts *noun*
a sweet dish eaten at the end of a meal.

■ say de-**zert**

destination
destinations *noun*
the place someone or something is going to.

*The plane's **destination** is Australia.*

destroy
destroys destroying destroyed *verb*
to ruin something completely.
*The fire **destroyed** the hut.*
destruction *noun*

detail
details *noun*
a small part of something.
*The news report gave few **details** of the robbery.*
detailed *adjective*

detective
detectives *noun*
a person who investigates crimes.

detergent
detergents *noun*
a soapy powder or liquid that is used for cleaning things such as clothes or dishes.
■ say de-**ter**-jent

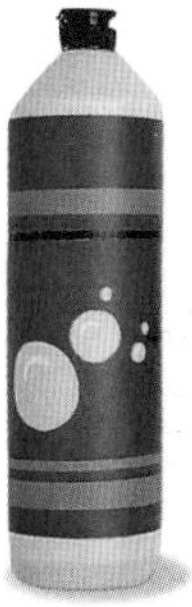

*bottle of **detergent***

determined
adjective
not letting anything stop you from doing something.

*He was **determined** to reach the top of the mountain.*
determination *noun*

develop
develops developing developed *verb*
to grow and become more complete.
*The bud **developed** into a beautiful flower.*
development *noun*

device
devices *noun*
a machine or tool invented for a special purpose.

*A corkscrew is a **device** for pulling corks out of bottles.*

dew
noun
small drops of water that form on cool surfaces outside during the night.

A B C D E F G H I J K L M N O P Q R S T U V W X Y Z

diagonal
adjective
sloping at an angle from one edge to another.

diagram
diagrams *noun*
a drawing or plan that shows or explains something.

*A **diagram** of the inside of a volcano.*

dial
dials *noun*
the face of a measuring device that has numbers on it.

diameter
diameters *noun*
the width of a circle, measured by a straight line.

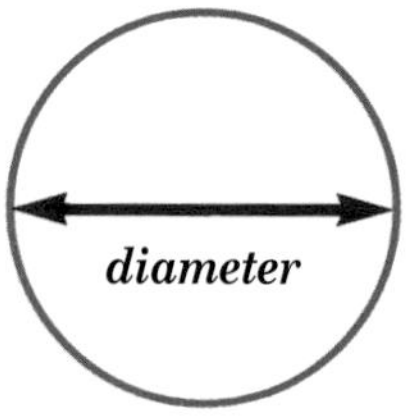

diary
diaries *noun*
a book in which you write down your thoughts and daily events (see **time** on page 216).

dice
noun
cubes with a different number of dots, from one to six, on each side. Dice are used in indoor games. A single cube is called a die.

dictionary
dictionaries *noun*
a book that contains an alphabetical list of words with their meanings.

die
dies dying died *verb*
to stop living.
death *noun*

diet
diets *noun*
the food that you usually eat.

*Fruit and vegetables are part of a healthy **diet**.*

different
adjective
not like something else.

*Two **different** shells.*
■ opposite **same**
difference *noun*

difficult
adjective
hard to do.
*It was **difficult** to cut the string with blunt scissors.*
■ opposite **easy**

dig
digs digging dug
verb
to make a hole in the ground.

digest
digests digesting digested *verb*
to break food down so that the body can use it.
■ say die-**jest**
digestion *noun*

digit
digits *noun*
1 a number from zero to nine, shown as a figure rather than written in words.
2 a finger or toe.

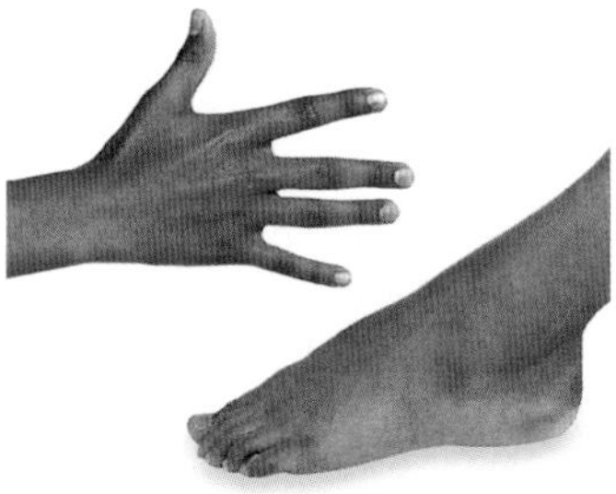

digital
adjective
1 showing number information in figures.
2 storing information using the digits zero and one.

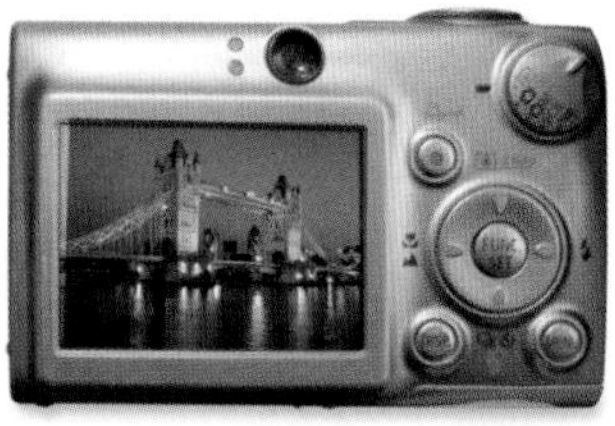

***digital** camera*

dilute
dilutes diluting diluted *verb*
to make thinner or weaker, often by adding water.
dilution *noun*

dim
adjective
not bright.
*A **dim** lightbulb.*
■ comparisons **dimmer dimmest**

dinghy
dinghies *noun*
a small, open sailing boat (see **boat** on page 31).
■ say **ding**-ee

dingo
dingoes *noun*
a wild dog that lives in Australia. Dingoes hunt alone or in small packs and eat birds, reptiles, and small animals.

dinner
dinners *noun*
the main meal of the day.

dinosaur
dinosaurs *noun*
one of a group of land reptiles that lived on Earth, at different times, for more than 150 million years. The last dinosaurs died out 65 million years ago.

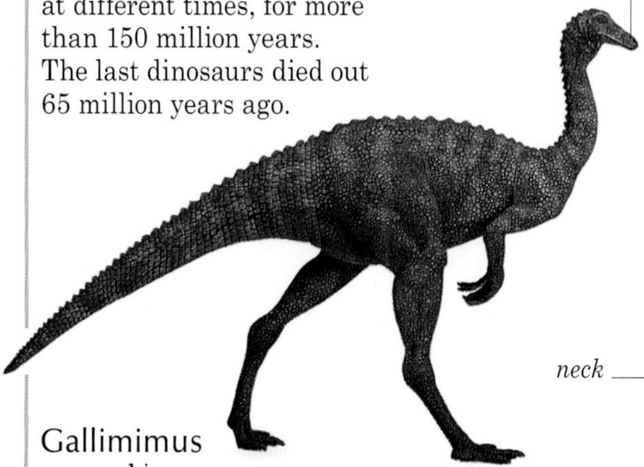

Gallimimus
■ say **gal**-i-**meem**-us

Triceratops
■ say try-**ser**-a-tops

Stegosaurus
■ say **steg**-uh-**sor**-rus

Barosaurus
■ say **bar**-oh-**soh**-rus

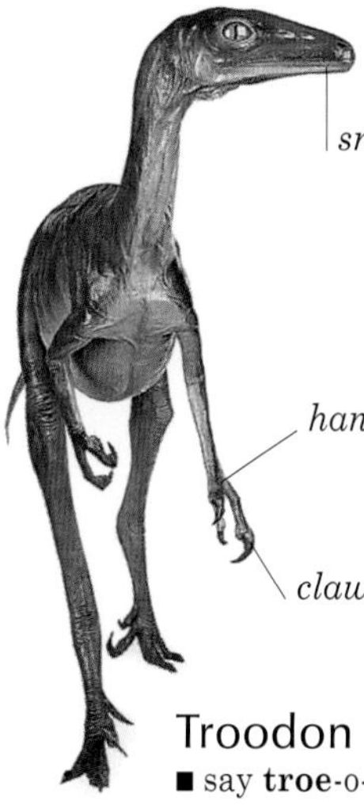

Troodon
■ say **troe**-o-don

Euoplocephalus
■ say **yoo**-oh-plo-**sef**-al-us

Deinonychus
■ say die-**non**-i-kus

Heterodontosaurus
■ say **het**-er-oh-**dont**-oh-**sor**-rus

Corythosaurus
■ say koh-rith-oh-**sor**-rus

Tyrannosaurus rex
■ say tie-**ran**-oh-**sor**-rus **reks**

A B C D E F G H I J K L M N O P Q R S T U V W X Y Z

dip
dips dipping dipped *verb*
1 to put something into a liquid or a soft substance and then take it out again immediately.

*Fruit **dipped** in chocolate.*
2 to slope downward.
*The road **dips** slightly here.*

direct
directs directing directed *verb*
1 to show or tell someone how to get to a particular place.

*He **directed** the tourist to the castle.*
direction *noun*
2 to be in charge of the making of a play or a movie.

***Directing** a movie.*

direct
adjective
going the shortest way.
*A **direct** route.*

directory
directories *noun*
a book that contains information about people and organizations, usually listed in alphabetical order.
*A telephone **directory**.*

dirty
adjective
not clean.

■ comparisons **dirtier dirtiest**
■ opposite **clean**

disabled
adjective
not having a limb, or being without power or strength, especially of movement, in part of your body because of injury or disease.
disability *noun*

disagree
disagrees disagreeing disagreed *verb*
to think differently from someone about something.
*We always **disagree**.*
■ opposite **agree**
disagreement *noun*

disappear
disappears disappearing disappeared *verb*
to go out of sight.

*The rabbit **disappeared** into its burrow.*
■ opposite **appear**
disappearance *noun*

disappoint
disappoints disappointing disappointed *verb*
to make someone sad by not doing something they expected.
*I **disappointed** my friends by not going to the game with them.*
disappointed *adjective*

disaster
disasters *noun*
a terrible event that may cause damage and suffering.

*Floods are natural **disasters**.*
■ say di-**zas**-tur
disastrous *adjective*

disc
discs *noun*
an object for recording sound.
*A compact **disc**.*

discover
discovers discovering discovered *verb*
to find or find out.

*The pirates **discovered** a chest of buried treasure on the island.*

discuss
discusses discussing discussed *verb*
to talk about something with someone else.
*We **discussed** where to go for our vacation.*
discussion *noun*

disease
diseases *noun*
an illness.
*Measles is an infectious **disease**.*

disgraceful
adjective
so bad that the person involved should be ashamed.
*Do this work again—it's **disgraceful**!*

disguise
disguises *noun*
an outfit that you wear to hide who you really are.

■ say dis-**gize**
disguise *verb*

disgusting
adjective
very unpleasant.
*There was a **disgusting** smell coming from the drains.*

dish
dishes *noun*
1 a plate or bowl that is used to hold food.

*A **dish** for serving vegetables.*

2 one part of a meal.

*The main **dish**.*

dishonest
adjective
telling lies or stealing.
■ opposite **honest**

disinfectant
disinfectants *noun*
a chemical that is used for killing germs.
disinfect *verb*

dislike
dislikes disliking disliked *verb*
to think someone or something is not very nice.

*She **disliked** the smell of the perfume.*
■ opposite **like**

disobey
disobeys disobeying disobeyed *verb*
to refuse to do something that someone tells you to do.
*You mustn't **disobey** orders.*
■ opposite **obey**
disobedient *adjective*

disperse
verb
to scatter widely.
*The dandelion seeds were **dispersed** by the wind.*
dispersal *noun*

disposable
adjective
for throwing away after use.

dissolve
dissolves dissolving dissolved *verb*
to mix something with water or another liquid so it becomes part of the liquid.

*A tablet **dissolving** in water.*

distance
distances *noun*
the space measured between two places.

*The signpost shows the **distance** between Denver and Atlanta.*

distinguish
distinguishes distinguishing distinguished *verb*
to be able to tell the difference between things.
*Can you **distinguish** between the twins?*
■ say di-**sting**-gwish

distract
distracts distracting distracted *verb*
to take someone's attention away from what they are doing.
*The noise outside **distracted** her from her work.*

distribute
distributes distributing distributed *verb*
to give something out.

*The teacher **distributed** the books to the children.*

district
districts *noun*
an area in a town, city, county, or country, which is sometimes marked out for a particular purpose.
*School **district**.*

disturb
disturbs disturbing disturbed *verb*
to interrupt the peace and quiet of a place or person.

*The noise of the drill **disturbed** her.*
disturbance *noun*

ditch
ditches *noun*
a long channel that drains away water.

diver
divers *noun*
a person who swims beneath the water, often taking an air supply to breathe with.

*scuba **diver***

divide
divides dividing divided *verb*
1 to split something up into parts.

*The cheese is **divided** into eight portions.*

2 to separate a number into equal parts.

8÷2=4

*Eight **divided** by two equals four.*
division *noun*

display
displays displaying displayed *verb*
to put something in a place where people can look at it.

***Displaying** paintings.*

dive
dives diving dived *verb*
to jump headfirst into water.

divorce
divorces divorcing divorced *verb*
to end a marriage legally.
divorce *noun*

dock
docks *noun*
1 a place where ships load and unload cargo.
dock *verb*

2 the place in a courtroom where the person on trial stands or sits.

doctor
doctors *noun*
a person who is trained to treat sick or injured people.

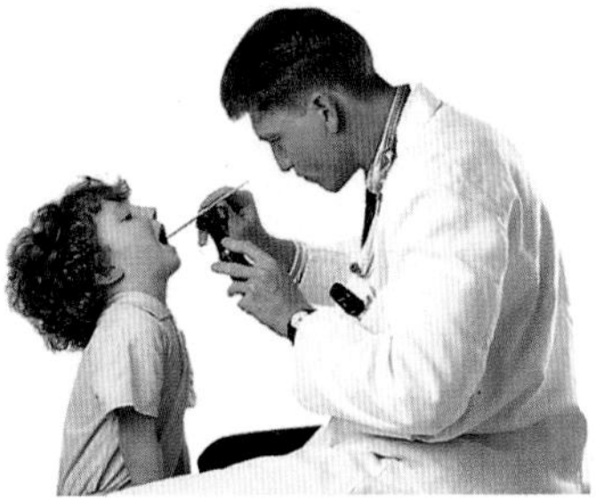

dodge
dodges dodging dodged *verb*
to avoid being hit by something by moving out of the way very quickly.
*She **dodged** the ball coming toward her.*

dog
dogs *noun*
a mammal that is often kept as a pet. Dogs mainly eat meat and can be trained to perform certain tasks, such as herding sheep. Dogs are related to wolves and foxes (see **pet** on page 148).

*collie **dog***

doll
dolls *noun*
a toy that is made to look like a human being.

dolphin
dolphins *noun*
a fish-eating sea mammal. Dolphins breathe air, so they must swim to the surface often. They are friendly animals and are known for their intelligence. Dolphins are a type of small whale.

■ say **doll**-fin

domino
dominoes *noun*
a small, flat piece of wood or plastic with dots marked on it. Dominoes are used in a table game, which is also called dominoes.

donation
donations *noun*
a gift, usually of money, that is made to a charity or another organization.
*He made a large **donation**.*

donkey
donkeys *noun*
a member of the horse family that has long ears and a soft, furry coat. Donkeys eat grass and in some countries are used for carrying people and goods.

door
doors *noun*
a piece of wood, glass, or metal that opens and shuts to provide a way into a room, cupboard, building, or vehicle.

dot
dots *noun*
a very small, round spot.
*Ladybugs have **dots** on them.*

double
adjective
twice as much.

*A **double** six.*
■ say **dub**-ul

doubtful
adjective
not sure, or unlikely.
*He was **doubtful** about his chances of winning.*
■ say **dout**-ful
doubt *verb*

dough
noun
a mixture of flour and either milk or water that is used to make bread or cakes.
■ say **doh**

doughnut
doughnuts *noun*
a sweet, round cake made from dough, which is fried in fat and covered in sugar.

■ say **doh**-nut

dove
doves *noun*
a bird that is a member of the pigeon family. Doves are often used as a symbol of peace.

down
adverb
to a lower place.

*The leaves floated **down**.*
■ opposite **up**

downcast
adjective
sad and upset.
*He looked **downcast**.*

downhill
adjective
sloping down.

***downhill** skiing*

downpour
downpours *noun*
a large, heavy amount of rain.

downstairs
adverb
to a lower floor.

*He ran **downstairs** to answer the phone.*

downstairs
adjective
on a lower floor than the one you are on.

*A noisy **downstairs** party.*

doze
dozes dozing dozed *verb*
to sleep lightly for a short time.
*She **dozed** in the chair.*

dozen
dozens *noun*
12 of something.

*A **dozen** candles.*

drag
drags dragging dragged *verb*
to pull something along the ground.

*He **dragged** his schoolbag behind him.*

dragon
dragons *noun*
a fierce, imaginary animal in myths and fairy tales, that breathes fire and has a large, scaly body and wings.

drain
drains *noun*
a pipe or channel that takes away waste water and other liquids.

drain
drains draining drained *verb*
to flow away slowly.
*The water **drained** away.*

drama
dramas *noun*
1 a play.
*My favorite **drama** is Shakespeare's* Hamlet.
2 plays, or the theater in general.
3 an exciting or frightening event.
*There was **drama** today when the school caught fire.*

draw
draws drawing drew drawn *verb*
1 to make a picture or diagram with a pencil or crayon.

2 to move together by pulling.
*He **drew** the curtains.*

dragonfly
dragonflies *noun*
a long, thin insect with two pairs of wings, often found near ponds and rivers. Dragonflies feed on small flying insects, which they catch with their legs while flying.

drawer
drawers *noun*
a box-shaped container that slides in and out of a piece of furniture. Drawers are used to store things in.

*A chest of **drawers**.*

dream
dreams dreaming dreamed or **dreamt** *verb*
1 to have thoughts and pictures going through your mind while you are asleep.

*I **dreamed** that I was petting a lion.*
2 to hope for something.
*She **dreamed** of traveling around the world.*
dream *noun*

drench
drenches drenching drenched *verb*
to soak with water.
*The rain **drenched** her.*

dress
dresses dressing dressed *verb*
to put on clothes.

*My little sister can **dress** herself.*
■ opposite **undress**

dress
dresses *noun*
a piece of clothing that has a top joined to a skirt.

dried
from the verb ***to dry***
He ***dried*** *his clothes outside.*

dried
adjective
with water or liquid removed.

dried *apricots*

drift
drifts drifting drifted *verb*
1 to move slowly without control.
The boat ***drifted*** *along.*
2 to be carried along by water or air.

drift
drifts *noun*
a pile of snow or sand made by the wind.

drill
drills drilling drilled *verb*
to bore a hole in something using a drill.

electric ***drill***

drill
drills *noun*
1 a tool used to make holes.
2 a practice.
Fire ***drill.***

drink
drinks drinking drank drunk *verb*
to swallow liquid.

drink *noun*

drip
drips dripping dripped *verb*
to fall slowly, drop by drop.
Water ***dripped*** *from the faucet.*

drip *noun*
dripping *adjective*

drive
drives driving drove driven *verb*
to make a car, train, or other vehicle move.
They ***drove*** *along the country roads.*
drive *noun*

drizzle
drizzles drizzling drizzled *verb*
to rain in small, fine drops, like a mist.
drizzle *noun*

droop
droops drooping drooped *verb*
to hang down in a weak or tired way.

The tulip ***drooped*** *over the edge of the vase.*
■ rhymes with **hoop**

drop
drops *noun*
1 a small amount of liquid.

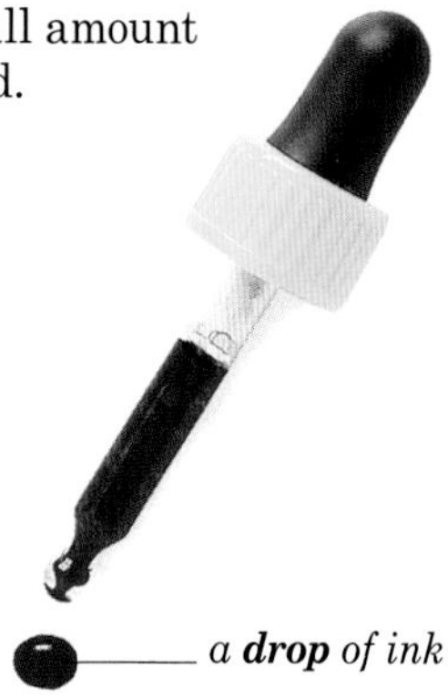

a ***drop*** *of ink*

2 a long way down.
It was a big ***drop*** *from the bridge to the river below.*

drop
drops dropping dropped *verb*
to let something fall.

He ***dropped*** *his sunglasses.*

drought
droughts *noun*
a period of time when there is not enough rain.

Many crops died during the ***drought.***
■ say **drout**

drown
drowns drowning drowned *verb*
to die because you have gone under water and have not been able to breathe.

drowsy
adjective
sleepy.

drug
drugs *noun*
1 a chemical substance used as a medicine to treat people who are sick or in pain.
2 an illegal chemical substance that people take to make them feel different. Taking this kind of drug is dangerous and can kill you.

drum
drums *noun*
a hollow musical instrument that has a covering across one or both ends. You hit the drum with sticks, special wire brushes, or your hands to make different sounds.

Japanese ***drum***

drum
drums drumming drummed *verb*
to tap or hit continuously, or to play a drum.

dry
adjective
not wet.
*They came in from the rain and changed into **dry** clothes.*
■ comparisons **drier driest**
■ opposite **wet**
dry *verb*

duck
ducks *noun*
a water bird that has oily, waterproof feathers and webbed feet for swimming. Ducks eat fish, small plants, and small animals. Male ducks are called drakes.

duck
(female)

drake
(male)

duet
duets *noun*
a piece of music to be played or sung by two people.

*A violin **duet**.*
■ say doo-**et**

dug
*from the verb **to dig***
*Our dog **dug** up part of the lawn this morning.*

dull
adjective
1 not bright.
*It was a **dull** day.*
2 not exciting.
*I thought the movie was very **dull**.*
■ comparisons **duller dullest**

dummy
dummies *noun*
a model of a person's body, often used for making or displaying clothes.

dressmaker's
dummy

dump
dumps dumping dumped *verb*
to put something down or throw it away carelessly.
*They **dumped** the shopping bags on the floor.*

dune
dunes *noun*
a hill of sand, near the sea or in a desert, that is made by the wind.

dungeon
dungeons *noun*
an underground prison cell in an old building, such as a castle.

■ say **dun**-jun

duplicate
duplicates *noun*
an exact copy.

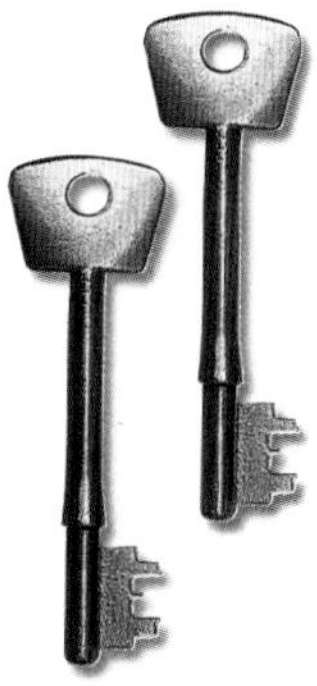

*One key is a **duplicate** of the other.*
■ say **doo**-pli-kat

during
preposition
1 at some time in.
*I fell asleep **during** the movie.*
2 the whole time of.
***During** the summer months we go swimming in the sea.*

dusk
noun
the time of evening when it starts to get dark.
■ opposite **dawn**

dust
noun
tiny pieces of dirt that float in the air and settle on surfaces.
dusty *adjective*

duty
duties *noun*
things that you ought to do or feel you should do.
*It is the guard's **duty** to make sure the doors are locked.*

dvd
noun
a plastic disc that contains digital recordings of sounds and images (see **abbreviations** on page 246).

dye
dyes dyeing dyed *verb*
to change the color of something by soaking it in colored liquids.

*These balls of yarn have been **dyed** different colors.*
dye *noun*

dynamite
noun
a powerful substance that explodes when it is burned.

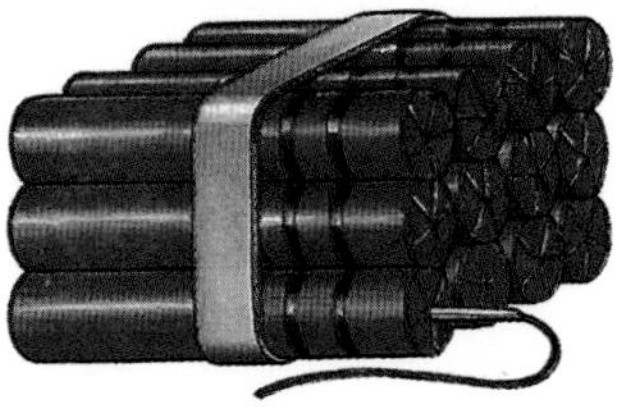

dynasty
dynasties *noun*
a series of rulers from the same family.
■ say **die**-nu-stee

dyslexia
noun
a learning difficulty that can affect reading, writing, or spelling.
■ say dis-**lek**-see-uh
dyslexic *adjective*

Ee

each
adjective
every single one.
*They **each** received a present.*

eager
adjective
wanting to do or have something very much.
*The riders were **eager** to start the race.*
eagerly *adverb*

eagle
eagles *noun*
a large bird of prey that lives in mountainous areas. Eagles eat animals and birds and have good eyesight for spotting prey a long way off.

golden ***eagle***

early
adverb
1 near the beginning.
*The hero dies **early** in the film.*
2 before the expected time.
*He arrived **early** for the show.*
■ comparisons **earlier earliest**
■ opposite **late**

earn
earns earning earned *verb*
to get something because you have worked for it or deserve it.
*They **earned** some extra money by washing cars.*

earring
earrings *noun*
a piece of jewelry that can be attached to, or hung from, the earlobe (see **jewelry** on page 112).

ear
ears *noun*
1 the part of your body that you hear with.

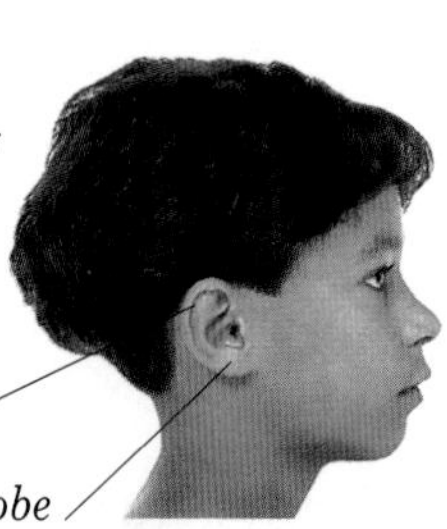

2 the top of a cereal stalk where the seeds grow.

***ear** of wheat*

Earth
noun
the planet that we live on.

earth
noun
1 the surface of the land or ground.
2 the material that plants grow in.

earthquake
earthquakes *noun*
a violent shaking of the ground, because of movement from within the Earth.

east
noun
one of the four main compass directions. East is the direction in which the Sun rises.

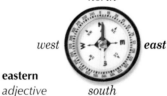

eastern
adjective

easy
adjective
simple, not difficult.
■ comparisons **easier easiest**
■ opposite **difficult**

eat
eats eating ate eaten *verb*
to take in food through your mouth.

echo
echoes *noun*
a sound that bounces off a surface and repeats itself.
*My voice **echoed** in the cave.*
■ say **eh**-ko
echo *verb*

eclipse
eclipses *noun*
1 a time when the Moon comes between the Earth and the Sun, hiding the Sun's light.

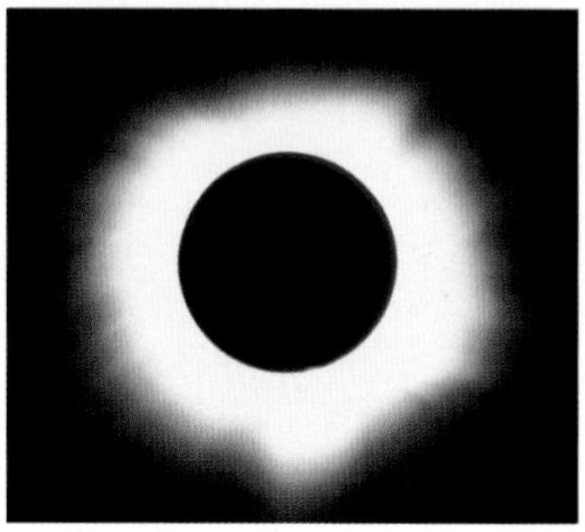
*An **eclipse** of the Sun.*

2 a time when the Earth comes between the Sun and the Moon, hiding the Moon's light.
*An **eclipse** of the Moon.*

ecology
noun
the study of how animals, plants, and humans affect one another and how they live in their environment.
■ say ee-**kol**-o-jee

edge
edges *noun*
the border of something.

*Flowers lined the path's **edge**.*

edible
adjective
safe to eat.
*Are these mushrooms **edible**?*

educate
educates educating educated
verb
to teach someone so that they learn and understand things.
education *noun*

eel
eels *noun*
a long, thin fish that lives in rivers and the sea. Eels eat tiny sea plants, animals called plankton and other fish.

ribbon ***eel***

effect
effects *noun*
the result of an action or event on another person or thing.
Seeing the crash on the news had a bad ***effect*** *on me.*

effort
efforts *noun*
the energy you need to do something.

It took a lot of ***effort*** *to lift the suitcase.*

egg
eggs *noun*
a rounded object that is produced by some female animals. Eggs contain the animal's babies, which hatch when developed.

crow's ***egg***

hen's ***egg***

elastic
noun
a stretchy fabric.

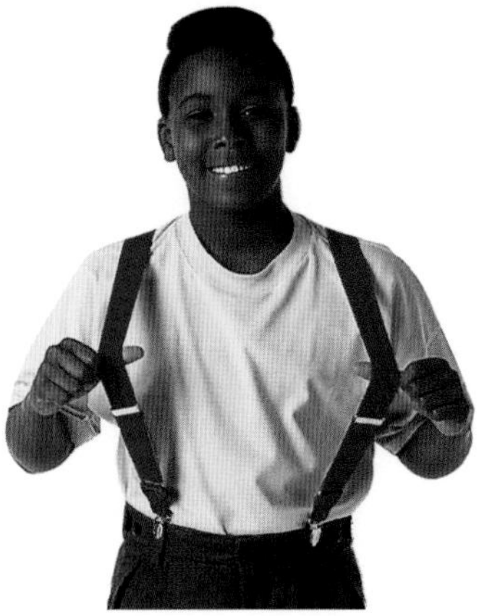
Suspenders made of ***elastic.***

elbow
elbows *noun*
the joint in the middle of your arm.

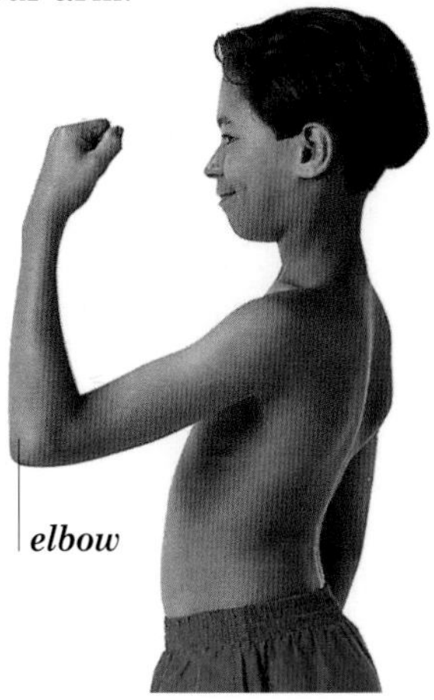

elderly
adjective
rather old.

elect
elects electing elected *verb*
to choose someone to do something by voting for them.

election
elections *noun*
the time when people vote for someone to be in charge.
Council ***elections.***

electric
adjective
powered by electricity.

electric *razor*

electricity
noun
a form of energy that is used for heating and lighting, and for making machines work. Electricity is produced at a power plant and carried along cables and wires.
electrical *adjective*

elephant
elephants *noun*
a huge mammal that lives in southern Asia and Africa. Elephants eat tree bark, roots, leaves, grass, and other plants. They use their trunks like hands to pick up or hold their food.

African ***elephant***

elevator
elevators *noun*
a large box or cage that carries people and goods between the floors of a building.

email
noun
messages sent electronically between computers.

embarrass
embarrasses embarrassing embarrassed *verb*
to make someone feel ashamed or shy.
It ***embarrasses*** *me to have to speak in public.*
embarrassment *noun*

emergency
emergencies *noun*
a sudden, dangerous event.

Helicopters are sometimes used in ***emergencies.***
■ say ee-**mer**-jen-see

emigrate
emigrates emigrating emigrated
verb
to leave your own country to go to live in another.
My best friend is ***emigrating*** *from Ireland to New Zealand.*
emigration *noun*

emotion
emotions *noun*
a strong feeling people have.
Love and hate are ***emotions.***

employ
employs employing employed
verb
to pay somebody to do a job.
I ***employ*** *six people in my office.*

empty
adjective
having nothing inside.

an ***empty*** *bottle*

A B C D E F G H I J K L M N O P Q R S T U V W X Y Z

emu
emus *noun*
a large bird that lives on the hot, grassy plains of Australia and eats leaves and insects. Emus can't fly, but they can run very fast.

■ say **ee**-mew

encourage
encourages encouraging encouraged *verb*
to help someone feel happy and confident about what they are doing.

Cheerleaders ***encourage*** *their team.*
■ say en-**kur**-rij

encyclopedia
encyclopedias *noun*
a book, or set of books, that contains facts and information about lots of different things.
■ say en-sy-kluh-**pee**-dee-uh

end
ends ending ended *verb*
to finish.
The movie ***ends*** *at 8:30 p.m.*

endangered
adjective
in danger of becoming extinct.

Turtles are ***endangered*** *animals.*

enemy
enemies *noun*
1 a person who dislikes you or would like to harm you.
2 the opposing country or army during a time of war.

energy
noun
1 the strength that makes a person or animal lively and active.

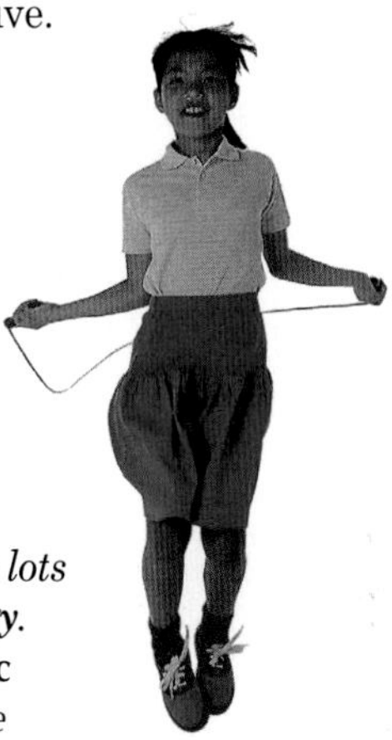

She has lots of ***energy****.*
energetic *adjective*

2 the power or ability of something to make something else work.

Wind ***energy****.*

end
ends *noun*
the place where something finishes.

There is an eraser at the ***end*** *of this pencil.*

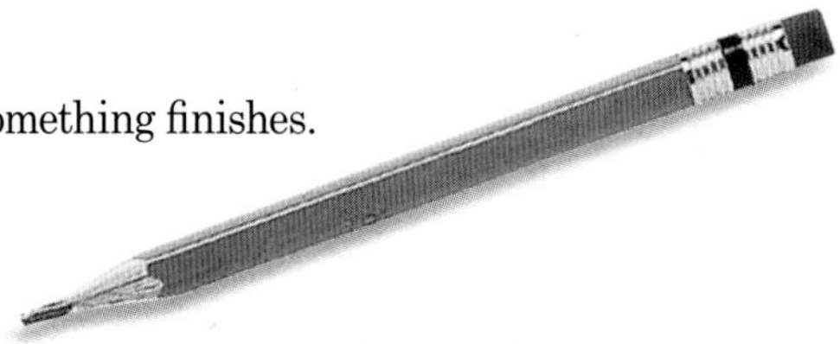

engine
engines *noun*
a machine that uses fuel to make something move.

jet ***engine***

engineer
engineers *noun*
a person who is trained to design, build, or repair things such as machines, buildings, or bridges.

enjoy
enjoys enjoying enjoyed *verb*
to like doing something.

enormous
adjective
very large.

An ***enormous*** *umbrella.*

enough
adjective
as much as is needed.
Do you have ***enough*** *money?*
enough *noun*

enter
enters entering entered *verb*
1 to go into a place.

The train ***entered*** *the tunnel.*
entrance *noun*
2 to take part in.
She ***entered*** *the diving competition with her friends.*
3 to write down, as for keeping a record.
I ***entered*** *my name at the top of the test paper.*

entertain
entertains entertaining entertained *verb*
to amuse people or provide a pleasant way to pass the time.

The juggler ***entertained*** *the children all afternoon.*
entertainment *noun*

enthusiastic
adjective
very interested in something.
He is an ***enthusiastic*** *skier.*
■ say en-thoo-zee-**as**-tik
enthusiasm *noun*

entire
adjective
whole.
The ***entire*** *class came to my party.*
entirely *adverb*

envelope
envelopes *noun*
a folded paper container for letters or cards.

environment
environments *noun*
the surroundings in which a person, plant, or animal lives.
*A city **environment** is often noisy and polluted.*
environmental *adjective*
■ say en-**vy**-run-munt

envy
envies envying envied *verb*
to feel unhappy because you want something that someone else has.
*I **envy** her long vacations.*
envious *adjective*
envy *noun*

episode
episodes *noun*
one part of a television or radio series.
*The first **episode** was so exciting that he couldn't wait to see the next one.*

equal
adjective
the same.

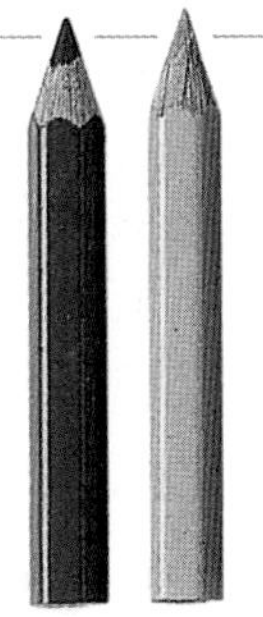

***Equal** in length.*
■ say **ee**-kwul

equator
noun
an imaginary line around the middle of the Earth that divides the northern half of the world from the southern half. The equator is drawn onto maps and globes.
■ say ee-**kway**-tor

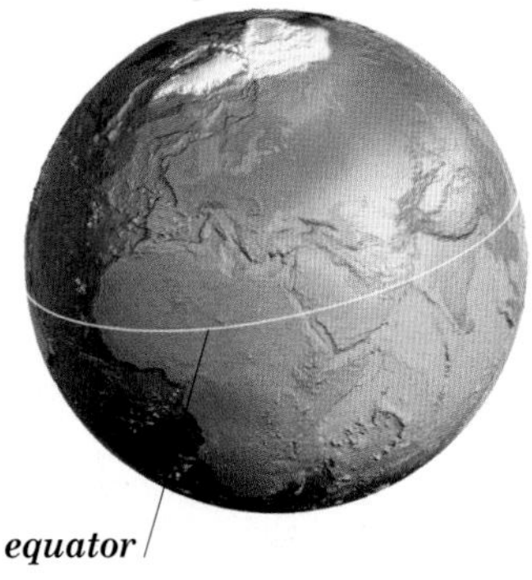

equator

equipment
noun
the things that you need for a job or an activity.

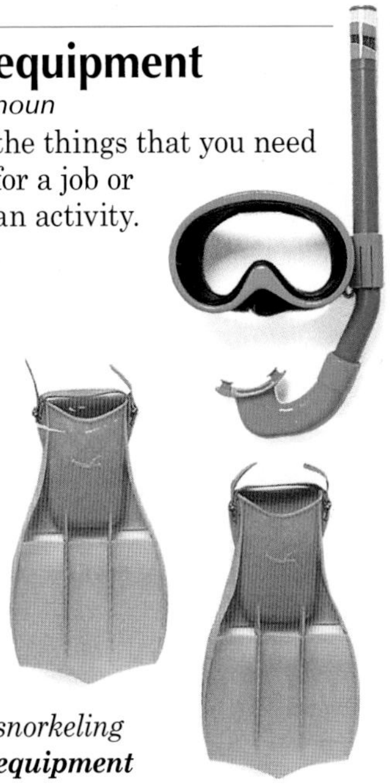

*snorkeling **equipment***

error
errors *noun*
a mistake.
*She failed the exam because her paper was full of **errors**.*

erupt
erupts erupting erupted *verb*
to explode suddenly.

*The volcano **erupted**.*
eruption *noun*

escalator
escalators *noun*
a moving staircase that carries people between levels or floors.

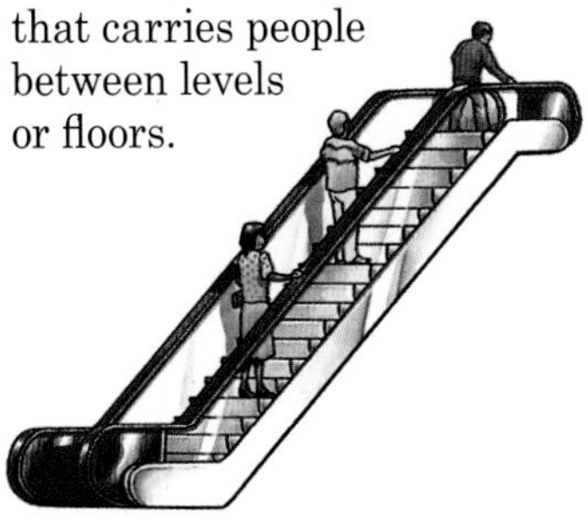

escape
escapes escaping escaped *verb*
to run away from somewhere or someone.

*The tiger **escaped** from his cage.*

establish
establishes establishing established *verb*
to organize or set up.
*They **established** a camp at the foot of the mountain.*

estimate
estimates estimating estimated *verb*
to make a thoughtful guess about something.
*We **estimated** that the journey would take 10 hours.*
estimate *noun*

evaporate
evaporates evaporating evaporated *verb*
to dry up gradually, changing from a liquid to a gas.
*The water slowly **evaporated**.*
evaporation *noun*

even
adjective
1 flat or level.

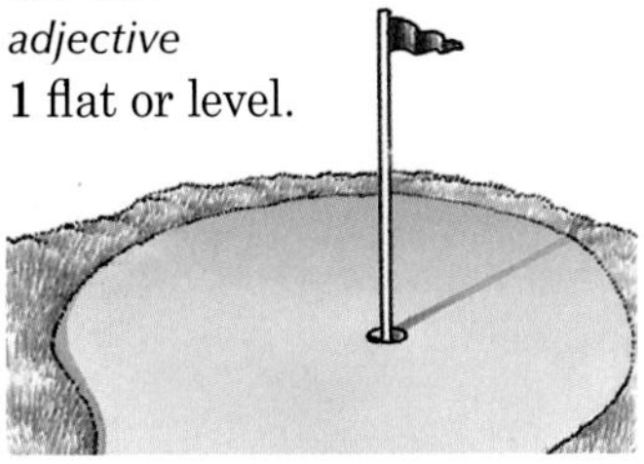

*Smooth and **even** grass.*
■ opposite **uneven**
2 a number that can be divided by two.
■ opposite **odd**

evening
evenings *noun*
the end of the day when the Sun sets and it grows dark.

event
events *noun*
something important that happens or is organized.

*The fireworks display is a big **event** each year.*

eventually
adverb
in the end or finally.
*After arguing for hours we **eventually** reached an agreement.*

evergreen
adjective
having green leaves all year round.

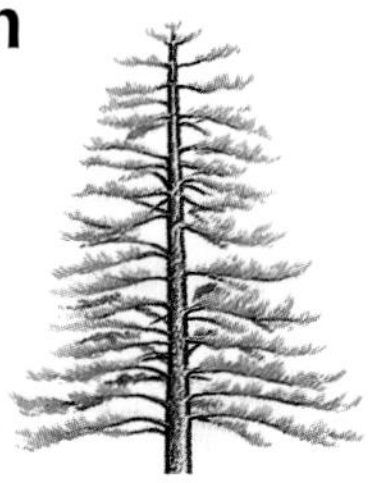

pine tree

pine branch

■ opposite **deciduous**

every
adjective
all, or each one.
◆ *We couldn't use the parking lot since **every** space was full.*
◆ ***Everybody** in the family loves chocolate.*
◆ *We can't take **every**one with us, since there are only four places on the bus.*
◆ ***Every**thing in the house was stolen.*
◆ *There were daffodils **every**where they looked.*

evidence
noun
proof that something has happened.

*The detectives looked for **evidence** at the scene of the crime.*

evil
adjective
wicked.

evolution
noun
the gradual development of animals and plants over a very long time.

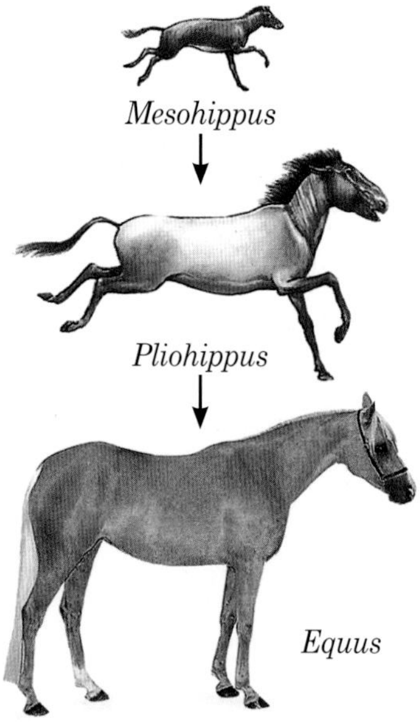

***Evolution** of the horse.*

ewe
ewes *noun*
a female sheep.
■ say **you**

exact
adjective
accurate or precise.

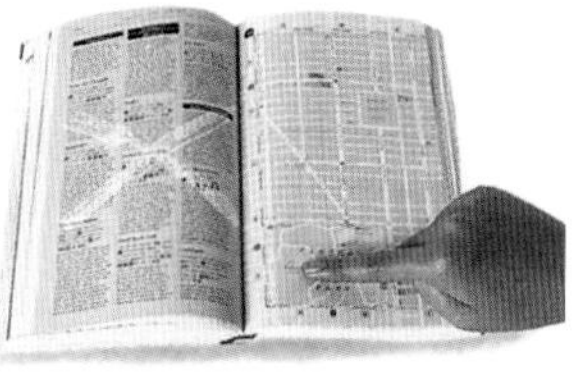

*She pointed to the **exact** place on the map.*
■ say egg-**zact**
■ opposite **approximate**
exactly *adverb*

exaggerate
exaggerates exaggerating exaggerated *verb*
to say more about something than is really true.

*She **exaggerated** the size of her catch.*
■ say ig-**za**-jur-rate
exaggeration *noun*

exam
exams *noun*
an important test to find out how much you know about something. Exam is short for examination.

examine
examines examining examined *verb*
to look at an object closely and carefully.

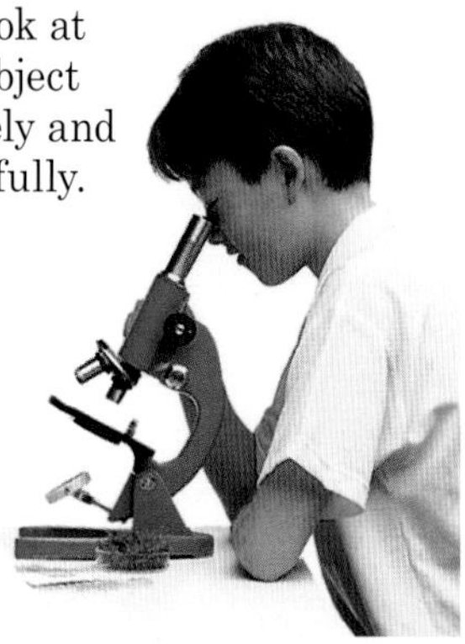

■ say ig-**zam**-in

example
examples *noun*
something that is typical of other similar things, or how a rule works.
*Can you think of an **example** of a plant that has blue flowers?*

excellent
adjective
extremely good.

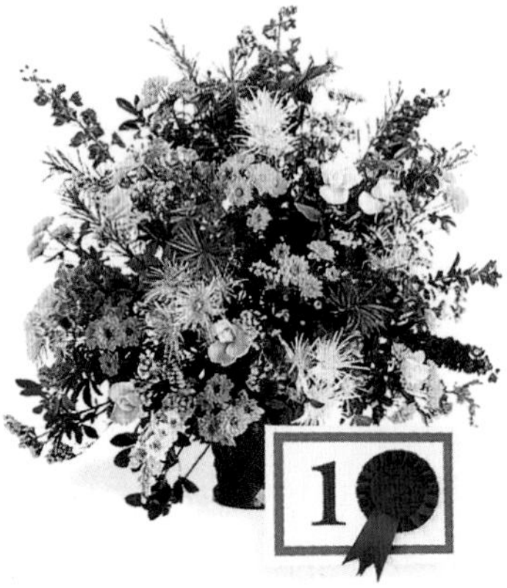

*The **excellent** flower arrangement won first prize.*

except
preposition
but, or other than.

*All the sheep were in the pen **except** one.*
exception *noun*

exciting
adjective
thrilling.

*The roller coaster ride was very **exciting**.*
excitement *noun*

excuse
excuses *noun*
a reason you give for not doing what you should have done.

*He had a good **excuse** for not washing the dishes.*
■ say ik-**skyoos**
excuse *verb*

exercise
exercises *noun*
1 activities or training that you do to become fit or to stay fit.

exercise *verb*
2 a piece of work that practices a skill or a person's knowledge of something.
*A math **exercise**.*

exhausted
adjective
extremely tired.

*She was **exhausted** after her long run.*
exhaustion *noun*

exhibition
exhibitions *noun*
an event where things are displayed for people to look at.

*A sculpture **exhibition**.*
■ say ek-suh-**bish**-un

exist
exists existing existed *verb*
to be or to live.
*Dinosaurs **existed** long before humans.*
existence *noun*

exit
exits *noun*
a way out of a building.

*We left by the nearest fire **exit**.*

expand
expands expanding expanded *verb*
to become larger.
*Water **expands** as it freezes.*
■ opposite **contract**
expansion *noun*

expect
expects expecting expected *verb*
to think that something is likely to happen.

*He was **expecting** rain.*

expedition
expeditions *noun*
an adventurous journey that is made for a special reason, such as exploring.

*They set off on an **expedition** to cross the Antarctic.*

expensive
adjective
costing a lot of money.
■ opposite **cheap**

*an **expensive** watch*

a cheap watch

experience
experiences *noun*
1 an important event that you remember for a long time.
*Traveling around the world was a fantastic **experience**.*
experience *verb*
2 knowledge or skill gained from doing something for a long time.
*She has years of **experience**.*
■ say ik-**speer**-ree-ens
experienced *adjective*

experiment
experiments *noun*
a test that you do in order to find out something.

expert
experts *noun*
a person who knows a lot about a subject.
*The space shuttle was designed by **experts**.*
expert *adjective*

explain
explains explaining explained *verb*
to help someone to understand something.
*Our teacher **explained** how rainbows occur.*
explanation *noun*

explode
explodes exploding exploded *verb*
to burst apart suddenly, often into many pieces.

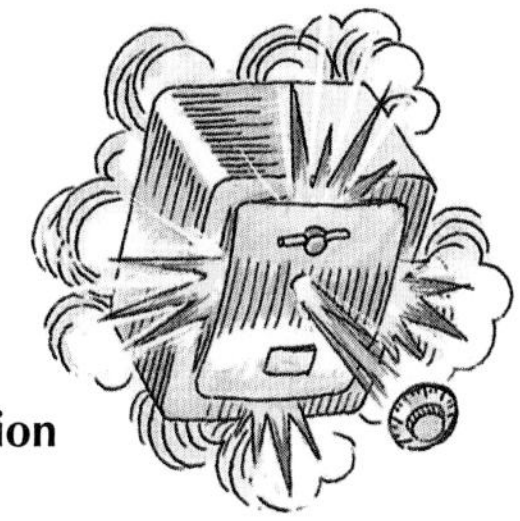

explosion *noun*

explore
explores exploring explored *verb*
to look around somewhere carefully for the first time.
*After we arrived on the island, we set off to **explore**.*
exploration *noun*

extinct
adjective
no longer existing.

*The dodo is an **extinct** bird.*

extra
adjective
more than is usual.

*An **extra** scoop of ice cream.*
extra *adverb*

extraordinary
adjective
very unusual.
*What an **extraordinary** car. It must be 30 feet long!*

extreme
adjective
very great, or much more than usual.
*He was in **extreme** danger.*

eye
eyes *noun*
the part of the body that you see with.

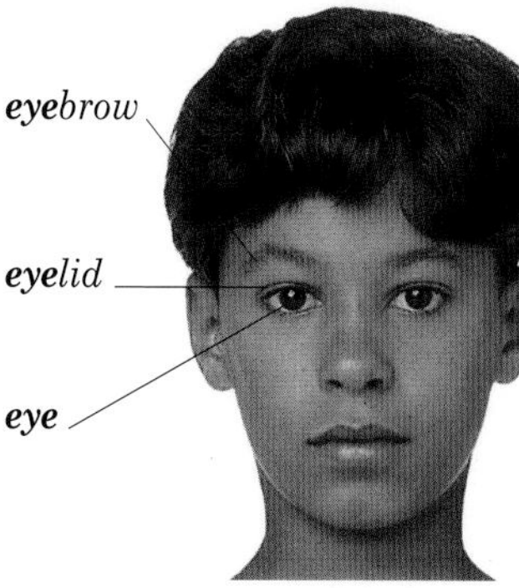

Ff

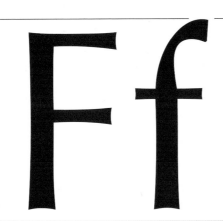

fable
fables *noun*
a story, often with animal characters, that tries to teach us in an amusing way.

fabric
fabrics *noun*
cloth.

façade
façades *noun*
the front of a building.

■ say fa-**sod**

face
faces *noun*
the front of your head, where your nose, eyes, and mouth are.

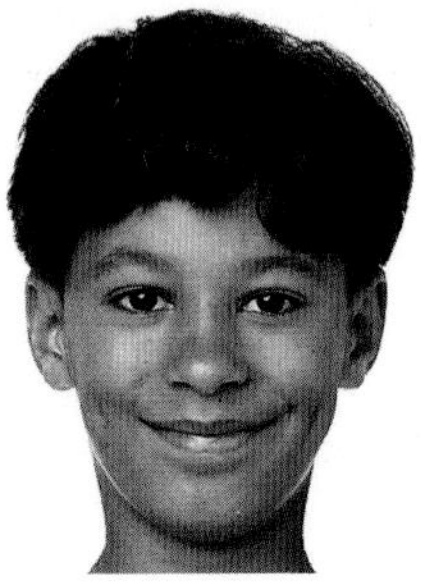

fact
facts *noun*
a piece of information that is known to be true.

factory
factories *noun*
a building where people make things using machines.

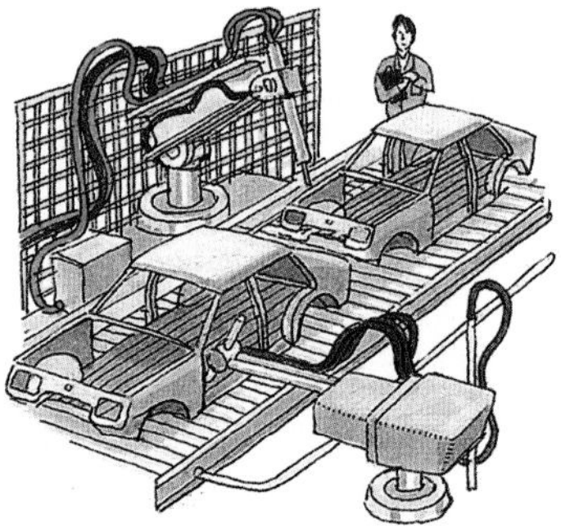

fade
fades fading faded *verb*
1 to lose color or strength.

*The photograph was old and had **faded**.*
2 to disappear slowly.
*The music **faded** away.*

fail
fails failing failed *verb*
to be unsuccessful at doing something.
*He **failed** his driving test.*
failure *noun*

faint
adjective
not very strong.
*She heard a **faint** noise coming from the cupboard.*

faint
faints fainting fainted *verb*
to become unconscious for a short time.

*He **fainted** in the heat.*
faint *noun*

fair
adjective
1 light in color.

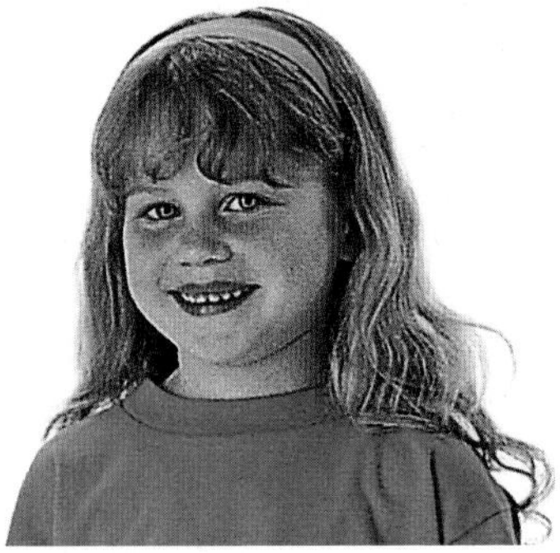

***Fair** hair.*
■ opposite **dark**
2 done in a way that is right and honest.
*Everyone gets a **fair** share.*
■ opposite **unfair**
3 dry and sunny.
***Fair** weather.*
■ comparisons **fairer fairest**

fair
fairs *noun*
an outdoor event with stalls, competitions, games, and other entertainments.

fairy
fairies *noun*
a small, imaginary creature from stories. Fairies often have magical powers.

faith
noun
a strong feeling of trust in someone or something.
*I have **faith** in my doctor.*

faithful
adjective
trustworthy or reliable.
*A **faithful** friend.*

fake
adjective
imitation, not real.

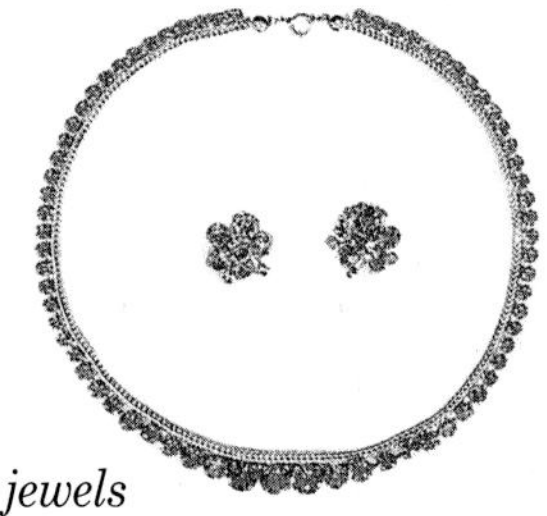

***fake** jewels*
fake *noun*

falcon
falcons *noun*
a bird with a sharp beak and claws that is related to the eagle. Falcons are good hunters and can fly very fast. They eat birds, reptiles, and small mammals.

■ say **fal**-kun

fall
falls falling fell fallen *verb*
to drop from a higher place to a lower place.

She was thrown from the horse and ***fell*** *into the water.*
fall *noun*

fall
falls *noun*
another name for autumn.

false
adjective
not real or true.
He wore a ***false*** *beard.*

familiar
adjective
well-known to you.
I saw a ***familiar*** *face in the crowd.*
■ opposite **unfamiliar**

family
families *noun*
1 a group of people who are closely related to each other.
I come from a large ***family*** *of five brothers and sisters.*
2 a group of animals or plants that are related to each other.

These butterflies belong to the same ***family****.*

famine
famines *noun*
a time when there is not enough to eat, usually because of a drought or a war.

famous
adjective
well-known to many people.

A ***famous*** *movie star.*

fan
fans *noun*
1 a device that moves air around to make you feel cooler.

electric ***fan***

2 a person who is very interested and enthusiastic about something.

They played to their ***fans****.*

fanatic
fanatics *noun*
someone who believes in something so strongly that it controls their life.
A football ***fanatic****.*

fang
fangs *noun*
1 a long, pointed tooth that meat-eating animals use for tearing up their food.

fang

2 a snake's long, sharp tooth that has poison in it.

fantastic
adjective
1 difficult to believe.
A ***fantastic*** *tale about giants.*
2 very pleasing or wonderful.
We had a ***fantastic*** *vacation.*

fantasy
fantasies *noun*
something that is imaginary and not real.

far
adverb
1 to or from a long way away.
Have you come ***far****?*
2 how distant something is.

She walked along a path ***far*** *from the city.*
■ comparisons **farther farthest**
■ opposite **near**

fare
fares *noun*
the money that you must pay to travel on a bus, train, or airplane.
What is the ***fare*** *to Glasgow?*

farm
farms *noun*
a place where crops are grown or animals are reared for food.

sheep ***farm***
farm *verb*

fascinate
fascinates fascinating fascinated *verb*
to interest someone so much that they think of nothing else.
Dinosaurs ***fascinate*** *me.*
■ say **fas**-uh-nate
fascination *noun*

fashion
fashions *noun*
a way of dressing that people like and want to copy at a particular time.

Long, straight dresses were the ***fashion*** *in the 1920s.*
fashionable *adjective*

fast
adjective
at great speed.
■ comparisons **faster fastest**
■ opposite **slow**
fast *adverb*

fast
adverb
firmly held.

Stuck ***fast*** *in the mud.*

A B C D E F G H I J K L M N O P Q R S T U V W X Y Z

fast
fasts fasting fasted *verb*
to go without food for a special reason.
*Muslims **fast** during the festival of Ramadan.*
fast *noun*

fasten
fastens fastening fastened *verb*
to join something together so that it holds.

***Fastening** her collar.*

fat
fats *noun*
1 the oily substance that is stored under the skin and in the cells of animals and people.
2 an oily, solid substance that is used in cooking. Lard, oil, butter, and margarine are all fats.

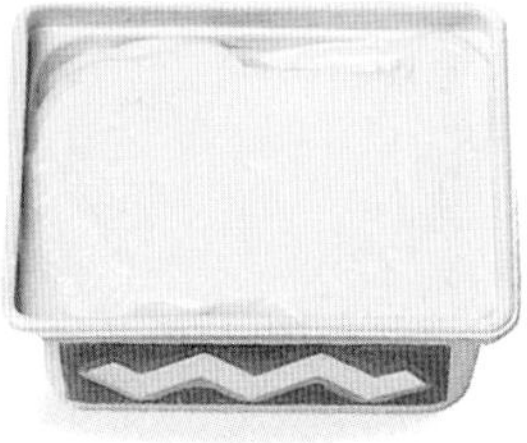

margarine

fat
adjective
having a lot of fat or flesh.

■ comparisons **fatter fattest**

fatal
adjective
resulting in death.
***Fatal** injuries.*
■ say **fay**-tuhl
fatally *adverb*

father
fathers *noun*
a male parent.

fault
faults *noun*
1 something that is wrong.
*A **fault** in the computer.*
2 a mistake that someone has made.
*It was my **fault** we were late.*
3 a split in the Earth's crust.
*The San Andreas **Fault** is in California.*
■ say **fall**-t

favor
favors *noun*
a kind and helpful action.
*Will you do me a **favor**?*

favorite
adjective
liked the best.

*Red is her **favorite** color.*
favorite *noun*

fawn
fawns *noun*
a young deer.

fax
faxes *noun*
a picture or message, that is recorded electronically on a fax machine. A fax is sent by telephone lines to another fax machine, where it is printed out.
fax *verb*

fear
fears *noun*
the feeling of being afraid.
*He had a **fear** of spiders.*
fear *verb*

feather
feathers *noun*
part of the soft, light covering that a bird has on its body (see **bird** on page 28).

fee
fees *noun*
money that you pay to a person or organization for a service.

feed
feeds feeding fed *verb*
1 to give someone or something food.

2 to eat food.

*Caterpillars **feed** on leaves.*

feel
feels feeling felt *verb*
1 to experience an emotion.
*I **feel** happy today.*
2 to experience something through touch.

feeling *noun*

fell
*from the verb **to fall***
*I **fell** off my bike last week.*

female
adjective
belonging to the sex that can give birth to babies, or produce eggs or seeds.
■ opposite **male**
female *noun*

feminine
adjective
of or like women or girls.
■ say **fem**-in-nin
■ opposite **masculine**

fence
fences *noun*
a barrier that separates one piece of land from another.

fern
ferns *noun*
a type of plant that has feathery leaves and doesn't produce flowers (see **plant** on page 151).

ferocious
adjective
fierce, dangerous, and cruel.
ferociously *adverb*

ferry
ferries *noun*
a boat or ship that regularly sails a short distance between two places, carrying vehicles, passengers, or cargo.

fertile
adjective
where something grows well.
Fertile *farmland.*

festival
festivals *noun*
a celebration or special event, often with music, dancing, and plays.

A dance ***festival.***

fetch
fetches fetching fetched *verb*
to go and get something and bring it back.

The dog ***fetched*** *the stick.*

fever
fevers *noun*
an illness when your body temperature is very high and your pulse is fast.

few
adjective
not many, or a small number of something.

There are a ***few*** *pencils in the jar.*
■ opposite **many**

fiancé / fiancée
fiancés / fiancées *noun*
someone who is engaged to be married.
■ say fee-**on**-say
■ a **fiancé** is a man and a **fiancée** is a woman

fiber
fibers *noun*
a fine thread of something.

rope ***fiber***

fiction
noun
a story or poem that has been made up and is not about real events.
I read a lot of crime ***fiction.***
■ opposite **nonfiction**

field
fields *noun*
an area of land where grass grows, crops are grown, or animals graze.

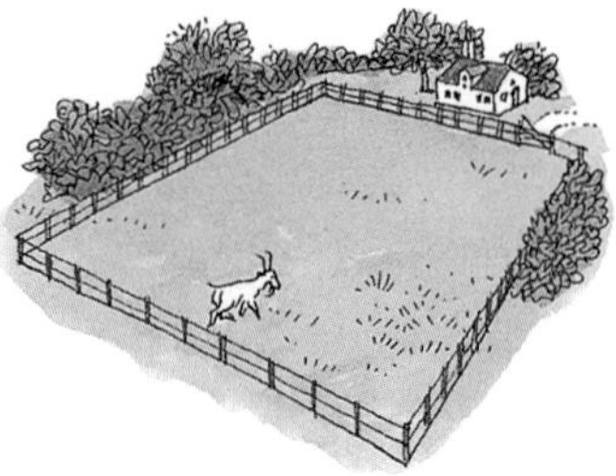

fierce
adjective
violent or dangerous.

A ***fierce*** *dog.*
■ comparisons **fiercer fiercest**
fiercely *adverb*

fig
figs *noun*
a small, soft fruit with a tough skin and sweet flesh, which is full of tiny seeds. Figs can be eaten fresh or dried.

fight
fights fighting fought *verb*
to struggle against a person or animal.

Fighting *with swords.*
fight *noun*

figure
figures *noun*
1 a symbol that represents a written number.

2 the shape of the human body.
He saw a shadowy ***figure*** *walking through the mist.*
■ say **fig**-yuhr

file
files *noun*
1 a folder for keeping paper and other pieces of information together.

2 a metal tool with rough sides that is used to smooth edges.

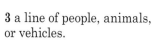

3 a line of people, animals, or vehicles.

The ducklings walked in single ***file.***

a b c d e f g h i j k l m n o p q r s t u v w x y z

fill
fills filling filled *verb*
to put as much of something into a container as it can hold.

film
films filming filmed *verb*
to use a movie or video camera to take moving pictures of something.

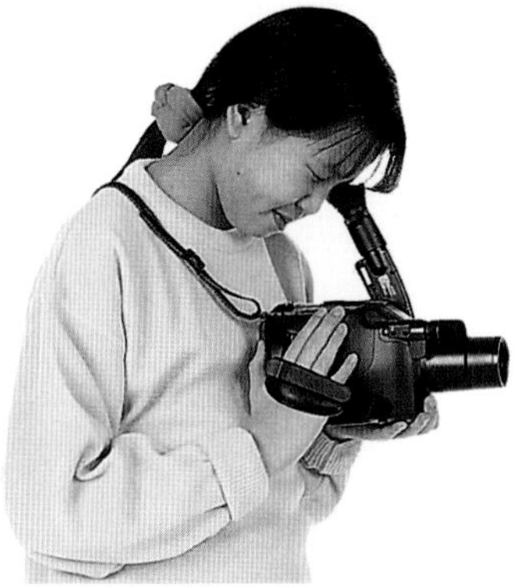

film
films *noun*
1 a series of moving pictures shown on a screen.
*We went to see a **film** at the movie theater.*
2 a long, thin piece of special plastic that is used in cameras for taking photographs.

3 a thin layer of something.
*A **film** of oil.*

filter
filters *noun*
a device that only allows some things, such as water or air, to pass through it.

filter
verb

fin
fins *noun*
1 the part of a fish that sticks out from its body and helps it to swim and keep its balance (see **fish** on page 79).
2 a device that helps vehicles keep steady while going fast (see **universe** on page 229).

Bluebird racing car

final
adjective
last in a series.
*This is the **final** call for the flight to Paris.*
finally *adverb*

find
finds finding found *verb*
to discover something.

*He **found** the key under the mat.*

fine
fines *noun*
money you have to pay as a punishment.
*A parking **fine**.*

fine
adjective
1 all right.
*I feel **fine**.*
2 dry and sunny.
***Fine** weather.*
3 very thin or delicate.
*The pen has a **fine** tip.*

4 having many small parts.
***Fine** sand.*
5 very good.
***Fine** food.*
■ comparisons **finer finest**

finger
fingers *noun*
one of the separate parts at the end of your hand.

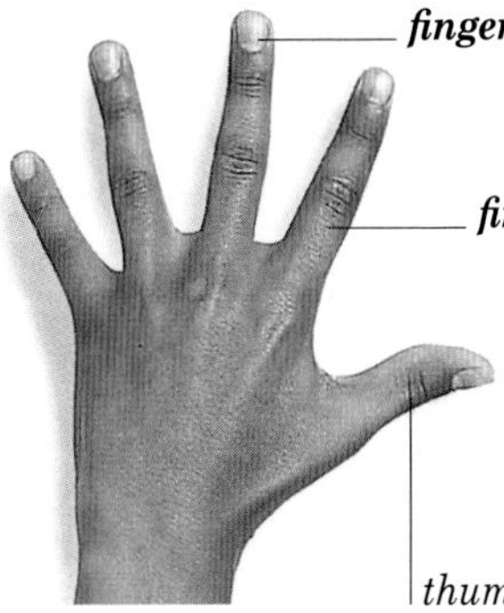

fingerprint
fingerprints *noun*
the mark that your finger or thumb makes when it touches something.

finish
finishes finishing finished *verb*
to come to the end of something.

*She **finished** the race ahead of him.*

fire
fires *noun*
the heat, light, and flames of something burning.

fire alarm
fire alarms *noun*
a bell that rings to warn people of a fire.

fire engine
fire engines *noun*
the vehicle that firefighters travel in to get to a fire.

fire extinguisher
fire extinguishers *noun*
a device filled with water, powder, or chemicals that is used for putting out fires.

firefighter
firefighters *noun*
someone whose job is to put out fires and rescue people in danger.

firework
fireworks *noun*
a device that burns or explodes when lit, creating a colorful display.

firm
adjective
1 solid.
*A **firm** mattress.*
2 fixed so it cannot move.
3 determined and definite.
*A **firm** decision.*
firmly *adverb*

fish

fish or **fishes** *noun*
a cold-blooded animal that lives in the water, breathes through gills, and is usually covered in scales. Most fish have streamlined shapes. Fish eat other water animals and plants (see **skeleton** on page 188).

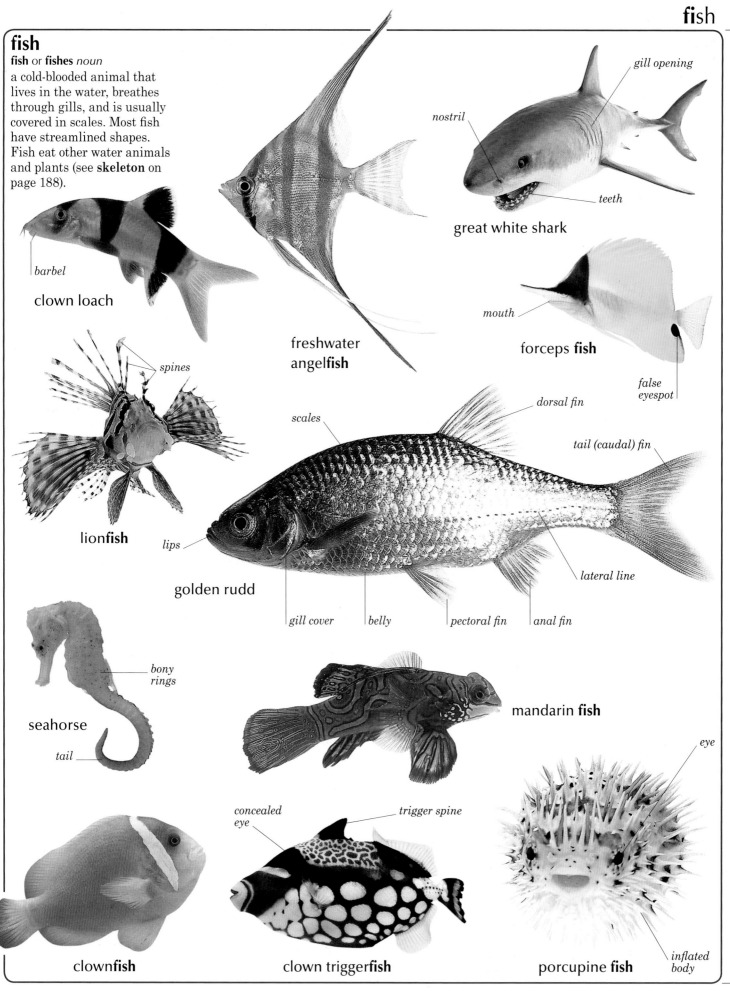

clown loach

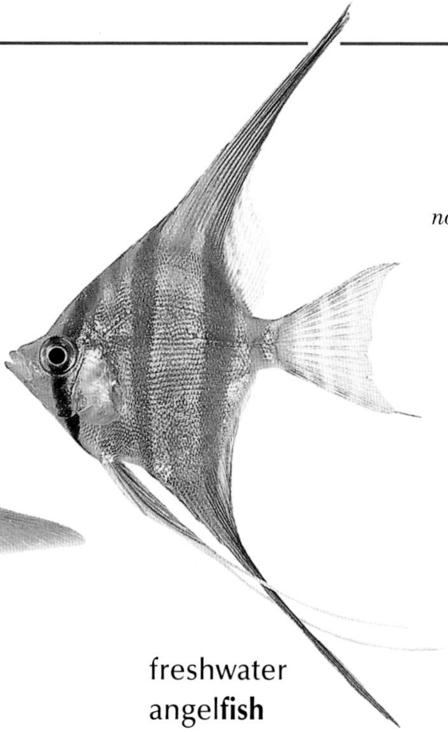

freshwater angel**fish**

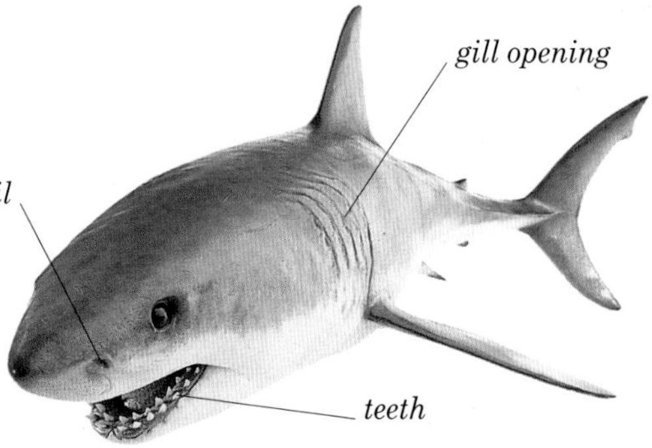

great white shark

forceps **fish**

lion**fish**

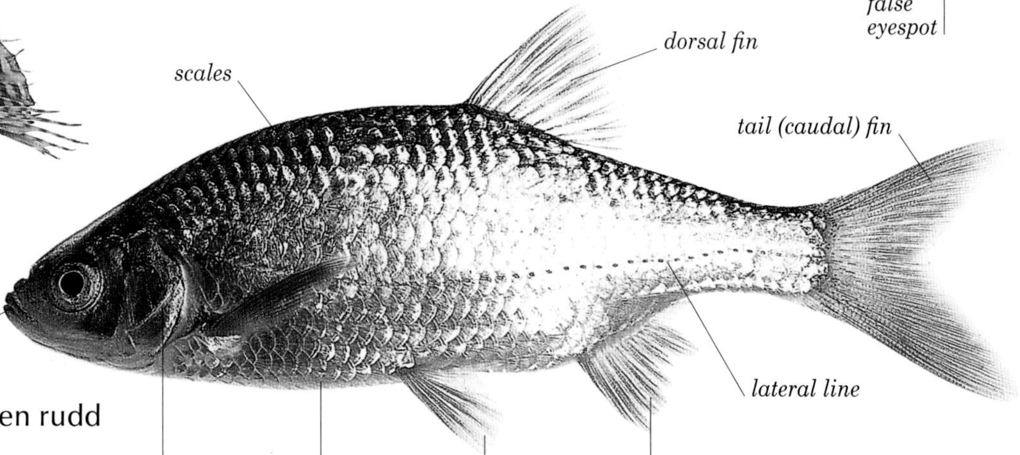

golden rudd

seahorse

mandarin **fish**

clown**fish**

clown trigger**fish**

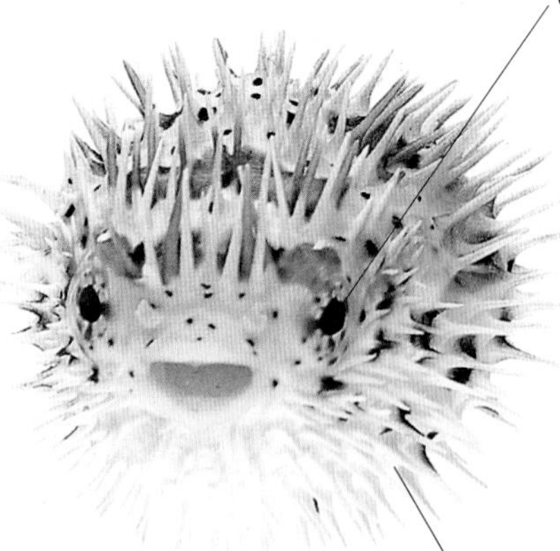

porcupine **fish**

fish
fishes fishing fished *verb*
to try to catch fish.
fishing *noun*

fist
fists *noun*
the shape your hand makes when you curl up your fingers and thumb tightly.

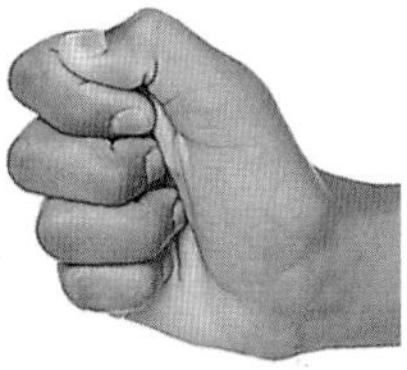

fit
fits fitting fit or **fitted** *verb*
1 to be the right size or shape.

*She checked to see if the skirt **fit** her.*

2 to put something in place.
*I **fitted** a lock to the door.*

fit
adjective
healthy.
■ comparisons **fitter fittest**

fix
fixes fixing fixed *verb*
1 to mend something.

***Fixing** a car engine.*
2 to make something secure.
*They **fixed** the shelf to the wall.*

fizzy
adjective
full of bubbles.

*A **fizzy** drink.*
fizz *verb*

flag
flags *noun*
a piece of cloth with a design that represents a country or an organization. Flags are often flown from flagpoles.

flagpole

*United Nations **flag***

flake
flakes *noun*
a small, thin piece of something.

***flakes** of pastry*
flake *verb*

flame
flames *noun*
a bright point of burning gas in a fire.

flammable
adjective
catching fire easily.
■ opposite **nonflammable**

flap
flaps flapping flapped *verb*
1 to hang or swing loosely.
*The laundry **flapped** in the wind.*
2 to move up and down.
*Birds **flap** their wings in order to fly.*

flash
flashes *noun*
1 a sudden, bright light.
*A **flash** of lightning.*
flash *verb*
2 a short period of time.
*It was all over in a **flash**.*

flask
flasks *noun*
a container for liquids that usually has a narrow top and a tight-fitting lid.

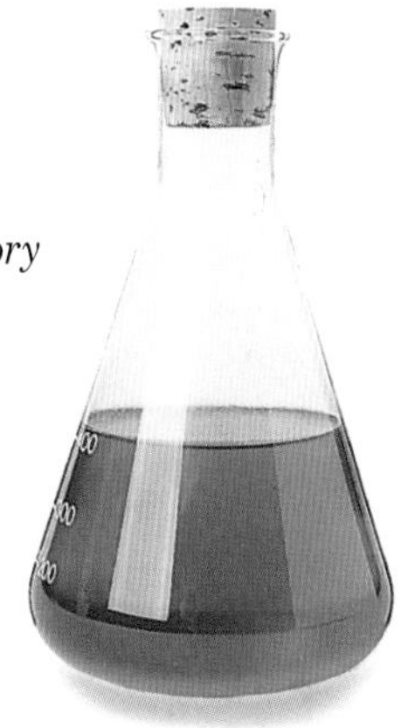

*laboratory **flask***

flat
adjective
1 level or even.
*A **flat** roof.*
2 without air inside it.

*A **flat** beach ball.*

flatten
flattens flattening flattened *verb*
to make something flat.
*The car ran over the can, **flattening** it.*

flavor
flavors *noun*
the taste of food or drink.

*This dessert has an orange **flavor**.*

flea
fleas *noun*
a very small, jumping insect without wings that sucks the blood of humans and animals.

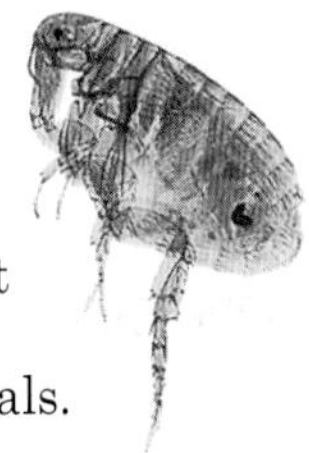

flew
*from the verb **to fly***
*He **flew** to France yesterday.*

flexible
adjective
easy to bend.

*A **flexible** ruler.*

flick
flicks flicking flicked *verb*
to touch or hit something in a quick, light way.

*The horse **flicked** the flies away with its tail.*
flick *noun*

flight
noun
1 the action of flying.

*A parakeet in **flight**.*
2 a journey through the air.
■ say **flite**

fling
flings flinging flung *verb*
to throw something suddenly and forcefully.
*He **flung** his shoes into the corner.*

float
floats floating floated *verb*
to rest on the surface of water or another liquid without sinking.

floating *adjective*

flock
flocks *noun*
a group of birds, or animals such as sheep or goats.
*A **flock** of geese.*

flood
floods flooding flooded *verb*
to cover an area that is normally dry with a large amount of water.
*The river burst its banks, **flooding** the town.*
flood *noun*

floodlight
floodlights *noun*
a large, bright lamp that is used at night to light up an open area, usually outside.

floodlit *adjective*

floor
floors *noun*
1 a surface that you walk on inside a building.
*A marble **floor**.*
2 a level of a building.
*I live on the sixth **floor** of this apartment building.*

florist
florists *noun*
a person who sells and arranges flowers.

flour
noun
a powder made by crushing grain such as wheat. Flour is used in baked goods such as bread and cakes.
■ say **flower**

flow
flows flowing flowed *verb*
to move along steadily.
*A steady **flow** of traffic.*

flower
flowers *noun*
the part of a plant that contains the seeds. Flowers often have colorful petals (see **plant** on page 151).

flu
noun
an infectious illness, caused by a virus, that often affects the nose and throat. Flu is short for "influenza."

fluff
noun
soft fibers or threads from a material.
fluffy *adjective*

fluid
fluids *noun*
a substance that flows. Gases and liquids are fluids.

fluorescent
adjective
giving off light.

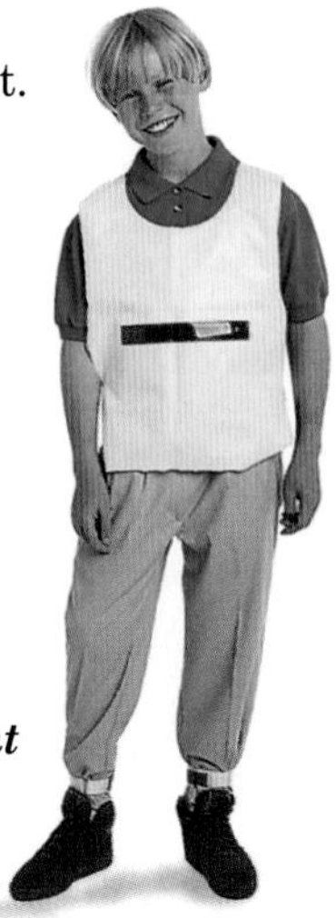

*His **fluorescent** top made him visible in the dark.*
■ say floo-**res**-sent

flush
flushes flushing flushed *verb*
1 to become red in the face.
*She **flushed** with anger when her friend shouted at her.*
2 to clean with a sudden and quick flow of water.
*He **flushed** the dirty water away.*

flute
flutes *noun*
a wind instrument made of wood or metal. You play it by covering holes with your fingers or special pads and blowing across a hole at one end.

flutter
flutters fluttering fluttered *verb*
to move or flap quickly.

*The butterflies **fluttered** around the bush.*

fly
flies *noun*
a flying insect with two wings and six legs. Most flies feed on rotting plants and animals. There are many different kinds of fly.

*bluebottle **fly***

fly
flies flying flew *verb*
to travel through the air.

foal
foals *noun*
a young horse.

foam
noun
lots of very small air bubbles. Foam can be liquid or solid.

*shaving **foam***

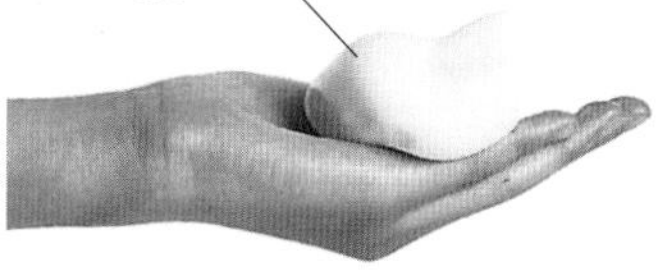

focus
focuses focusing focused *verb*
to adjust something to make a clearer and sharper image.
*He **focused** his camera on the flower.*
focus *noun*

fog
noun
a thick cloud of tiny water droplets and dust that hangs in the air, close to the ground.
foggy *adjective*

fold
folds folding folded *verb*
to bend one part of something over another.

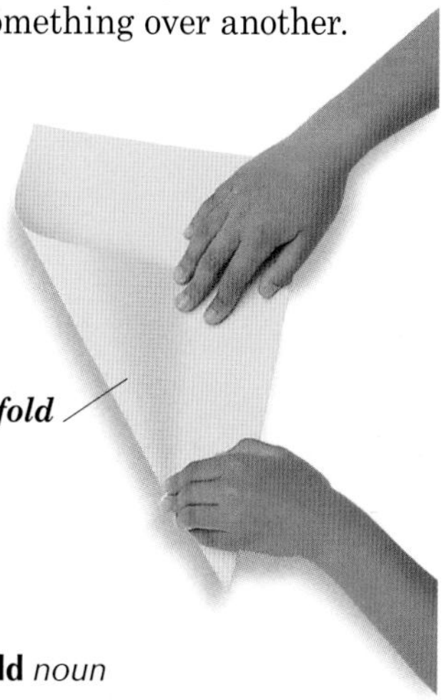

*a **fold***

fold *noun*

follow
follows following followed *verb*
to go behind or after someone or something.
*The dog **followed** him all the way home.*

food
noun
all the things that humans and animals eat to help them live and grow.

*Pasta is an Italian **food**.*

foolish
adjective
not sensible.

*He was **foolish** to walk under the ladder.*
foolishly *adverb*

foot
feet *noun*
the part of your body that you stand on.

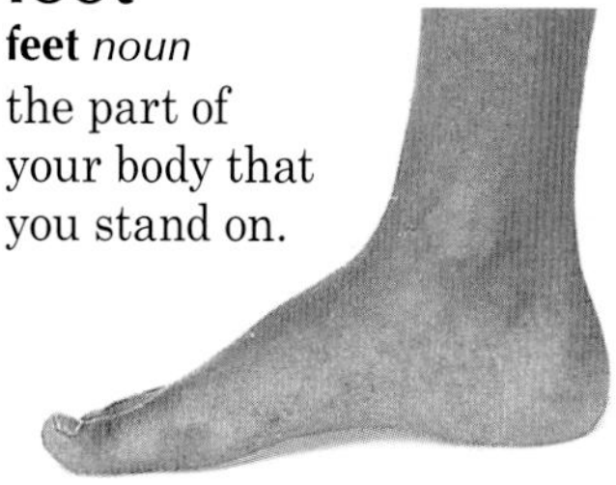

football
noun
1 a game for two teams of 11 players. Points are scored by carrying the ball over the other team's goal line, or kicking it through the other team's goalposts.

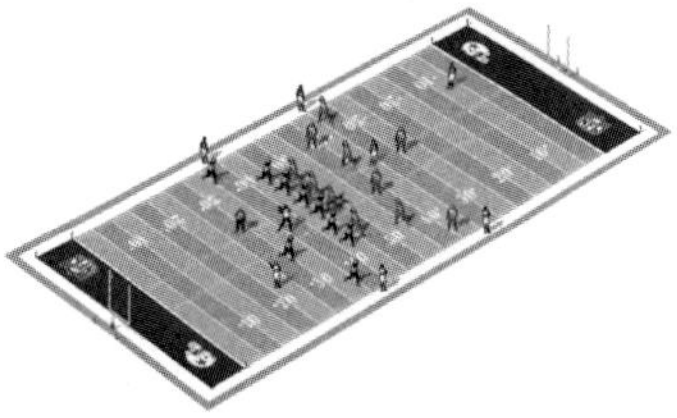

2 an oval-shaped ball that is used in football games.

*a **football***

footprint
footprints *noun*
the mark left by a foot or shoe.

footstep
footsteps *noun*
the sound of someone walking.
*I heard **footsteps** behind me.*

forbid
forbids forbidding forbade forbidden *verb*
to tell a person that they must not do something.
*I **forbid** you to drive.*
■ opposite **allow**
forbidden *adjective*

force
forces forcing forced *verb*
1 to make a person do something.
*I was **forced** to make a choice.*
2 to push strongly.
*They **forced** the safe open.*

force
forces *noun*
1 a power.

*The **force** of the wind blew her hat off.*
2 a group of people who together have power.
*The armed **forces**.*

forearm
forearms *noun*
the part of your arm between your elbow and your wrist.

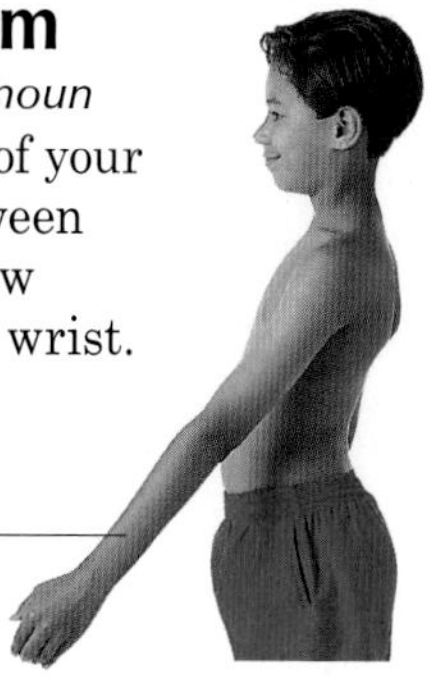

forearm

forecast
forecasts forecasting forecast *verb*
to predict that something will happen in the future.

***Forecasting** the weather.*
forecast *noun*

forehead
foreheads *noun*
the part of your face above your eyes and below your hair.

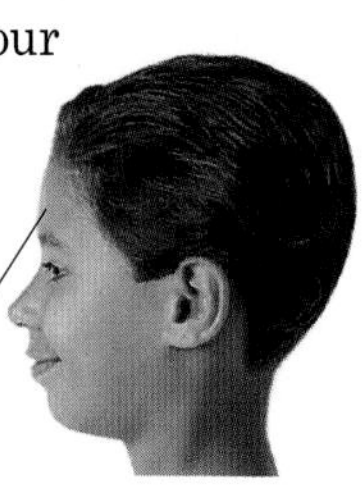

forehead

foreign
adjective
belonging to another country.
***Foreign** languages.*
■ say **for**-in
foreigner *noun*

forest
forests *noun*
a very large area of trees.

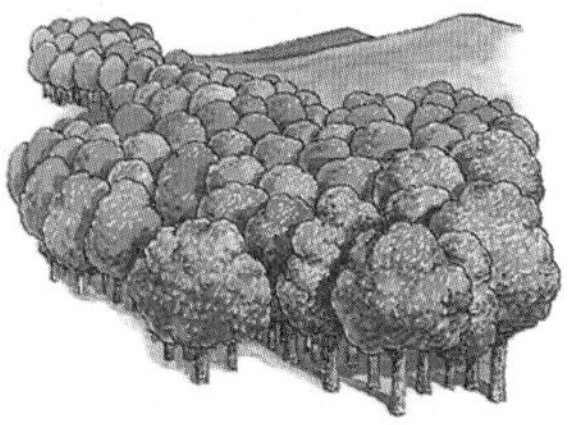

forget
forgets forgetting forgot forgotten *verb*
to not remember something.
*I **forgot** my sister's birthday.*
■ opposite **remember**

forgive
forgives forgiving forgave forgiven *verb*
to stop blaming or being angry with someone for something they said or did.
*I **forgave** my brother for losing my favorite CD.*
forgiveness *noun*

fork
forks *noun*
1 a tool with two or more narrow spikes that is used for lifting things.

*table **fork***

2 the place where something divides into two parts.

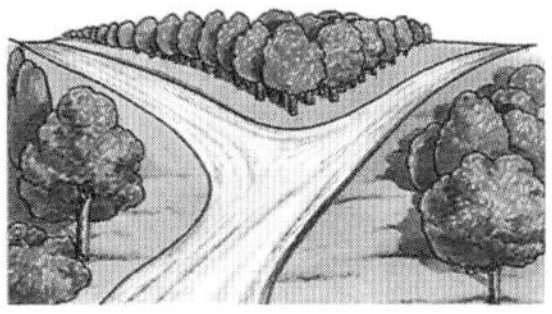

*A **fork** in the road.*

form
forms *noun*
1 the shape or the type of something.
*Trains are a **form** of transportation.*
2 a printed piece of paper with spaces in which you write information.
*I filled in the **form**.*

formula
formulas or **formulae** *noun*
1 a type of recipe or code that shows chemists what chemicals are made of.

$$H_2O$$

*chemical **formula** for water*
2 instructions or a recipe for making or doing something.

fortnight
noun
a period of time lasting two weeks.
fortnightly *adjective*
fortnightly *adverb*

fortune
noun
1 luck.
*He had the good **fortune** to be rescued from the wreck.*
■ opposite **misfortune**
2 a lot of money.

*She won a **fortune**.*

forward
adverb
moving toward the front.
*He fell **forward** onto his hands.*

fossil
fossils *noun*
the remains or print of a plant or animal that died many years ago. Fossils are found preserved in rocks.
fossilized *adjective*

foster
fosters fostering fostered *verb*
to give a home for a period of time to a child who comes from another family.
*They have **fostered** three children in the past two years.*

fought
*from the verb **to fight***
*The team **fought** back, but in the end they lost the game.*
■ say **fawt**

found
*from the verb **to find***
*She **found** her wallet this morning.*

fountain
fountains *noun*
a statue or structure that sprays water up into the air.

fox
foxes *noun*
a mammal that belongs to the dog family and lives in the countryside and in towns. Foxes eat small animals, birds, and scraps from garbage cans.

fraction
fractions *noun*
1 a number that is part of a whole number.

$$\frac{1}{3}$$

*One-third is a **fraction**.*
2 a very small part of something.
*You can fly there in a **fraction** of the time it takes to drive.*

fracture
fractures fracturing fractured *verb*
to break.

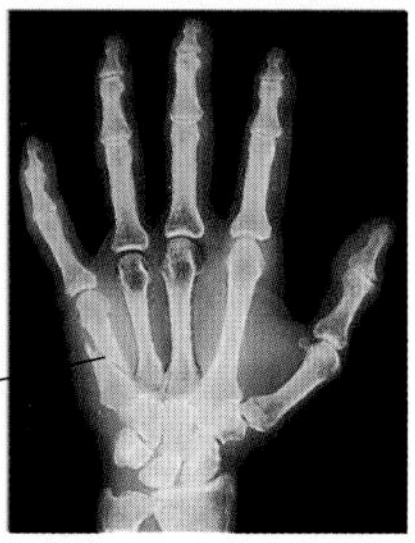

fracture

*The X-ray showed where the bone had **fractured**.*
fracture *noun*

fragile
adjective
delicate and easily broken.

***fragile** coral*
■ say **fraj**-uhl

frame
frames *noun*
a structure that surrounds the edge of something, holding it in place.

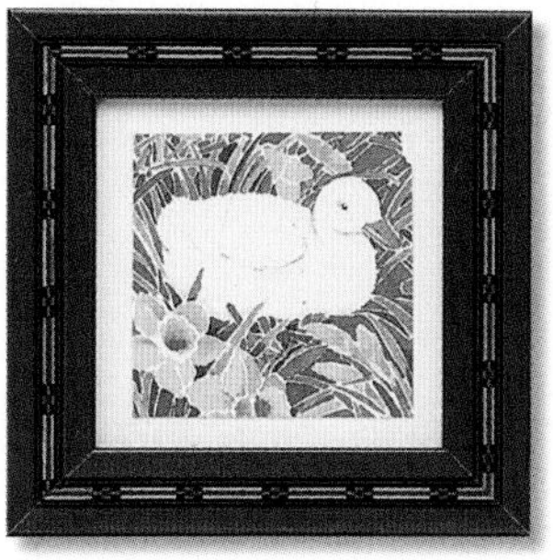

*A picture **frame**.*

frantic
adjective
very upset and excited, because of fear, worry, or pain.
*The **frantic** animal tried to escape from its cage.*
frantically *adverb*

freckle
freckles *noun*
a small, light brown spot on the skin.

freckle

free
adjective
1 costing no money.
*Please accept this **free** gift.*
2 not restricted by rules or limits.
*Do you have any **free** time this week?*
free *adverb*
free *verb*

freedom
noun
being free.
*The **freedom** to do as you like.*

freeze
freezes freezing froze frozen *verb*
to reach such a low, cold temperature that a liquid becomes a solid.

*The lake **froze** in winter.*

freezer
freezers *noun*
a machine that freezes food so that it can be stored for a long time without spoiling.

freight
noun
goods that are carried by road, rail, sea, or air.
■ rhymes with **mate**

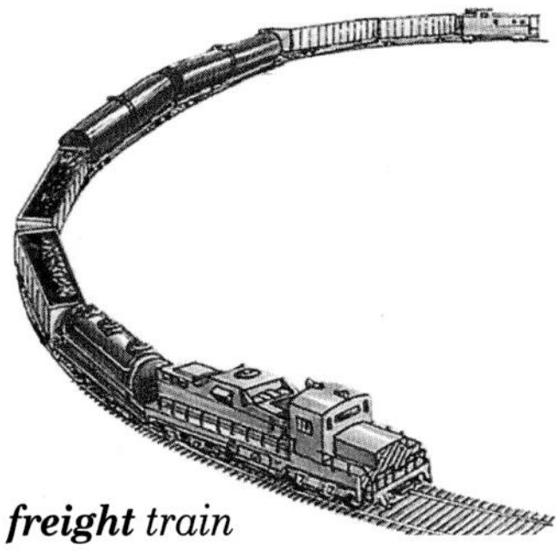

***freight** train*

frequent
adjective
happening often.
*There is a **frequent** train service to the city.*
■ say **free**-kwent
frequently *adverb*

fresh
adjective
new, not stale or preserved.

***fresh** parsley*

dried parsley

friend
friends *noun*
someone whom you like and who likes you.
friendly *adjective*

frighten
frightens frightening frightened *verb*
to make someone feel afraid.
*She was always trying to **frighten** her brother.*
frightening *adjective*

fringe
fringes *noun*
a border made up of loose, hanging pieces of material or thread.

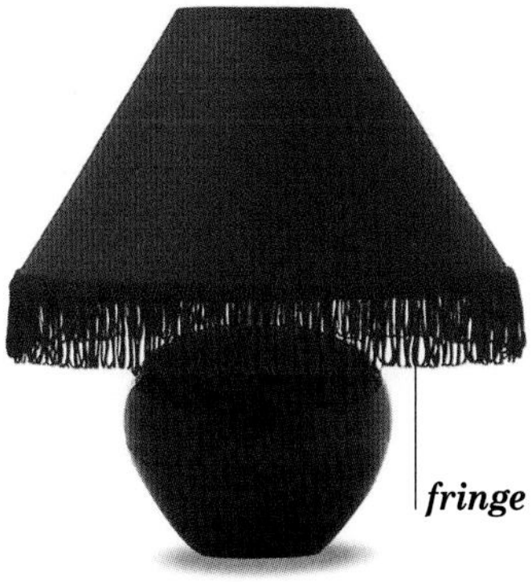

fringe

frog
frogs *noun*
an amphibian with no tail that lives in or near water. Frogs eat spiders, worms, small fish, and insects. They begin life as fishlike tadpoles.

front
fronts *noun*
the part of something that faces forward.

***front** of a truck*

frontier
frontiers *noun*
the border between two regions or countries, especially if one of them is wild and unknown.
■ say fron-**tee**-er

frost
frosts *noun*
tiny ice crystals that form on surfaces outside in very cold weather.
frosty *adjective*

frown
frowns frowning frowned *verb*
to pull your eyebrows together and wrinkle your forehead to show that you are not happy about something.

frozen
adjective
preserved by being kept very cold.

***frozen** peas*

fruit

fruits *noun*
the part of a plant that contains the seeds. Many fruits are edible.
■ rhymes with **boot**

greengage plums

lychees

black currants

passion fruit

mango

red currants

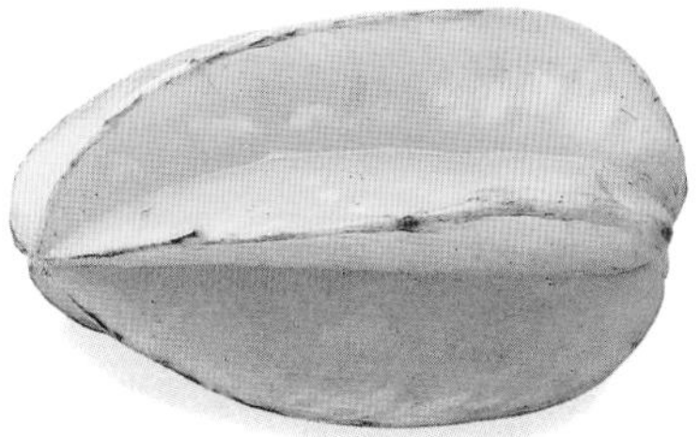
star fruit *(side view)*

(end view)

green olives

red raspberries

kiwi **fruit**

pomegranates

pineapple

mandarin oranges

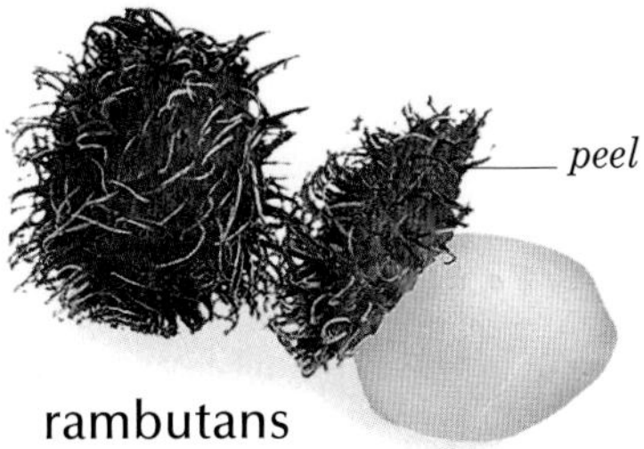

rambutans

tomatoes

ugli **fruit**

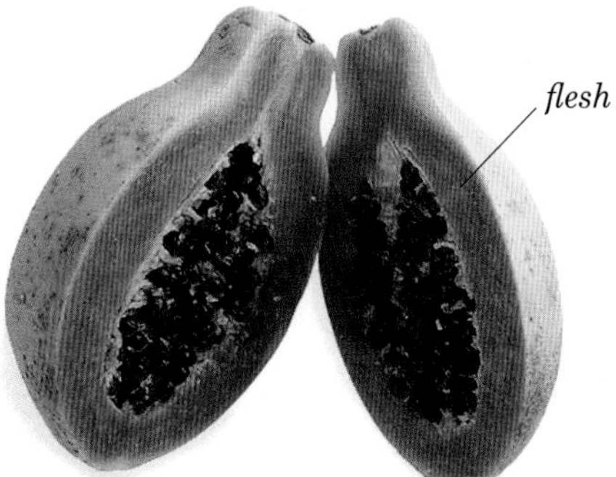

papaya

A B C D E F G H I J K L M N O P Q R S T U V W X Y Z

frustrate
frustrates frustrating frustrated *verb*
to upset someone by keeping them from doing something they want to do.
*It was **frustrating** that the last tickets for the concert had already been sold.*
frustration *noun*

fry
fries frying fried *verb*
to cook something in hot oil.

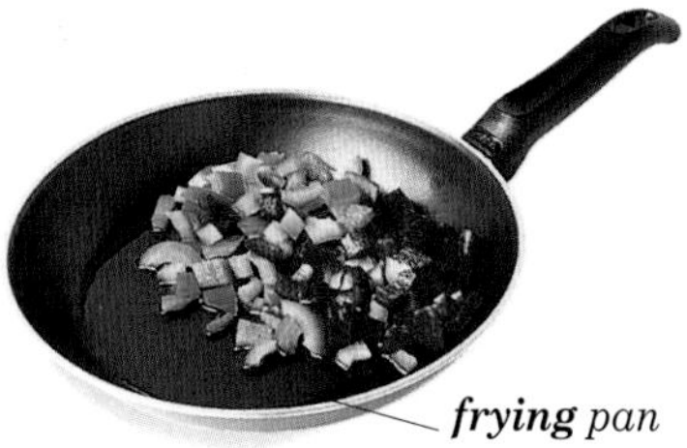

frying pan

fuel
fuels *noun*
something that is burned to give heat or power.
*Wood, coal, and gasoline are types of **fuel**.*

full
adjective
without space for any more.

*This box is **full** of beads.*

fumes
noun
smoke or gas that is often strong-smelling and unpleasant. Some fumes are poisonous.
*Exhaust **fumes**.*

fun
noun
an enjoyable activity.
*The treasure hunt was lots of **fun**.*

fund
funds *noun*
an amount of money collected for a special reason.

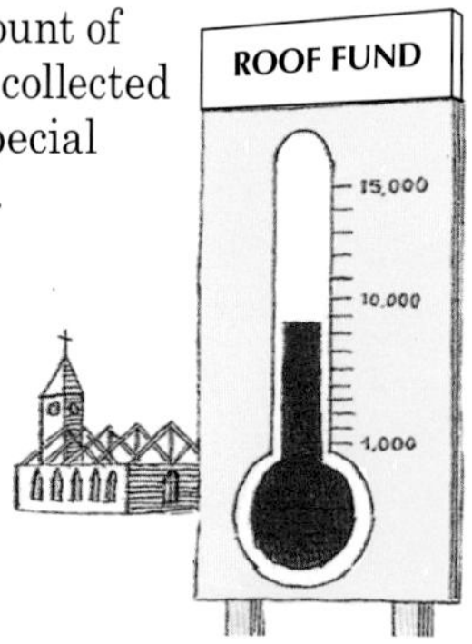

*The church has started a **fund** to repair the roof.*

funeral
funerals *noun*
a formal occasion during which the body of someone who has died is buried or burned.

fungus
fungi or **funguses** *noun*
a plant with no flowers or leaves. Fungus grows in damp places and has seeds called spores.

fly agaric

funnel
funnels *noun*
1 a tube that is wide at one end and narrow at the other. Funnels are used for pouring liquids through small openings.

2 the smokestack on a ship.

funnel

funny
adjective
1 making you laugh or smile.

2 strange or odd.
*What's that **funny** noise?*
■ comparisons **funnier funniest**

fur
noun
the soft, hairy covering that some animals have on their bodies.

furry *adjective*

furious
adjective
very angry.
*She was **furious** to discover that her wallet was missing.*
■ say **fyoor**-ee-us

furnace
furnaces *noun*
a device in which fuel is burned to heat buildings, or to melt metals.
■ say **fur**-nis

*steel-making **furnace***

furniture
noun
chairs, beds, cupboards, and other movable things that you have in the place where you live or work.

cupboard

armchair

double bed

furrow
furrows *noun*
a groove in the ground made by a plow.

fuse
fuses *noun*
a safety device for electrical machines that stops the current from flowing if it is too strong.

fuss
fusses fussing fussed *verb*
to be more anxious than is necessary about something.
*Don't **fuss** with my hair!*
fussy *adjective*

future
noun
the time that is to come.
*In the **future**, people might travel to Mars.*
■ opposite **past**

Gg

gadget
gadgets *noun*
a small, useful tool.
■ say **ga**-jit

galaxy
galaxies *noun*
a large group of stars.
*The Milky Way is a **galaxy**.*

gale
gales *noun*
a strong wind.

gallop
gallops galloping galloped *verb*
to move in the way that a horse does when it runs as fast as it can.

gamble
gambles gambling gambled *verb*
to bet money on the result of a race, game, or competition.

game
games *noun*
an activity that you play for fun, or a sport. Many games have rules and a scoring system.

bowling pins

gang
gangs *noun*
a group of people who do things together.
*A **gang** of road workers.*

gangster
gangsters *noun*
someone who belongs to a group of criminals.

gap
gaps *noun*
a space between two things.

*A **gap** in the hedge.*

gape
gapes gaping gaped *verb*
to stare at something with your mouth open.
*They **gaped** at the acrobat on the tightrope.*

garage
garages *noun*
1 a place where cars and other vehicles are stored.

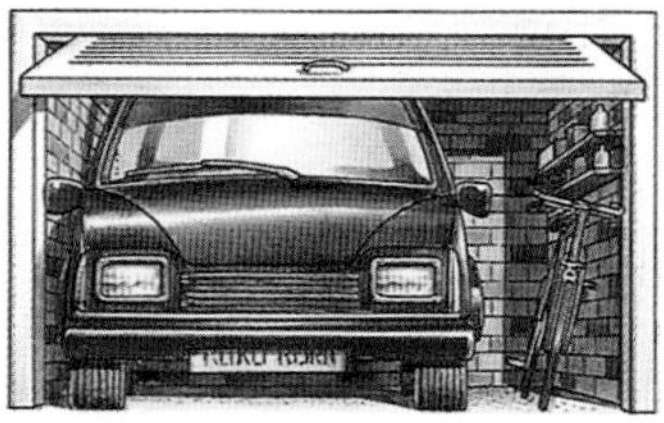

2 a place where cars and other vehicles are repaired.
■ say guh-**razh**

garbage
noun
things that have been thrown away.
■ say **gar**-bij

garden
gardens *noun*
a piece of ground where fruit, flowers, vegetables, and other plants are grown.

*The **garden** looked beautiful in the summer.*

garlic
noun
a plant with an onion-shaped bulb, made up of sections called cloves. Garlic is used in cooking to add flavor to food.

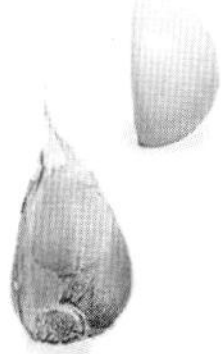

***garlic** cloves*

*string of **garlic***

gas
gases *noun*
1 a substance that is not a liquid or a solid.

*This stove is powered by a **gas** called butane.*

2 the fuel used in cars; short for "gasoline."

gash
gashes *noun*
a long, deep cut.

gasp
gasps gasping gasped *verb*
to struggle to breathe, taking in air in short, quick breaths.
*He rose to the surface of the water, **gasping** for air.*
gasp *noun*

gate
gates *noun*
a type of outside door that is fitted into walls or fences.

gather
gathers gathering gathered *verb*
to collect together.

***Gathering** leaves.*

gave
from the verb ***to give***
She ***gave*** *me a kite for my birthday last week.*

gaze
gazes gazing gazed *verb*
to stare at something for a long time.
He ***gazed*** *out of the window.*

gem
gems *noun*
a jewel or precious stone.

emerald

aquamarine

fire opal

heliodor

yellow sapphire

general
adjective
1 usual, or true of most people.
The ***general*** *opinion is that exercise is good for you.*
2 having to do with the main parts, but not the details.
The newspaper reported the ***general*** *points of the president's speech.*
generally *adverb*

generation
generations *noun*
all the people who are in approximately the same age group. There is usually a period of about 30 years between one generation and the next.

Three different ***generations.***
child *parent* *grandparent*

generous
adjective
kind and ready to give.
It was ***generous*** *of him to lend us the car.*
generously *adverb*

genius
geniuses *noun*
a person who is extremely intelligent.
Many people think that Albert Einstein was a ***genius.***
■ say **jeen**-nyus

gentle
adjective
kind and careful.

Be ***gentle*** *with the kitten.*
■ comparisons **gentler gentlest**
gently *adverb*

genuine
adjective
real, or not imitation.
A ***genuine*** *leather bag.*
■ say **jen**-yoo-in

geography
noun
the study of the Earth's surface and its inhabitants.
■ say jee-**og**-ra-fee

geometry
noun
the study of shapes, surfaces, and angles.
■ say jee-**om**-e-tree

germ
germs *noun*
a tiny plant or animal that can cause illness.

germinate
germinates germinating germinated *verb*
to start to grow.

a seed ***germinating***

gesture
gestures *noun*
a sign that you make with your hands or body.

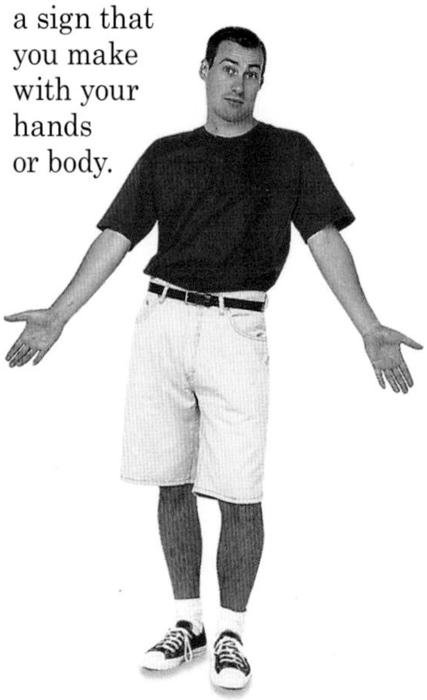

ghost
ghosts *noun*
the spirit of a dead person.

■ say **goest**
ghostly *adjective*

giant
giants *noun*
a huge, imaginary person from fairy tales or legends.

giant
adjective
very large.

gift
gifts *noun*
a present.

gigantic
adjective
huge or enormous.
A ***gigantic*** *house with 20 bedrooms.*
■ say jie-**gan**-tik

giggle
giggles giggling giggled *verb*
to laugh in a nervous or silly way.

gill
gills *noun*
the organ that a fish uses to breathe (see **fish** on page 79).

gimmick
gimmicks *noun*
a way of making people aware of something or somebody.
*Free gifts are often given away as a **gimmick** to draw attention to a new product.*

ginger
noun
a spicy root that is used to add flavor to food.

*ground **ginger***

*root **ginger***

giraffe
giraffes *noun*
a very tall mammal that lives on dry plains in Africa. Giraffes eat leaves on trees, which they can reach with their long necks.

girl
girls *noun*
a young female person.

give
gives giving gave given *verb*
to let somebody have something.
*He **gave** her a book as a prize.*

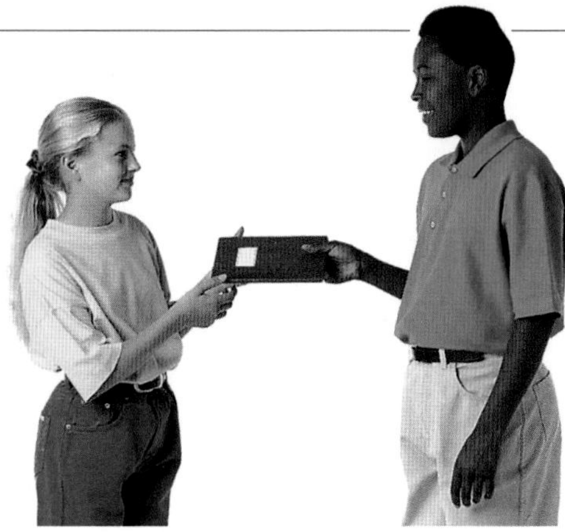

glacier
glaciers *noun*
a huge river of ice that moves very slowly.

glad
adjective
pleased and happy.
*I am **glad** to be back home.*

gladiator
gladiators *noun*
a man who was trained to fight as entertainment for spectators in ancient Rome.

glance
glances glancing glanced *verb*
to take a quick look at something.
*She **glanced** at the clock to see if it was time to go out.*

gland
glands *noun*
one of the parts of your body that makes the chemicals your body needs.
***Glands** near your eyes make tears.*

glare
glares glaring glared *verb*
1 to look at someone in an angry way.
2 to shine very brightly.
*The sun **glared** down.*
glare *noun*

glass
noun
1 a transparent, fragile substance that is used to make things such as windows and bottles.

*stained **glass***

2 a container that is used to drink from.

*wine**glass***

glasses
noun
a pair of lenses in frames. People wear glasses to help them see better.

gleam
gleams gleaming gleamed *verb*
to shine or glow.

glider
gliders *noun*
a very light aircraft with no motor that flies using air currents.

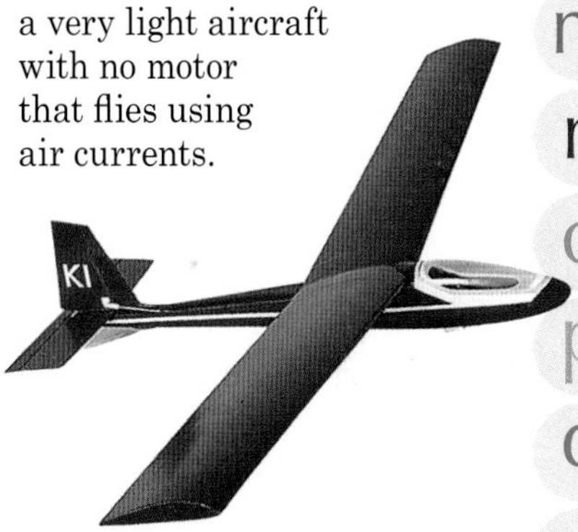

glimpse
glimpses glimpsing glimpsed *verb*
to see something or someone for just a few moments.
*He **glimpsed** his friend in the crowd.*

glitter
glitters glittering glittered *verb*
to shine with a bright, sparkling light.

globe
globes *noun*
the world, or a model of the world.

gloomy
adjective
dull and dark.
*A **gloomy** winter day.*

glossy
adjective
shiny.
***Glossy** paper.*
■ comparisons **glossier glossiest**

glove
gloves *noun*
a piece of clothing that you wear on your hands.

glow
glows glowing glowed *verb*
to give off a steady light.

*The fire **glowed** brightly in the dark.*

glue
glues *noun*
a substance that is used to stick things together.

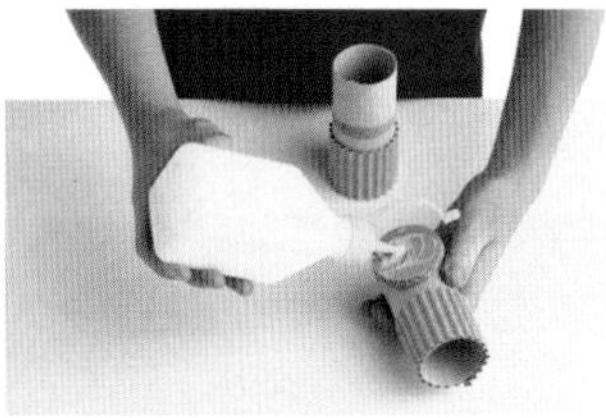

glue *verb*

gnat
gnats *noun*
a small, biting insect with wings and long, fine legs.
*A mosquito is a type of **gnat**.*
■ say **nat**

gnaw
gnaws gnawing gnawed *verb*
to chew something.

*The mouse **gnawed** the wood.*
■ say **naw**

goal
goals *noun*
1 the target that you have to aim the ball at in some games.
*An ice hockey **goal**.*
2 a point scored for sending a ball into a net.

*She scored a **goal** in the last minute of the game.*
3 an aim or an ambition.
*My **goal** in life is to become a doctor.*

goat
goats *noun*
a mammal with horns from the same animal group as sheep. Goats eat grass and other plants and are often kept on farms for their milk. A baby goat is called a kid.

gobble
gobbles gobbling gobbled *verb*
to eat something quickly and in a greedy way.

God
noun
the being that Christians, Jews, and Muslims worship and believe made the world.

god
gods *noun*
a being that people worship and believe has power over their lives.

*Shiva, a Hindu **god***

*Vishnu, a Hindu **god***

goggles
noun
special glasses worn to protect the eyes.

*swimming **goggles***

gold
noun
a soft, bright, yellow metal that is very valuable.

***gold** ore*

***gold** ring*

goldfish
noun
an orange fish that is often kept in aquariums and ponds as a pet.

golf
noun
a game played on a grass course, with a ball, and sticks called clubs. Players hit the ball into holes around the course. The player who completes the course in the fewest shots is the winner.

gong
gongs *noun*
a metal disk that you hit to make a loud noise.

good
adjective
1 pleasant or of high quality.
*That was a **good** movie!*
2 useful.
*This knife is **good** for cutting.*
3 kind or well-behaved.
*A **good** child.*
4 skillful.
*She's very **good** at math.*
■ comparisons **better best**

good-bye
interjection
a word that you say when someone leaves.

goods
noun
things that can be bought and sold.

goose
geese *noun*
a large bird that lives on or near water. Geese eat grasses and grain. A male goose is called a gander. Some types of geese are kept by farmers for their eggs, meat, and feathers.

gorge
gorges *noun*
a deep, narrow valley.

gorgeous
adjective
very nice to look at or taste.
*The long, sandy beach looked **gorgeous** in the photograph.*
■ say **gor**-jus

gorilla
gorillas *noun*
a large mammal covered in dark hair that lives in rain forests in Africa. Gorillas eat fruits, nuts, and leaves. They are the largest and strongest apes in the world.

*baby **gorilla***

gossip
gossips gossiping gossiped *verb*
to talk about someone or something without always knowing whether what you say is true or not.
*People often **gossip** about movie stars.*

government
governments *noun*
a group of people who run a country.
■ say **guv**-ern-ment
govern *verb*

grab
grabs grabbing grabbed *verb*
to take hold of something in a quick, rough way.

*He **grabbed** his coat and ran to the station.*

graceful
adjective
moving in a beautiful way.

*Ballet dancers are very **graceful**.*
gracefully *adverb*

grade
grades *noun*
1 a year at school
2 a mark to show how well you have done in your schoolwork.
grade *verb*

graffiti
noun
writing and drawing on walls in public places.

■ say gruh-**fee**-tee

grain
grains *noun*
1 a seed of a cereal crop such as wheat or barley, or a quantity of these seeds.

*barley **grains***

2 a small, hard piece of something.
*Sand is made up of many tiny **grains**.*
3 the pattern in wood.

*different wood **grains***

grammar
noun
the rules for writing and speaking a language.

grand
adjective
large and impressive.
*The **grand** house had a huge, iron gate.*
■ comparisons **grander grandest**

A B C D E F G H I J K L M N O P Q R S T U V W X Y Z

grandchild
grandchildren *noun*
a son or daughter's child.
*A **grandchild** can be a granddaughter or a grandson.*

grandfather
grandfathers *noun*
the father of a parent.
*A **grandfather** can also be called granddad or grandpa.*

grandmother
grandmothers *noun*
the mother of a parent.
*A **grandmother** can also be called grandma or granny.*

grape
grapes *noun*
a small, round fruit with a smooth green or black skin and soft, juicy flesh. Grapes can be used to make wine.

*bunch of **grapes***

grapefruit
grapefruit or **grapefruits** *noun*
a large, round, juicy fruit with a thick skin and a sour taste.

graph
graphs *noun*
a diagram that shows how amounts and numbers of things compare with each other.

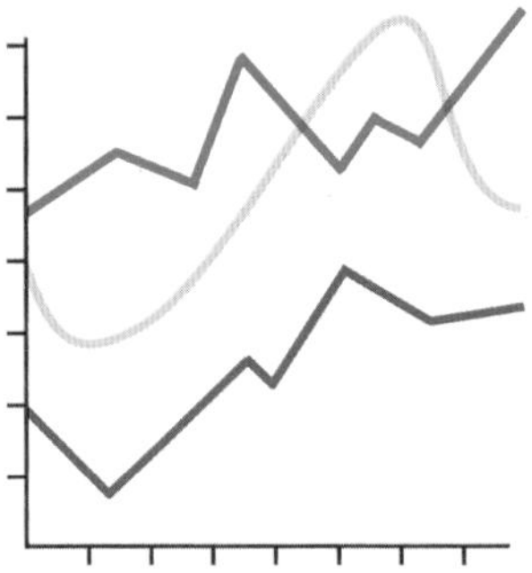

■ say **graf**

grasp
grasps grasping grasped *verb*
1 to take hold of something firmly.

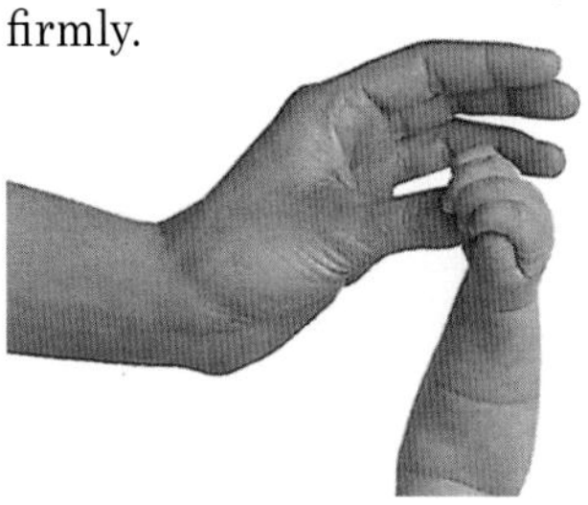

2 to understand something.
*They couldn't **grasp** how the computer worked.*

grass
grasses *noun*
a plant with long, thin, green leaves. Grass is an important food for many animals.

grasshopper
grasshoppers *noun*
a jumping insect that feeds on plants. Grasshoppers have two sets of wings and strong back legs.

grateful
adjective
feeling thankful to someone because they have done something for you.

*She was **grateful** for one of his sandwiches.*
gratefully *adverb*

grave
graves *noun*
a hole in the ground in which a dead body is buried.

grave
adjective
very serious and important.

gravel
noun
a mixture of tiny pieces of stone, used for covering paths and roads.

gravity
noun
1 the natural force that pulls everything down toward Earth.

*Apples fall downward rather than upward because of **gravity**.*
2 seriousness.
*A criminal's punishment depends on the **gravity** of a crime.*
■ say **grav**-it-ee

gray
noun
a color that is a mixture of black and white.

graze
grazes grazing grazed *verb*
1 to move around eating grass and plants, in the way that cattle and other animals do.

***grazing** antelopes*

2 to touch lightly in passing.
*Her skirt **grazed** the flowers on the path.*

grease
noun
a soft, thick oil or fat.
greasy *adjective*

great
adjective
1 very big.
*The **great** trees grew over the road.*

2 important or powerful.
*A **great** leader.*
■ say **grayt**
■ comparisons **greater greatest**

greedy
adjective
wanting much more of something than you need.
*A **greedy** person.*
■ comparisons **greedier greediest**

green
noun
a color.

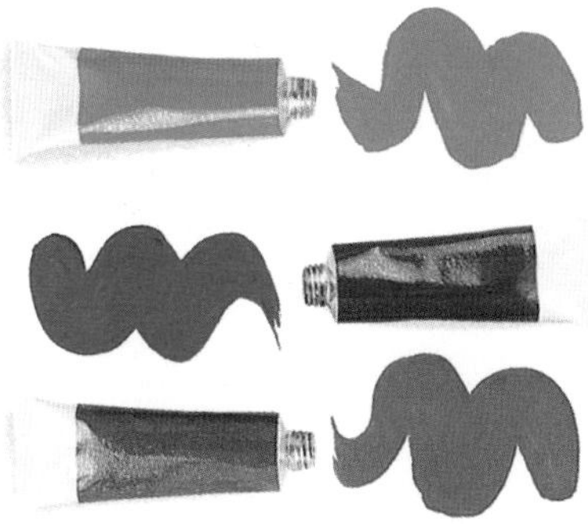

greenhouse
greenhouses *noun*
a building made mainly of glass, used for growing plants.

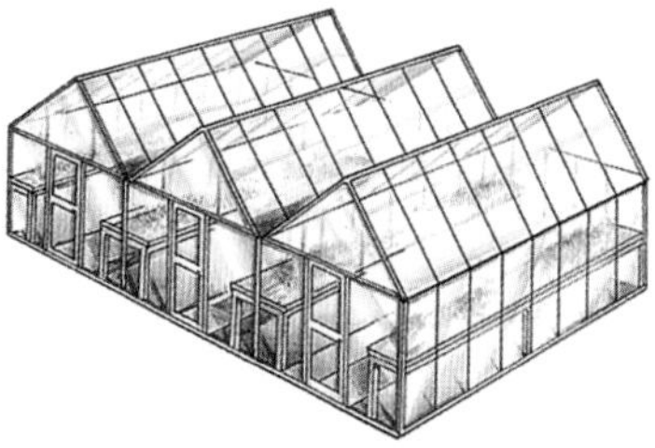

greet
greets greeting greeted *verb*
to welcome someone.

greeting
greetings
noun
an action, or words, used when meeting someone.

*When we arrived, she gave us a traditional Indian **greeting**.*

grief
noun
great unhappiness.

grill
grills *noun*
a set of metal bars for cooking food on.
grill *verb*

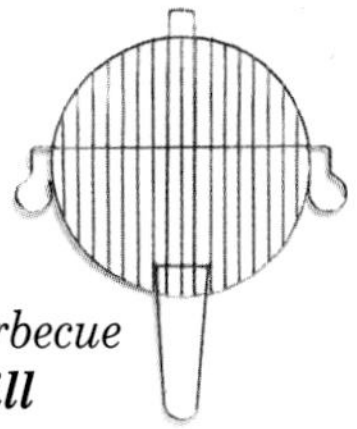

*barbecue **grill***

grin
grins grinning grinned *verb*
to have a big smile.

grin *noun*

grind
grinds grinding ground *verb*
to crush something into a powder by rubbing it.

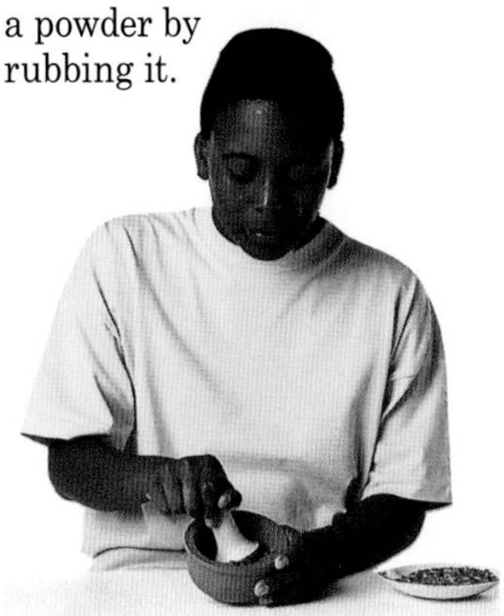

***Grinding** spices.*

grip
grips gripping gripped *verb*
to hold on to something very firmly.
*She **gripped** her briefcase.*

groan
groans groaning groaned *verb*
to make a long, deep sound because you are unhappy or in pain.

groceries
noun
food, cleaning supplies, and other things that you buy regularly to use at home.

■ say **grow**-sir-reez

groom
grooms grooming groomed *verb*
to make an animal clean by brushing it.

groove
grooves *noun*
a long, fine line that is cut into a flat surface.

grotesque
adjective
ugly and strange.
■ say grow-**tesk**

ground
noun
1 the surface of the Earth.

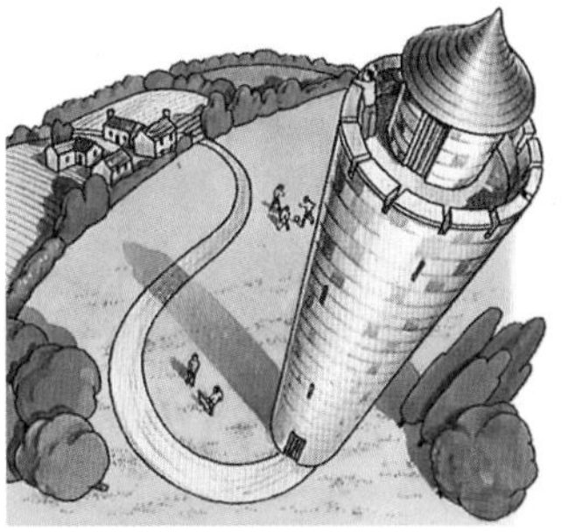

*You could see the **ground** from the top of the tower.*
2 a piece of land around a building.
*Hospital **grounds**.*

group
groups *noun*
people, animals, or things that are connected in some way.

*A **group** of schoolchildren.*

grow
grows growing grew grown *verb*
1 to become bigger.

*The plant **grew** a little more every day.*

2 to become something gradually.
***Growing** older.*

growl
growls growling growled *verb*
to make a long, low, angry sound deep down in the throat.
*The dog **growled** every time I came near.*

A B C D E F G H I J K L M N O P Q R S T U V W X Y Z

growth

noun

the way in which things change as they become older and bigger. The growth of animals and plants happens in many different ways.

Snake

egg — hatchling — adult rat snake

Butterfly

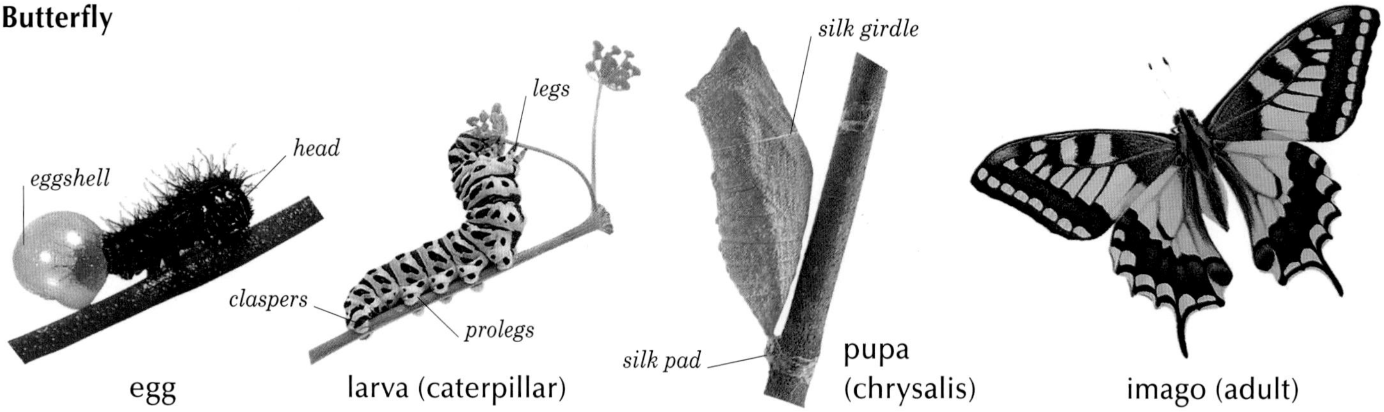

egg — larva (caterpillar) — pupa (chrysalis) — imago (adult)

Sunflower

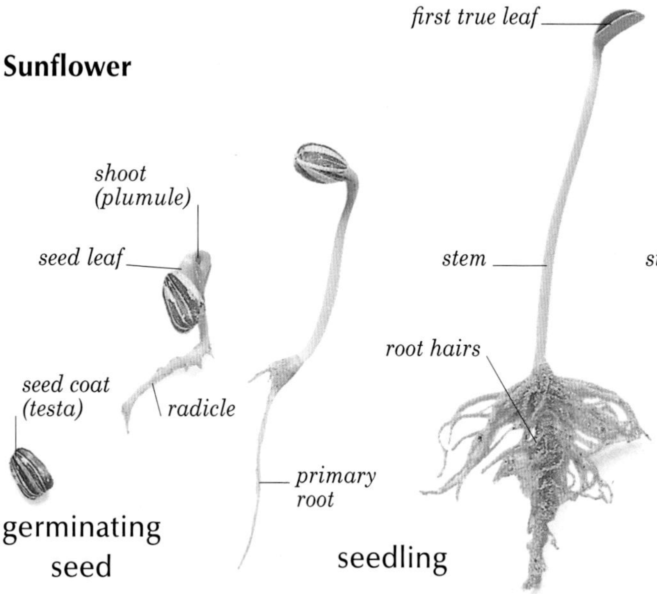

germinating seed — seedling — flower

Human being

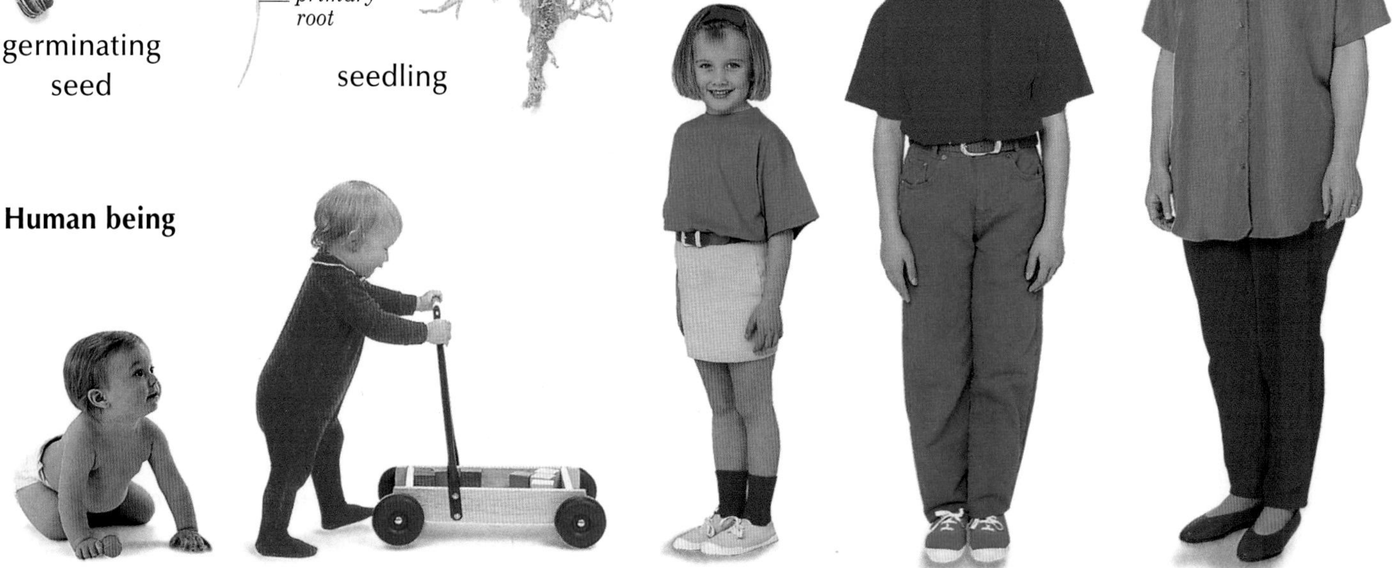

baby — toddler — child — teenager — adult

grub
grubs *noun*
the larva of a newly hatched insect before it becomes an adult. A grub looks like a thick, soft worm.

grumble
grumbles grumbling grumbled *verb*
to complain in an angry way, usually in a quiet voice.

grunt
grunts grunting grunted *verb*
to make a short sound like the noise a pig makes.

guarantee
guarantees *noun*
1 a promise from a company that if one of their products breaks or goes wrong they will fix or replace it.
*A one-year **guarantee**.*
2 a promise that something will happen.
■ say ga-run-**tee**

guard
guards guarding guarded *verb*
to watch over something to keep it safe.
*The building was **guarded** at night.*
■ say **gard**

guess
guesses guessing guessed *verb*
to suggest an answer to a question, without being sure it is the right one.

*She had to **guess** what she was holding.*
guess *noun*

guest
guests *noun*
someone who stays at a house or a hotel.
■ rhymes with **best**

guide
guides *noun*
1 someone whose job is to show people around places.
*The **guide** took us around the museum.*
2 a book with maps and information about a place.
guide *verb*

guard
guards *noun*
1 someone who watches over and protects something or someone.

*security **guard***

2 something that prevents damage or injury.

*face **guard***

guilty
adjective
having done something wrong.

guilt *noun*

guitar
guitars *noun*
a musical instrument with six or twelve strings. You pull the strings with your fingers to make different sounds.

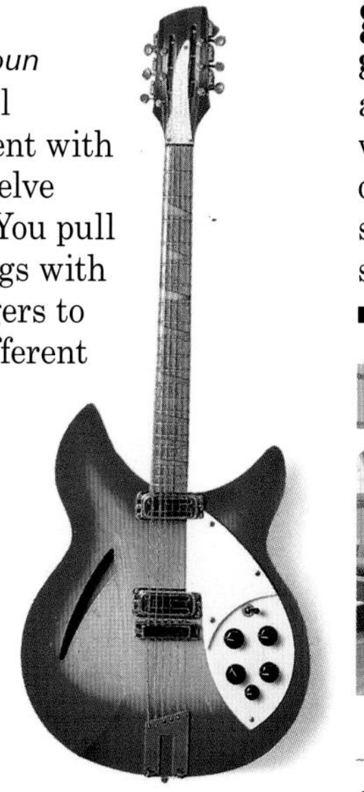

*electric **guitar***

gulp
gulps gulping gulped *verb*
to swallow something fast or in large amounts.
*He **gulped** the drink quickly.*

gum
gums *noun*
1 the firm part inside your mouth around your teeth.
2 a sticky substance that is usually made from plants.
*Chewing **gum**.*

gun
guns *noun*
a weapon that shoots bullets.

*18th-century **gun***

gurgle
gurgles gurgling gurgled *verb*
to make small bubbling sounds in the throat.
*The baby **gurgled** when his mother tickled him.*

gust
gusts *noun*
a sudden, strong rush of wind.
*A **gust** of wind blew off his hat.*

gym
gyms *noun*
a large room or building where people can play sports or exercise, often using special equipment. Gym is short for "gymnasium."
■ say **jim**

gymnast
gymnasts *noun*
a person who is skilled in gymnastics.
■ say **jim**-nast

gymnastics
noun
a sport in which people perform exercises that develop physical strength and ability.
■ say jim-**nass**-ticks

Hh

habit
habits *noun*
1 something that you usually do without thinking.

*Biting your nails is a bad **habit**.*

2 a type of clothing worn by monks and nuns.

*monk's **habit***

habitat
habitats *noun*
the natural place where an animal, bird, or plant lives and grows.

hail
noun
frozen rain that falls in small, hard balls.

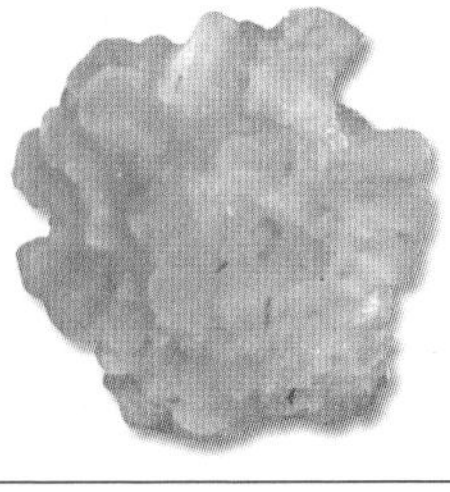

hair
noun
1 thin strands that grow on the skin of animals and people.
2 a mass of thin strands that covers your head.

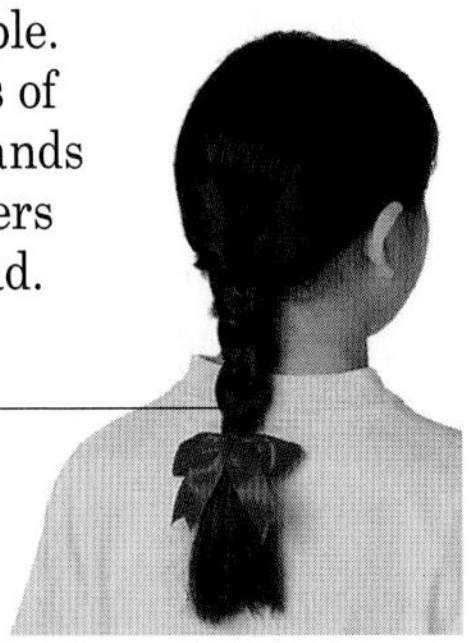

*braided **hair***

hairy *adjective*

hairbrush
hairbrushes *noun*
a brush for hair.

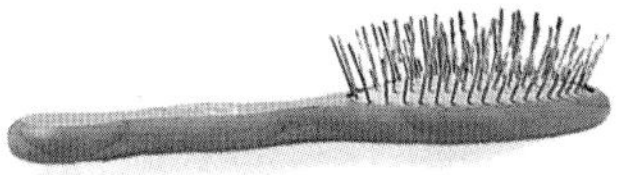

haircut
haircuts *noun*
a style in which hair is cut.
*Have you seen his new **haircut**?*

hairdresser
hairdressers *noun*
someone whose job it is to cut hair.

half
halves *noun*
one of two equal parts of something.

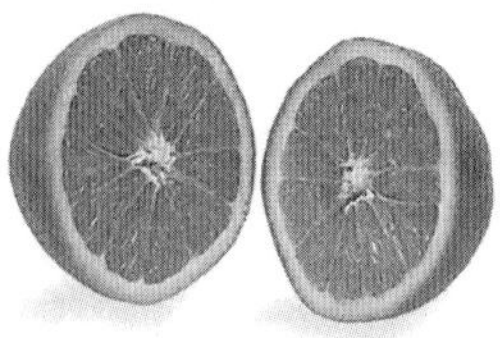

halve *verb*

hall
halls *noun*
1 a corridor or small room at the entrance of a house.
2 a large, open room in a building, used for meetings or other group activities.

halt
halts halting halted *verb*
to stop walking or moving forward.
■ say **hawlt**

ham
noun
meat from the leg of a pig that has been preserved with salt or smoke.

hamburger
hamburgers *noun*
a flat piece of chopped beef, grilled and served in a roll.

hammer
hammers *noun*
a tool with a metal end that is used to knock nails into wood and for shaping metals.
hammer *verb*

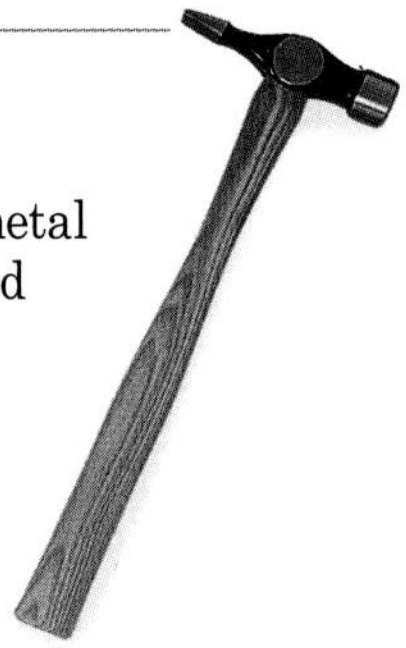

hammock
hammocks *noun*
a bed made of cloth or net hung by rope and fastened at two ends.

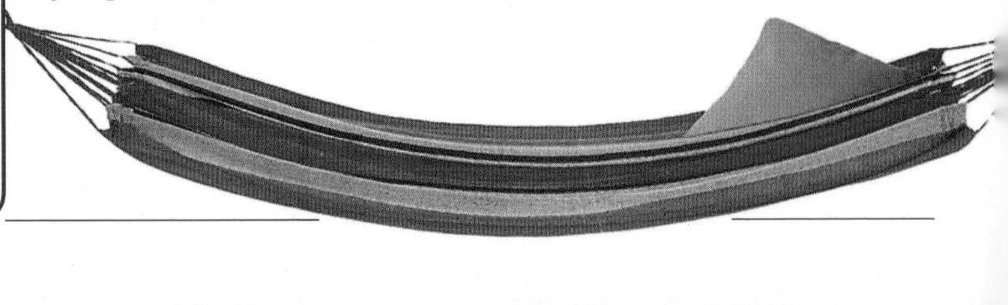

hand
hands *noun*
the part of your body at the end of your arm that has four fingers and one thumb.

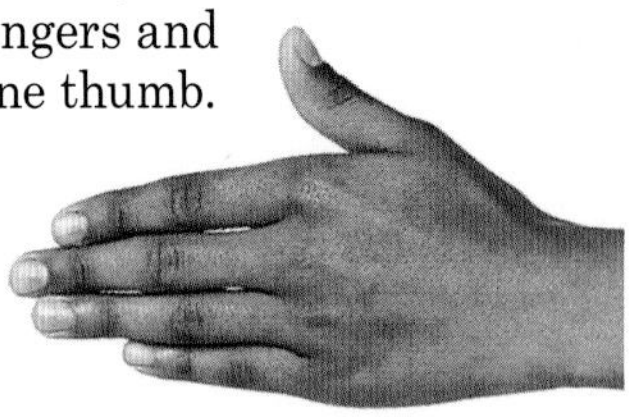

hand
hands handing handed *verb*
to give something to someone with your hand.
***Hand** the hammer to me.*

handkerchief
handkerchiefs *noun*
a small piece of cloth or paper used for blowing your nose.

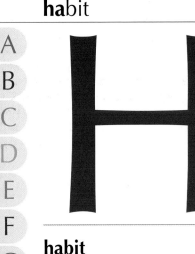

handle
handles *noun*
a part of something that is designed to be grasped or held by the hand.

*door **handle***

handle
handles handling handled *verb*
to touch or hold something.
*Please **handle** that vase carefully!*

handlebar
handlebars *noun*
a bar at the front of a bicycle that you turn to steer (see **transportation** on page 221).

handsome
adjective
attractive and pleasant to look at.
*A **handsome** man.*

handstand
handstands *noun*
an upside-down position, standing on your hands, with your legs in the air.

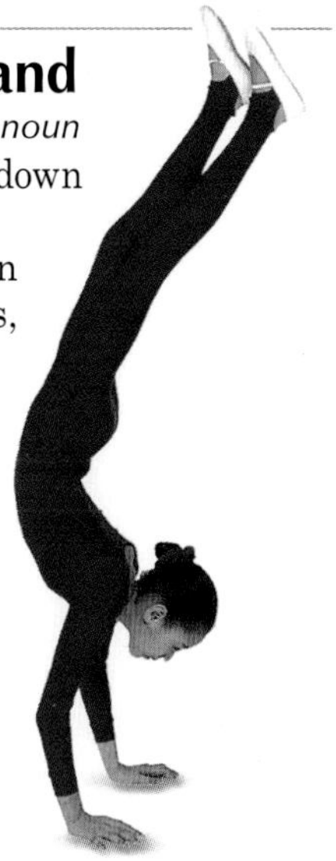

handwriting
noun
writing done by hand, not typed or printed.

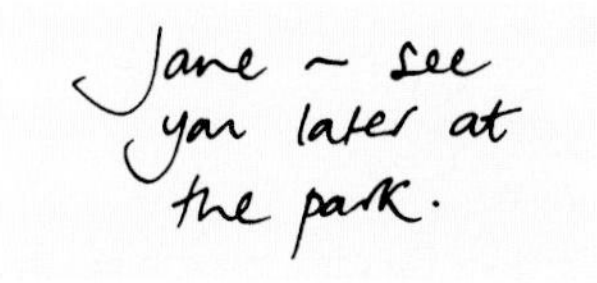

hang
hangs hanging hung *verb*
to support something from above.

***Hanging** up her clothes.*

hangar
hangars *noun*
a very large building where aircraft are stored.

hang glider
hang gliders *noun*
a huge kite that a person can hang from. The hang glider rides on currents of air in the same way as a glider.

happen
happens happening happened *verb*
to take place.
*What **happened** to your car?*

happy
adjective
pleased and content.
*He felt **happy** on his birthday.*
■ comparisons **happier happiest**
happiness noun

harbor
harbors *noun*
a sheltered place where ships can anchor and unload safely.

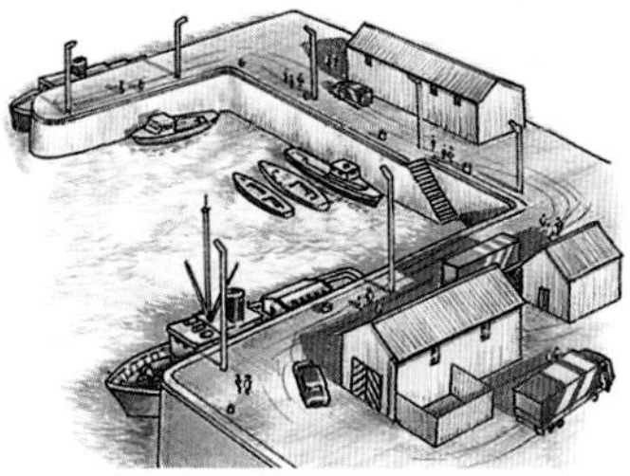

hard
adjective
1 solid and firm to touch.
***Hard** ground.*
2 difficult to understand or do.
*These puzzles are **hard**.*
■ comparisons **harder hardest**
hard *adverb*

hare
hares *noun*
a furry, plant-eating mammal that belongs to the same animal group as rabbits. Hares can run fast and have very good hearing. Males are called jacks and females are called jills.

harm
harms harming harmed *verb*
to damage or injure something or someone.

harmful
adjective
able to damage or injure someone or something.
■ opposite **harmless**

harmony
harmonies *noun*
a collection of musical notes played or sung together to make a pleasant sound.
*They sang in perfect **harmony**.*

harp
harps *noun*
a musical instrument that has a large frame with strings stretched across it. Harps are played by pulling the strings with your fingers.

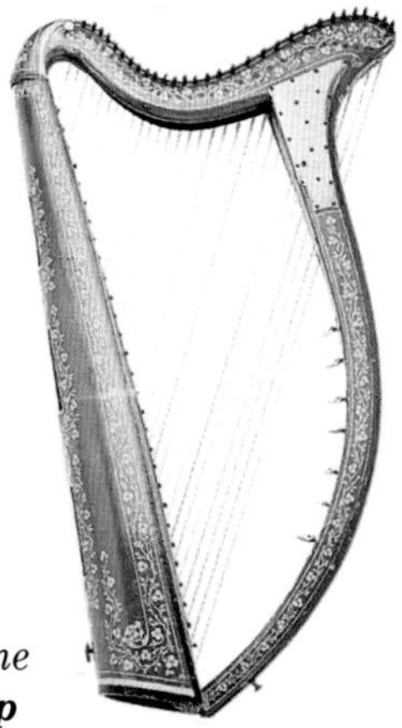

frame
harp

harvest
harvests harvesting harvested *verb*
to gather a crop, such as fruit or wheat, when it is ready to be used or eaten.

combine
harvester

***Harvesting** wheat.*
harvest *noun*

hat
hats *noun*
something that is worn on the head.

hatch
hatches hatching hatched *verb*
to be born by coming out of an egg.

hate
hates hating hated *verb*
to dislike something or someone very much.
hatred *noun*

haul
hauls hauling hauled *verb*
to pull with force.

***Hauling** a boat.*

a b c d e f g h i j k l m n o p q r s t u v w x y z

haunted
adjective
having ghosts or other spirits in it.
*A **haunted** house.*

hawk
hawks *noun*
one of a group of birds that hunt animals for food. Falcons, buzzards, and vultures are all hawks.

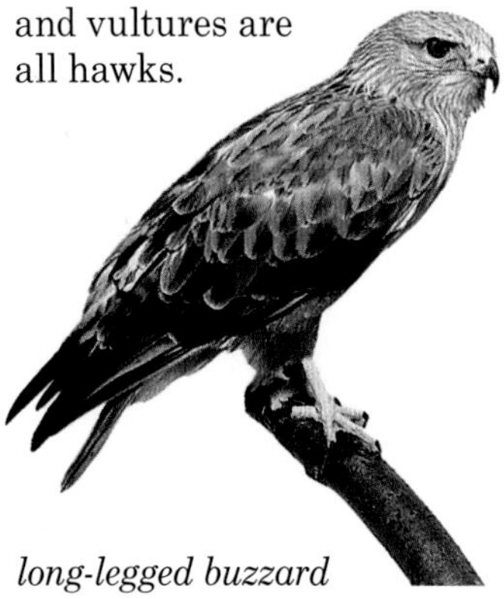

long-legged buzzard

hay
noun
grass that has been cut and dried to be fed to animals. Hay is often stored in large heaps called haystacks.

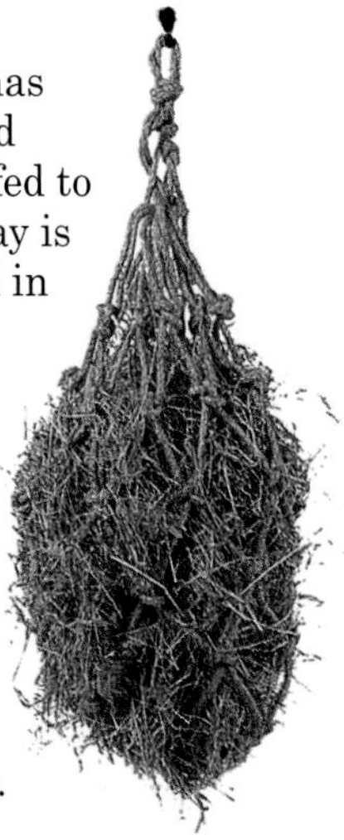

***Hay** is often hung in a net for horses to eat.*

hazard
hazards *noun*
a risk or dangerous obstacle.

*Icy pavements are a **hazard** to pedestrians in winter.*
hazardous *adjective*

head
heads *noun*
1 the part of your body that contains your brain, and is where your ears, eyes, nose, and mouth are.

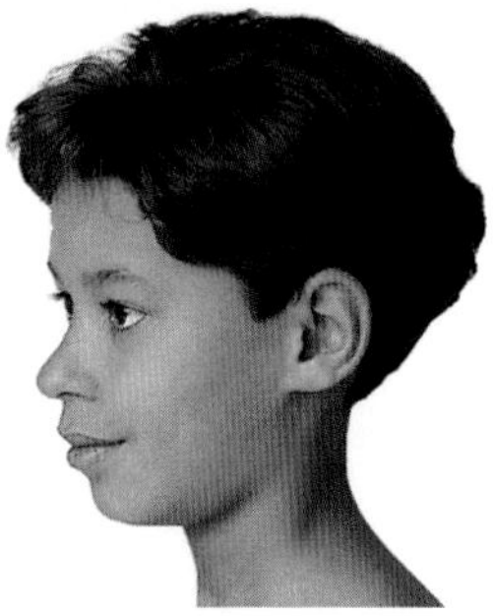

2 a leader of a group.
*She is the **head** of a large company.*

headache
headaches *noun*
a pain in your head.

headlight
headlights *noun*
a light at the front of a vehicle, used when driving at night.

headlight

headline
headlines *noun*
the title of a report in a newspaper.
*Have you seen the **headlines** today?*

headphones
noun
a device worn over the ears that is used for listening to the radio or to recorded music.

healthy
adjective
well and strong.
■ say **hell**-thee
■ comparisons **healthier healthiest**
health *noun*

heap
heaps *noun*
a collection of things lying on top of each other.

*She left her clothes in a **heap** on the chair.*

hear
hears hearing heard *verb*
1 to notice a sound.
*Did you **hear** that bird?*
2 to listen to.
*I'd like to **hear** you play the piano.*

heart
hearts *noun*
1 the organ in your chest that pumps blood around your body.

heart

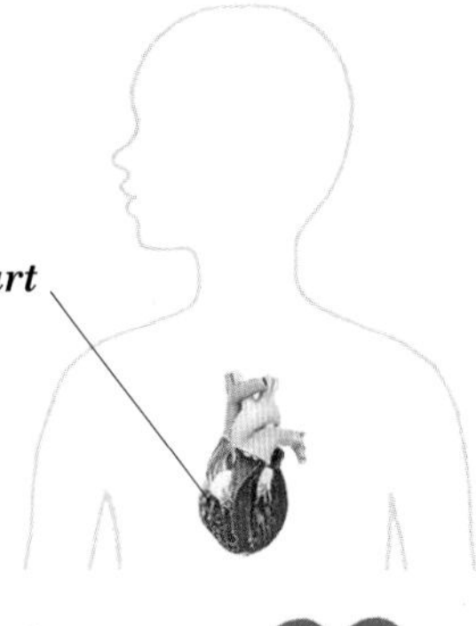

2 a shape.

■ say **hart**

heat
heats heating heated *verb*
to make or become warmer.
*We **heated** some water.*
heat *noun*

heave
heaves heaving heaved *verb*
to lift, pull, or throw something with a lot of effort.

*He **heaved** the sack onto the back of the truck.*

heavy
adjective
weighing a large amount.

*a **heavy** stone*

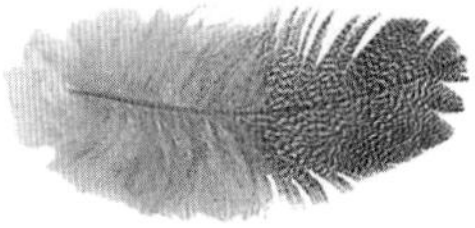

a light feather

■ say **hev**-ee
■ comparisons **heavier heaviest**
■ opposite **light**

hedge
hedges *noun*
a line of bushes grown so that they make a boundary between two places.

hedgehog
hedgehogs *noun*
a small, noctural mammal covered in spines. Hedgehogs hunt for insects and small animals. They roll into a ball when they feel threatened.

A B C D E F G H I J K L M N O P Q R S T U V W X Y Z

heel
heels *noun*
1 the back part of your foot.

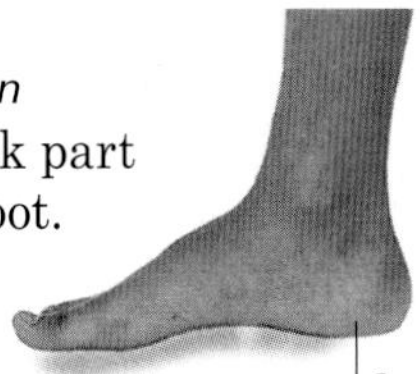
heel

2 the higher back part of a shoe.

heel

height
heights *noun*
the measurement of how tall or high someone or something is.

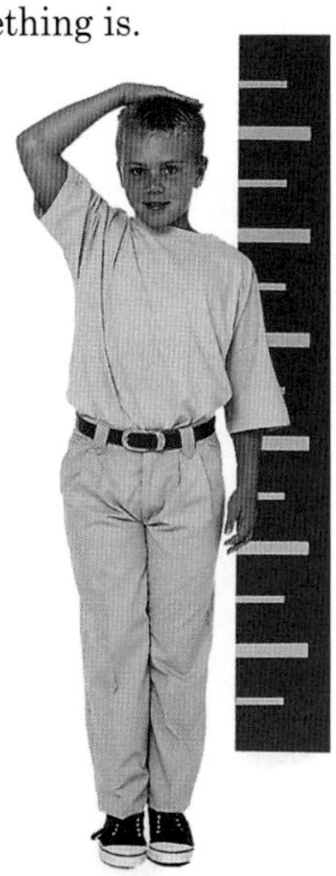

*He measured his **height**.*
■ say **hite**

held
*from the verb **to hold***
*I **held** a snake when we went to the zoo yesterday.*

helicopter
helicopters *noun*
a type of aircraft that uses rotating blades to make it fly and hover.

helmet
helmets *noun*
a strong hat, worn to protect the head.

*cycling **helmet***

help
helps helping helped *verb*
to make something easier or better for someone.
help *noun*

helpless
adjective
unable to take care of yourself.
*A baby is completely **helpless**.*

hemisphere
hemispheres *noun*
one half of the world.

*northern **hemisphere***

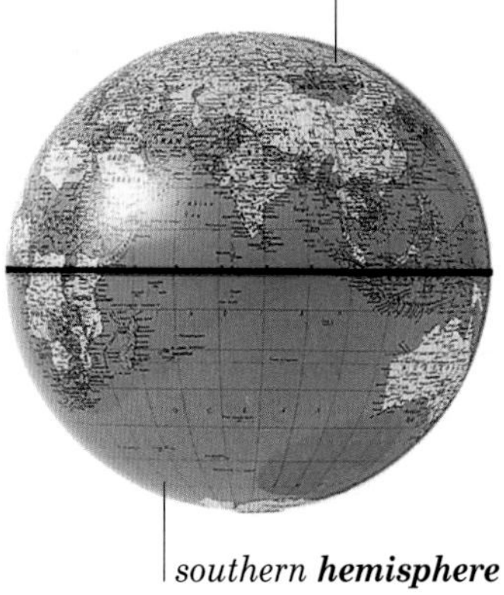

*southern **hemisphere***

herb
herbs *noun*
a plant that is used fresh or dried to flavor food or to make medicines.
*Two different types of **herb**.*

herbal *adjective*

rosemary

oregano

herd
herds *noun*
a group of large, grazing animals.

*A **herd** of bison.*

here
adverb
in this place.
*Is there a doctor **here**?*

hero / heroine
heroes / heroines *noun*
1 a very brave person.
2 the main character in a story, movie, or play.
■ **hero** is male and **heroine** is female

hesitate
hesitates hesitating hesitated *verb*
to pause because you are not sure what to do.

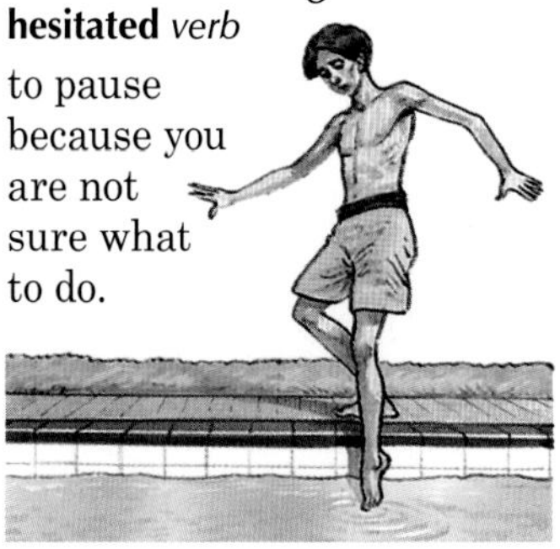

*He **hesitated** before jumping into the icy pool.*
hesitation *noun*

hexagon
hexagons *noun*
a shape with six sides (see **shape** on page 182).

hibernate
hibernates hibernating hibernated *verb*
to go to sleep for the winter.

*A fieldmouse **hibernating**.*
■ say **hie**-ber-nate
hibernation *noun*

hiccup
hiccups *noun*
a sudden movement in your chest that causes a quick breath and a short gulp.
■ also spelled **hiccough**
hiccup *verb*

hide
hides hiding hid hidden *verb*
to put yourself or something out of sight.

hieroglyphics
noun
a type of writing that uses pictures to represent sounds, words, and letters.

*ancient Egyptian **hieroglyphics***
■ say **hie**-roh-**gli**-fiks

high
adjective
tall or a long way up.

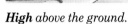

***High** above the ground.*
■ say **hye**
■ comparisons **higher highest**

highway
highways *noun*
a main road.

hijack
hijacks *noun*
a crime in which a vehicle or an aircraft is seized by force, and people are held prisoner.
hijack *verb*

hill
hills *noun*
an area of high ground.
hilly *adjective*

Hindu
Hindus *noun*
a follower of Hinduism (cultural and religious beliefs and practices that originated in India centuries ago).

hinge
hinges *noun*
a metal device that holds doors and gates in place, allowing them to open and close.

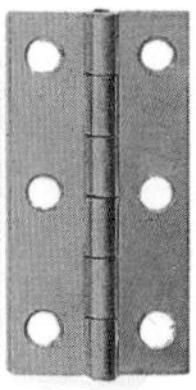

hint
hints hinting hinted *verb*
to suggest something in a vague way.
*He **hinted** that he knew about my secret.*

hip
hips *noun*
a joint at the top of each of your legs, between your waist and your thigh.

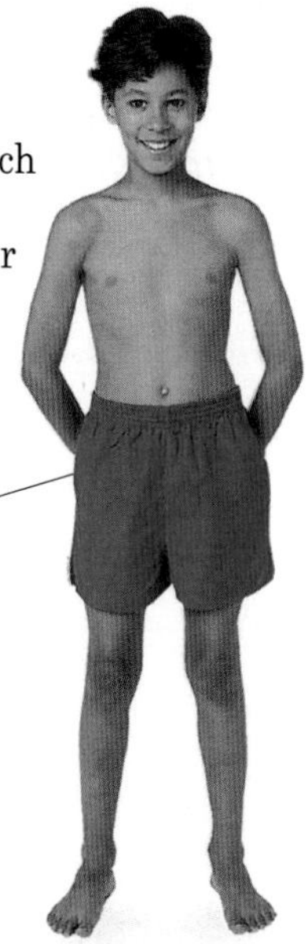

hip

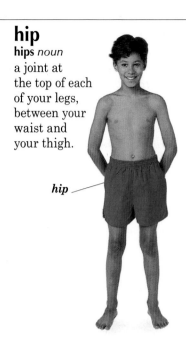

hippopotamus
hippopotamuses or **hippopotami**
noun
a large mammal that lives in Africa. Hippopotamuses spend most of the time in lakes or rivers and eat water plants.

hire
hires hiring hired *verb*
to pay money so you can use someone's services.
*They **hired** two girls to help clean the yard.*

hiss
hisses hissing hissed *verb*
to make a noise like air escaping from a tire.

*Snakes **hiss**.*
hiss *noun*

history
noun
the study of things that have happened to people in the past.
*We are studying the **history** of the United States.*
historical *adjective*

hit
hits hitting hit *verb*
to come into contact with someone or something in a forceful way.

*The tennis player **hit** the ball over the net.*

hit
hits *noun*
a success.
*The song was a big **hit**.*

hoax
hoaxes *noun*
an unpleasant trick or a joke where a person tries to make someone believe something that isn't really true.
*A **hoax** phone call.*
■ say **hoeks**

hobble
hobbles hobbling hobbled *verb*
to walk with difficulty and pain.

hobby
hobbies *noun*
an activity that you do for enjoyment in your spare time.

*Stamp collecting is a popular **hobby**.*

hold
holds holding held *verb*
1 to have or keep something in a certain position.

***Holding** a cup and saucer.*
2 to contain.

*This container **holds** kitchen utensils.*

hold
holds *noun*
a place inside a ship or an aircraft where cargo is stored.
*The cars were driven into the ferry's **hold**.*

hole
holes *noun*
a hollow place or gap.

holiday
holidays *noun*
a period of time off from school or work, often to celebrate a special event.

hollow
adjective
with a space inside.

*The mouse ran through the **hollow** pipe.*

home
homes *noun*
the place where a person or an animal lives or comes from.

honest
adjective
truthful or able to be trusted.
■ say **on**-nist
■ opposite **dishonest**
honesty *noun*

honey
noun
a sweet, sticky food, made by bees from the nectar of flowers.
■ say **hun**-ee

*jar of **honey***

***honey**comb*

hood
hoods *noun*
1 a part of a coat, jacket, or sweatshirt that covers your head.
2 the metal engine covering on the front of a car.

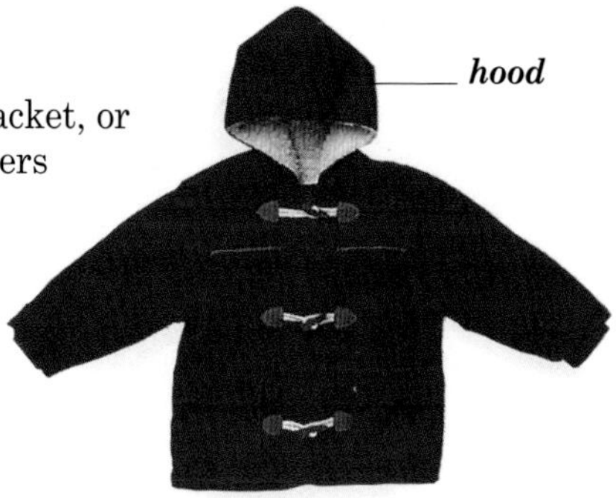

hood

hoof
hoofs or **hooves** *noun*
the hard, nail-like part of the foot of a horse, deer, or similar animal.

*horse's **hoof***

hook
hooks *noun*
a curved metal object used for hanging things on or for catching things.

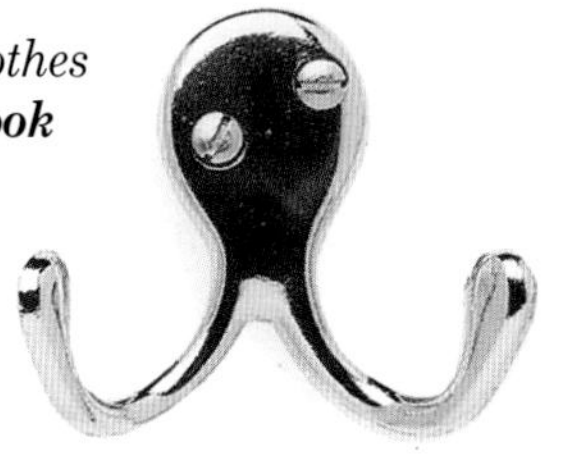

*clothes **hook***

hoop
hoops *noun*
a round strip of plastic, wood, or metal.

hoot
hoots hooting hooted *verb*
1 to make a sound like the noise an owl makes.
2 to blow a horn or whistle.
hoot *noun*

hop
hops hopping hopped *verb*
to jump on one leg.
hop *noun*

hope
hopes hoping hoped *verb*
to want something to happen, and think that it might.
*I **hope** I'll make the team.*
hopeful *adjective*

horizon
horizons *noun*
the line in the distance where the land or the sea seems to meet the sky.

■ say hor-**ize**-on

horizontal
adjective
parallel to the ground.
*A tabletop is **horizontal.***
■ opposite **vertical**
horizontally *adverb*

horn
horns *noun*
1 a tough, pointed, bony part on the head of some animals.

*goat's **horn***

2 a brass wind instrument that you play by holding down valves with your fingers and blowing through the narrow end of the tube.

*French **horn***

3 a device that is used to make a warning signal.

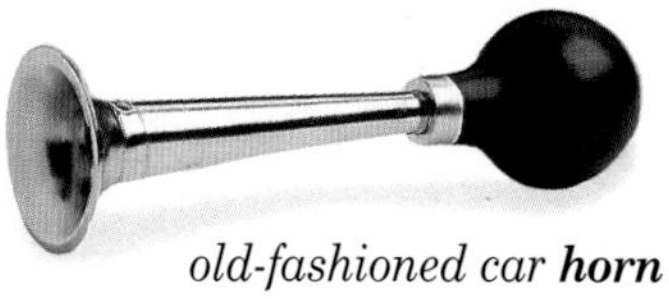

*old-fashioned car **horn***

horoscope
horoscopes *noun*
a prediction of what might happen to you in the future, made from the position of the stars and your date of birth.

horrible
adjective
very unpleasant or frightening.
horribly *adverb*

horror
noun
a feeling of shock and fear.
*They watched in **horror** as the house burned down.*

A B C D E F G H I J K L M N O P Q R S T U V W X Y Z

horse

horses *noun*

a large, plant-eating mammal that is often used for riding and pulling equipment. There are many different breeds of horse, and their coats can be a variety of colors.

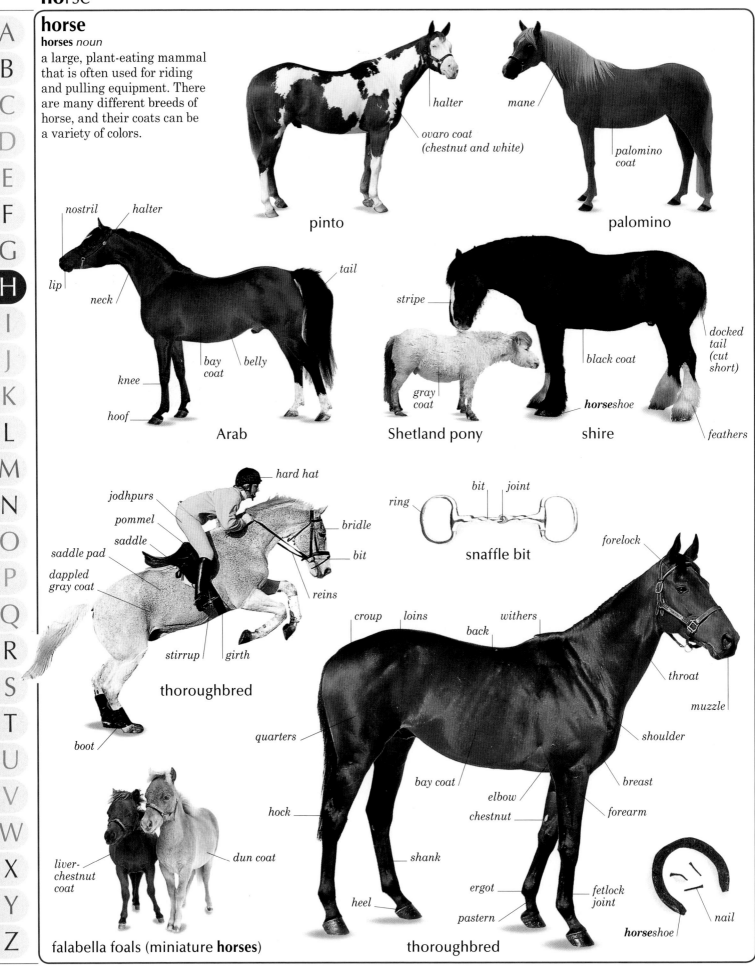

pinto

palomino

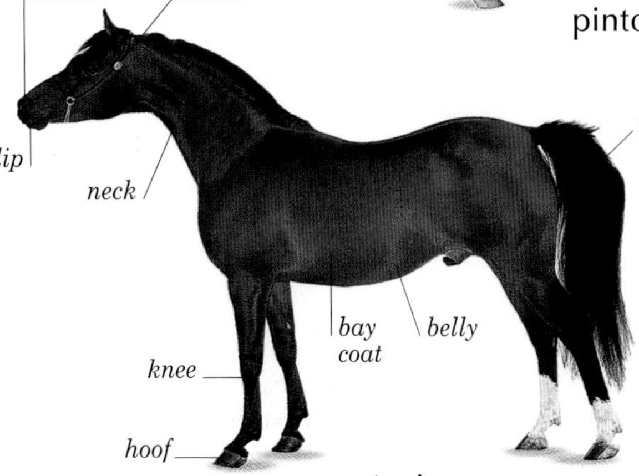

Arab

Shetland pony

shire

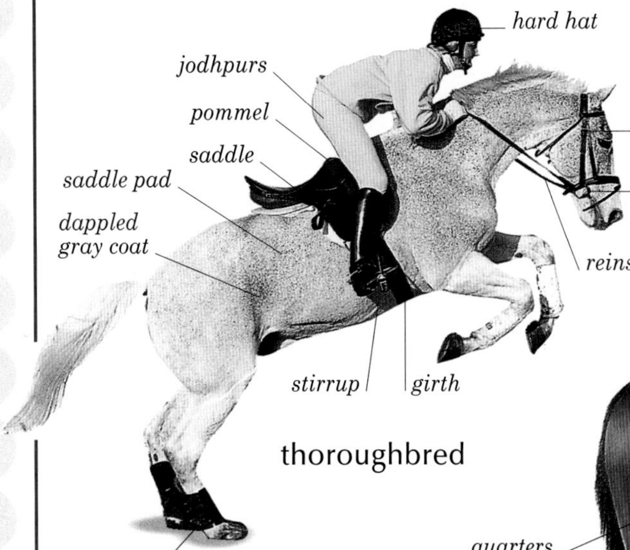

thoroughbred

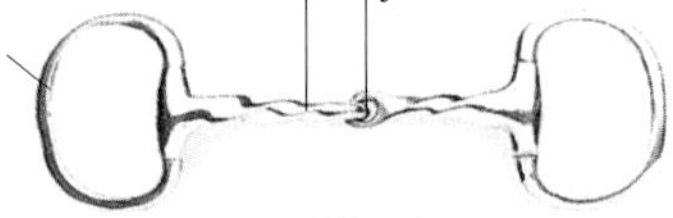

snaffle bit

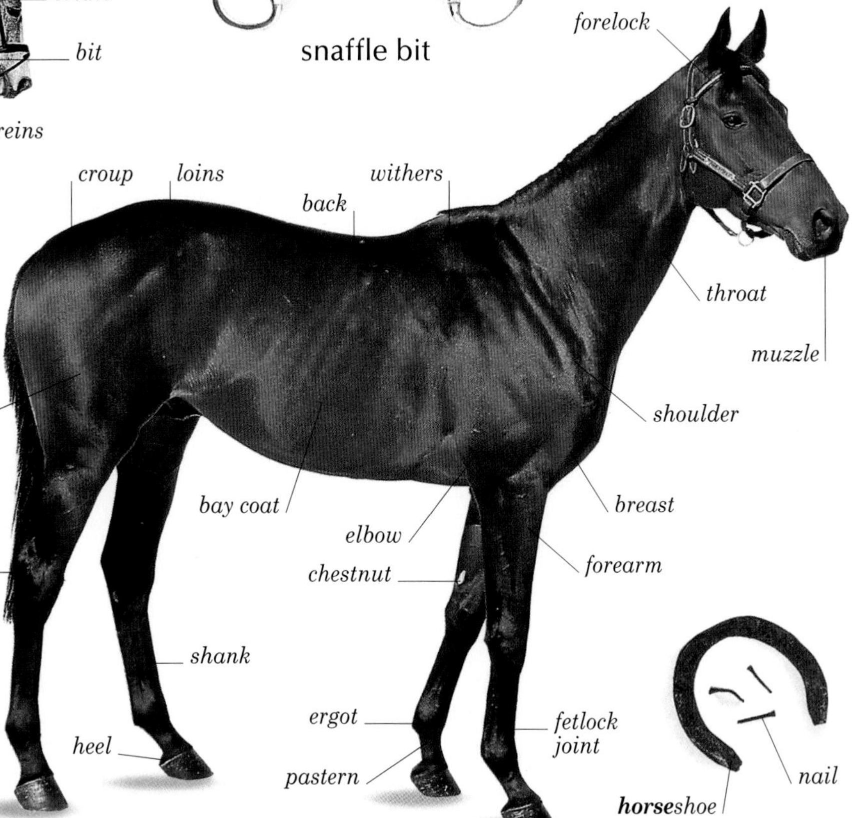

thoroughbred

horseshoe

falabella foals (miniature **horses**)

hose
hoses *noun*
a long, narrow tube, through which liquids can be sent.

garden hose

hospital
hospitals *noun*
a place where sick or injured people are treated.

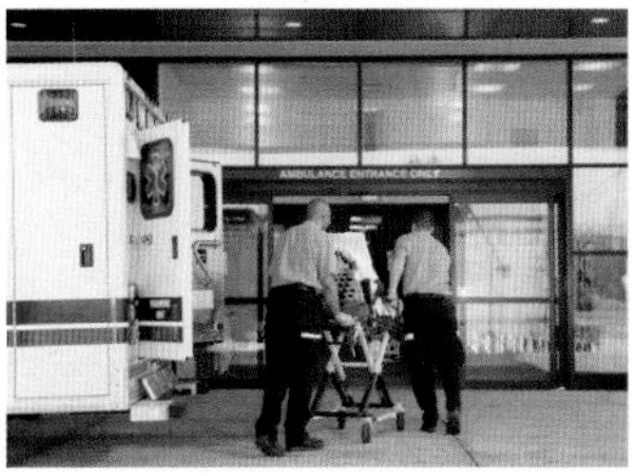

hostage
hostages *noun*
a person who is taken prisoner by someone who demands something in return for the prisoner's safety.

hot
adjective
1 very warm.

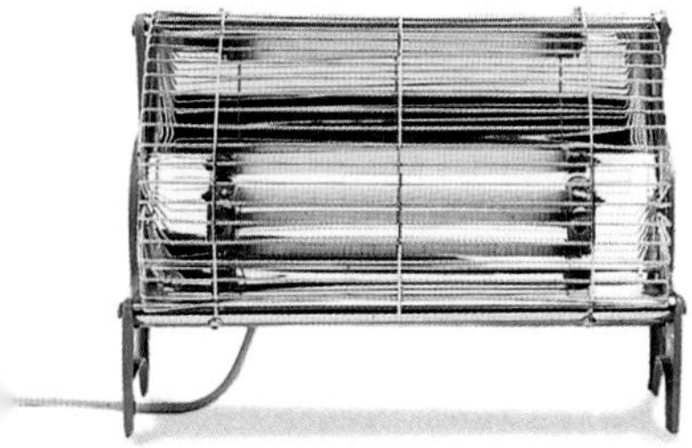
The bars of the heater are very ***hot****.*
2 very spicy.

Chili peppers taste very ***hot****.*
■ comparisons **hotter hottest**

hotel
hotels *noun*
a building with bedrooms that people pay to stay in. Most hotels have a restaurant and a bar.

hotel *building*

hour
hours *noun*
a period of time lasting 60 minutes. There are 24 hours in a day.
■ say **ow**-er
hourly *adjective*

house
houses *noun*
a building that people live in.

houseboat
houseboats *noun*
a small boat that people live on.

household
households *noun*
all the people that live together in one home.

hover
hovers hovering hovered *verb*
to stay in one place in the air.

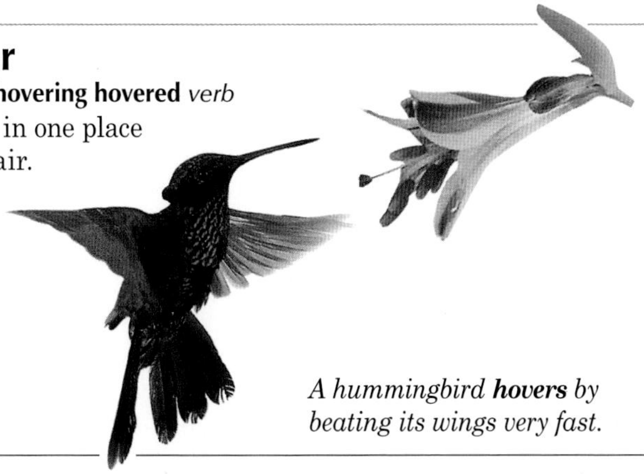
A hummingbird ***hovers*** *by beating its wings very fast.*

hovercraft
hovercraft *noun*
a vehicle that rides on a cushion of air. A hovercraft can travel across land and sea.

how
adverb
in what way.
How does this work?

howl
howls howling howled *verb*
to make a long, whining sound like a wolf.

huddle
huddles huddling huddled *verb*
to push or squeeze together.
They ***huddled*** *under the shelter.*

hug
hugs hugging hugged *verb*
to hold someone close in a loving way.

huge
adjective
very large or enormous.
He was so hungry that he ate a ***huge*** *plateful of food.*

hum
hums humming hummed *verb*
to make a musical sound with your lips closed.
humming *noun*

human being
human beings *noun*
a man, woman, or child.

■ say **hew**-mun
human *adjective*

humane
adjective
kind and merciful.
■ say hew-**mane**
humanely *adverb*

humid
adjective
warm and damp.
*The weather was **humid**.*

humiliate
humiliates humiliating humiliated *verb*
to make someone feel ridiculous or ashamed.
■ say hew-**mil**-lee-ate

humor
noun
the ability to see or show that something is funny.
*A good sense of **humor**.*
■ say **hew**-mer
humorous *adjective*

hump
humps *noun*
a large, round lump.

*This camel has two **humps**.*

hung
*from the verb **to hang***
*I **hung** my coat up when I arrived this morning.*

hungry
adjective
wanting or needing something to eat.

***hungry** chicks*
■ comparisons **hungrier hungriest**
hunger *noun*

hunt
hunts hunting hunted *verb*
1 to chase an animal, often to kill it for food.

*Lions **hunt** in packs.*
2 to search for something in many places.

*I **hunted** all over the house for my key.*
hunt *noun*

hurl
hurls hurling hurled *verb*
to throw something as hard as you can.

*She **hurled** the cushion across the room.*

hurricane
hurricanes *noun*
a violent storm with very strong winds.

hurry
hurries hurrying hurried *verb*
to act quickly because there is not a lot of time.

*He had to **hurry** to deliver the package on time.*

hurt
hurts hurting hurt *verb*
1 to cause pain or injury.
*I **hurt** my leg when I fell.*
2 to be painful.
*My broken arm **hurts**.*

husband
husbands *noun*
a married man.
■ opposite **wife**

hush
noun
silence.
*There was a **hush** as the teacher came into the room.*

hut
huts *noun*
a small shelter.

*Tourists stayed in **huts** on the beach.*

hutch
hutches *noun*
a large box made of wood and wire for a small pet to live in.

*rabbit **hutch***

hydrogen
noun
a gas that is lighter than air, burns easily, and has no taste, color, or smell.
■ say **hy**-dro-jen

hyena
hyenas *noun*
a fierce mammal from Africa and Asia that looks like a large dog. Hyenas hunt for food and have a strange bark that sounds like a laugh.

■ say hy-**ee**-nuh

hygiene
noun
cleanliness and health.

*Good **hygiene** is important in the kitchen.*
■ say **hy**-jeen

hysterical
adjective
crying or laughing wildly.
■ say his-**ster**-i-kuhl

Ii

ice
noun
frozen water.

iceberg
icebergs *noun*
a huge piece of ice floating in cold seas.

ice cream
ice creams *noun*
a sweet, frozen food made mainly from cream or milk.

ice cube
ice cubes *noun*
a small block of ice used in drinks.

ice rink
ice rinks *noun*
a surface of ice where people skate; also called a "skating rink."

ice skate
ice skates *noun*
a boot with a metal blade on the sole, used for skating on ice.

icicle
icicles *noun*
a hanging piece of ice, formed by dripping water that has frozen.

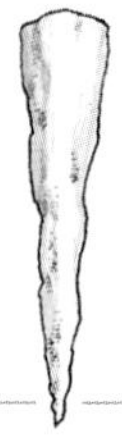

idea
ideas *noun*
a thought or suggestion about something.
*Do you have any better **ideas**?*

ideal
adjective
perfect in every way.
*That's an **ideal** solution.*
ideal *noun*

identical
adjective
exactly the same.

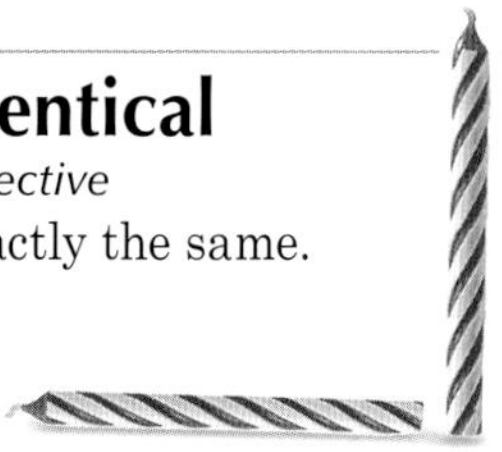

***identical** candles*

identify
identifies identifying identified *verb*
to recognize something or someone by name.

*Can you **identify** which tree these leaves come from?*
identification *noun*

identity
identities *noun*
who someone is or what something is.

*The card around his neck shows his **identity**.*

idle
adjective
lazy, or doing nothing.

igloo
igloos *noun*
a round building made of snow and ice.

ignorant
adjective
not knowing about something.
ignorance *noun*

ignore
ignores ignoring ignored *verb*
to take no notice of someone or something.

iguana
iguanas *noun*
a large lizard found mainly in Central and South America. The common iguana lives near rivers and streams. It eats plants, insects, and small animals.

*common **iguana***

ill
adjective
feeling sick or unwell.
illness *noun*

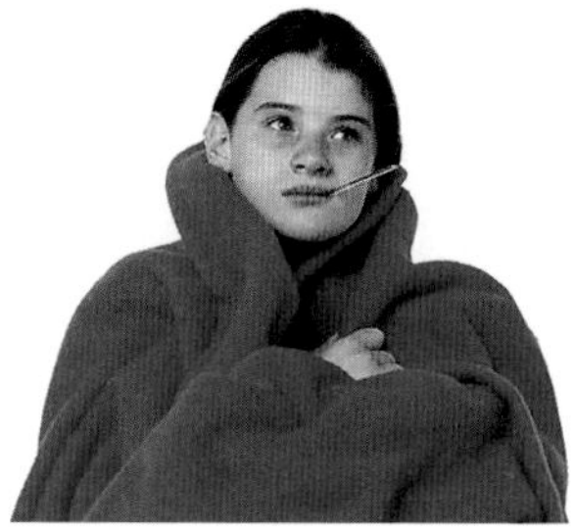

illegal
adjective
not allowed by law.
*It is **illegal** to park there.*
■ opposite **legal**
illegally *adverb*

illustrate
illustrates illustrating illustrated *verb*
to supply with pictures.

***Illustrating** a book.*
illustration *noun*

image
images *noun*
a picture of something or someone, or a picture in your mind.

imaginary
adjective
not real.

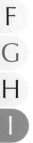

*The unicorn is an **imaginary** animal.*
■ say i-**maj**-i-nar-ee

imagine
imagines imagining imagined *verb*
to create a picture of something in your mind.
■ say i-**ma**-jin
imagination *noun*

imitate
imitates imitating imitated *verb*
to copy the way that someone talks or does something.

imitation
imitations *noun*
a copy.

*These **imitations** of fruit don't look real.*
imitation *adjective*

immediately
adverb
without delay.
*Go home **immediately**!*
immediate *adjective*

immigrate
immigrates immigrating immigrated *verb*
to go to a country in order to live there permanently.
immigration *noun*

impact
impacts *noun*
1 the action of one object hitting another with force.

*The **impact** of the crash wrecked both cars.*
2 something that has enough power to create strong feelings in someone.
*Traveling abroad had a great **impact** on me.*

impatient
adjective
1 not willing to wait.

*He became **impatient** when the bus didn't come.*
2 easily annoyed.
*She was often **impatient** with her little brother.*
impatience *noun*

important
adjective
1 meaning a lot.
*Winning this competition is very **important** to me.*
2 having great power or influence.
*An **important** visitor.*
importance *noun*

impossible
adjective
not able to be done.

*It is **impossible** for people to fly like birds.*
■ opposite **possible**

impress
impresses impressing impressed *verb*
to make someone have a good opinion of something.
*His cooking skills **impressed** the judges.*

improve
improves improving improved *verb*
to make or become better.

*We **improved** the flowerpot by decorating it.*
improvement *noun*

include
includes including included *verb*
to put something in as part of a whole.
*The travel brochure **includes** pictures of the hotels.*
inclusion *noun*

inconvenient
adjective
not easy or not suitable.
*Steep stairs are **inconvenient** for a lot of people.*
■ say in-kun-**veen**-nyent
■ opposite **convenient**
inconvenience *noun*

increase
increases increasing increased *verb*
to become bigger in size or number.
■ opposite **decrease**
increase *noun*

incredible
adjective
difficult to believe.
*He tells some **incredible** stories.*

independent
adjective
not controlled by anyone or anything.
■ opposite **dependent**
independently *adverb*

index
indexes or **indices** *noun*
an alphabetical list of subjects and page numbers, usually found at the back of a book.

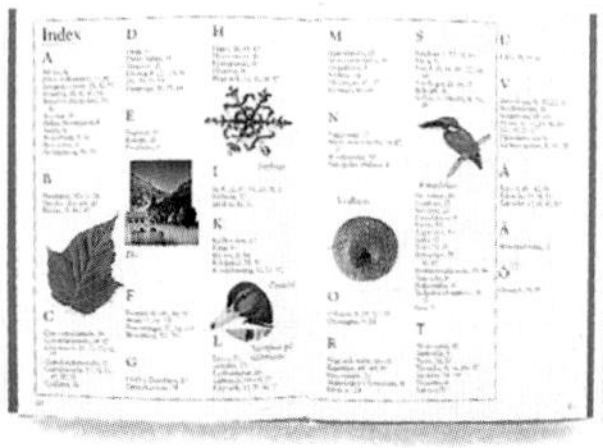

indignant
adjective
upset and annoyed because something is unfair.
*They were **indignant** about the way they were treated.*
indignantly *adverb*

individual
adjective
separate or for just one person.

***Individual** teaching.*
individual *noun*

indoors
adverb
inside a building.
*Let's go **indoors** now.*
■ opposite **outdoors**

industry
industries *noun*
a trade or business, and all the people and processes involved in it.

*The food **industry**.*
industrial *adjective*

infant
infants *noun*
a very young child.

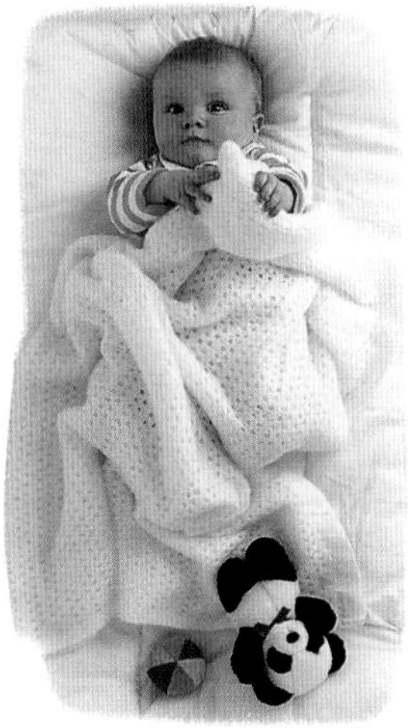

infancy *noun*

infection
infections *noun*
a disease caused by germs, which can be passed from one person to another.
infect *verb*
infectious *adjective*

infinite
adjective
with no end.
infinity *noun*

inflate
inflates inflating inflated *verb*
to make something bigger by filling it with air or gas.

inflatable *adjective*

influence
influences influencing influenced *verb*
to have an effect on someone so that they change their ideas or behavior.
■ say **in**-floo-ens
influence *noun*

information
noun
useful facts about something.

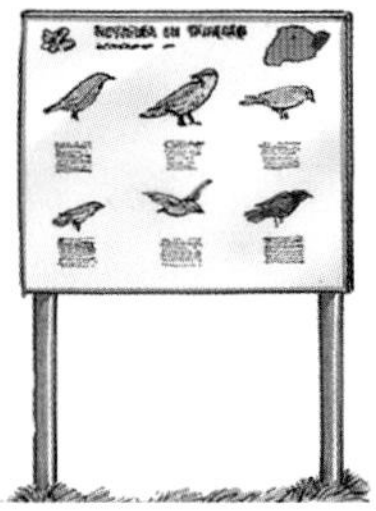

*The board gave **information** about the birds in the area.*

infuriate
infuriates infuriating infuriated *verb*
to make someone very angry.
■ say in-**fyoor**-ee-ate

ingredient
ingredients *noun*
one of the parts of a mixture.

***Ingredients** for a salad.*
■ say in-**gree**-dee-ent

inhabitant
inhabitants *noun*
a person who lives in a place.
*The desert has very few **inhabitants**.*
inhabit *verb*

initial
initials *noun*
the first letter of a word or name.

R.A.

*Robert Anderson's **initials**.*
■ say i-**nish**-uhl

inject
injects injecting injected *verb*
to put a substance into your body using a hollow needle and a syringe.
injection *noun*

injure
injures injuring injured *verb*
to hurt yourself or someone else.

*He **injured** his leg when he fell down the stairs.*
injured *adjective*
injury *noun*

ink
inks *noun*
a black or colored liquid used for writing or drawing.

inland
adjective
away from the sea, toward the middle of the country.

inlet
inlets *noun*
a small opening or bay along the coast.

*An **inlet**.*

innocent
adjective
not guilty.
*He was arrested for stealing, but was found to be **innocent**.*
innocence *noun*
innocently *adverb*

inquire
inquires inquiring inquired *verb*
to ask for information.

*He **inquired** at the stand about the way to the museum.*
■ say in-**kwire**
inquiry *noun*

insect

insects *noun*

a small animal with six legs and a body divided into three parts. Insects usually have two pairs of wings and do not have a backbone.

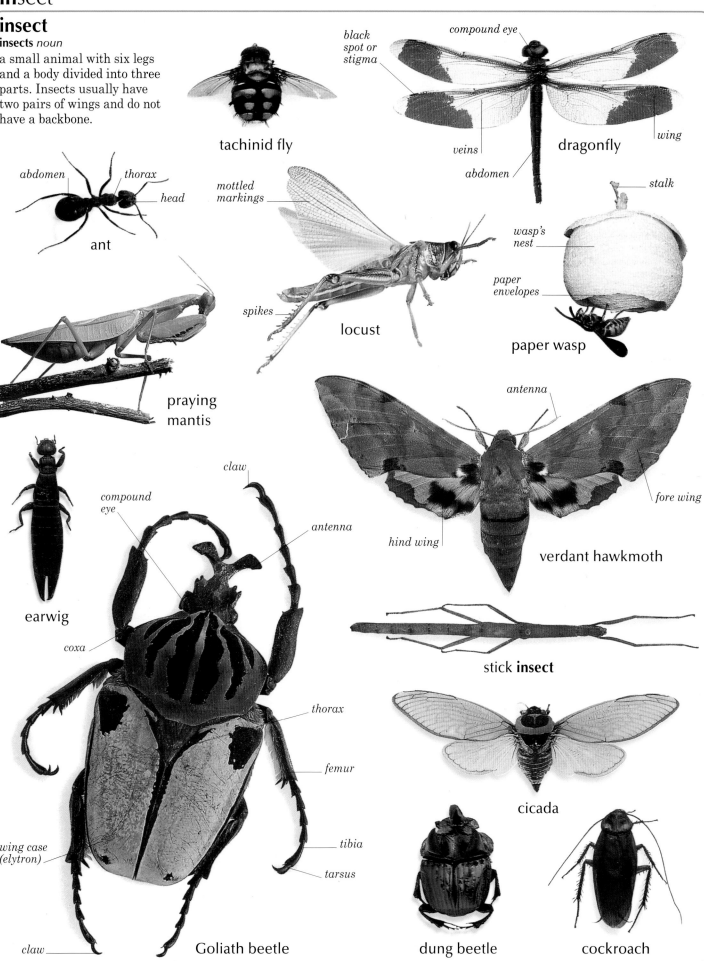

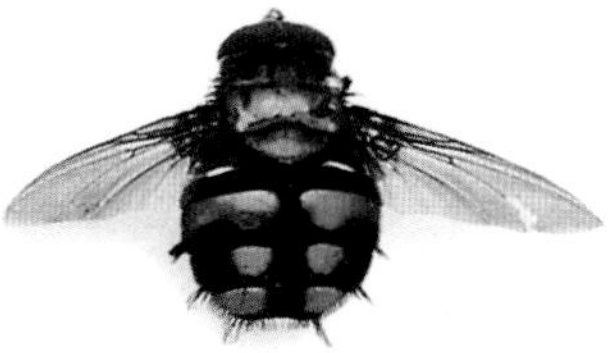

tachinid fly

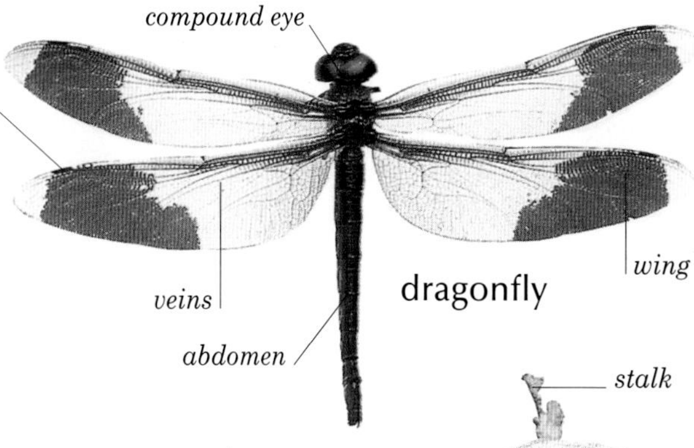

dragonfly

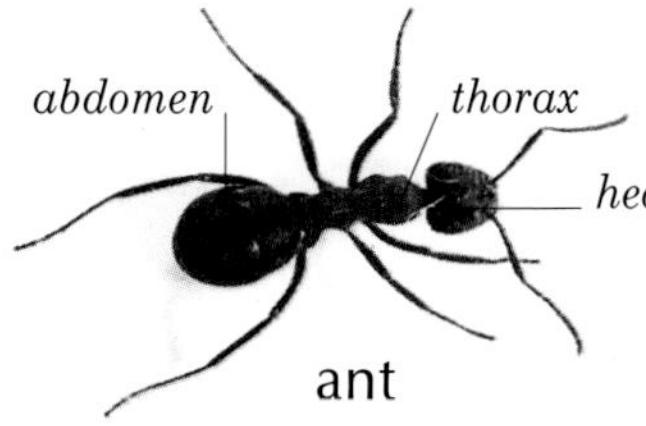

ant

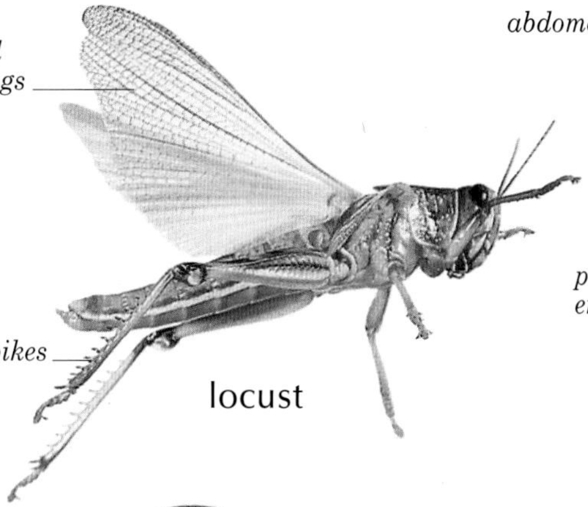

locust

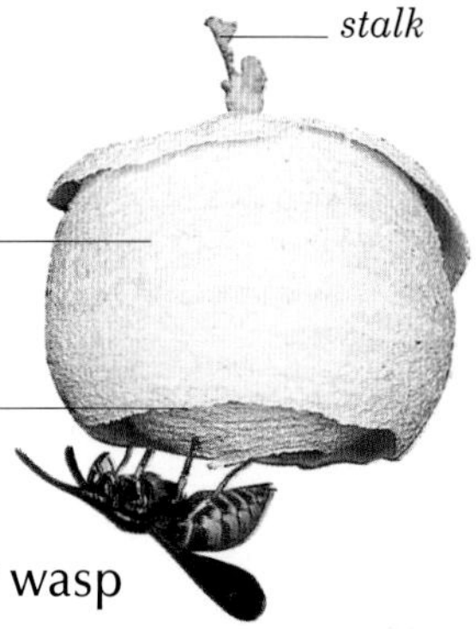

paper wasp

praying mantis

verdant hawkmoth

earwig

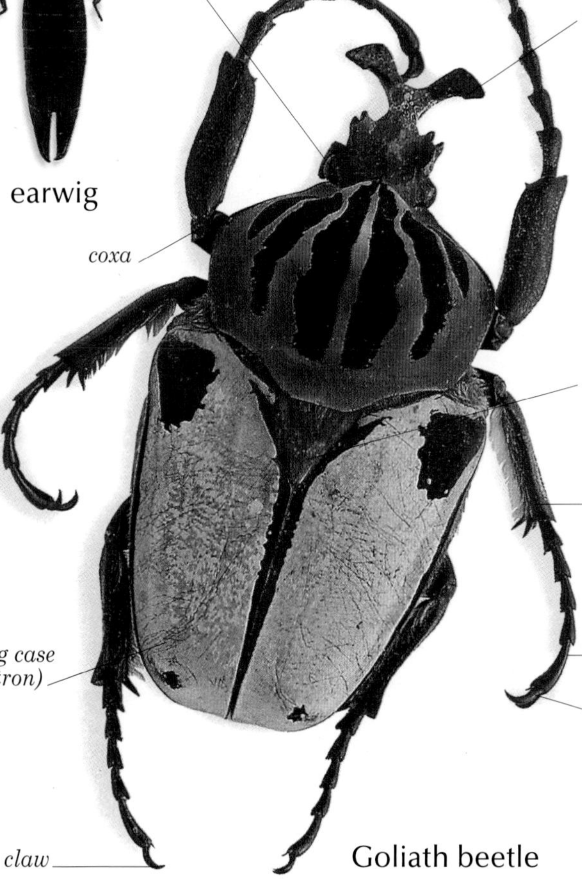

Goliath beetle

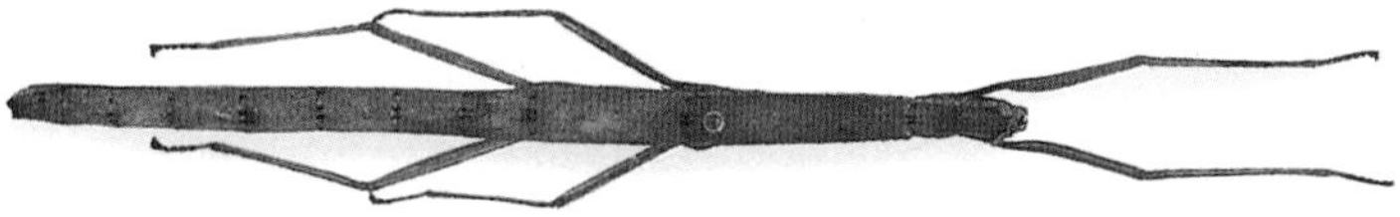

stick **insect**

cicada

dung beetle

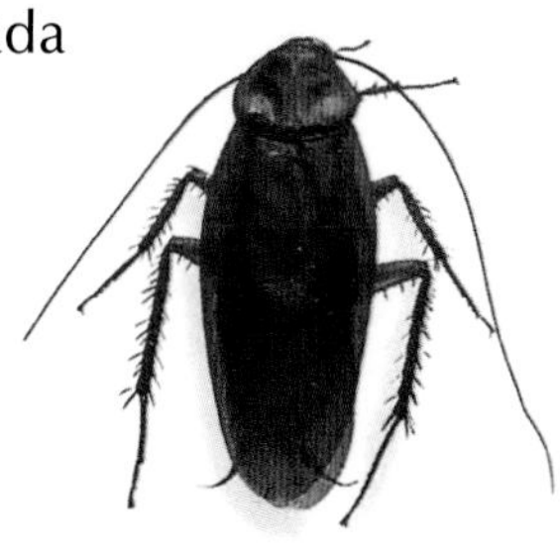

cockroach

insert
inserts inserting inserted *verb*
to put one thing inside another.

inside
preposition
in the interior of.

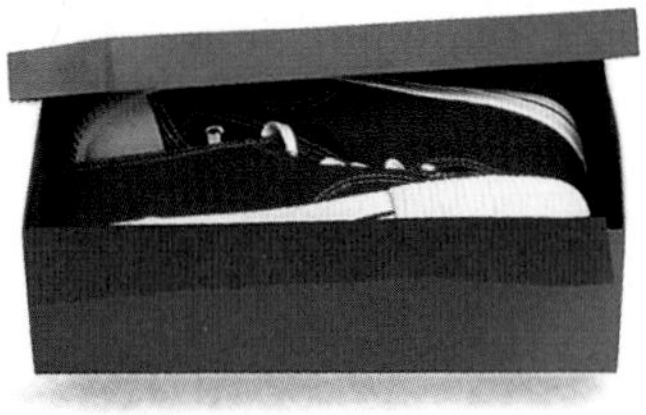

Inside *the box.*

inside
adverb
in or into something.
Come ***inside!***
inside *noun*

insist
insists insisting insisted *verb*
to say something very firmly.
She ***insisted*** *that she had seen a ghost.*
insistence *noun*
insistent *adjective*

inspect
inspects inspecting inspected *verb*
to check something carefully.

Cars are ***inspected*** *for faults before leaving the factory.*
inspection *noun*

instant
adjective
immediate.
She was an ***instant*** *success.*

instead
adverb
in place of.
I chose the red pen ***instead*** *of the blue one.*

instinct
instincts *noun*
a strong, natural feeling that makes animals or people do things that they haven't learned.
Birds have a pecking ***instinct.***

instruction
instructions *noun*
information about something.
Read the ***instructions*** *before you use the machine.*
instruct *verb*

instrument
instruments *noun*
a device or tool that has a special use.

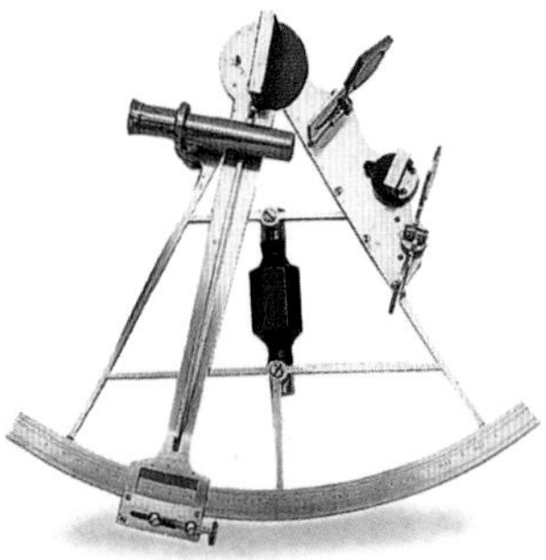

A navigational ***instrument.***

insult
insults insulting insulted *verb*
to upset someone by saying unpleasant things to them or about them.
insult *noun*

intelligent
adjective
quick to learn, think, and understand.

She was ***intelligent****, so she solved the puzzle quickly.*
intelligence *noun*

interest
interests interesting interested *verb*
to hold the attention of.
Anything to do with space ***interests*** *me.*
interesting *adjective*

interfere
interferes interfering interfered *verb*
to involve yourself in something that doesn't have anything to do with you.

She kept ***interfering*** *as he tried to prepare lunch.*

interior
interiors *noun*
the part that is inside something.

interior *of a doll's house*
interior *adjective*

interjection
interjections *noun*
a word such as "good-bye" or "hey" that can be used on its own.

internal
adjective
on the inside.

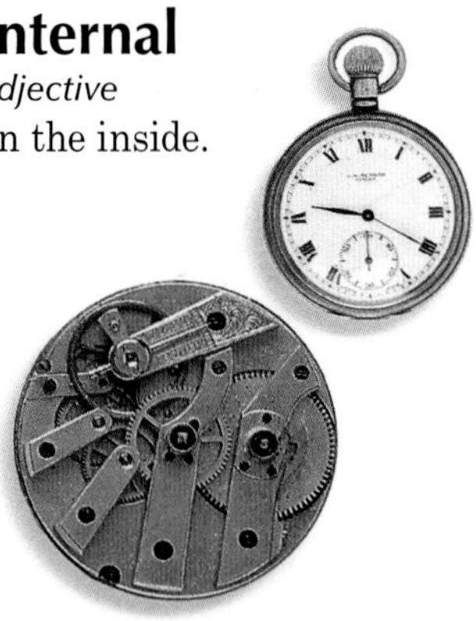

The ***internal*** *workings of a pocket watch.*
■ opposite **external**
internally *adverb*

international
adjective
involving several countries.
An ***international*** *event.*

internet
noun
a worldwide computer network for sharing information and sending messages.

interrupt
interrupts interrupting interrupted *verb*
1 to stop someone from talking by breaking into the conversation.
Please don't ***interrupt*** *while I'm speaking!*
2 to stop something from happening temporarily.
The tennis match was ***interrupted*** *by rain.*

intersection
intersections *noun*
a place where lines or roads cross each other.

A busy road ***intersection.***

A B C D E F G H I J K L M N O P Q R S T U V W X Y Z

interval
intervals *noun*
a period of time between events.
*There was a short **interval** between the two acts.*

interview
interviews *noun*
a meeting where someone is questioned.

*A job **interview**.*
interview *verb*

intestine
intestines *noun*
an organ that is connected to the stomach. Food is digested in the intestine as well as in the stomach.
■ say in-**tes**-tin

introduce
introduces introducing introduced *verb*
to present a person or idea to someone for the first time.
***Introduce** me to your friend.*
introduction *noun*

invade
invades invading invaded *verb*
to enter a place as an enemy.
invasion *noun*

invent
invents inventing invented *verb*
to design an original device or process.
*This device was **invented** to record sound and play it back.*
invention *noun*

investigate
investigates investigating investigated *verb*
to look at a situation carefully to find out what is happening or what has happened.
*The police are **investigating** yesterday's robbery.*
investigation *noun*

invisible
adjective
unable to be seen.
■ opposite **visible**

invitation
invitations *noun*
a written or spoken request asking someone to come and be with you.

*A party **invitation**.*
invite *verb*

involve
involves involving involved *verb*
to include or affect something.
*Two cars were **involved** in the accident.*

involved
adjective
complicated.
*An **involved** plan.*

iris
irises *noun*
1 a tall, flowering plant that grows from a bulb or a rootlike stem.

2 the round, colored part of the eye.

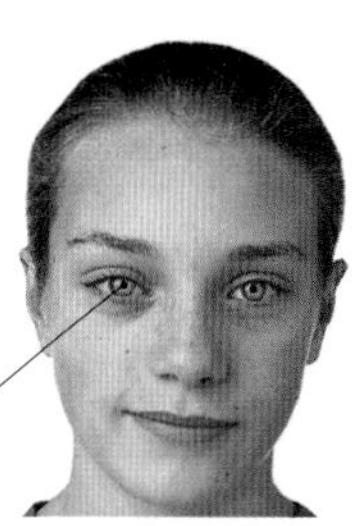

■ say **eye**-ris

iron
noun
1 a strong, heavy metal found in rocks; it is used to make things such as tools and gates.

*wrought-**iron** gate*

2 a piece of electrical equipment that heats up and is used to remove creases in clothing.

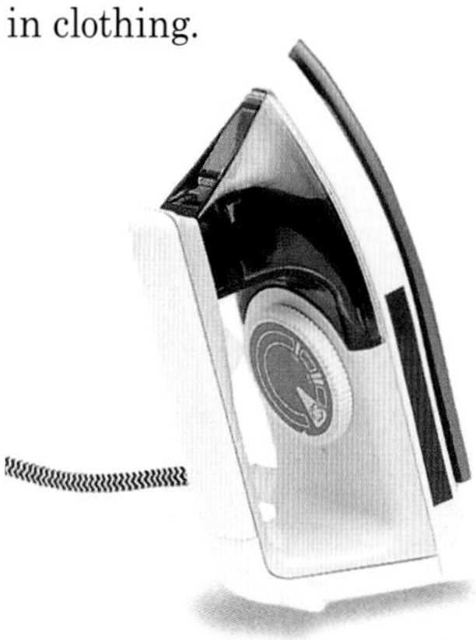

irrigate
irrigates irrigating irrigated *verb*
to supply land with water.
irrigation *noun*

irritate
irritates irritating irritated *verb*
to annoy someone.
irritation *noun*

Islam
noun
the Muslim religion. Muslims believe there is one God, Allah, and that Mohammed is his prophet.
Islamic *adjective*

island
islands *noun*
a piece of land completely surrounded by water.

■ say **eye**-land

itch
itches itching itched *verb*
to have a feeling in your skin that makes you want to scratch.

*She scratched her hand because it was **itching**.*
itch *noun*

ivy
ivies *noun*
an evergreen climbing plant.

■ say **eye**-vee

Jj

jab
jabs jabbing jabbed *verb*
to push a finger or a pointed tool into something in a quick, sharp way.
*He **jabbed** his finger into his friend's ribs.*
jab *noun*

jacket
jackets *noun*
a short coat.

jagged
adjective
having rough, sharp edges.
***Jagged** rocks.*

jaguar
jaguars *noun*
a meat-eating mammal that belongs to the cat family. Jaguars live in forests and marshes of North and South America.

jail
jails *noun*
a place where criminals are kept locked up.

jam
jams *noun*
1 a sweet food made from boiled fruit and sugar.

*strawberry **jam***

2 a group of people or things that are squashed together.

*traffic **jam***

jar
jars jarring jarred *verb*
to make an unpleasant sound or a jolt.
jarring *adjective*

jar
jars *noun*
a glass container with a wide top, used for storing foods.

javelin
javelins *noun*
a long, pointed stick that is thrown like a spear in athletic competitions.

jaw
jaws *noun*
the U-shaped bone that supports your mouth, allowing it to open and close.

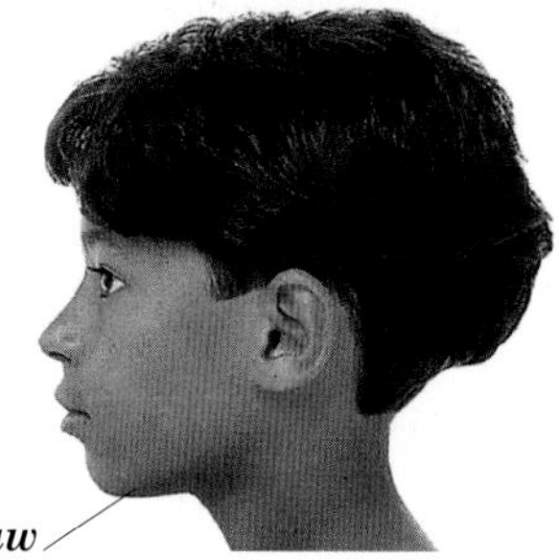

jaw

jazz
noun
a type of popular music with strong rhythms, first played in the United States.

jealous
adjective
annoyed and unhappy because others have something you would like.
*He was **jealous** of his friend's computer.*
■ say **jell**-us
jealousy *noun*

jeans
noun
pants made of denim.

jeep
jeeps *noun*
a small, open vehicle for driving over rough ground (see **car** on page 39).

jelly
jellies *noun*
a soft, firm, clear food made from fruit juice and sugar.

jellyfish
jellyfish or **jellyfishes** *noun*
a sea animal that has a transparent, soft body. Jellyfish feed on fish and tiny sea animals, which they catch by stinging them with their long tentacles.

*mangrove **jellyfish***

jet
jets *noun*
1 a sudden spray or stream of liquid or gas.
*The water was thrown up in a huge **jet**.*
2 a fast aircraft that is powered by an engine that sucks in air, heats it, and then pushes it out again.

*supersonic **jet***

Jew
Jews *noun*
a person whose ancestors were Hebrew or whose religion is Judaism.
Jewish *adjective*

jewel
jewels *noun*
1 a precious stone that has been cut and polished. Diamonds, rubies, and emeralds are all jewels.
2 an ornament made of gems and precious metals that people wear.

jewelry

noun

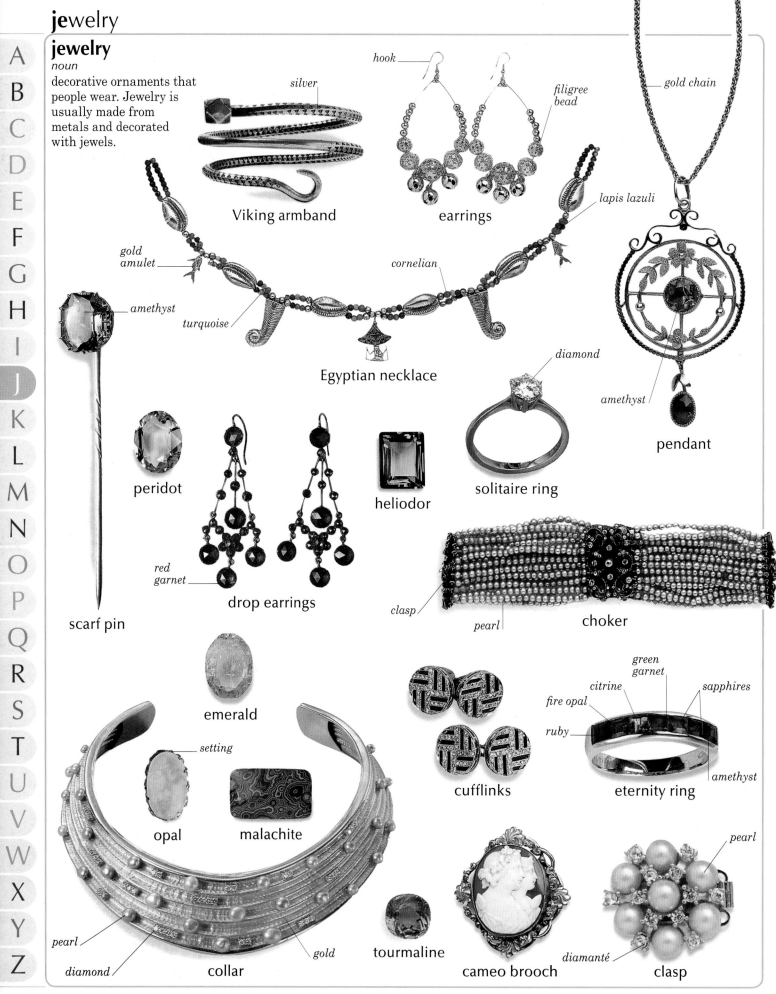

decorative ornaments that people wear. Jewelry is usually made from metals and decorated with jewels.

Viking armband

earrings

pendant

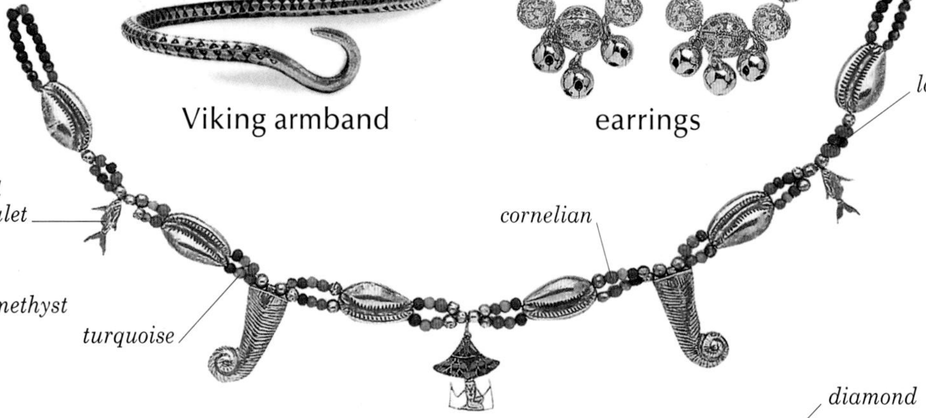

Egyptian necklace

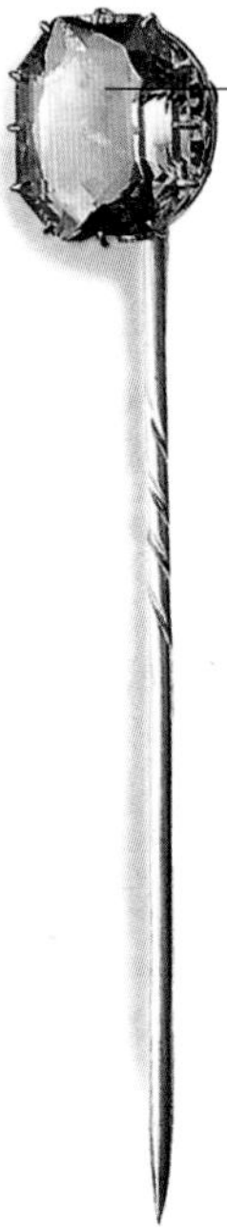

scarf pin

peridot

drop earrings

heliodor

solitaire ring

choker

emerald

cufflinks

eternity ring

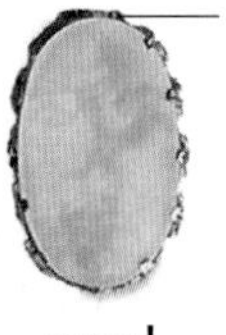

opal

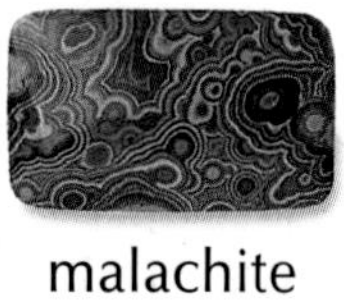

malachite

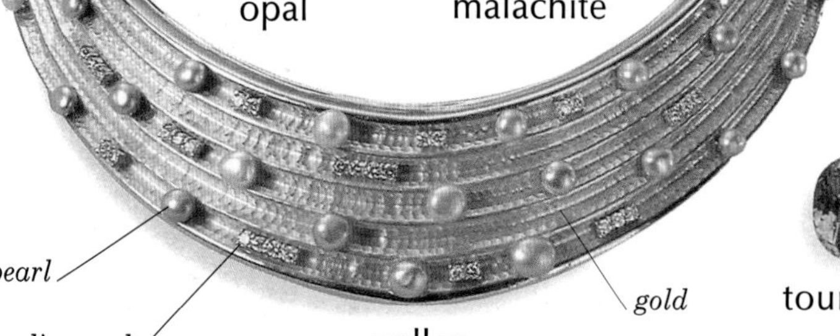

collar

tourmaline

cameo brooch

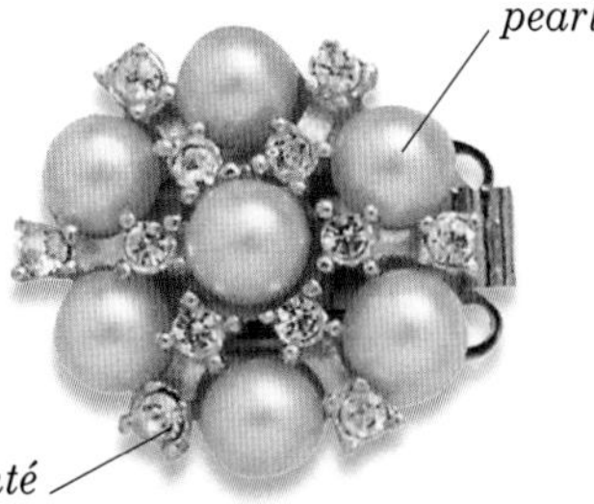

clasp

jigsaw puzzle
jigsaw puzzles *noun*
a puzzle with oddly shaped pieces that fit together to make a picture.

job
jobs *noun*
1 a task or some work that you have to do.
Jobs to do around the house.
2 work that someone is paid to do.
*I have an outdoor **job**.*

jockey
jockeys *noun*
a person who rides a horse in races.

jog
jogs jogging jogged *verb*
to run steadily and slowly.

join
joins joining joined *verb*
1 to put two things together.

***Joining** the two ends of a strip of paper.*
2 to become a member of something, such as a club.

joint
joints *noun*
the place where two pieces of something join together.
The bones in your body meet at joints to help you move around.

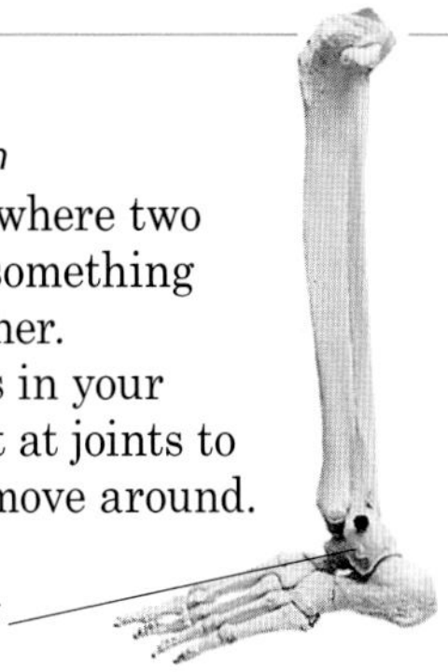

*ankle **joint***

joke
jokes *noun*
something that someone says or does to make people laugh.
joke *verb*

jolt
jolts jolting jolted *verb*
to shake or move in a bumpy way.

***Jolting** along a bumpy track.*
jolt *noun*

journalist
journalists *noun*
a person who gathers and writes news.
■ say **jur**-nuhl-list

journey
journeys *noun*
a distance traveled.
■ say **jur**-nee

Judaism
noun
the religion of Jewish people. Jews believe in one God, and in the teachings of the Old Testament and the Talmud, the Jewish holy books.
■ say **joo**-dee-iz-uhm

judge
judges judging judged *verb*
to decide whether something is right or wrong, good or bad.
judgment *noun*

judge
judges *noun*
1 a person in charge of a court who decides the punishment of those people that the jury finds guilty.
2 a person who decides the winner of a competition or contest.

judo
noun
a sport from Japan in which two people fight using special movements to try and throw the other player to the ground.

jug
jugs *noun*
an open container that is used to hold liquids and that has a handle and a narrow mouth.

juggle
juggles juggling juggled *verb*
to keep several objects in the air at the same time by throwing and catching.

juice
juices *noun*
a liquid from fruit or meat.
juicy *adjective*

jump
jumps jumping jumped *verb*
to throw yourself into the air.

junction
junctions *noun*
a place where several things join, such as roads or railroads.

jungle
jungles *noun*
a dense, tropical forest.

junior
adjective
younger or less experienced.

jury
juries *noun*
a group of 12 people, chosen from the public, who sit in court and decide whether the person on trial is guilty or not guilty.

justice
noun
a fair and honest judgment.
■ say **jus**-tis

A B C D E F G H I J K L M N O P Q R S T U V W X Y Z

Kk

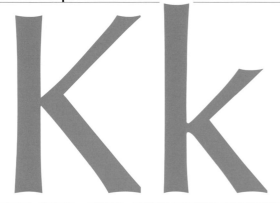

kaleidoscope
kaleidoscopes *noun*
a tube with mirrors and small pieces of colorful plastic inside that you can look through. When the tube is turned, the pieces move, making a pattern of colors.
■ say kuh-**ly**-duh-skope

kangaroo
kangaroos *noun*
a marsupial mammal from Australia that eats leaves and plants. Kangaroos can hop fast on their strong back legs. The females carry their young in a stomach pouch.

karate
noun
a sport from Southeast Asia in which people fight with their hands and feet using special movements.

■ say ka-**rah**-tee

kayak
kayaks *noun*
a covered canoe for one person, originally made from sealskins.
■ say **ky**-yak

kebab
kebabs *noun*
pieces of meat and vegetables, usually cooked over a grill on a sharp spike of wood or metal called a skewer.

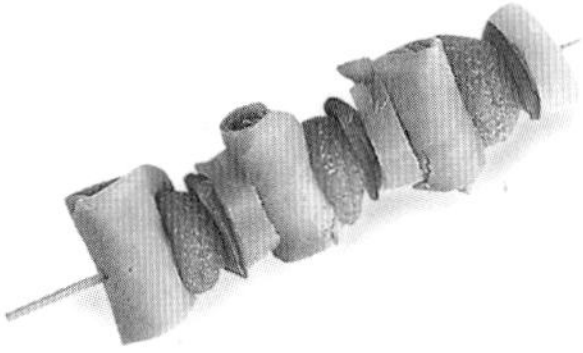

keep
keeps keeping kept *verb*
1 to have something and not give it away.
*She wanted to **keep** the doll.*
2 to remain.
***Keep** still!*
3 to continue.
*He **kept** walking.*

kennel
kennels *noun*
a shelter outdoors for a dog.

key
keys *noun*
1 a piece of metal that has been cut so that it will lock and unlock a door or padlock.

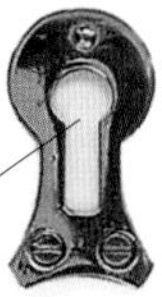

keyhole

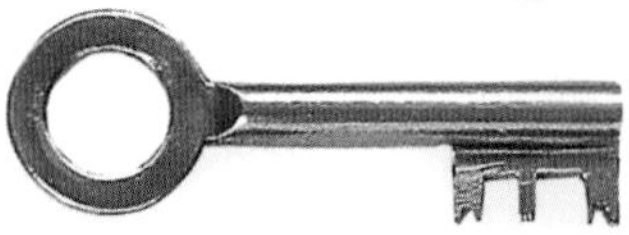

2 a small lever that you press with your finger.
*Computer **keys**.*

keyboard
keyboards *noun*
a row of keys that you use to play a musical instrument, or to use a computer or a typewriter.

*computer **keyboard***

kick
kicks kicking kicked *verb*
to hit something or someone with your foot.

kick *noun*

kidnap
kidnaps kidnapping kidnapped *verb*
to take someone away against their will and keep them prisoner.
kidnapping *noun*

kidney
kidneys *noun*
one of two organs in your body that filters your blood and helps to keep it clean.

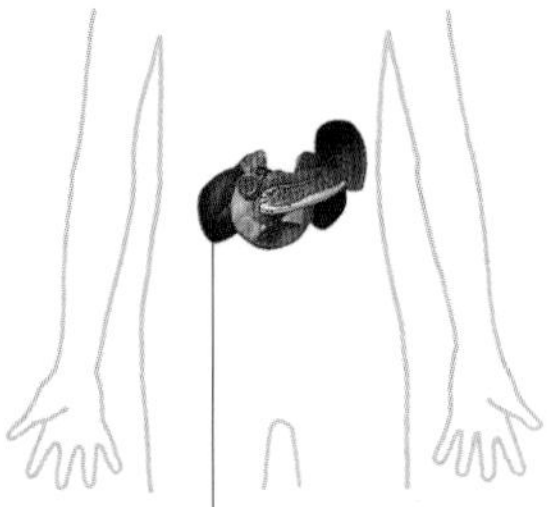

kidney

kill
kills killing killed *verb*
to make someone or something die.
*She **killed** the wasp with a rolled-up newspaper.*

kind
kinds *noun*
a type or sort of something.

*Different **kinds** of brush.*

kind
adjective
helpful and generous to other people.
■ comparisons **kinder kindest**
■ opposite **unkind**

king
kings *noun*
a male ruler of a country.

kingfisher
kingfishers *noun*
a bird with a long, straight bill and a small body. Kingfishers eat insects or fish and live in river banks or holes in trees.

kiss
kisses kissing kissed *verb*
to touch someone with your lips in an affectionate way.

kiss *noun*

kitchen
kitchens *noun*
a room in which food is prepared and cooked.

kite
kites *noun*
a light, material-covered frame that is flown in the air. Kites are attached to a string held by a person on the ground.

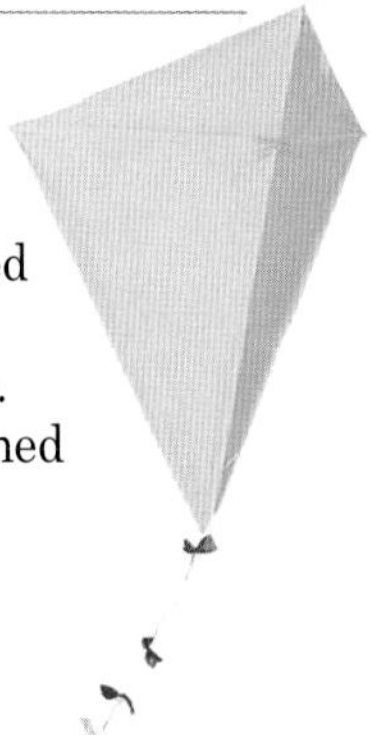

kitten
kittens *noun*
a young cat.

kiwi
kiwis *noun*
a nocturnal bird from New Zealand. Kiwis have hairlike feathers but they cannot fly. They have long, curved bills, which they use to hunt for insects and worms (see **bird** on page 28).
■ say **kee**-wee

knee
knees *noun*
the joint between the upper and lower bones of your leg.

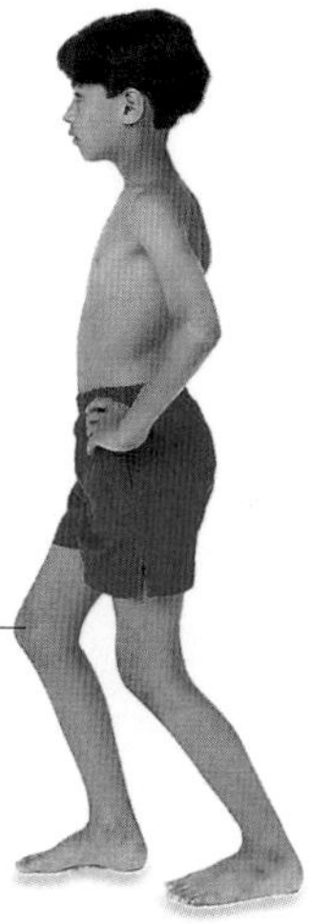

■ say **nee**

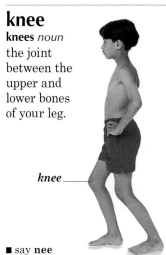

kneel
kneels kneeling kneeled or **knelt** *verb*
to go down on your knees.
■ say **neel**

knew
from the verb ***to know***
I ***knew*** *the answers to the test this morning.*
■ say **new**

knife
knives *noun*
a sharp blade with a handle, that is used for cutting.
■ say **nife**

knight
knights *noun*
a soldier from medieval times who rode a horse. A knight fought on behalf of a lord, or for the king or queen.
■ say **nite**

knit
knits knitting knitted *verb*
to make clothes and blankets from thread or yarn using large plastic or metal needles.
■ say **nit**
knitting *noun*

knob
knobs *noun*
a round handle made of metal, china, plastic, or wood that is fitted to a piece of furniture.
■ say **nob**

knock
knocks knocking knocked *verb*
to strike something sharply and quickly.
She ***knocked*** *on the door.*
■ say **nok**

knot
knots *noun*
a twisted or tied piece of string, rope, or other cord.

■ say **not**
knot *verb*

know
knows knowing knew known *verb*
1 to understand something or to be sure about something.
Do you ***know*** *her name?*
2 to have met someone before.
I have ***known*** *him for years.*
■ say **no**

knowledge
noun
the things that someone knows, or all the things that are known.
■ say **noll**-ij
knowledgeable *adjective*

knuckle
knuckles *noun*
one of the bony joints at the base of your fingers.

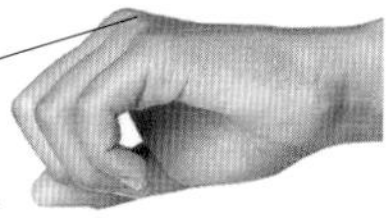

■ say **nu**-kuhl

koala
koalas *noun*
a marsupial from Australia. Koalas eat the leaves and bark of the eucalyptus trees in which they live.

kosher
adjective
food that is prepared according to the rules of the Jewish religion.
Kosher *meat.*
■ say **koh**-shur

Ll

label
labels *noun*
a small notice attached to something that gives you information about it.

laboratory
laboratories *noun*
a place where scientists work.

lace
noun
1 a material with a pattern of small holes.

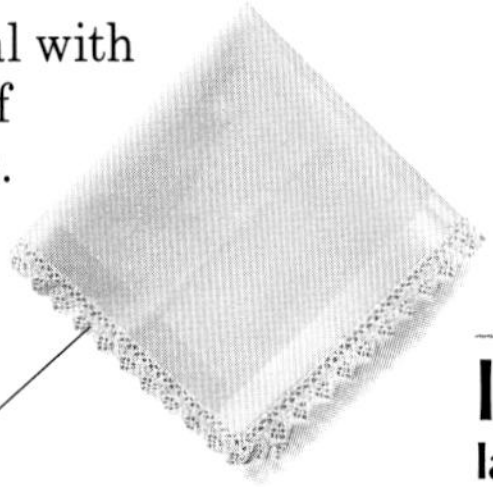

2 a cord that is used to fasten things.

lace
laces lacing laced *verb*
to thread a lace through holes.

lack
noun
a state of not having enough or any of something.
*The plants died from **lack** of water.*
lack *verb*

ladder
ladders *noun*
a wooden or metal frame with rungs or steps, which you use for climbing up or down.

ladle
ladles *noun*
a large, deep, round spoon used to serve soup and other liquids.

ladybug
ladybugs *noun*
a small flying insect with spotted wing covers. Ladybugs eat other small insects.

lagoon
lagoons *noun*
a shallow lake, cut off from the sea or a larger lake by coral, rocks, or sand banks.

laid
*from the verb **to lay***
*1 He **laid** his paintings on the table so we could see them.*
*2 Our hen **laid** two eggs this morning.*

lake
lakes *noun*
a large area of water surrounded by land.

lamb
lambs *noun*
1 a young sheep.

2 meat from a young sheep.

lamp
lamps *noun*
a light that works by using electricity, oil, or gas.

land
lands landing landed *verb*
to arrive on the ground after flying.

*The plane **landed** on the runway.*

land
lands *noun*
1 the parts of the world that are not covered by sea.
2 a country, or an area of ground.
*The farmer owns all the **land** around the village.*

language
languages *noun*
the words or movements that people use to communicate with each other.

*The word "language" in sign **language**.*
■ say **lan**-gwij

lantern
lanterns *noun*
a light that is inside a transparent case to protect it from winds.

lap
laps *noun*
1 the top of your legs when you are sitting down.

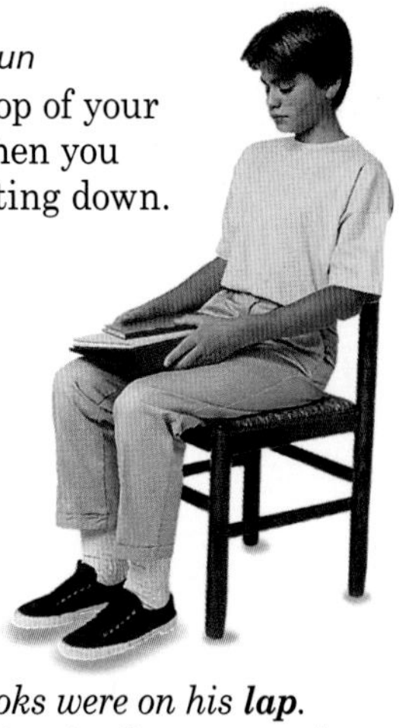

*The books were on his **lap**.*
2 one circuit of a race track.
*The runners were on the last **lap** of the track.*

lap
laps lapping lapped *verb*
1 to splash gently against something.
*The waves **lapped** against the beach.*
2 to drink using the tongue, in the way an animal does.

*The kittens **lapped** up the milk.*

large
adjective
great in size.

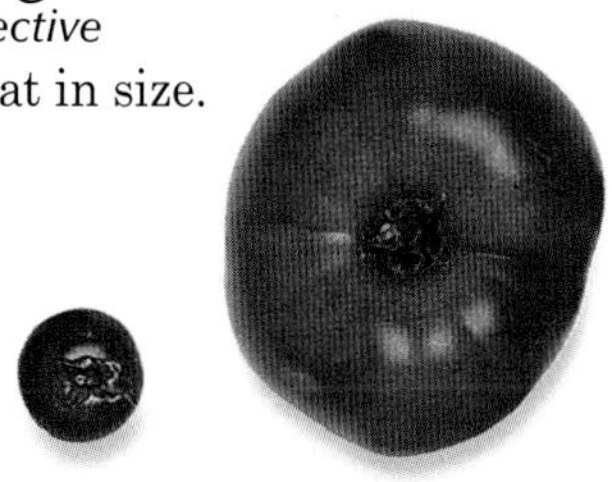

*a small tomato a **large** tomato*

■ comparisons **larger largest**
■ opposite **small**

larva
larvae *noun*
an insect after it has hatched out of its egg, but before it has become an adult (see **growth** on page 94).

laser
lasers *noun*
a machine that produces a beam of powerful light. Lasers are used to cut metal, to perform surgery, or for light shows.

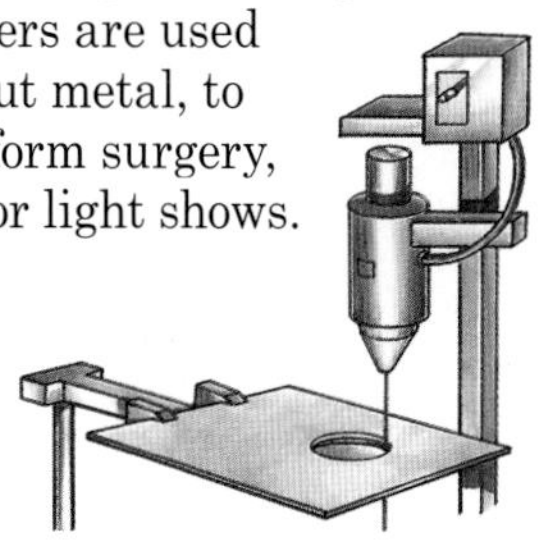

last
adjective
1 the only one left.
*The **last** roll on the plate.*
■ opposite **first**
2 the most recent.
*We stayed in **last** night.*

last
lasts lasting lasted *verb*
to take a certain amount of time.
*My riding lesson **lasts** an hour.*

late
adjective
after the correct time.
*They were **late** for dinner.*
■ comparisons **later latest**
■ opposite **early**

laugh
laughs laughing laughed *verb*
to make a noise with your voice because you think that something is funny.

■ say **laf**
laughter *noun*

launch
launches launching launched *verb*
1 to put a boat or ship into the water.

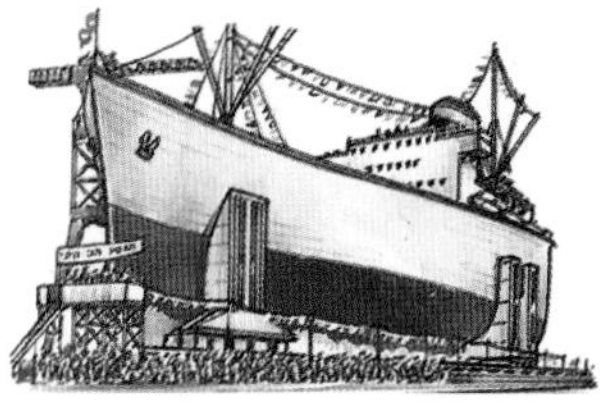

2 to start something off.

*They **launched** the rocket successfully.*

law
laws *noun*
a set of rules that people live by, usually made by the government of a country.
*It is against the **law** to litter.*

lawn
lawns *noun*
an area of grass that is regularly cut in a park or a garden.

lay
lays laying laid *verb*
1 to arrange or put something down on a surface carefully.

***Lay** the cards on the table.*
2 to produce an egg.

lay
*from the verb **to lie***
*He **lay** down on the bed.*

layer
layers *noun*
a single thickness of something.

*There is a **layer** of nuts on top of the cake.*

lazy
adjective
not wanting to work or do anything energetic.
■ comparisons **lazier laziest**

lead
leads leading led *verb*
1 to go first to show someone the way.
*Our tour guide **led** us to the bus.*
■ opposite **follow**
2 to be in charge of something.
*She **led** the expedition to the South Pole.*
3 to go in the direction of something.
*The road **leads** to the house.*

lead
leads *noun*
1 the first place in a race.
*She was in the **lead** all the way around the race track.*
2 a clue.
*The police followed up every **lead**.*
■ rhymes with **feed**

lead
noun
a soft, heavy metal used in building and for making weights.

■ rhymes with **bed**

leaf
leaves *noun*
one of the thin, flat, green parts of a plant that grows out from the stem or shoots.

leak
leaks *noun*
a hole or crack in a container through which liquid or gas can escape.
*There is a **leak** in this bottle.*
leak *verb*

lean
leans leaning leaned
verb
to rest on something or tilt to one side.

leap
leaps leaping leaped or **leapt**
verb
to jump a long distance, or to jump high into the air.

leap year
leap years *noun*
a year that has 366 days, instead of 365. A leap year happens once in every four years. The extra date in a leap year is February 29.

learn
learns learning learned
verb
to find out about something, and to understand it.
*We **learned** about magnetism at school today.*
learning *noun*

leather
noun
a material made from the skin of an animal, usually a cow.

***leather** bag*

leave
leaves leaving left *verb*
1 to go away.
*We'll **leave** after lunch.*
2 to let something stay as it is.
***Leave** those cookies alone!*

lecture
lectures *noun*
a talk given by one person to an audience.

leek
leeks *noun*
a long vegetable with layers of tight leaves. Leeks are part of the onion family.

left
adjective
the side that is opposite to the right.

*She writes with her **left** hand.*
left *noun*

leg
legs *noun*
1 the part of your body between your hip and your foot.

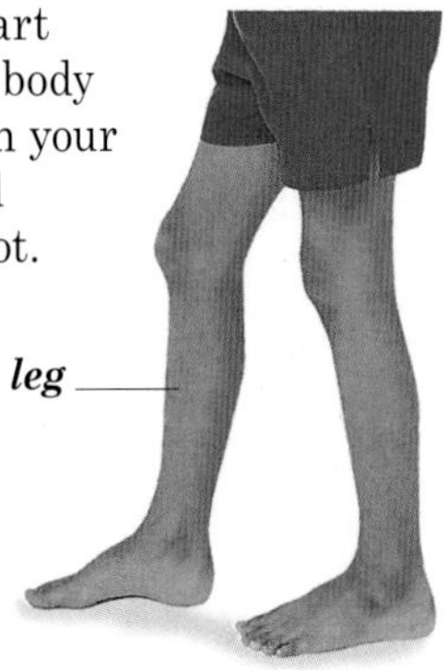

2 a support for furniture.

*table **leg***

legal
adjective
allowed by law, or having to do with the law.
■ say **lee**-gal
■ opposite **illegal**

legend
legends *noun*
a well-known old story that may or may not be true.
■ say **lej**-und

leisure
noun
a time when you don't have to work.
■ say **lee**-zhur or **leezh**-ur

lemon
lemons *noun*
a sour, juicy fruit with a tough, yellow skin.

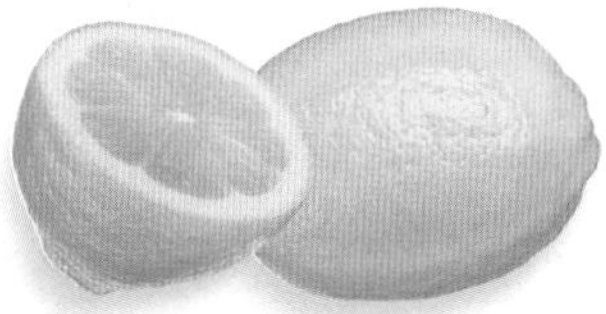

lend
lends lending lent *verb*
to give something to someone for a short time.
*He **lent** me his umbrella because it was raining.*
■ opposite **borrow**

length
lengths *noun*
1 the measurement of something from one end to the other.
*Twelve inches in **length**.*
2 a piece cut from a longer piece.

*A **length** of ribbon.*

lens
lenses *noun*
a curved piece of plastic or glass that is used to help you to see things in a clearer way. Lenses are an important part of telescopes, cameras, and eyeglasses.

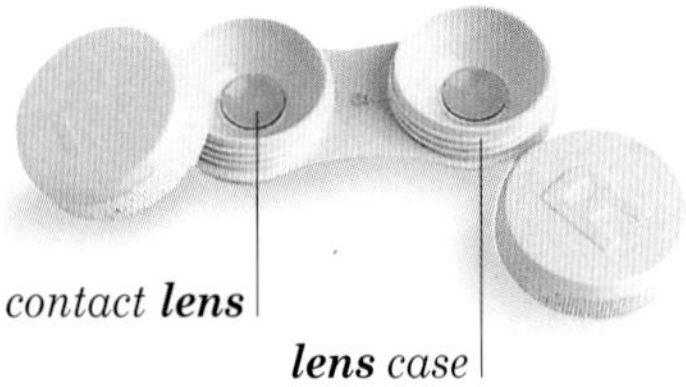

■ say **lenz**

leopard
leopards *noun*
a large mammal that lives in Africa and Asia and belongs to the cat family. Leopards hunt at night and are good at climbing trees.

■ say **lep**-ard

leotard
leotards *noun*
a tight piece of clothing worn for dancing and other kinds of exercise.

■ say **lee**-uh-tard

less
adjective
not as much.
*Three is **less** than four.*
■ opposite **more**

lesson
lessons *noun*
a period of time for teaching and learning.
*A piano **lesson**.*

let
lets letting let *verb*
to allow someone to do something.
*The farmer **let** the children pet the donkey.*

letter
letters *noun*
1 a written symbol that is part of the alphabet (see **alphabet** on page 16).
2 a written message that you send to someone by mail.

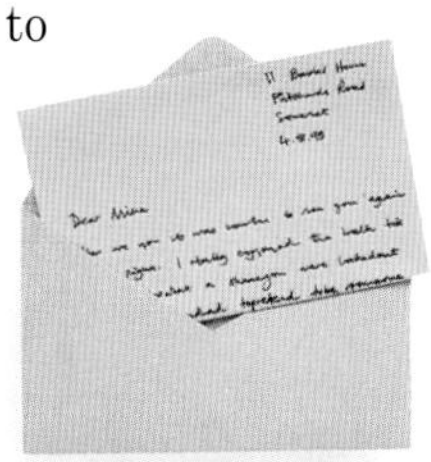

lettuce
lettuces *noun*
a green vegetable with large leaves around a short, central stem. Lettuce is often used in salads.

■ say **let**-iss

level
adjective
smooth and flat.
*A sports field should be **level**.*

lever
levers *noun*
1 a bar that is used to lift heavy weights or to force things open.
2 a long bar or handle for operating a machine.

lever

espresso coffee machine

liberty
liberties *noun*
freedom.
*The prisoner's relatives campaigned for his **liberty**.*

library
libraries *noun*
a place where books and other sources of information are collected and may be borrowed.

license
licenses *noun*
an official certificate that shows you have permission to do something.
*A driving **license**.*
■ say **lie**-sens
license *verb*

lick
licks licking licked *verb*
to touch something with your tongue to eat it or make it wet.

***Licking** an ice pop.*

lid
lids *noun*
the top of a container.

*saucepan **lid***

lie
lies lying lied *verb*
to say something that you know is untrue.
lie *noun*

lie
lies lying lay lain *verb*
to be in a horizontal position.
***Lying** down.*

life
lives *noun*
1 all things that are living.
***Life** on Earth.*
2 the time that you are alive.
*My grandmother had a long, happy **life**.*

lifeboat
lifeboats *noun*
a boat for rescuing people who are in trouble at sea.

lifeguard
lifeguards *noun*
a person whose job it is to rescue people who are in trouble in the sea or in a swimming pool.

lift
lifts lifting lifted *verb*
to pick something up.

lift
lifts *noun*
1 a machine that carries people up to or down from high places.

*A ski **lift**.*
2 a ride in a vehicle that you don't have to pay for.
*Can I give you a **lift** into town?*

light
lights lighting lit *verb*
to make something catch fire, or to turn on a light.
***Lighting** a candle.*

light
lights *noun*
something that shines to help you see in the dark.
*I had to turn on the **light** so I could see the way.*

A B C D E F G H I J K L M N O P Q R S T U V W X Y Z

light
adjective
1 weighing little.

*a **light** balloon* *a heavy bucket*

■ comparisons **lighter lightest**
■ opposite **heavy**
2 not dark in color.
*Her dress was **light** blue.*

lighthouse
lighthouses *noun*
a tall tower with a bright, flashing light that guides or warns ships around dangerous areas of coast.

lightning
noun
a flash of light in the sky during a thunderstorm.

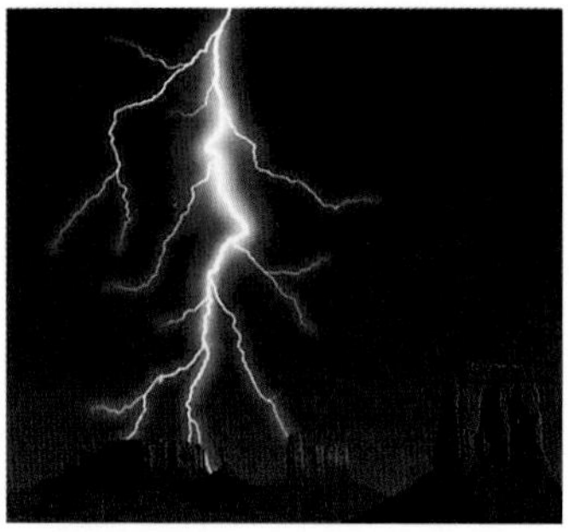

like
likes liking liked *verb*
to think that someone or something is pleasant.
■ opposite **dislike**
likeable *adjective*

like
adjective
similar to.
*He looks **like** his brother.*

lily
lilies *noun*
a tall plant that grows from a bulb, with large, trumpet-shaped blooms.

lime
limes *noun*
a juicy fruit with a sour flavor, similar to that of a lemon.

limit
limits *noun*
the point where something ends.
*The **limits** of the town.*

limp
limps limping limped *verb*
to walk with difficulty because your leg or your foot is injured or stiff.
*The dog **limped** because it had a thorn in its paw.*
limp *noun*

limp
adjective
not stiff.

*A **limp** flag.*

line
lines *noun*
1 a piece of rope or thread.
*A fishing **line**.*
2 a long, thin mark.

*A wavy **line**.*

3 a straight row of something.

*A **line** of cars.*

liner
liners *noun*
a large passenger ship.

link
links *noun*
1 one of the individual sections that make up a chain.

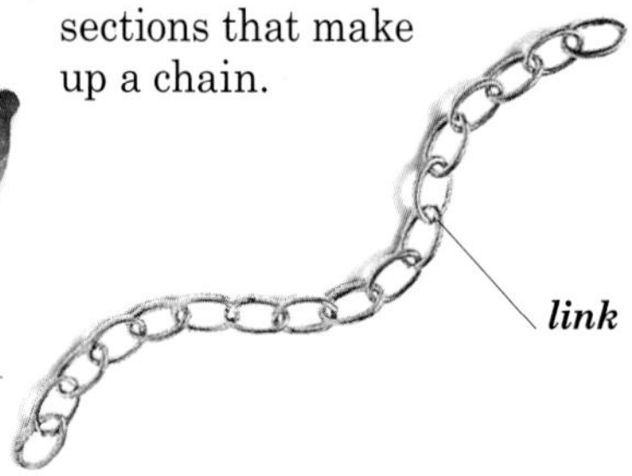

2 a connection between two things.
*The new highway provides a **link** between the two cities.*

liquid
liquids *noun*
a substance that flows and is not a gas.

list
lists *noun*
the names of several people or things written in columns.
*A shopping **list**.*

lion
lions *noun*
a large mammal that is found in Africa and India. Lions belong to the cat family. They live together in groups called prides. The females, called lionesses, hunt at night for large animals such as antelope and zebra.

lioness

listen
listens listening listened *verb*
to hear and pay attention to something, such as music.

lip
lips *noun*
1 one of the two soft, pink edges of your mouth.

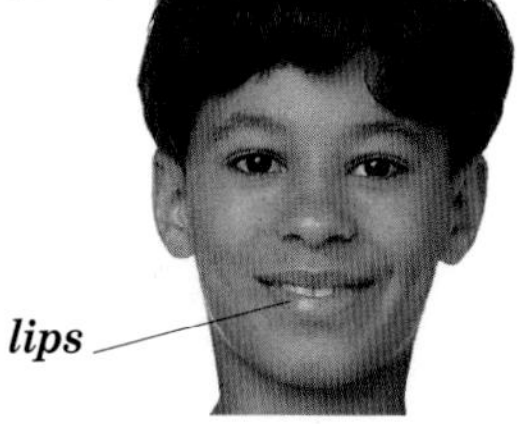

2 the top edge of a container.

lit
from the verb **to light**
They ***lit*** *a fire last night.*

literature
noun
novels, plays, poems, and other written material.

litter
noun
1 garbage left lying around.
2 baby animals born to the same mother at one time.

A ***litter*** *of puppies.*

little
adjective
1 small in size.

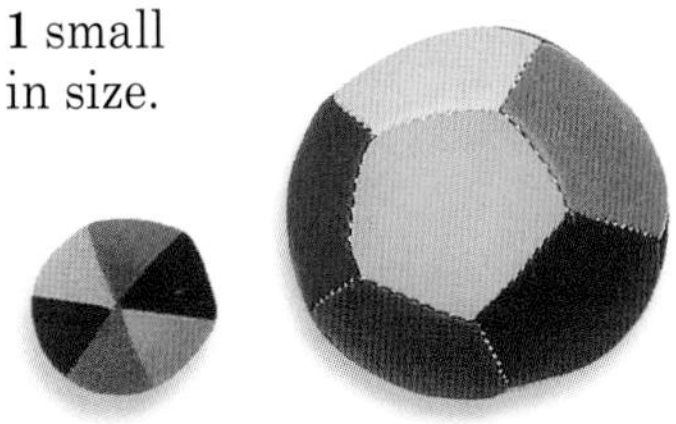

a ***little*** *ball* *a big ball*

■ comparisons **littler littlest**
■ opposite **big**
2 not much.
I only have a ***little*** *time.*
■ comparisons **less least**

live
lives living lived *verb*
1 to be alive.
He ***lived*** *to an old age.*
2 to stay in a place.

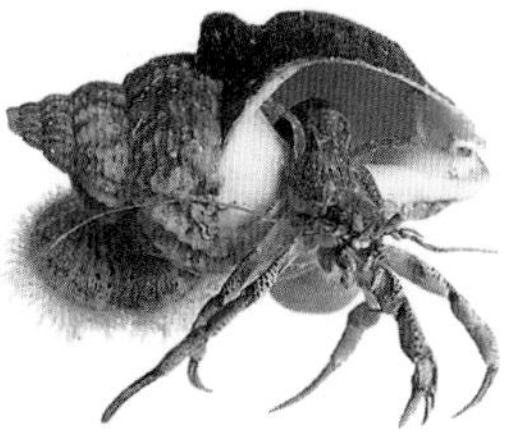

Hermit crabs ***live*** *in shells.*
■ rhymes with **give**
living *adjective*

live
adjective
1 having life.
A ***live*** *snake.*
2 shown while the event is taking place.
A ***live*** *television show.*
■ rhymes with **dive**

liver
livers *noun*
an organ in the body that cleans the blood and helps to digest food.

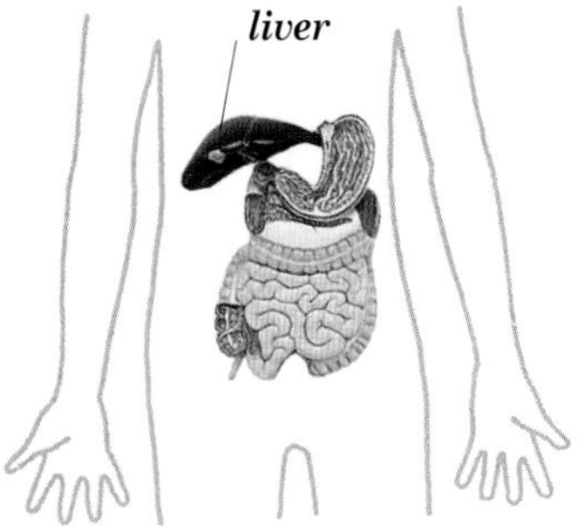

living
noun
the way a person lives or earns money.
He earns his ***living*** *as a chef.*

lizard
lizards *noun*
a reptile with scales. Most types of lizard have four legs and a long tail. Many lizards live in warm regions and eat insects.

A gecko is a type of ***lizard.***

load
loads *noun*
an amount of something that is carried.

A ***load*** *of gravel.*

load
loads loading loaded *verb*
to put things into a vehicle.
Loading *the ship with cargo.*

loaf
loaves *noun*
a lump of bread baked as one piece that can be cut into slices.

loaf *of bread*

lobster
lobsters *noun*
a large shellfish that lives in the sea and has five pairs of legs. One pair of legs are claws, which lobsters use for cutting up dead fish and crushing shellfish to eat.

European ***lobster***

local
adjective
having to do with the area near to a place.
The ***local*** *paper showed a picture of the flood.*
locally *adjective*

locate
locates locating located *verb*
1 to be in a particular place.
The company has ***located*** *its main office in the city.*
2 to find where something is.
He finally ***located*** *the garage down a side street.*

location
locations *noun*
the place or position of something.

lock
locks *noun*
1 a device that keeps something shut.

combination ***lock***

lock *verb*
2 a device on a canal that raises or lowers the water level so that boats can move up and down.

locker
lockers *noun*
a small, narrow cupboard with a lock that is used for storing clothes or books.

log
logs *noun*
a thick piece of tree trunk or branch.

lonely
adjective
feeling sad and alone.
He was ***lonely*** *with no one to play with.*
■ comparisons **lonelier loneliest**
loneliness *noun*

A B C D E F G H I J K L M N O P Q R S T U V W X Y Z

long
adjective
1 having great length.

a short string of beads

*a **long** string of beads*

■ comparisons **longer longest**
■ opposite **short**
2 being a certain length.
*The fish was one foot **long**.*

look
looks looking looked *verb*
1 to use your eyes to see something.

***Looking** up.*
2 to appear a certain way.
*He **looked** tired after a sleepless night.*

loose
adjective
not firmly fastened or held.

loose scarf

■ say **loos**
■ comparisons **looser loosest**
loosely *adverb*
loosen *verb*

lose
loses losing lost *verb*
1 to no longer have something.

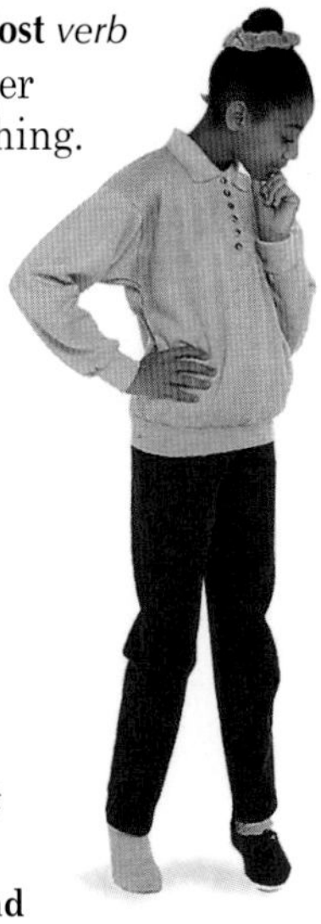

*She has **lost** her shoe.*
■ opposite **find**
2 to be defeated in a game or battle.
*He **lost** the tennis match.*
■ say **looz**
■ opposite **win**

loud
adjective
noisy.
***Loud** music.*
■ comparisons **louder loudest**

loudspeaker
loudspeakers *noun*
a device that turns electrical signals into sound.

love
loves loving loved *verb*
to like someone or something very much.
love *noun*

low
adjective
near the ground.

*A **low** table.*
■ comparisons **lower lowest**

lower
lowers lowering lowered *verb*
to let something down to the ground carefully.

*The load was **lowered** onto the pile.*

luck
noun
something that happens to you by chance, without being planned.
*I had the good **luck** to win a free vacation.*
lucky *adjective*

luggage
noun
cases and bags containing your clothes and other things that you carry when you travel.

■ say **lug**-ij

lukewarm
adjective
not very warm.
*The hot water system wasn't working properly, so he had to have a **lukewarm** shower.*

lull
lulls lulling lulled *verb*
to calm someone.
*He **lulled** the baby to sleep.*

lullaby
lullabies *noun*
a song that is sung to help children to fall asleep.

luminous
adjective
glowing in the dark.

*A deep-sea fish with **luminous** markings.*
■ say **loo**-min-us

lump
lumps *noun*
a rough piece of something.
*A **lump** of coal.*

lunch
lunches *noun*
a meal eaten in the middle of the day.

lung
lungs *noun*
one of a pair of organs inside your body that you use for breathing.

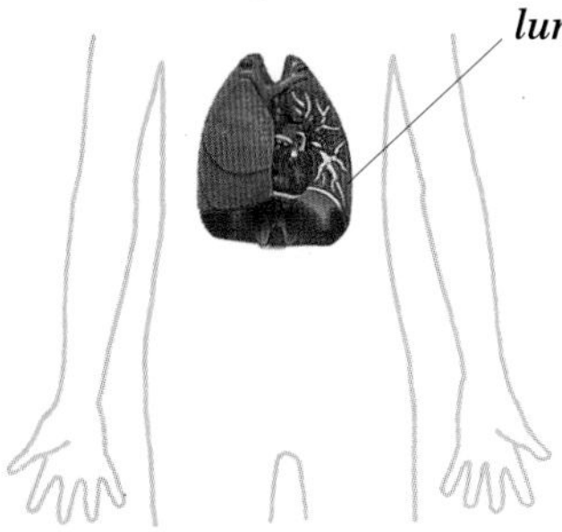

lung

luxury
luxuries *noun*
something that is expensive.
*The new car was a **luxury**.*
■ say **lug**-zhur-ee or **luk**-zhur-ee
luxurious *adjective*

lyrics
noun
the words to a song.
■ say **lir**-iks

Mm

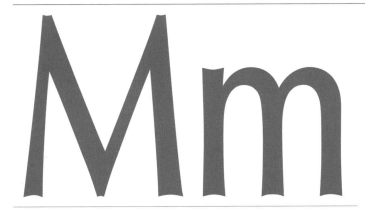

machine
machines *noun*
a piece of equipment that is made up of several parts. The parts move together to do a particular job.

*A food processor is a useful **machine**.*

machinery
noun
machines in general.

mad
adjective
1 very angry.
2 crazy or foolish.
*She is **mad** to swim in the sea during winter.*
■ comparisons **madder maddest**

magazine
magazines *noun*
a collection of news, stories, pictures, and advertisements with a paper cover.

magic
noun
tricks that a person performs that seem to make impossible and surprising things happen.
magical *adjective*

magician
magicians *noun*
someone who performs magic tricks.

magnet
magnets *noun*
a piece of iron that attracts metals with iron or steel in them.

magnetic *adjective*
magnetism *noun*

magnificent
adjective
grand and wonderful.
*A **magnificent** fountain.*

magnify
magnifies magnifying magnified *verb*
to make something look bigger than it really is.

***magnifying** glass*

mail
noun
letters and packages that are collected and delivered.

mail *verb*

main
adjective
most important.
*The **main** road.*
mainly *adverb*

major
adjective
big or important.
*Scientists have made a **major** discovery.*
■ opposite **minor**
majority *noun*

make
makes making made *verb*
1 to create, produce, build, or do something.

*She **made** some musical pipes out of straws and tape.*

2 to cause something to happen.

*The stone **made** ripples in the pond.*
3 to force someone to do something.
*Our teacher **made** us straighten up the classroom.*

makeup
noun
a substance that people put on their faces to change the way that they look.

male
adjective
belonging to the sex that can be a father, but cannot give birth to babies or produce eggs or seeds.
■ opposite **female**
male *noun*

A B C D E F G H I J K L M N O P Q R S T U V W X Y Z

mammal

mammals *noun*

one of a group of animals that usually have hair or fur and a backbone and are warm-blooded. Most female mammals give birth to live babies and feed them on milk.

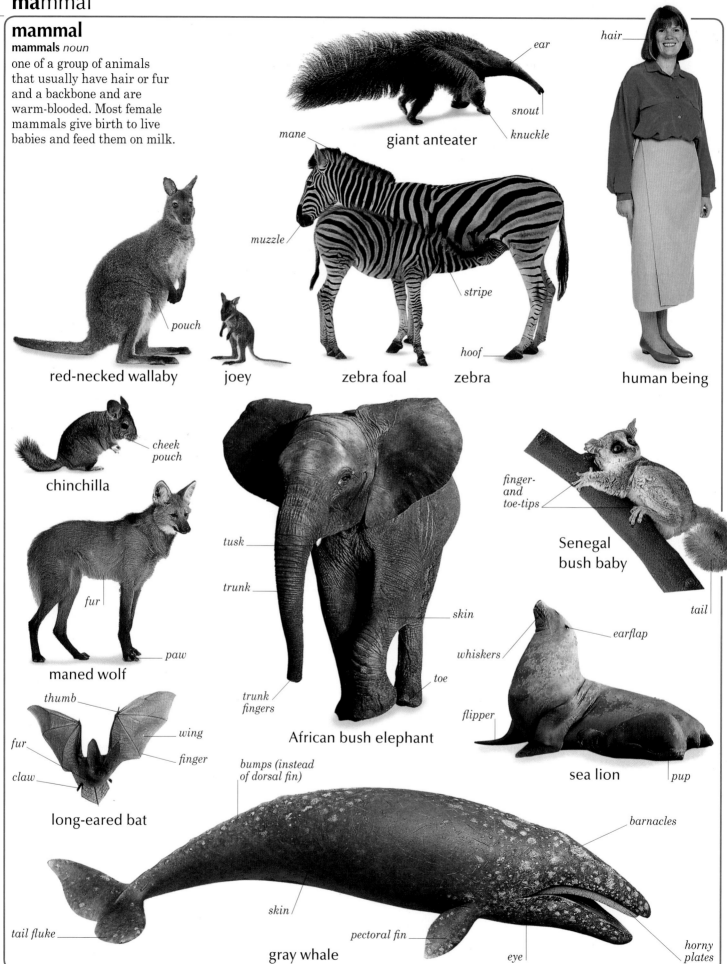

giant anteater

red-necked wallaby

joey

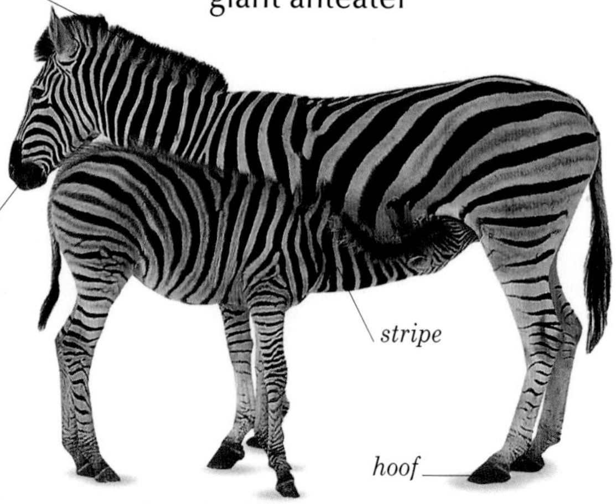

zebra foal

zebra

human being

chinchilla

maned wolf

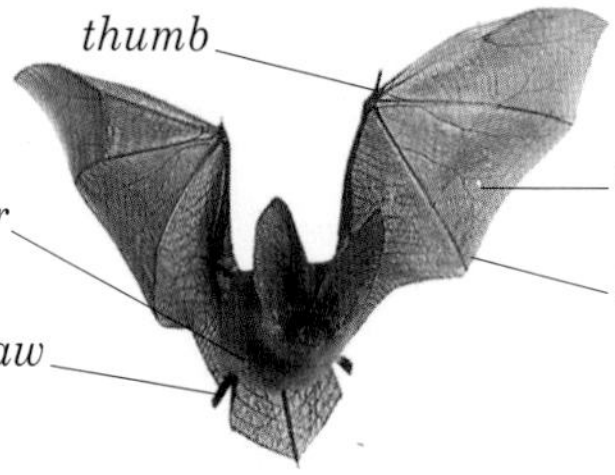

long-eared bat

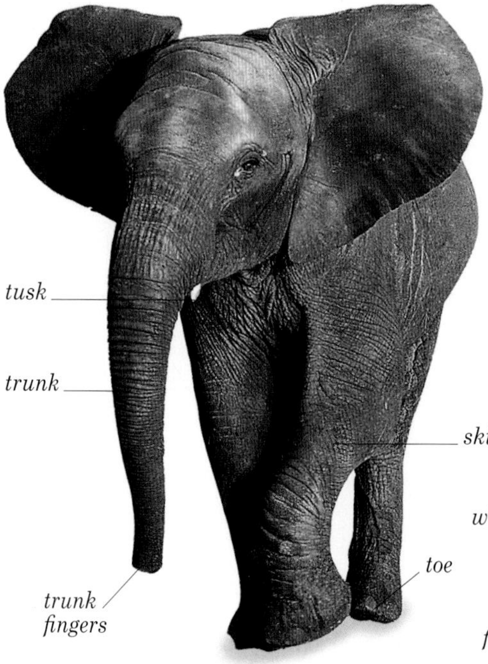

African bush elephant

Senegal bush baby

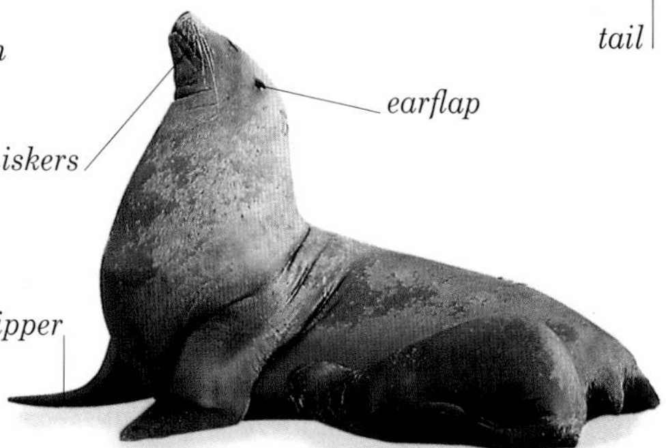

sea lion

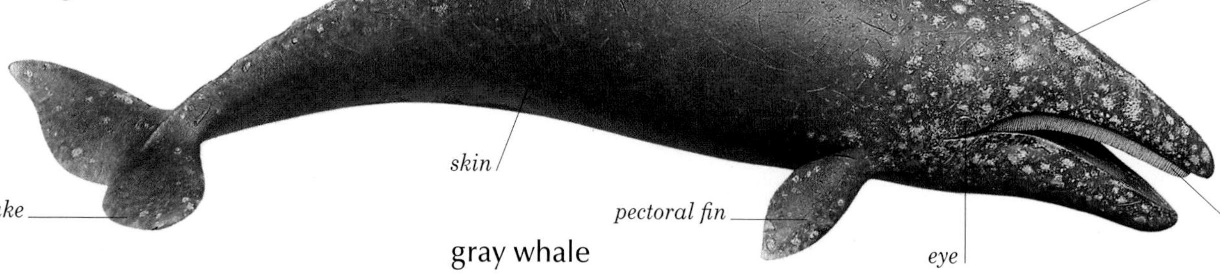

gray whale

man
men *noun*
an adult male person.

man
noun
people in general.
*Apes are related to **man**.*

manage
manages managing managed *verb*
1 to be in charge of a business or part of a business.
*She **manages** a store and has two assistants to help her.*
2 to be able to do something that is difficult.
*She **managed** to swim across the bay.*

manner
noun
a way that a person acts, or a way something is done.
*She always greets us in a friendly **manner**.*

manners
noun
the way a person behaves.

*He has good **manners**.*

manufacture
manufactures manufacturing manufactured *verb*
to make something in large quantities with a machine.
***Manufacturing** cars.*
■ say man-yu-**fak**-chur

many
adjective
a large number.
*There were so **many** people, I couldn't find her.*
■ comparisons **more most**
■ opposite **few**

map
maps *noun*
a drawing of all, or part of, Earth's surface. Maps often show where towns, rivers, and other geographical features are.

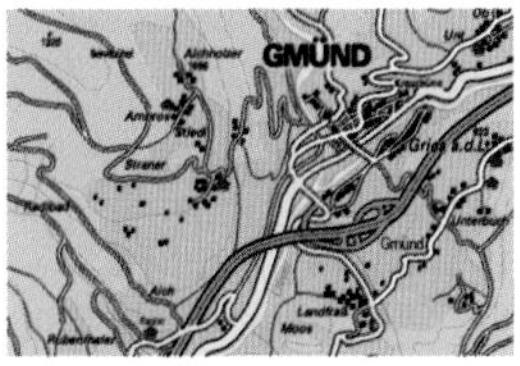

*road **map***

marathon
marathons *noun*
a very long running race. A marathon is 26 miles and 385 yards (42.2 km) long.

marble
noun
1 a hard rock that is used in buildings to make floors or for decoration.

***marble** slab*
2 a small, glass ball that is used to play a children's game called marbles.

march
marches marching marched *verb*
to walk with quick, regular steps.

march *noun*

margarine
noun
a food made of vegetable oil that is used for cooking or spreading on bread.
■ say **mar**-jer-in

margin
margins *noun*
a space that forms a border at the edge of a piece of paper.

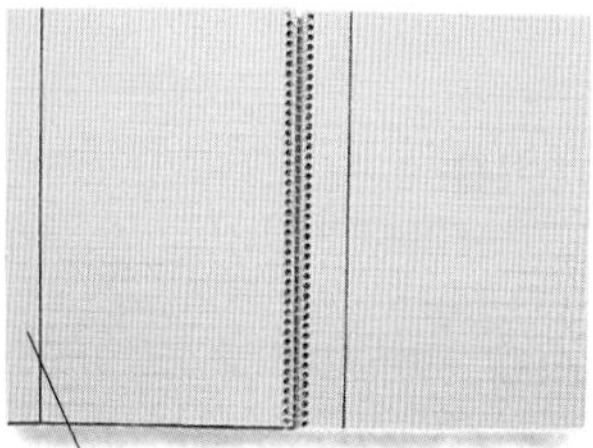

margin

marine
adjective
living in the sea, or having something to do with the sea.

***marine** life*
■ say ma-**reen**

mark
marks *noun*
1 a line or a stain on something.
*A chalk **mark**.*
2 a score that shows how well you have done at something.
*I got high **marks** in French.*

market
markets *noun*
a place with stalls for buying and selling goods, often outside.

*open **market***

marmalade
marmalades *noun*
a type of jam made from fruit such as oranges or limes.

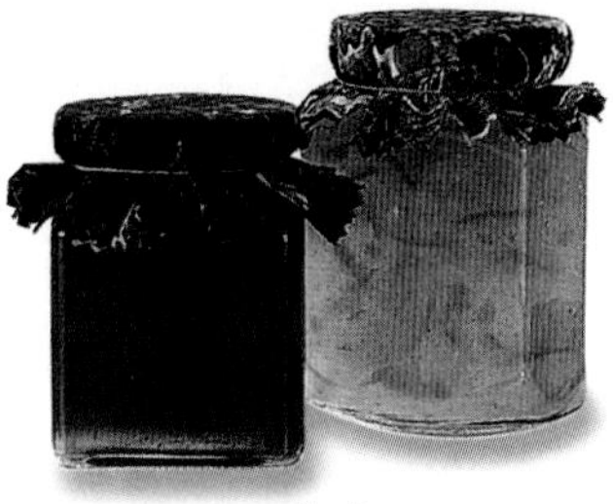

*orange **marmalade***

marry
marries marrying married *verb*
to become someone's husband or wife at a wedding.
marriage *noun*

marsh
marshes *noun*
a low area of land that is always wet.

A B C D E F G H I J K L M N O P Q R S T U V W X Y Z

marsupial
marsupials *noun*
one of a group of mammals that carry their babies in pouches. Kangaroos and koalas are marsupials (see **mammal** on page 124).
■ say mar-**soo**-pee-al

masculine
adjective
of, or like, men or boys.
■ say **mas**-kul-lin
■ opposite **feminine**

mask
masks *noun*
something that hides or protects the face.

*party **mask***
mask *verb*

mass
masses *noun*
a very large number of people or things.

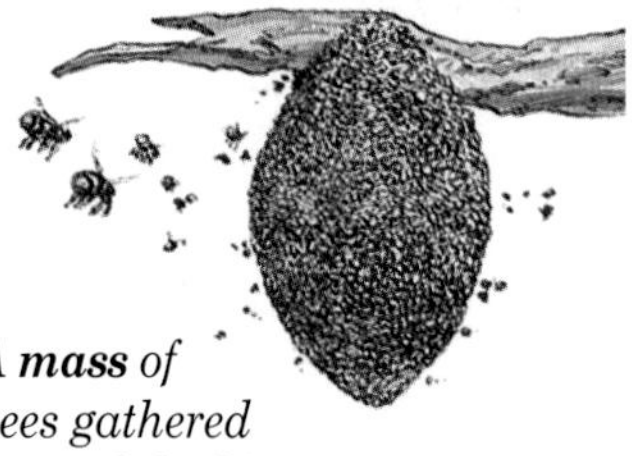

*A **mass** of bees gathered around the hive.*

mast
masts *noun*
an upright pole that holds the sails on a boat or ship (see **boat** on page 31).

mat
mats *noun*
a covering for a floor or to put under dishes on a table.

match
matches matching matched *verb*
to be similar to, or to go well with, something else.

*His pants **matched** his hat and scarf.*
matching *adjective*

match
matches *noun*
1 a sports competition between two people or teams.
*A tennis **match**.*
2 a small stick of wood or cardboard that you strike against a rough surface to make a flame.

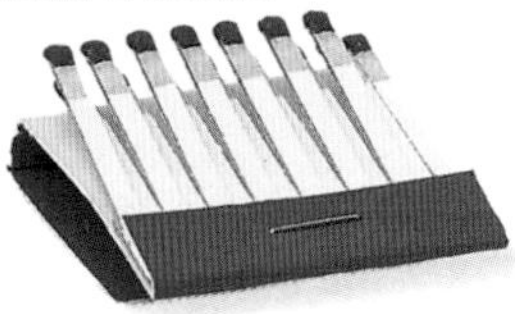

mate
mates mating mated *verb*
to join together as males and females to produce babies.
*Many animals **mate** in the spring and have their babies in the summer.*
mate *noun*

material
materials *noun*
1 cloth.

*woven **material***

2 things that are used to make or do something.

*building **materials***

mathematics
noun
the study of numbers, quantities, shapes, and sizes. Mathematics is often shortened to "math."

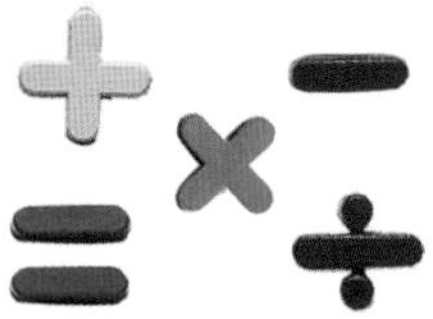

*Symbols that are used in **mathematics**.*
mathematical *adjective*

matter
noun
1 any substance that takes up space and has weight, such as solids, liquids, and gases.
*Everything is made up of **matter**.*
2 a subject that needs to be discussed or decided.
*It was an urgent **matter**.*

mattress
mattresses *noun*
a soft, thick pad that you lie on in a bed.

mature
adjective
fully grown or developed.
mature *verb*
maturity *noun*

maximum
noun
the greatest possible amount.

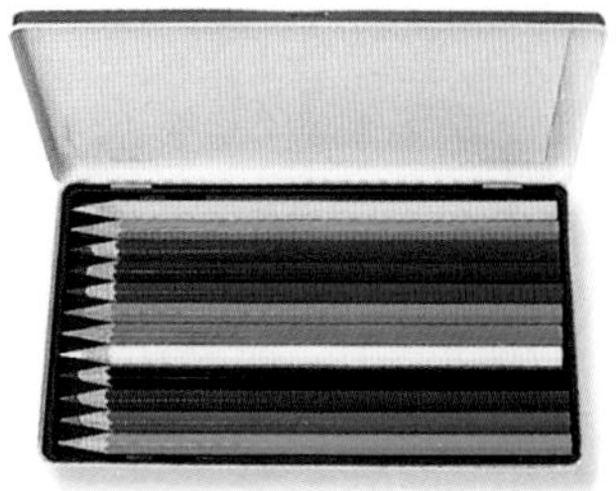

*This box holds a **maximum** of 12 pencils.*
■ opposite **minimum**

may
might *verb*
1 to ask or have permission to do something.
***May** I go now?*
2 to suggest that something is possible.
*It **may** rain later.*
■ always used with another verb

mayonnaise
noun
a creamy sauce made from eggs, vegetable oil, and vinegar and eaten with salads.

■ say **may**-uh-nayz

maze
mazes *noun*
a system of paths in which it is difficult to find your way around.

meadow
meadows *noun*
a field of grass, often with wild flowers growing in it.
■ say **med**-oh

meal
meals *noun*
food eaten at a particular time of the day.

*An evening **meal**.*

mean
adjective
1 unkind or unpleasant.

mean
mean meaning meant *verb*
to have in your mind as your purpose.
*What did you **mean** by that?*

meaning
meanings *noun*
the explanation behind what something says or what it is about.
*She didn't understand the **meaning** of the joke.*

meanwhile
adverb
at the same time.
*Put the pasta on to boil, and **meanwhile**, make the sauce.*

measure
measures measuring measured *verb*
to find out how big or how heavy something is.

■ say **mezh**-ur
measurement *noun*

meat
noun
the parts of an animal that can be eaten.

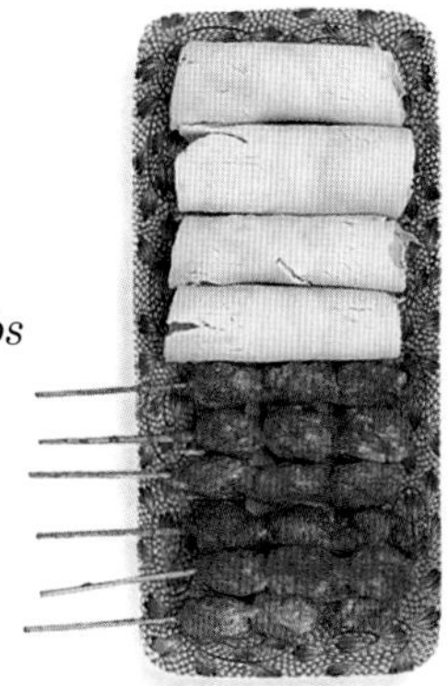

***meat** kebabs*

mechanic
mechanics *noun*
a person who makes and repairs engines and machines.

mechanical
adjective
worked by a machine.

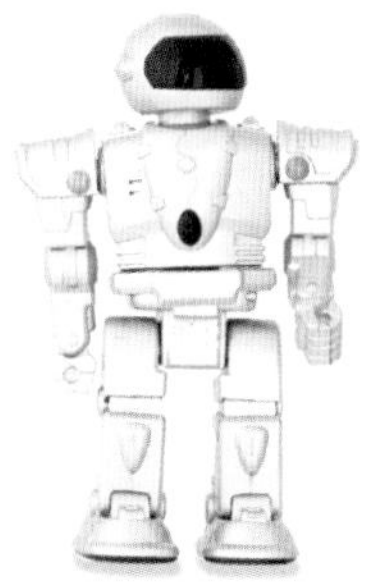

*A **mechanical** toy.*

medal
medals *noun*
a piece of metal that looks like a large coin hanging on a ribbon. Medals are awarded to people for something special that they have done.

*war **medal***

medical
adjective
having to do with medicine or doctors.
***Medical** school.*

medicine
medicines *noun*
a substance given to a sick person to help make them better.

■ say **med**-i-sin

medieval
adjective
coming from the historical period between the 12th and 15th centuries.

***medieval** costume*

■ say med-ee-**ee**-val

medium
adjective
an average size, not particularly large or small.

small ***medium*** *large*

meet
meets meeting met *verb*
to come face-to-face with another person.
*I **meet** my friend at the bus stop every day.*
meeting *noun*

melody
melodies *noun*
a tune.
*Do you recognize this **melody**?*
melodic *adjective*

melon
melons *noun*
a round yellow or green fruit with a tough skin, soft flesh, and many seeds.

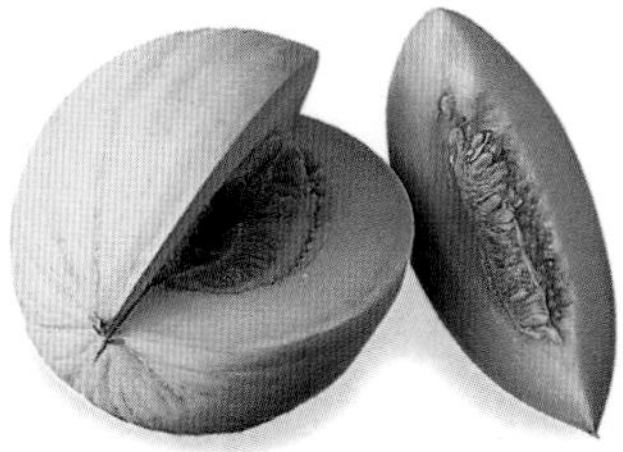

melt
melts melting melted *verb*
to turn from a solid to a liquid when heated.

*The butter **melted** quickly in the hot pan.*

member
members *noun*
a person who belongs to a club or an organization.

memorial
memorials *noun*
a structure that is built to remind us of people who have died.

*A war **memorial**.*

memorize
memorizes memorizing memorized *verb*
to learn something so that you can remember it in detail.
***Memorize** the directions before you begin your trip.*

memory
memories *noun*
1 the ability to remember things.
*I have a terrible **memory** for people's names.*
2 what you remember of something that has happened in the past.
*The photos brought back happy **memories**.*

mend
mends mending mended *verb*
to repair something that is broken.

mental
adjective
having to do with the mind.
*A test of **mental** abilities.*

menu
menus *noun*
a list of dishes in a restaurant.

■ say **men**-yoo

mercury
noun
a heavy, silver-colored metal that is usually in a liquid form. Mercury is often used in thermometers.

mercury

mercy
noun
the ability to forgive someone or to treat them sympathetically.
*The prisoners were shown **mercy** and released.*
merciful *adjective*

merit
merits meriting merited *verb*
to deserve something.
*Her actions **merited** a special award for bravery.*
merit *noun*

mermaid
mermaids *noun*
a sea creature from legends that has the upper body of a woman and the tail of a fish.

merry
adjective
happy and cheerful.
■ comparisons **merrier merriest**

mess
messes *noun*
things that are dirty or in the wrong place and look untidy.
*There was a big **mess** after they had finished cooking.*
messy *adjective*

message
messages *noun*
a piece of information or an instruction that you send to someone or leave for them.

met
*from the verb **to meet***
*I **met** my friend in town yesterday.*

metal
metals *noun*
a substance that is found in rocks and can be hammered or stretched into a shape. Iron, gold, and copper are all metals. Electricity and heat can be passed through metals.

tin can

gold watch

metallic *adjective*

meteorite
meteorites *noun*
a piece of rock that falls to Earth from space without burning up. Pieces of rock that burn up as they enter Earth's atmosphere are called meteors.

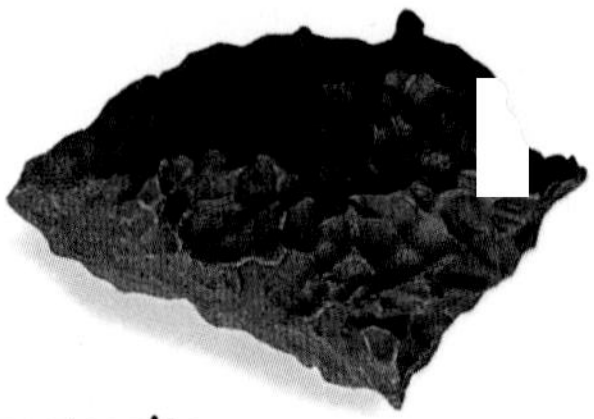

meteorite
■ say **meet**-ee-or-ite

method
methods *noun*
a way of doing something.
*Organic farming **methods**.*

microphone
microphones *noun*
a device that is used to send sound over a distance or to make it louder.

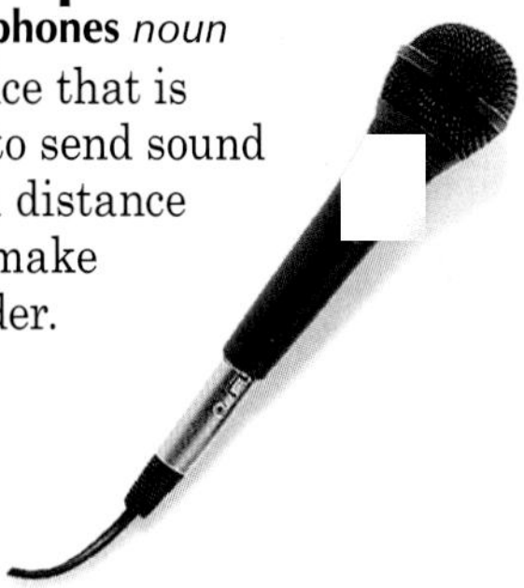

microscope
microscopes *noun*
an instrument that magnifies very tiny things so that they can be seen in detail.

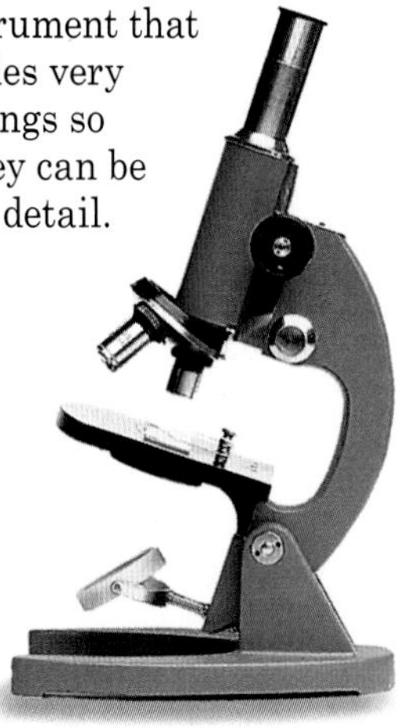

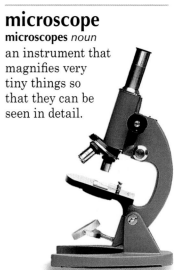

microwave oven
microwave ovens *noun*
an oven that cooks food very quickly by passing electrical signals through it.

midday
noun
12 o'clock, in the middle of the day.
■ opposite **midday** → **midnight**

middle
middles *noun*
the center, or the part between the outer edges of something.

*She sat in the **middle** of the bench, between her two friends.*

midnight
noun
12 o'clock at night.
■ opposite **midday**

might
*from the verb **may***
*It **might** snow later.*
■ say **mite**

migrate
migrates migrating migrated *verb*
1 to go from one place to another to live there.
***Migrating** from the country to the city.*
2 to go from one place to another every year at the same time.

*Birds **migrate** huge distances.*
■ say **my**-grate
migration *noun*

military
adjective
to do with an army, navy, or air force.

***military** hat*

milk
noun
the liquid that female mammals produce to feed their babies. People also drink goat's and cow's milk.

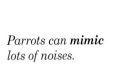

mill
mills *noun*
1 a building where materials are manufactured.

*saw**mill***

2 a device that grinds or crushes.

*pepper **mill***

millionaire
millionaires *noun*
a very rich person with money and property worth more than a million dollars.

mime
mimes *noun*
a type of acting that uses movements instead of words.

mime *verb*

mimic
mimics mimicking mimicked *verb*
to imitate what someone says or does.

*Parrots can **mimic** lots of noises.*

mind
minds minding minded *verb*
1 to object to something.
*Do you **mind** if I sit here?*
2 to take care of someone for a time.
*I had to **mind** the baby while my sister went out.*

mind
minds *noun*
1 the thoughts, feelings, and memory of a person.
*I've changed my **mind**.*
2 intelligence.
*She has a quick **mind**.*

mine
mines *noun*
1 a deep hole in the ground from which minerals are dug out of rock.
miner *noun*
2 a type of bomb that can float in the sea or be buried in the ground.

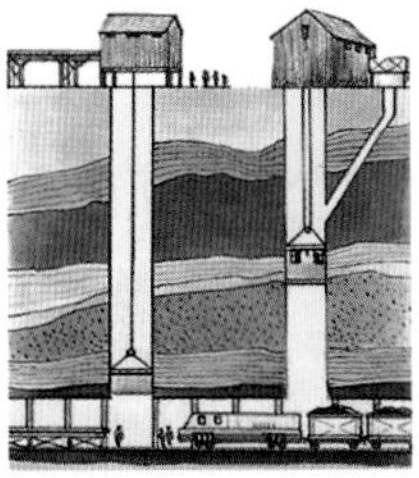

*coal **mine***

mineral
minerals *noun*
a natural substance, such as coal or gold, that is found in rocks and in the ground.

lapis lazuli

miniature
adjective
very small, or made to a small scale.

***miniature** china*
■ say **min**-i-cher
miniaturize *verb*

minimum
noun
the smallest possible amount or number.
*The **minimum** age for driving a car is 16.*
■ opposite **maximum**

minister
ministers *noun*
1 a person who holds religious services in a church.
2 someone in charge of a government department.
*The British health **minister**.*

a b c d e f g h i j k l m n o p q r s t u v w x y z

minor
adjective
small or unimportant.
*A **minor** fault delayed the plane's departure.*
■ opposite **major**
minority *noun*

minus
preposition
subtract or less.
*8 **minus** 5 equals 3.*
■ opposite **plus**

minus
minuses *noun*
a symbol in mathematics that means subtract.

minus *adjective*

minute
minutes *noun*
a measurement of time that lasts 60 seconds. There are 60 minutes in an hour.
■ say **min**-it

minute
adjective
extremely small.

*A **minute** bead.*
■ say my-**noot**

miracle
miracles *noun*
a sudden, wonderful event that sometimes makes a bad situation better.
*Her recovery after the accident was a **miracle**.*
■ say **mir**-u-kuhl
miraculous *adjective*

mirage
mirages *noun*
something that looks real from far away, but is not there when you get closer to it.
*The lake that they saw in the desert was only a **mirage**.*
■ say -mi-**razh**

mirror
mirrors *noun*
a shiny surface, usually made of glass. Mirrors reflect the images of things placed in front of them.

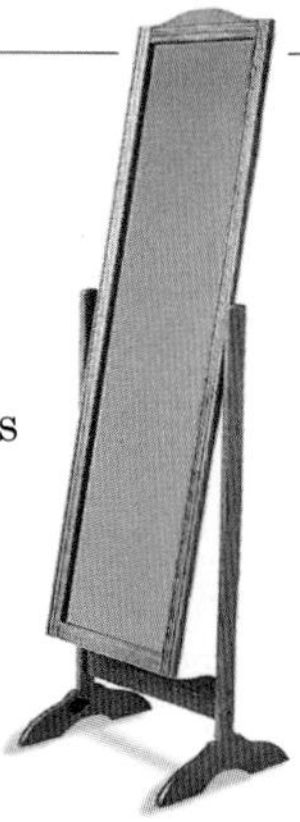

mischievous
adjective
playful in a way that can be annoying.

*The **mischievous** cat knocked over the plant.*
■ say **mis**-chuh-vus
mischievously *adverb*

miserable
adjective
very sad or unhappy.

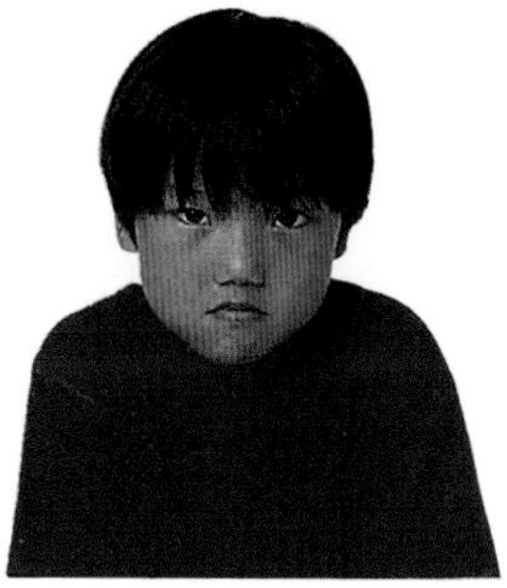

miss
misses missing missed *verb*
1 to fail to meet, reach, or hit something that you are aiming at.
*He threw the ball at the target, but **missed** it.*
2 to be sad because someone is not there.
*I will **miss** you.*
3 to fail to keep, have, or attend something.
*She has **missed** school for three weeks now.*

mist
mists *noun*
a cloud of tiny water drops in the air.
misty *adjective*

mistake
mistakes *noun*
something that someone does wrong.

8-5=1

mistaken *adjective*

mix
mixes mixing mixed *verb*
to combine two or more things together.

mixture *noun*

moan
moans moaning moaned *verb*
to complain or to make a long, low, groaning noise because of pain or sadness.

moat
moats *noun*
a deep ditch filled with water that surrounds a castle.

mobile
adjective
able to move or be carried around.
*A **mobile** library.*

mobile
mobiles *noun*
a decoration made of small objects hanging on strings.

model
models *noun*
1 a small copy of something larger.

*A **model** of an airplane.*
model *adjective*
2 a person who demonstrates clothes or other things that are for sale.

*A fashion **model**.*
3 a person who poses for photographs or for an artist.

modern
adjective
of the present time.
*A **modern** house.*

modest
adjective
not boasting about your talents and actions.
*He was too **modest** to say he had won first prize.*

moist
adjective
slightly wet.
moisture *noun*

mole
moles *noun*
1 a small, furry mammal that lives in underground tunnels. Moles eat worms and insects and they are almost blind.

2 a small, dark patch on your skin.

moment
moments *noun*
a short time.
*I'll be back in a **moment**.*

money
noun
the coins and paper bills used to buy things.

mongrel
mongrels *noun*
a dog that is a mixture of more than one breed.

monk
monks *noun*
a man who lives in a religious community.

*Buddhist **monk***

■ say **munk**

monkey
monkeys *noun*
a furry mammal that usually lives in hot regions. Most monkeys live in trees and eat fruit, although some eat small insects and mammals. There are many different species of monkey.

macaque

■ say **mung**-kee

monster
monsters *noun*
a fierce, frightening creature from myths and fairy tales.

month
months *noun*
a period of between 28 and 31 days. A year is divided into 12 months.

mood
moods *noun*
a way you feel at a particular time.
*The sunny day put us all in a good **mood**.*

moon
moons *noun*
a ball-shaped natural satellite made of rock that revolves around a planet (see **universe** on page 229).

mop
mops *noun*
a tool for cleaning floors, used with water and a bucket.

more
adjective
greater in number or quantity.
■ opposite **less**

morning
mornings *noun*
the early part of the day, ending at noon.
*School starts at 8:30 in the **morning**.*

mosaic
mosaics *noun*
a picture or pattern made of small squares of colored stone.

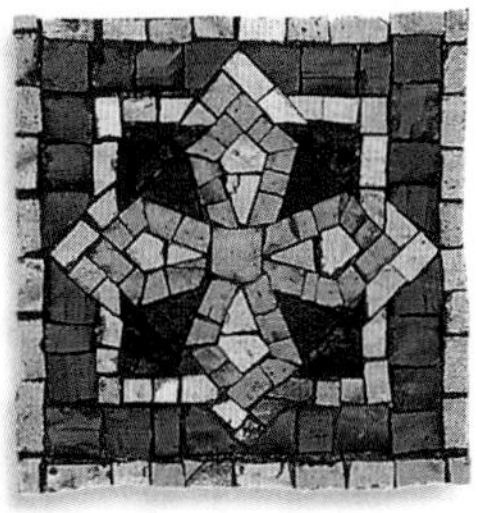

■ say mo-**zay**-ik

mosque
mosques *noun*
a building where Muslims go to pray.
■ say **mosk**

mosquito
mosquitoes or **mosquitos** *noun*
a small, flying insect found in hot, wet regions. Female mosquitoes bite and feed on the blood of people and animals and can infect them with serious illnesses, such as malaria.

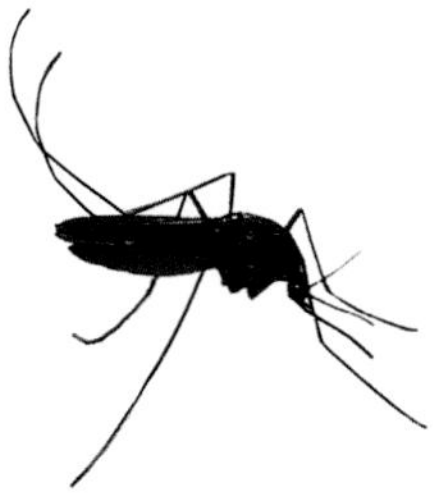

■ say muh-**skee**-toe

most
adjective
greatest in number or quantity.
■ opposite **least**

motel
motels *noun*
a hotel specially built for guests with cars.

moth
moths *noun*
a flying insect with wings covered in fine scales. Moths belong to the same animal group as butterflies, but they usually fly at night.

*pine emperor **moth***

mother
mothers *noun*
a female parent.

motion
motions *noun*
movement.
*The rocking **motion** of the boat made me feel sick.*

motor
motors *noun*
a machine that supplies power to objects to move them or make them work.

motorcycle
motorcycles *noun*
a two-wheeled vehicle that is powered by a motor.

motorist
motorists *noun*
a person who drives a car regularly.

mound
mounds *noun*
a small hill, or a pile.
*There is a **mound** of dirt at the end of the mole's tunnel.*

mountain
mountains *noun*
an area of land that rises up to a great height.
mountainous *adjective*

mourn
mourns mourning mourned *verb*
to be sad because someone has died.
■ say **morn**

mouse
mice *noun*
1 a small, furry mammal from the rodent family. Mice have large front teeth that they use to gnaw food. Mice mainly eat plants, but sometimes they eat small animals and insects, too.

2 a control switch for a computer that can be used to move things around on a computer screen.

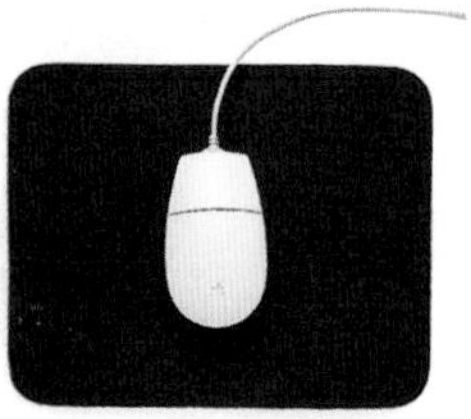

mouth
mouths *noun*
1 the opening in your face that you use for eating and talking.

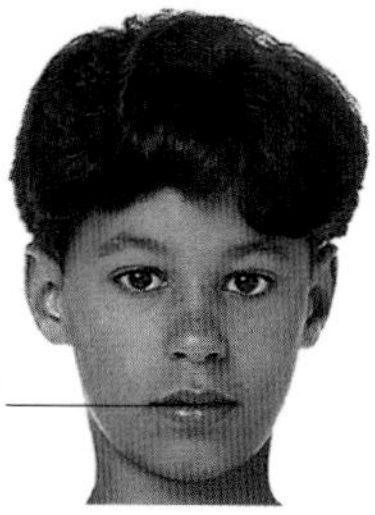

2 the end of a river where it meets the sea.

move
moves moving moved *verb*
to go from one place to another, or to make something change position.
movement *noun*

moving
adjective
making you feel emotions, especially sympathy.

movie
movies *noun*
a moving picture.

mow
mows mowing mowed *verb*
to cut grass.

***Mowing** the lawn.*
■ rhymes with **go**

mud
noun
soft, wet earth.
muddy *adjective*

muddle
muddles *noun*
a confusing or messy situation.
muddle *verb*

mug
mugs *noun*
a large cup without a saucer.

multiply
multiplies multiplying multiplied *verb*
to increase a number or an amount of something by adding it to itself several times.

9x5=45

*Nine **multiplied** by five equals forty-five.*
multiplication *noun*

munch
munches munching munched *verb*
to make a crunching noise while eating something.
***Munching** lettuce.*

murder
murders murdering murdered *verb*
to kill someone deliberately.

murmur
murmurs *noun*
a quiet, whispering sound.
murmur *verb*

muscle
muscles *noun*
the fleshy parts of your body that help it to move.

■ say **mus**-suhl
muscular *adjective*

museum
museums *noun*
a place where objects from other times and places, or of special interest, are displayed.
■ say myoo-**zee**-um

mushroom
mushrooms *noun*
a common fungus that grows in warm, damp areas. Some mushrooms can be eaten, but others are poisonous.

*field **mushrooms***

music
noun
the sound that people make when they sing or play musical instruments.

musical instrument

musical instruments *noun*
an instrument for making music, usually played by hitting, blowing, or pulling or hitting strings.

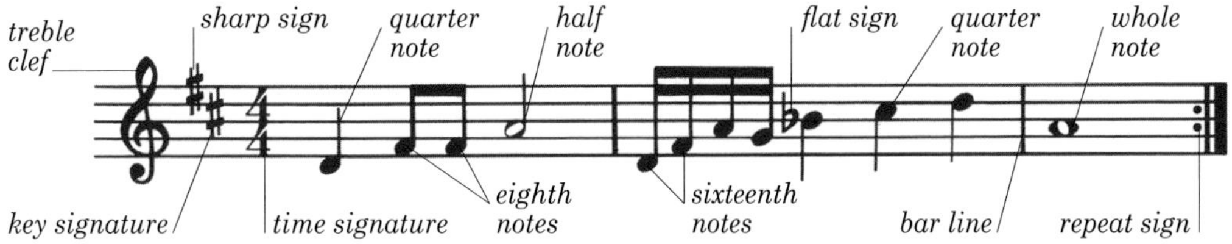

Musical symbols

Wind instruments

didgeridoo
(Australian Aboriginal pipe)

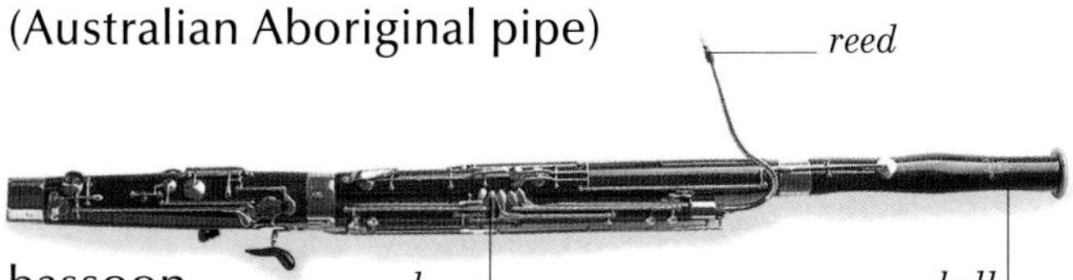

bassoon

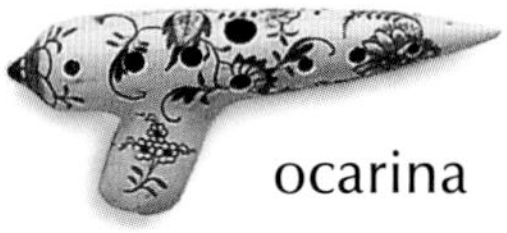

ocarina

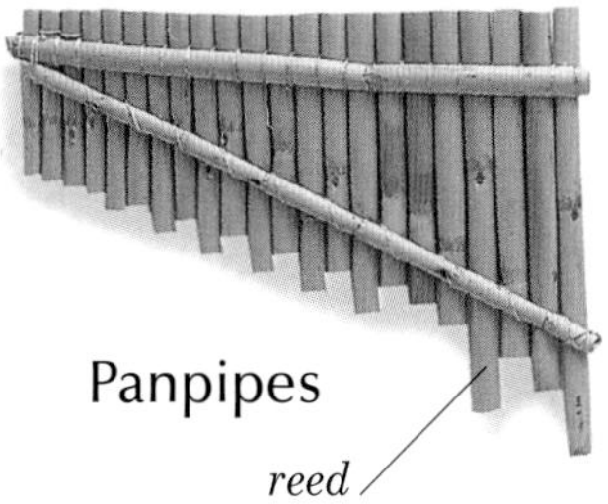

Panpipes

Brass instruments

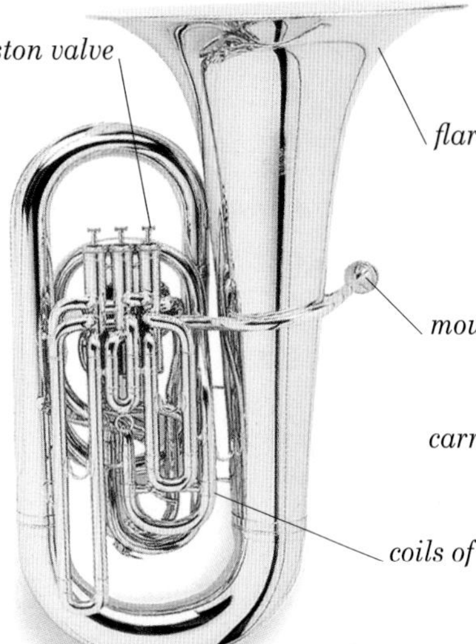

tuba

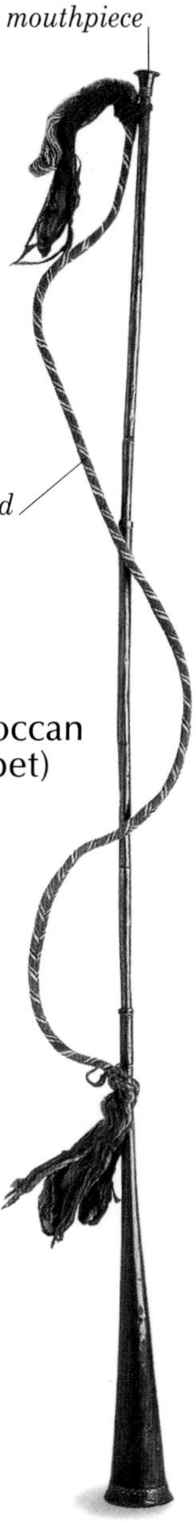

nfîr
(Moroccan trumpet)

String instruments

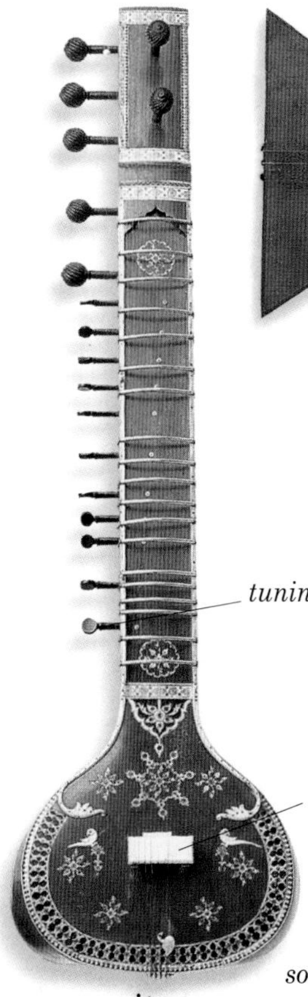

sitar

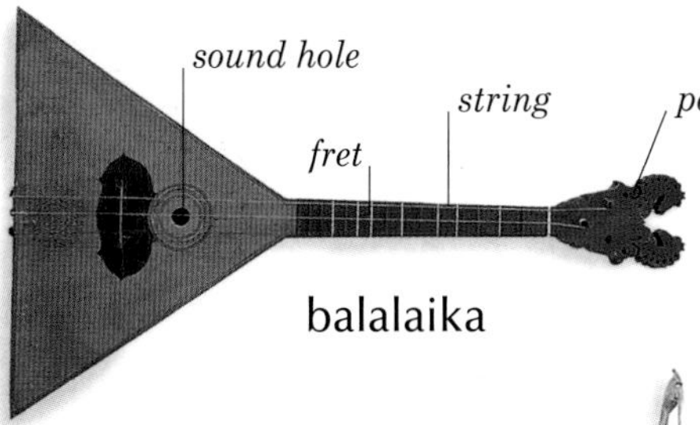

balalaika

fiddle

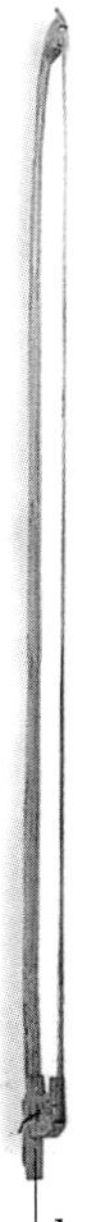

Percussion instruments

castanets

cabaca (rattle)

djeme (African drum)

mu-yus (Chinese temple blocks)

musician
musicians *noun*
a person who sings, plays a musical instrument, or writes music.

■ say myoo-**zish**-un

Muslim
Muslims *noun*
a person who believes in and follows the Islamic religion.
■ also spelled **Moslem**

mussel
mussels *noun*
a type of shellfish that is edible. Some mussels live in the sea, while others live in lakes and streams.

must
verb
to have to do something.
*I **must** mail her birthday present today.*
■ opposite **must not** or **mustn't**
■ always used with another verb

mustard
noun
a spicy powder or sauce made from mustard seeds and used to add flavor to food.

mutiny
mutinies *noun*
a rebellion by the crew of a ship or by soldiers in an army against the people in charge.
■ say **myoot**-n-ee
mutiny *verb*

mutter
mutters muttering muttered *verb*
to talk in a low voice.
*I can't hear when you **mutter**.*

mutual
adjective
shared by two or more.
*A **mutual** friend.*
■ say **myoo**-tyoo-ul

muzzle
muzzles *noun*
1 the mouth and nose of an animal.
2 a cage or straps put over an animal's mouth to stop it from biting.

mystery
mysteries *noun*
an unusual and puzzling event.
*His disappearance is still a **mystery**.*
mysterious *adjective*

myth
myths *noun*
an ancient story that tries to explain how the world became the way it is.

*Zeus was the god of light, clear skies, and thunder in Greek **myths**.*
mythical *adjective*

Nn

nail
nails *noun*
1 a long, thin, pointed metal spike that is hammered into pieces of wood to fasten them together.
nail *verb*

2 a hard substance that grows at the ends of your fingers and toes.

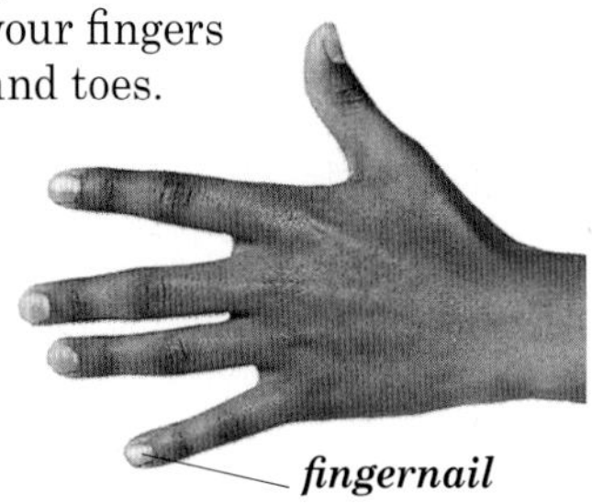

naked
adjective
not wearing any clothes.
■ say **nay**-kid

name
names *noun*
a word that a person or thing is known by.
*My dog's **name** is Rover.*

nap
naps *noun*
a short sleep.

*He took a quick **nap** before supper.*

narrator
narrators *noun*
someone who tells a story, either by writing it or by reading it aloud.

narrate *verb*

narrow
adjective
with sides or edges that are very close together.

*The path was very **narrow**.*
■ comparisons **narrower narrowest**
■ opposite **wide**

nasty
adjective
unpleasant or cruel.
■ comparisons **nastier nastiest**

nation
nations *noun*
a group of people who usually share the same history, language, and way of life and live in the same country.
national *adjective*

natural
adjective
produced by nature.

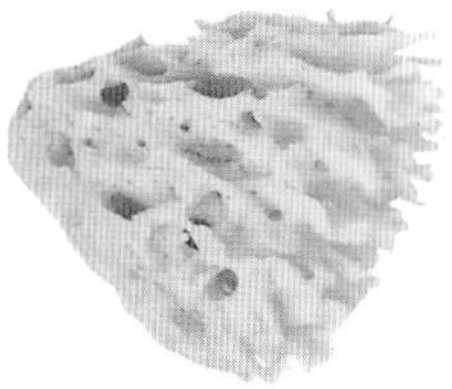

***natural** sponge*

nature
noun
all the things in the world that are not made by humans, such as the weather, animals, plants, and the sea.
■ say **nay**-cher

naughty
adjective
disobedient or badly behaved.

*It is very **naughty** to draw on walls.*
■ say **naw**-tee
■ comparisons **naughtier naughtiest**

nautical
adjective
relating to ships, sailors, or sailing.

ship's register

map dividers

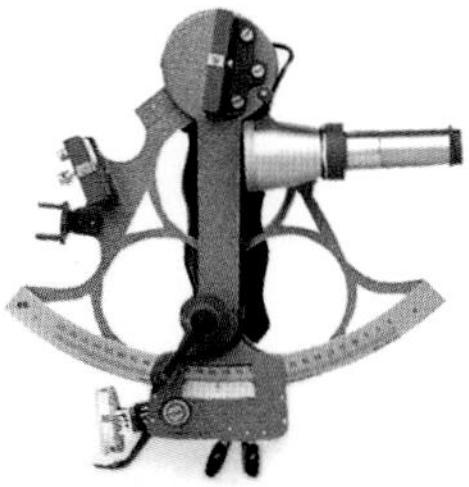

sextant

***Nautical** instruments.*

navigate
navigates navigating navigated
verb
to steer a boat, ship, or aircraft in a particular direction using special instruments and maps.

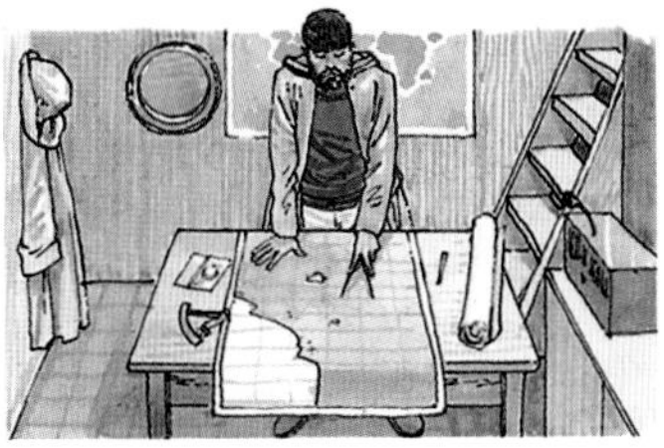

navigation *noun*

navy
noun
1 a country's warships and sailors.
2 a dark blue color.

near
preposition
close to or not far from.

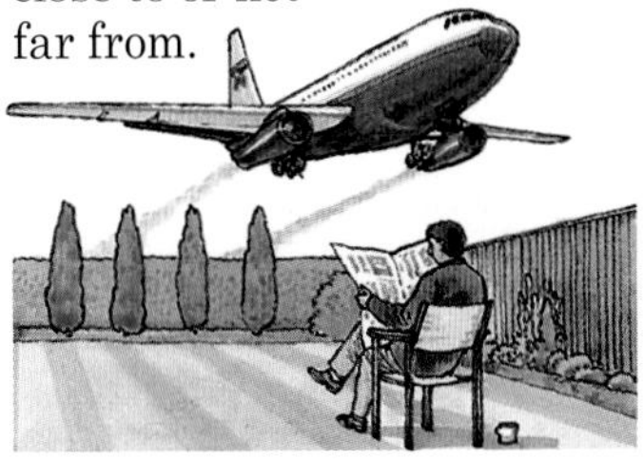

*They lived **near** the airport.*
■ opposite **far**
near *adjective*
near *adverb*

nearby
adverb
not far away.
*Do you live **nearby**?*

nearly
adverb
not quite, but almost.
*It's **nearly** bedtime.*

necessary
adjective
needed.
***Necessary** equipment for survival at sea.*
■ say **nes**-i-sair-ee
■ opposite **unnecessary**
necessarily *adverb*

handheld flare

parachute flare

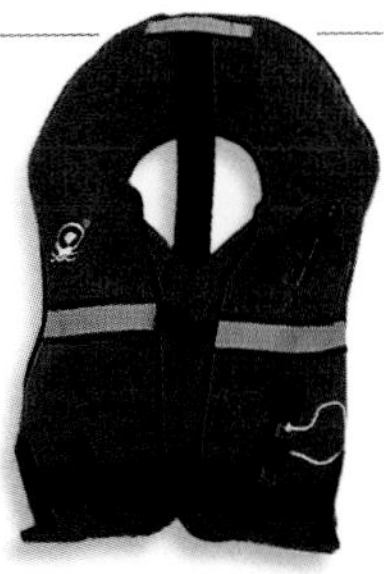

life jacket

neck
necks *noun*
the part of the body that supports your head and joins it to the rest of your body.

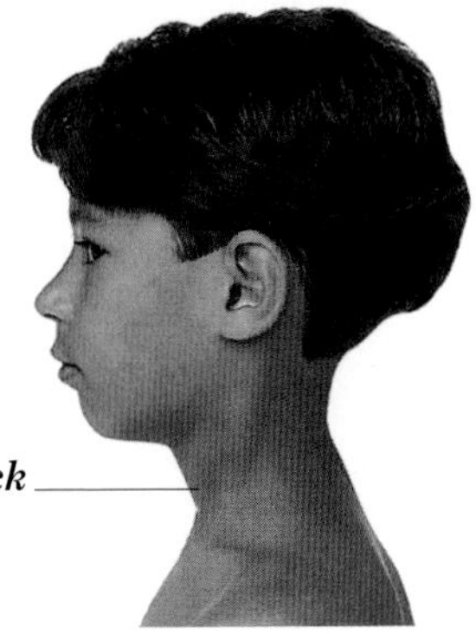

neck

necklace
necklaces *noun*
a chain or beads worn around the neck as a piece of jewelry.

nectar
noun
a sweet liquid that bees and some birds collect from flowers. Bees use nectar to make honey.

need
needs needing needed *verb*
to want something because you have to have it.
*Do you **need** anything from the store?*

needle
needles *noun*
1 a small, thin piece of pointed steel.

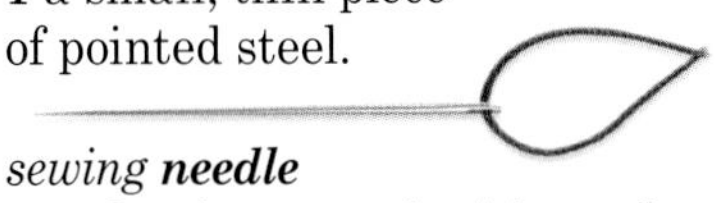

*sewing **needle***
2 a plastic or metal stick used for knitting.

3 a thin, pointed leaf of some plants, such as pine trees.
4 a part that points on a dial.
*A compass **needle**.*

negative
adjective
1 saying or meaning no.
*A **negative** answer.*
2 smaller than zero.
*A **negative** number.*
■ opposite **positive**

neglect
neglects neglecting neglected
verb
to pay too little or no attention to someone or something.

*They **neglected** their yard.*
neglect *noun*

negotiate
negotiates negotiating negotiated *verb*
to discuss something in order to reach an agreement.
■ say neg-**oh**-she-ate
negotiation *noun*

neighbor
neighbors *noun*
someone who lives near you.
■ say **nay**-bur

neighborhood
neighborhoods *noun*
the people and the area where you live.
■ say **nay**-bur-hood

nephew
nephews *noun*
the son of a person's brother, sister, brother-in-law, or sister-in-law.
■ say **nef**-yoo

nerve
nerves *noun*
1 a thin fiber that connects your brain to all parts of your body. Nerves carry messages to and from your brain so that you can feel and move.

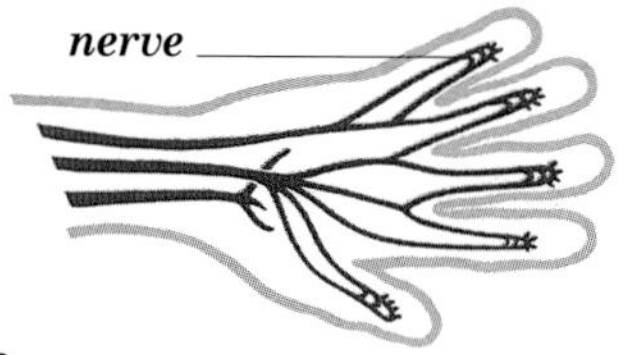

2 courage.
*To lose your **nerve**.*

nervous
adjective
slightly worried or frightened about what is happening or going to happen.

*He was **nervous** about speaking in public.*
nervously *adverb*

nest
nests *noun*
the home that a bird or animal builds out of leaves, grass, and other materials.

*squirrel's **nest***
nest *verb*

net
nets *noun*
a material made of knotted threads, string, or rope. Nets are often used to catch fish.

nettle
nettles *noun*
a plant with stinging hairs on its stems and leaves. These hairs can cause a rash on your skin if you touch the plant.

network
networks *noun*
1 a system of connected lines, roads, people, computers, or organizations.

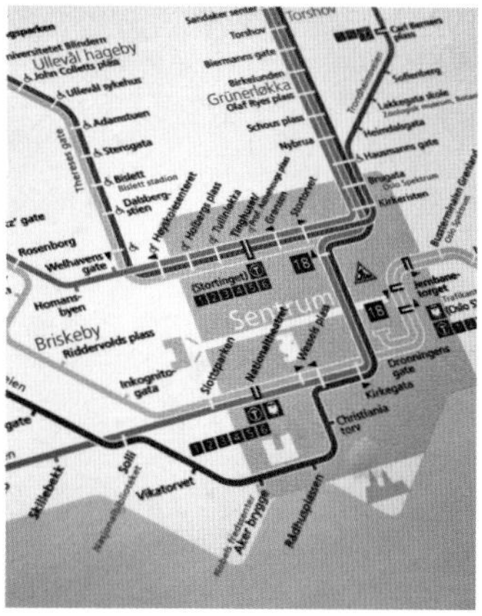

*Plan of a rail **network**.*

2 a group of connected radio or television stations that can broadcast the same programs.

neutral
adjective
1 not being on anyone's side.
*A **neutral** country.*
2 not very definite.
*Gray is a **neutral** color.*
■ say **noo**-trul

never
adverb
not ever.
*I've **never** been here before.*

new
adjective
1 recently made, or unused.

*I bought a **new** shirt today.*
2 unfamiliar or recently changed.
*A **new** job.*
■ comparisons **newer newest**
■ opposite **old**

news
noun
information about recent events around the country or around the world.
*Have you heard the **news**?*

newspaper
newspapers *noun*
large sheets of paper, printed with pictures and news reports.

*daily **newspapers***

next
adjective
1 coming immediately after.
*The **next** day.*
2 nearest.
*It's in the **next** room.*
next *adverb*

nib
nibs *noun*
the point at the end of an ink pen where the ink comes out.

nibble
nibbles nibbling nibbled *verb*
to eat by taking quick, small bites out of something.

***Nibbling** some nuts.*
nibble *noun*

nice
adjective
1 pleasant or delightful.
*A **nice** day.*
2 kind.
*He is a **nice** person.*
■ comparisons **nicer nicest**

nickel
noun
1 a 5-cent piece.
2 a strong, silvery-white metal. Nickel doesn't rust easily.

***nickel** ore*

nickname
nicknames *noun*
a shortened form of a name or an extra name that people may use instead of a person's full name.
*She was so smart that she earned the **nickname** "Brains."*

niece
nieces *noun*
the daughter of a person's brother, sister, brother-in-law, or sister-in-law.
■ rhymes with **peace**

night
nights *noun*
the time between sunset and sunrise, when the sky is dark.

■ opposite **day**

nightmare
nightmares *noun*
an unpleasant and frightening dream.

*A **nightmare** about a ghost.*

nimble
adjective
able to move quickly and easily.
***Nimble** fingers.*

nitrogen
noun
a gas with no taste or smell. All living things contain nitrogen, and air is mainly made of nitrogen.
■ say **ny**-troh-jin

nobody
noun
no person.
***Nobody** came to the party.*

nocturnal
adjective
active at night.

*Bats are **nocturnal** animals.*

nod
nods nodding nodded *verb*
to move your head up and down.
nod *noun*

noise
noises *noun*
any kind of sound, especially a sound that is too loud or unpleasant.

*He was making a lot of **noise**.*

noisy
adjective
making loud sounds.
noisily *adverb*

nonfiction
noun
information that is written about real events, things, and people.
■ opposite **fiction**

nonsense
noun
words that are silly or do not make sense.

noodle
noodles *noun*
a type of pasta that is made in long, flat, narrow strips.

noon
noun
12 o'clock midday.

noose
nooses *noun*
a circle of rope with a sliding knot. The loop tightens when the rope is pulled.

normal
adjective
usual or ordinary.
*Come at the **normal** time.*
normally *adverb*

north
noun
one of the four main compass directions. North is to your right when you are facing the setting Sun.

northern *adjective*

nose
noses *noun*
the part of your face that you smell and breathe with through two openings called nostrils.

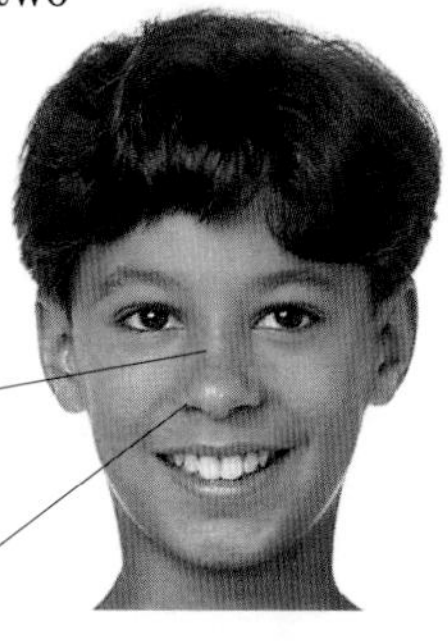

note
notes *noun*
1 a short, written message to remind you of something, or a short letter.

2 a piece of paper money.

3 a single sound in a piece of music.

nothing
noun
1 not anything.
*There's **nothing** to worry about.*
2 zero.

notice
notices noticing noticed *verb*
to see or be aware of something and pay attention to it.

*He **noticed** that he had a mark on his sleeve.*
noticeable *adjective*

a b c d e f g h i j k l m n o p q r s t u v w x y z

notice
notices *noun*
1 a written or printed sign that provides information.

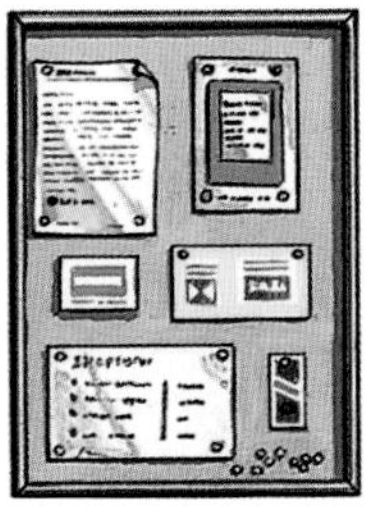

***Notices** on a board.*
2 attention.
*Take no **notice** of them.*

noun
nouns *noun*
a word that is used as a name. A noun can name a person, a place, a thing, or an idea.

novel
novels *noun*
a fictional written story in book form.

nowhere
adverb
not in any place.

*His dog was **nowhere** to be seen.*

nozzle
nozzles *noun*
a spout attached to the open end of a pipe or hose, through which water or other liquids are sprayed.

nuclear energy
noun
energy that is released by splitting the center, or nucleus, of particular atoms.
■ say **noo**-klee-ur

nude
adjective
with no clothes on.

nudge
nudges nudging nudged *verb*
to push or poke someone gently to draw their attention to something.

nudge *noun*

nugget
nuggets *noun*
a lump of something, usually a mineral.

*A gold **nugget**.*

nuisance
nuisances *noun*
an annoying person or thing.

*The cat was being a **nuisance**.*
■ say **noo**-suhns

numb
adjective
unable to feel anything.
*His fingers were **numb** with cold.*
■ say **num**

number
numbers *noun*
a figure used in counting that shows the quantity or total of something.

848

*848 is a three-figure **number**.*

numeral
numerals *noun*
a symbol that stands for a number.
*VI is the Roman **numeral** for 6.*

VI

numerous
adjective
very many.
*Too **numerous** to count.*

nun
nuns *noun*
a woman who lives in a religious community.

nurse
nurses *noun*
a person who is trained to care for and treat sick people, usually in a hospital.

nursery
nurseries *noun*
1 a room or building where young children are looked after.

2 a place where trees and plants are grown and sold.

nut
nuts *noun*
1 a tree fruit that consists of a seed, or kernel, surrounded by a hard shell.

2 a small piece of metal with a hole in it that is screwed onto a bolt.

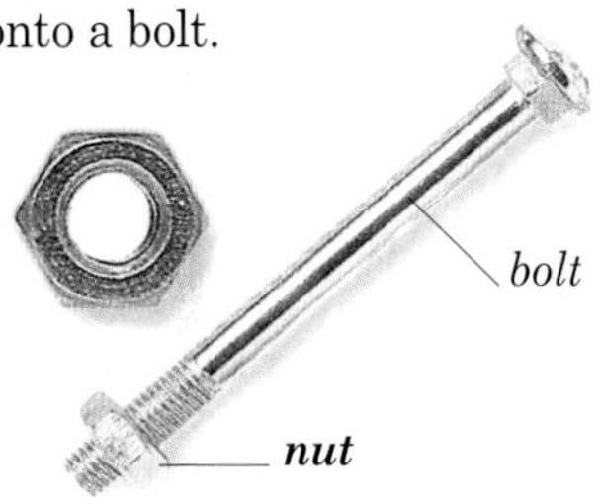

nutmeg
nutmegs *noun*
the hard seed of the tropical, evergreen nutmeg tree. Nutmegs can be used as a spice in cooking.

nutrient
nutrients *noun*
a part of a food that gives living things what they need to be healthy or to grow.

Oo

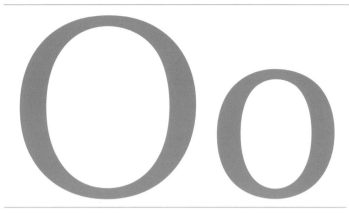

oak
oaks *noun*
a large deciduous tree that has fruit called acorns. Oak wood is often used for making furniture (see **tree** on page 223).

***oak** leaf*

oar
oars *noun*
a long pole with a wide, flat end used for rowing a boat.
■ say **or**

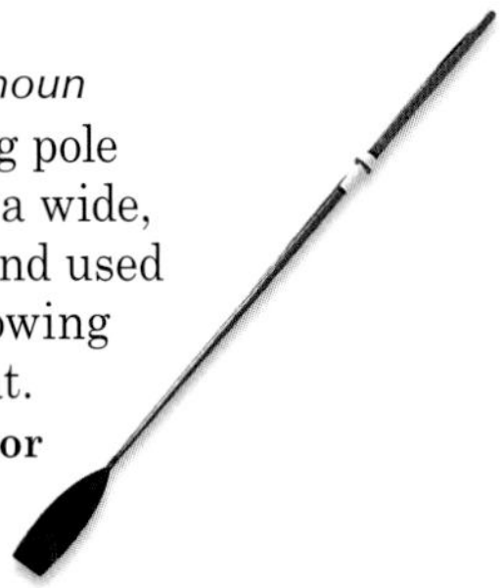

oasis
oases *noun*
a place in the desert where there is water and where plants and trees can grow.

■ say oh-**ay**-sis

oats
noun
a type of cereal crop grown on farms. Oats are used to make food and to feed cattle, horses, and other animals.

obey
obeys obeying obeyed *verb*
to do something that someone tells or orders you to do.

*She taught the dog to **obey** her commands.*
■ opposite **disobey**
obedient *adjective*

object
objects *noun*
anything you can see or touch that isn't alive.
■ say **ob**-jekt

object
objects objecting objected *verb*
to dislike or disagree with something.
*He **objected** to people dropping litter in the street.*
■ say ub-**jekt**

oblong
adjective
longer than it is wide, with sides nearly parallel.

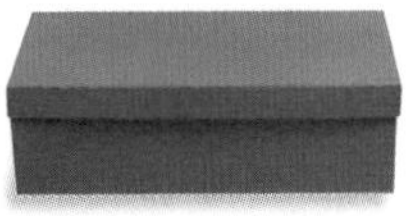
*An **oblong** box.*
oblong *noun*

observatory
observatories *noun*
a building from which people observe stars, the planets, and the weather, using powerful telescopes.

observe
observes observing observed *verb*
to watch something.
observation *noun*

obstacle
obstacles *noun*
a thing that blocks your way.
*He had to jump over 10 **obstacles** to win the race.*

obstinate
adjective
difficult to persuade.

*He was very **obstinate** and refused to pick up his room.*
obstinately *adverb*

obstruct
obstructs obstructing obstructed *verb*
to block or to prevent something or someone from passing.

*She **obstructed** his path.*
obstruction *noun*

obvious
adjective
easy to see or understand.
■ say **ob**-vee-us
obviously *adverb*

occasion
occasions *noun*
1 a special event.

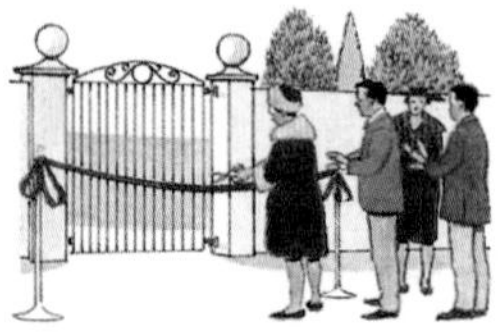
*The park opening was a grand **occasion.***
2 a time when something happens.
*I have flown in an airplane on two **occasions.***

occupation
occupations *noun*
the work that someone does to earn a living.

occupy
occupies occupying occupied *verb*
1 to be busy.
*I was **occupied** with my book when the doorbell rang.*
2 to take up a space or live in a place.
*The company **occupied** the top two floors of the building.*
3 to control a place by force.
*The army **occupied** the city.*

occur
occurs occurring occurred *verb*
1 to happen or exist.
*When did the problem **occur**?*
2 to come into your mind.
*That never **occurred** to me.*

ocean
oceans *noun*
a very large area of sea, usually separating continents.

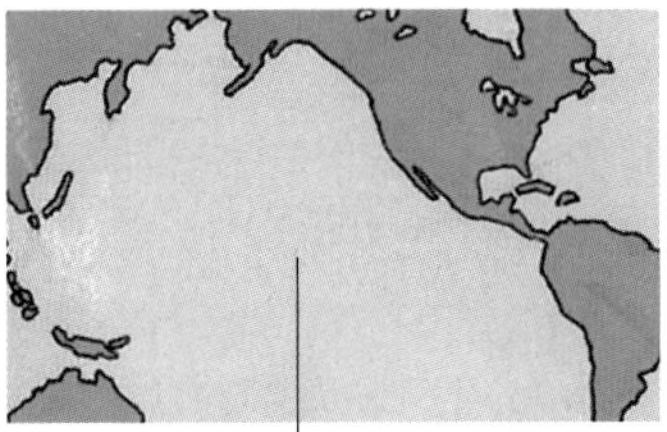

Pacific ***Ocean***

octagon
octagons *noun*
a flat shape with eight straight sides (see **shape** on page 182).

octopus
octopuses or **octopi** *noun*
a sea animal that does not have a backbone. Octopuses have eight arms, which they use for catching crabs, shellfish, and fish. They have good eyesight and are thought to have the ability to learn things.

odd
adjective
1 strange or unusual.
That's a very ***odd*** *thing to do!*
■ comparisons **odder oddest**
2 not belonging to a pair or a set of things.

Wearing ***odd*** *socks.*
3 any number that cannot be divided exactly by two.
■ opposite **even**

odor
odors *noun*
a strong smell.

There was a strange ***odor*** *coming from the garbage.*
■ say **oh**-der

offend
offends offending offended *verb*
1 to upset or annoy someone.
offensive *adjective*
2 to break a law.

offer
offers offering offered *verb*
to ask someone if they would like something, or if you can do something for them.

He ***offered*** *her some grapes.*
offer *noun*

office
offices *noun*
a place where people organize and run a business.

official
adjective
properly approved by someone in charge.
■ say uh-**fish**-al
officially *adverb*

often
adverb
many times.
I ***often*** *go to school by bus.*

oil
noun
1 a thick liquid that occurs naturally underground. Oil is used to make products such as fuel and plastics.
2 a greasy substance that is found in the seeds and fruits of some plants. This type of oil is often used for cooking.

Sunflower ***oil.***

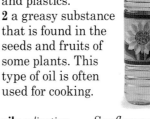

oily *adjective*

oil rig
oil rigs *noun*
a structure and machinery used for drilling into the ground in search of oil and gas. Some oil rigs are used at sea, while others are used on land.

oil slick
oil slicks *noun*
a patch of oil, usually spilled accidentally, that floats on the surface of the sea.

oil tanker
oil tankers *noun*
a ship that transports huge amounts of oil.

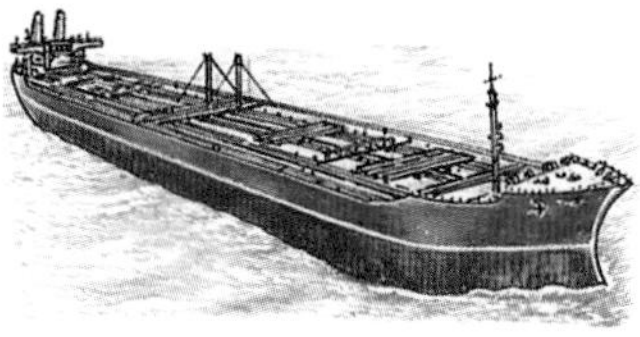

ointment
ointments *noun*
a substance that you put on your skin or on a wound to make it better.

old
adjective
1 having been in use for a long time.

An ***old*** *teddy bear.*
■ opposite **new**
2 having existed for a long time.
■ opposite **young**
■ comparisons **older oldest**

olive
olives *noun*
a small, oval fruit that grows in countries near the Mediterranean Sea. Olives are eaten in salads and crushed to make olive oil.

Olympic Games
noun
a sporting competition for athletes from countries all over the world that is held every four years.

omit
omits omitting omitted *verb*
to leave something out, or not to do something.
His name was ***omitted*** *from the list.*

onion
onions *noun*
a small, round root vegetable with a strong taste. Onions have a thin, papery skin with many layers inside.

only
adjective
without any others.
*He's the **only** person wearing green.*

only
adverb
1 just.

*There were **only** a few beads left in the box.*
2 no more than.
***Only** five of us went to the park.*

open
adjective
1 not closed or shut, so that people or things can go in and out.

***Open** car doors.*
■ opposite **shut**
2 with plenty of space, or not closed in.
***Open** fields.*

opera
operas *noun*
a musical play where the words are sung instead of spoken.

***opera** singer*

operate
operates operating operated *verb*
1 to work a piece of machinery.

*You must be careful when **operating** machinery.*
2 to perform surgery in a hospital.

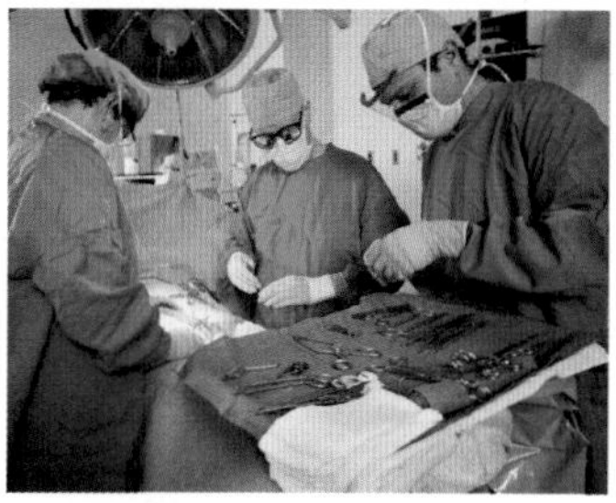

operating *adjective*
operation *noun*

opinion
opinions *noun*
a person's belief or judgment about something.
*Who is the best football player, in your **opinion**?*

opponent
opponents *noun*
someone who is on the opposite side in a fight or competition.

*Chess **opponents**.*

opportunity
opportunities *noun*
a chance, or a suitable time to do something.
*He had the **opportunity** to go to Europe for a year.*

oppose
opposes opposing opposed *verb*
to argue or fight against someone or something.
*They **opposed** the decision to close the park.*
opposition *noun*

opposite
adjective
1 on the other side.

*He saw his friend on the **opposite** side of the river.*
2 completely different.
*Tall is the **opposite** of short.*
opposite *noun*

optician
opticians *noun*
a person whose job is to test peoples' sight and to sell eyeglasses and contact lenses.
■ say op-**tish**-un

optimistic
adjective
expecting or hoping that things will go well.
***Optimistic** about the future.*
■ opposite **pessimistic**
optimism *noun*

option
options *noun*
a choice.
*You have several **options**: you can travel by car, train, or plane.*
optional *adjective*

orange
oranges *noun*
1 a color made by mixing red and yellow together.

2 a juicy fruit with a tough skin.

orangutan
orangutans *noun*
a large ape that lives in tropical forests in Southeast Asia. Orangutans eat mainly fruit, but also eat leaves, bark, and birds' eggs. They live in nests called platforms, which they build in trees.

■ say or-**rang**-a-tang

orbit
orbits orbiting orbited *verb*
to move around a planet, a moon, or the Sun in space.
*The Earth **orbits** the Sun.*
orbit *noun*

orchard
orchards *noun*
an area of land where fruit trees are grown.

*They were picking apples in the **orchard**.*

orchestra
orchestras *noun*
a large group of musicians who play together.
■ say **or**-kes-tra

orchid
orchids *noun*
a type of plant with flowers that are an unusual shape.
■ say **or**-kid

order
orders *noun*
1 an instruction telling someone to do something.

*He gave them **orders** to stop.*
2 a request for something in a store or restaurant.

order *verb*
3 a way that things are placed or arranged.
*Alphabetical **order**.*
4 a peaceful, lawful state.
*Law and **order**.*

ordinary
adjective
not different or unusual in any way.

*His sandwich was fairly **ordinary**, but she had a special one.*

organ
organs *noun*
1 a musical instrument with a keyboard and large air pipes. The pipes make a noise when air is forced into them.
2 a part inside your body that does a particular job. Your heart is an organ.

organism
organisms *noun*
any living animal or plant.

organization
organizations *noun*
a group of people with common goals or business.

organize
organizes organizing organized *verb*
to arrange or plan something.

***Organizing** work into folders.*
organization *noun*

origin
origins *noun*
the beginning of something, or where something or someone comes from.
*The pot was of Roman **origin**.*
■ say **o**-rij-in

original
adjective
earliest or first.
*An **original** design.*
■ say or-**rij**-in-nal

ornament
ornaments *noun*
an object that is used as a decoration.

orphan
orphans *noun*
someone whose parents have died.
■ say **or**-fan

ostrich
ostriches *noun*
a tall bird from Africa that can run very fast, but cannot fly. Ostriches live in dry, open countryside and eat plants, fruit, insects, and small animals.

other
adjective
the remaining one, usually of two.

*She tried on the **other** hat.*

ought
verb
to do something because it is necessary or should be done.
*You **ought** to be in bed.*
■ say **awt**
■ always used with another verb

out
adverb
1 away from a place or not in a place.

*The bird pulled the worm **out** of the ground.*
2 into view.
*The Sun came **out** from behind the cloud.*
■ opposite **in**
3 no longer lit.
*Blow the candle **out**.*

outcome
outcomes *noun*
the result of something.
*What was the **outcome** of the football game?*

outdoors
adverb
not inside a building.
*Shall we eat **outdoors** today?*
■ opposite **indoors**

outfit
outfits *noun*
a set of clothes worn for a particular occasion.

outgrow
outgrows outgrowing outgrew outgrown *verb*
to grow too big for something.
*He had **outgrown** his clothes.*

outline
outlines *noun*
a line that shows the shape of something.
***Outline** of a leaf.*

outside
outsides *noun*
a part of something that faces out.
*They painted the **outside** of the house green.*
outside *adverb*

oval
ovals *noun*
a flat, round shape like a zero.
oval *adjective*

oven
ovens *noun*
a space for cooking food, heating, or drying things, usually inside a stove.

over
preposition
above or across.
She threw the ball ***over*** *the wall.*

overboard
adverb
over the side of a ship or boat.

The fishermen threw their nets ***overboard****.*

overgrown
adjective
covered in plants that have been left to grow wild.
An ***overgrown*** *garden.*

overhear
overhears overhearing overheard *verb*
to hear people talking about things accidently.

overlap
overlaps overlapping overlapped *verb*
to cover the edge of something.
Fish scales ***overlap*** *each other.*

overtake
overtakes overtaking overtaken overtook *verb*
to catch up with and pass by.
The car ***overtook*** *the truck.*

owe
owes owing owed *verb*
to have to pay back money or something else you have borrowed.
You ***owe*** *me $5.*

owl
owls *noun*

a nocturnal bird that hunts for mice and other small animals. Owls have good hearing and can see well in the dark. They can turn their heads around to see behind them.

own
owns owning owned *verb*
to have something that belongs to you.

ox
oxen *noun*
a bull used for carrying or pulling things.
A zebu is a type of ***ox****.*

oxygen
noun
a gas found in air and water. You cannot see, smell, or taste oxygen. All living things need oxygen in order to live.
■ say **ox**-i-jen

oyster
oysters *noun*

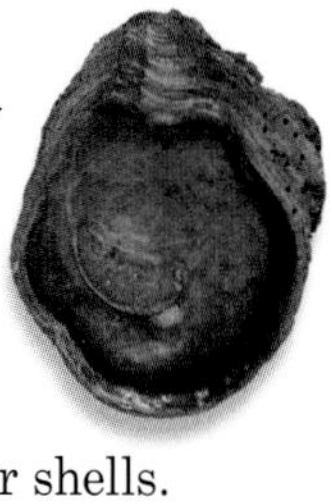

a shellfish that lives in shallow water. Oysters feed on tiny bits of food that they filter through the edge of their shells.

ozone layer
noun
a layer of ozone gas in the Earth's atmosphere that protects the Earth from the more harmful rays of the Sun.

Pp

pack
packs packing packed *verb*

to put things into a suitcase, box, or other container.
■ opposite **unpack**
2 to fit in as much as possible.
The hall was ***packed*** *with people.*

pack
packs *noun*
1 a bundle that you carry.
2 a group of similar animals or objects.
Pack *of cards.*

package
packages *noun*
a wrapped parcel or bundle.

pad
pads *noun*
1 a pile of sheets of paper joined at one end.
2 a thick piece of soft material.
3 the soft, fleshy parts on an animal's paw.
4 a place where helicopters land and take off.

paddle
paddles *noun*
a pole with a flat blade at one or both ends. You hold the paddle and use it to move a boat or canoe through water (see **boat** on page 31).

paddle
paddles paddling paddled *verb*
1 to move a boat through water using a paddle.

2 to walk around in shallow water.

paddock
paddocks *noun*
a fenced area of grass, often where animals are kept.

padlock
padlocks *noun*

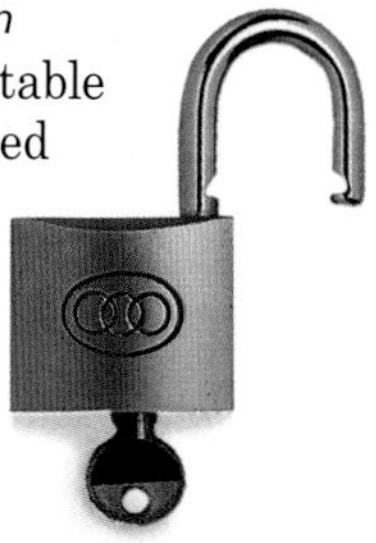

a type of portable lock often used on gates.

page
pages *noun*
one side of a single piece of paper forming part of a book, newspaper, or magazine.

A B C D E F G H I J K L M N O P Q R S T U V W X Y Z

paid
from the verb ***to pay***
I ***paid*** *for the movie tickets.*

pail
pails *noun*
a bucket, usually made of wood or metal.

pain
pains *noun*
suffering caused by an injury, disease, or sadness.
painful *adjective*

paint
paints *noun*
a colored liquid used for decorating or for making pictures.

paint*brush*

paint
paints painting painted *verb*
to cover a surface with color, either for decoration or to create a picture.

painting
paintings *noun*
a painted picture.

pair
pairs *noun*
a set of two things that match each other, or belong together.
A ***pair*** *of socks.*

palace
palaces *noun*
a large, grand home belonging to an important person.

pale
adjective
of faint color, almost white.
He painted the hall ***pale*** *blue.*
■ comparisons **paler palest**

palm
palms *noun*
1 the flat, middle part on the inside of your hand.

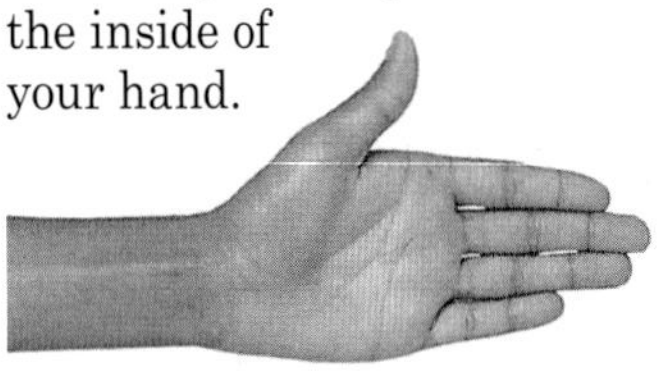

2 a tree without branches that grows in hot regions. Palms have long leaves that grow from the top of the trunk (see **tree** on page 223).

pan
pans *noun*
a metal container with a handle, used for cooking.

pancake
pancakes *noun*
a flat, fried cake made of eggs, flour, and milk.

panda
pandas *noun*
a large, bearlike mammal that lives in the mountain forests of China. Pandas mainly eat bamboo shoots, but sometimes eat other plants and small animals.

panic
panics panicking panicked *verb*
to lose control suddenly because you are frightened or do not know what to do.
The chickens ***panicked*** *when they saw the fox.*
panic *noun*

pant
pants panting panted *verb*
to breathe quickly through your mouth because you are hot or out of breath.

panther
panthers *noun*
a black leopard.

pantomime
pantomimes *noun*
a traditional children's play with music, songs, and dancing.

paper
papers *noun*
a material made from wood, and mainly used for writing, printing, and drawing on.

parachute
parachutes *noun*
an apparatus made of material that helps people and objects fall to the ground safely from an aircraft.

■ say **pair**-uh-shoot

parade
parades *noun*
a procession of people, animals, or vehicles, either for display or inspection.

paragraph
paragraphs *noun*
a section in a piece of writing. Paragraphs start on a new line.

parallel
adjective
being side by side and at the same distance from each other.

parallel *lines*

paralyze
paralyzes paralyzing paralyzed *verb*
to be unable to move a part of the body because of an injury or disease.
paralysis *noun*

parcel
parcels *noun*
an object wrapped up with paper.

parent
parents *noun*
a father or mother.

park
parks *noun*
an area of grass and trees that the public may use.

park
parks parking parked *verb*
to drive a vehicle into a position where it can be left.

parliament
parliaments *noun*
a group of people who have been elected to govern and make the laws of their nation.
■ say **par**-luh-ment

parrot
parrots *noun*
a large bird that lives in tropical forests and eats fruit and seeds. Parrots are often kept as pets. In the wild, parrots live in large flocks.

part
parts *noun*
1 a piece of something.

*The **parts** of an electric guitar.*
2 a role in a play.

*She played the **part** of the queen in the play.*

particular
adjective
1 a specific one.
*Which **particular** one do you mean?*
2 special, or careful.
*Take **particular** care of that!*

partner
partners *noun*
one of a pair of people who do something together, such as dancing or playing a game.
*A business **partner**.*

party
parties *noun*
1 a group of people invited to celebrate a special occasion.
2 an organized group of people who have the same political beliefs.

pass
passes passing passed *verb*
1 to go by someone or something.
2 to give something to someone with your hand.

*He **passed** the bowl to her.*
3 to be successful in an examination or test.

passenger
passengers *noun*
someone traveling in or on a vehicle that is controlled by another person.

passport
passports *noun*
an official certificate that you need for traveling to other countries.

past
noun
the time before now.
past *adjective*

past
adverb
by or beyond.
*He walked **past** the store.*

pasta
noun
an Italian food, usually made from wheat flour and water.

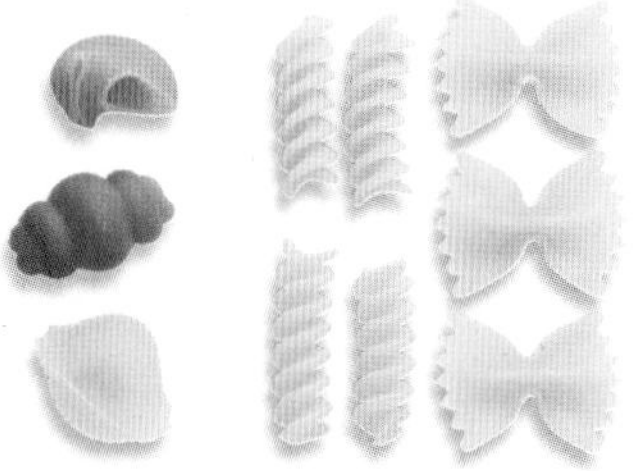

*Different shapes of **pasta**.*

paste
pastes *noun*
1 a soft, moist, and usually sticky substance.
2 a type of glue made of flour and water.

pasteurize
pasteurizes pasteurizing pasteurized *verb*
to heat and then cool something to kill the bacteria in it. Milk is usually pasteurized.
■ say **past**-yoor-ize

pastry
pastries *noun*
a dough made of flour, water, and fat that is baked to make small cakes called pastries, or shells for pies.

*cheese **pastries***

pasture
pastures *noun*
a field of grass where animals graze.

patch
patches *noun*
1 a small piece of material that is placed over a hole to repair it.

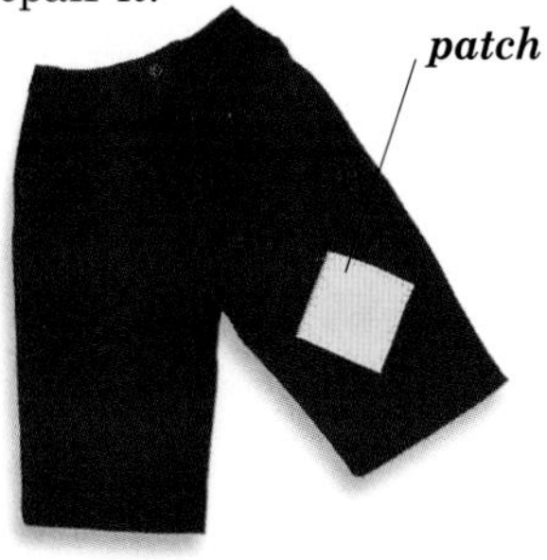

2 a small area of something.
*A **patch** of grass.*

path
paths *noun*
a narrow track for walking along, or a route.

patient
adjective
able to wait calmly.
■ say **pay**-shent
patience *noun*

patient
patients *noun*
a person being treated by a doctor, nurse, or dentist.

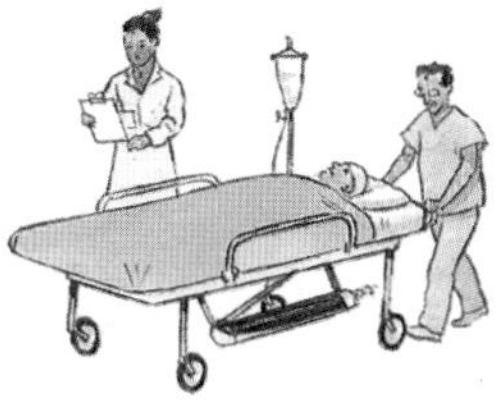

patrol
patrols patrolling patrolled *verb*
to guard a place by moving around it and checking it regularly.
patrol *noun*

pattern
patterns *noun*
1 a decorative shape or design.

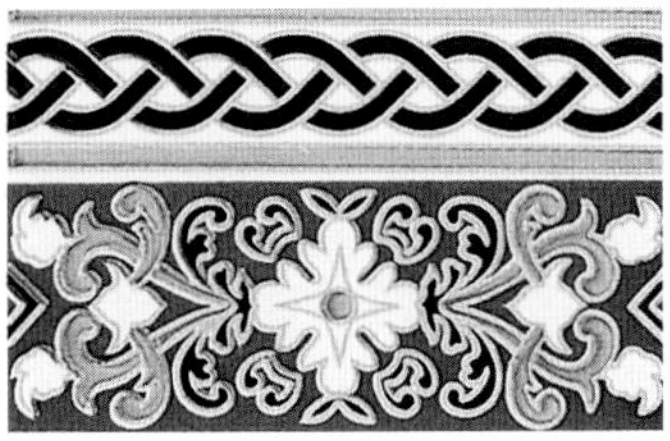

patterned *adjective*

2 a guide for making things, such as toys or clothes.

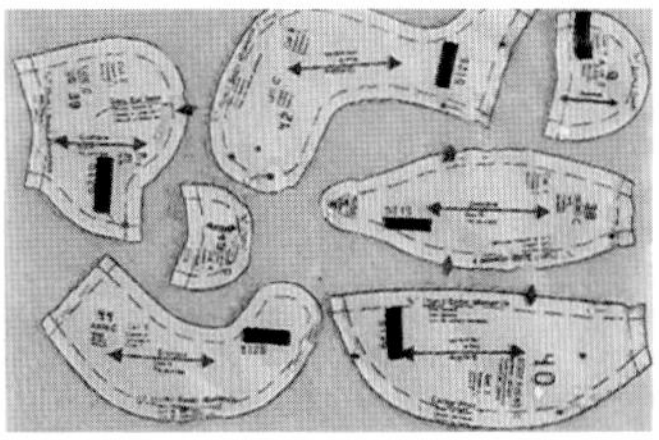

teddy bear ***pattern***

pause
pauses pausing paused *verb*
to stop what you are doing for a short time.
■ say **pawz**
pause *noun*

pave
paves paving paved *verb*
to cover a road with stone or concrete to make it smooth.

paw
paws *noun*
a soft, padded animal foot with claws or nails.

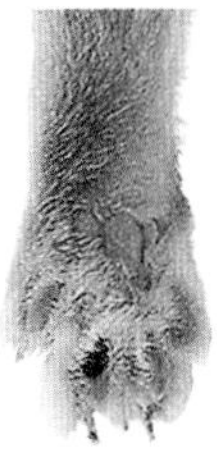

cat's ***paw***

pay
pays paying paid *verb*
to give money in return for something.
payment *noun*

pea
peas *noun*
a small, round, sweet-tasting vegetable that grows in a pod.

peace
noun
a period of quietness and calm.
peaceful *adjective*

peach
peaches *noun*
a round fruit with a velvety skin and a large pit inside.

peacock
peacocks *noun*
a large bird that is also called a peafowl. Peacocks live in forests in Africa and India and eat insects, grains, plants, and small animals. The males are known for their beautiful tail feathers (see **bird** on page 28).

peak
peaks *noun*
the pointed top of a mountain.

peanut
peanuts *noun*
a small, edible nut that grows in pods under the ground.

pear
pears *noun*
a pale green or brown fruit with a thin skin, pale, juicy flesh, and pits.

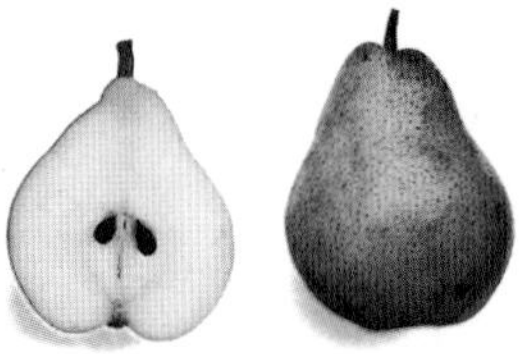

■ rhymes with **hair**

pearl
pearls *noun*
a smooth, shiny, rounded object that grows inside an oyster. Pearls are often used for making jewelry.

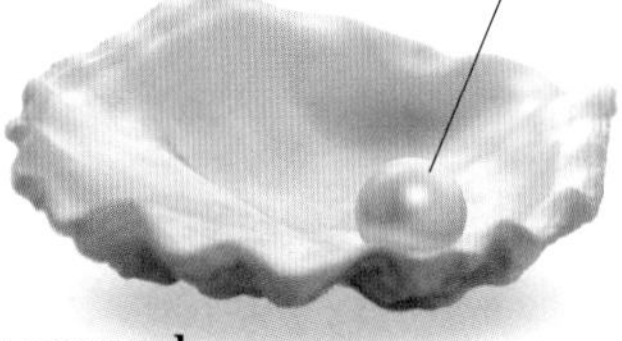

■ say **purl**

pebble
pebbles *noun*
a small, smooth, rounded stone.

peck
pecks pecking pecked *verb*
to bite or strike with a beak.

The bird ***pecked*** *at the food.*

peculiar
adjective
strange, odd, or unusual.

pedal
pedals *noun*
a lever that you work with your foot to move or control something (see **transportation** on page 221).

pedestrian
pedestrians *noun*
a person traveling on foot.

peel
peels peeling peeled *verb*
to remove or strip something off.

Peeling *a banana.*

peep
peeps peeping peeped *verb*
to look quickly and secretly at something or someone.

peer
peers peering peered *verb*
to look closely at something or someone.

peg
pegs *noun*
a hook on the wall for hanging things on.
He hung his coat on the ***peg****.*

pelican
pelicans *noun*
a large bird that lives in or near water in warm regions. It has a pouch beneath its bill that it uses to catch and hold fish.

pen
pens *noun*
1 a tool filled with ink, used for writing.

2 a small area with a fence for keeping animals in.
*A cattle **pen**.*

penalty
penalties *noun*
a fine or a punishment for breaking a law or rule, or for breaking a rule during a sports game.
*The referre gave a **penalty** to our team.*

pencil
pencils *noun*
a tool with an erasable material inside, used for writing and drawing.

penguin
penguins *noun*
a large, fish-eating seabird found in the cold seas of the southern hemisphere. Penguins cannot fly, but are good underwater swimmers (see **bird** on page 28).

penknife
penknives *noun*
a small knife that folds into a case.

pentagon
pentagons *noun*
a flat shape with five sides of equal length (see **shape** on page 182).

people
noun
1 human beings in general.
2 members of a particular race, culture, or nation.

pepper
peppers *noun*
1 the dried berries of the pepper plant used to flavor foods.

***pepper**corns*

*ground **pepper***

2 a bright green, yellow, orange, or red vegetable (see **vegetable** on page 233).

percent
noun
a fraction of a whole written as part of 100. Fifty percent means 50 parts of 100. Percent is also written as percentage. The sign for percent is "%."

*27% (**percent**) of 100 is 27.*

perch
perches perching perched *verb*
to sit on a branch or other place like a bird.

***Perching** on a branch.*
perch *noun*

perfect
adjective
having nothing wrong, or just right.
perfectly *adverb*

perform
performs performing performed *verb*
to put on a show for other people.

***Performing** in the street.*
performance *noun*

perfume
perfumes *noun*
1 a sweet-smelling liquid that you put on your skin.

2 any sweet or pleasant smell.

perhaps
adverb
maybe or possibly.

perimeter
perimeters *noun*
the outer edge or boundary of something.
■ say puh-**rim**-i-ter

period
periods *noun*
a length or portion of time.
*A fortnight is a **period** of two weeks.*

permanent
adjective
lasting a long time or forever.
*A **permanent** job.*
■ opposite **temporary**

permission
noun
the act of allowing someone to do something.

*The teacher gave him **permission** to leave the room.*
permit *verb*

perpendicular
adjective
crossing at or forming a right angle.
■ say pur-pen-**dik**-yuh-lur

person
persons or **people** *noun*
a human being.

personal
adjective
belonging to, or meant for one person.

***Personal** belongings.*

personality
personalities *noun*
1 your character or the kind of person you are.
*My sister has a friendly **personality**.*
2 someone famous.
*A sports **personality**.*

persuade
persuades persuading persuaded *verb*
to make someone believe or do something by giving good reasons.
*She **persuaded** me to go skiing with her.*
persuasion *noun*
■ say pur-**swade**

pest
pests *noun*
an insect or animal that is harmful or a nuisance.

Colorado beetle

a b c d e f g h i j k l m n o p q r s t u v w x y z

pet

pets *noun*

a tame animal that is kept because it is loved rather than because it is useful. Pets are often kept in the home.

Siamese cat

green budgerigar

zebra finches

Jack Russell puppy

giant Flemish rabbit

Abyssinian guinea pig

Peruvian guinea pig

grooming brush

Manx cat

golden retriever

Persian cat

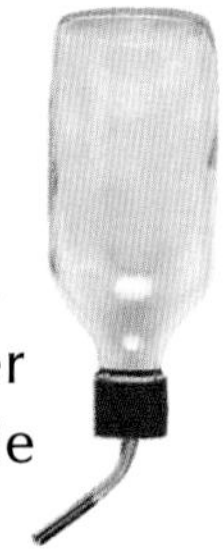

water bottle

Angora rabbit

self golden guinea pig

fox terrier

whippet

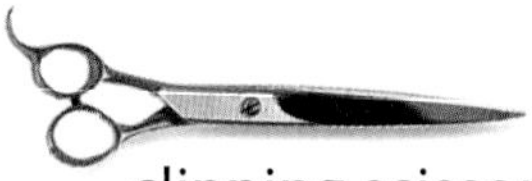

clipping scissors

lop-eared French rabbit

shorthaired cat

petal
petals *noun*
the colored outer parts of a flower that are not green (see **plant** on page 151).

petroleum
noun
a natural liquid that can be made into gasoline.

photocopy
photocopies *noun*
an exact copy of words or pictures made by a machine.

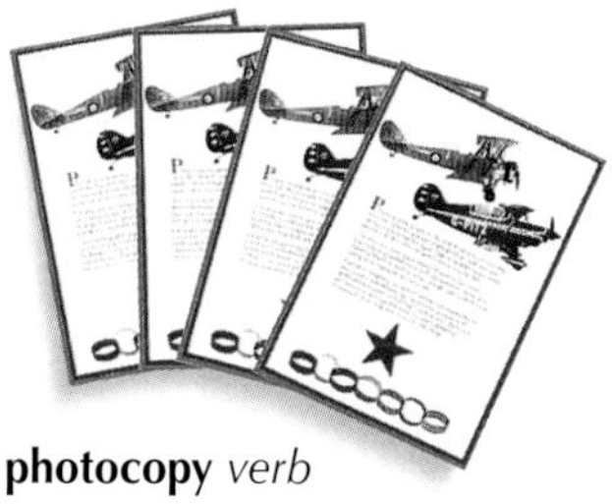

photocopy *verb*

photograph
photographs *noun*
a picture made using a camera. Photograph can be shortened to photo.

*Taking a **photograph**.*

photographer
photographers *noun*
a person who takes photographs.

physical
adjective
to do with the body.
***Physical** exercise.*
■ say **fiz**-i-kul

pianist
pianists *noun*
a person who plays the piano.
■ say **pee**-uh-nist

piano
pianos *noun*
a large, stringed, musical instrument with black and white keys. Different musical notes are produced by pressing the keys.

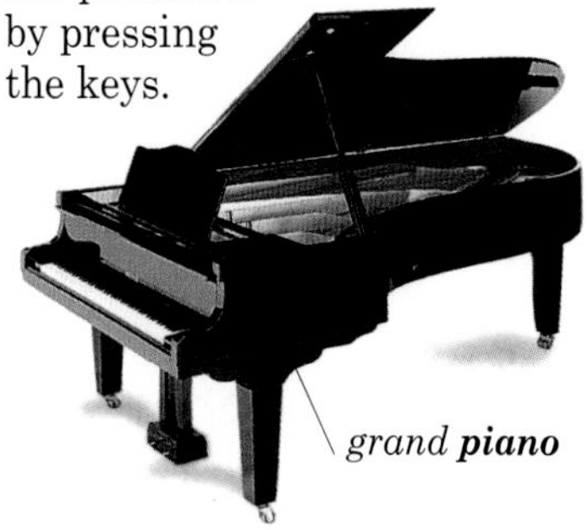

*grand **piano***

pick
picks picking picked *verb*
1 to choose something.

*She asked him to **pick** a card.*
2 to remove a flower, fruit, or leaf from a plant.

***Picking** a flower.*

picnic
picnics *noun*
a meal that is eaten in the open air, away from home.

picnic *verb*

picture
pictures *noun*
an image of something, such as a painting or a photograph.

pie
pies *noun*
a pastry case filled with vegetables, meat, fish, or fruit and baked in an oven.

*apple **pie***

piece
pieces *noun*
a bit or a part of something.

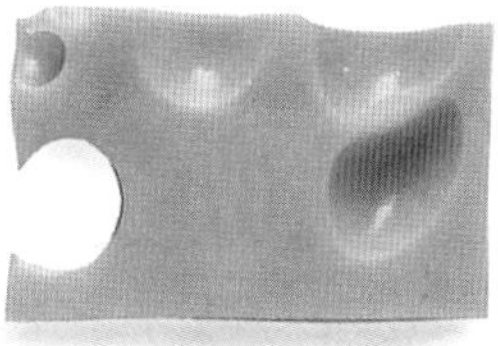

*A **piece** of cheese.*

pier
piers *noun*
a long platform built out into the sea for people to walk along or to tie boats to.

pig
pigs *noun*
an animal with a blunt snout and a curly tail that is kept on farms to provide meat, such as pork, ham, and bacon.

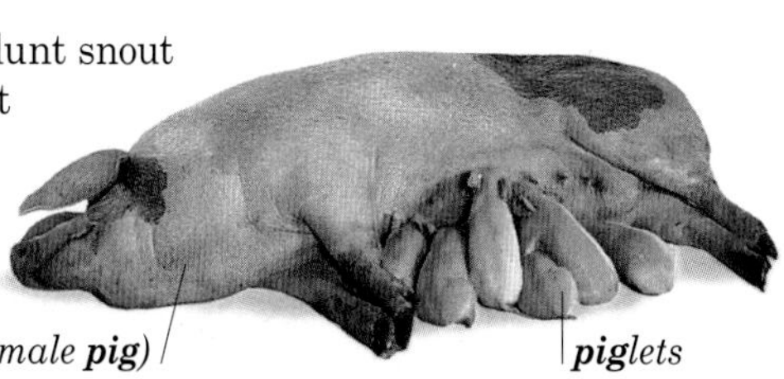

*sow (female **pig**)*
***pig**lets*

pigeon
pigeons *noun*
a bird that is common in both town and countryside. Pigeons mainly eat berries, fruits, and seeds. Some pigeons can be trained to deliver messages.

■ say **pij**-in

pigment
pigments *noun*
1 a colored powder that is mixed with other substances to make paint.

windsor red *cadmium yellow*

2 the substance that gives coloring to the skin of animals and vegetables.

pile
piles *noun*
a group of things resting or lying one on top of the other.

pill
pills *noun*
a small piece of medicine that is swallowed whole.

pillow
pillows *noun*
a soft pad for resting your head on in bed.

pilot
pilots *noun*
a person who controls and flies an aircraft.

pin
pins *noun*
a small piece of metal with a sharp point at one end, used to fasten pieces of cloth together.

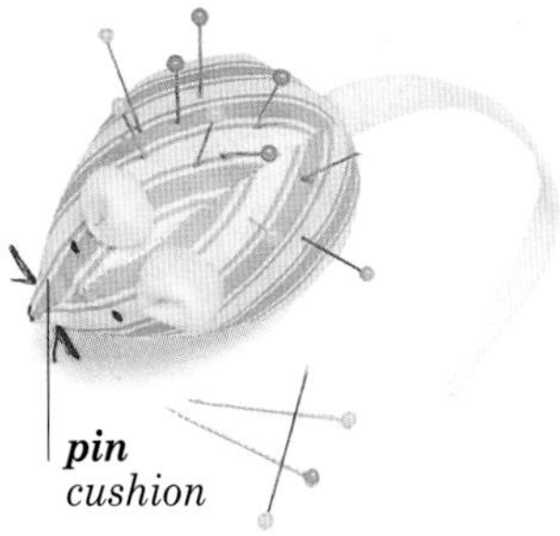

pinch
pinches pinching pinched *verb*
to squeeze someone's skin between your finger and thumb.

pine
pines *noun*
an evergreen tree that has needle-shaped leaves and produces cones.

Arolla ***pine***

pineapple
pineapples *noun*
a tropical fruit with a tough, scaly skin and a sprout of spiky, green leaves at the top (see **fruit** on page 85).

pink
noun
a color made by mixing red and white together.

pipe
pipes *noun*
a tube through which liquids and gases can flow.

pipe*line*

pirate
pirates *noun*
someone who attacks and robs ships or boats at sea.

pit
pits *noun*
1 a deep hole in the ground.
2 a coal mine.

pitch
pitches *noun*
1 a throw of a ball, or the throw to a batter in baseball.
2 the highness or lowness of a musical note, musical instrument, or a human voice.
pitch *verb*

pitiful
adjective
making you feel sad or full of pity.
*A **pitiful** sight.*

pity
noun
a feeling of sadness for someone because they are unhappy or in pain.
pity *verb*

pizza
pizzas *noun*
a round, flat piece of dough with tomato, cheese, and other foods on top that is baked in an oven.

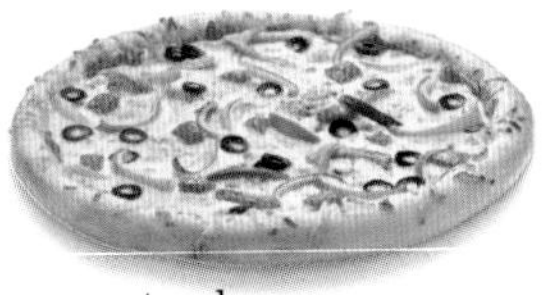

■ say **peet**-suh

place
places *noun*
1 a particular area.
2 a position in a competition or race.

*They won the first, second, and third **places** in the race.*

place
places placing placed *verb*
to put something in a position.
*He **placed** the vase in the center of the table.*

plain
adjective
1 ordinary, or not fancy.
*Her dress was very **plain**.*
2 understandable or clear.
*His meaning was **plain**.*

plain
plains *noun*
a large area of flat land.

plan
plans *noun*
a map or drawing of an area, such as a room, building, or town.

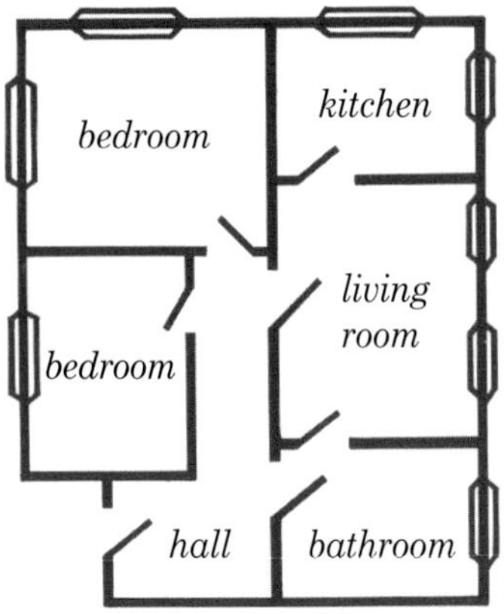

*A **plan** of an apartment.*

plan
plans planning planned *verb*
to decide how you are going to do something.
plan *noun*

planet
planets *noun*
one of the huge spheres of rock and gas that revolve around the Sun. The eight planets in our solar system are Mercury, Venus, Earth, Mars, Jupiter, Saturn, Uranus, and Neptune (see **universe** on page 229).

plant
plants planting planted *verb*
to put a seed, bulb, or plant into the soil so that it will grow.

Planting *a window box.*

plant

plants *noun*

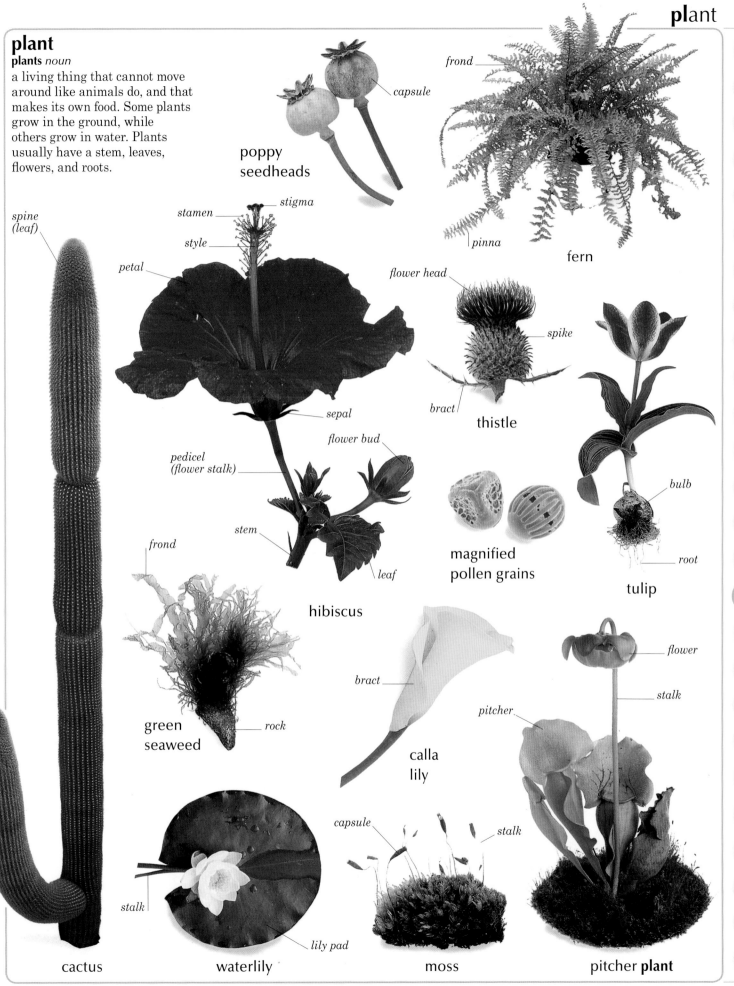

a living thing that cannot move around like animals do, and that makes its own food. Some plants grow in the ground, while others grow in water. Plants usually have a stem, leaves, flowers, and roots.

poppy seedheads

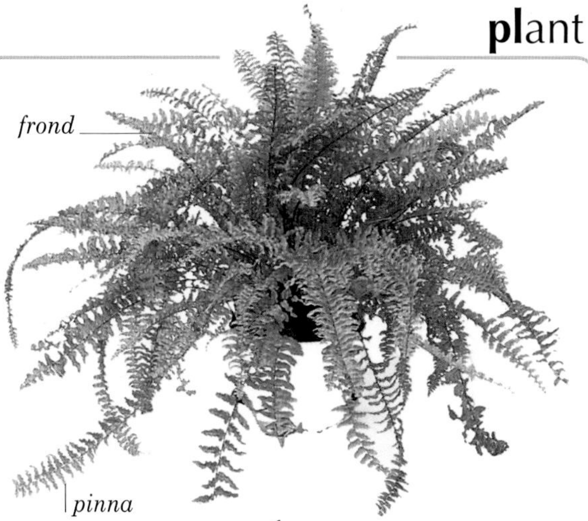

fern

cactus

hibiscus

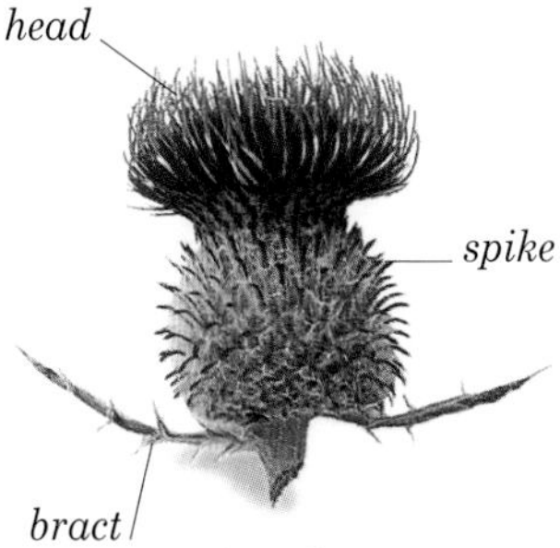

thistle

tulip

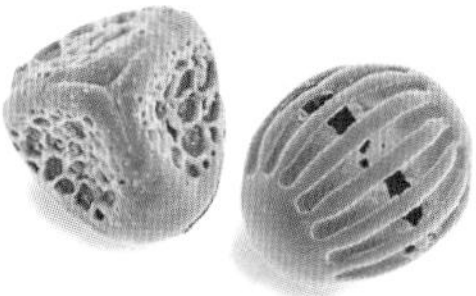

magnified pollen grains

green seaweed

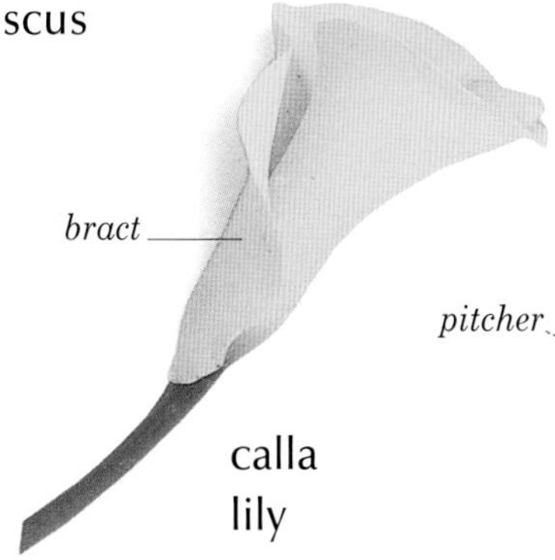

calla lily

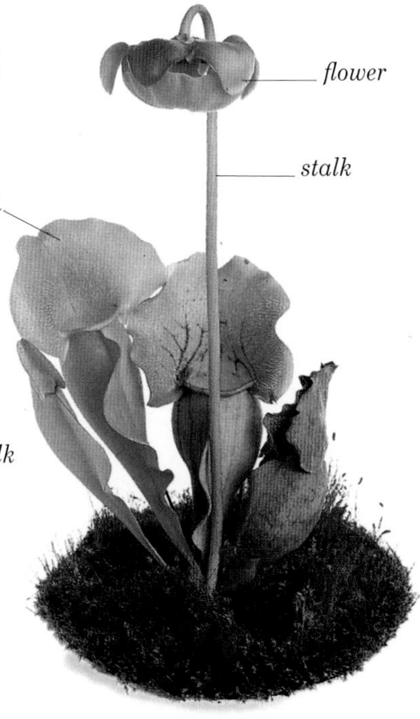

pitcher **plant**

waterlily

moss

plaster
plasters *noun*
a powder mixed with water that is spread on walls and ceilings to make them smooth.

plastic
plastics *noun*
a light, manufactured material made from chemicals. Many types of plastic can be heated up and molded into different shapes and products.

plastic duck

plate
plates *noun*
a flat dish that is used for serving food on.

dinner ***plate***

plateau
plateaus or **plateaux** *noun*
a high, wide, flat area of ground.
■ say **pla**-toh

platform
platforms *noun*
1 the flat, raised area at a train station where people get on and off trains.
2 a flat, raised area in a hall where speakers or performers stand so they can be seen.

platypus
platypuses or **platypi** *noun*
an Australian mammal with a bill like a duck's, webbed feet, and a long, flat tail. Platypuses live in water and, unusually for a mammal, lay eggs. They eat plants, worms, insects, and water animals.
■ say **plat**-uh-pus

play
plays playing played
verb
1 to take part in a game, usually with other people.

Playing *with a balloon.*
2 to make music on a musical instrument.

Playing *an accordion.*
3 to act a part.
She ***played*** *the fairy.*
play *noun*

pleasant
adjective
enjoyable or well-liked.
A ***pleasant*** *evening.*
■ opposite **unpleasant**

please
interjection
a word used when you ask for something politely.

pleasure
pleasures *noun*
enjoyment or satisfaction.
■ say **plezh**-ur

pleat
pleats *noun*
a fold that is pressed or sewn into cloth.

pleat *verb*

plenty
noun
a large amount of something.
Do you want some candy? I have ***plenty.***
plentiful *adjective*

plot
plots plotting plotted *verb*
to make a secret plan.
The thieves ***plotted*** *to rob the bank.*
plot *noun*

plot
plots *noun*
1 the story of a book, play, or movie.
The book has a complicated ***plot.***
2 a small piece of ground.

plug
plugs *noun*
1 a circular piece of plastic or other material used to keep water in a bath or sink.
2 an electrical device that connects the wire from a piece of electrical equipment to a source of electricity.

plum
plums *noun*
a fruit that grows on trees, and has a smooth, thin skin and soft, juicy flesh.

plumber
plumbers *noun*
a person who fits water and heating pipes into buildings and repairs them when they go wrong.

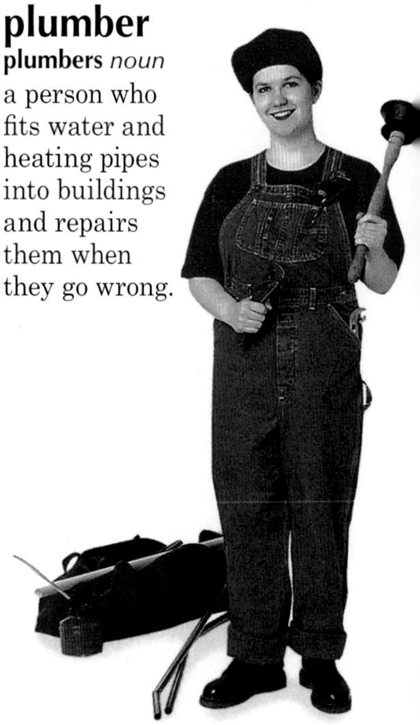

plow
plows *noun*
a farm tool that has large blades for cutting and turning the soil. Plows are used to prepare the soil for planting crops and are pulled by a tractor or an animal.

■ rhymes with **now**
plow *verb*

plunge
plunges plunging plunged *verb*
to fall or dive very quickly.

*The bridge broke in two and **plunged** into the river.*
plunge *noun*

plural
plurals *noun*
a word used to describe two or more things or people.
*The **plural** of baby is babies.*

plus
preposition
added to.
*4 **plus** 2 equals 6.*
■ opposite **minus**

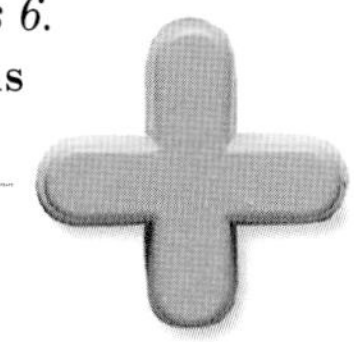

plus
pluses *noun*
a symbol in mathematics that means add.

pocket
pockets *noun*
a small pouch or fold sewn into clothing or a bag where you can put your belongings.

pocket

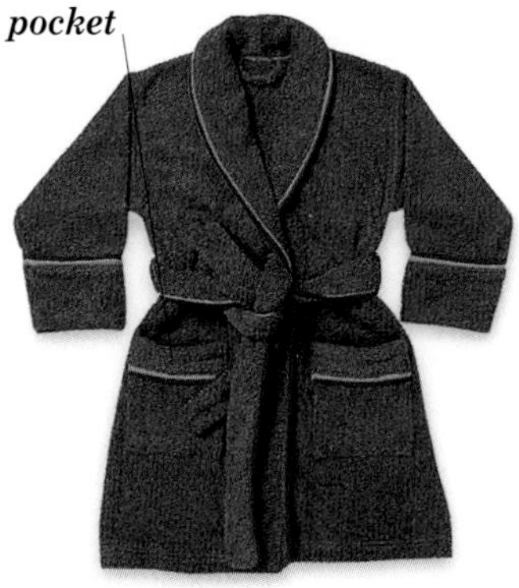

pod
pods *noun*
a long seed case that holds the seeds of some plants.

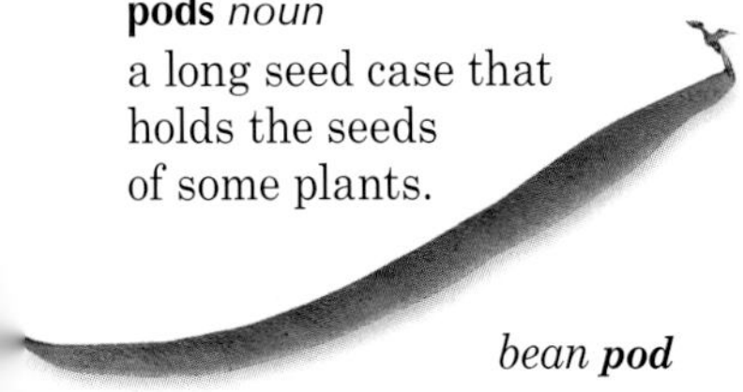

*bean **pod***

poem
poems *noun*
a piece of writing, set out in lines that sometimes rhyme. Poems describe things in a thoughtful and imaginative way.

poet
poets *noun*
a person who writes poetry.

poetry
noun
a general name for poems.

point
points *noun*
1 the sharp end of an object.

*Each star has six **points**.*
2 a score in a game or competition.
*How many **points** did you get?*
3 the main goal or purpose.
*What's the **point** of this story?*
4 the level, time, or place at which something happens.
*The freezing **point** of water is 32°F (0°C).*
5 a dot.

point
points pointing pointed *verb*
to show where something is with your finger.

poison
poisons *noun*
a substance that can kill or harm animals or plants.

***poison** arrow frog*

*A deadly **poison** can be made from this frog's skin.*
poisonous *adjective*

poke
pokes poking poked *verb*
to push something with a stick, your finger, or another pointed object.

*He **poked** the fire with a stick.*

polar bear
polar bears *noun*
a large mammal that lives in Arctic regions. Polar bears eat animals such as seals and fish. Their white fur camouflages them against the snow and ice where they live.

police
noun
an organization that is responsible for keeping law and order and making sure that a country's laws are not broken.

polish
polishes polishing polished *verb*
to rub something so that it shines.

***Polishing** shoes.*

polish
polishes *noun*
a substance that is rubbed into something to make it shine.

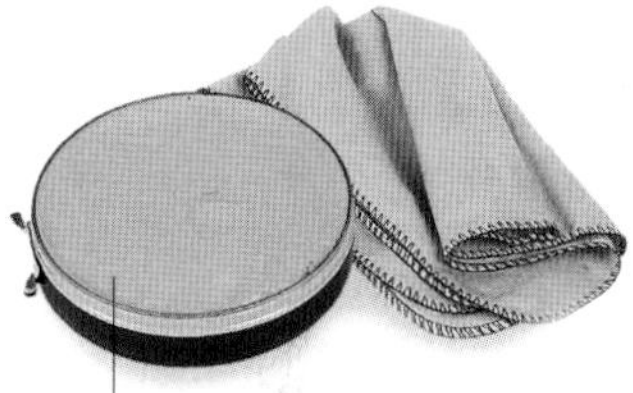

*furniture **polish***

polite
adjective
well-mannered and pleasant to other people.
■ opposite **rude**
politely *adverb*

pole
poles *noun*
1 a long, rounded rod made from wood, metal, or plastic.

*A row of flag**poles**.*

2 the most northern and southern end of an imaginary line, or axis, that passes through Earth's center.

*North **Pole***

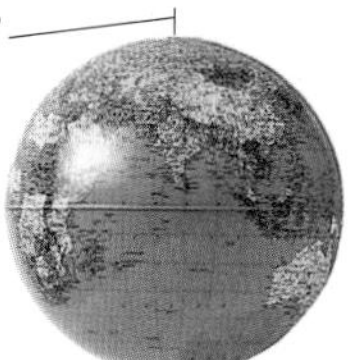

*South **Pole***

3 either end of a magnet.

A B C D E F G H I J K L M N O P Q R S T U V W X Y Z

politics
noun
the work of government.
political *adjective*

pollen
noun
a fine, yellow powder found in the middle of flowers. Pollen is made by the male parts of a flower.

pollinate
pollinates pollinating pollinated
verb
to transfer pollen from the male to the female parts of a plant so that a seed can grow.

*The bee **pollinated** the flower.*

pollute
pollutes polluting polluted *verb*
to make a thing or a place dirty, unclean, or harmful.
*Chemicals from the factory **polluted** the river.*
pollution *noun*

pond
ponds *noun*
an area of fresh water that is smaller than a lake.

*duck **pond***

pony
ponies *noun*
a small horse (see **horse** on page 102).

pool
pools *noun*
a small area of water, especially one that is made for people to swim in.

*swimming **pool***

poor
adjective
1 not having enough money to live on.
*The family was very **poor**.*
■ opposite **rich**
2 of low or bad quality.
*The house was in a **poor** condition.*
3 unfortunate.
*The **poor** child was soaking wet.*
poor *noun*

popcorn
noun
a snack made by heating grains from the corn plant until they burst open and puff up.

poppy
poppies *noun*
a wild flower with delicate, petals. When the flowers die, they leave behind a round seed head (see **plant** on page 151).

popular
adjective
liked by many people.

population
populations *noun*
all the people living in a district or country.

porch
porches *noun*
a shelter built around the entrance to a building.

porcupine
porcupines *noun*
a large rodent that is covered in lots of sharp spines called quills. A porcupine can raise the quills to protect itself from its enemies. Porcupines eat bark, buds, twigs, and leaves.

pork
noun
meat from a pig.

porpoise
porpoises *noun*
a sea mammal that belongs to the whale family. Porpoises eat shrimp, fish, squid, and other sea animals.

■ say **poor**-pus

port
ports *noun*
a place on a coast or river, where ships load and unload.

portable
adjective
easily carried or moved.

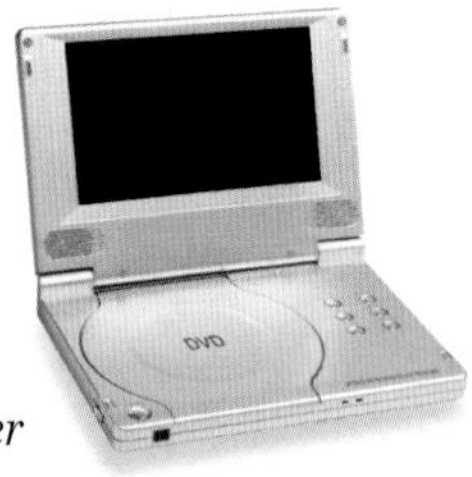

portable *DVD player*

portion
portions *noun*
a part or share of something.

*A **portion** of fisherman's pie.*

portrait
portraits *noun*
a picture of a person or animal, especially their face.

pose
poses posing posed *verb*
to arrange yourself or a thing in a particular position, especially for a painting or a photograph.
pose *noun*

position
positions *noun*
1 the way in which a person or thing is placed or arranged.
*A sitting **position**.*
2 a place or location.
*He found the **position** of his house on the map.*

positive
adjective
definite or certain.
■ opposite **negative**

possess
possesses possessing possessed *verb*
to own or have something.
possession *noun*

possible
adjective
able to be done or happen.
*Is it **possible** to walk there?*
■ opposite **impossible**
possibly *adverb*

post
noun
1 the delivery of letters and other mail, or the letters themselves.
2 an upright pole of wood, stone, or metal set in the ground.

*gate-**post***

3 the place where a person is supposed to be when working.

poster
posters *noun*
a large notice or picture that is displayed on a wall as an ad or for decoration.

post office
post offices *noun*
a place where you go to buy stamps and to send letters and packages.

postpone
postpones postponing postponed *verb*
to put something off until later.
*The game was **postponed** because of the rain.*

posy
posies *noun*
a small bunch of flowers.

pot
pots *noun*
a container with high sides.

*coffee **pot***

potato
potatoes *noun*
a common root vegetable that can be boiled, roasted, fried, or baked.

pottery
noun
a general name for containers and ornaments made from clay, then baked in a kiln.
*kitchen **pottery***

pouch
pouches *noun*
1 a small, open bag or sack that is used for carrying things like money.
2 a part of the body that is shaped like a bag or pocket (see **mammal** on page 124).

pounce
pounces pouncing pounced *verb*
to spring forward suddenly and grab hold of something.

*The cat **pounced** on the leaf.*

pour
pours pouring poured *verb*
to tip a container up so that its contents flow out.

poverty
noun
the situation of not having enough money to live on.
*The family lived in **poverty**.*

powder
noun
a mass of very fine, dry grains of a substance.

*washing **powder***

power
powers *noun*
1 the ability to do something.
2 the ability to control what someone else does.
3 energy or force.

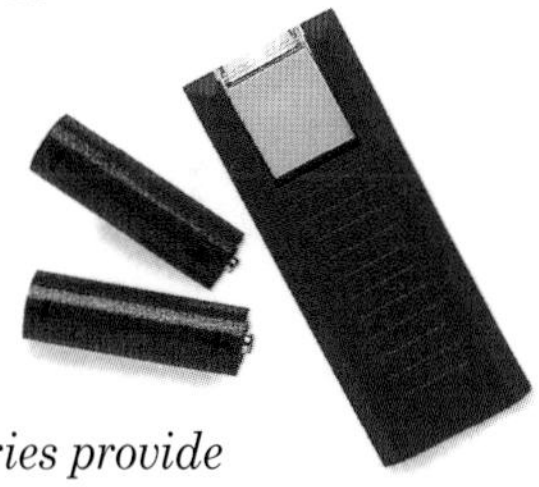

*Batteries provide the **power** for this flashlight.*
■ rhymes with **our**

practical
adjective
1 sensible and useful.
*Gloves are very **practical** in cold weather.*
■ opposite **impractical**
2 having practice at doing something.
*You need **practical** experience for this job.*

practice
practices practicing practiced *verb*
to do something over and over again in order to be good at it.

***Practicing** the piano.*
practice *noun*

A B C D E F G H I J K L M N O P Q R S T U V W X Y Z

praise
praises praising praised *verb*
to tell someone that what they have done is very good.
praise *noun*

pray
prays praying prayed *verb*
to talk to a god, prophet, or saint.
prayer *noun*

precaution
precautions *noun*
care or action taken in advance to prevent something from happening.
Locks are a ***precaution*** *against theft.*
■ say pre-**kaw**-shun

precious
adjective
very valuable or special to someone.

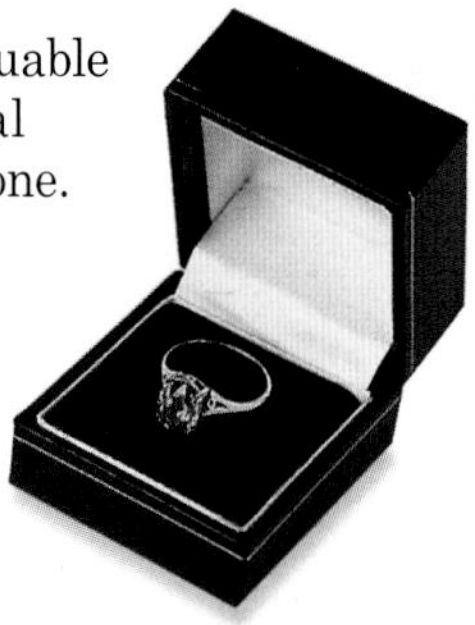

The ring was very ***precious.***
■ say **presh**-us

precise
adjective
exact or accurate.

Stopwatches measure the ***precise*** *time.*
■ say pri-**sise**

predict
predicts predicting predicted *verb*
to say what is going to happen in the future.
prediction *noun*

preen
preens preening preened *verb*
to clean and arrange feathers with the beak. Birds preen themselves.

prefer
prefers preferring preferred *verb*
to like something or someone better than another.

She pointed to the pair of skates she ***preferred.***
preferable *adjective*

pregnant
adjective
expecting a baby.
pregnancy *noun*

prehistoric
adjective
belonging to the time before any records were written.

prejudice
prejudices *noun*
a strong feeling about something, which has been formed unfairly or before all the facts are known.
■ say **pre**-joo-dis

prepare
prepares preparing prepared *verb*
to make something or yourself ready.

Preparing *sandwiches for lunch.*

preposition
prepositions *noun*
a word such as "on" that relates a noun or pronoun to another word in the sentence.
The bird was ***on*** *the chair* ***in*** *the backyard.*

prescription
prescriptions *noun*
an order for medicine written by a doctor.

present
noun
1 the time now.
The story takes place in the ***present.***
present *adjective*
2 a gift to someone.

■ say **prez**-unt

present
presents presenting presented *verb*
to award or give something to someone.
The judge ***presented*** *the rider with a cup.*
■ say pri-**zent**

preserve
preserves preserving preserved *verb*
1 to keep something the way it is.
2 to keep food so that it lasts.

Fruit ***preserved*** *in a jar.*

press
presses pressing pressed *verb*
to squeeze or push something down, often in order to flatten it.

Pressing *flowers.*

pretend
pretends pretending pretended *verb*
1 to try to make people believe something that isn't true.
2 to believe something for fun.

He ***pretended*** *to be a cowboy.*
pretence *noun*

pretty
adjective
nice to look at.
■ comparisons **prettier prettiest**

prevent
prevents preventing prevented *verb*
to stop something from happening.
*The barrier **prevented** anyone from falling down the hole.*
prevention *noun*

previous
adjective
happening or existing before.
*The **previous** day.*
■ say **pree**-vee-us

prey
noun
creatures that are hunted and eaten by other animals.

*The owl swooped down on its **prey**.*
■ say **pray**
prey *verb*

price
prices *noun*
the amount of money needed to buy something.

prickly
adjective
having many little sharp points or needles.

*A **prickly** cactus.*
■ comparisons **pricklier prickliest**
prick *verb*

priest
priests *noun*
a person who is trained to lead religious services.

prince / princess
princes / princesses *noun*
a son or daughter of a king or queen. The wife of a prince is also a princess.
■ **prince** is male and **princess** is female

principle
principles *noun*
a general rule, belief, or truth.
*Scientific **principles**.*

print
prints printing printed *verb*
1 to write the letters of words separately, rather than with linked letters.

2 to put words, pictures, or patterns onto paper, using paint or ink, and printing blocks.

***Printing** a picture.*
printed *adjective*

printer
noun
a machine that prints on paper, usually linked to a computer.

prison
prisons *noun*
a secure place in which criminals are kept as punishment.

private
adjective
belonging only to one person or a few people, or not open to the public.
*My diary is **private**.*
■ say **pry**-vit
privately *adverb*

prize
prizes *noun*
a reward for winning something.

*The **prize** was a silver cup.*

probable
adjective
likely to happen.
probably *adverb*

problem
problems *noun*
something that is difficult to do or hard to understand.

process
processes *noun*
the method of making or doing something.
■ say **prah**-ses

procession
processions *noun*
a line of people or vehicles following each other.

*A **procession** of musicians.*

prod
prods prodding prodded *verb*
to poke or push something, often with something sharp.

produce
produces producing produced *verb*
1 to make something happen.
*The magician **produced** a rabbit out of his hat.*
2 to make, grow, manufacture, or create something.

*The orange trees **produced** a large crop of fruit this year.*
■ say pruh-**doos**
product *noun*
production *noun*

produce
noun
things that are grown or made.

*farm **produce***
■ say **pro**-doos

profession
professions *noun*
1 a job or occupation where special knowledge of a subject is needed.
2 all the people who do such a job.
*The medical **profession**.*

professional
adjective
1 having to do with a profession.
*He took **professional** advice.*
2 earning a living from an occupation that is not usually thought of as a job.
*A **professional** actor.*

profile
profiles *noun*
the side view of a face or object.

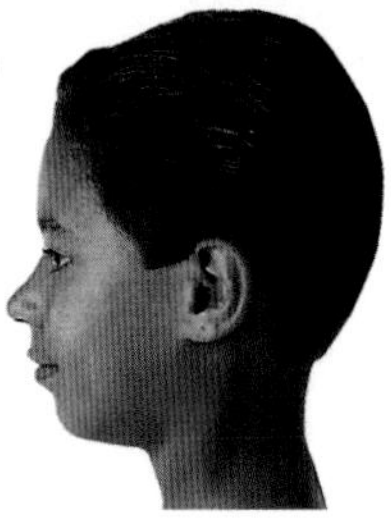

profit
profits *noun*
the extra money made when something is sold for more than it cost to make or buy.
■ opposite **loss**
profitable *adjective*

program
programs *noun*
1 a television or radio show.
2 a list of planned events.
3 a small book of information about a play or concert.
*There are two pianists on the **program**.*
4 a set of instructions that tells a computer how to do something.
*This **program** sorts for me.*

progress
noun
the process of moving forward or improving.

*She made slow **progress** through the swamp.*
progress *verb*

prohibit
prohibits prohibiting prohibited *verb*
to ban or to forbid someone from doing something.

*Smoking is **prohibited**.*

project
projects *noun*
a piece of work involving research and study of a particular subject.

*He is doing a **project** on plants.*
■ say **prah**-jekt

project
projects projecting projected *verb*
to stick out or throw outward.

*The rock **projected** over the valley.*
■ say pro-**jekt**

promise
promises promising promised *verb*
to say and mean that you will, or will not, do something.
promise *noun*

promotion
promotions *noun*
1 a campaign to improve the sale of a product or event by advertising it.

*The **promotion** for a new yogurt.*
2 a change to a more important job or position.
promote verb

prompt
prompts prompting prompted *verb*
to encourage someone to do or say something.

prompt
adjective
on time, or without delay.

*A **prompt** delivery.*

pronoun
pronouns *noun*
a word such as "he" or "she" that is used in a sentence to replace a noun.
*Jane was sick today, so **she** didn't go to school.*

pronunciation
pronunciations *noun*
the way a word is said.
■ say pro-nun-see-**ay**-shun
pronounce *verb*

proof
noun
a thing or happening that shows something is true.

*The footprint was **proof** that someone had been there.*

propeller
propellers *noun*
a device with revolving blades. Propellers spin around to move a boat through the water, or to power an airplane through the air (see **boat** on page 31 and **transportation** on page 221).

proper
adjective
suitable and correct.

*This is the **proper** way to hit a golf ball so that it rolls along the ground.*
properly *adverb*

property
noun
1 the things that belong to a person.
2 a general name for the buildings and land owned by someone.

prosecute
prosecutes prosecuting prosecuted *verb*
to accuse someone of a crime in a court of law.
■ say **pros**-i-kyoot
prosecution *noun*

protect
protects protecting protected *verb*
to keep someone or something from being harmed.

*Gardening gloves **protect** your hands from thorns.*
protection *noun*

protest
protests protesting protested *verb*
to say very clearly that you disagree with something.

*They **protested** against the building of a new road.*
■ say **pro**-test
protest *noun*

proud
adjective
feeling very pleased or satisfied.

*She was **proud** of her new outfit.*
■ say **prowd**
proudly *adverb*

prove
proves proving proved *verb*
to show that something is true.
■ say **proov**

proverb
proverbs *noun*
a short common saying that comments on life.
*"Many hands make light work" is a **proverb**.*

provide
provides providing provided *verb*
to supply something that is useful or needed.

*The runners were **provided** with drinks along the route.*

prowl
prowls prowling prowled *verb*
to move around quietly while searching for something.

*The tiger **prowled** around the tree.*

public
adjective
open to everybody.

publish
publishes publishing published *verb*
to produce and print a book, newspaper, or magazine.

puddle
puddles *noun*
a shallow pool of liquid on the ground.

puff
puffs *noun*
a small, sudden gust of smoke, air or breath.

*a **puff** of smoke*

pull
pulls pulling pulled *verb*
to move something with force toward you or in the same direction as you are going.

***Pulling** on a rope.*

pulley
pulleys *noun*
a device made of a wheel with a rope or a chain around it that is used for lifting heavy objects.

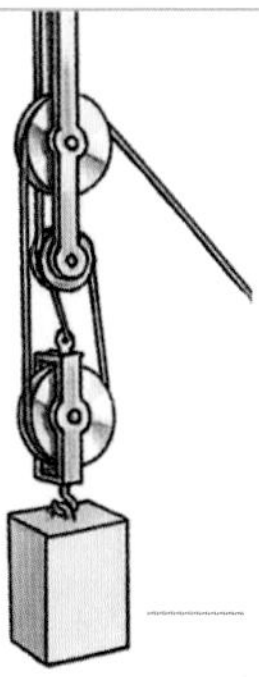

pulp
noun
the soft, inside part of a plant, particularly fruits (see **fruit** on page 85).

pulse
pulses *noun*
the regular sound of your blood as the heart pumps it through your body.

*Feeling her **pulse**.*

pump
pumps pumping pumped *verb*
to fill or inflate something by forcing air or liquids into it.

***Pumping** up a balloon.*

pump
pumps *noun*
a device that pushes liquids or gases into or out of something.

*bicycle **pump***

punch
punches *noun*
1 a hard blow made with your fist.

punch *verb*
2 a machine that stamps holes, letters, or patterns in something.

*hole **punch***
3 a sweet drink made by mixing fruit juices and other liquids together. Punch is usually served from a large bowl.

puncture
punctures *noun*
a hole or wound, often made by a sharp pointed object or instrument.
*My tire has a **puncture**.*
puncture *verb*

a b c d e f g h i j k l m n o p q r s t u v w x y z

punish
punishes punishing punished
verb
to make someone suffer in some way for things they have done wrong.
punishment *noun*

pupa
pupae *noun*
the stage of an insect's development when it changes from a larva to a winged insect inside a rounded case (see **growth** on page 94).
■ say **pyoo**-puh

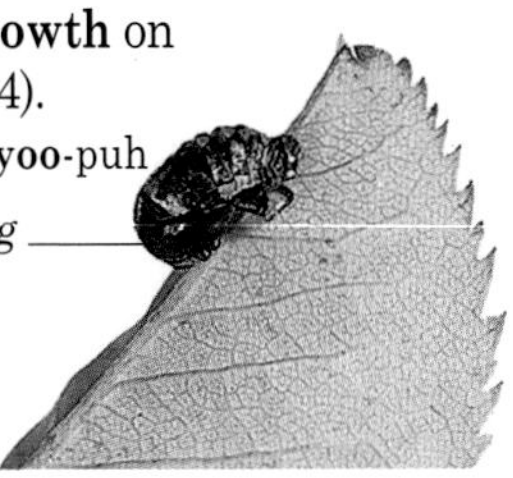

ladybug ***pupa***

pupil
pupils *noun*
1 a student at school.

2 the small, dark part at the center of your eye that expands or contracts to let in the right amount of light.

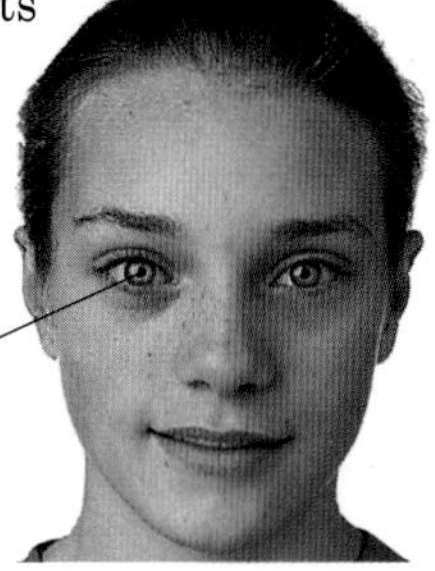

pupil

puppy
puppies *noun*
a young dog (see **pet** on page 148).

purchase
purchases purchasing purchased *verb*
to buy something.

■ say **pur**-chis

pure
adjective
clean, or not mixed with anything.
Pure gold.
■ comparisons **purer purest**

purple
noun
a color made by mixing red and blue together.

puppet
puppets *noun*
a doll or animal figure that is moved by pulling on its strings or by making hand movements inside it.

finger ***puppet***

string ***puppet***

purpose
purposes *noun*
a reason for doing something, or a goal.

purr
purrs purring purred *verb*
to make a low, rumbling noise like a cat makes.

purse
purses *noun*
a small bag for carrying money and personal things.

push
pushes pushing pushed *verb*
to move something away from you by pressing hard against it.

*He had to **push** the car to a garage when it broke down.*

put
puts putting put *verb*
to place or position something somewhere.

*She **put** her books into her schoolbag.*

puzzle
puzzles *noun*
1 a problem or question that it is difficult to find the answer to.
2 a game in which you have to find the answers to a problem.

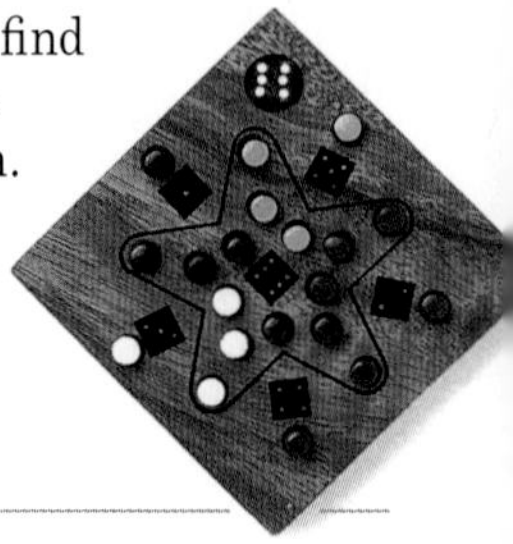

puzzle
puzzles puzzling puzzled *verb*
1 to try to figure out something you do not understand.
2 to confuse.
*The strange noises **puzzled** us.*
■ say **puz**-l
puzzling *adjective*

pyramid
pyramids *noun*
1 a solid shape with a square base and four triangular faces that meet in a point (see **shape** on page 182).
2 an ancient tomb or temple shaped like a pyramid.

*The **pyramids** of Egypt.*
■ say **pir**-a-mid

python
pythons *noun*
a large snake that is found in hot regions. Pythons kill by wrapping themselves around their prey and squeezing. They eat small mammals.

■ say **pie**-thon

Qq

quake
quakes quaking quaked *verb*
to shake or tremble.

*He **quaked** with fear when he saw the crocodile.*
■ say **kwake**

qualify
qualifies qualifying qualified *verb*
to prove that you are fit or suitable for something.
*I hope I **qualify** for the team!*
■ say **kwol**-uh-fie
qualification *noun*

quality
qualities *noun*
1 a judgment of how good or bad something is.
*High **quality**.*
2 something that is special about someone or something.
*She has many good **qualities**.*
■ say **kwol**-i-tee

quantity
quantities *noun*
an amount or number.

*A large **quantity** of crates.*
■ say **kwon**-ti-tee

quarrel
quarrels quareling quareled *verb*
to have an argument or disagreement with someone.
■ say **kwor**-rul
quarrel *noun*

quarry
quarries *noun*
a place where stone, sand, or gravel is cut out of the ground.

*A stone **quarry**.*
■ say **kwor**-ee

quarter
quarters *noun*
1 one of four equal pieces of a whole.

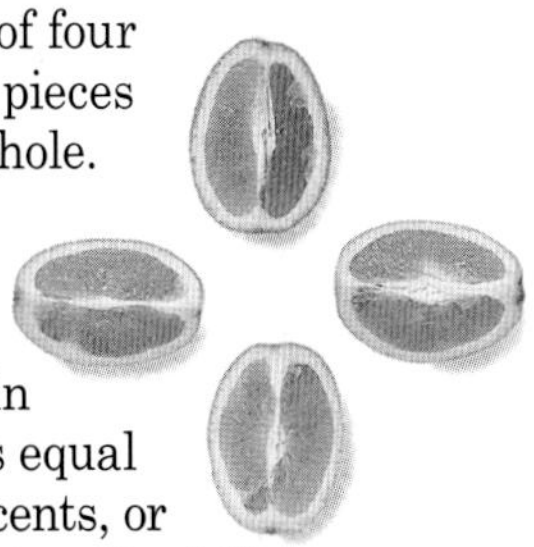

2 a coin that is equal to 25 cents, or a quarter of a dollar.

quartz
noun
a hard mineral, often found in crystal form.
■ say **kworts**

quay
quays *noun*
an area by a harbor where ships are loaded and unloaded.
■ say **kee**

queen
queens *noun*
a female ruler of a country or the wife of a king.

query
queries *noun*
a question, because you have a doubt or problem about something.

*The teacher helped to answer the student's **query**.*
■ say **kweer**-ree
query *verb*

question
questions questioning questioned *verb*
to ask someone for information or an answer.
■ opposite **answer**
question *noun*

questionable
adjective
doubtful or suspicious.
*His reasons for leaving so quickly were **questionable**.*

quick
adjective
fast or sudden.
*A **quick** movement.*
■ comparisons **quicker quickest**
■ opposite **slow**
quickly *adverb*

quiet
adjective
silent and peaceful.
■ comparisons **quieter quietest**

quill
quills *noun*
a large feather, especially one that has been made into an ink pen.
■ say **kwil**

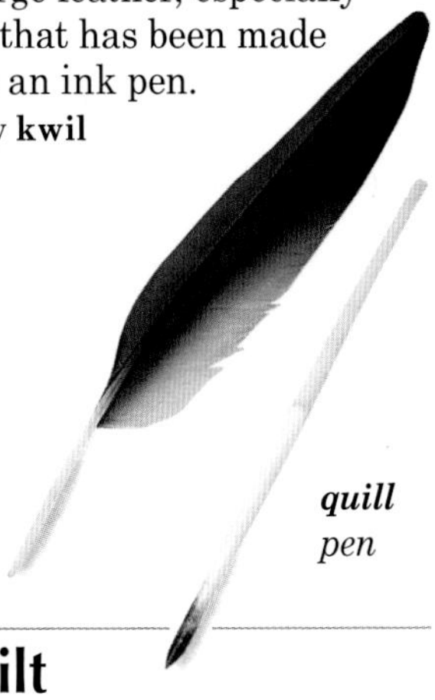

quill pen

quilt
quilts *noun*
a thick, soft cover for a bed.

*patchwork **quilt***

quite
adverb
1 fairly.
*I am **quite** good at running.*
2 completely.
*You are **quite** right.*

quiz
quizzes *noun*
a game in which you are asked questions to find out how much you know.

quote
quotes quoting quoted *verb*
to repeat something that someone else has said or written.
quotation *noun*

a b c d e f g h i j k l m n o p q r s t u v w x y z

Rr

rabbi
rabbis *noun*
a teacher of the Jewish religion and law.
■ say **rab**-eye

rabbit
rabbits *noun*
a small mammal with long front teeth that lives underground in burrows. Rabbits are normally active in the evening or at night. They eat grass, roots, and leaves.

race
races *noun*
1 a competition of speed.

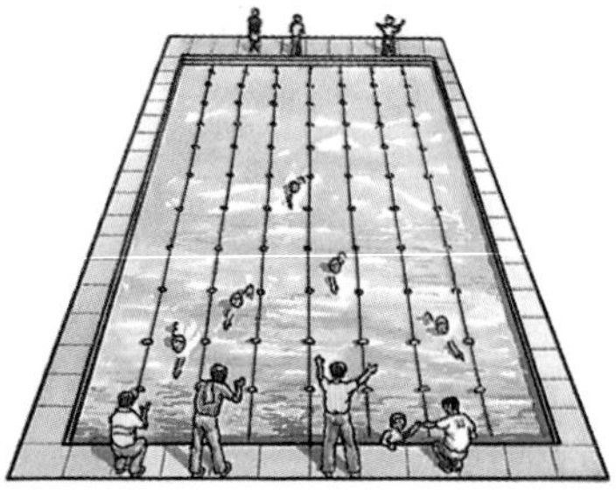

A swimming ***race****.*
race *verb*
2 a group of people who share the same ancestors and may share some physical characteristics.
racial *adjective*

racket
rackets *noun*
1 a bat with strings used for playing sports such as tennis and badminton (see **sport** on page 197).

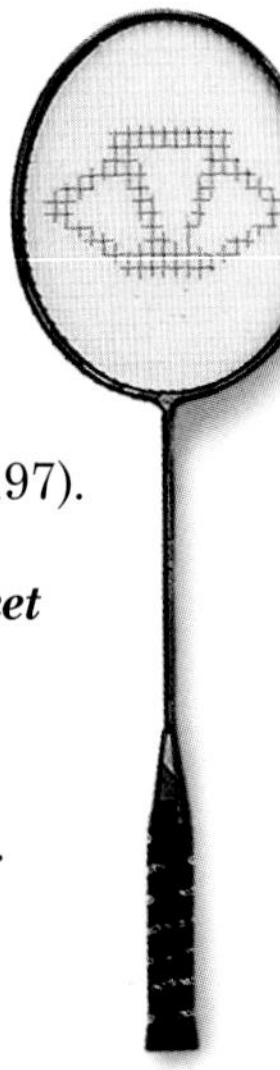

badminton ***racket***

2 a loud, annoying noise.
He was making a ***racket*** *with his drums.*

radar
noun
a device that tells you the position and speed of ships, cars, and aircraft by sending out radio waves.

An airport ***radar*** *screen.*
■ say **ray**-dar

radiator
radiators *noun*
1 a thin, metal tank with hot water flowing through it that heats a room.
2 a metal tank that allows air to cool the hot water in the engine of a vehicle.
■ say **ray**-dee-ay-tor

radio
radios *noun*
a device that sends or receives electrical signals and changes them into sound.

radioactivity
noun
the energy released by the center of atoms breaking up in some substances. High amounts of radioactivity can be harmful to living things.

They tested for ***radioactivity*** *outside the nuclear power plant.*
■ say **ray**-dee-oh-ak-**tiv**-i-tee
radioactive *adjective*

radius
radii or **radiuses** *noun*
a straight line drawn from the center of a circle to its outer edge.

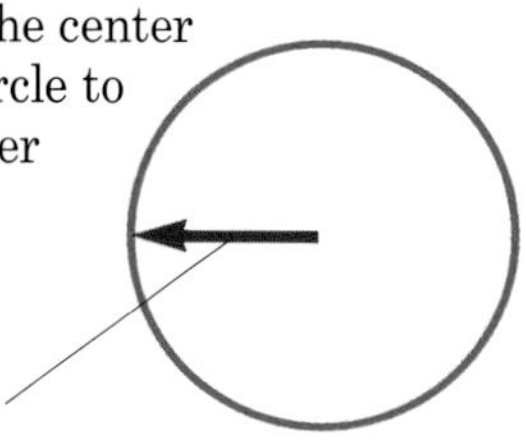

radius

raft
rafts *noun*
1 a floating platform made of logs that have been tied tightly together.

2 a hollow mat made of rubber or plastic and filled with air that can be used as a boat.

life ***raft***

rag
rags *noun*
a small, torn piece of cloth.

rage
rages *noun*
anger or uncontrolled temper.
In her ***rage****, she slammed the door shut.*

raid
raids *noun*
a sudden surprise attack by a group of people.
The police made a ***raid*** *on the house, arresting two women.*
raid *verb*

rail
rails *noun*
1 a long bar for holding on to, or for hanging clothes on.
Use the ***rail*** *to help you climb the stairs.*
2 a long line of metal track that trains run along.

3 the railroad.
We traveled by ***rail*** *around Europe.*

railroad
railroads *noun*
1 a network of tracks that trains run on.
2 a transportation system that uses rail tracks, together with trains, stations, and land.

rain
rains *noun*
water that falls from the clouds in drops.

rain *verb*
rainy *adjective*

rainbow
rainbows *noun*
an arch of colors that appears in the sky when the sun shines while it's raining.

raindrop
raindrops *noun*
a single drop of rain.

rainfall
noun
the amount of rain that falls over a particular area.
The chart shows the annual ***rainfall*** *in South America.*

rain forest
rain forests *noun*
a dense, hot, wet jungle that grows in tropical areas.

rake
rakes raking raked *verb*
to gather up leaves into a pile or to smooth over soil.

rally
rallies *noun*
1 a large, public meeting held to discuss something that is important or worrying to people.

The party held a political ***rally*** *in the park.*
2 a long-distance car race that tests drivers' skills.

ram
rams *noun*
1 a male sheep.

2 a device for pushing against something with force.

They used the log as a ***ram*** *to break down the door.*
ram *verb*

ran
from the verb ***to run***
1 *Last week, he* ***ran*** *a 400-meter race.*
2 *She* ***ran*** *a bookstore.*

ranch
ranches *noun*
a huge farm where cattle or other animals are reared.

rang
from the verb ***to ring***
He ***rang*** *the doorbell.*

ranger
rangers *noun*
a person who looks after a forest or a wildlife park.
■ say **rain**-jer

rapid
adjective
quick or swift.

rare
adjective
unusual or not common.
A ***rare*** *blue morpho butterfly.*

■ comparisons **rarer rarest**
■ opposite **common**

rascal
rascals *noun*
a mischievous person.

rash
rashes *noun*
a patch of red, itchy spots on your skin.

raspberry
raspberries *noun*
a juicy, red fruit that grows on a bush with thorns.

■ say **raz**-bair-ee

rat
rats *noun*
a common rodent that looks like a large mouse. Some kinds of rat eat plants, while others eat small animals. They can gnaw through stone, wood, and even metal with their strong front teeth.

rate
rates *noun*
1 a speed.
Ostriches can run at a ***rate*** *of 30 miles (50 km) per hour.*
2 a level of payment.
The vacation resort charges high ***rates*** *for its apartments.*

rather
adverb
1 fairly or quite.
*It was **rather** hot the other day.*
2 preferably.

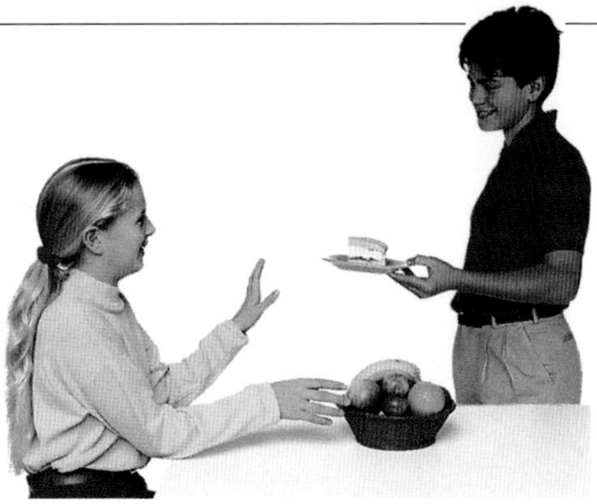

*She'd **rather** have fruit than cake.*

ration
rations *noun*
a fixed amount of something that someone is allowed.
*Food **rations**.*
■ say **rash**-un
ration *verb*

raw
adjective
1 in its natural condition, not processed or cooked.

***raw** carrot*
2 not experienced.
*A **raw** recruit.*
3 painful to touch.
*A **raw** wound.*

ray
rays *noun*
a long, narrow beam of light, heat, or other powerful force.

***rays** of light*

razor
razors *noun*
a device with a blade that people use to shave.

reach
reaches reaching reached *verb*
1 to stretch out your hand and arm to touch something.

2 to arrive at a place.
*After a long trek they **reached** the other side of the island.*

react
reacts reacting reacted *verb*
to say or do something in response to an event.
*He **reacted** badly to the news.*
■ say ree-**akt**
reaction *noun*

read
reads reading read *verb*
to look at and understand written words.
■ rhymes with **seed**

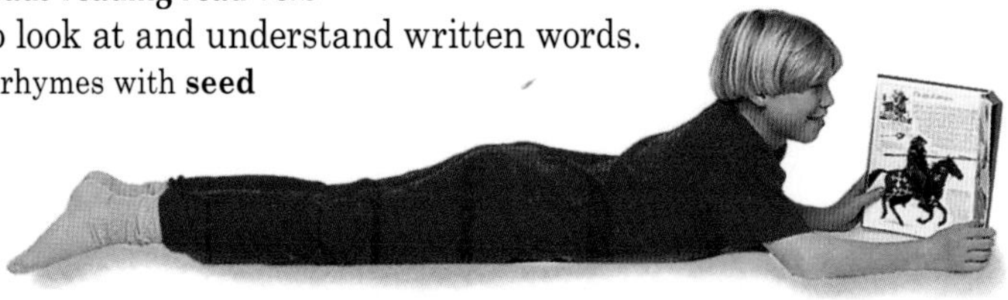

ready
adjective
prepared, or able to start.
■ say **red**-ee

real
adjective
actually existing, or genuine.

realize
realizes realizing realized *verb*
to become aware, or to understand completely.

*She did not **realize** the puddle was so deep.*

really
adverb
very, or actually.
*The trip was **really** fun.*

rear
rears rearing reared *verb*
1 to feed and care for young animals as they grow up.
*Our cat has **reared** 10 kittens.*
2 to rise up on the back legs.
*A **rearing** horse.*

rear
noun
the back of something, or the part that is opposite or behind the front.

*The **rear** of a car.*
rear *adjective*

reason
reasons *noun*
an explanation of why or how something has happened.

rebel
rebels *noun*
someone who fights against those in charge.
■ say **reb**-ul
rebellion *noun*

receipt
receipts *noun*
a written or printed piece of paper that shows you have received and paid for something.
■ say ri-**seet**

receive
receives receiving received *verb*
to take something given or sent to you.

*She **received** lots of presents for her birthday.*

recent
adjective
not long ago.
*A **recent** storm.*
■ say **ree**-sunt
recently *adverb*

recipe
recipes *noun*
instructions that tell you how to make and cook food, or how to make a drink.

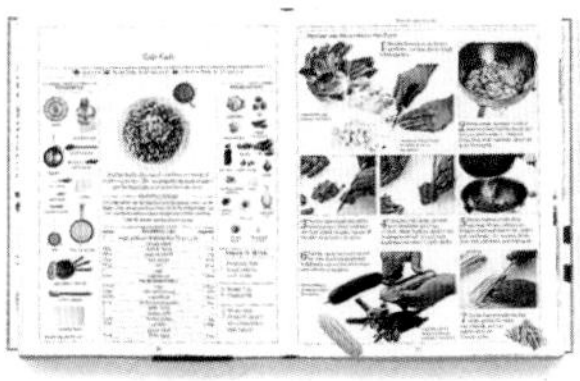

***recipe** book*
■ say **res**-uh-pee

recite
recites reciting recited *verb*
to say aloud something that you have learned by heart.

reckon
reckons reckoning reckoned *verb*
1 to suppose or think something.
*What do you **reckon** that is?*
2 to work out the amount of something.
■ say **rek**-un

recognize
recognizes recognizing recognized *verb*
to see someone or something and know who they are or what it is.

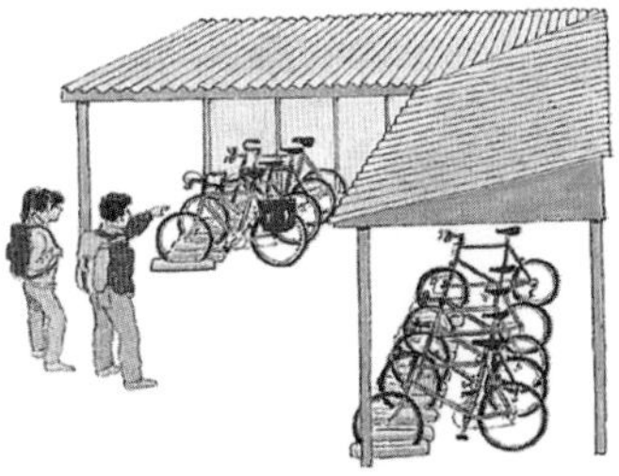

*He **recognized** his friend's bike because of the red bags.*
recognition *noun*

record
records *noun*
1 a round plastic disc with tiny grooves in the surface, on which sounds are recorded.
2 information that is written or printed.

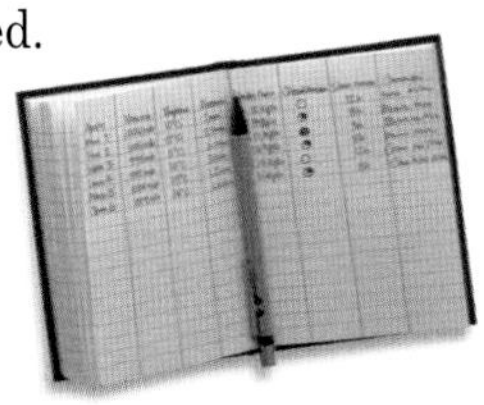

*She kept a **record** of the day's events in her diary.*
3 the fastest or best performance in an activity or sport.
*They tried to beat the **record** for the number of people who can stand on a chair.*
■ say **rek**-urd

recorder
recorders *noun*
a small wooden or plastic wind instrument that you blow into. The air is forced out through holes, which you cover with your fingers to make different sounds.

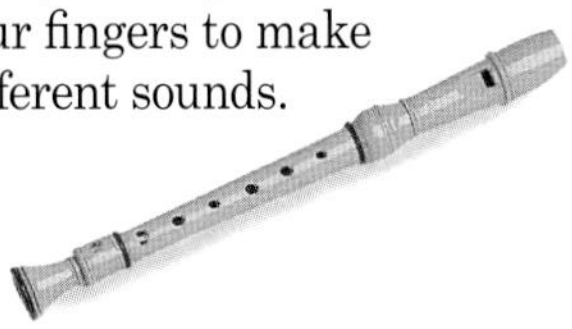

recover
recovers recovering recovered *verb*
1 to get better after being ill.
2 to get something back.

*He **recovered** his hat from the lake.*

record
records recording recorded *verb*
1 to store sounds or pictures, on tape, film, record, compact disc (CD), or digital versatile/video disc (DVD).
2 to write down information on paper.
■ say ree-**kord**

***Recording** a song.*

recreation
noun
the things we like to do in our spare time, such as playing sports and having hobbies.

recruit
recruits *noun*
a new member of an organization or group.
■ say ree-**kroote**

rectangle
rectangles *noun*
a flat four-sided shape with four right angles in its corners (see **shape** on page 182).

recycle
recycles recycling recycled *verb*
to use things again, often by turning garbage into new products. Glass, plastics, paper, and metal can all be recycled.

*materials for **recycling***

red
noun
a color.

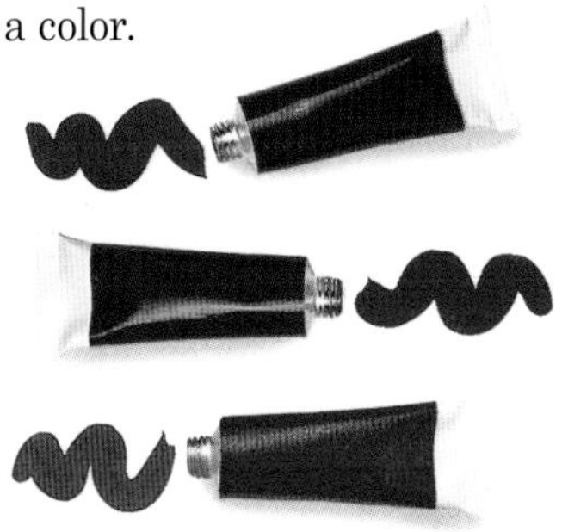

reduce
reduces reducing reduced *verb*
to make something smaller in size or amount.
*The store **reduced** the price of hats by half.*
■ say re-**doos**
reduction *noun*

reed
reeds *noun*
a tall plant with a long, stiff, straight stem that grows in wet areas. Reeds are used to make house roofs and paper.

*common **reed***

reef
reefs *noun*
a raised, narrow ridge of rock, sand, or coral, just above or below the surface of the sea.

*coral **reef***

referee
referees *noun*
someone who watches over a game or contest to see that people play by the rules.

reference
adjective
providing information.
*The **reference** book was full of interesting facts.*
reference *noun*

refinery
refineries *noun*
a large factory where natural substances are processed into other products. Oil is made into gasoline at a refinery.

*oil **refinery***

reflect
reflects reflecting reflected *verb*
1 to throw back light, heat, or sound that has come from somewhere else.
*Shiny surfaces **reflect** light.*
2 to give back, or show, an image of something or someone.

*His face was **reflected** in the mirror.*
reflection *noun*

refrigerator
refrigerators *noun*
a machine that keeps food and beverages cool and fresh. A refrigerator is sometimes called a fridge for short.

refugee
refugees *noun*
someone who leaves their home and belongings and escapes to another place, usually because he or she is in danger.
■ say ref-yoo-**jee**

refuse
refuses refusing refused *verb*
to say that you will not do something.

*He **refused** to give her the ball.*

region
regions *noun*
an area or district of a country.

*A mountain **region**.*
■ say **ree**-jun

regret
regrets regretting regretted *verb*
to be sorry or sad about something that has happened.
*He **regretted** being angry with his sister.*

regular
adjective
1 normal, or happening at certain times.
*A **regular** bus service.*
2 even in shape or sound.

*These wooden cubes are **regular** shapes.*
■ opposite **irregular**
regularly *adverb*

rehearse
rehearses rehearsing rehearsed *verb*
to practice doing something before giving a performance in public.

***Rehearsing** for a play.*
■ say ree-**hurs**
rehearsal *noun*

reign
reigns reigning reigned *verb*
to rule a country or region as a queen or king.
■ say **rain**
reign *noun*

rein
reins *noun*
a long, thin, leather strap that a rider uses to control a horse (see **horse** on page 102).
■ say **rain**

reindeer
reindeer or **reindeers** *noun*
a deer with large antlers that lives in cold, Arctic regions. Reindeer herds migrate great distances every summer and winter in search of plants to eat. Some reindeer are tamed and used to pull sleighs.

relative
relatives *noun*
a member of someone's family.

relax
relaxes relaxing relaxed *verb*
to rest and feel comfortable.

*She **relaxed** with her favorite book.*

relay
relays *noun*
a team race in which runners take turns carrying a baton and completing parts of a course.

release
releases releasing released *verb*
to let someone or something go free.

*They **released** balloons in the park to celebrate the event.*

reliable
adjective
able to be trusted.

relief
noun
1 the removal of worry, pain, or unhappiness.
*It was a **relief** when the exam was over.*
2 help given to people who need it.
■ say ri-**leef**

religion
religions *noun*
a belief in God or gods, and the way people express this belief in their life and worship.
religious *adjective*

reluctant
adjective
unsure or unhappy about doing something.

*He was **reluctant** to cross the old bridge.*

rely
relies relying relied *verb*
to depend on someone for something with complete trust.
*Young birds **rely** on their mothers for food.*
■ say **re**-lie

remain
remains remaining remained *verb*
1 to stay behind.

*He **remained** there alone.*
2 to be left behind.
remains *noun*
3 to stay unchanged.
*She **remained** calm while everyone else panicked.*

remember
remembers remembering remembered *verb*
to think about a place, person, object, or past event again.
*She suddenly **remembered** she had left her bag on the bus.*

remind
reminds reminding reminded *verb*
to make someone remember something.

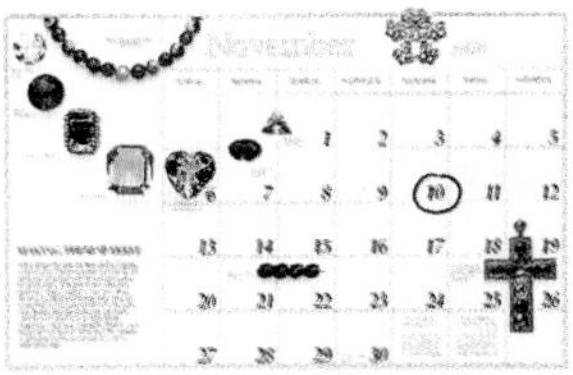

*A calendar **reminds** you of future events.*

remote
adjective
far away, distant.
*A **remote** farmhouse.*

remove
removes removing removed *verb*
to take something off or away.

*She **removed** her shoe to get a pebble out.*

renew
renews renewing renewed *verb*
to begin, make, or get again.
*He **renewed** his bus pass.*

rent
rents *noun*
a regular payment that you make to the owner of something so that you can use it.
rent *verb*

repair
repairs repairing repaired *verb*
to fix something that is broken.

***Repairing** a bicycle.*
repair *noun*

repeat
repeats repeating repeated *verb*
to say or do something again.
repetition *noun*

replace
replaces replacing replaced *verb*
1 to put something back where it came from.

*She **replaced** the book on the shelf.*
2 to exchange or renew.
*He **replaced** his bicycle with a bigger, more expensive one.*
replacement *noun*

replay
replays replaying replayed *verb*
1 to play a sports match again.
2 to play a recording of something again.

replica
replicas *noun*
an exact copy of something.
*She made a **replica** of the ship out of matchsticks.*

reply
replies replying replied *verb*
to answer.
*He **replied** to the invitation immediately.*
reply *noun*

report
reports *noun*
a spoken or written account of a situation or event.

reporter
reporters *noun*
a person who gathers information on events and writes or speaks about them for a television program, newspaper, or radio station.

represent
represents representing represented *verb*
to mean or show something.

*Sailors use this flag to **represent** the word "yes" when they signal to other ships.*

reptile

reptiles *noun*

one of a group of cold-blooded animals that have a backbone, lungs for breathing, dry, scaly skin, and clawed fingers or toes. Reptiles lay their eggs on dry land.

crested water dragon

milk snake

tokay lizard

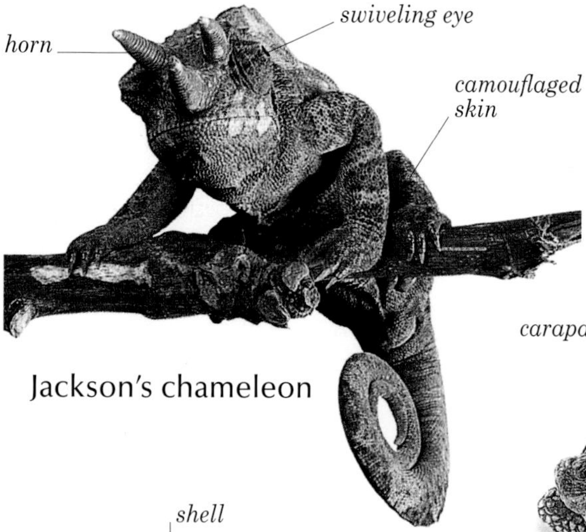

Jackson's chameleon

tortoise hatching

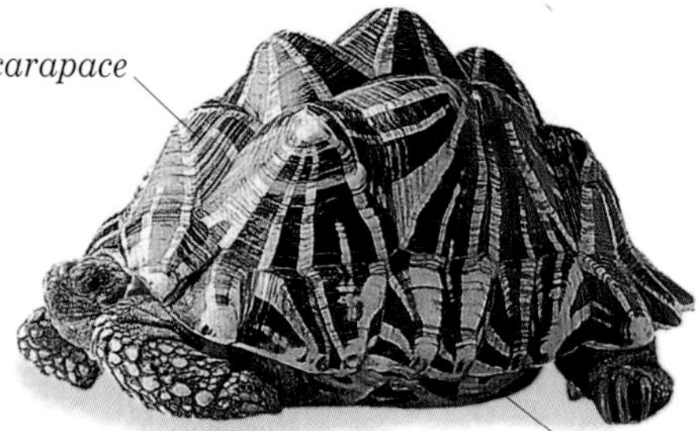

starred tortoise

rattlesnake

red-eared terrapin

leopard gecko

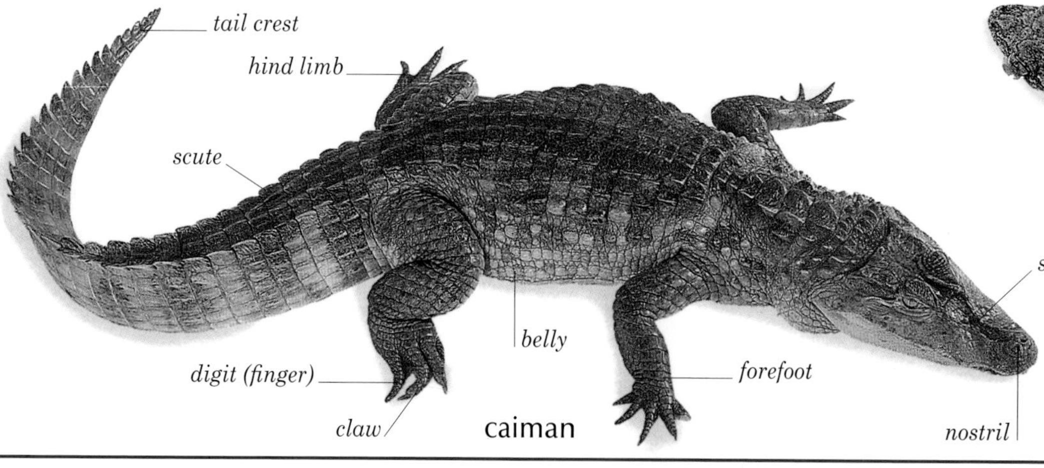

caiman

flying gecko

request
requests requesting requested *verb*
to ask for something formally.
The prisoner ***requested*** *a visit to his mother.*
■ say ri-**kwest**
request *noun*

rescue
rescues rescuing rescued *verb*
to save someone who is injured or in danger.

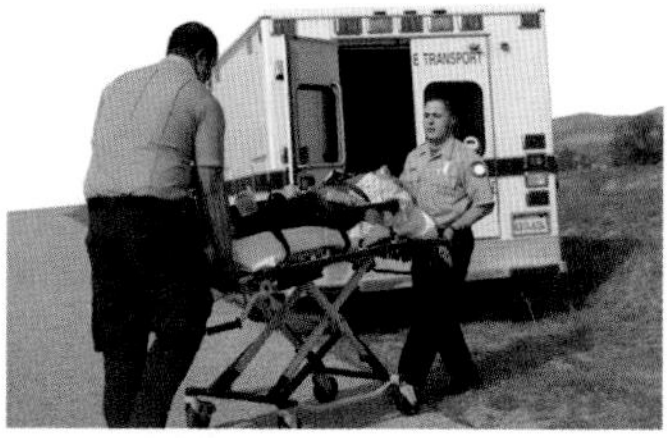

■ say **res**-kyoo

research
researches researching researched *verb*
to study a subject in order to learn new facts or develop new ideas.

Researching *objects found on the seashore.*
research *noun*

reserve
reserves reserving reserved *verb*
to arrange to have something kept for a later time.
They ***reserved*** *a table at the restaurant for 8 o'clock.*
reservation *noun*

resign
resigns resigning resigned *verb*
to give up your job.
■ say ri-**zine**

resist
resists resisting resisted *verb*
to try to stop something from happening.
He ***resisted*** *temptation.*

resort
resorts *noun*
a place where many people go for a vacation.

A ski ***resort****.*

resource
resources *noun*
a supply of something useful or valuable, such as oil or gas.
The country is rich in natural ***resources****.*
■ say **ree**-sors

respect
noun
1 admiration for someone.
I have great ***respect*** *for her.*
2 politeness.
respect *verb*
respectful *adjective*

response
responses *noun*
a reply, in actions or words, to something.
respond *verb*
responsive *adjective*

reservoir
reservoirs *noun*
a large storage area where water is collected and stored for future use.
■ say **rez**-ur-vwar

responsible
adjective
1 sensible and dependable.
2 in charge of something.

The boy was ***responsible*** *for feeding his dog.*

rest
noun
1 the time when you are relaxing.
rest *verb*
2 something that is left over.
Most people left yesterday, but the ***rest*** *went this morning.*
3 when something is still.
The ball came to ***rest*** *at the teacher's feet.*

restaurant
restaurants *noun*
a place where people go to buy and eat a meal.

■ say **res**-tur-ont

restless
adjective
unable to stay still or relax.

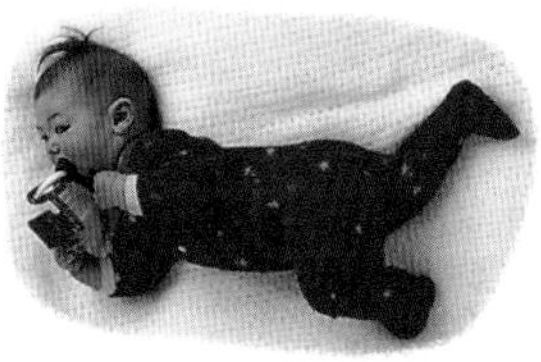

The baby had a ***restless*** *night.*

restore
restores restoring restored *verb*
to fix something old or worn, so that it looks new or can be used again.

result
results *noun*
the effect of certain actions or events.
What was the ***result*** *of the experiment?*
result *verb*

retire
retires retiring retired *verb*
to give up working, usually because of old age or illness.

return
returns returning returned *verb*
1 to come back from somewhere.

The boomerang ***returned*** *easily to his hand.*
2 to give something back to a person.
She ***returned*** *the book he had lent her.*
return *noun*

revenge
noun
harm or injury that a person does to another, in return for something unpleasant previously done to them.

reverse
reverses reversing reversed *verb*
to go backward, usually in a vehicle.

*She **reversed** her motorcycle into the parking space.*

reverse
adjective
at the opposite side, inside, or back of an object.

*The **reverse** side of the coat is lined with white material.*
reverse *noun*

revise
revises revising revised *verb*
to look back over work to make extra changes.
revision *noun*

revolution
revolutions *noun*
1 one complete turn.
2 a time when people fight to change the government of their country.
*The French **Revolution**.*
■ say rev-uh-**loo**-shun

reward
reward *noun*
a prize given because of a good thing someone has done.

*They offered a **reward** to anyone who found their cat.*

rhinoceros
rhinoceroses *noun*
a heavy mammal that lives in hot regions. Rhinoceroses have one or two horns and thick skin with hardly any hair.

■ say ry-**noss**-er-rus

rhubarb
noun
a large-leaved plant. Its long stems can be cooked and eaten as a dessert.

■ say roo-**barb**

rhyme
rhymes *noun*
words that have the same or similar sound and are often found in a poem.
■ say **rime**

rhythm
rhythms *noun*
a regular pattern of sound, such as beats in music.
■ say **rith**-um

rib
ribs *noun*
one of the bones that curves around from your spine to the front of your chest. Ribs protect your internal organs (see **skeleton** on page 188).

ribbon
ribbons *noun*
a thin strip of decorative material often used for tying hair or wrapping presents.

rice
noun
a grasslike plant that grows in warm, wet regions. The small white or brown grains can be cooked and eaten.

*cooked **rice***

rich
adjective
1 having a lot of money.
2 having a lot of something.
*Milk is **rich** in calcium.*
■ comparisons **richer richest**
■ opposite **poor**

riddle
riddles *noun*
a word puzzle in which you have to guess the answer from clues.

ride
rides riding rode ridden *verb*
1 to travel on the back of a horse.

2 to travel on anything that moves.

***Riding** on a Ferris wheel.*
ride *noun*

ridiculous
adjective
crazy, funny, or not making sense.

*She looked **ridiculous**.*
■ say ri-**dik**-yuh-lus

right
adjective
1 the opposite direction to left.
*My **right** hand.*
2 correct or lawful.
*The **right** answer.*
right *noun*

right angle
right angles *noun*
an angle that measures 90 degrees, formed by two lines that are perpendicular to one another (see **shape** on page 182).
*The four inside corners of a square are **right angles**.*

rim
rims *noun*
the edge or border of something.

*He looked over the **rim** of the volcano into the crater.*

ring
rings ringing rang rung *verb*
1 to strike metal or play a bell so that it makes a pleasant sound.

2 to sound or press a doorbell.
*I **rang** the doorbell three times but no one answered the door.*

ring
rings *noun*
a piece of jewelry that is worn on your finger (see **jewelry** on page 112).

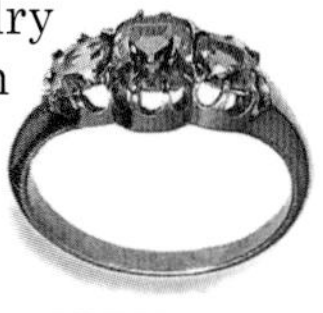

rinse
rinses rinsing rinsed *verb*
to wash something in water with no soap in it.

riot
riots *noun*
uncontrolled fighting among a crowd of people who are angry or protesting about something.
■ say **ry-ut**

rip
rips ripping ripped *verb*
to tear something, usually cloth or paper.

*He **ripped** the piece of paper in half.*

ripe
adjective
ready to pick or eat, usually used about fruit.
■ comparisons **riper ripest**
■ opposite **unripe**

ripple
ripples *noun*
a small wave on the surface of water.

*When the duck dived, it made **ripples** on the water's surface.*

rise
rises rising rose risen *verb*
to go upward or become higher.
*Heat **rises**.*
rising *adjective*

risk
risks risking risked *verb*
to take the chance of harming or losing something.
*He **risked** his life to save her.*
risk *noun*
risky *adjective*

river
rivers *noun*
a large stream of water that flows into another river, a lake, or the ocean.

road
roads *noun*
a path for vehicles to travel on, usually with a hard, smooth surface.

roar
roars roaring roared *verb*
to make a loud, deep, rumbling noise like the noise a lion makes.

roast
roasts roasting roasted *verb*
to cook food in a hot oven or over a fire.

rob
robs robbing robbed *verb*
to steal from someone, often by using violence.
*They **robbed** the bank.*
robbery *noun*

robber
robbers *noun*
a person who robs you of something, usually money or goods.

robot
robots *noun*
a machine that can imitate some human actions. Robots are often used in factories, but can also be used in homes.

*A toy **robot** runs on batteries.*

rock
rocks *noun*
a hard, natural, nonliving substance.
*Mountains are made up mostly of **rock**.*

*granite **rock***
rocky *adjective*

rock
rocks rocking rocked *verb*
to move gently backward and forward, or from side to side.

***rocking** chair*

a b c d e f g h i j k l m n o p q r s t u v w x y z

rocket
rockets *noun*
1 an engine that powers a spacecraft. Hot gases are released from the rear of the engine, causing the craft to move forward.

2 a type of firework that shoots into the sky and explodes.

rode
from the verb ***to ride***
She ***rode*** *her horse last week.*

rodent
rodents *noun*
a small, usually nocturnal mammal with long front teeth for gnawing food. Some rodents eat insects and plants, while others only eat plants. Rats, mice, and squirrels are rodents.
■ say **road**-nt

roll
rolls rolling rolled *verb*
1 to move by turning over and over.

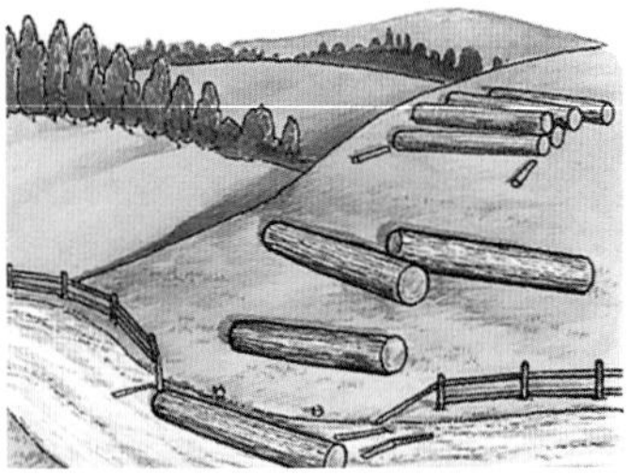

The logs ***rolled*** *down the hill.*
2 to move on wheels.
3 to tilt from side to side, like a ship on a rough sea.

4 to flatten something by moving a tool over it.

roll
rolls *noun*
1 paper, cloth, film, or other material that has been wound onto a tube.

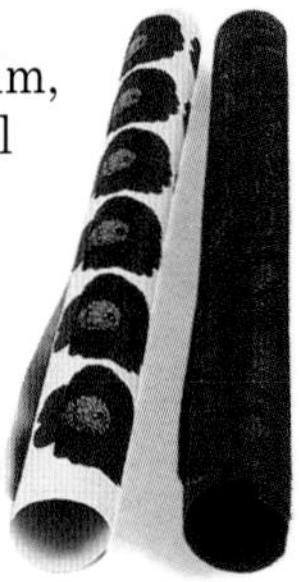

rolls *of wrapping paper*

2 a rounded piece of bread or pastry.

bread ***rolls***

roof
roofs *noun*
1 the outside covering on top of a vehicle or a building.
2 the highest surface inside your mouth or a cave.

room
rooms *noun*
1 one of the separate areas inside a building.

*bath****room***
2 space.
Is there any ***room*** *in the car for me?*

roost
roosts roosting roosted *verb*
to settle down for the night, usually done by birds.

root
roots *noun*
the part of a plant that usually grows underground. A plant's roots supply it with water and minerals from the soil.

rope
ropes *noun*
a strong, thick piece of twisted string or wire.

coil of ***rope***

rose
roses *noun*
a plant with thorns along its stem and flowers with many petals.

rose
from the verb ***to rise***
The Sun ***rose*** *in the sky.*

rot
rots rotting rotted *verb*
to go bad, or to weaken and break down.
rotten *adjective*

rotate
rotates rotating rotated *verb*
to turn around a central point like a wheel does.

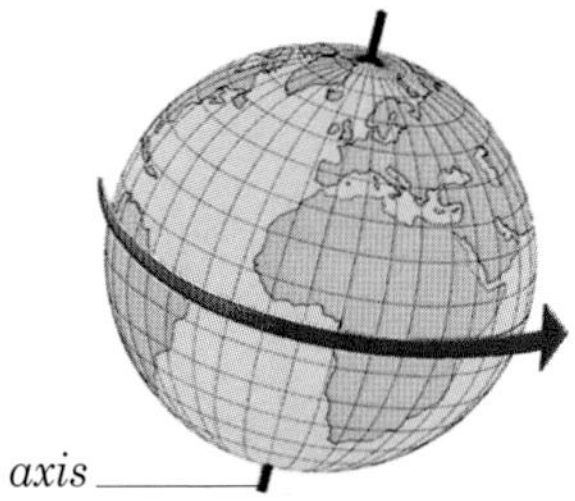

The Earth ***rotates*** *on its axis.*
rotation *noun*

rough
adjective
1 uneven, or not smooth.
A ***rough*** *sea.*
2 approximate, or not exact.
A ***rough*** *guess.*
■ comparisons **rougher roughest**

round
adjective
shaped like a circle, with no corners.

route
routes *noun*
the path you take to get from one place to another.

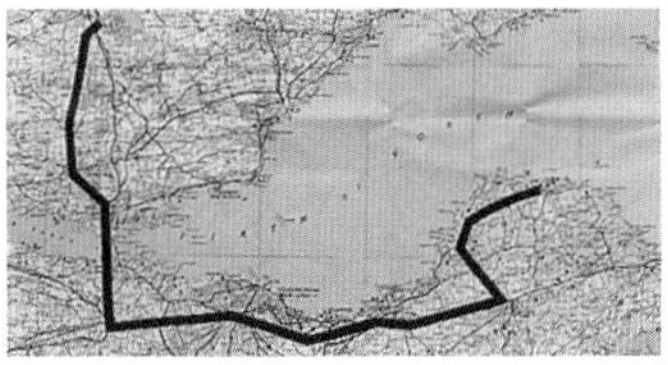

We drew our ***route*** *on the map in red.*
■ say **root**

routine
routines *noun*
a regular activity.
■ say roo-**teen**

row
rows *noun*
a line of several things next to each other.

■ rhymes with **toe**

row
rows rowing rowed *verb*
to make a boat move forward by pulling it through the water with oars.

royal
adjective
to do with a king, queen, or members of his or her family.

rub
rubs rubbing rubbed *verb*
to press something backward and forward over the surface of something else.

*She **rubbed** her wet hair with a towel.*

rubbish
noun
the things that people throw away because they no longer have use for them.

rude
adjective
speaking or behaving in a way that does not show respect.
■ opposite **polite**

rug
rugs *noun*
a small carpet made of thick material.

*a cotton bath **rug***

rugged
adjective
1 having a rough, uneven surface.
*A **rugged** landscape.*

2 not regular, or tough and strong.
*The actor had a **rugged** face.*
3 stormy.
***Rugged** weather.*
■ say rug-**id**

ruin
ruins *noun*
the broken remains of a building.

ruined *adjective*

ruin
ruins ruining ruined *verb*
to spoil or damage something.

*She **ruined** her top by spilling ink on it.*

rule
rules *noun*
an instruction of what must or must not be done, for example, in a game.

rule
rules ruling ruled *verb*
to govern a country or a group of people.

ruler
rulers *noun*
1 a straight piece of wood, metal, or plastic that is used for measuring and drawing straight lines.
2 a person, such as a king or queen, who rules a country.

rumble
rumbles rumbling rumbled *verb*
to make a long, low sound, like the noise thunder makes.
rumble *noun*

rumor
rumors *noun*
a tale passed from one person to another about something that may not be true.

run
runs running ran *verb*
1 to move quickly on your legs.

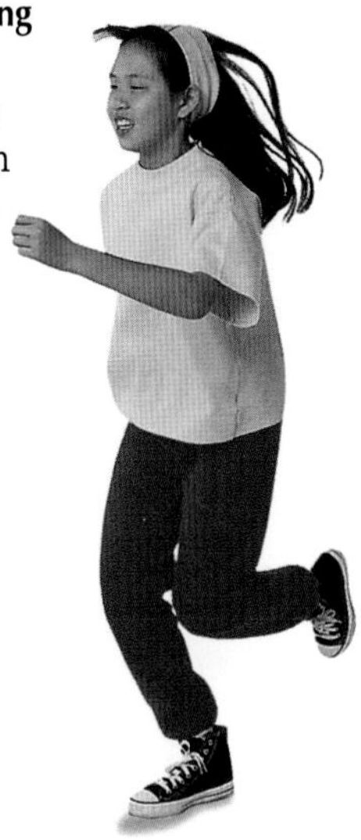

2 to organize something.
*He **runs** a swim club.*

runway
runways *noun*
a long, flat strip of ground with a hard surface from which aircraft take off and land.

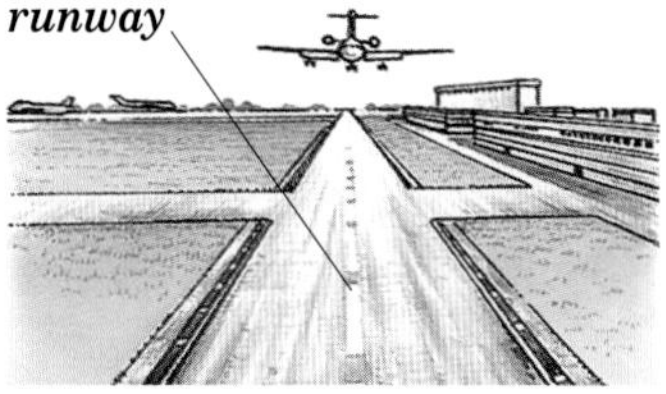

rural
adjective
to do with the countryside or farms.
*A **rural** village.*
■ say **roor**-ul

rush
rushes rushing rushed *verb*
to hurry, or to do something quickly.

rust
noun
the red-brown coating that forms on some metals when they get wet.

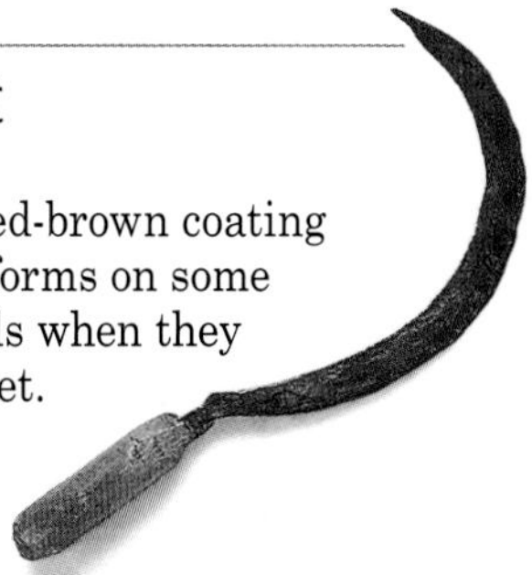

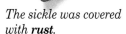

*The sickle was covered with **rust**.*

rustle
rustles rustling rustled *verb*
to make a soft, whispering sound.
*The leaves on the tree **rustled** in the wind.*

rye
noun
a grass with light-brown grains, grown to make bread and food for cattle.

A B C D E F G H I J K L M N O P Q R S T U V W X Y Z

Ss

sack
sacks *noun*
a large, strong bag made of cloth, plastic, or paper that is used for carrying or storing things.

sacred
adjective
holy, or connected with the worship of God or gods.
*The Qur'an is the **sacred** book of Muslims.*
■ say **say**-krid

sad
adjective
not feeling happy.
■ comparisons **sadder saddest**
■ opposite **happy**

saddle
saddles *noun*
a seat for a rider on a horse or a bicycle (see **horse** on page 102 and **transportation** on page 221).

*horse **saddle***

safari
safaris *noun*
an expedition to hunt or observe wild animals, usually in Africa.

■ say sa-**far**-ree

safe
adjective
1 protected from harm or danger.
***Safe** on dry land.*
2 not dangerous.
*A **safe** driver.*
■ comparisons **safer safest**
safety *noun*

safe
safes *noun*
a lockable metal box that is used for storing money and valuable things.

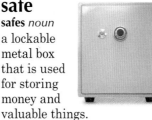

sag
sags sagging sagged *verb*
to bend or sink, especially in the middle.
*The sofa **sagged** in the middle.*

said
*from the verb **to say***
1 *She **said** "Good morning."*
2 *The clock **said** half past four.*

sail
sails sailing sailed *verb*
to travel across water in a ship or boat.

sail
sails *noun*
a piece of material attached to the mast of a boat or ship that catches the wind and helps to move the vessel along (see **boat** on page 31).

salad
salads *noun*
a mixture of vegetables, fruit, or other foods, usually served cold.

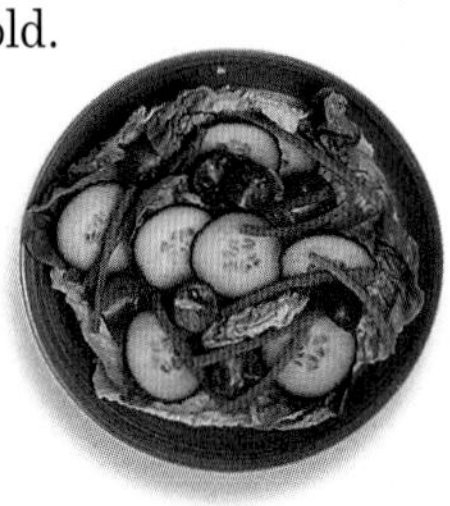

*mixed **salad***

salary
salaries *noun*
an amount of money regularly paid to someone for work they have done.
*A monthly **salary**.*

sale
sales *noun*
1 the act of offering something to be sold.

*The house is for **sale**.*
2 an event where things are sold at reduced prices.
*Half-price **sale**!*

saliva
noun
the fluid that is produced in your mouth to help you to chew and digest food.

salmon
noun
a large, edible fish. Salmon hatch in rivers, but then swim to the sea to live. They swim back up rivers to lay their eggs.

■ say **sam**-un

salt
noun
a substance made of small, white crystals that we put on food in order to add flavor.

***salt** mill*
salty *adjective*

salute
salutes saluting saluted *verb*
to give a sign of respect by raising the right hand to the forehead or by firing guns into the air.
salute *noun*

same
adjective
1 matching exactly.
*She was wearing the **same** dress as me.*
2 mentioned or seen before.
*He looks like the **same** person who was there yesterday.*
■ opposite **different**

sample
samples *noun*
a small part of something that shows what the rest is like.

*The supermarket was giving away free **samples** of cheese.*
sample *verb*

sand
noun
very small grains of broken rock, found on beaches or in deserts.

sandal
sandals *noun*
a shoe with a top made of straps, usually worn in warm weather.

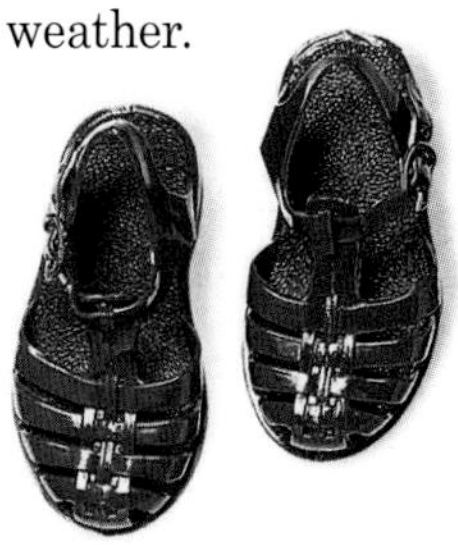

sandwich
sandwiches *noun*
slices of bread with another food in between.

sang
*from the verb **to sing***
*The blackbird **sang** loudly outside my window.*

sank
*from the verb **to sink***
1 *The ship **sank** at sea.*
2 *The balloon **sank** slowly.*

sari
saris *noun*
a long, light cloth wrapped around the body and shoulder that is worn mainly by women of India, Bangladesh, Nepal, and Sri Lanka.

sarong
sarongs *noun*
a traditional Asian skirt worn by men and women and made from a piece of cloth wrapped around the waist or chest.

sash
sashes *noun*
a band of fabric worn around the waist or over the shoulder.

sash

sat
*from the verb **to sit***
1 *I **sat** down on the floor.*
2 *She **sat** for a painter.*

satellite
satellites *noun*
1 an object in orbit around a larger object in space. Planet satellites are called moons.
2 an artificial device in space that receives and transmits information around the world.
*An Earth observation **satellite**.*
■ say **sat**-i-lite

satisfy
satisfies satisfying satisfied *verb*
to please someone or give someone what they want or need.
*His answer didn't **satisfy** the teacher.*
satisfaction *noun*

sauce
sauces *noun*
a liquid or soft food that is eaten with a meal.

*raspberry **sauce***
■ say **sawss**

saucepan
saucepans *noun*
a metal container with a handle, used for cooking.

■ say **sawss**-pan

saucer
saucers *noun*
a small, shallow plate that is placed beneath a cup.

■ say **sawss**-ser

sausage
sausages *noun*
a food made from a mixture of chopped meat, fat, and cereal inside a tube of thin skin.
■ say **saw**-sij

save
saves saving saved *verb*
1 to rescue.
*The firefighter **saved** him from the burning house.*
2 to not waste.
***Save** power—turn off the light!*
3 to keep something to use later.
*He **saved** all his allowance.*

saw
saws *noun*
a tool for cutting wood that has a handle and a blade with sharp teeth.

saw
saws sawing sawed *verb*
to use a saw.

***Sawing** a plank of wood.*

saw
*from the verb **to see***
*I **saw** my face in the mirror.*

say
says saying said *verb*
1 to speak words out loud.
*"Hurry up!" I **said**.*
2 to give a message or some information.
*The sign **says** "No Entry."*

scald
scalds scalding scalded *verb*
to burn with hot liquid or steam.
■ say **skawld**

scale
scales *noun*
1 a series of regular marks along a line used for measuring.
Thermometers have a ***scale*** *for measuring temperature.*
2 a set sequence of musical notes going from the highest to the lowest, or from the lowest to the highest.

3 a small, hard plate on the skin of a fish, insect, or reptile (see **fish** on page 79, **insect** on page 108, **reptile** on page 168).
4 the size of a map or a model compared with the actual size of the object.

This model of a building has been made to ***scale****.*

scales
noun
a machine that is used to weigh things.

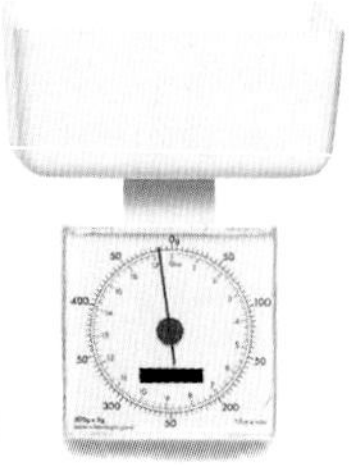

kitchen ***scales***

scar
scars *noun*
a mark left on the skin after a wound has healed.
scar *verb*

scarce
adjective
not great in amount, or not often found.
Snow is ***scarce*** *in May.*
■ say **skairs**

scare
scares scaring scared *verb*
1 to become frightened.
2 to make someone else frightened.

The bear appeared suddenly and ***scared*** *him.*

scarecrow
scarecrows *noun*
a figure made from sticks and old clothes that is used to scare birds away from crops.

scarf
scarves *noun*
a piece of cloth that you wear around your shoulders, neck, or head for decoration or to keep warm.

scatter
scatters scattering scattered *verb*
to spread in many different directions.
The wind ***scattered*** *the seeds.*

scavenger
scavengers *noun*
an animal that feeds on rotting meat and garbage.

scavenge *verb*

scene
scenes *noun*
1 the place where something happened.
The ***scene*** *of the crime.*
2 a part of a play or film, set in a particular time or place.
3 a view.

A winter ***scene****.*
■ say **seen**

scenery
noun
1 the way a place looks.
The ***scenery*** *in the mountains was amazing.*
2 an artificial background used in a play or a film.

■ say **see**-nuh-ree

scent
scents *noun*
1 a trail of smell left by an animal or a person.
The dog followed the ***scent****.*
2 perfume.
■ say **sent**

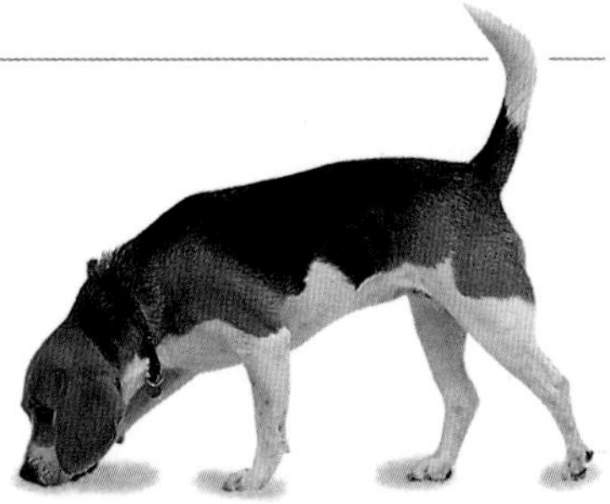

scheme
schemes *noun*
1 a secret plan.
2 a way of arranging things.
A color ***scheme****.*
■ say **skeem**

school
schools *noun*
a place where children go to learn.
■ say **skool**

science
sciences *noun*
the study of things in the world; it involves observing, measuring, and experimenting to test ideas.
■ say **sy**-uns
scientific *adjective*

scientist
scientists *noun*
someone who does scientific work.
■ say **sy**-un-tist

scissors
noun
a tool with handles and two blades joined together. Scissors are used for cutting things, such as paper and hair.

■ say **siz**-urz

scold
scolds scolding scolded *verb*
to speak to someone angrily because they have done something wrong.
My father ***scolded*** *me for being late.*

scoop
scoops scooping scooped *verb*
to lift something up using your hand or a tool shaped like a deep spoon.

***Scooping** pasta out of a jar.*

score
scores scoring scored *verb*
to win points in a game.

scorn
scorns scorning scorned *verb*
to show by words or your expression that you do not think much of something or someone.
*The journalist **scorned** the plans for the power plant.*
scornful *adjective*

scorpion
scorpions *noun*
a small, nocturnal animal that is part of the same animal group as spiders. Scorpions usually live in hot regions. They eat insects and spiders that they kill with the poisonous stingers on their tails.

*imperial **scorpion***

scowl
scowls scowling scowled *verb*
to frown in an angry or bad-tempered way.
*She **scowled** when she was given extra homework.*
scowl *noun*

scramble
scrambles scrambling scrambled *verb*
1 to crawl or climb fast, using your hands.

*He **scrambled** back up the riverbank.*
2 to mix together.
***Scrambling** an egg.*

scrap
noun
1 a small piece of something.

***scraps** of paper*

2 anything that is worn out or no longer of any use.

*The cars were sold as **scrap**.*
scrap *verb*

scrape
scrapes scraping scraped *verb*
to drag an object across something, often removing part of the surface.

***Scraping** wallpaper off the walls.*

scratch
scratches scratching scratched *verb*
1 to make a mark on the surface of something with a sharp object.

*The cat **scratched** the tree.*
2 to rub skin with fingernails or claws to stop it from itching.
scratch *noun*

scream
screams screaming screamed *verb*
to cry out in a loud, high voice because you are frightened or in pain.
scream *noun*

screen
screens *noun*
1 a flat surface onto which moving images are projected.
*Some movie theaters have six **screens**.*
2 a barrier that is used to hide, separate, or protect something.

*She dressed behind a **screen**.*
3 the part of a computer or television on which the picture or text appears.

screw
screws *noun*
a metal pin used for fastening things together.

screwdriver
screwdrivers *noun*
a tool for turning screws.

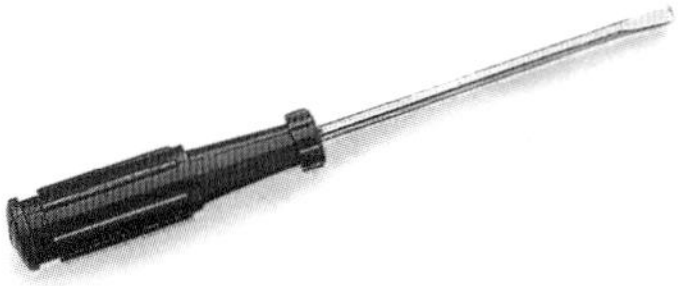

script
scripts *noun*
1 a written version of a play, film, radio, or television show.
2 handwriting.

scrub
scrubs scrubbing scrubbed *verb*
to clean by rubbing hard.

***Scrubbing** a rabbit hutch.*

sculpture
sculptures *noun*
a piece of art made from wood, stone, metal, or another solid material.

sea
seas *noun*
the salt water that covers two-thirds of the Earth's surface.

sea life

noun

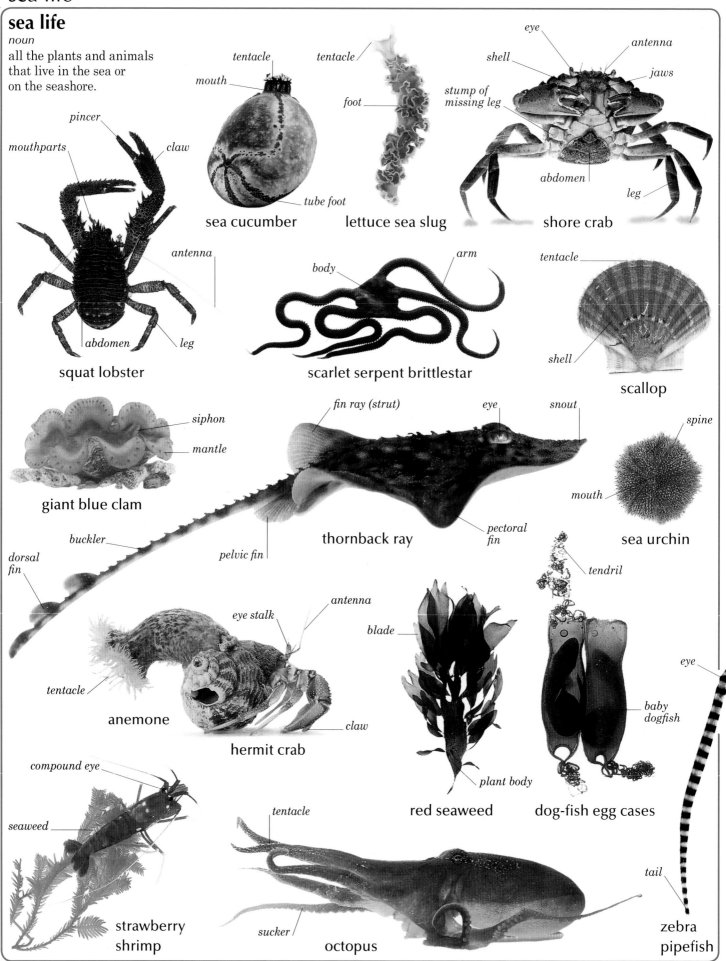

all the plants and animals that live in the sea or on the seashore.

sea cucumber

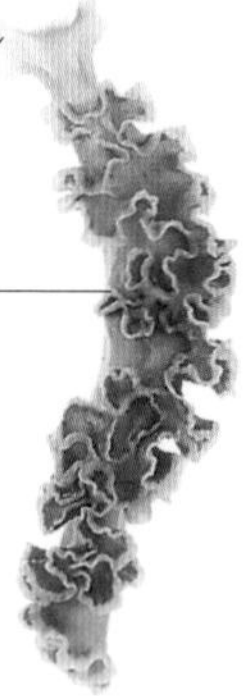

lettuce sea slug

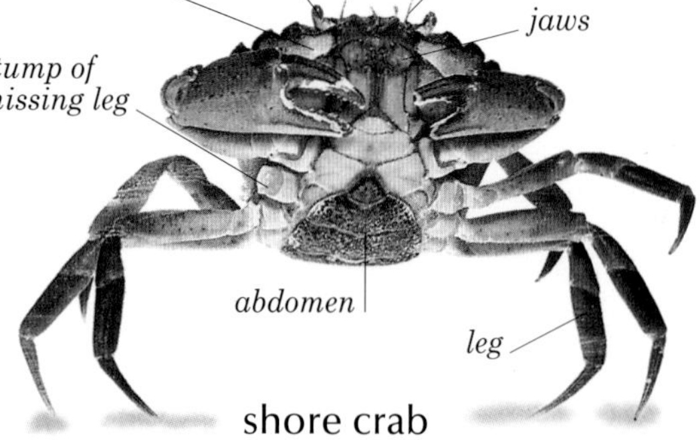

shore crab

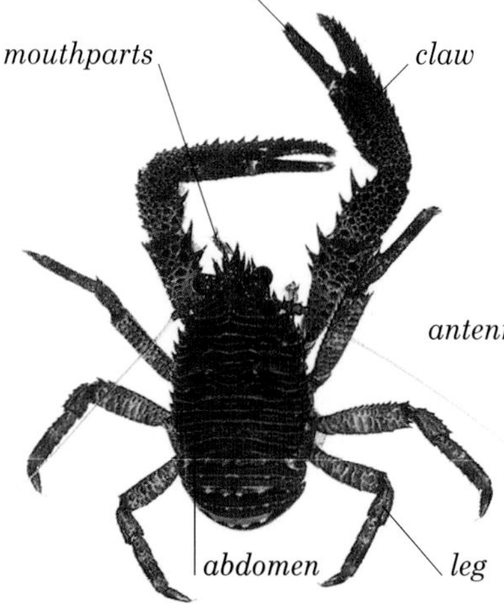

squat lobster

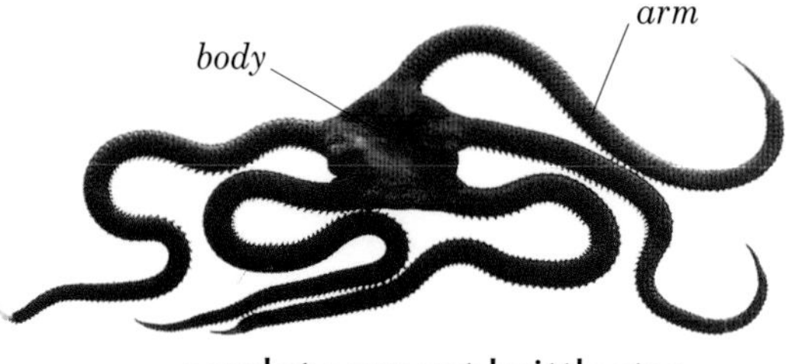

scarlet serpent brittlestar

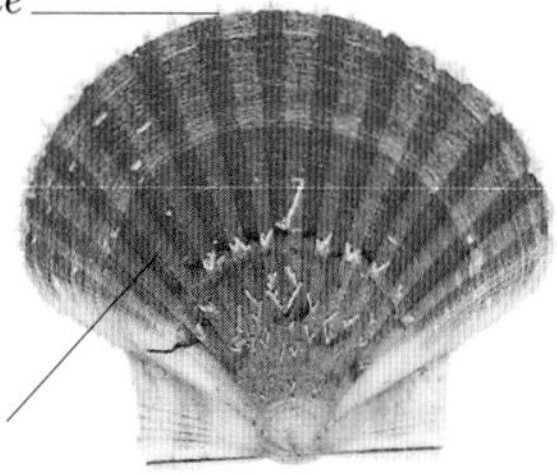

scallop

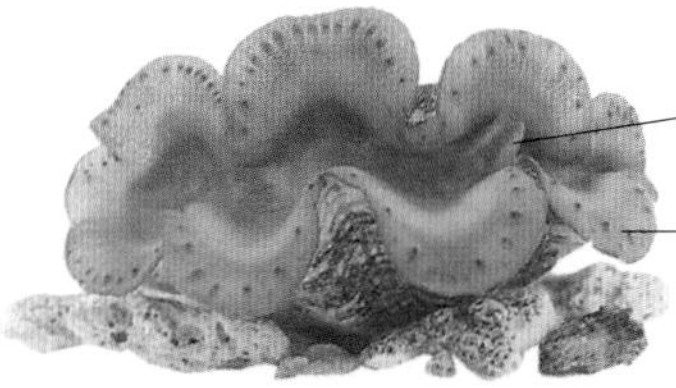

giant blue clam

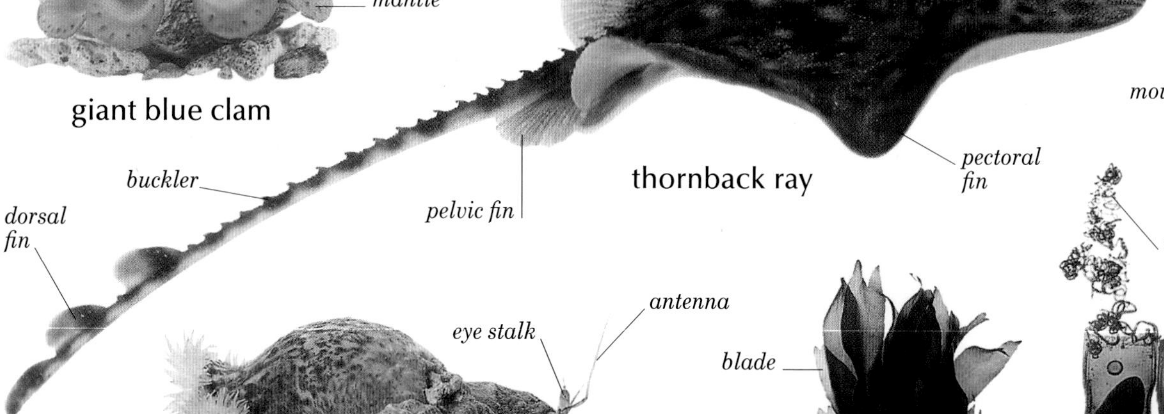

thornback ray

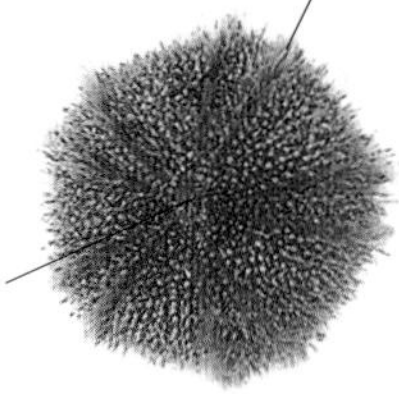

sea urchin

anemone

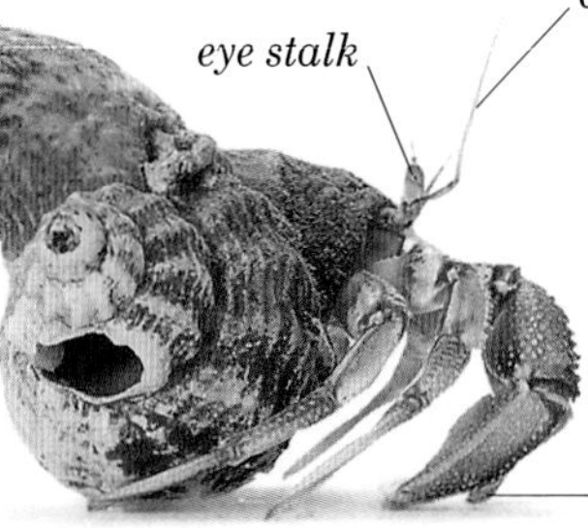

hermit crab

red seaweed

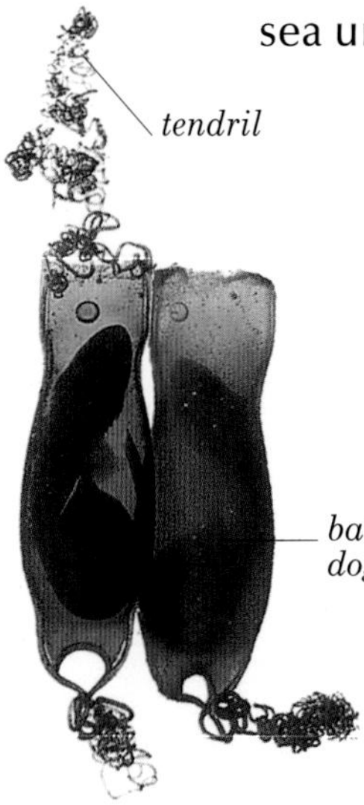

dog-fish egg cases

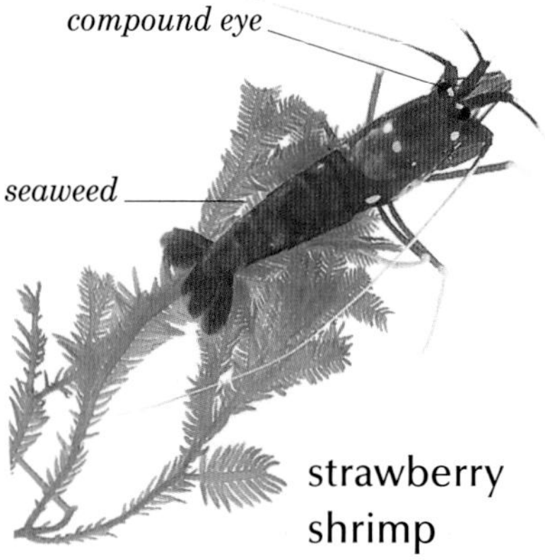

strawberry shrimp

octopus

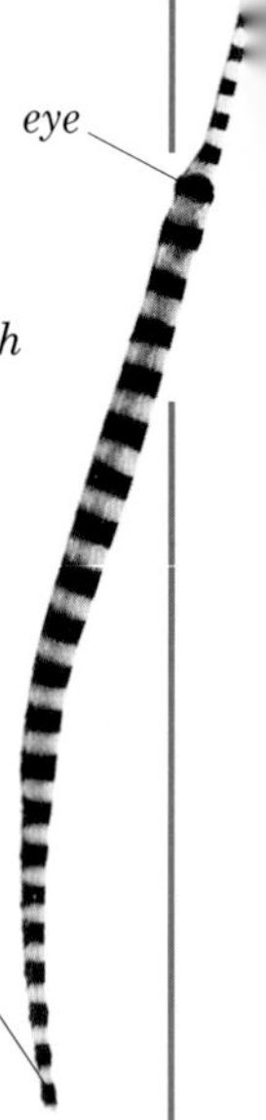

zebra pipefish

seal
seals *noun*
1 a sea mammal usually found in cold seas. Seals eat fish and are excellent swimmers. Some seals are clumsy on land, where they move by rolling or sliding along.

2 a piece of paper or wax that is used to mark something or to close it so that you can tell whether it has been opened.

wax ***seal***

seal
seals sealing sealed *verb*
to close something securely or tightly.
Seal *the envelope.*

search
searches searching searched *verb*
to look hard for something.

He ***searched*** *for his ball in the long grass.*
search *noun*

season
seasons *noun*
1 one of the four divisions of the year marked by particular kinds of weather.
Our ***seasons*** *are spring, summer, fall, and winter.*
2 a particular part of the year.
The football ***season*** *starts next week.*

seat
seats *noun*
anything that is used for sitting on.

child's car safety ***seat***
seat *belt*

second
seconds *noun*
a very short period of time. There are 60 seconds in one minute.

secret
secrets *noun*
something that is not known by everyone.
Can you keep a ***secret****?*
secret *adjective*

secretary
secretaries *noun*
a person whose job is to assist other people by making business appointments, writing letters, and keeping records.

section
sections *noun*
a separate part or portion of something.
The library has a children's ***section****.*

secure
adjective
1 well fastened.
A ***secure*** *door.*
secure *verb*

2 safe and confident.
My baby brother needs his teddy bear to help him feel ***secure****.*

see
sees seeing saw seen *verb*
to notice something with your eyes.

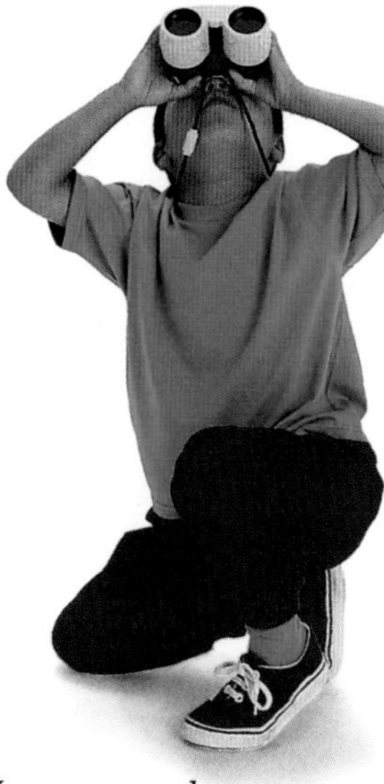

You can ***see*** *a long way with binoculars.*

seed
seeds *noun*
a small, hard part of some flowering plants, from which new plants may grow (see **growth** on page 94).

sunflower ***seeds***

seek
seeks seeking sought *verb*
to search for something, or try to achieve something.
Seeking *help.*

seem
seems seeming seemed *verb*
to appear to be.
She ***seems*** *worried about something.*

seesaw
seesaws *noun*
a balancing toy. Children play on a seesaw by sitting at either end of a board and rocking up and down.

seize
seizes seizing seized *verb*
to take hold of something suddenly.
The thief ***seized*** *her bag.*
■ say **seez**

seldom
adverb
not often, or rarely.
I ***seldom*** *get home before six.*

select
selects selecting selected *verb*
to choose something you want from a number of things.

She ***selected*** *a pot of paint from the tray.*
selection *noun*

selfish
adjective
only caring about yourself.
He was very ***selfish*** *and never shared his toys.*

sell
sells selling sold *verb*
to give something to someone in return for money.
They ***sell*** *all kinds of vegetables at the market.*

a b c d e f g h i j k l m n o p q r s t u v w x y z

semaphore
noun
a way of sending messages by signaling with two flags. The flags are held in different positions to represent each letter of the alphabet.

The letter "x" in ***semaphore****.*
■ say **sem**-uh-for

send
sends sending sent *verb*
to make someone or something go to another place.
Send *me a postcard!*

senior
adjective
older, more experienced, or more important.
Senior *club members set the rules.*
■ say **seen**-yur

sense
senses *noun*
1 one of the five ways in which we can receive information about the world. The five senses are sight, hearing, touch, smell, and taste.

You need your ***sense*** *of hearing to use a telephone.*
2 a feeling.
A ***sense*** *of disappointment.*
3 reasonable decisions or good judgment.
She has a lot of ***sense****.*
4 a meaning that can be understood.
It makes ***sense****.*

sensible
adjective
thinking clearly or in a practical way.

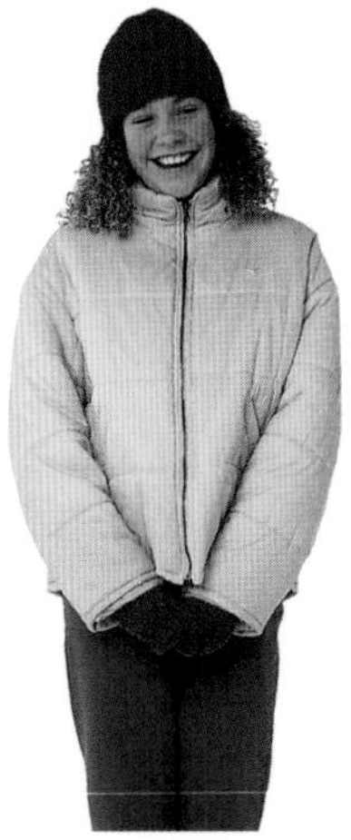

She was ***sensible*** *about dressing for the cold weather.*
sensibly *adverb*

sensitive
adjective
1 quick to feel, understand, or react to something.

Sensitive *hairs on this plant make the leaves close when they are touched.*
2 easily upset or hurt.
His skin was very ***sensitive*** *where he had been burned.*

sentence
sentences *noun*
1 a group of words that make sense together. Sentences start with a capital letter and end with a period. They usually include a verb.
2 a punishment decided by a judge in a court of law.
He received a four-year prison ***sentence****.*

separate
separates separating separated *verb*
to set apart from each other.

He ***separated*** *the yellow marbles from the green ones.*
separate *adjective*
separately *adverb*

sequel
sequels *noun*
something that follows an earlier event, or continues a story from a previous book or movie.
A movie ***sequel****.*
■ say **see**-kwul

sequence
sequences *noun*
a number of things that follow in a particular order.
■ say **see**-kwens

sequin
sequins *noun*
a small, shiny, metal or plastic disk that is sewn onto material as a decoration.
■ say **see**-kwin

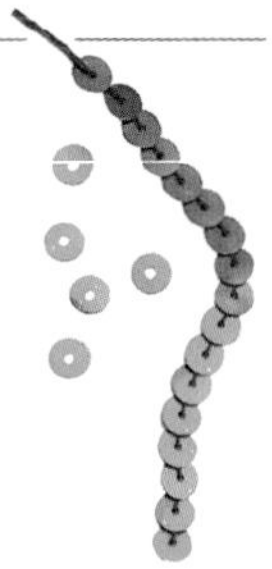

serial
serials *noun*
a story that is broadcast or published in a series of parts.

serious
adjective
1 requiring careful thought.
A ***serious*** *question.*
2 not smiling or laughing.
A ***serious*** *expression.*
3 worrying or dangerous.

The fallen tree caused ***serious*** *damage to the roof.*

servant
servants *noun*
a person whose job it is to work for someone in that person's home.

serve
serves serving served *verb*
1 to help someone, usually by giving them something they want or need.
2 to start play in games such as tennis by hitting the ball to your opponent.

series
noun
1 a group of similar things that follow one another in order.
A ***series*** *of books on nature.*

2 a television or radio show that is broadcast in regular episodes, or a set of novels about the same characters.

service
services *noun*
1 the act of serving.
*Good restaurant **service**.*
2 employment in the armed forces or in a public organization.
*Military **service**.*
3 the supply of something that helps or serves people.
*A telephone **service**.*
4 religious worship.
*A church **service**.*
5 the act of checking and repairing machinery so that it continues to work well.
*A car **service**.*

set
sets *noun*
a group of things that belong together.

*A toy construction **set**.*

set
sets setting set *verb*
1 to put in position or arrange something.
*She **set** the vase on the table.*
2 to decide or determine a limit, time, or date.
*She **set** the party for Friday.*
3 to go below the horizon.
*The Sun **sets** in the west.*
4 to go hard.
*The cement took a long time to **set**.*

settle
settles settling settled *verb*
1 to calm down or stop moving.

*The dog **settled** down to sleep.*
2 to decide or agree about something without any doubts.
***Settle** an argument.*

several
adjective
a number, usually three or more, but not many more.
***Several** people waved as they walked past.*

severe
adjective
1 extremely bad.
*A **severe** accident.*
2 strict or hard.
*The rock face was a **severe** test for the climbers.*
severely *adverb*

sew
sews sewing sewn *verb*
to join something together using a needle and thread.

***Sewing** on a shirt button.*
■ say **so**

sewer
sewers *noun*
a large, underground pipe or channel that takes dirty water and waste matter away.
■ say **soo**-er

sex
sexes *noun*
one of two groups, male or female, that people, animals, and plants are divided into.

shade
shades *noun*
1 a cool place where the Sun's direct light doesn't reach.

*She sat in the **shade** to read.*
shady *adjective*
2 a slight difference in color.

*Different **shades** of paint.*

shadow
shadows *noun*
a dark shape made by something that is blocking the light.

shaft
shafts *noun*
1 a long, vertical passageway.
*A lift **shaft**.*
2 a long, straight part of something.
*A **shaft** of light.*

shaggy
adjective
having long, rough, untidy hair.

■ comparisons **shaggier shaggiest**

shake
shakes shaking shook shaken *verb*
1 to move something rapidly up and down, or from side to side.

***Shaking** hands.*
2 to tremble with fear, shock, or cold.

shall
verb
a word used to show that something will happen in the future.
*I **shall** go shopping later.*
■ always used with another verb

shallow
adjective
not deep.

*They played in **shallow** water.*

shame
shames *noun*
1 a sad thing that happens.
*It's a **shame** you can't come.*
2 an uncomfortable, guilty feeling about something you have done.
ashamed *adjective*

shampoo
shampoos *noun*
a soapy liquid that is used for washing hair.

shampoo *verb*

A B C D E F G H I J K L M N O P Q R S T U V W X Y Z

shape

shapes *noun*

the outline or form of an object. Everything has a shape. Some shapes are two-dimensional, because they have width and length, but no height. Some shapes are three-dimensional, because they have width, length, and height.

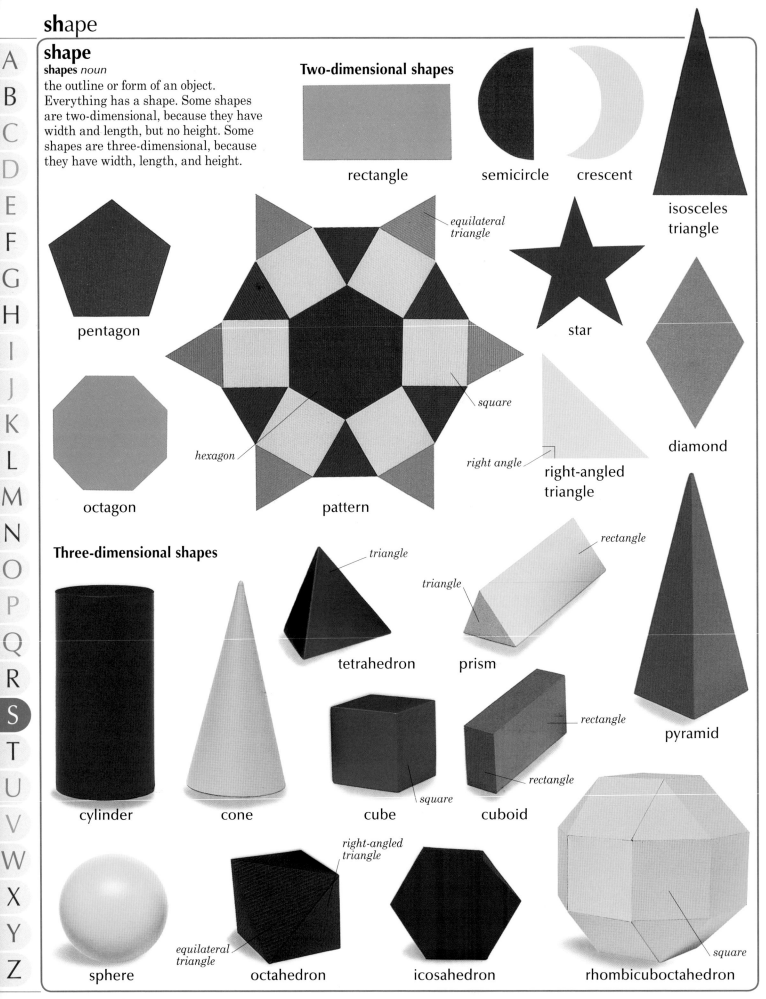

Two-dimensional shapes

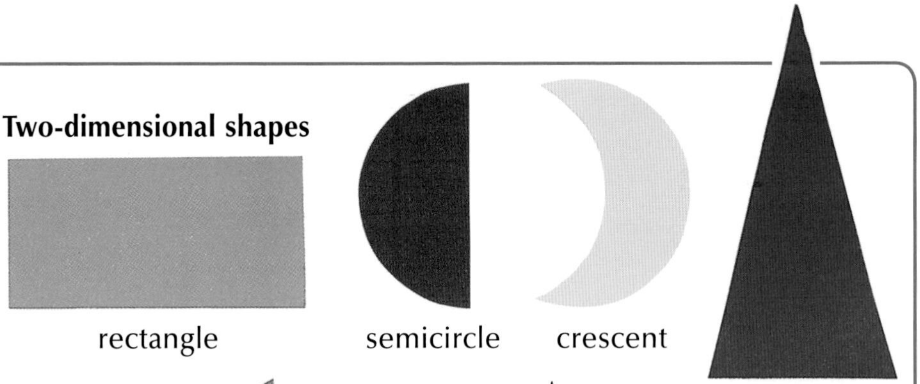

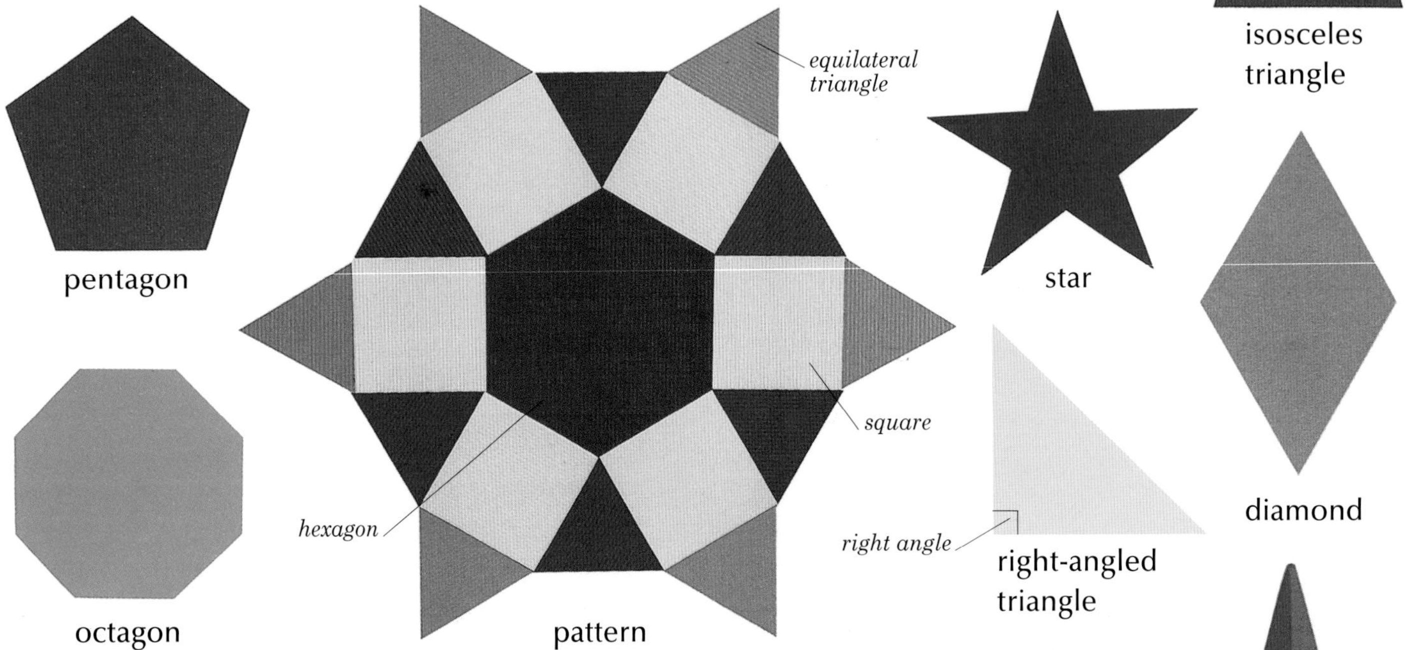

Three-dimensional shapes

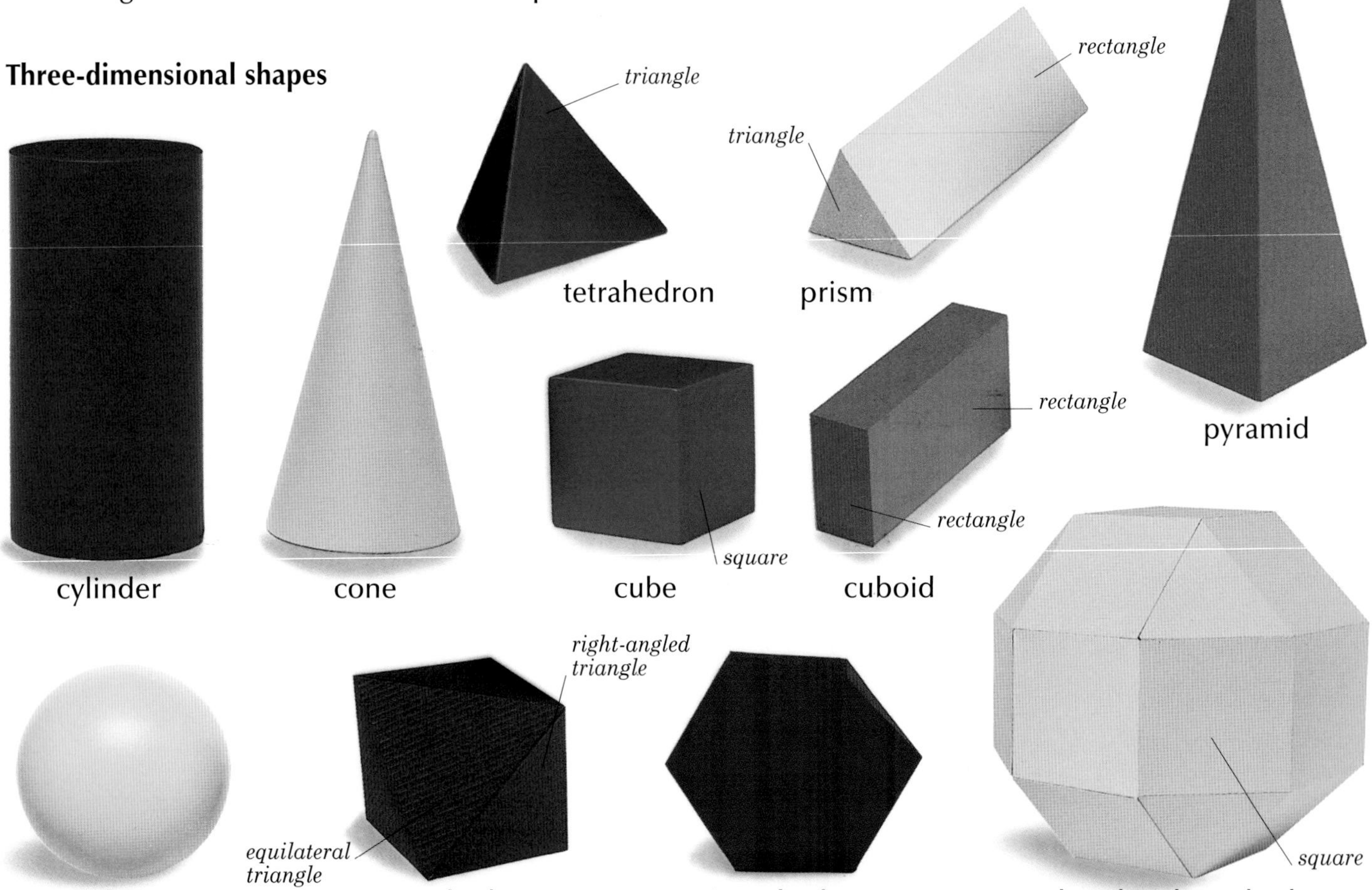

share
shares sharing shared *verb*
1 to have or use together.
2 to divide something into parts to give to others.

*They **shared** the melon.*

shark
sharks *noun*
a large fish with rows of sharp teeth that lives in both cold and warm oceans. Sharks eat fish or small water animals and are able to detect smells and sounds at great distances.

*leopard **shark***

sharp
adjective
with a thin edge or a fine point that may be used for cutting things.
*Careful—that knife is **sharp**!*
■ comparisons **sharper sharpest**

shatter
shatters shattering shattered *verb*
1 to break into many pieces.

*When she sang the top notes, the glass **shattered**.*
2 to ruin someone's plans, or to make someone upset.
*The loss of their jobs **shattered** their dreams of buying a home.*

shave
shaves shaving shaved *verb*
to remove hair from the skin with a razor.

shawl
shawls *noun*
a large piece of cloth worn over the shoulders.

shear
shears shearing sheared shorn *verb*
to cut off wool or fur.
*We **shear** sheep for their wool.*

shed
sheds *noun*
a small building for storing things such as garden tools.

shed
sheds shedding shed *verb*
to drop, lose, or separate from something.

*Snakes **shed** their skins.*

sheep
sheep *noun*
a farm animal reared for its wool and meat.

sheer
adjective
1 very steep.
*It was a **sheer** drop.*
2 complete or absolute.
***Sheer** exhaustion.*

sheet
sheets *noun*
a large, thin, flat piece of cloth, paper, plastic, or metal.
*A **sheet** of steel.*

shelf
shelves *noun*
a horizontal piece of wood or metal for storing things on.

shell
shells *noun*
the hard, outer covering that protects some living things. Eggs, nuts, and animals such as snails, crabs, and tortoises have shells (see **reptile** on page 168).

*egg **shell***

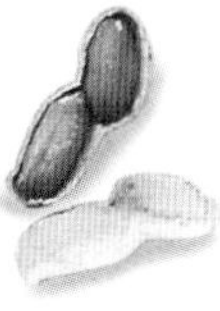

*nut **shell***

*crab's **shell***

shellfish
noun
any small, edible water animal that has a shell.

shelter
shelters *noun*
a thing that protects someone or something from the weather or from danger.

*The doorway was a **shelter** from the rain.*
shelter *verb*
sheltered *adjective*

sheriff
sheriffs *noun*
a law officer whose job is to see that people obey the law in a particular area.

shield
shields *noun*
a strong piece of metal or leather that soldiers used to carry in battle to protect their bodies from their opponents' weapons.

*an ancient Indian **shield***

shield
shields shielding shielded *verb*
to protect.

*She **shielded** her eyes from the sun.*

shin
shins *noun*
the front part of your leg below the knee.

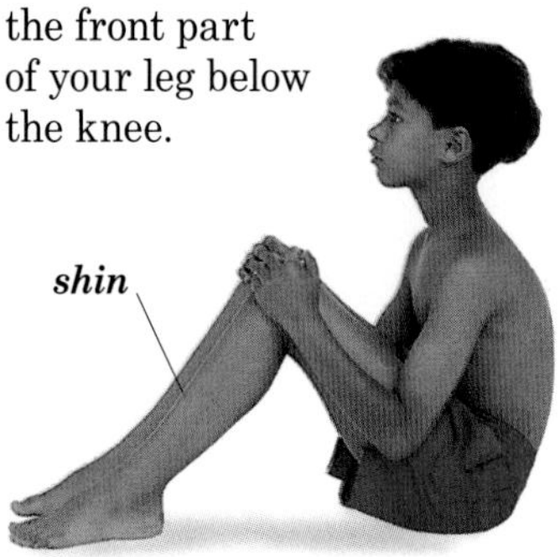

shine
shines shining shone *verb*
to give out or reflect light.

*The car headlights **shone** on the road ahead.*
shiny *adjective*

ship
ships *noun*
a large vessel for transporting people and cargo by sea. A ship is powered by a motor or sails and is bigger than a boat.

shipwreck
shipwrecks *noun*
1 the destruction of a ship at sea.
*The whole of the ship's cargo was lost in the **shipwreck**.*
2 the remains of a ship that was destroyed at sea.

■ say **ship**-rek

shirt
shirts *noun*
a piece of clothing for covering the top half of your body. Shirts have sleeves and usually have a collar and buttons down the front.

shiver
shivers shivering shivered *verb*
to tremble with cold or fear.

*He **shivered** in the cold wind.*

shock
shocks *noun*
1 an unpleasant experience.
shock *verb*
shocking *adjective*
2 pain and injury caused by a flow of electricity through a person's body.
3 a state of weakness caused by injury or pain, or by an unpleasant experience.
*He was in **shock** after the accident.*

shoe
shoes *noun*
a protective covering worn on your feet, often made of leather.

shook
*from the verb **to shake***
*The dog **shook** himself dry.*

shoot
shoots shooting shot *verb*
1 to fire a bullet from a gun or another weapon.

*She **shot** at the ducks in the fairground booth, hoping she would win a prize.*
2 to wound or kill with a bullet or other weapon.
*The hunters **shot** the birds.*
3 to take pictures with a camera.
*She **shoots** lots of animal photographs.*

shop
shops shopping shopped *verb*
to visit a store to look at and buy things.
*Let's go **shopping** today.*
shop *noun*

shore
shores *noun*
the edge of an ocean, sea, or lake.

*sea**shore***

short
adjective
1 not long in measurement.

2 not lasting a long time.
*The movie was very **short**.*
■ comparisons **shorter shortest**
■ opposite **long**
3 not having enough of something.
*We are one playing card **short**.*

shortage
shortages *noun*
a situation where there is not enough of something.
*There is a **shortage** of bread in the supermarket.*

shorten
shortens shortening shortened *verb*
to make something shorter.

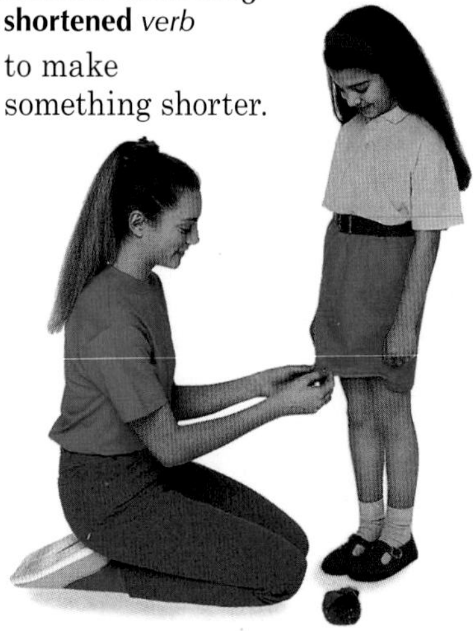

*She **shortened** the little girl's skirt for her.*

shorts
noun
a pair of short pants that usually do not reach below the knees.

shot
shots *noun*
an injection.
*The doctor gave her a **shot** to make her feel better.*

should
verb
a word used to show that something must be done, ought to be done, or is expected to happen.
*I **should** do my homework.*
■ opposite **should not / shouldn't**
■ always used with another verb

shoulder
shoulders *noun*
the place below your neck where your arms join your body.

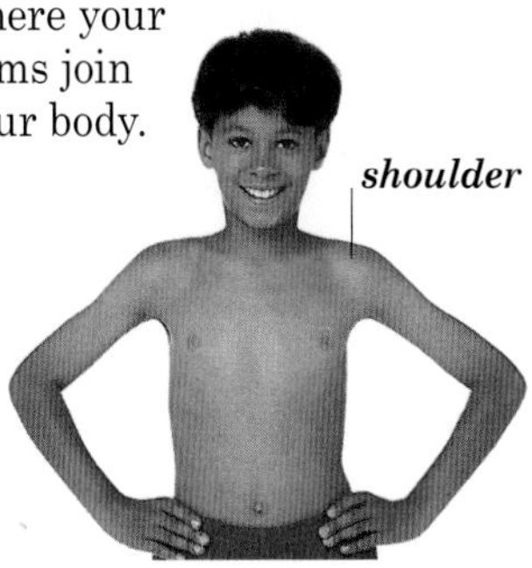

shout
shouts shouting shouted *verb*
to call out loudly.
shout *noun*

shovel
shovels *noun*
a broad spadelike tool that you use to move something, like earth or snow, by scooping it up.

show
shows showing showed *verb*
to allow something to be seen, or to make something clear to other people.

*He **showed** the class his favorite photograph in the book.*

show
shows *noun*
a public performance or exhibition.

shower
showers *noun*
1 a device that sends out a fine spray of water, used for washing your body.

2 a short, sudden rain.
3 a sudden fall of something in large quantities.
*A **shower** of meteors.*
■ rhymes with **our**
shower *verb*

shred
shreds *noun*
a small, narrow strip that has been cut or torn off something.

***shreds** of paper*

shriek
shrieks shrieking shrieked *verb*
to cry out in a high-pitched voice because you are excited or afraid.
*He **shrieked** when he saw the mouse.*
■ say **shreek**
shriek *noun*

shrill
adjective
making a sharp, high sound.
*A **shrill** whistle.*
■ comparisons **shriller shrillest**

shrink
shrinks shrinking shrank shrunk *verb*
to become smaller.

*His sweater had **shrunk** in the wash.*

shrivel
shrivels shriveling shriveled *verb*
to become small and wrinkled, or dry out.
*Water your plants or they will **shrivel** and die.*

shrub
shrubs *noun*
a large plant that is smaller than a tree, often with many stems and little or no trunk.

shrug
shrugs shrugging shrugged *verb*
to raise your shoulders to show that you do not care or do not know.

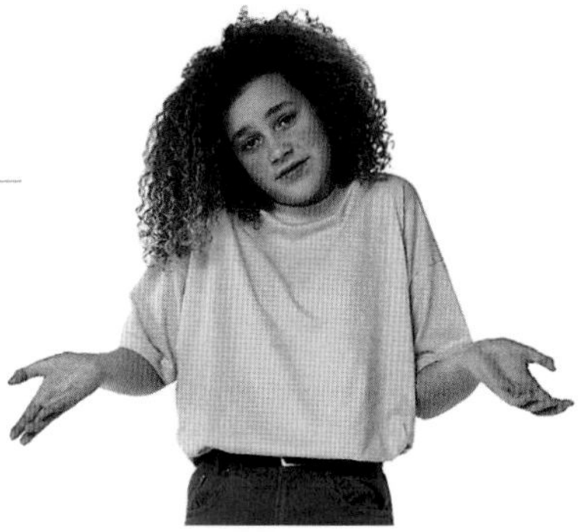

shudder
shudders shuddering shuddered *verb*
to shake or tremble violently for a short time.
*The thought of spiders makes me **shudder**.*

shuffle
shuffles shuffling shuffled *verb*
1 to mix things up to change their order.

*He **shuffled** the cards.*
2 to move by dragging your feet along the ground.

shut
shuts shutting shut *verb*
to close something.
*He **shut** the book carefully.*
■ opposite **open**
shut *adjective*

shutter
shutters *noun*
1 a hard cover for a window.

*The house has **shutters** on every window.*
2 the part of a camera inside the lens that opens and closes to allow light to fall onto the film.

shy
adjective
timid and lacking confidence with people.
■ comparisons **shier shiest**
shyly *adverb*

sick
adjective
ill, or not healthy.
■ comparisons **sicker sickest**

A B C D E F G H I J K L M N O P Q R S T U V W X Y Z

side
sides *noun*

1 the edge of something.
*Triangles have three **sides**.*
2 the outside surfaces of something, but not the front or back.

*A car viewed from the **side**.*
3 a team or group of people that is against another group.
*Which **side** are you on?*

sideways
adverb

toward the side or from the side.
*Crabs walk **sideways**.*

siege
sieges *noun*

the action of surrounding a place to try to force the people inside to surrender.
■ say **seej**

sieve
sieves *noun*

a container made of plastic or metal that has mesh or small holes for sorting solids from liquids, or fine grains from larger pieces.

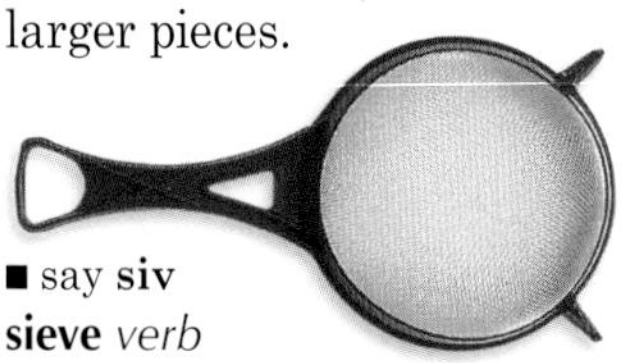

■ say **siv**
sieve *verb*

sift
sifts sifting sifted *verb*

to sort through something carefully in order to separate larger pieces from smaller pieces.

***Sifting** for gold.*

sigh
sighs sighing sighed *verb*

to let out a long, deep breath slowly.
■ say **sye**

sight
noun

1 the ability to see.
*She lost her **sight** in an accident.*
2 something that can be seen.
*The ship was a fine **sight** as it sailed up the river.*
■ say **site**

sign
signs signing signed *verb*

1 to write your signature.

*The boy **signed** his friend's cast.*
2 to use sign language to communicate with people who have hearing difficulties.
■ say **sine**

sign
signs *noun*

1 a symbol that represents something.
*The **sign** for dollar is "$."*
2 a movement that expresses a meaning.
*He nodded his head as a **sign** that he wanted to leave.*
3 a public notice that gives information.

*A road **sign**.*
4 anything that indicates something is going to happen.
*Is there any **sign** of snow?*

signal
signals *noun*

1 an action or object that is used to send a message without words.

*He put his right arm out as a **signal** that he wanted to turn right.*
2 the electrical current by which sounds and pictures are transmitted to radios, televisions, and telephones.

signature
signatures *noun*

your special way of writing your own name.

■ say **sig**-nuh-chur

significant
adjective

very important, or having a special meaning.
*A **significant** event.*

Sikh
Sikhs *noun*

a person who follows Sikhism, an Indian religion. Sikhs believe in a single God.
■ say **seek**

silent
adjective

not making any sound.
silence *noun*
silently *adverb*

silhouette
silhouettes *noun*

a dark outline of something seen against a pale background.
■ say sil-oo-**et**

silk
silks *noun*

a thin, soft fabric made from threads spun by a silkworm.

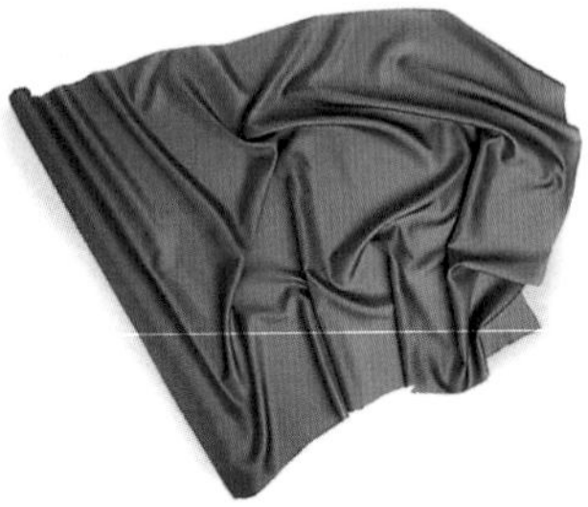

silly
adjective

not sensible.
*What a **silly** idea!*
■ comparisons **sillier silliest**

silver
noun

1 a precious metal found in the ground that is used in making coins and jewelry.

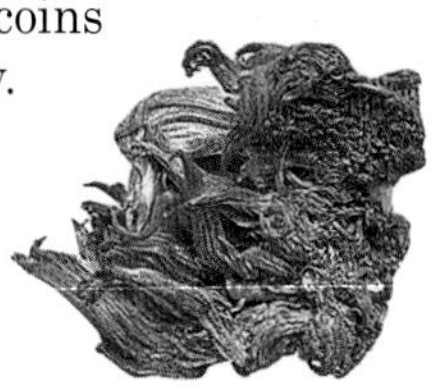

silver

***silver** ring*

2 the color of the metal silver.
silver *adjective*

similar
adjective

almost, but not exactly, the same.

*These mugs are **similar**.*

simmer
simmers simmering simmered *verb*
to cook something so that it bubbles very gently.
*Leave the soup to **simmer** for 20 minutes.*

simple
adjective
1 easy to understand or solve.
*A **simple** solution.*
■ opposite **complicated**
2 plain.

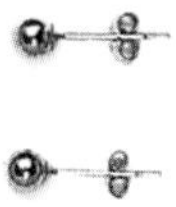
***simple** earrings*

ornate earrings

■ comparisons **simpler simplest**

simplify
simplifies simplifying simplified *verb*
to make something easier.

sincere
adjective
honest, or not pretending.
*She was **sincere** when she said she was sorry.*
■ say sin-**seer**
sincerely *adverb*

sing
sings singing sang sung *verb*
1 to make a musical sound with your voice.

*She likes to **sing**.*

2 to perform by singing.
*She is **singing** in an opera.*

single
adjective
something that is only for one person, or only one of something.

***single** bed*

sink
sinks sinking sank sunk *verb*
1 to go down below the surface of water.
*The boat was **sinking** fast.*
2 to go down slowly.
*The Sun **sank** below the horizon.*

sink
sinks *noun*
a basin with a water supply, faucets, and a drain.

*kitchen **sink***

sip
sips sipping sipped *verb*
to drink in small amounts.

*He **sipped** his coffee slowly.*
sip *noun*

siren
sirens *noun*
a device that makes a loud noise and is used as a warning signal.
*A fire engine's **siren**.*
■ say **sy**-run

sister
sisters *noun*
a female person who has the same mother and father as someone else.

sit
sits sitting sat *verb*
1 to rest your body by supporting your weight on your bottom, rather than on your feet.

2 to rest or be positioned.
3 to pose for something.
*She **sat** for her portrait.*

site
sites *noun*
an area of ground used for a particular purpose.

*A construction **site**.*

situation
situations *noun*
what is happening in a particular place at a particular time.

*He found himself in a desperate **situation**.*
■ say sich-oo-**ay**-shun

size
sizes *noun*
a measurement of how large or small something is.

*These shoes are the wrong **size**.*

sizzle
sizzles sizzling sizzled *verb*
to make a hissing sound during cooking.
*The sausages **sizzled** under the broiler.*

skate
skates skating skated *verb*
to slide along on a hard surface wearing special shoes with blades or wheels.

skating *noun* | *roller **skate***

skateboard
skateboards *noun*
a small board on wheels that people stand on to ride along.

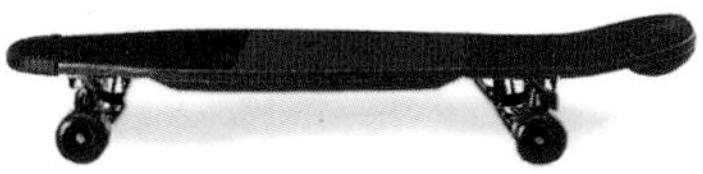

skeleton

skeletons *noun*

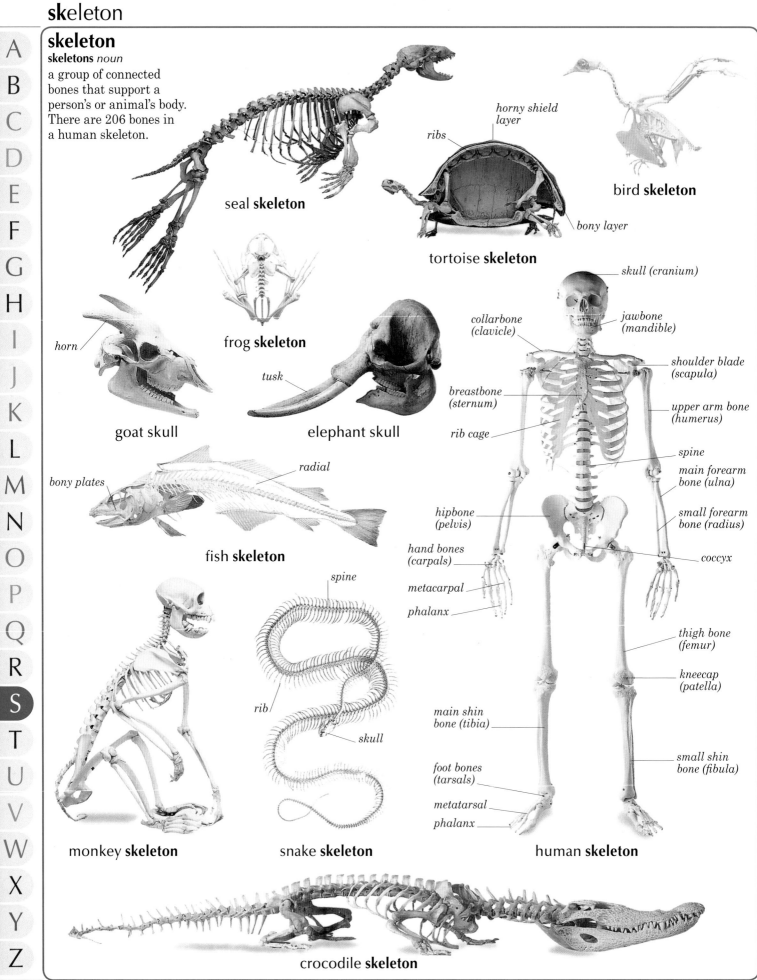

a group of connected bones that support a person's or animal's body. There are 206 bones in a human skeleton.

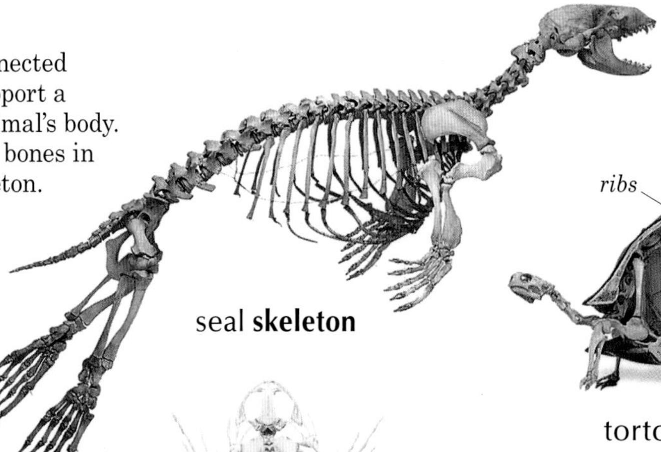

seal **skeleton**

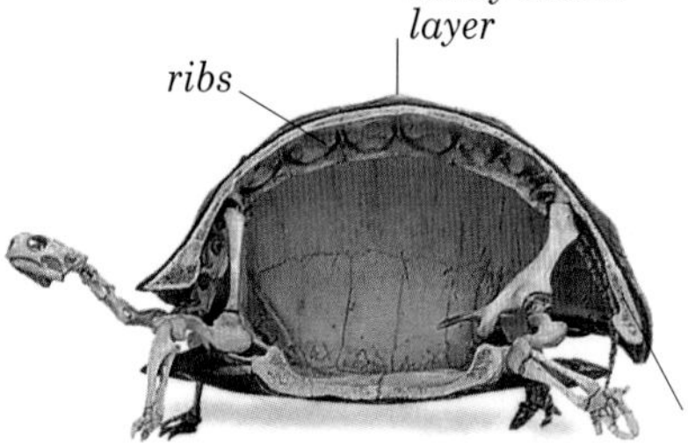

tortoise **skeleton**

bird **skeleton**

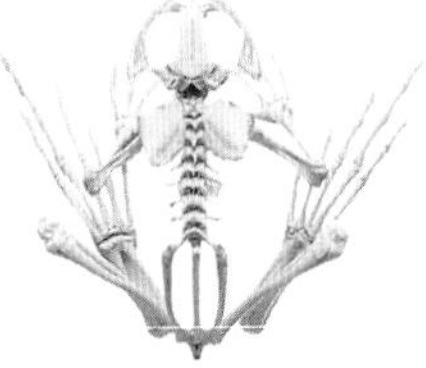

frog **skeleton**

goat skull

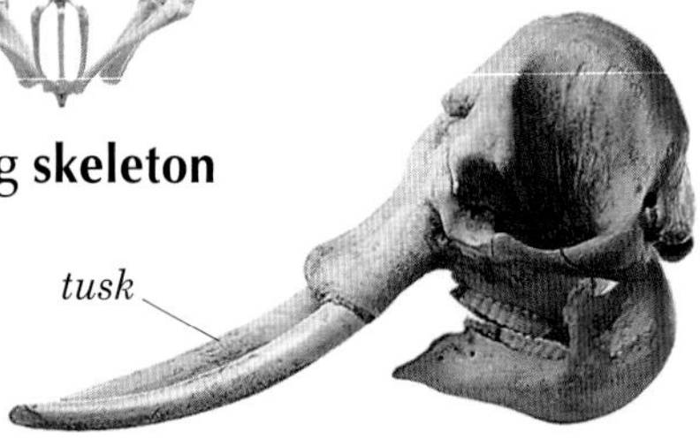

elephant skull

fish **skeleton**

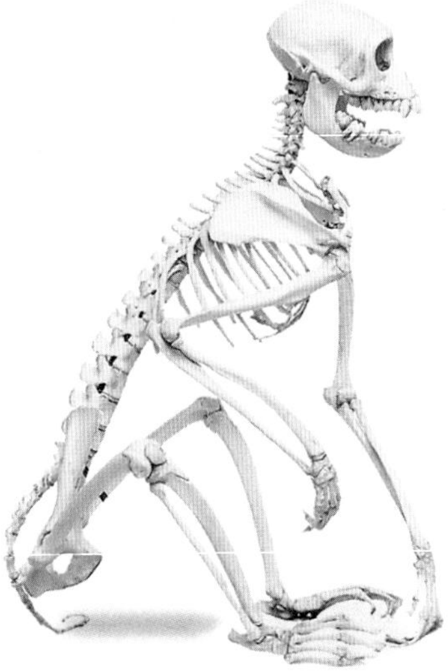

monkey **skeleton**

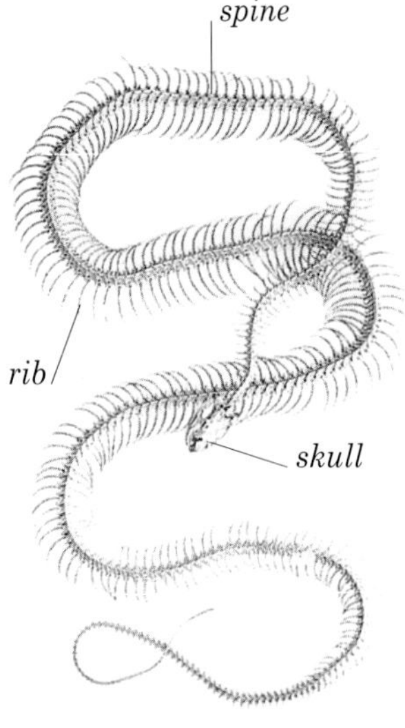

snake **skeleton**

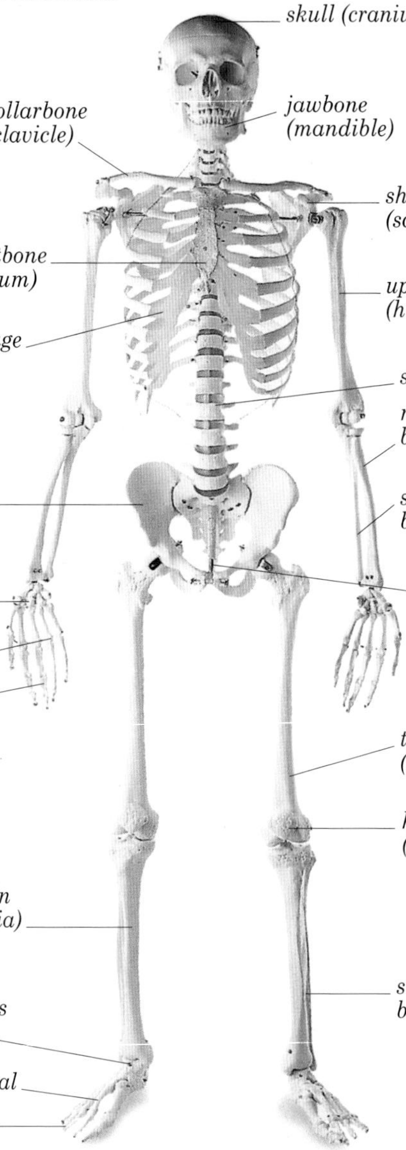

human **skeleton**

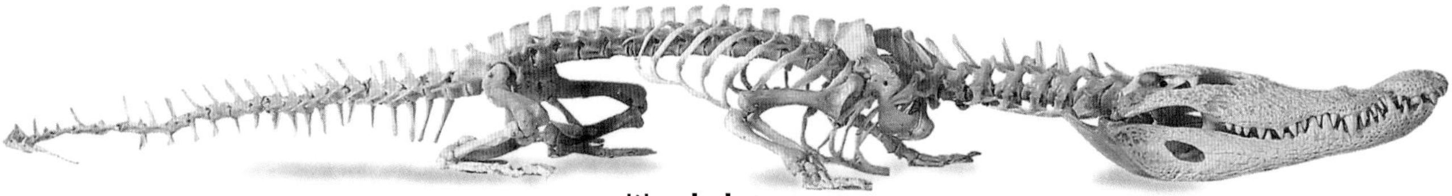

crocodile **skeleton**

sketch
sketches *noun*
1 a quick drawing.

*A **sketch** of a ship.*
2 a short play.

ski
skis skiing skied *verb*
to move over snow or ice on two long pieces of wood, metal, or plastic attached to special boots.

■ say **skee**
ski *noun*

skid
skids skidding skidded *verb*
to slide out of control.

*The car **skidded** on the icy road.*

skill
skills *noun*
an ability to do something.
*Juggling is a difficult **skill** to learn.*
skilful *adjective*

skin
skins *noun*
1 the thin, protective layer that animals and people have on the outside of their bodies (see **mammal** on page 124).
2 a thin layer that covers the flesh of vegetables and fruit (see **fruit** on page 85).

skip
skips skipping skipped *verb*
1 to move along, hopping lightly from one foot to another.
*She **skipped** down the road.*
2 to jump over a turning rope.

3 to pass over or leave something out deliberately.
*We'll **skip** the next question.*

skirt
skirts *noun*
a piece of clothing worn by a girl or woman that hangs down from the waist.

skull
skulls *noun*
the bone frame of the head that protects the brain and supports the face (see **skeleton** on page 188).

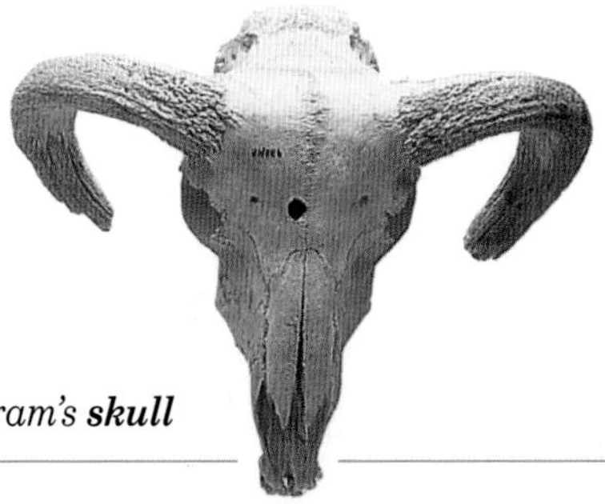

*ram's **skull***

sky
skies *noun*
the air around the Earth as we see it. The sky usually looks blue.
*Not a cloud in the **sky**.*

skyscraper
skyscrapers *noun*
a very tall building with many stories.

slam
slams slamming slammed *verb*
to shut something with a bang.
***Slam** the door.*

slang
noun
everyday words and phrases that are not normally used in writing or formal speaking.

slant
slants slanting slanted *verb*
to slope sideways.

*The wooden shelf **slanted** to the right.*

slap
slaps slapping slapped *verb*
to hit quickly with the palm of your hand.
slap *noun*

slave
slaves *noun*
someone who is forced to work without being paid and is not free to leave.

sled
sleds *noun*
a low platform with curved strips of metal or wood underneath. Sleds are used to carry people and things over snow and ice.

sleek
adjective
smooth and shiny.
*Seals have **sleek** fur.*

sleep
sleeps sleeping slept *verb*
to rest your body and mind with your eyes closed.

sleep *noun*

sleeve
sleeves *noun*
the part of a piece of clothing that covers the arm.

sleigh
sleighs *noun*
a large sled, usually pulled by an animal and used for traveling over snow or ice.

■ say **slay**

slender
adjective
long and thin.
*A **slender** branch.*

slice
slices *noun*
a thin, flat piece cut from something.

*a **slice** of bread*

slice *verb*

slide
slides sliding slid *verb*
to move smoothly over a surface.
*She **slid** across the ice on her skates.*

slide
slides *noun*
1 a piece of children's play equipment for sliding down.

2 a transparent photo in a cardboard or plastic frame.

slight
adjective
very small in amount.
*There's a **slight** chance he'll come.*
■ say **slite**
■ comparisons **slighter slightest**
slightly *adverb*

slim
adjective
fairly thin.
■ comparisons **slimmer slimmest**

slime
noun
an unpleasantly wet and slippery substance.
*Snails leave a trail of **slime** as they move along.*
slimy *adjective*

sling
slings *noun*
a piece of material used to support an injured arm.

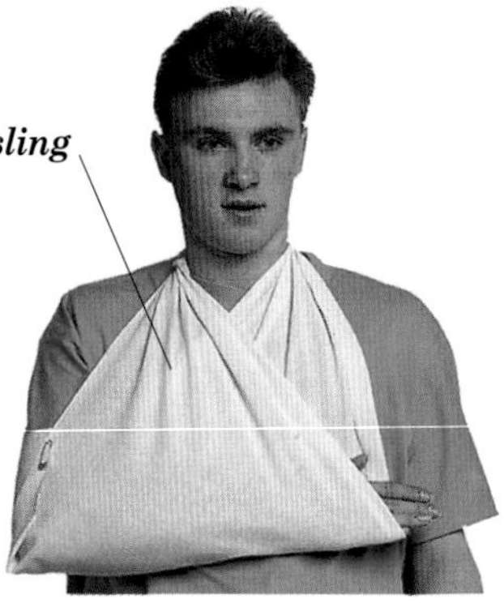

sling

slip
slips slipping slipped *verb*
1 to move, or to move something easily or quietly.
*She **slipped** the note under the door.*
2 to slide or fall over by accident.
*He **slipped** in the mud.*

slipper
slippers *noun*
a soft, comfortable, loose shoe worn indoors.

slippery
adjective
smooth and difficult to grip.
*She couldn't hold on to the **slippery** fish.*

slit
slits *noun*
a long, narrow, straight cut.
slit *verb*

slither
slithers slithering slithered *verb*
to slide along.
*Snakes **slither** over sand.*

slope
slopes *noun*
ground that slants.

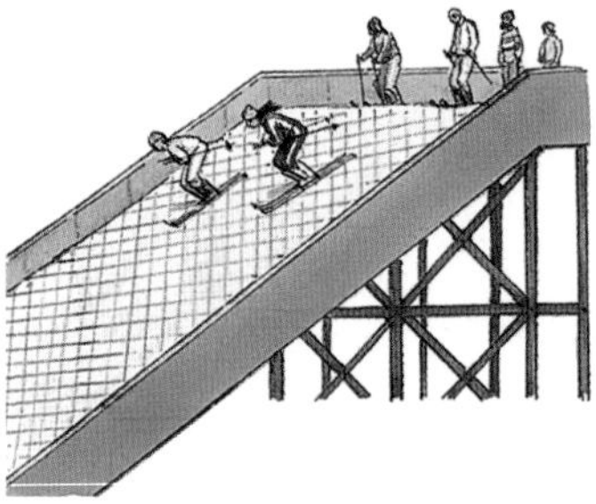

*They practiced on the artificial ski **slope**.*
slope *verb*

slot
slots *noun*
a small, narrow opening for putting something in.

*She put a coin in the **slot**.*
slot *verb*

slouch
slouches slouching slouched *verb*
to sit, stand, or walk so that your shoulders are bent over and your back is not straight.
■ rhymes with **ouch**

slow
adjective
1 taking a long time, or not hurrying.

*Tortoises are very **slow**, while rabbits move quickly.*
2 behind the time.
*This watch is 5 minutes **slow**.*
■ comparisons **slower slowest**
■ opposite **fast**
slowly *adverb*

sly
adjective
doing something in a sneaky or secretive way.
*She had a **sly** plan to trick her brother.*
■ comparisons **slier sliest**
slyly *adverb*

smack
smacks smacking smacked *verb*
to open and close your lips noisily.

small
adjective
little in size, or not great or big.

***small** can of paint* *big can of paint*
■ comparisons **smaller smallest**
■ opposite **big**

smart
adjective
1 quick and intelligent.
*A **smart** idea.*
2 well-dressed.

*He looked very **smart** in his new suit.*
■ comparisons **smarter smartest**

smash
smashes smashing smashed *verb*
to break something into pieces.

*The plates **smashed** on the ground.*

smear
smears smearing smeared *verb*
to spread something sticky or messy.

*He **smeared** glue onto the back of the picture.*
■ say **smeer**
smear *noun*

smell
smells smelling smelled
verb
1 to use your nose to notice odors.

***Smelling** a rose.*
2 to have an odor.
*The barn **smelled** of hay.*

smell
smells *noun*
1 the sense you use to notice odors through your nose.
***Smell** is one of the five senses.*
2 the odor of something, usually unpleasant.
*What a **smell**!*

smile
smiles smiling smiled *verb*
to show you are happy by widening your mouth and turning up the corners of your lips.

smile *noun*

smoke
noun
the cloud of gas and small ash particles that rises from a fire.
smoke *verb*

smolder
smolders smoldering smoldered
verb
to burn very slowly, without any flames.
■ say **smole**-dur

smooth
adjective
having an even surface, without sharp edges or lumps.
*As **smooth** as glass.*
■ opposite **rough**

smudge
smudges *noun*
a dirty mark made by rubbing or smearing something onto a surface.

*She had a **smudge** of chalk on her cheek.*
smudge *verb*

smuggle
smuggles smuggling smuggled
verb
to take something into a place secretly and illegally.

*They **smuggled** their cargo into the country under cover of darkness.*

snack
snacks *noun*
a small amount of food eaten between meals or instead of a meal.

snail
snails *noun*
a slow-moving animal with a spiral shell. Snails live on land or in water and eat mainly plants. When in danger, snails pull their soft bodies back into their shells.

snake
snakes *noun*
a long, thin reptile with no legs. Snakes eat insects, eggs, fish, or animals. Some snakes are poisonous, while others kill by squeezing their prey tightly.

*vine **snake***

snap
snaps snapping snapped *verb*
1 to make a sudden cracking noise.
***Snap** your fingers.*
2 to break suddenly.

*She **snapped** the stick in half.*
3 to talk in a quick, angry way.
*"Why haven't you done your homework?" he **snapped**.*

snarl
snarls snarling snarled *verb*
to growl fiercely, showing the teeth.
*The guard dog **snarled** at the burglar.*

snatch
snatches snatching snatched
verb
to take hold of something suddenly.
*I **snatched** my coat and ran out of the house.*

sneak
sneaks sneaking sneaked *verb*
to move or act in a quiet or secret way.

*He **sneaked** out of the room when no one was looking.*
sneaky *adjective*

sneer
sneers sneering sneered *verb*
to show scorn about something or someone.
*"My bike is better than yours," she **sneered**.*
sneer *noun*

sneeze
sneezes sneezing sneezed *verb*
to force air out of your nose in a sudden, uncontrolled way.

sneeze *noun*

sniff
sniffs sniffing sniffed *verb*
1 to breathe in noisily through your nose.
*Stop **sniffing** and blow your nose!*
2 to breathe in through your nose, trying to smell something.
*Dogs find out about things by **sniffing** them.*

snip
snips snipping snipped *verb*
to cut something with scissors in one, quick movement.

***Snipping** the top off the box.*

snore
snores snoring snored *verb*
to breathe noisily as you sleep.

snorkel
snorkels *noun*
a short tube that a swimmer holds in his or her mouth in order to breathe underwater.

snorkel
snorkels snorkeling snorkeled
verb
to swim using a snorkel.

snout
snouts *noun*
an animal's long nose and jaws (see **dinosaur** on page 61, **mammal** on page 124, and **reptile** on page 168).

snow
noun
soft, white flakes of ice that fall from the clouds in cold weather.
snow *verb*
snowy *adjective*

snowball
snowballs *noun*
a ball shape made by pressing snow together.

snowdrift
snowdrifts *noun*
snow that has been blown into a pile by the wind.

snowflake
snowflakes *noun*
a group of ice crystals that falls as a tiny piece of snow.

snowman
snowmen *noun*
a figure that you build with snow.

snowplow
snowplows *noun*
a machine used to clear snow off the roads or off other surfaces.

snowstorm
snowstorms *noun*
a storm during which a lot of snow falls.

snug
adjective
comfortable and warm.

*The cat looked very **snug** curled up inside the basket.*

snuggle
snuggles snuggling snuggled *verb*
to lie close together in order to keep warm.

soak
soaks soaking soaked *verb*
to make or become thoroughly wet.

*The rain had **soaked** her hair.*

soap
soaps *noun*
a substance used for washing.

soar
soars soaring soared *verb*
to fly high in the air.

*The eagle **soared** over the valley.*

sob
sobs sobbing sobbed *verb*
to cry noisily, catching your breath.

*The little boy was **sobbing** in the corner.*

soccer
noun
a game played with a round ball that players may move with any part of their bodies except their hands and arms. Players score by moving the ball into the other team's goal.

social
adjective
to do with people living together in communities.
***Social** history.*
■ say **so**-shul

society
societies *noun*
1 all the people who live in a group or in a country, and their way of life.
*Laws protect **society**.*
2 a club or an organization.
*An animal welfare **society**.*
■ say suh-**sy**-i-tee

sock
socks *noun*
a piece of clothing that covers your foot and the lower part of your leg.

socket
sockets *noun*
a hole that something, such as a plug or bulb, fits into.
*An electric **socket**.*

soft
adjective
1 easy to put out of shape by touching, or not firm or hard.
*A **soft** pillow.*
■ opposite **hard**
2 gentle or smooth to the touch.

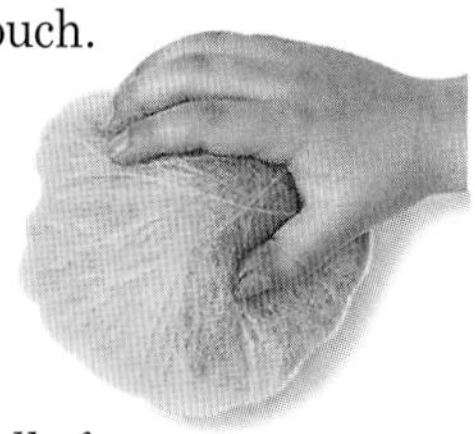

*A **soft** ball of yarn.*
■ opposite **rough**
3 not harsh or loud.
*A **soft** sound.*
■ comparisons **softer softest**

software
noun
programs that are put into a computer to make it work.

soil
soils *noun*
the top layer of earth in which plants can grow.

*You can grow some vegetables in pots of **soil**.*

solar
adjective
having to do with the power of the Sun or any other light.

*A **solar**-powered calculator.*

sold
*from the verb **to sell***
*She **sold** her bike when she grew too big for it.*

soldier
soldiers *noun*
a person who is part of an army.

*a Roman **soldier***
■ say **sole**-jur

sole
soles *noun*
1 the bottom part of your foot.

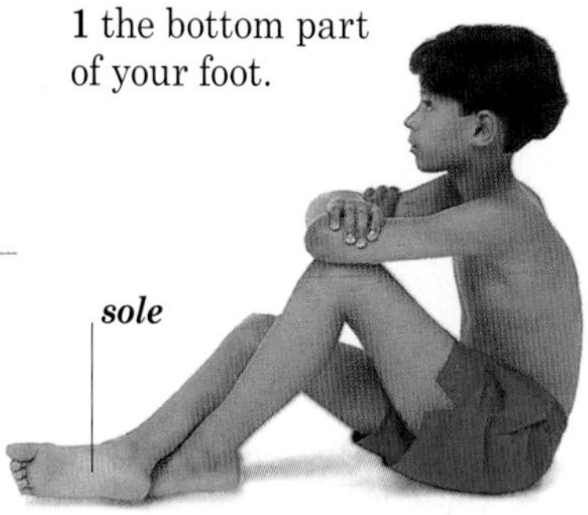

2 the bottom of a shoe.

3 an edible type of flat fish.

sole
adjective
one or only.
*He was the **sole** survivor of the crash.*

solemn
adjective
serious.
*A **solemn** promise.*
■ say **sol**-em

solid
solids *noun*
a substance that keeps its shape, and is not a liquid or a gas.
*Ice, rock, and jelly are **solids**.*

solid
adjective
1 made of the same thing all the way through.

*This cat is carved from a **solid** block of wood.*
2 firm or strongly made.
*They built a **solid** wall around the castle.*

solo
adjective
on your own.
*She made a **solo** flight around the world.*
■ say **so**-low

solo
solos *noun*
a piece of music that is played or sung by one person.

*She played a violin **solo**.*

solution
solutions *noun*
1 the answer to a problem.
*The **solution** to the crossword.*
2 a liquid that has something dissolved in it.
*A **solution** of salt and water.*
■ say suh-**loo**-shun

solve
solves solving solved *verb*
to find the answer to a problem or mystery.

*To **solve** the puzzle you must end up with one marble in the middle.*

some
adjective
1 several or a few, but not a definite number or amount.
*Could you buy **some** apples, please?*
2 part of, but not all.
*I ate **some** cake.*
◆ ***Some**body has taken my ruler.*
◆ *I must get there **some**how.*
◆ *Will **some**one set the table please.*
◆ *Let's get **some**thing to eat.*
◆ ***Some**times I go to the swimming pool after school.*
◆ *You must have put it **some**where.*

somersault
somersaults somersaulting somersaulted *verb*
to roll or leap forward or backward so that your whole body turns over.

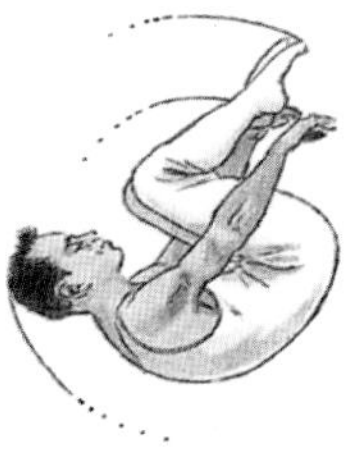

■ say **summer**-salt
somersault *noun*

son
sons *noun*
a person's male child.
■ say **sun**

sonar
noun
a device that finds and records the depth of water. Sonar works by sending out sound waves and measuring how long it takes for the echo to return. Submarines use sonar to navigate at sea.

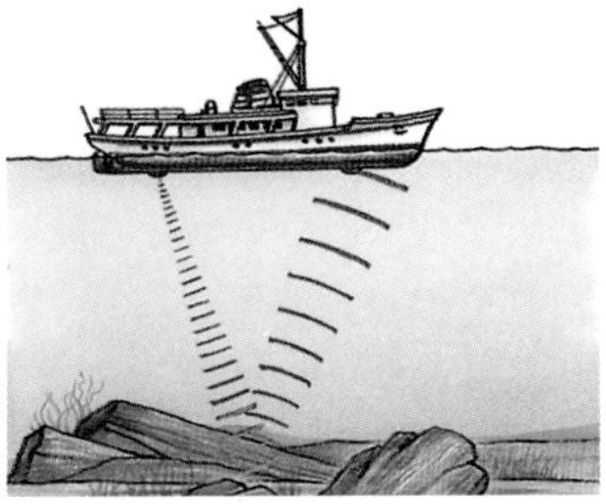

■ say **so**-nar

song
songs *noun*
a piece of music with words that you sing.

soon
adverb
after a short time.
*It will **soon** be lunchtime.*

sore
adjective
aching or hurting.

*His head was **sore** where he had bumped it.*
■ comparisons **sorer sorest**

sorry
adjective
feeling sad or unhappy about what has happened.
*I am **sorry** that I stepped on your toe.*
■ comparisons **sorrier sorriest**
■ opposite **pleased**

sort
sorts *noun*
a group of similar things, or a type of something.
*What **sort** of vacation will you take this year?*

sort
sorts sorting sorted *verb*
to arrange things into different types or groups.

*He **sorted** the socks and put them in pairs.*

sought
*from the verb **to seek***
*The two countries **sought** peace.*
■ say **sawt**

soul
souls *noun*
the spiritual part of a person. Some people believe that the soul continues after a person's body is dead.

sound
sounds *noun*
something that can be heard.

soup
soups *noun*
a liquid food made from fish, meat, or vegetables, cooked in water or milk.

*vegetable **soup***
■ say **soop**

sour
adjective
with a sharp taste, like vinegar or a lemon.
■ rhymes with **power**

source
sources *noun*
the place where something comes from or is found.
*The **source** of a river.*

south
noun
one of the four main directions on a compass. South is to your right when you are facing the rising Sun.

north
west

east
south

southern *adjective*

souvenir
souvenirs *noun*
something that you keep to remind you of a person, place, or event.
*Holiday **souvenirs**.*
■ say soo-vuh-**neer**

sow
sows sowing sowed sown *verb*
to put seeds in the soil so that they will grow into plants.

*She **sowed** some seeds in a window box.*
■ say **so**

soybean
noun
a vegetable seed used for food or crushed for its oil.

space
noun
1 the place where all the stars and planets are found.
2 an empty area or gap.

spacecraft
spacecrafts *noun*
a vehicle for traveling in space.

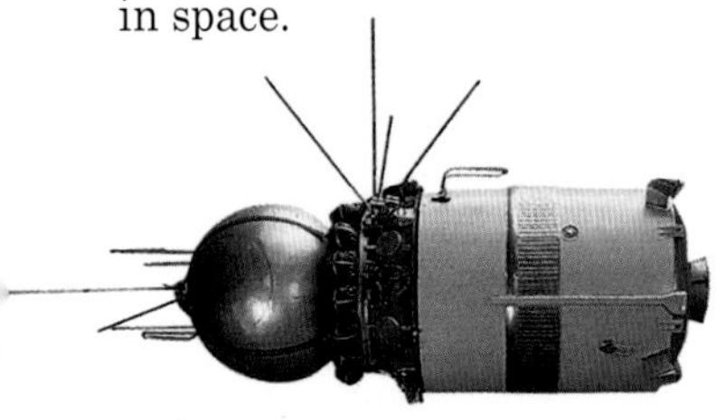

Vostok 1 *was the first manned* ***spacecraft****.*

spade
spades *noun*
a shovel or tool that is used for digging.

spaghetti
noun
a type of long, thin pasta.

■ say spu-**get**-ee

span
spans *noun*
1 a period of time.
2 the distance between two objects.

spare
adjective
more than is needed.

spare *tire*

spark
sparks *noun*
a small, burning piece of material that is thrown up from a fire.

sparkle
sparkles sparkling sparkled *verb*
to reflect tiny flashes of bright light.

Diamonds ***sparkle****.*
sparkling *adjective*

speak
speaks speaking spoke spoken *verb*
to say words, or to talk.

spear
spears *noun*
a long weapon with a sharp point that is thrown by hand.

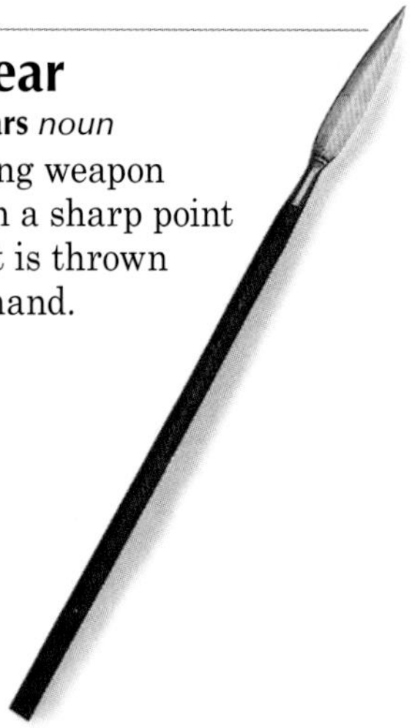

special
adjective
different from the rest, usually because it is better.
■ say **spesh**-ul
■ opposite **ordinary**

species
species *noun*
a group of animals or plants that usually look similar or behave in a similar way.
There are about 320 ***species*** *of salamander in the world.*
■ say **spee**-sheez

specific
adjective
definite or precise.
Can you be more ***specific****?*
■ say spi-**sif**-ik

speck
specks *noun*
a very small piece or spot.
A ***speck*** *of dust.*

speckled
adjective
covered with tiny marks or spots.

A ***speckled*** *egg.*

spectator
spectators *noun*
a person who watches an event but does not take part.

The ***spectators*** *cheered for their favorite team.*

speech
speeches *noun*
1 the ability to speak and the way people speak.
Speech *is a power only humans have.*
2 a talk given to an audience.

speed
speeds *noun*
a measurement of how fast something is moving.

spell
spells spelling spelled or **spelt** *verb*
to say or write the letters of a word in the correct order.
How do you ***spell*** *"special"?*

spell
spells *noun*
words that are supposed to have a magic power.
The magician cast a ***spell*** *on the frog.*

spend
spends spending spent *verb*
1 to use money to buy things.
I ***spent*** *my money on a book.*
2 to pass time.
We ***spent*** *two weeks camping in the forest.*

sphere
spheres *noun*
a solid, round shape, like a ball (see **shape** on page 182).
■ say **sfeer**

spice
spices *noun*
a substance made from dried parts of a plant and used to add flavor to food.

cayenne pepper

paprika

cinnamon stick

spicy
adjective
strongly flavored with spice.

A B C D E F G H I J K L M N O P Q R S T U V W X Y Z

spider
spiders *noun*
a small animal with eight legs. Spiders spin nets of thin, sticky threads called webs, which they use to trap insects for food. They kill their prey with poison.

spike
spikes *noun*
a sharp point, often made of metal or wood, or a pointed part of an animal or plant.

spill
spills spilling spilled or **spilt** *verb*
to let something drop or overflow from a container.

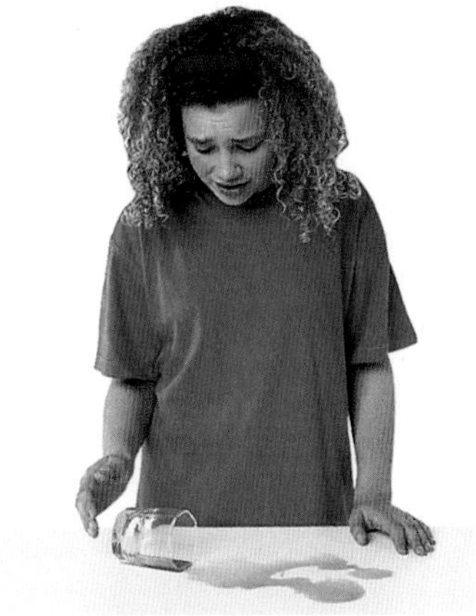

*She **spilled** her drink.*

spin
spins spinning spun *verb*
1 to turn around quickly, or to make something turn quickly.

2 to produce threads. Spiders and silkworms spin threads by producing them from their bodies. People spin raw cotton and wool to make threads.

spine
spines *noun*
1 the column of bones that makes up the backbone of a skeleton (see **skeleton** on page 188).

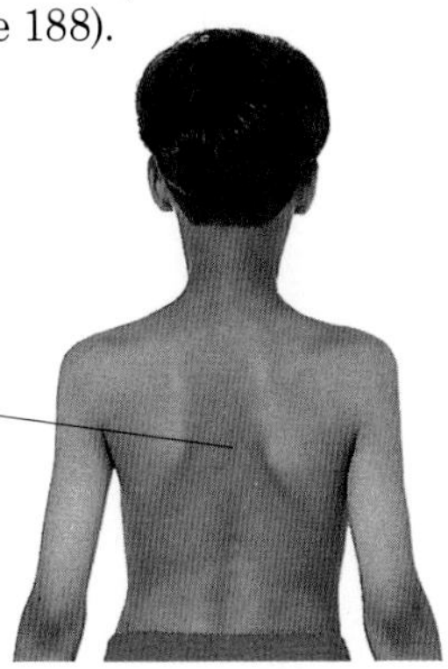

spine

2 one of the stiff, sharp points on an animal, like a porcupine, or on a plant, like a cactus (see **fish** on page 79, **plant** on page 151, and **sea life** on page 178).
3 the part of a book where the pages are joined and that holds the book together.

spiral
spirals *noun*
an object shaped in a curve that turns around a central point.

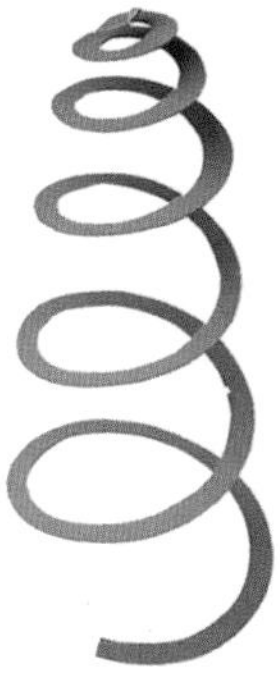

spire
spires *noun*
a tall, pointed structure at the top of a tower.

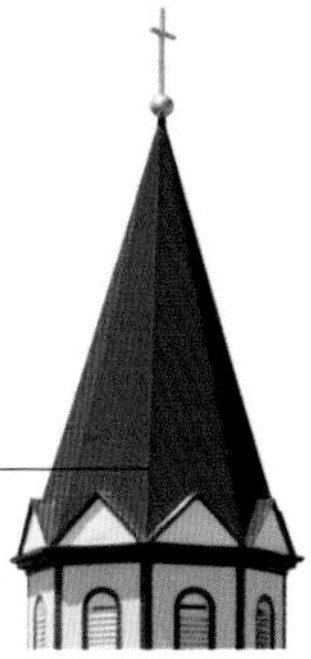

*church **spire***

spirit
spirits *noun*
1 a person's mind and feelings.
*In good **spirits**.*
spiritual *adjective*
2 a being, such as a ghost, that does not have a body.

spit
spits spitting spat *verb*
to force saliva or something else out of your mouth.
*She **spat** out the rotten apple.*

spite
noun
deliberate nastiness.
*He ignored him out of **spite**.*
spiteful *adjective*

splash
splashes splashing splashed *verb*
to scatter water or another liquid.

*The children **splashed** around in the pool.*
splash *noun*

splinter
splinters *noun*
a thin, sharp piece that has broken off something hard, such as wood or glass.

split
splits splitting split *verb*
1 to divide into parts.

*She **split** the logs with an ax.*
2 to tear or crack, perhaps by mistake.
*The bag **split** open.*

splutter
splutters spluttering spluttered *verb*
to speak quickly in a confused way.
*She knocked over the display and **spluttered** an apology.*

spoil
spoils spoiling spoiled *verb*
1 to destroy or damage something.
*Don't draw on that—you'll **spoil** it.*
2 to give a child so much that he or she becomes demanding and unpleasant.

spoke
*from the verb **to speak***
*They **spoke** in a whisper in case anyone was listening.*

sponge
sponges *noun*
a soft, flexible material used for washing and cleaning. Some sponges are made of plastic, but real sponges are made from the skeletons of sea creatures.
■ say **spunj**

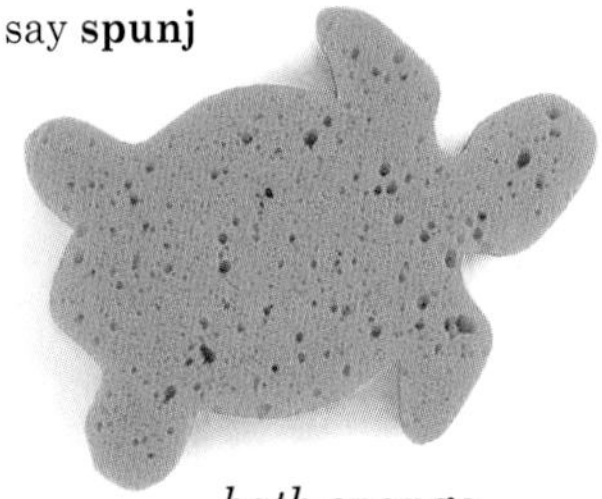

*bath **sponge***

sponsor
sponsors sponsoring sponsored *verb*
to give money to support a charity or event. Sometimes money is given in return for a person completing an activity.
*The sporting goods store **sponsored** the race.*
sponsor *noun*

spoon
spoons *noun*
a small utensil with a curved bowl at one end. Spoons are used for eating or stirring.

*plastic **spoon***

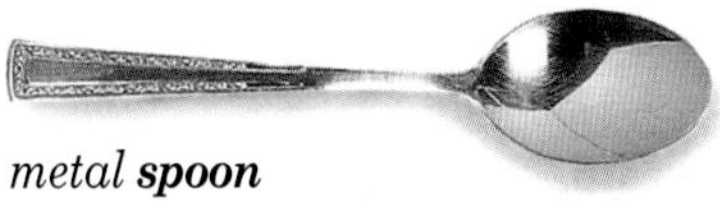

*metal **spoon***

sport

sports *noun*

an activity or game that requires physical effort or skill. People play sports for exercise or pleasure.

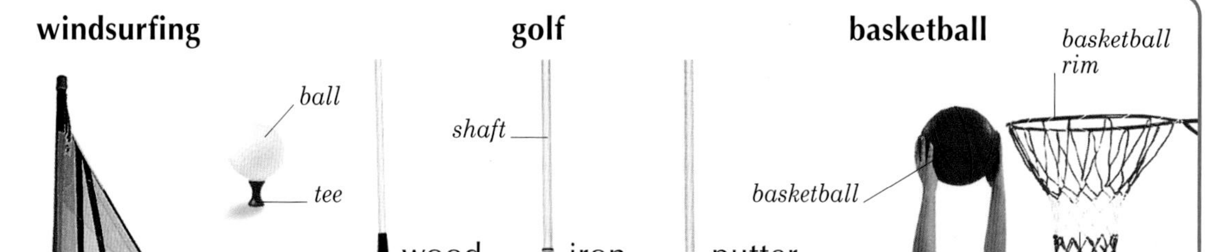

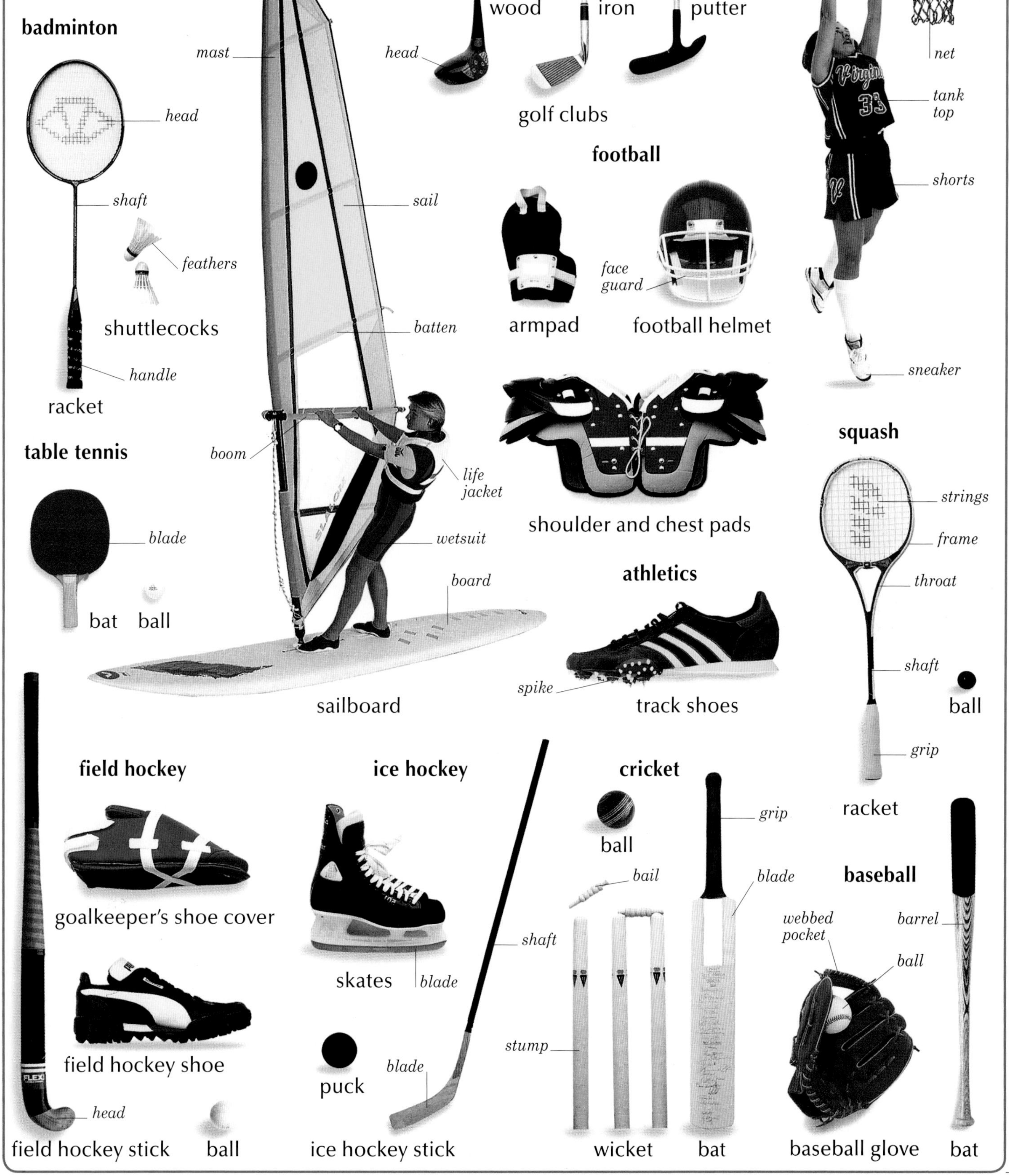

a b c d e f g h i j k l m n o p q r s t u v w x y z

A B C D E F G H I J K L M N O P Q R S T U V W X Y Z

spot
spots *noun*
1 a small, round area that is a different color from the area around it.
This cup and saucer are covered in white ***spots****.*
2 a place.
It was a perfect picnic ***spot****.*

spot
spots spotting spotted *verb*
to notice or see.
Can you ***spot*** *my car?*

spotlight
spotlights *noun*
a strong light pointed at a small area, usually on a stage.

spout
spouts *noun*
the part of a container that a liquid is poured from.

teapot ***spout***

spray
sprays spraying sprayed *verb*
to scatter a fine shower of liquid onto something.

He ***sprayed*** *the plant with water.*
spray *noun*

spread
spreads spreading spread *verb*
to open something out or make it cover a bigger area.

He ***spread*** *the blanket out on the ground.*
■ say **spred**

spring
springs *noun*
1 the season between winter and summer when the weather becomes warmer and many plants start to grow.
2 a coil of thin metal that jumps back into shape after it has been pressed together or pulled apart.

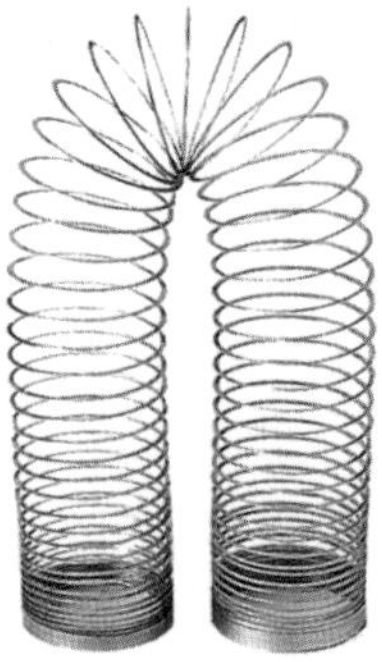

3 a place where water flows out of the ground.

spring
springs springing sprang sprung *verb*
1 to jump upward in a lively way.

She ***sprang*** *over the gymnastic apparatus.*
spring *noun*
2 to appear or grow quickly.
New houses ***sprang*** *up all over the hillside.*

sprint
sprints sprinting sprinted *verb*
to run very fast for a short distance.

sprint *noun*

sprout
sprouts sprouting sprouted *verb*
to begin to grow.

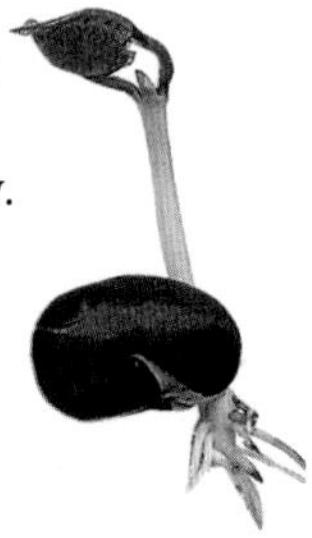

Green shoots ***sprouted*** *from the bean.*
sprout *noun*

spy
spies *noun*
a person who gathers information in secret.
spy *verb*

square
squares *noun*
a shape with four equal sides and four right angles (see **shape** on page 182).
square *adjective*

squash
squashes squashing squashed *verb*
1 to crush something so that it becomes flat.
2 to squeeze together.

We all ***squashed*** *onto the sofa.*
■ say **skwosh**

squeak
squeaks squeaking squeaked *verb*
to make a short, high-pitched sound like a mouse.
squeak *noun*

squeal
squeals squealing squealed *verb*
to make a long, high-pitched sound like a piglet.
squeal *noun*

squeeze
squeezes squeezing squeezed *verb*
to press hard, often in order to push something out.

She ***squeezed*** *the paint out of the tube.*

squirm
squirms squirming squirmed *verb*
to twist the body from side to side, or to wriggle.
The rabbit ***squirmed*** *under the fence.*
■ say **skwurm**

squirrel
squirrels *noun*
a small, furry rodent. Some types of squirrel live in trees, while others live on the ground. Squirrels eat nuts, berries, fruits, and insects.

squirt
squirts squirting squirted *verb*
to shoot out a thin jet of liquid.

*He **squirted** the dishwashing liquid into the bowl.*
■ rhymes with **dirt**

stab
stabs stabbing stabbed *verb*
to pierce or wound with a knife or other pointed object.
*She **stabbed** the potato with a fork to see if it was cooked.*

stable
stables *noun*
a building where horses or other animals are kept.

*a **stable** for horses*

stack
stacks *noun*
a pile of things, one on top of another.

*A **stack** of plates.*
stack *verb*

stadium
stadiums or **stadia** *noun*
a sports ground surrounded by seats for spectators.

staff
noun
a group of people who work together in a business, school, or other organization.

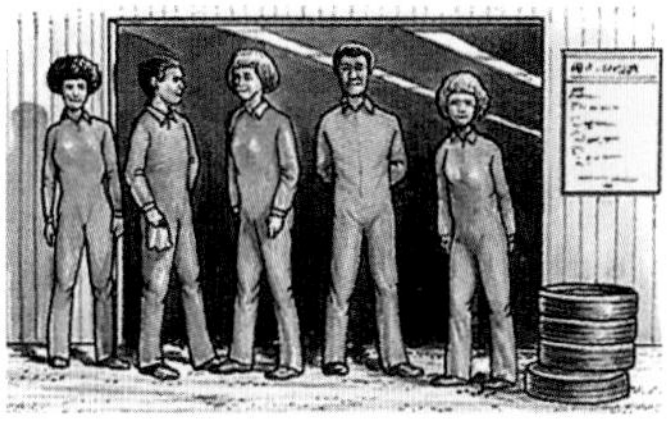

*The **staff** at the garage wear uniforms.*

stag
stags *noun*
a male deer, especially a red deer that is over four years old.

stage
stages *noun*
1 a platform used for plays and other performances.
2 a point reached in the progress of something.
*They made the long journey in several **stages**.*

stagger
staggers staggering staggered *verb*
to walk in an unsteady way.
*They **staggered** home after the long walk.*

stain
stains *noun*
a dirty mark that is difficult to remove.

*coffee **stain***
stain *verb*

stair
stairs *noun*
one of a series of steps, set one after the other.

*A flight of **stairs**.*

stalactite
stalactites *noun*
a spike of rock that is formed from dripping water and hangs down from the roof of a cave.
■ say stuk-**lak**-tite

stalagmite
stalagmites *noun*
a spike of rock that is formed by dripping water and builds up on the floor of a cave.
■ say stu-**lag**-mite

stale
adjective
no longer fresh.
***Stale** bread is hard and dry.*

stalk
stalks *noun*
1 the stem of a plant or a leaf (see **plant** on page 151).
2 a long, thin part of an animal (see **sea life** on page 178).

*leaf **stalk***

stall
stalls *noun*
1 an area divided off in a stable or barn for one animal.

2 a table used to display and sell goods, usually at a market.

■ rhymes with **call**

stall
stalls stalling stalled *verb*
to come to a stop suddenly, without meaning to.
*The old car **stalled** at the traffic light.*

stammer
stammers stammering stammered *verb*
to stutter or speak with difficulty, often stopping in the middle of words and repeating sounds.
stammer *noun*

stamp
stamps *noun*
a sticker you put on an envelope or package to show that you have paid for it to be delivered.

stamp
stamps stamping stamped *verb*
to bring your foot down very hard.

stamp *noun*

stand
stands standing stood *verb*
to be in an upright position.

She ***stood*** *on a box to look over the fence.*

standard
standards *noun*
a level of quality that is considered acceptable, or how good something is.
The ***standard*** *of spelling in this class is very high.*

standard
adjective
ordinary or usual.
Headlights are ***standard*** *equipment on all cars.*

stank
from the verb ***to stink***
The boat ***stank*** *of fish.*

staple
staples *noun*
a small, thin strip of metal used to join sheets of paper together.
■ say **stay**-pul

star
stars *noun*
1 an object in the sky that appears as a ball of light. The Sun is the nearest star to Earth.

2 a shape with five or more points (see **shape** on page 182).
3 a famous actor, actress, or other performer.

stare
stares staring stared *verb*
to look for a long time at something with your eyes wide open.

The cat ***stared*** *at the mouse.*

starfish
starfish *noun*
a star-shaped sea animal, usually with five arms. Starfish eat plants and sea animals, such as crabs and other shellfish. They sense things through tentacles on their arms (see **sea life** on page 178).

start
starts starting started *verb*
to begin.

The runners lined up, ready to ***start*** *the race.*
start *noun*

startle
startles startling startled *verb*
to give someone a surprise or a shock.

His son ***startled*** *him.*

starve
starves starving starved *verb*
to suffer or die from lack of food.
starvation *noun*

state
states *noun*
1 the condition of something, or what it is like.
In an untidy ***state****.*
2 a group of people under one government. A state can be a whole country or part of a country.
The United ***States*** *of America.*

state
states stating stated *verb*
to say something clearly.
statement *noun*

station
stations *noun*
1 a place where buses and trains stop so that people can get on and off.
2 a building used by a public service, such as the police.
A police ***station****.*
■ say **stay**-shun

statue
statues *noun*
a figure of a person or animal made from stone, wood, or another hard material.

Statue *of Liberty*

■ say **stach**-oo

stay
stays staying stayed *verb*
1 to remain in one place.
Dad ***stayed*** *at home while we went to the show.*
2 to live somewhere for a short time.
I went to ***stay*** *with my cousin during the summer vacation.*
3 to continue to be in one state.
It ***stayed*** *sunny all week.*

steady
adjective
1 firm.
He held the ladder ***steady****.*
2 continuous or unchanging.
A ***steady*** *fall of snow.*

■ say **sted**-ee
■ comparisons **steadier steadiest**
steadily *adverb*

steak
steaks *noun*
a thick slice of fish or meat, usually beef.
■ say **stake**

steal
steals stealing stole stolen *verb*
to take something that does not belong to you without the owner's permission.

*Magpies **steal** shiny things.*

steam
noun
the gas that water turns into when it boils. Steam can be used as a source of power.

steel
noun
a hard, strong metal made from iron mixed with a small amount of carbon. Steel can also be combined with other metals. Stainless steel is a mixture of steel, chromium, and nickel.

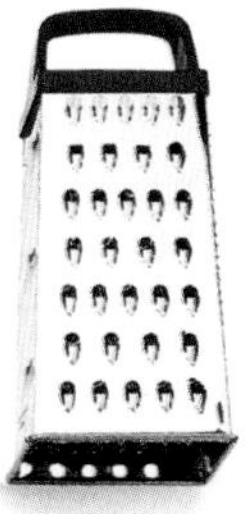

grater

hand whisk

*Many kitchen utensils are made of **steel**.*

steep
adjective
slanting up or down sharply.
*A **steep** hill.*
■ comparisons **steeper steepest**

steer
steers steering steered *verb*
to control the direction something is going in.
*She **steered** her car into the driveway.*

stem
stems *noun*
the main stalk of a plant that grows up out of the soil (see **growth** on page 94 and **plant** on page 151).

step
steps *noun*
1 the movement made by lifting your foot and putting it down when you walk along or dance.
step *verb*
2 a level surface for putting your foot on to help you climb up or down, usually as part of a staircase or ladder.

3 a stage in a series of things to do.
*The first **step** in learning to swim is to enjoy being in the water.*

stepladder
stepladders *noun*
a portable ladder with flat steps that can stand up without leaning on anything.

stereo
stereos *noun*
equipment for playing recorded sound. The sound comes from two different directions so that it sounds natural.
■ say **stair**-ee-oh
stereo *adjective*

stern
adjective
firm or strict.
*A **stern** warning.*

stern
noun
the back part of a ship or boat (see **boat** on page 31).

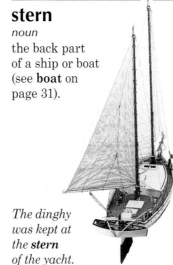

*The dinghy was kept at the **stern** of the yacht.*

stethoscope
stethoscopes *noun*
an instrument used by doctors for listening to the heart and lungs.

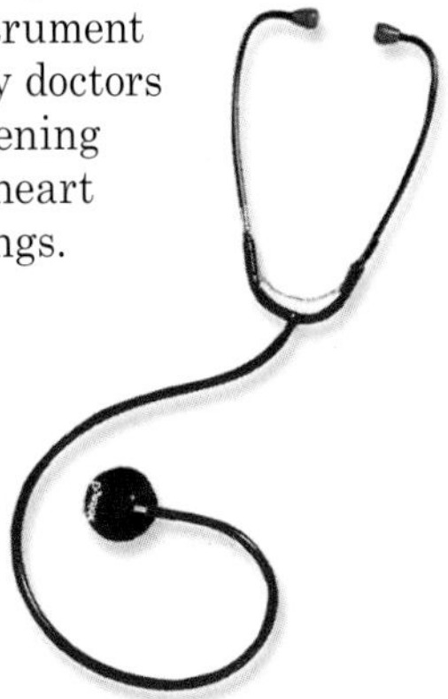

stick
sticks *noun*
1 a thin piece of wood.
2 something long and thin.
*A **stick** of chalk.*

stick
sticks sticking stuck *verb*
1 to glue or fasten one thing to another.
*She **stuck** the model airplane together with glue.*
sticky *adjective*
2 to press a sharp point into something.
*He **stuck** a pin into the balloon.*
3 to project out.

*The bread **stuck** out of the basket.*

stiff
adjective
not easy to bend or move.

*This folder is made of **stiff** plastic cardboard.*
■ comparisons **stiffer stiffest**

still
adverb
1 up until now.
*He is **still** there.*
2 even so, or nevertheless.
*I don't like rice pudding, but I **still** have to eat it.*
3 an even larger amount.
***Still** more snow fell.*

still
adjective
not moving or without sound.

stilt
stilts *noun*
one of a pair or set of long poles used to support a person or thing high off the ground.

*pair of **stilts***

A B C D E F G H I J K L M N O P Q R S T U V W X Y Z

sting
stings stinging stung *verb*
to prick the skin, or to cause a sharp pain. Some insects sting when they are frightened or angry, injecting a poison into the skin.

stink
stinks stinking stank stunk *verb*
to have a strong, bad smell.
*This garbage **stinks**!*
stink *noun*

stir
stirs stirring stirred *verb*
to mix something by moving it around with a spoon or similar tool.

stitch
stitches *noun*
a loop of thread or wool made with a needle in sewing or knitting.

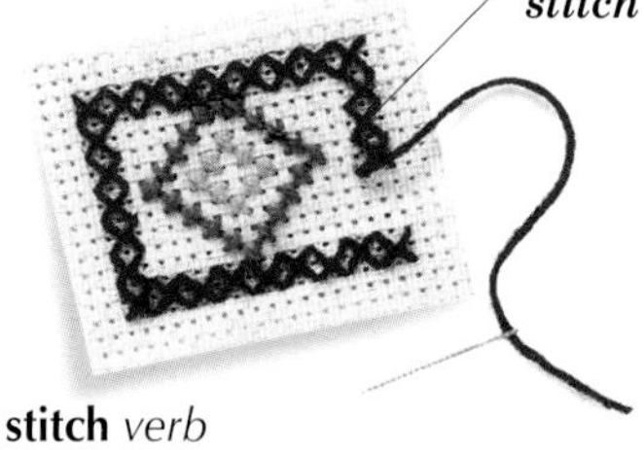

stitch *verb*

stock
stocks stocking stocked *verb*
to keep a supply of something.
*Do you **stock** writing paper in this store?*
stock *noun*

stolen
*from the verb **to steal***
*A painting was **stolen** from the gallery.*

stomach
stomachs *noun*
1 the part of your body where food goes after you have eaten it, to be partly digested.

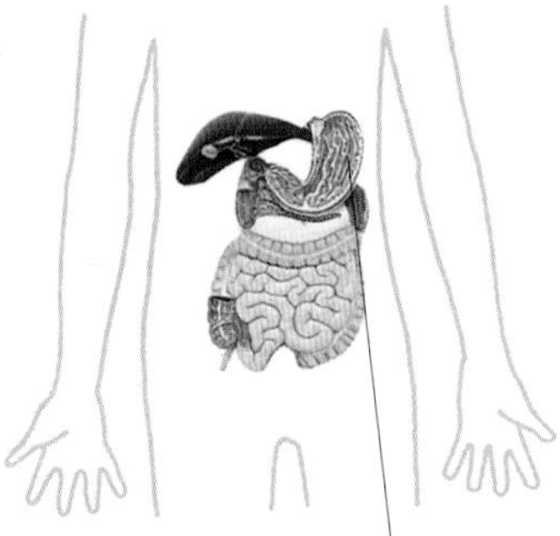

2 the outside part of your body at the front between your ribs and your hips.
■ say **stum**-ik

stone
stones *noun*
1 the hard material that rocks are made of.

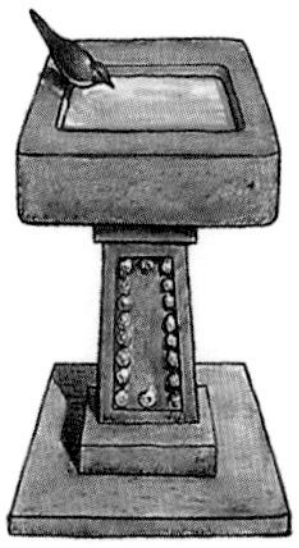

*A bird table made of **stone**.*

2 a small, loose piece of rock.

*The field was full of **stones**.*

stood
*from the verb **to stand***
*They **stood** at the bus stop for an hour.*

stool
stools *noun*
a seat without a back or arms.

*kitchen **stool***

stop
stops stopping stopped *verb*
1 to come, or bring, to an end.
*The rain **stopped**.*
2 to prevent something from happening.

*The man **stopped** the boy from running into the road.*

stopwatch
stopwatches *noun*
a watch that can be started and stopped to measure how much time something takes (see **time** on page 216).

store
stores storing stored *verb*
to put something away for when you need it.

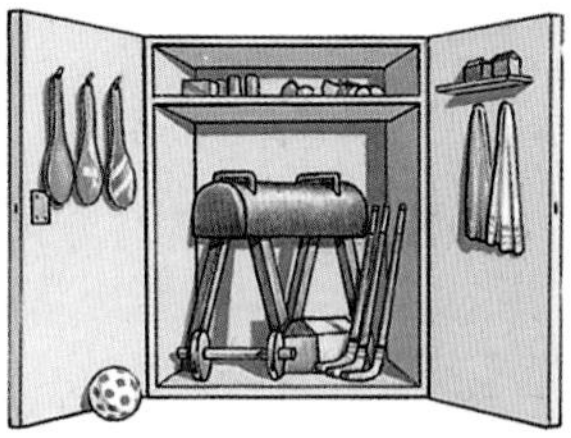

*They **stored** the sports equipment in the cupboard.*

store
stores *noun*
a large shop or warehouse.
*A department **store**.*

stork
storks *noun*
a large bird with a long beak and long legs that lives near shallow water. Storks eat fish, insects, rodents, and snakes. They live in large nests built in trees and on cliffs.

marabou ***stork***

storm
storms *noun*
a period of bad weather with strong winds and thunder and lightning, or snow.

story
stories *noun*
a tale, or a description of an event, either real or imaginary.
*Tell me a **story**.*

stove
stoves *noun*
a piece of equipment used for cooking or heating.

straight
adjective
not bent or curved.

*She drew a **straight** line.*
■ say **strate**
■ comparisons **straighter straightest**

strain
strains straining strained *verb*
1 to try so hard that it hurts or tires you.
*Be careful not to **strain** yourself when you exercise.*
strain *noun*
2 to pass something through a sieve in order to filter out larger pieces.

strand
strands *noun*
1 any thread that is twisted together with others to make a stronger line.
2 anything that looks like a rope or string.
*A **strand** of hair.*

stranded
adjective
unable to leave somewhere.

*He was left **stranded** on the island.*

strange
adjective
unusual or unfamiliar.
■ comparisons **stranger strangest**

stranger
strangers *noun*
a person you have not seen before or who is new to a place.

strap
straps *noun*
a strip of leather or other material, used for fastening or holding things.

*shoulder **strap***

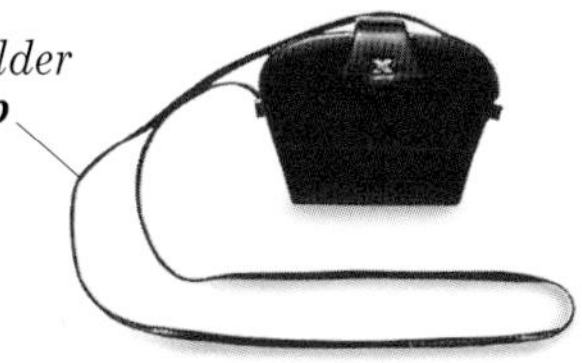

strawberry
strawberries *noun*
a small, red fruit that is soft and sweet and grows on a plant.

stray
strays straying strayed *verb*
to wander away from someone or somewhere.

*One duckling **strayed** from its mother.*

streak
streaks *noun*
a long, thin mark or smear.
*After the football game his clothes were covered with **streaks** of mud.*

stream
streams *noun*
1 a small river.

2 a steady flow of something.
*A **stream** of cars rushed along the street.*

straw
straws *noun*
1 stalks of dried wheat or other cereal plants. Straw is used for farm animals and pets to lie on.

2 a hollow tube used for drinking liquids through.

streamlined
adjective
having a smooth shape that allows quick and easy movement through air or water.

*This cycling helmet has a **streamlined** shape.*
streamline *verb*

street
streets *noun*
a road in a city or town.
*What is the name of the **street** you live in?*

strength
strengths *noun*
the quality of being strong or powerful.

*The weight lifter had incredible **strength** in his arms.*

strengthen
strengthens strengthening strengthened *verb*
to make something strong or stronger.
*You can **strengthen** your muscles by exercising.*

stress
stresses *noun*
1 a strain on a person or thing.
*He is under a lot of **stress**.*
2 an extra force laid on part of a word when speaking. In the word "stretcher," the stress is on the first syllable.

stretch
stretches stretching stretched
verb
1 to pull something so that it becomes longer or bigger.
2 to straighten or reach out as much as you can with part of your body.

*She **stretched** out her arms.*

3 to reach one place from another.

*The road **stretches** all the way to the mountains.*

stretcher
stretchers *noun*
a light bed with handles that is used to carry someone who is hurt.

strict
adjective
keeping closely to the rules.
*The teacher was very **strict**.*
■ comparisons **stricter strictest**

a b c d e f g h i j k l m n o p q r s t u v w x y z

A B C D E F G H I J K L M N O P Q R S T U V W X Y Z

stride
strides striding strode *verb*
to walk with long steps.

stride *noun*

strike
strikes *noun*
the action of stopping work in order to get better pay and working conditions, or to protest about something.
On ***strike****.*

strike
strikes striking struck *verb*
1 to hit something hard.

The tree was ***struck*** *by lightning.*
2 to stop work in order to protest about something.

string
strings *noun*
a long, narrow cord used for fastening or as part of a musical instrument (see **musical instrument** on page 133).

strip
strips *noun*
a long, narrow piece of something.
A ***strip*** *of paper.*

stripe
stripes *noun*
a long, narrow band of color.

This swimsuit has blue ***stripes****.*
striped *adjective*

stroke
strokes stroking stroked *verb*
to rub gently with the hand.

He ***stroked*** *the rabbit.*

stroll
strolls strolling strolled *verb*
to walk slowly in a relaxed way.
They ***strolled*** *through the woods.*
stroll *noun*

strong
adjective
1 tough.
A ***strong*** *rope.*
2 powerful.
Elephants are very ***strong****.*
■ comparisons **stronger strongest**
■ opposite **weak**

structure
structures *noun*
1 something that has been built.

The Eiffel Tower is a tall, steel ***structure****.*
2 the way that something is put together or organized.
A company's ***structure****.*

struggle
struggles struggling struggled *verb*
to try hard, or to fight hard.
He ***struggled*** *with the math problem for a long time.*

stubborn
adjective
determined to have your own way.

A ***stubborn*** *mule.*
■ say **stub**-urn

stuck
from the verb ***to stick***
1 *I* ***stuck*** *the label on the jar.*
2 *The thorn* ***stuck*** *in her leg.*

student
students *noun*
a person who is studying at some kind of school.
■ say **stoo**-dnt

studio
studios *noun*
1 a room where an artist or photographer works.
2 a room or building where television programs or movies are made.
■ say **stoo**-dee-oh

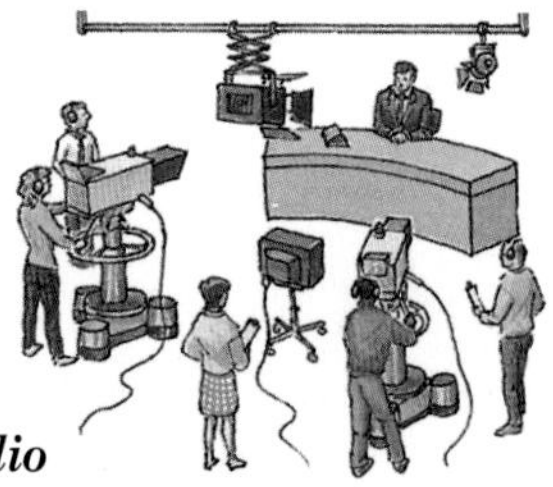

television ***studio***

study
studies studying studied *verb*
1 to look at something carefully.

She ***studied*** *the flower through a magnifying glass.*
2 to learn about a subject from books and classes.
She ***studied*** *for her exams.*

stuffy
adjective
without fresh air.
The room was ***stuffy*** *so she opened the window to let in some fresh air.*

stumble
stumbles stumbling stumbled *verb*
to trip and almost fall.

stump
stumps *noun*
a short part of something left behind after the rest has been cut or worn away.

tree ***stump***

stunt
stunts *noun*
a dangerous action that is done as part of a film or performance.

*The **stunt** involved jumping over the cars on a motorcycle.*

stupid
adjective
foolish, or not intelligent.
■ say **stoo**-pid
■ comparisons **stupider stupidest**
■ opposite **clever**

sturdy
adjective
strong and well made.
*A **sturdy** table.*
■ comparisons **sturdier sturdiest**

stutter
stutters stuttering stuttered *verb*
to stammer or speak with difficulty, often stopping in the middle of words or repeating sounds.
stutter *noun*

style
styles *noun*
1 the way that something is done or made.
*Which **style** of tennis racket do you prefer, wooden or metal?*
2 a fashion or design.

*What **style** of car is this?*
■ say **stile**

subject
subjects *noun*
something you are talking, writing, or learning about.

submarine
submarines *noun*
a vessel that can travel underwater.

■ say **sub**-muh-reen

substance
substances *noun*
a material or object that can be seen or felt.
*There was a sticky **substance** on the table.*

substitute
substitutes *noun*
someone or something that is used in place of another person or thing.

*Margarine is used as a **substitute** for butter.*
■ say **sub**-sti-toot

subtract
subtracts subtracting subtracted *verb*
to take one number away from another number.

8-5=3

*Five **subtracted** from eight equals three.*
subtraction *noun*

subway
subways *noun*
an underground railroad system.

succeed
succeeds succeeding succeeded *verb*
to manage to do what you were trying to do.
*They **succeeded** in moving the heavy piano up the stairs.*
■ say suk-**seed**

success
successes *noun*
a thing that works out well.
*His magic act was a complete **success**.*
■ say suk-**sess**
successful *adjective*

such
adjective
1 of a particular kind.
*Pins, needles, and **such** things.*
2 so much.

*There was **such** a lot of decorating to do, that he didn't know where to begin.*

suck
sucks sucking sucked *verb*
to pull liquid into your mouth, or to hold something in your mouth and lick it.

*He **sucked** his drink through a straw.*

suddenly
adverb
quickly and without warning.

***Suddenly** she had an idea.*
sudden *adjective*

suffer
suffers suffering suffered *verb*
to feel pain, or to be ill.
*She is **suffering** from the flu.*

suffocate
suffocates suffocating suffocated *verb*
to die because you are unable to breathe.
■ say **suf**-uh-kate

sugar
noun
a sweet substance made from plants and used in food and drinks.

■ say **shoog**-ur

suggest
suggests suggesting suggested *verb*
to mention a new idea or plan to someone.
*I **suggested** going to the park to ride our bikes.*
■ say sug-**jest**
suggestion *noun*

suicide
noun
killing yourself deliberately.
■ say **soo**-i-side

suit
suits *noun*
a jacket and skirt or pants, designed to be worn together.

■ rhymes with **boot**

suit
suits suiting suited *verb*
to look good on someone.
*Does this **suit** me?*

suitable
adjective
right for a particular purpose or occasion.

*These boots are **suitable** for walking over rough ground.*
■ say **soo**-tuh-bull

suitcase
suitcases *noun*
a large bag with a handle that is used for carrying clothing and other things when you travel.

sulk
sulks sulking sulked *verb*
to be silent because you are in a bad mood.
sulky *adjective*

sum
sums *noun*
1 a total made by adding two or more numbers together.

3+49=52

*The **sum** of 3 and 49 is 52.*
2 an amount of money.
*A new bike will cost you a large **sum** of money.*

summary
summaries *noun*
a short form of a story or a piece of information that just gives the main points.
*They gave a **summary** of the news at the end of the program.*

summer
summers *noun*
the warmest season of the year. Summer comes between spring and fall.

summit
summits *noun*
the highest point of something.

*The two climbers finally reached the **summit** of the mountain.*

Sun
noun
the star that is the center of our solar system (see **universe** on page 229).

sun
noun
the light and heat that we get from the Sun.
*The cat was sitting in the **sun**.*

sunflower
sunflowers *noun*
a tall plant with large, yellow flowers. The seeds can be eaten or used to make cooking oil.

sunglasses
noun
glasses with dark lenses that you wear to protect your eyes from sunlight.

sunlight
noun
the light from the Sun.

sunrise
sunrises *noun*
the time when the Sun is coming up over the horizon in the morning.

sunset
sunsets *noun*
the time when the Sun is going down below the horizon in the evening.

sunshine
noun
bright sunlight.

superb
adjective
extremely good.
*A **superb** performance.*
■ say soo-**purb**

superior
adjective
higher in rank or position.
*Soldiers must salute their **superior** officers.*
■ say soo-**peer**-ee-ur
■ opposite **inferior**

supermarket
supermarkets *noun*
a large store that sells food and other items. People select the goods they want and pay for them at the exit.

supersonic
adjective
faster than the speed of sound.

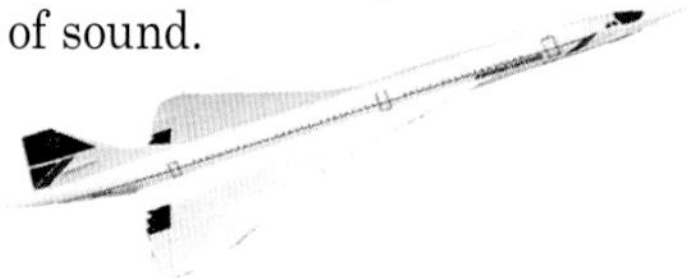

*The Concorde was a **supersonic** aircraft.*
■ say soo-per-**son**-ic

superstition
superstitions *noun*
a false belief based on fear or lack of knowledge about something.
*A common **superstition** is that it is unlucky to walk under ladders.*
■ say soo-per-**stish**-un
superstitious *adjective*

supper
suppers *noun*
a meal eaten in the evening.

A B C D E F G H I J K L M N O P Q R S T U V W X Y Z

supply
supplies *noun*
a quantity of something that may be needed.

*The farmer kept a **supply** of grain in the barn.*
supply *verb*

support
supports supporting supported *verb*
to hold something or someone up to stop it, or them, from falling.

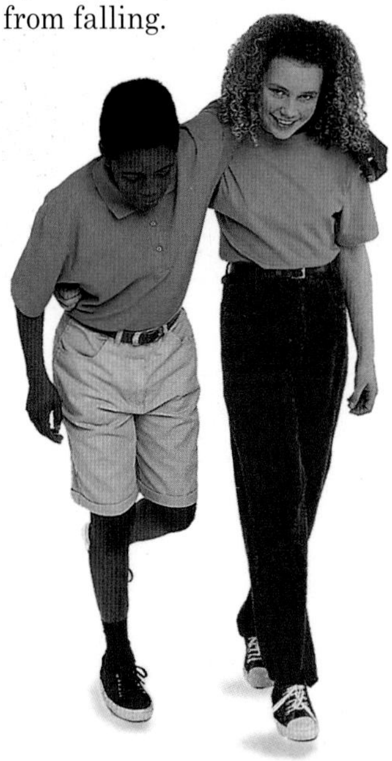

*She **supported** her friend who had hurt his leg.*
support *noun*

suppose
supposes supposing supposed *verb*
to think that something is true or likely.
*I **suppose** you are right.*

sure
adjective
certain, or with no doubt.
*I am **sure** you will enjoy your stay here.*
■ say **shoor**

surf
surfs surfing surfed *verb*
1 to balance on a special board while riding on waves as they begin to break near the seashore.
2 to explore the internet.

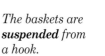

surface
surfaces *noun*
the outside or top of something.

*These buttons have shiny **surfaces**.*
■ say **sur**-fus

surgeon
surgeons *noun*
a doctor who treats patients by doing operations.

■ say **sur**-jun

surgery
surgeries *noun*
1 a medical operation that involves cutting open part of a patient's body.
2 a place where you go to see a doctor or dentist for treatment.
■ say **sur**-juh-ee

surname
surnames *noun*
the last part of someone's name that shows which family they belong to.

surprise
surprises *noun*
something that happens when you do not expect it.
*She got a **surprise** when she received the package!*
surprise *verb*
surprising *adjective*

surrender
surrenders surrendering surrendered *verb*
to give yourself up.

*The kidnappers finally **surrendered** to the police.*

surround
surrounds surrounding surrounded *verb*
to be or to go on all sides of something.

*The bench **surrounded** the tree trunk.*

survive
survives surviving survived *verb*
to continue to live after an event in which you might have died.
*They all **survived** the crash.*

survivor
survivors *noun*
a person who is still alive after experiencing an event that might have killed them.
*He was one of three **survivors** of the shipwreck.*
■ say sur-**vy**-vur

suspect
suspects suspecting suspected *verb*
1 to think that someone is guilty of something.
*I **suspect** her of being a thief.*
suspect *noun*
2 to suppose that something is likely.
*I **suspect** it will rain.*

suspend
suspends suspending suspended *verb*
to attach something by its top so that it hangs down.

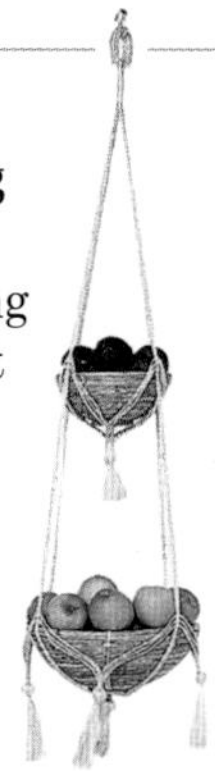

*The baskets are **suspended** from a hook.*

suspense
noun
the feeling of being anxious or excited about what might happen next.
*This movie is full of **suspense**.*

suspicious
adjective
1 suspecting something bad.
*I became **suspicious** when my friends didn't answer the telephone for a week.*
2 behaving in a way that makes people suspect you.

*A **suspicious** character was climbing into the house.*
■ say su-**spish**-us

swallow
swallows swallowing swallowed *verb*
to make your food go down your throat and into your stomach.

*The snake **swallowed** the egg whole.*

swallow
swallows *noun*
a small bird with long wings and a forked tail. Swallows eat mainly insects and are found in most parts of the world.

swam
*from the verb **to swim***
*I **swam** across the pool.*

swamp
swamps *noun*
an area of wet or marshy land.

*A mangrove **swamp**.*

swan
swans *noun*
a large bird that lives in and around water. Swans feed on water plants, which they grasp with their sharp-edged bills. Swans are related to geese.

■ say **swon**

swap
swaps swapping swapped *verb*
to give one thing in return for something else.
*He **swapped** his toy for her tennis racket.*

swarm
swarms *noun*
a large number of insects moving together.
*A **swarm** of bees.*
■ say **sworm**

sway
sways swaying swayed *verb*
to swing or lean from side to side.

*The trees **swayed** in the wind.*

swear
swears swearing swore sworn *verb*
1 to make a solemn promise.
*She **swears** that she didn't do it.*
2 to speak rude or unpleasant words.

sweat
noun
the salty liquid that comes out of your skin when you are hot.
*She was covered in **sweat** after the race.*
sweat *verb*

sweatshirt
sweatshirts *noun*
a thick, cotton shirt with long sleeves.

sweep
sweeps sweeping swept *verb*
1 to clean up dust, dirt, or other mess using a brush.

2 to push away.
*The flood **swept** the car off the road.*

sweet
adjective
1 containing sugar or tasting like sugar.
*Grapes are very **sweet**.*
2 very pleasant or kind.
*It was **sweet** of you to bring me flowers.*
■ comparisons **sweeter sweetest**

sweet
sweets noun
a small piece of snack food, made mostly of sugar, and also called candy.

swell
swells swelling swelled swollen *verb*
to become larger.

*The male frigate bird's throat **swells** up to attract females.*

swelling
swellings *noun*
a swollen place on the body.
*She had a **swelling** where she had bumped her head.*

swerve
swerves swerving swerved *verb*
to turn quickly to one side when you are moving.

*The cyclist **swerved** to avoid the hole.*

swift
adjective
moving quickly.
■ comparisons **swifter swiftest**

swim
swims swimming swam swum *verb*
to move through water using arms, legs, or fins.

swim *noun*

swimming pool
swimming pools *noun*
a large, artificial area of water for swimming in.

swing
swings swinging swung *verb*
to move backward and forward, usually while hanging from a support.

swing *noun*

swirl
swirls swirling swirled *verb*
to move with a twisting or circular motion.

The boat and leaves ***swirled*** *around as they floated downstream.*

switch
switches *noun*
a lever or button used to turn equipment or a machine on and off.
switch *verb*

swivel
swivels swiveling swiveled *verb*
to turn around on a central point.

Swiveling *around on a chair.*

swoop
swoops swooping swooped *verb*
to move downward through the air in a curving movement.

The stunt plane ***swooped*** *down out of the sky.*

sword
swords *noun*
a weapon with a long blade and a handle.

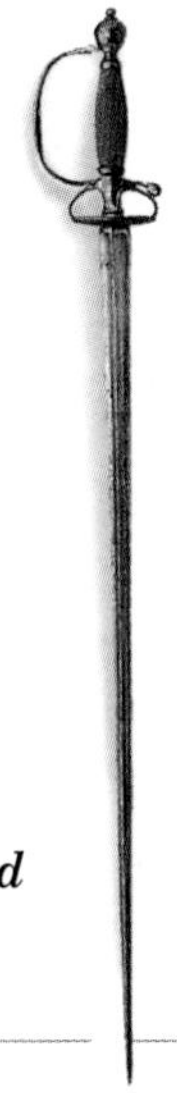

18th-century ***sword***
■ say **sord**

swore
from the verb ***to swear***
She ***swore*** *she was telling the truth.*

syllable
syllables *noun*
a word or part of a word made up of a single sound. The word "once" has one syllable and the word "single" has two.
■ say **sil**-uh-bul

symbol
symbols *noun*
a sign or object that reminds you of something else, or represents something else.

A dove is a ***symbol*** *of peace.*
■ say **sim**-bul

symmetrical
adjective
having two halves that match each other.

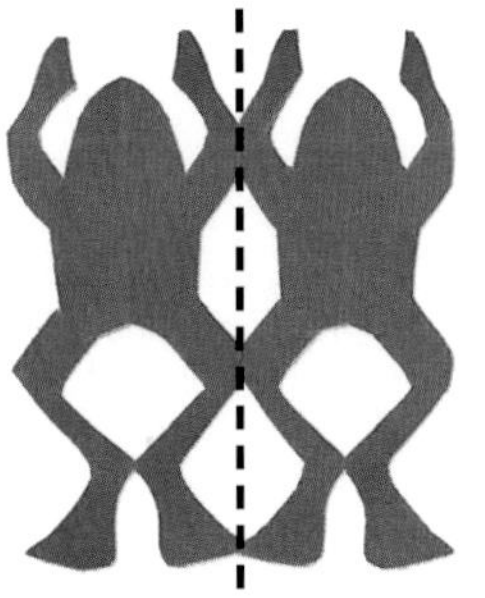

This cut-out shape is ***symmetrical*** *through its middle.*
■ say si-**met**-ri-kul
symmetry *noun*

sympathy
noun
a caring feeling shown by someone for someone else. *When you're hurt, it's nice to get* ***sympathy****.*
■ say **sim**-puh-thee
sympathetic *adjective*

symptom
symptoms *noun*
a sign that shows you have a particular illness or disease. *One of the* ***symptoms*** *of measles is red spots.*
■ say **simp**-tum

synagogue
synagogues *noun*
a building where Jews go to worship.
■ say **sin**-uh-gog

synthetic
adjective
made with artificial materials, not natural ones.

This frog is made from ***synthetic*** *fur.*
■ say sin-**thet**-ik

syringe
syringes *noun*
a tube with a nozzle or hollow needle attached that is used for sucking up and squirting out liquid. Doctors use syringes to give injections.

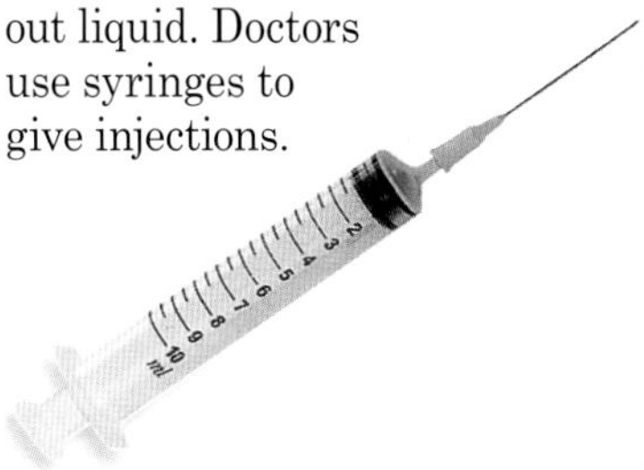

■ say suh-**rinj**

syrup
syrups *noun*
a sweet, sticky liquid food, often made from sugar.

maple ***syrup***
■ say **sur**-up

system
systems *noun*
a group of things that work together in an organized way.
■ say **sis**-tum

Tt

table
tables *noun*
1 a piece of furniture with a flat surface and legs underneath to support it.

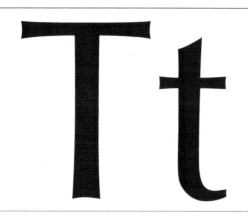

2 a list of facts or figures written in columns.
*A multiplication **table**.*

tablet
tablets *noun*
a small, hard piece of medicine.

tackle
tackles tackling tackled *verb*
1 to try to solve something.
*They had to **tackle** some difficult math problems.*
2 to seize and try to throw someone to the ground, usually in a sport such as football.

tactful
adjective
trying to avoid hurting someone's feelings.
*She was very **tactful** when talking about his new haircut.*
■ opposite **tactless**
tactfully *adverb*

tactics
noun
methods used to make something happen.
*The team's **tactics** helped to win the game.*
tactical *adjective*

tadpole
tadpoles *noun*
a young frog or toad. Tadpoles live in water. As they grow their tails get smaller and they grow legs.

tail
tails *noun*
the part that sticks out beyond the back end of an animal's body.

tailor
tailors *noun*
a person who makes or mends clothes. Tailors usually make clothes to fit a particular person.

take
takes taking took taken *verb*
1 to get hold of or carry.
*She **took** her coat off the rack.*
2 to bring or lead.
*My parents **took** me to the movie theater.*
3 to make use of something.
***Take** the first turn on the left.*
4 to require or need.
*It **takes** three hours to cook.*
5 to travel by or on something.
*Let's **take** the bus.*
6 to remove or steal.

*The thief **took** a wallet from someone's coat pocket.*

tale
tales *noun*
a story about things that may not be true.
*A fairy **tale**.*

talent
talents *noun*
a special natural skill or ability.

*She showed a **talent** for dancing at an early age.*

talk
talks talking talked *verb*
to say words, or to speak.
*He **talked** to his sister on the telephone for an hour.*
■ say **tawk**
talk *noun*

talkative
adjective
talking a lot.
*Our parrot is very **talkative**.*

tall
adjective
1 very high.

*The **tall** office building was surrounded by shorter ones.*
■ opposite **short**
2 having a particular height.
*He is 4 feet **tall**.*
■ comparisons **taller tallest**

tambourine
tambourines *noun*
a musical instrument that is held in the hand and shaken or tapped to provide a rhythm.

■ say tam-buh-**reen**

tame
adjective
used to living or working with human beings.
*The bird they rescued from the cat became very **tame**.*
■ comparisons **tamer tamest**
■ opposite **wild**

tan
tans *noun*
the color of your skin after you've been in the sun.
tan *verb*

tangle
tangles tangling tangled *verb*
to twist into an untidy mass of knots.

*The kittens **tangled** the yarn.*
tangle *noun*

tank
tanks *noun*
1 a large container for liquid or gas.
2 a heavy vehicle with guns that moves along on metal belts instead of wheels.

tanker
tankers *noun*
a vehicle or large ship that carries oil or other liquids.

tantrum
tantrums *noun*
a noisy display of bad temper.

*He had a **tantrum** when he was told to clean his room.*

tap
taps tapping tapped *verb*
to hit gently with your fingers.

*She **tapped** on his shoulder.*
tap *noun*

tap
taps *noun*
a device that you turn to control the flow of liquid or gas from a pipe.

tape
tapes *noun*
1 a long, narrow strip of material such as paper, plastic, or metal.

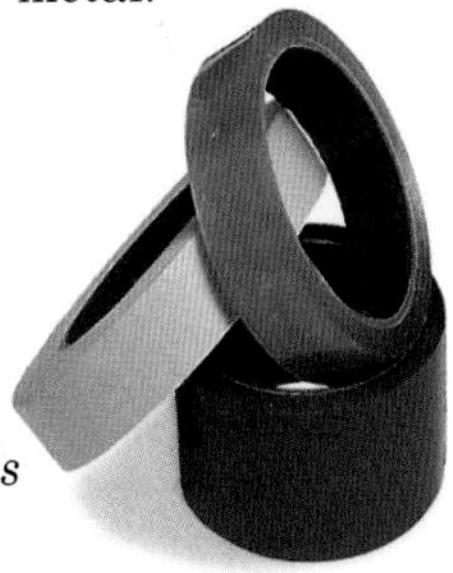

*three kinds of **tape***

2 a strip of plastic coated with magnetic powder that is used for recording sounds, video pictures, and computer information.

tape measure
tape measures *noun*
a tape marked in centimeters and inches that is used for measuring length.

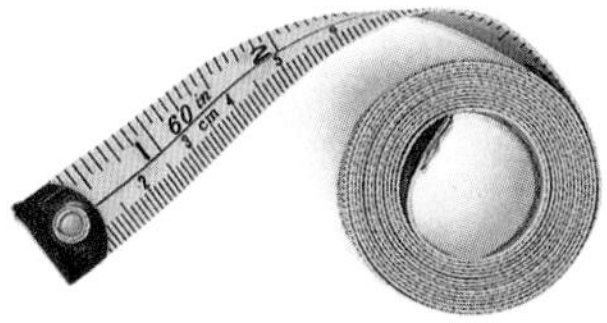

tar
noun
a thick, dark, sticky liquid that is made from coal or wood. Tar is used in making road surfaces.

target
targets *noun*
an object that you try to hit when shooting or throwing something.

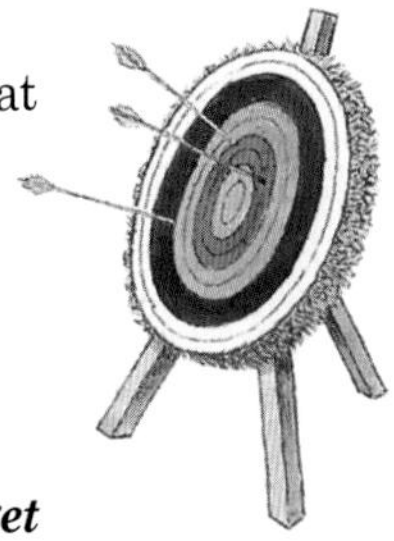

*archery **target***

tartan
adjective
decorated with a special pattern of lines and squares. Tartan patterns originally came from Scotland.

***tartan** scarf*

task
tasks *noun*
a piece of work or a duty.
*My **task** was cleaning the car.*

taste
noun
1 one of the body's five senses that we use to find out the flavor of something.
2 the flavor of something when you have licked it or put it in your mouth.

*She tried the soup to see if she liked the **taste**.*
taste *verb*
tasty *adjective*

tattoo
tattoos *noun*
a permanent picture or design printed on someone's skin using needles filled with colored ink.

tax
taxes *noun*
money that people have to pay to a government that is used to provide public services.
tax *verb*

taxi
taxis *noun*
a car that you can hire to travel in by paying the driver money (see **car** on page 39).
■ say **tak**-see

tea
noun
a drink made by pouring boiling water onto the chopped, dried leaves of the tea plant.

***tea** plant leaves*

*cup of **tea***

teach
teaches teaching taught *verb*
to help someone learn about a subject or learn a skill.
*He has **taught** history for three years.*

teacup
teacups *noun*
a cup used for drinking tea.

team
teams *noun*
a group of people who work or play sports together.

*football **team***

teapot
teapots *noun*
a container with a spout, lid, and handle that is used for making and serving tea.

tear

tears tearing tore torn *verb*
to make a hole or split in something by pulling hard.

The dog ***tore*** *his pant leg.*
■ rhymes with **care**
tear *noun*

tear

tears *noun*
a drop of salty water that comes from your eyes when you cry.

■ rhymes with **deer**

tease

teases teasing teased *verb*
to bother someone by saying or doing things in a playful, but annoying way.
He ***teased*** *his little sister about her dolls.*

technology

noun
science that is put to use in everyday life.
Medical ***technology****.*
■ say tek-**nol**-uh-jee
technological *adjective*

teenager

teenagers *noun*
a person between the ages of 13 and 19 (see **growth** on page 94).

telephone

telephones *noun*
an instrument that allows you to talk to and hear people who are far away, by means of electrical signals. Telephone is often shortened to phone.

telescope

telescopes *noun*
an instrument with lenses inside it. When you look through it distant things appear closer and larger.

television

televisions *noun*
a piece of electrical equipment that receives pictures and sound that are broadcast by a television station. Television is often shortened to TV.

flat-screen ***television***

tell

tells telling told *verb*
to put something into words, or let someone know something.
Tell *me a story.*

temper

tempers *noun*
1 a mood.
Are you in a good ***temper*** *today?*
2 an angry mood.
She threw the book across the room in a ***temper****.*

temperature

temperatures *noun*
a measurement of how hot or cold something is.

She took the child's ***temperature****.*
■ say **tem**-pur-uh-chur

temple

temples *noun*
a building where people go to worship.

Buddhist ***temple***
■ say **tem**-pul

temporary

adjective
lasting for only a short time.

The box was a ***temporary*** *bed for the cat.*
■ say **tem**-puh-rare-ee
■ opposite **permanent**
temporarily *adverb*

tempt

tempts tempting tempted *verb*
to try to persuade someone to do something that they wouldn't usually do or shouldn't do.
Can I ***tempt*** *you to take another slice of cake?*
■ say **temt**
temptation *noun*

tendency

tendencies *noun*
the way that a person or thing usually or often behaves.
She has a ***tendency*** *to be late.*
tend *verb*

tender

adjective
1 easy to chew or cut.
A ***tender*** *piece of steak.*
2 feeling sore when touched.

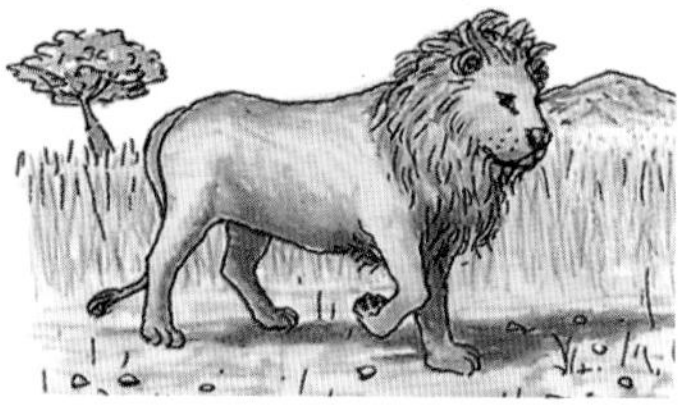

The lion had a ***tender*** *paw after stepping on a thorn.*
3 gentle and loving.
He gave his baby a ***tender*** *smile.*
tenderly *adverb*

tennis

noun
a game that is played with a racket and ball on a court divided by a net. The players try to hit the ball over the net in a way that makes it hard for their opponent to return it (see **sport** on page 197).

tennis *court*

tense
adjective
1 nervous.
2 stretched tight.
Tense muscles.
■ opposite **relaxed**

tense
noun
a form of a verb that shows whether the action is taking place in the past, present, or future.

tent
tents *noun*
a portable shelter made of waterproof material stretched over a frame of poles.

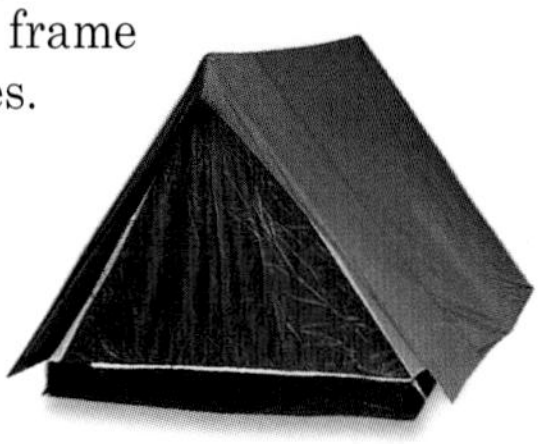

term
terms *noun*
one of the periods of time during a year when a school or university is open for teaching.

terminal
terminals *noun*
a building at the end of a travel route where passengers arrive and depart.

terrible
adjective
very bad or unpleasant.
*It was a **terrible** day.*

terrify
terrifies terrifying terrified *verb*
to frighten very badly.

*Heights **terrified** him.*

territory
territories *noun*
an area of land that is controlled by a country's laws or lived in by an animal.
*The pride of lions never left their own **territory**.*
■ say **tear**-i-tor-ee

terror
noun
great fear.

terrorist
terrorists *noun*
a person who uses or threatens to use violence to force people to do something, usually for a political cause.
terrorism *noun*
terrorize *verb*

test
tests testing tested *verb*
to try something out.

*She **tested** the liquid to see if it was an acid.*
test *noun*

text
noun
the words of something written or printed.

text message
noun
a written message sent between cell phones.

textile
textiles *noun*
a cloth or fabric made by weaving or knitting.

texture
textures *noun*
the way something feels when you touch it.

*Sandpaper has a rough **texture**.*
■ say **teks**-chur

thank
thanks thanking thanked *verb*
to say that you are grateful for something.
*They **thanked** him for their presents.*
thank you *interjection*

thaw
thaws thawing thawed *verb*
to melt or to make something melt.
*The snow started to **thaw** in the sunshine.*
thaw *noun*

theater
theaters *noun*
a building where plays and shows are performed.
■ say **thee**-uh-tur

theft
thefts *noun*
the act of stealing.
*He reported the **theft** of the painting to the police.*

theme
themes *noun*
a main subject, idea, or topic.

*The **theme** of the costume party was cartoon characters.*

theory
theories *noun*
an idea about how or why something happens.
*She tested her **theory** with scientific experiments.*
■ say **thee**-uh-ree or **theer**-ee

thermometer
thermometers *noun*
a device that measures temperature.
■ say thur-**mom**-i-tur

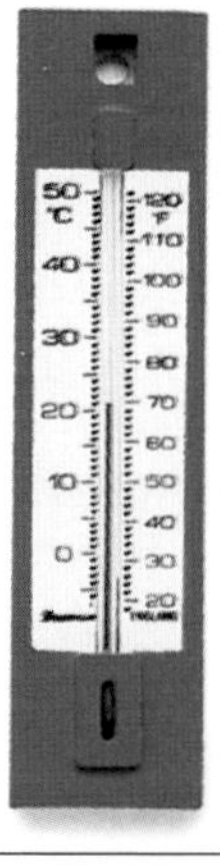

*wall **thermometer***

thesaurus
thesauruses or **thesauri** *noun*
a book that groups words that have similar meanings together.
■ say thi-**saur**-rus

thick
adjective
1 large in width or depth.

***thick** candle*

2 packed closely together.
*A **thick** forest.*
■ opposite **thin**
3 having a certain measurement in width or depth.
*The plank was three inches **thick**.*
■ comparisons **thicker thickest**

thief
thieves *noun*
a person who steals things.
■ rhymes with **beef**

thigh
thighs *noun*
the part of your leg between your knee and your hip.

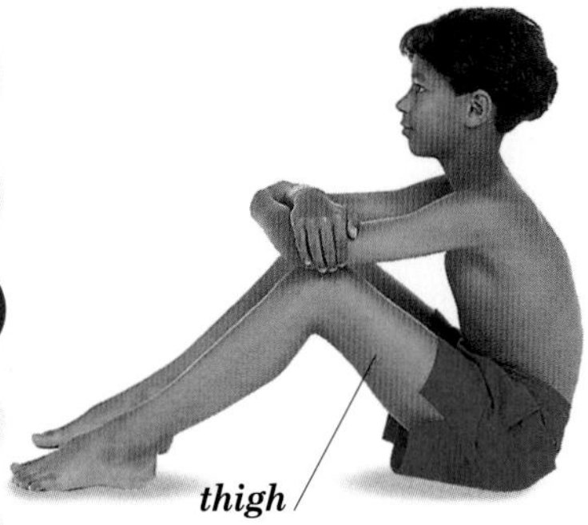

■ rhymes with **sky**

thimble
thimbles *noun*
a small, hard covering worn on the end of your finger when you are sewing.
The thimble protects your finger and helps you push the needle through the fabric.

thin
adjective
1 small in width or depth.

***thin** candle*

2 hardly covered.
*A **thin** layer of snow covered the ground.*
■ opposite **thick**
3 not having much fat.
*A **thin** man.*
■ opposite **fat**
■ comparisons **thinner thinnest**

thing
things *noun*
1 an object that is not alive.
2 an idea or an action.
*There are four **things** I want to do this evening.*

think
thinks thinking thought *verb*
to use your mind to create ideas or opinions.

*She **thought** about what she could eat for lunch.*

thirsty
adjective
needing something to drink.

*He was very **thirsty** after a day without water.*
■ comparisons **thirstier thirstiest**

thistle
thistles *noun*
a wild plant with prickly leaves and purple, white, or yellow flowers.

thorn
thorns *noun*
a sharp spike on the stem of a plant.

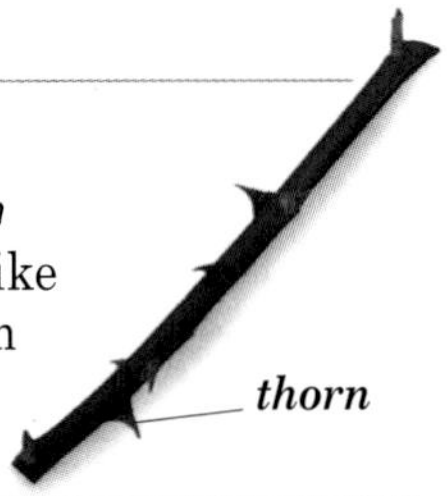

thorough
adjective
complete in every way.
*He had a **thorough** search for his book.*
■ say **thur**-oh
thoroughly *adverb*

thought
thoughts *noun*
an idea or opinion that you have been thinking about.
■ say **thawt**

thoughtful
adjective
caring about other people's feelings and needs.

*It was **thoughtful** of her to help him.*
■ say **thawt**-ful
■ opposite **thoughtless**

thread
threads *noun*
a thin yarn such as cotton or silk, that is used for sewing.
■ say **thred**

thread
threads threading threaded *verb*
to pass a length of thread or rope through a hole in something.

***Threading** beads onto a string.*

threat
threats *noun*
a warning that something may happen.
*There's a **threat** of rain in the air.*
■ say **thret**
threaten *verb*

thrill
thrills *noun*
an excited feeling.
*It was a real **thrill** to ride on the roller coaster.*
thrilling *adjective*

throat
throats *noun*
the tube that leads from your mouth, through your neck, to your stomach and lungs.
■ rhymes with **boat**

throne
thrones *noun*
a special chair used by a ruler of a country.

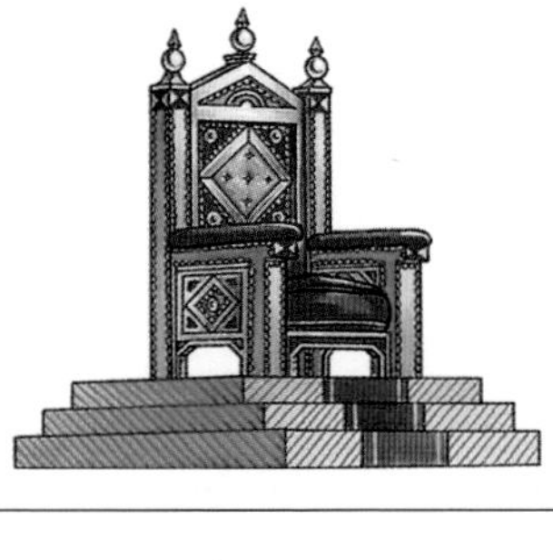

through
preposition
from one side or end to the other.
*She drove **through** the tunnel.*
■ say **throo**

throw
throws throwing threw thrown *verb*
to send something out of your hand and through the air forcefully.

thud
thuds *noun*
a dull sound made when a heavy object falls on something.
*The book dropped to the floor with a **thud**.*

thumb
thumbs *noun*
the short, thick finger set apart from your other fingers at the side of your hand.

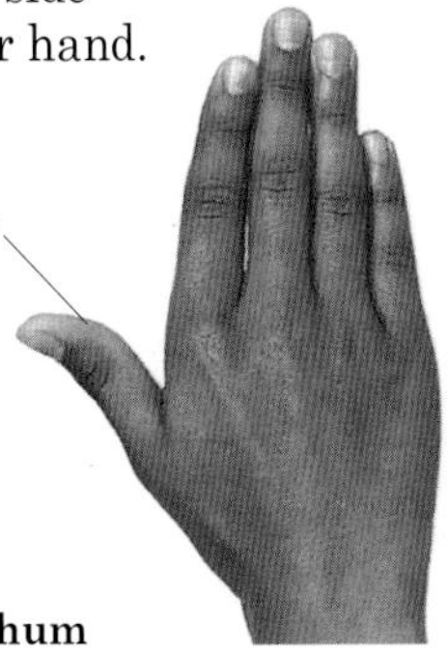

■ say **thum**

thunder
noun
a loud, rumbling sound that comes after a flash of lightning during a storm.

thunderstorm
thunderstorms *noun*
a storm that has thunder and lightning.

tick
ticks *noun*
1 a small animal that feed on the blood of animals.
2 the clicking sound of a clock.
*Each clock **tick** made me more nervous.*
tick *verb*

ticket
tickets *noun*
a piece of paper that shows that you have paid to do something, such as travel on a bus or go into a theater.

tickle
tickles tickling tickled *verb*
to touch someone's skin lightly, making them laugh or squirm.

tide
tides *noun*
the regular change in the level of the sea that happens twice a day.

*The **tide** is out.*

tidy
tidies tidying tidied *verb*
to put in order.

*He **tidied** up his room.*

tie
ties tying tied *verb*
1 to fasten something with a knot or bow.

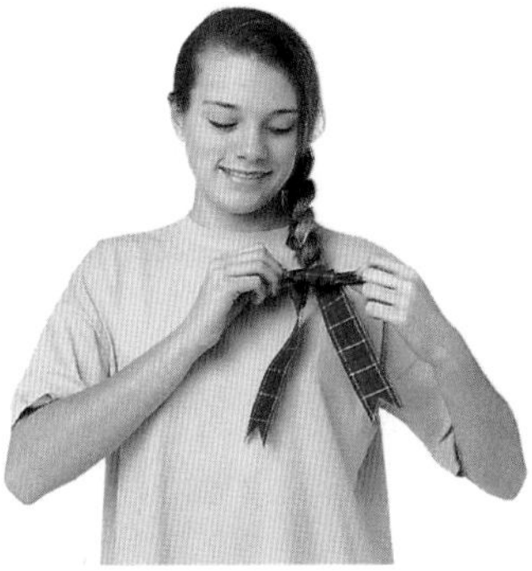

*She **tied** a ribbon in her hair.*
2 to score the same number of points as someone else in a contest.
*They **tied** for first place.*
tie *noun*

tie
ties *noun*
a thin strip of fabric worn around the neck and knotted under the collar of a shirt.

tiger
tigers *noun*
a large, wild mammal that is part of the cat family. Tigers live in many regions of Asia, from tropical forests to cold plains. They hunt at night for their food.

tight
adjective
fitting closely.
*A **tight** fit.*
■ say **tite**
■ comparisons **tighter tightest**
■ opposite **loose**
tighten *verb*
tightly *adverb*

tightrope
tightropes *noun*
a rope stretched high above the ground that acrobats balance on.

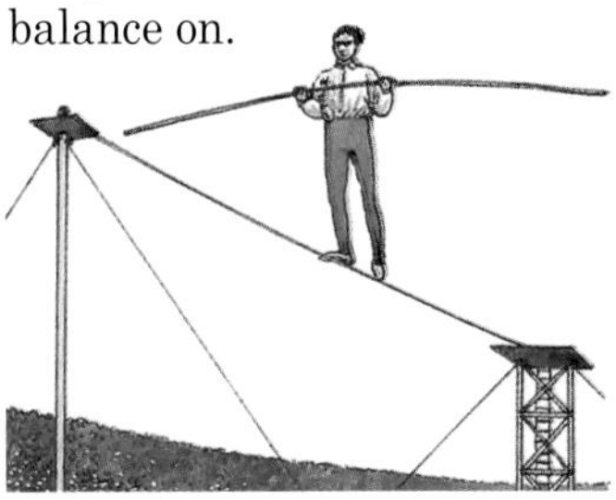

tile
tiles *noun*
a thin piece of decorated baked clay or other material that is used as a wall or floor covering.

till
tills tilling tilled *verb*
to prepare land for planting.
*The farmer **tilled** his fields before planting the new season's crops.*
tillable *adjective*

tilt
tilts tilting tilted *verb*
to move or be moved into a sloping or leaning position.
*The huge pile of books **tilted** dangerously.*

timber
noun
cut wood that is used for building and making things.

time

times *noun*

1 all of the past, present, and future. Time is measured in periods such as centuries, years, months, weeks, days, and hours.

2 a particular point in the day.
*What **time** is it?*

3 a period in the past, present, or future.
*In Roman **times**, many roads were built throughout Europe.*

4 an occasion or event.
*I go swimming three **times** a week.*

Telling the time

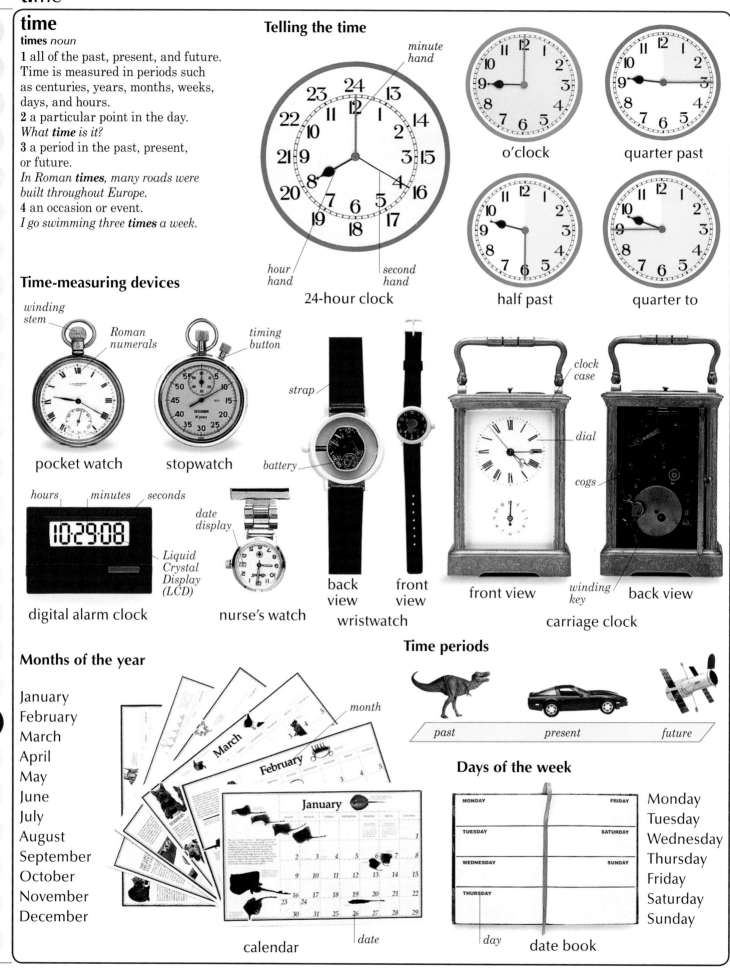

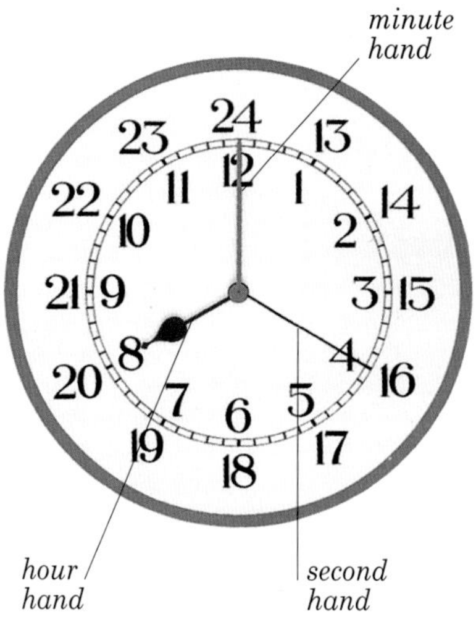

24-hour clock

o'clock

quarter past

half past

quarter to

Time-measuring devices

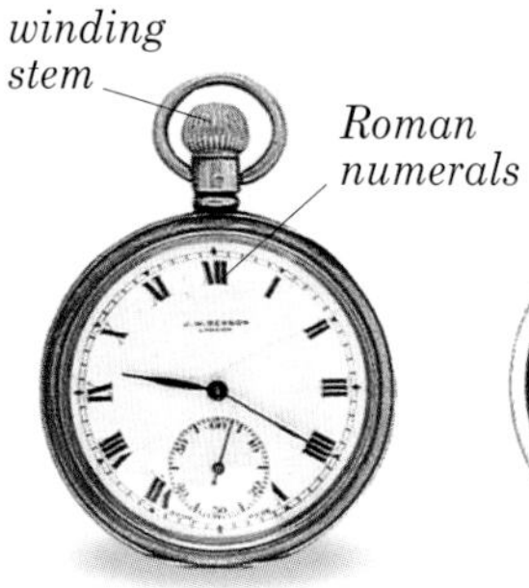

pocket watch

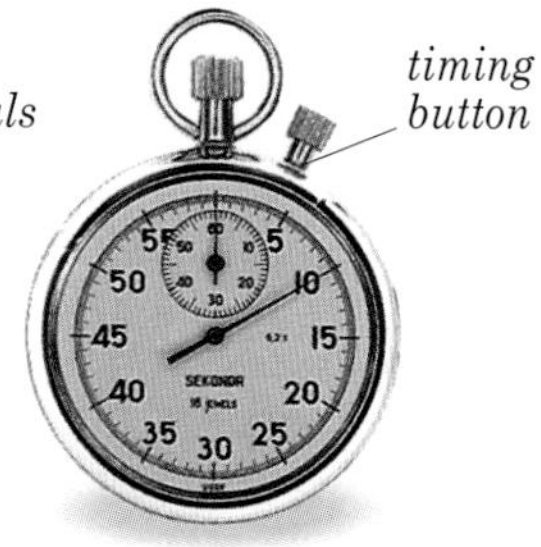

stopwatch

wristwatch

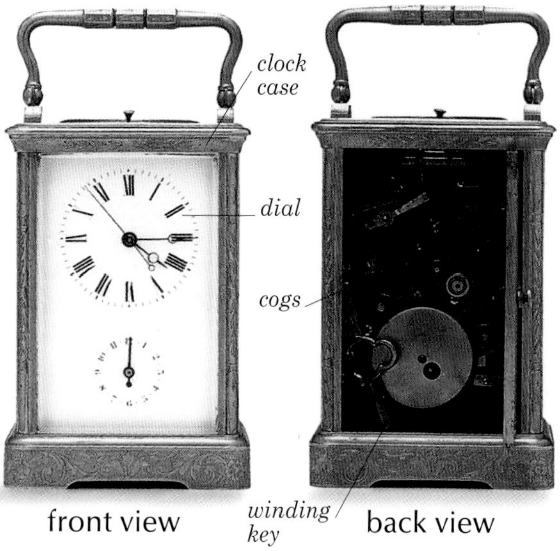

carriage clock

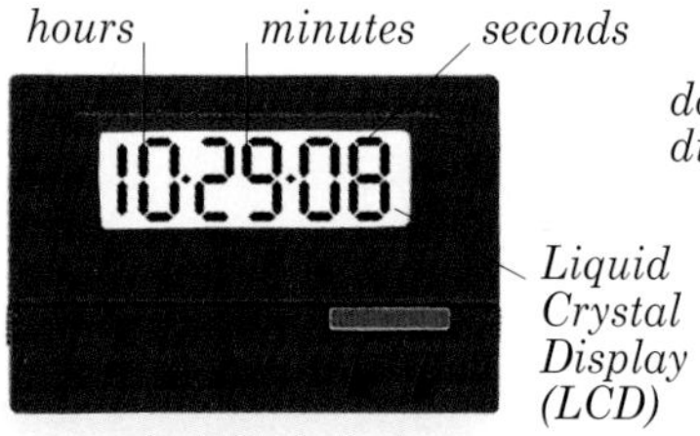

digital alarm clock

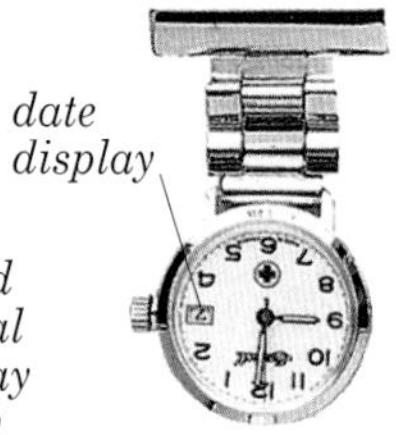

nurse's watch

Months of the year

January
February
March
April
May
June
July
August
September
October
November
December

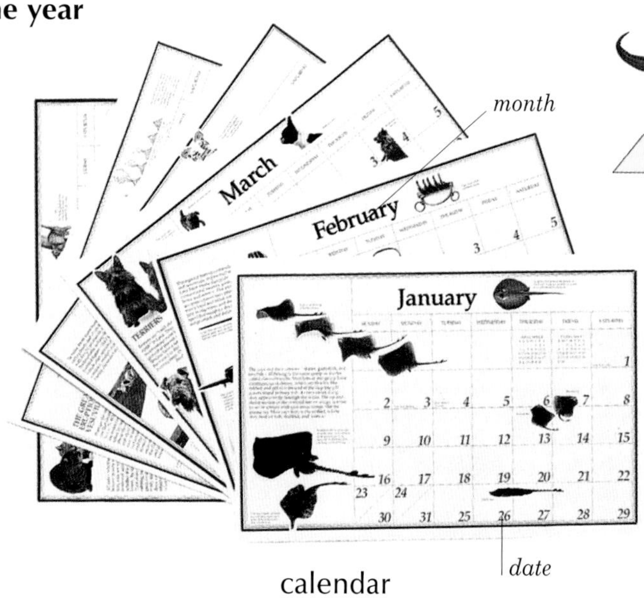

calendar

Time periods

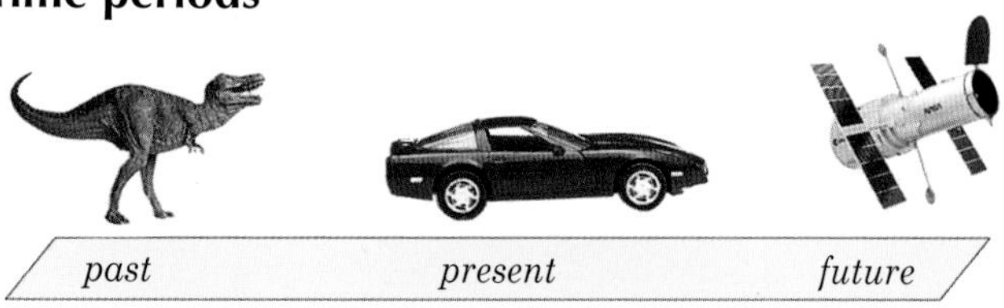

Days of the week

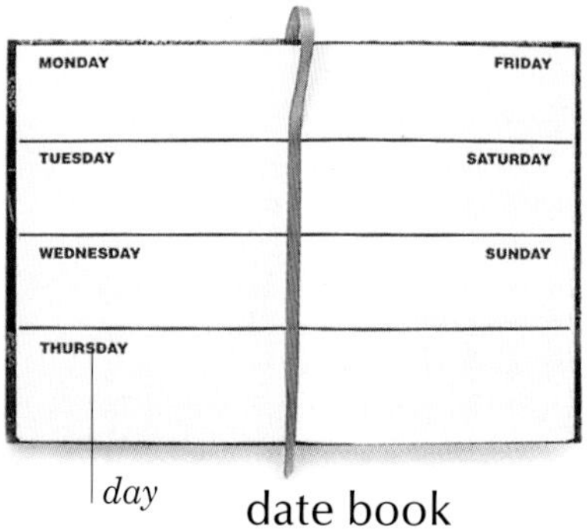

date book

Monday
Tuesday
Wednesday
Thursday
Friday
Saturday
Sunday

timetable
timetables *noun*
a chart that shows the times when events should happen, or when jobs should be done.

*He checked the **timetable** to find out when the bus left.*

timid
adjective
easily frightened or shy.
*The bird was very **timid** and flew away when I moved.*
timidly *adverb*

tin
tins *noun*
1 a light, soft, silvery metal.

***tin** ore*

***tin** can*

2 a metal container for putting things in or for preserving food.

tingle
tingles tingling tingled *verb*
to have a slight stinging feeling in a part of your body.
*Carbonated drinks make my mouth **tingle**.*

tinkle
tinkles tinkling tinkled *verb*
to make a light, ringing sound.
*The bells **tinkled** as the sleigh moved along.*

tiny
adjective
very small.
■ comparisons **tinier tiniest**

tip
tips tipping tipped *verb*
1 to move something so that it is not upright.
2 to turn something over so that the contents fall out.
*She **tipped** the dirty water out of the bucket.*

tip
tips *noun*
1 the narrow, pointed end of something.

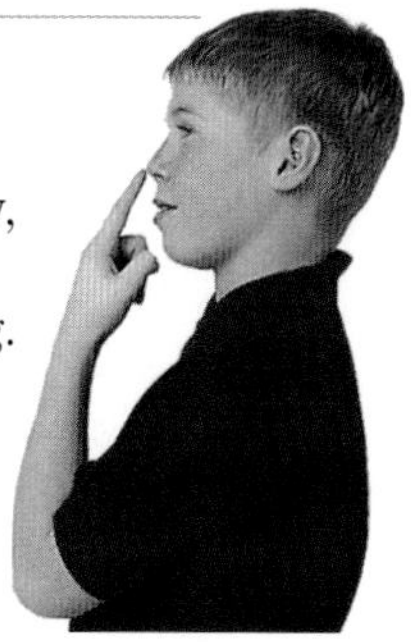

*Touching the **tip** of his nose.*
2 a helpful hint or piece of useful information.
*Do you have any **tips** for getting rid of stains?*
3 a small, extra gift of money, given in return for a service.
*I left the waiter in the restaurant a **tip**.*

tiptoe
tiptoes tiptoeing tiptoed *verb*
to walk slowly and quietly on your toes.

tired
adjective
feeling that you would like to sleep or rest.
*She felt **tired** after working in the garden all day.*

tissue
tissues *noun*
1 a thin, soft paper used for wiping skin.

2 a material that makes up a part of a living thing.
*Brain **tissue**.*
■ say **tish**-yoo

title
titles *noun*
1 the name of a creative piece of work such as a book, movie, or painting.
2 a person's professional position.
*Her **title** was Senior Editor.*
■ say **tite**-l

toad
toads *noun*
an amphibian similar to a frog, but with a rougher, dryer skin. Toads eat insects, usually live on land, and move along with short hops. They hibernate in winter.

*green **toad***

toadstool
toadstools *noun*
a poisonous fungus with an umbrella-shaped top.

toast
noun
1 bread that is grilled on both sides until it is crisp and brown.
2 the action of wishing someone well by raising your glass and drinking.
*Let's drink a **toast** to the bride and groom.*
toast *verb*

tobacco
noun
a plant whose leaves are dried and used in cigarettes and pipes.

toboggan
toboggans *noun*
a flat sled that is used for sliding down slopes.

today
adverb
on this day.
*I'm going to the zoo **today**.*
today *noun*

toddler
toddlers *noun*
a young child who is learning or has just learned to walk (see **growth** on page 94).

toe
toes *noun*
one of the five separate parts at the end of your foot.

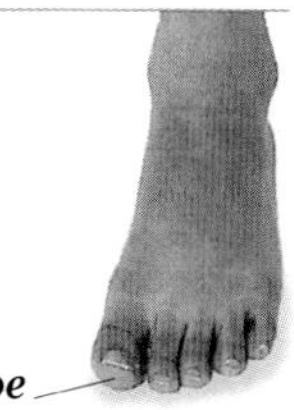

toe

toffee
toffees *noun*
a chewy sweet made from sugar and butter.

together
adverb
with each other.
*Shall we go **together**?*

toilet
toilets *noun*
a bowl with a seat that is connected to a drain and flushed with water. People use toilets to dispose of waste from the body.

A B C D E F G H I J K L M N O P Q R S T U V W X Y Z

told
from the verb ***to tell***
She ***told*** *her friends what she had done over the weekend.*

tomato
tomatoes *noun*
a soft, juicy, red fruit that can be eaten raw in salads or cooked (see **fruit** on page 85).

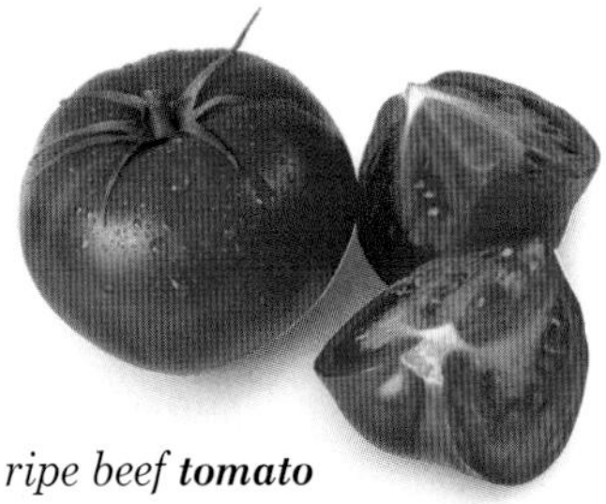

ripe beef ***tomato***

tomorrow
adverb
on the day after today.
I'm going away ***tomorrow.***
tomorrow *noun*

tone
tones *noun*
the quality of a sound or a voice.
He spoke in a low ***tone.***
■ rhymes with **own**

tongue
tongues *noun*
a flexible flap of muscle in your mouth that you use to eat, taste, and speak.

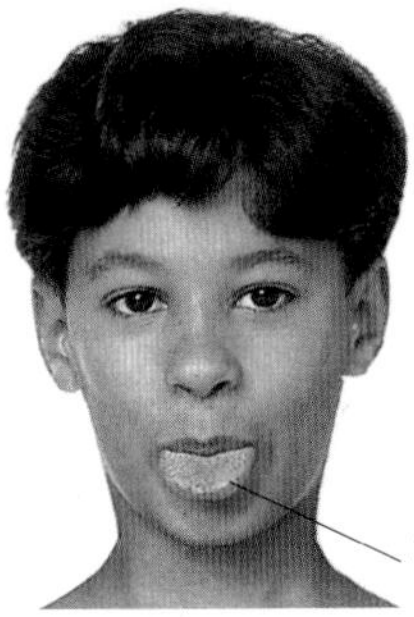

■ say **tung**

tonight
adverb
on the evening and night of the present day.
Let's go to the concert ***tonight.***
tonight *noun*

tonsil
tonsils *noun*
one of two small lumps of tissue at the back of your throat.

took
from the verb ***to take***
He ***took*** *the can out of the cupboard.*

tool
tools *noun*
a piece of equipment that helps you do a job.

tooth
teeth *noun*
1 one of the hard, white, bonelike structures inside your mouth that you use for biting and chewing.

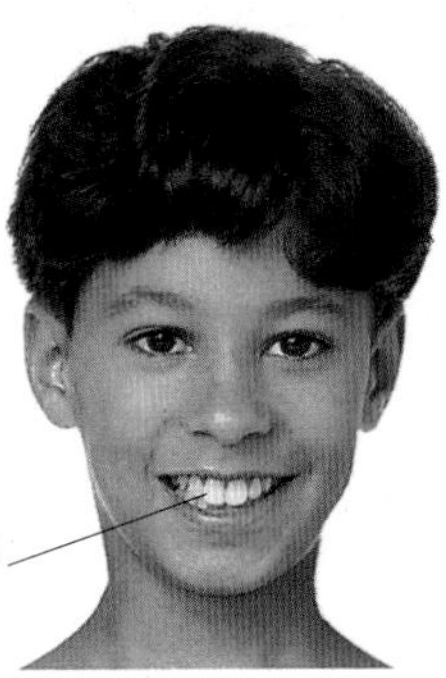

2 one of the pointed parts on an object such as a saw or a comb.

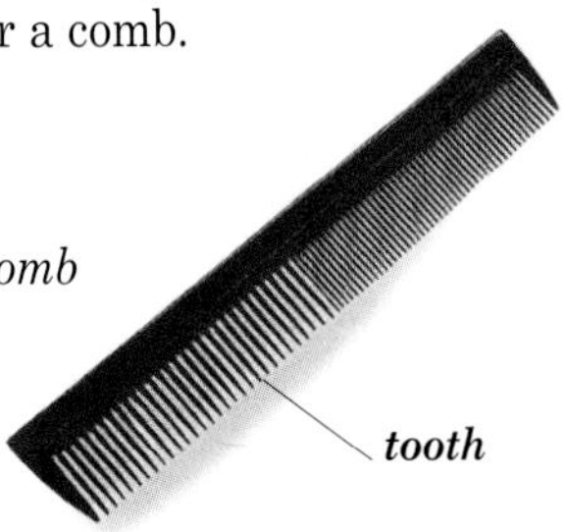

toothbrush
toothbrushes *noun*
a small brush with a long handle that you use for cleaning your teeth.

top
tops *noun*
1 the highest point of something.

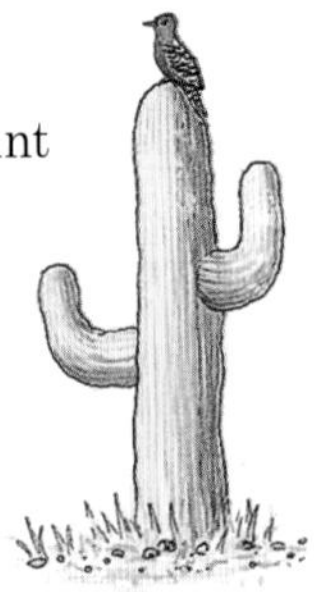

The bird sat on the very ***top*** *of the cactus.*
■ opposite **bottom**
2 a lid.

3 a spinning toy.
4 a piece of clothing worn on the upper part of your body.

pajama ***top***

topic
topics *noun*
a subject that is spoken or written about.
The fire was the main ***topic*** *of conversation for weeks.*

topple
topples toppling toppled *verb*
to fall over.
The dominoes ***toppled*** *over.*

torch
torches *noun*
a burning piece of wood carried as a light.

Olympic ***torch***

tore
from the verb ***to tear***
She ***tore*** *her sleeve on a nail.*

tornado
tornadoes or **tornados** *noun*
a violent, whirling wind that causes great damage to the land and buildings.

■ say tor-**nay**-doh

tortoise
tortoises *noun*
a slow-moving reptile with a hard shell. Tortoises live in hot regions. They eat grass and other plants and can live a long time (see **reptile** on page 168).
■ say **tort**-us

toss
tosses tossing tossed *verb*
1 to throw with a quick, easy motion.
We ***tossed*** *the ball around before the game.*
2 to throw a coin and guess which side will face up in order to decide something.
We ***tossed*** *a coin to see who should have the first turn.*
toss *noun*

total
totals *noun*
the entire amount of everything added together.
The ***total*** *of 2, 3, and 4 is 9.*
■ say **tote**-l

total
adjective
complete.
Total *darkness.*

toucan
toucans *noun*
a colorful bird with a large beak that lives in the rain forests of South America. Toucans nest in holes in trees and feed on fruit, insects, small lizards, and eggs.
■ say **too**-kan

touch
touches touching touched *verb*
to put your hand or another part of your body on something.

Can you ***touch*** *the floor with your hands, while keeping your legs straight?*
■ say **tuch**
touch *noun*

tough
adjective
1 strong and not easy to break or damage.

Crash helmets are made of ***tough*** *plastic.*
■ opposite **weak**
2 very difficult.
A ***tough*** *problem.*
■ opposite **easy**
■ say **tuff**
■ comparisons **tougher toughest**

tour
tours *noun*
a journey that takes you to see several places.
We went on a sightseeing ***tour*** *of the city.*
■ say **toor**

tourist
tourists *noun*
a person who travels and visits places for pleasure.

tournament
tournaments *noun*
a series of contests or matches in a sport or game.
A chess ***tournament****.*

tow
tows towing towed *verb*
to pull something along behind.
The truck ***towed*** *the car to the garage.*
■ say **toe**

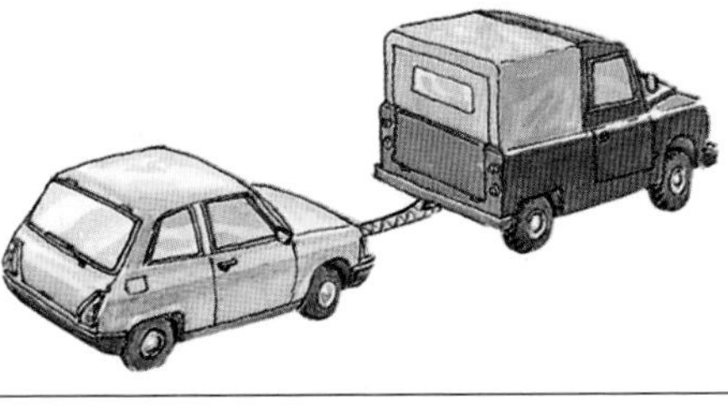

toward
preposition
in the direction of.

The horse trotted across the field ***toward*** *her.*

towel
towels *noun*
a piece of soft, thick cloth or paper that is used for drying things.

tower
towers *noun*
a tall, narrow structure.
The Eiffel ***Tower****.*
■ rhymes with **our**

town
towns *noun*
a place with houses and other buildings, where people live, work, and shop. A town is smaller than a city but larger than a village.

toy
toys *noun*
an object to play with.

jack-in-the-box

trace
traces tracing traced *verb*
1 to copy a picture by placing a sheet of thin paper over it and drawing around the outline.

She ***traced*** *the picture of a tiger from a book.*
2 to follow or discover something by observing marks or clues.
She ***traced*** *her family's history back three centuries.*

trace
traces *noun*
a small mark or track left behind by something.
There were ***traces*** *of a fire in the cave.*

track
tracks *noun*
1 a mark or marks left by someone or something that is moving.

The fox left ***tracks*** *in the fresh snow.*
2 a path or rough road.
They drove the truck up a bumpy ***track****.*
3 a course used for races.
They did four laps around the running ***track****.*
4 rails laid on the ground for trains to run on.

a b c d e f g h i j k l m n o p q r s t u v w x y z

tractor
tractors *noun*
a farm vehicle with large wheels that is used for pulling heavy loads or machinery over rough ground.

trade
trades trading traded *verb*
to exchange one thing for another.

tradition
traditions *noun*
a special event, belief, or way of doing something that has continued in the same way for many years.
*It is a **tradition** to celebrate the New Year with a party.*
■ say truh-**dish**-un
traditional *adjective*

traffic
noun
vehicles, ships, or aircraft moving along a route.

*There was a lot of **traffic** on the bridge.*

tragedy
tragedies *noun*
1 a very sad and unfortunate event.
*The train crash was a terrible **tragedy**.*
2 a play with a sad ending.
Shakespeare's Romeo and Juliet *is a **tragedy**.*
■ say **traj**-i-dee

tragic
adjective
bringing great sadness.
*A **tragic** accident.*
■ say **traj**-ik
tragically *adverb*

trail
trails trailing trailed *verb*
1 to drag something along behind or let something hang loosely.

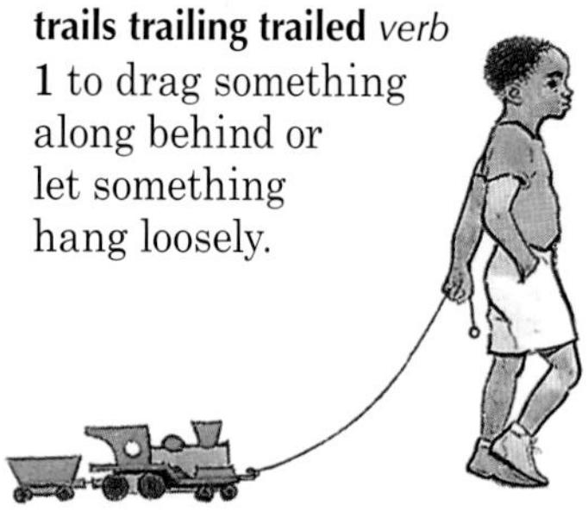

*He **trailed** his toy train behind him.*
2 to walk or move slowly behind someone.
*The children **trailed** along behind their mother.*

trail
trails *noun*
1 a path or track.
*A nature **trail**.*
2 a track, scent, or other sign left by something that has passed by.

*He left a **trail** of garbage behind him.*

trailer
trailers *noun*
a small vehicle or container that can be towed behind a car, truck, or tractor.

train
trains *noun*
a vehicle that runs on tracks. Train cars are pulled along by an engine in front.

train
trains training trained *verb*
1 to practice doing exercises or skills for a sport.
*She **trains** for three hours a day.*

2 to teach or to learn a skill.
*He **trained** his dog to sit.*
training *noun*

traitor
traitors *noun*
a person who turns against his or her country or friends by helping an enemy.

trample
tramples trampling trampled *verb*
to crush something by stepping on it.

*The dog **trampled** all over the flowers.*

trampoline
trampolines *noun*
a piece of gymnastic equipment made of strong fabric and attached to a frame by springs.

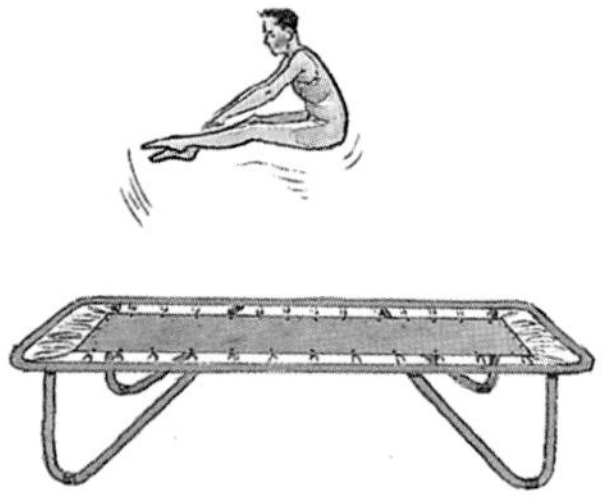

■ say tram-puh-**leen**

trance
trances *noun*
a kind of sleep, or a dazed state, when you are not completely conscious.
■ say **trans**

transfer
transfers transferring transferred *verb*
to move something from one person or place to another.
*He **transferred** his money to a savings account.*

translate
translates translating translated *verb*
to turn words in one language into words of another language.
*She **translated** the French poem into English.*

transparent
adjective
able to be seen through.

*This pitcher is **transparent**.*
■ say trans-**pair**-unt

transplant
transplants *noun*
an operation to move an organ or tissue from one person or part of the body to another.
*A heart **transplant**.*

transportation

noun

a way of carrying goods or people from one place to another. Different methods of transportation are used to travel on land, on water, or in the air.

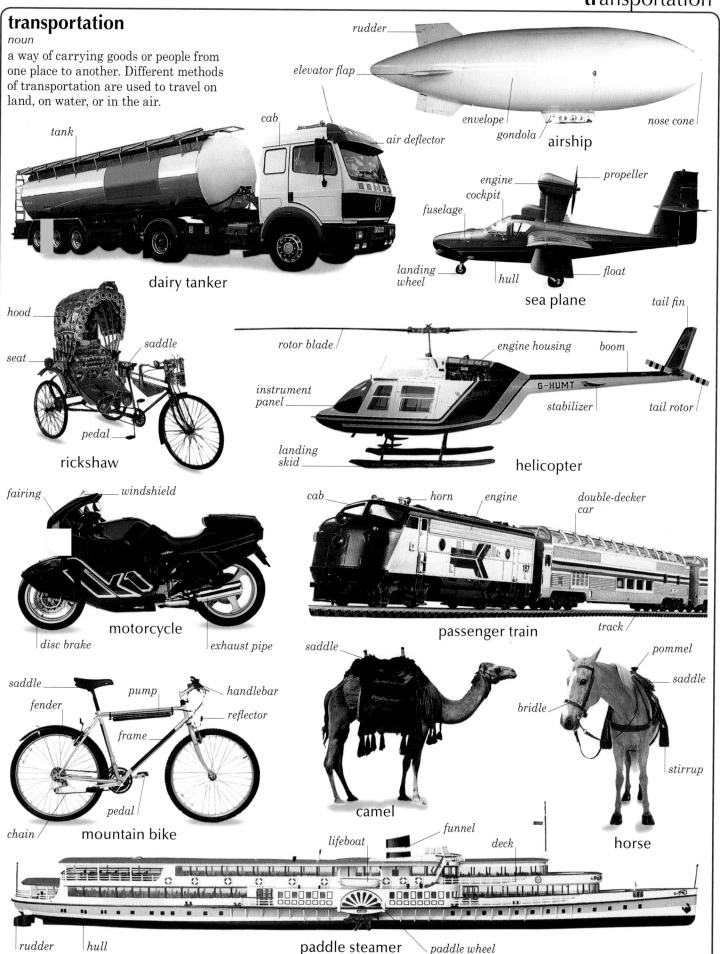

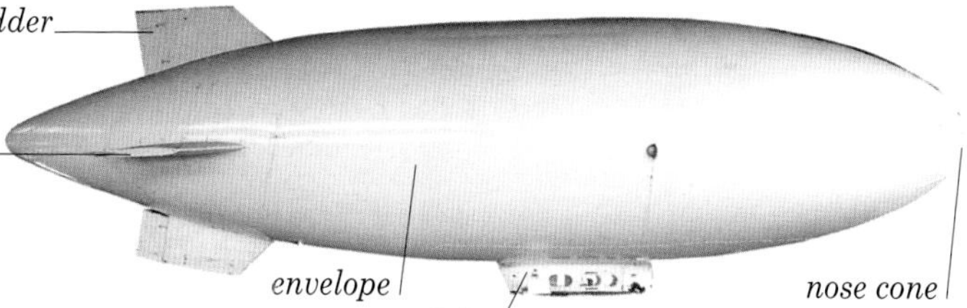

airship

dairy tanker

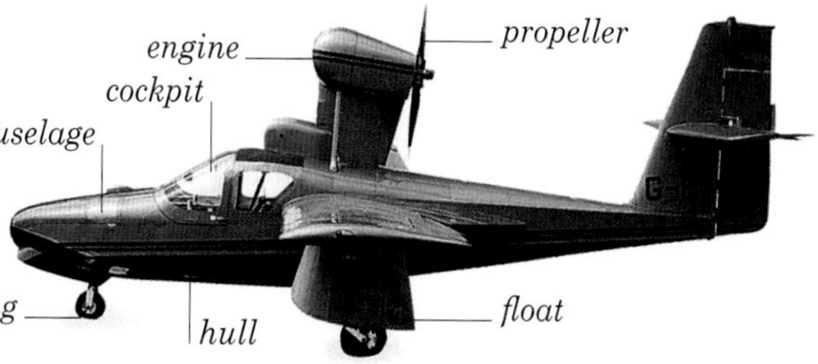

sea plane

rickshaw

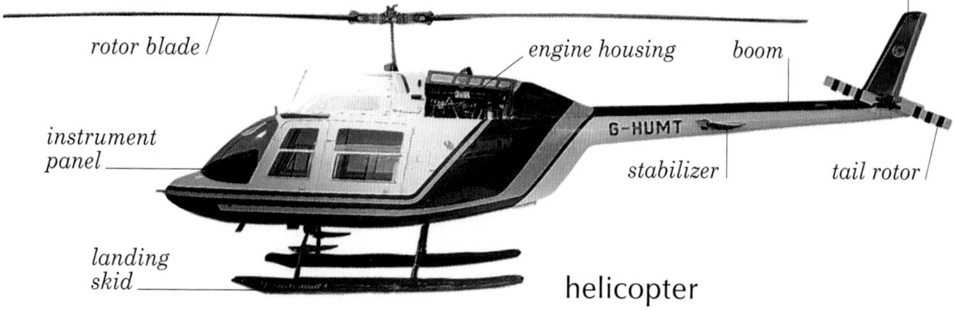

helicopter

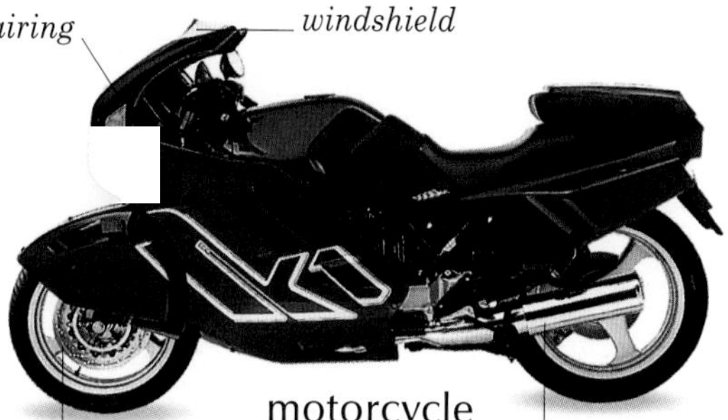

motorcycle

passenger train

camel

horse

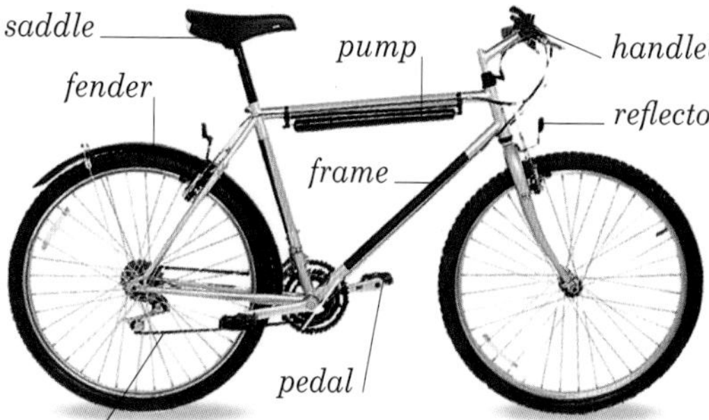

mountain bike

paddle steamer

transport
transports transporting transported *verb*
to carry people or things from one place to another.
*The goods were **transported** by train.*
transportation *noun*

trap
traps trapping trapped *verb*
to catch an animal or person and hold them in some way so that they cannot get away.
trap *noun*

trapdoor
trapdoors *noun*
a small door cut into a floor, on a stage, or in the ceiling.

trapeze
trapezes *noun*
a high swing used by acrobats for performing stunts.

trash
noun
garbage, or something that is worthless or useless.

traumatic
adjective
upsetting enough to have a long-lasting effect on someone.
*Giving evidence in the trial was very **traumatic**.*
■ say **traw**-ma-tik
trauma *noun*

travel
travels traveling traveled *verb*
to go from one place to another.

*We **traveled** around the lakes and mountains on vacation.*
travel *noun*

trawler
trawlers *noun*
a boat that is used to catch fish by dragging a large net behind it along the bottom of the sea.

tray
trays *noun*
a flat board, often with a rim, that is used for carrying food and drinks.

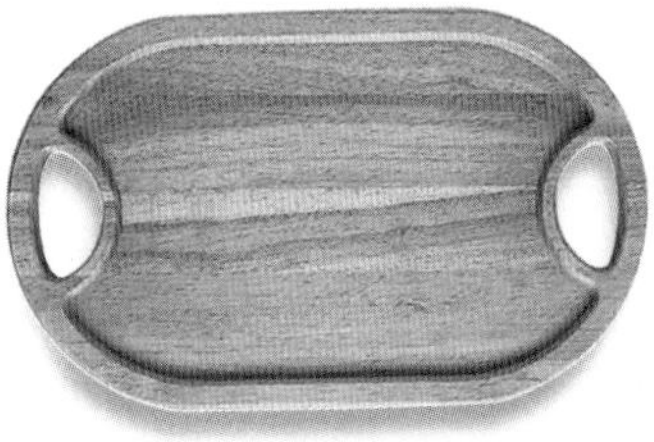

treacherous
adjective
very dangerous.

*The sea can be **treacherous** for a small boat.*
■ say **trech**-ur-us

tread
treads *noun*
the raised part of a tire.
■ say **tred**

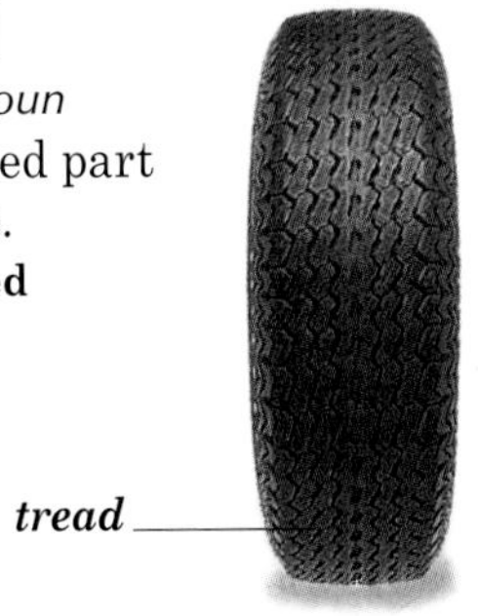

tread
treads treading trod trodden *verb*
to put your foot on something.

*The elephant **trod** on his foot.*

treason
noun
the act of being a traitor to your country by trying to destroy the government or the ruler, or by helping the enemy during a war.
■ say **tree**-zun

treasure
treasures *noun*
a large amount of gold, jewels, or other valuable things.

■ say **trezh**-ur

treasurer
treasurers *noun*
a person who looks after the money and accounts of a government, a club, or a company.

treat
treats *noun*
a special thing that gives someone pleasure.

*They were taken to the fair as a birthday **treat**.*
■ say **treet**

treat
treats treating treated *verb*
1 to behave in a certain way toward people, animals, or things.
*She **treats** her pet hamster very well.*
2 to try to make someone well.

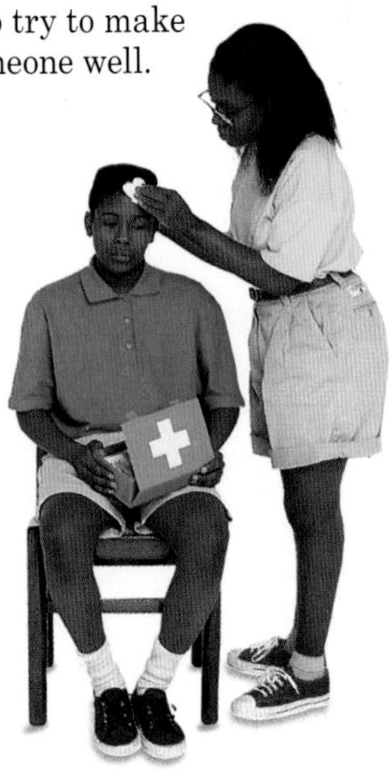

*She **treated** the cut on his head.*
treatment *noun*

treaty
treaties *noun*
an agreement made between countries.

*Signing a peace **treaty**.*

tree

trees *noun*

a tall plant with branches, leaves, and a main stem called a trunk. Trees are either deciduous or evergreen.

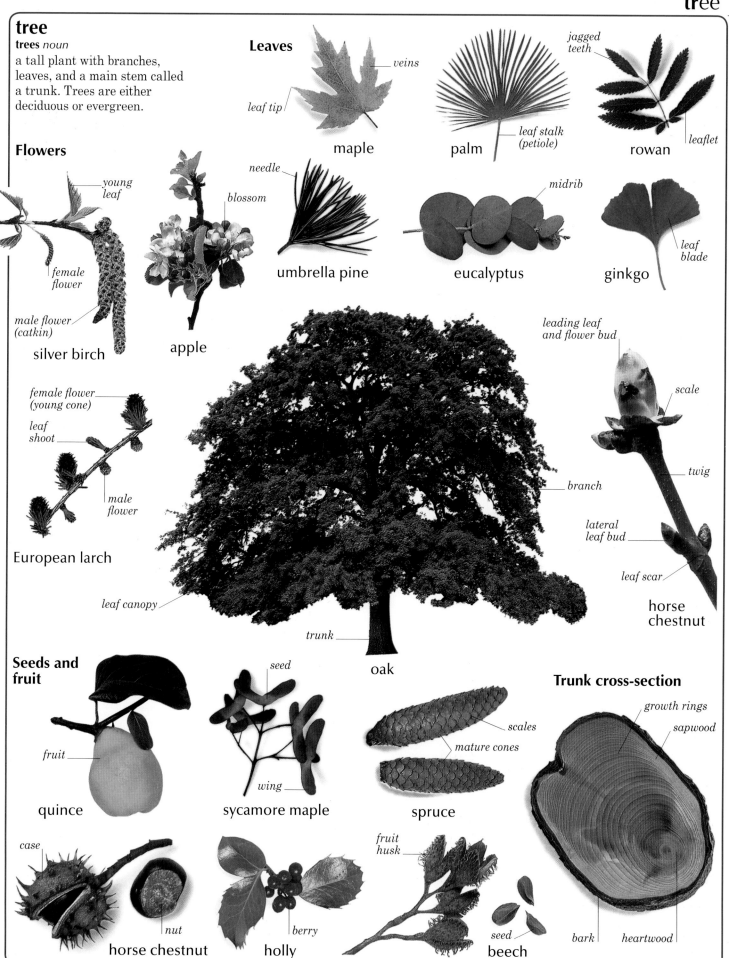

Leaves

maple

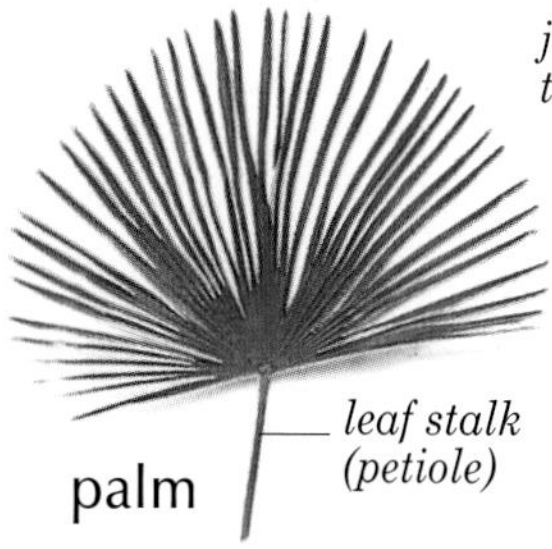

palm

rowan

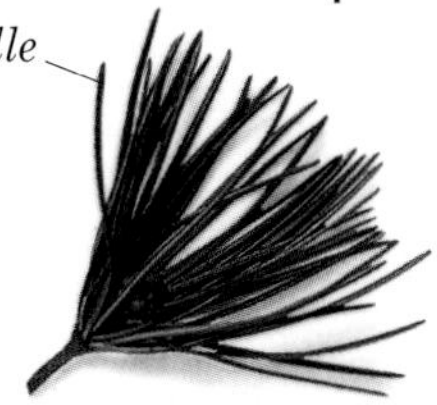

umbrella pine

eucalyptus

ginkgo

Flowers

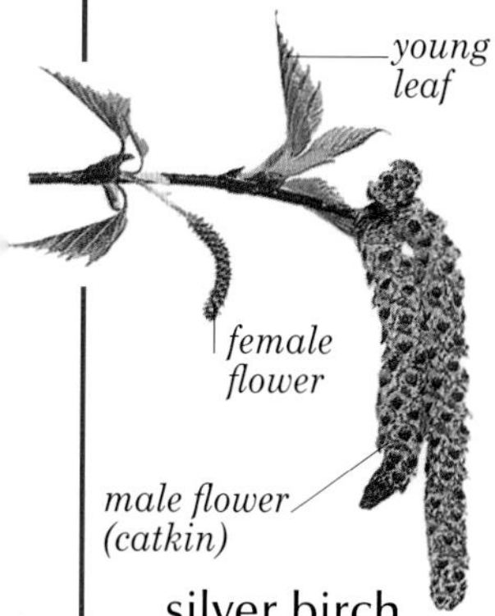

silver birch

apple

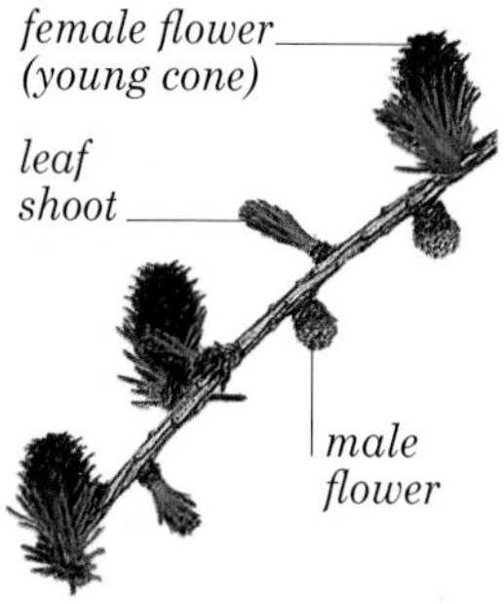

European larch

oak

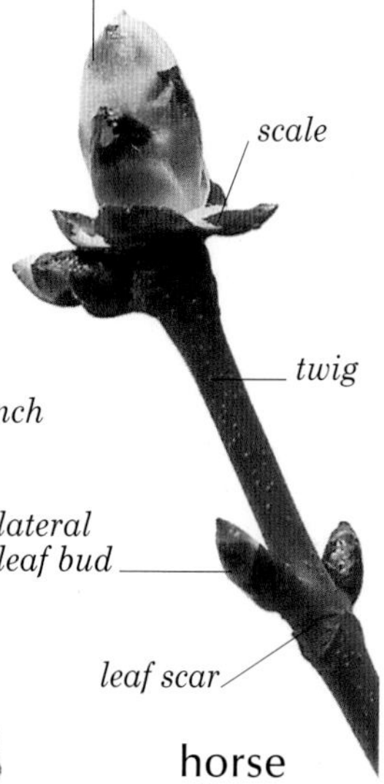

horse chestnut

Seeds and fruit

quince

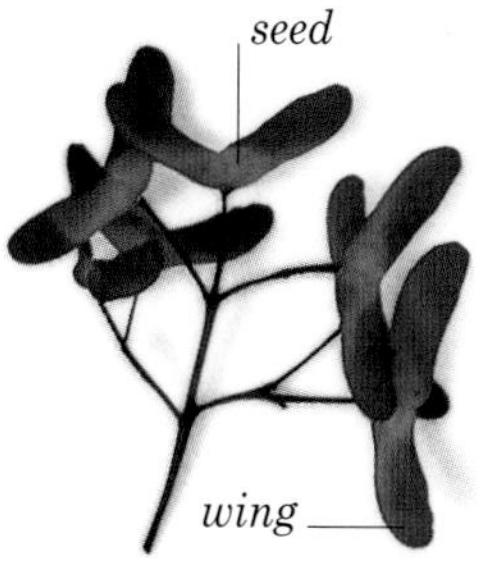

sycamore maple

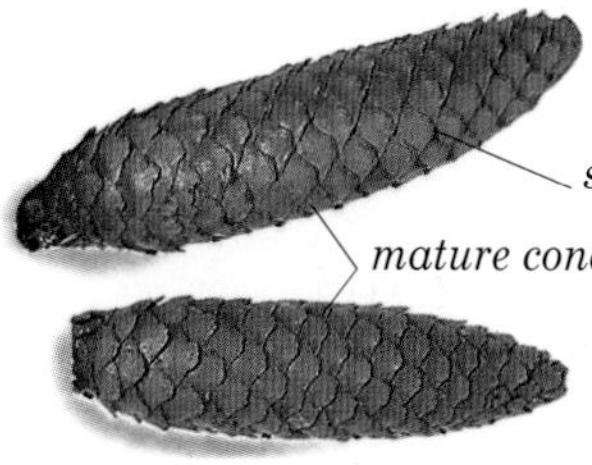

spruce

horse chestnut

holly

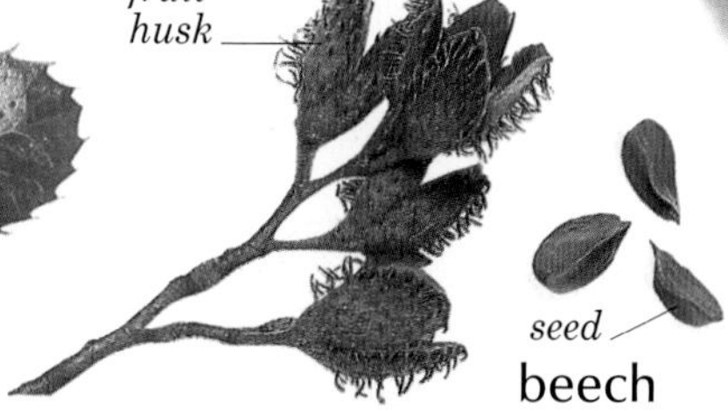

beech

Trunk cross-section

tremble
trembles trembling trembled *verb*
to shake with fear or cold.

trial
trials *noun*
1 the legal process by which a judge and jury decide whether a person is guilty or innocent of a crime.
She is on ***trial*** *for theft.*
2 an experiment or test to see what something is like or to see if it works.
The new sports car passed its ***trials*** *successfully.*
■ say **try**-ul

triangle
triangles *noun*
1 a shape with three sides (see **shape** on page 182).
triangular *adjective*
2 a musical instrument. A triangle is played by hitting one of the metal sides with a small metal rod.

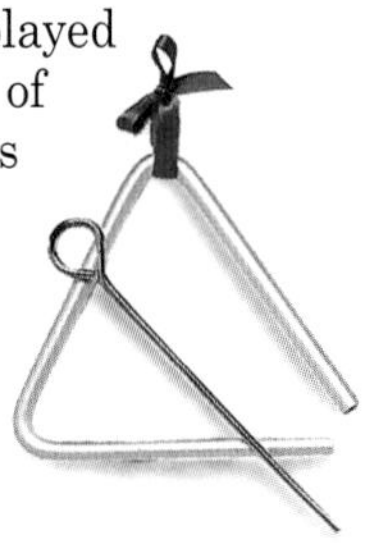

trick
tricks *noun*
1 a skillful action that is done to entertain someone.

A magic ***trick****.*
2 something done to fool someone.
trick *verb*

trickle
trickles trickling trickled *verb*
to flow very slowly.
The raindrops ***trickled*** *down the window.*

tricycle
tricycles *noun*
a vehicle with three wheels that is moved by turning the pedals around, like a bicycle.

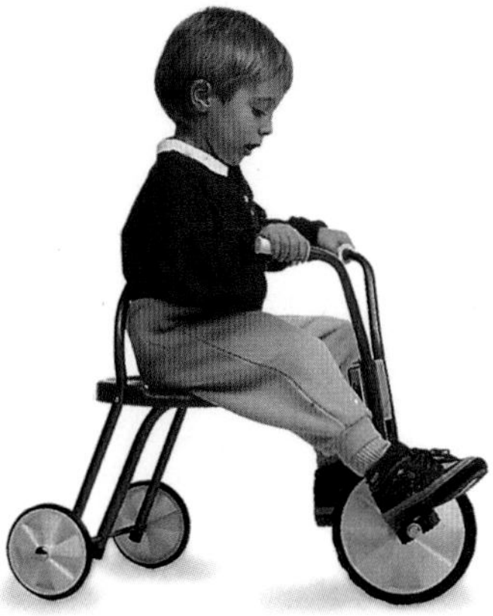

child's ***tricycle***
■ say **try**-sik-ul

trim
trims trimming trimmed *verb*
to cut the edges or ends off something, such as hair, in order to make it neat.

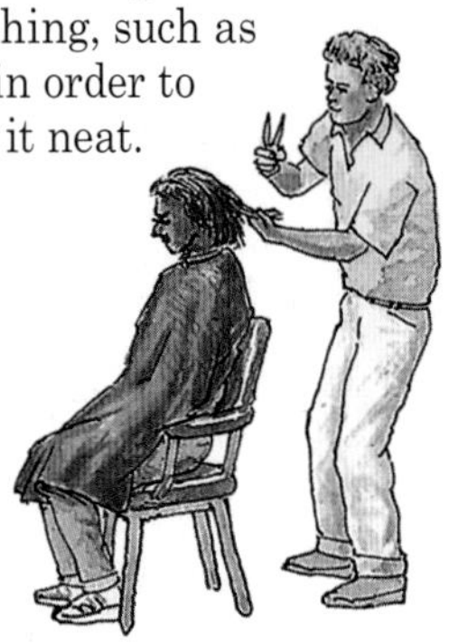

The hairdresser ***trimmed*** *his hair.*

trip
trips tripping tripped *verb*
to stumble and fall.
I ***tripped*** *over the book that she'd left on the floor.*

trip
trips *noun*
a journey.
We went on a school ***trip*** *to the museum.*

tripod
tripods *noun*
a frame with three legs that is used as a support for a camera.

■ say **try**-pod

triumph
triumphs *noun*
a great success.
Winning the race was a ***triumph****.*
■ say **try**-umf
triumphant *adjective*

trod
from the verb ***to tread***
She ***trod*** *in a puddle and splashed her clothes.*

trolley car
trolley cars *noun*
a vehicle that runs on tracks in streets and is powered by an electric current from an overhead wire.

trombone
trombones *noun*
a large, brass musical instrument, played by blowing through a mouthpiece. The notes are produced by sliding a long, bent tube backward and forward.

tenor ***trombone***

trophy
trophies *noun*
a cup, medal, or other prize that is given to the winner of a contest.

tennis ***trophy***
■ say **tro**-fee

tropical
adjective
from the hot, wet area of the world near the equator.
Tropical *fruit.*

trot
trots trotting trotted *verb*
to move the way a horse does when it is walking fast. One of the horse's front hooves and the opposite back hoof are on the ground at the same time.

trot *noun*

trouble
troubles *noun*
a situation or problem that is worrying or difficult.
If you smash that window, you'll be in ***trouble****!*
■ say **trub**-ul

trough
troughs *noun*
a narrow, open container for animals to eat or drink from.
■ say **trof**

trousers
noun
pants; a piece of clothing that you wear on your legs.

trout
trout *noun*
a type of edible fish that is part of the same family as the salmon. Most trout live in fresh water, but some species migrate to the sea after laying their eggs. They feed on insects, small fish, and shrimp.

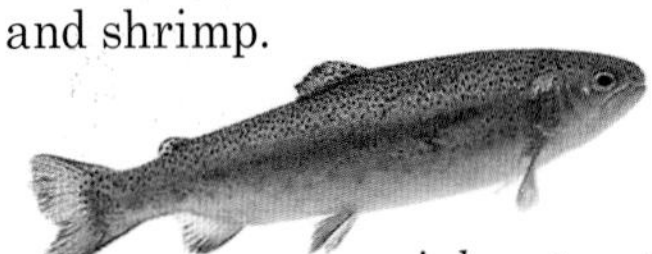

rainbow ***trout***

trowel
trowels *noun*
a small hand tool similar to a shovel. Curved trowels are used for gardening. Flat ones are used for spreading cement.

gardening ***trowel***
■ rhymes with **owl**

truce
truces *noun*
an agreement to stop fighting for a short time.
The armies called a ***truce****.*
■ rhymes with **noose**

truck
trucks *noun*
a large vehicle used for carrying goods from one place to another.

trudge
trudges trudging trudged *verb*
to walk in a tired way.

They ***trudged*** *home through the snow.*

true
adjective
real and accurate.
A ***true*** *story.*
■ opposite **false**

trumpet
trumpets *noun*
a small, brass musical instrument made of a long, curved, narrow tube with an end like a funnel. Notes are produced by pressing valves down and blowing through a mouthpiece.

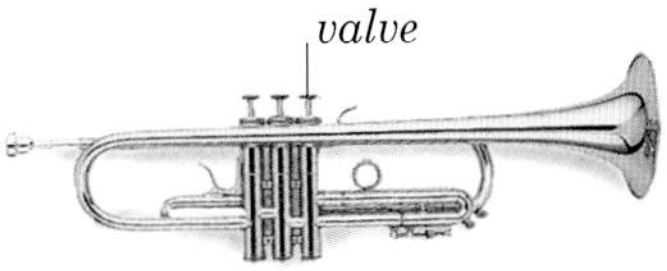

trunk
trunks *noun*
1 the main stem of a tree (see **tree** on page 223).
2 the main part of the body of a person or animal, not including the head, arms, and legs.

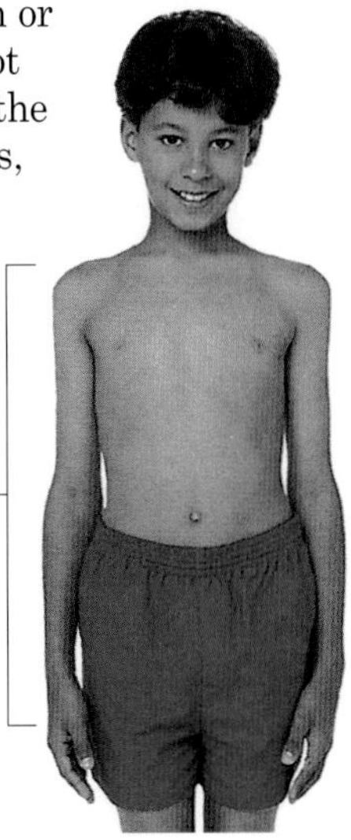

3 the long nose of an elephant (see **mammal** on page 124).
4 a large box with a hinged lid, used for storing things.

trust
trusts trusting trusted *verb*
to believe that someone or something is honest and reliable.
I ***trusted*** *my friend not to give away the secret.*
trust *noun*
trustworthy *adjective*

truth
noun
something that is true.
Do you always tell the ***truth****?*
■ say **trooth**

try
tries trying tried *verb*
1 to make an effort to do something.
He ***tried*** *to climb up the tree.*
2 to test something to see if it works, or to put something on to see if it fits.

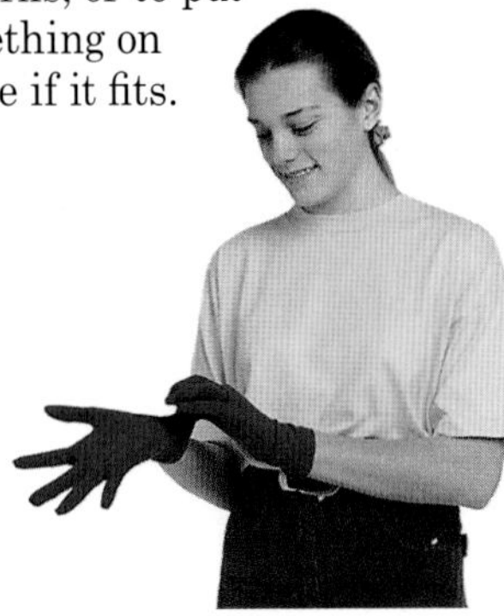

She ***tried*** *on the gloves.*
3 to decide in a trial, within a court of law, whether someone is innocent or guilty of a crime.
The court ***tried*** *him for theft.*

T-shirt
T-shirts *noun*
a shirt made from knitted cotton with short sleeves and no collar.

tub
tubs *noun*
a rounded, open container that is used to store things or wash things.

tube
tubes *noun*
1 a long, hollow pipe.
A cardboard ***tube****.*
2 a long, narrow container made of plastic or thin metal. The contents are removed by squeezing.

tube *of toothpaste*

tuck
tucks tucking tucked *verb*
1 to fold or push into place.

Tuck *your shirt into your pants.*
2 to cover up in a snug way.
I like being ***tucked*** *in bed.*

tuft
tufts *noun*
a bunch of grass, threads, hair, or feathers that grows or is tied closely together.

tug
tugs tugging tugged *verb*
to give something a quick, hard pull.
My sister ***tugged*** *at my sleeve.*

tulip
tulips *noun*
a plant with a large, cup-shaped flower that grows from a bulb.

■ say **too**-lip

tumble
tumbles tumbling tumbled *verb*
to fall and roll over.
She ***tumbled*** *down the hill.*

tuna
tuna or **tunas** *noun*
a large, edible sea fish. Tuna feed on squid and other fish. They are fast swimmers and migrate long distances every year.
■ say **too**-nuh

A B C D E F G H I J K L M N O P Q R S T U V W X Y Z

tune
tunes *noun*
a series of musical notes put together in a certain order to form a melody.
*He sang a song and I played the **tune** on the piano.*

tunnel
tunnels *noun*
an underground passage.

turban
turbans *noun*
a head covering consisting of a long strip of cloth wrapped around the head, worn especially by Muslim and Sikh men.

turkey
turkeys *noun*
a large bird that lives wild in the forests of North America. Turkeys feed on acorns, seeds, berries, and insects. Turkeys are reared on farms for their meat in many parts of the world.

turn
turns turning turned *verb*
1 to go around.
*The watch hands **turn** clockwise.*
2 to change direction.
*He **turned** to see what was happening behind him.*
3 to become.
*His fingers **turned** blue with the cold.*

turn
turns *noun*
a chance or duty that comes to each of a number of people in order.
*It's your **turn** to do the dishes.*

turnip
turnips *noun*
a type of plant with a round root that is eaten as a vegetable.

turquoise
noun
1 a green-blue stone that is often used in jewelry.

2 the color of the stone turquoise.
■ say **tur**-koiz

turtle
turtles *noun*
a reptile that is part of the same family as the tortoise. Turtles live in water and feed on plants and small animals. Some turtles lay their eggs on land.

*green **turtle***

tusk
tusks *noun*
a long, pointed tooth that sticks out of the mouth of certain animals (see **mammal** on page 124).

twig
twigs *noun*
a small branch of a tree or shrub (see **tree** on page 223).

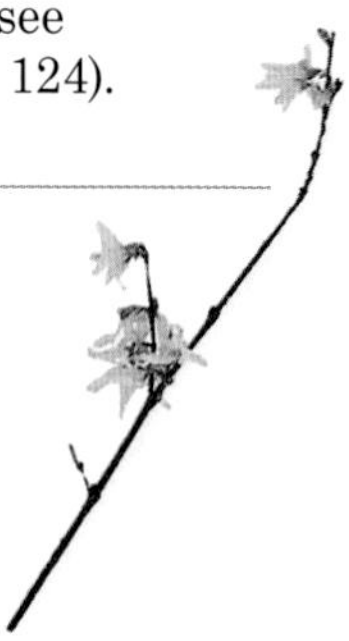

twin
twins *noun*
1 one of a pair of children or animals born to their mother at the same time.
*Identical **twins**.*
2 one of two things that are exactly the same.
twin *adjective*

twinkle
twinkles twinkling twinkled *verb*
to shine with small flashes of light.
*The stars **twinkled** in the sky.*

twirl
twirls twirling twirled *verb*
to spin in a quick, light way.

*She **twirled** around to show them her new skirt.*

twist
twists twisting twisted *verb*
to turn or wind something.

*She **twisted** her head around.*

type
types typing typed *verb*
to write using the letter and number keys on a typewriter or other keyboard.
■ say **tipe**

type
types *noun*
1 a group of people or things that are alike in some way.
*The store sold two **types** of boot.*
2 printed letters.
*This book has small **type**.*

typewriter
typewriters *noun*
a machine with a keyboard, used for printing letters and numbers on paper.

typical
adjective
being a good example of something, or showing all its usual qualities.
*They lived in a **typical** city street.*
■ say **tip**-i-kul
typically *adverb*

Uu

ugly
adjective
unpleasant to look at.
■ say **ug**-lee
ugliness *noun*

ulcer
ulcers *noun*
a sore patch on your skin or in your stomach.
■ say **ul**-ser

umbrella
umbrellas *noun*
a covered frame, held up by a stick that is used to protect a person from the rain, or as a shade from the sun. Umbrella frames are covered with cloth or plastic and can be folded up when not in use.

umpire
umpires *noun*
someone who makes sure that players follow the rules of a game or sport.
umpire *verb*

unanimous
adjective
agreed by everyone.
*The leader was elected by a **unanimous** vote.*
■ say yoo-**nan**-uh-mus

uncle
uncles *noun*
the brother of someone's parent, or their aunt's husband.

uncomfortable
adjective
1 not able to relax.

*She was too **uncomfortable** to go to sleep.*
2 causing an unpleasant feeling or slight pain.
***Uncomfortable** shoes.*
■ opposite **comfortable**

unconscious
adjective
1 not able to think and feel, possibly because of an illness or accident.
*The falling brick knocked him **unconscious**.*
2 done without thinking.
*He has an **unconscious** habit of scratching his chin.*
■ say un-**kon**-shus
■ opposite **conscious**

uncover
uncovers uncovering uncovered *verb*
to remove the cover, unwrap, or reveal something.

*The archeologists **uncovered** a Roman mosaic.*

under
preposition
below or beneath something, or to a lower place.

*She is holding the ball **under** her arm.*

undercover
adjective
done in secret to obtain information.
*The police were working on an **undercover** investigation.*

underdone
adjective
not cooked for long enough.

underground
adjective
below the ground.

*An **underground** cave.*
underground *adverb*

underline
underlines underlining underlined *verb*
to draw a line under something, usually to stress it or to show that it is important.

You <u>must</u> reply.

underneath
preposition
below something, or in a lower place.

*The children played **underneath** the table.*
underneath *adverb*

understand
understands understanding understood *verb*
to know what something means.
*Did you **understand** the question?*

understudy
understudies *noun*
a person who learns a part in a play or performance so that he or she can take over if the usual actor cannot perform.
understudy *verb*

underwater
adjective
found under the surface of the water, or used under the surface of the water.

*The diver swam among the **underwater** plants and animals.*
underwater *adverb*

underwear
noun
the clothes that you wear next to your skin and under your other clothes.

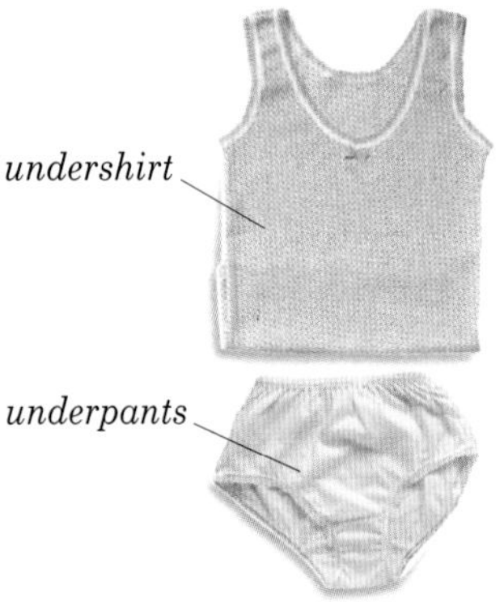

undo
undoes undoing undid undone *verb*
to unfasten or untie.

Undoing a knot in a rope.
■ say un-**doo**

undress
undresses undressing undressed *verb*
to take clothes off.

■ opposite **dress**

uneasy
adjective
not feeling comfortable or happy.
*She felt **uneasy** about leaving the door unlocked.*
uneasily *adverb*

unemployed
adjective
without a job.
*He's been **unemployed** for almost a year.*
■ opposite **employed**
unemployment *noun*

uneven
adjective
not smooth or level.

*The road had a very **uneven** surface.*
■ opposite **even**
unevenly *adverb*

unexpected
adjective
surprising, or happening when you do not think it will.

*The **unexpected** rain made everyone leave the beach.*
■ opposite **expected**
unexpectedly *adverb*

unfair
adjective
not right or honest.
*That's **unfair**! You have more than me!*
■ opposite **fair**

unfortunate
adjective
having or bringing bad luck.

*It was **unfortunate** that he'd left a roller skate on the floor.*
■ opposite **fortunate**
unfortunately *adverb*

unhappy
adjective
sad or miserable.
*She felt **unhappy** when she failed the exam.*
■ opposite **happy**

unhealthy
adjective
1 not well or not fit.
*You look **unhealthy**.*
2 bad for your health.
*It's **unhealthy** to eat snacks all the time.*
■ say un-**hel**-thee
■ opposite **healthy**

unicorn
unicorns *noun*
an imaginary animal in myths and fairy tales. A unicorn is like a horse, but has a long, spiraled horn on its forehead.
■ say **yoo**-ni-korn

unicycle
unicycles *noun*
a machine for riding on, with pedals, a saddle, and one wheel. Unicycles are sometimes used for performing acrobatic tricks.

■ say **yoo**-ni-sy-kul

uniform
uniforms *noun*
special clothes worn by members of a group to show that they belong to that group. People in the armed forces, the police force, and some students wear uniforms.

*19th-century army general's **uniform***
■ say **yoo**-ni-form

union
unions *noun*
1 two or more people, places, or things that are joined together to become one.
*Russia was once a part of the **Union** of Soviet Socialist Republics.*
2 a group of workers that join together to take care of the concerns of employees.
■ say **yoon**-yun

unique
adjective
being the only one of its kind.

*Every snowflake is **unique**.*
■ say yoo-**neek**

unit
units *noun*
1 a single part of something.
*A kitchen **unit**.*
2 a fixed amount used as a standard by which other things are measured.
*A foot is a **unit** of length.*

unite
unites uniting united *verb*
to join together or to do something together.
*The towns **united** in their fight against the factory's pollution.*
■ say yoo-**nite**

universe
noun
all of space, and everything that exists in it. The universe includes Earth, the other planets, and all the stars.

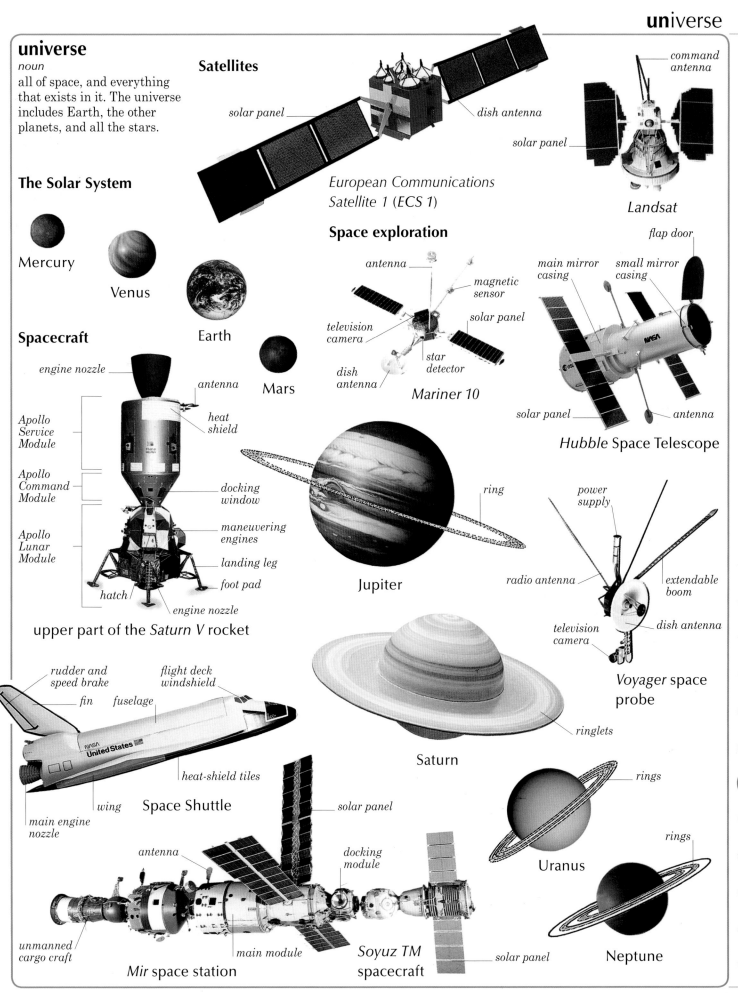

Satellites

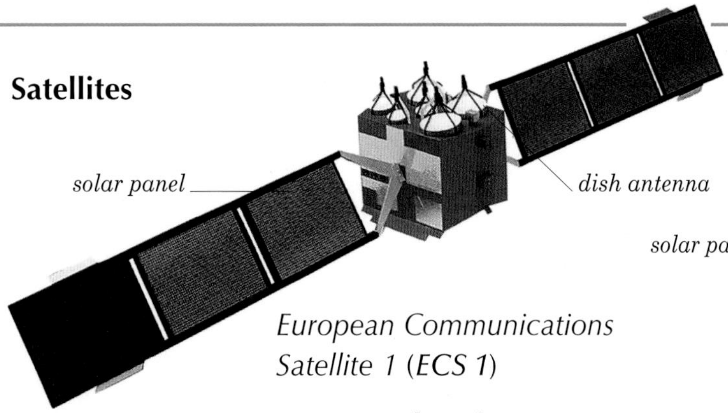

European Communications Satellite 1 (ECS 1)

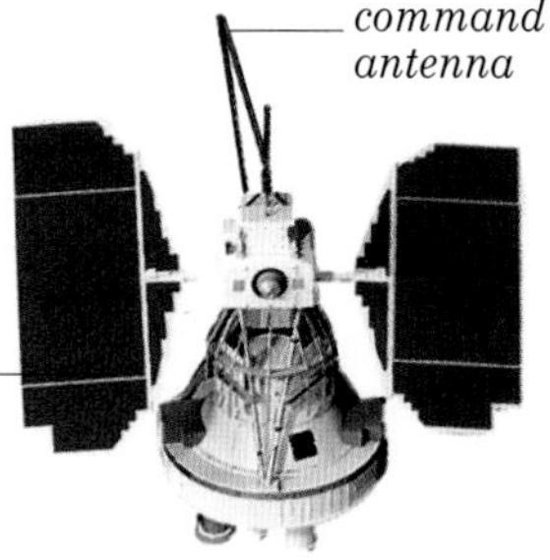

Landsat

The Solar System

Mercury

Venus

Earth

Mars

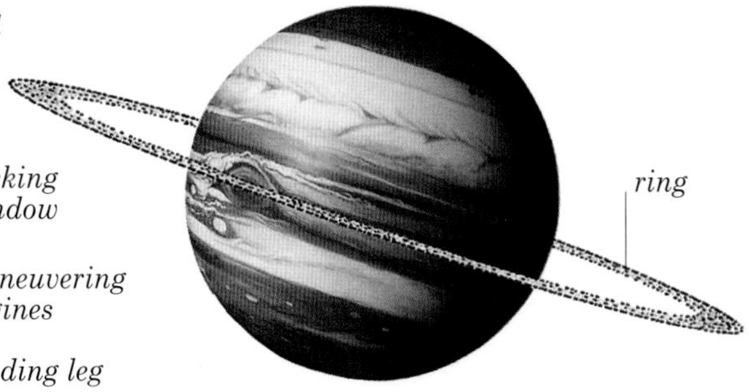

Jupiter

Saturn

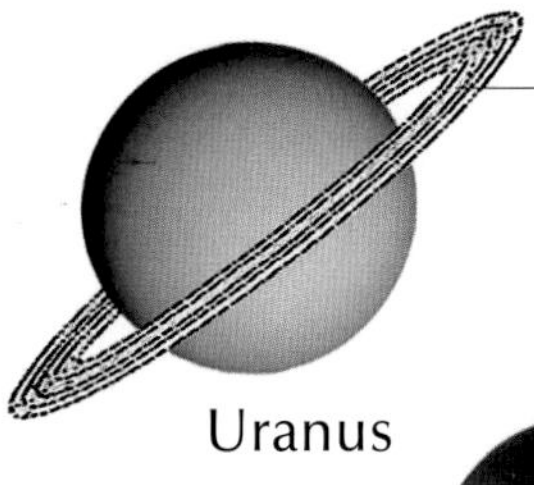

Uranus

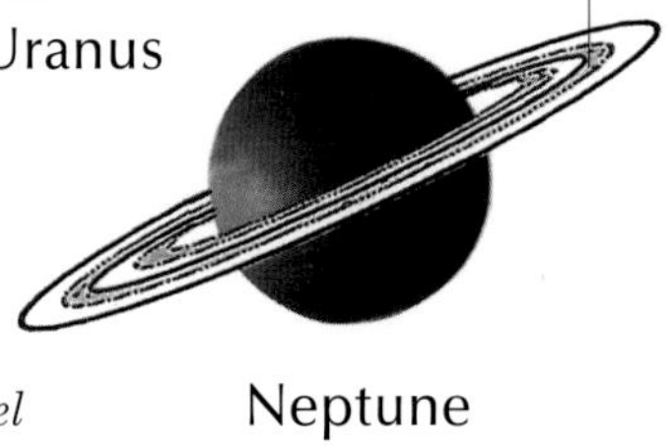

Neptune

Space exploration

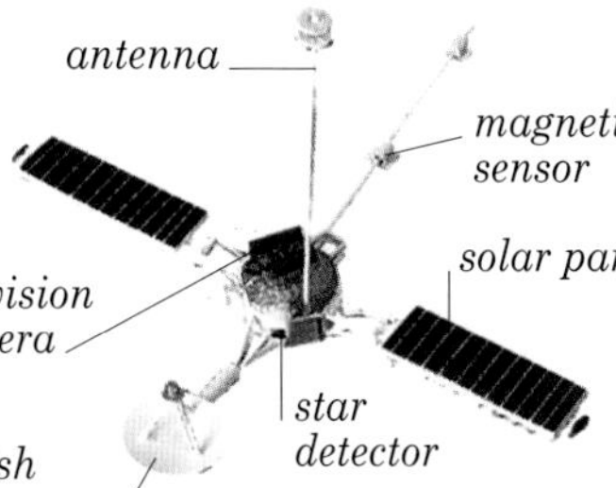

Mariner 10

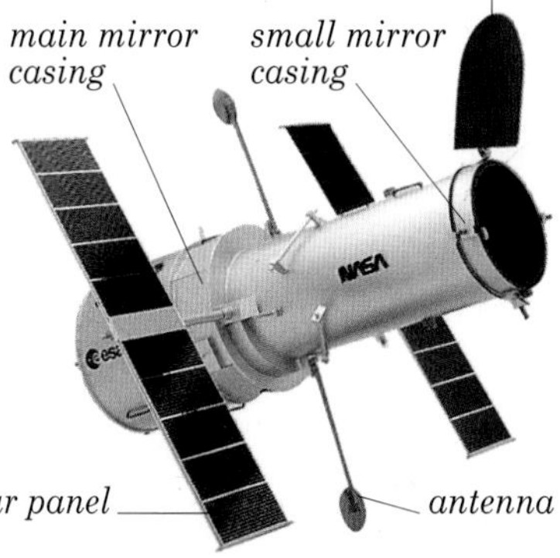

Hubble Space Telescope

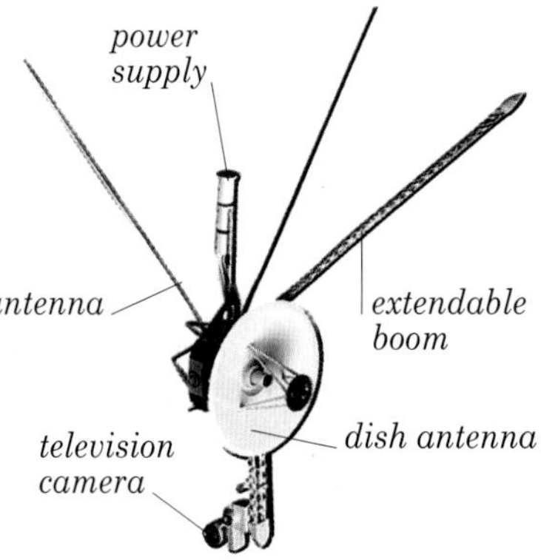

Voyager space probe

Spacecraft

upper part of the *Saturn V* rocket

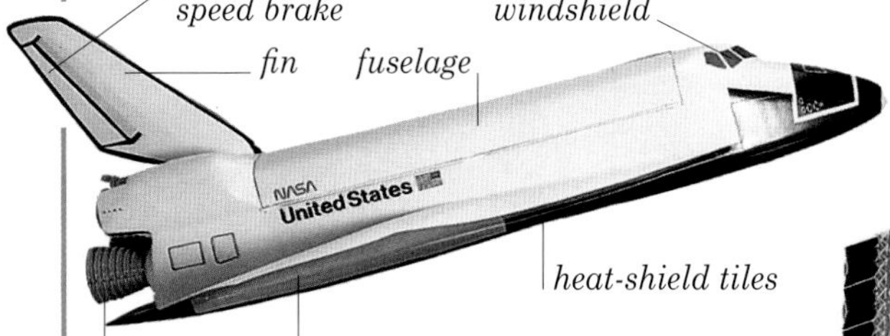

Space Shuttle

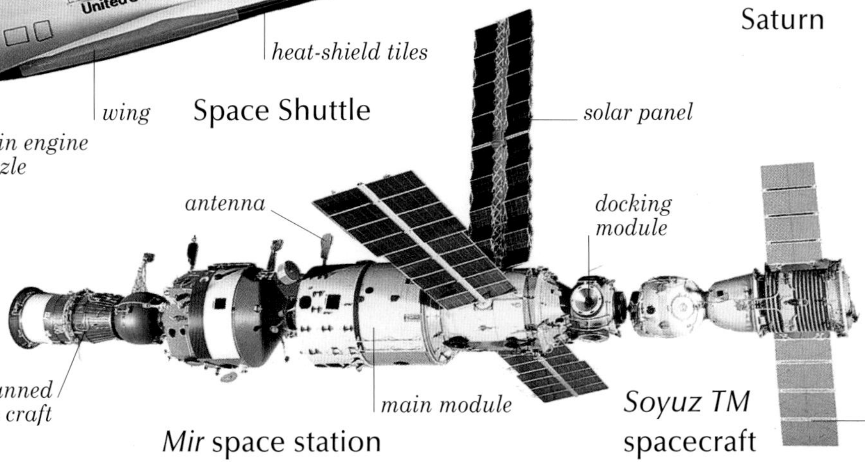

Mir space station

Soyuz TM spacecraft

university
universities *noun*
a place where students go for the highest level of education.

*Graduating from **university** with advanced degrees.*
■ say yoo-nuh-**vur**-si-tee

unkind
adjective
cruel or not caring.

*She was very **unkind** to her little sister.*
■ opposite **kind**

unknown
adjective
never seen or heard of.
*Highways were **unknown** in the 19th century.*
■ say un-**noen**

unlikely
adjective
not probable.
*An **unlikely** story.*
■ opposite **likely**

unload
unloads unloading unloaded
verb
to take things out of a vehicle or container.

*He **unloaded** the groceries from the shopping cart.*
■ opposite **load**

unlock
unlocks unlocking unlocked *verb*
to open something by undoing a lock.

*He **unlocked** his bicycle.*
■ opposite **lock**

unlucky
adjective
having bad luck, or bringing bad luck.
*It's thought to be **unlucky** to walk under ladders.*
■ comparisons **unluckier unluckiest**
■ opposite **lucky**

unnecessary
adjective
not needed.
*It's **unnecessary** to wear a coat in very hot weather.*
■ say un-**nes**-i-sair-ee
■ opposite **necessary**

unoccupied
adjective
vacant, or not being used.

*The house had been **unoccupied** for months.*
■ opposite **occupied**

unorganized
adjective
with no order or plan.
*The trip was very **unorganized**.*
■ opposite **organized**

unpack
unpacks unpacking unpacked *verb*
to take things out of a container.

Unpacking a suitcase.
■ opposite **pack**

unpleasant
adjective
not pleasing, or not nice.
*An **unpleasant** smell.*
■ opposite **pleasant**

unscrew
unscrews unscrewing unscrewed
verb
to loosen by turning, or to undo screws.

*She **unscrewed** the numbers from the door.*

untidy
adjective
in a mess.
*Her room was always **untidy**.*
■ say un-**ty**-dee
■ opposite **tidy**

untie
unties untying untied *verb*
to undo something that is knotted, such as rope or thread.

*She **untied** the rope and rowed away.*
■ opposite **tie**

until
preposition
up to the time of.
*We were awake **until** midnight.*

untrue
adjective
false or not based on facts.
*The story about the two-tailed dog was **untrue**.*
■ opposite **true**

unused
adjective
not in use or never used.
*An **unused** notebook.*
■ say un-**yoozd**
■ opposite **used**

unusual
adjective
rare or not ordinary.

*A very **unusual** guitar.*
■ say un-**yoo**-zhoo-al

unwise
adjective
foolish or not smart.
*It was **unwise** to play catch in the house.*
■ opposite **wise**

unwrap
unwraps unwrapping unwrapped *verb*
to take the wrapping or covering off something.

*She **unwrapped** her present.*
■ say un-**rap**
■ opposite **wrap**

up
preposition
toward a higher position.
*I walked **up** the hill to the house at the top.*
■ opposite **down**

up
adverb
to or in a higher position.
*Stand **up**!*
■ opposite **down**

upright
adverb
sitting or standing up straight rather than bent over.

*The dog stood **upright** on its hind legs.*
■ say **up**-rite
upright *adjective*

uproar
noun
a state of noisy activity.
*The crowd was in an **uproar**.*

upset
upsets upsetting upset *verb*
1 to make someone sad or anxious.
*The accident **upset** him.*
2 to knock something over.
*The cat **upset** the vase of flowers.*
upset *adjective*

upside down
adverb
with the top part underneath, or turned the wrong way up.

*He hung **upside down** from the bar.*
upside-down *adjective*

upstairs
adverb
to or on an upper story.

*The lights are on **upstairs**.*
■ opposite **downstairs**
upstairs *adjective*

upward
adverb
toward a higher position.

*She let go and the balloons drifted **upward**.*
■ opposite **downward**

uranium
noun
a silvery white, radioactive metal used for producing nuclear energy.

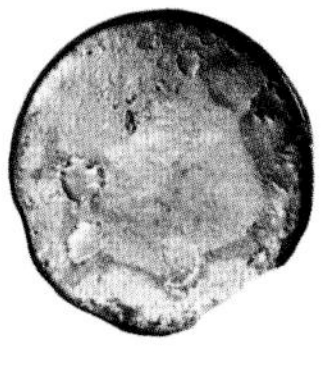

■ say yoo-**ray**-nee-um

urge
urges urging urged *verb*
to try to persuade someone to do something.
*He **urged** them to be careful when playing by the river.*
■ say **urj**

urge
urges *noun*
a powerful feeling that makes you want to do something.
*A sudden **urge** to sneeze.*

urgent
adjective
needing immediate action or attention.
*An **urgent** message.*
■ say **ur**-junt
urgently *adverb*

urine
noun
liquid waste from the body.
■ say **yoor**-in

use
uses using used *verb*
to put something into action.

*The cat **uses** a cat flap to come in and go out of the house.*
■ say **yooz**

use
uses *noun*
1 the value of something for a certain purpose.

*This penknife has many **uses**.*
2 the state of being used.
*Steam trains are still in **use** in some areas.*
■ say **yoos**

useful
adjective
able to be used for all kinds of tasks, or good for a certain task.

*This gadget is **useful** for unscrewing lids.*
■ say **yoose**-ful
■ opposite **useless**
usefully *adverb*

usual
adjective
most often done or seen.
*I left work at the **usual** time.*
■ say **yoo**-zhoo-ul
usually *adverb*

utensil
utensils *noun*
a tool used for a particular job, especially one used in the kitchen.

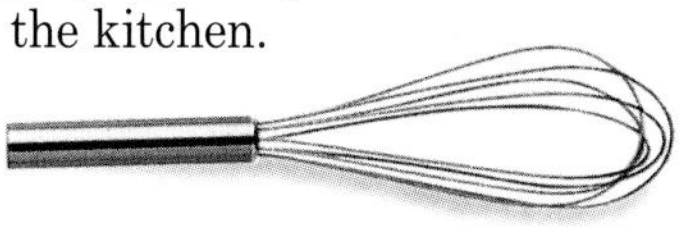

*A whisk is a kitchen **utensil**.*
■ say yoo-**ten**-sul

Vv

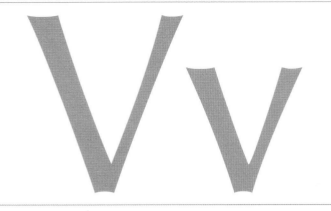

vacant
adjective
empty or not used.
*She parked in the **vacant** space.*
■ say **vay**-kunt

vaccination
vaccinations *noun*
an injection of a substance called a vaccine that prevents you from getting a particular disease.

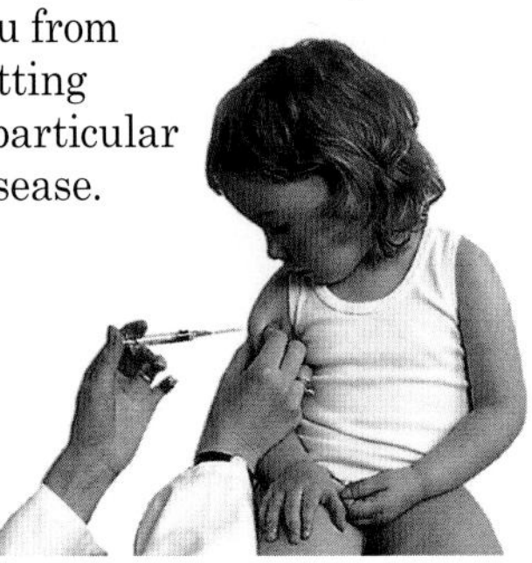

■ say vak-suh-**nay**-shun

vacuum
vacuums *noun*
a space from which all, or almost all, of the air has been removed.
■ say **vak**-yoom

vacuum cleaner
vacuum cleaners *noun*
a machine that cleans by sucking up dirt.

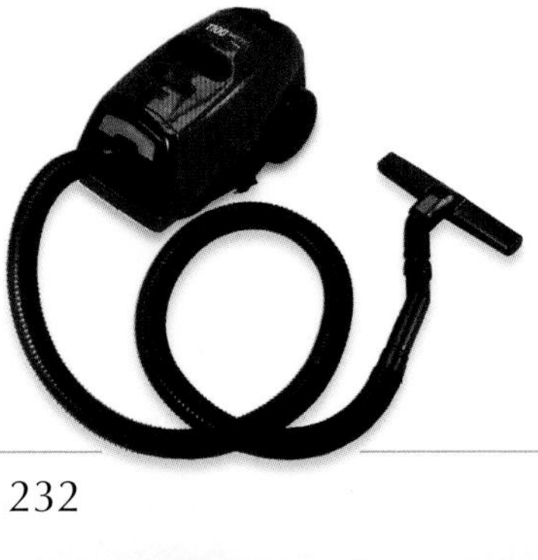

vacuum flask
vacuum flasks *noun*
a container used for keeping liquids hot or cold. Flasks have double walls with a vacuum between them. We commonly call this a thermos.

vague
adjective
not clear or not definite.
*A **vague** idea.*
■ say **vayg**
vaguely *adverb*

vain
adjective
1 too proud of what you can do, what you look like, or what you own.
Vain people look in the mirror all the time.
■ comparisons **vainer vainest**
2 unsuccessful.
*They made a **vain** attempt to put out the fire.*
vainly *adverb*

valley
valleys *noun*
an area of lowland between hills, often with a river or stream flowing through it.

valuable
adjective
1 precious, or worth a lot of money.

*This **valuable** Chinese ornament once belonged to an emperor.*
2 useful or worthwhile.
***Valuable** help.*
■ say **val**-yoo-uh-bul
■ opposite **worthless**
value *noun*

van
vans *noun*
a boxy road vehicle that is bigger than a stations wagon and smaller than a bus.

vandal
vandals *noun*
a person who deliberately damages things.
vandalize *verb*

vanilla
noun
a sweet food flavoring made from the pods of a tropical orchid, also called vanilla.

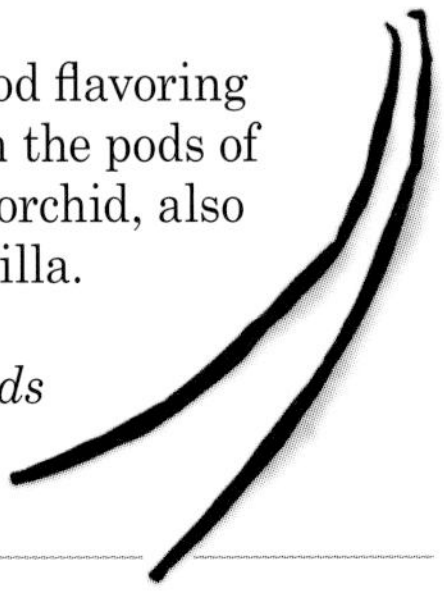

***vanilla** pods*

vanish
vanishes vanishing vanished *verb*
to disappear suddenly.
*The magician waved his wand and the rabbit **vanished**.*

vapor
vapors *noun*
1 the gas that certain liquids or solids give off when they are heated.
2 steam, mist, or smoke in the air.
■ say **vay**-pur

variety
varieties *noun*
1 change or difference.
*It is important to have **variety** in your work, or you will be bored.*
2 a selection of different things.
*The store had a **variety** of mugs for sale.*
3 a particular type.
*What **variety** of fruit is that?*
■ say vuh-**ry**-i-tee

various
adjective
of several different kinds.
*I bought **various** things at the mall.*
■ say **vair**-ee-us

varnish
varnishes *noun*
a type of clear paint that makes a surface tough and shiny when it is dry.

*wood **varnish***
varnish *verb*

vase
vases *noun*
a jar used as an ornament for displaying flowers.

■ say **vayz**

a b c d e f g h i j k l m n o p q r s t u v w x y z

vegetable

vegetables *noun*

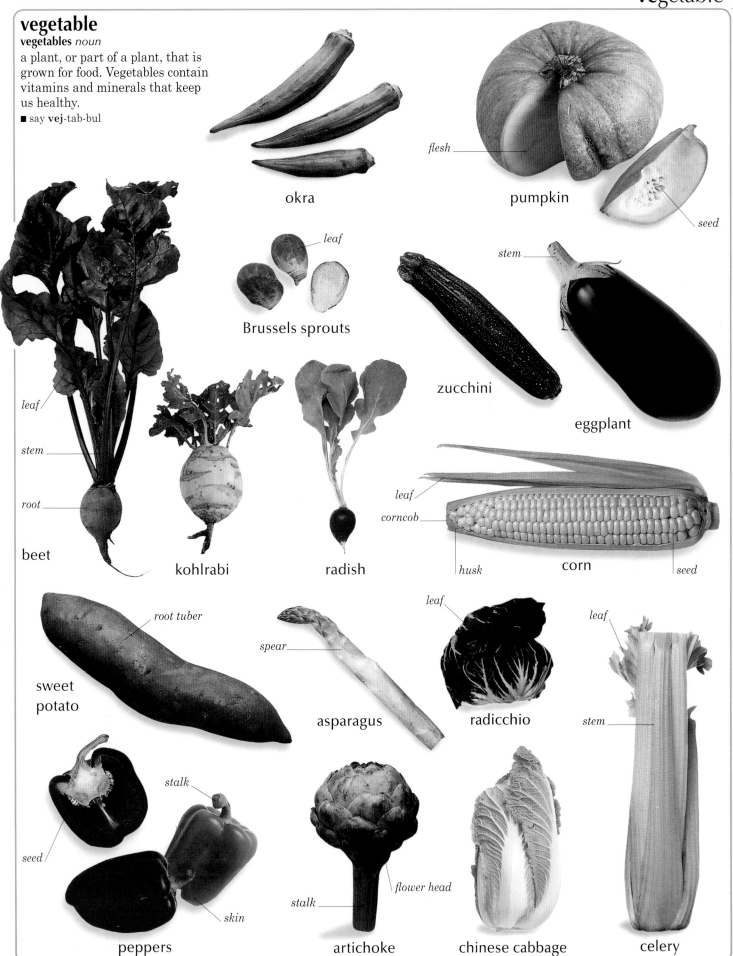

a plant, or part of a plant, that is grown for food. Vegetables contain vitamins and minerals that keep us healthy.

■ say **vej**-tab-bul

okra

pumpkin

beet

Brussels sprouts

zucchini

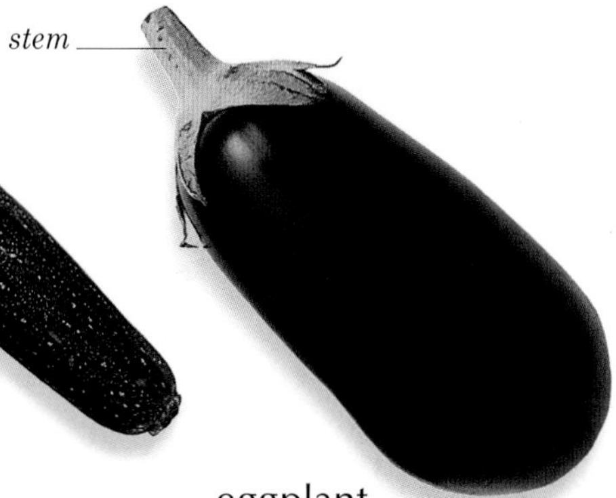

eggplant

kohlrabi

radish

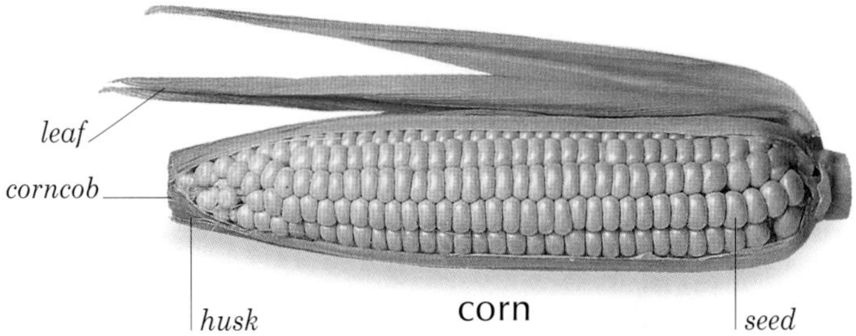

corn

sweet potato

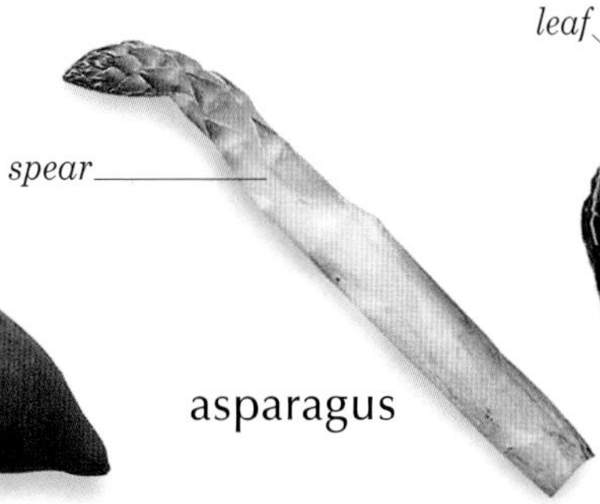

asparagus

radicchio

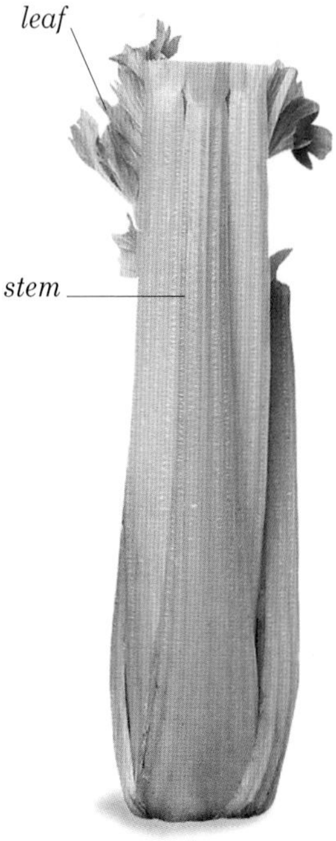

celery

peppers

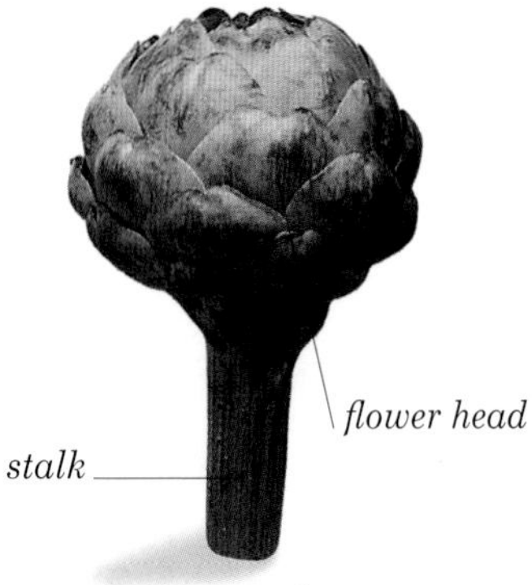

artichoke

chinese cabbage

vegetarian
vegetarians *noun*
someone who does not eat meat or fish.
■ say vej-it-**tear**-ee-an

vehicle
vehicles *noun*
something that is used to transport people or things on land, in the air, or in space.

■ say **vee**-i-kul

veil
veils *noun*
a covering for the face or head that is made of thin fabric.

■ rhymes with **pale**

vein
veins *noun*
1 any one of the tubes that carries blood from other parts of the body to the heart. The vena cava is the major vein in the body.

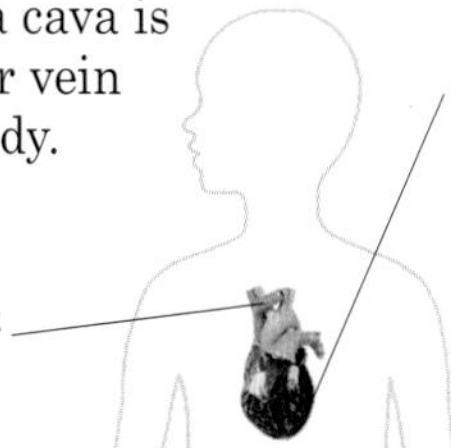

2 one of the fine tubes in a leaf or in an insect's wings.

■ say **vane**

velvet
noun
a type of fabric covered in short, soft fibers.

velvet *adjective*

ventriloquist
ventriloquists *noun*
a person who can speak without moving his or her lips. Most ventriloquists use dolls and make it seem as if the doll is talking.

■ say ven-**tril**-uh-kwist

verb
verbs *noun*
a word that describes what a person or thing is doing. A sentence usually needs a verb in order to make sense.

verse
verses *noun*
1 a section of a poem or song.
2 a general name for poetry.
*He wrote a book of **verse**.*

version
versions *noun*
A different kind or form of the same thing.
*I like this **version** of the story.*

vertical
adjective
standing straight up, at right angles to the horizon.

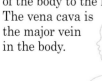

*a **vertical** line*

very
adverb
extremely, or by a great amount.
*This book is **very** long.*

vessel
vessels *noun*
1 a craft that is used for water transportation; usually anything larger than a boat.

2 any kind of hollow container, usually for food.
*When it rained, they filled the **vessels** with water.*
■ say **ves**-ul

vest
vests *noun*
a piece of underwear worn on the top half of the body.

veterinarian
veterinarians *noun*
a person who is trained to treat sick animals. Veterinarian can be shortened to vet.

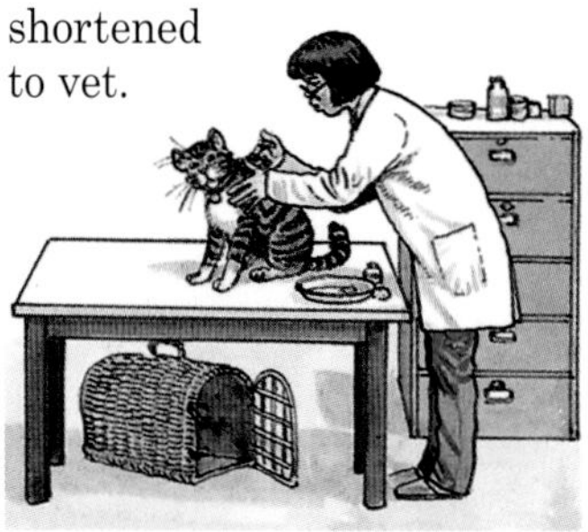

vibrate
vibrates vibrating vibrated *verb*
to make tiny, rapid, shaking movements.
*The drill **vibrated** noisily.*
■ say **vy**-brate
vibration *noun*

vicious
adjective
likely to hurt people or things.
*A **vicious** dog attacked him.*
■ say **vish**-us

victim
victims *noun*
a person who has been harmed or killed by something or someone.
*The **victim** of an accident.*

victory
victories *noun*
success in a contest or battle.

*The race-car driver was thrilled with his **victory**.*
■ say **vik**-tor-ee

view
views *noun*
1 everything that you can see from a certain place.

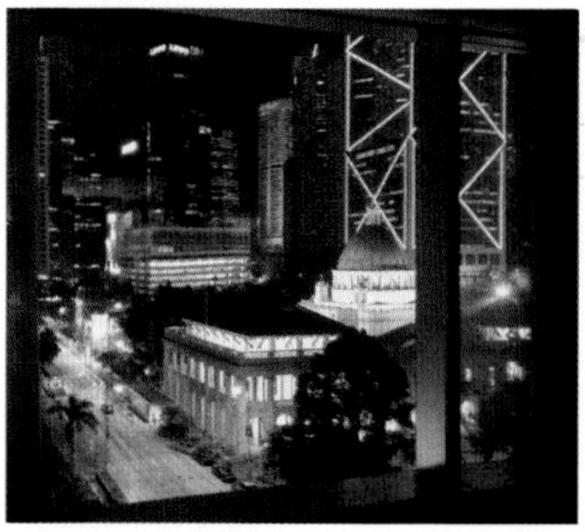

*There was a good **view** of the city from the window.*
2 an opinion.
*In my **view**, more people ought to travel by train.*
■ say **vyoo**

A B C D E F G H I J K L M N O P Q R S T U V W X Y Z

village
villages *noun*
a community in the country that is smaller than a town.

vinegar
noun
a sour liquid used to flavor or preserve food.
■ say **vin**-i-gur

vintage
adjective
old and of good quality (see **car** on page 39).

violent
adjective
using strong and damaging force.
*The **violent** storm threw cars across the street.*
violence *noun*
violently *adverb*

violin
violins *noun*
a wooden musical instrument with four strings. The violin body is held below the chin and played with a bow.

bow

violin

virus
viruses *noun*
a type of germ that causes a disease such as the flu.
■ say **vye**-rus

visible
adjective
able to be seen.
*The mountain was **visible** for miles.*
■ opposite **invisible**

visit
visits visiting visited *verb*
to go to see a person or a place.

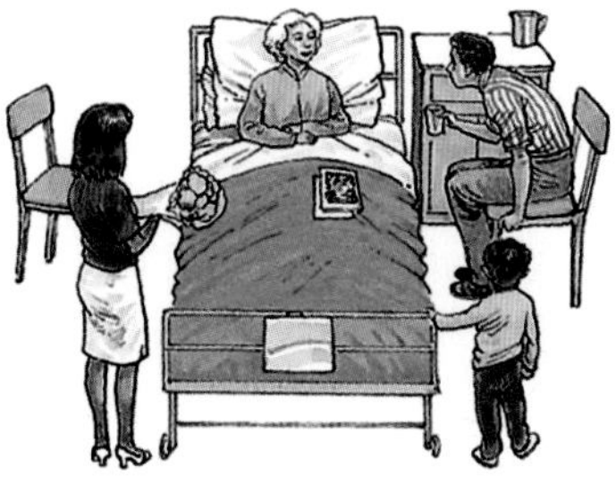

*I went to **visit** her in the hospital.*
visit *noun*

vitamin
vitamins *noun*
one of a group of natural substances found in foods that we need to eat to keep healthy.

parsley

pepper

*Foods containing **vitamin** C.*

vocabulary
vocabularies *noun*
1 all the words in a language.
2 all the words that are known and used by a person.
■ say vo-**kab**-yoo-lar-ee

voice
voices *noun*
the sound that comes out of your mouth when you speak or sing.
*He's lost his **voice**.*
■ say **voys**

volcano
volcanoes *noun*
a mountain that is created by lava from inside the Earth. Volcanoes sometimes erupt, sending lava and ash down onto the surrounding country.

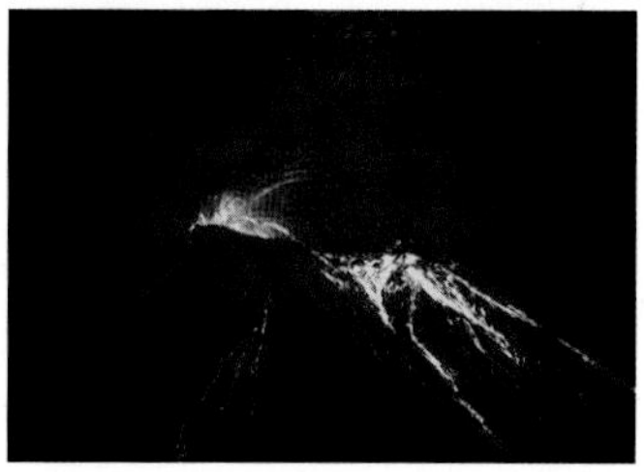

volcanic *adjective*

volume
volumes *noun*
1 a book, usually one of a series.

*The fourth **volume** of an encyclopedia.*
2 the amount of space inside something, or the amount of space that something fills.

*This pitcher's **volume** is one quart.*
3 an amount.
*This road has a huge **volume** of traffic traveling along it.*
4 the loudness of a sound.
*Can you turn up the **volume** on the television?*

volunteer
volunteers *noun*
a person who offers to do something without being told or paid to do it.
volunteer *verb*

vomit
vomits vomiting vomited *verb*
to throw up the contents of your stomach.
vomit *noun*

vote
votes voting voted *verb*
to show your choice or opinion by putting up your hand or by marking a name on a piece of paper.

*He **voted** for the candidate by putting an "X" on the paper.*
vote *noun*

vow
vows *noun*
a solemn promise.
vow *verb*
■ rhymes with **how**

vowel
vowels *noun*
a sound represented by the letters a, e, i, o, or u (see **alphabet** on page 16).
■ rhymes with **owl**

vulture
vultures *noun*
a large bird of prey that feeds on dead animals. Vultures have a good sense of smell and good eyesight. Their feet are adapted for walking rather than holding onto branches.

*Egyptian **vulture***

A B C D E F G H I J K L M N O P Q R S T U V W X Y Z

Ww

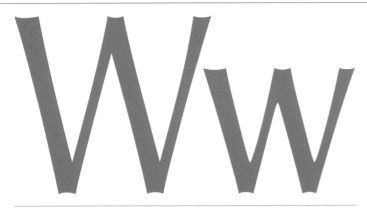

wade
wades wading waded *verb*
to walk through water.
*We **waded** across the stream.*

wafer
wafers *noun*
a thin, crisp cookie that is often eaten with ice cream.
■ say **way**-fur

waffle
waffles *noun*
a crisp, thick pancake with squares pressed into it. Waffles are made from eggs and flour.

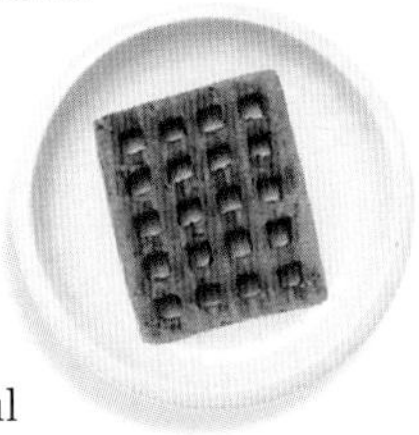

■ say **wof**-ul

wage
wages *noun*
the money paid to some in return for work.
*He collects his weekly **wages** every Friday.*
■ say **wayj**

waist
waists *noun*
the narrower part of your body between your chest and your hips.

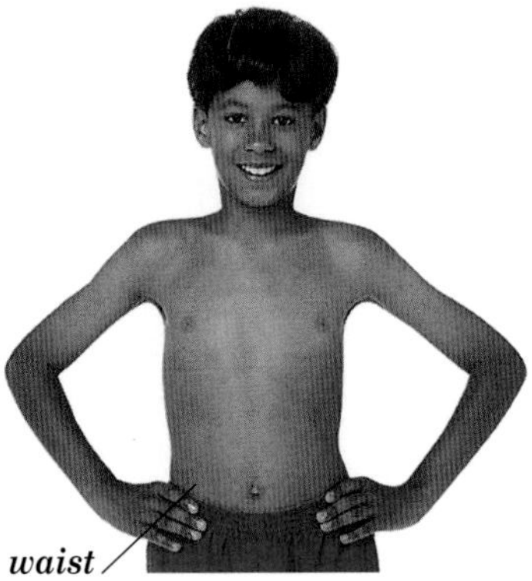

wait
waits waiting waited *verb*
to stay in a place or delay doing something until a certain event happens.
***Wait** for me!*
wait *noun*

waiter / waitress
waiters / waitresses *noun*
someone whose job it is to serve you with a meal.
■ **waiter** is male and **waitress** is female.

wagon
wagons *noun*
a vehicle with four wheels used for transporting heavy loads. A wagon can be pulled by a train or a horse.

wake
wakes waking woke woken *verb*
to stop sleeping or to stop someone else from sleeping.
*I **woke** up early this morning.*
awake *adjective*

walk
walks walking walked *verb*
to move along on foot.
■ say **wawk**

walker
walkers *noun*
a framework, usually waist-high, that a baby or handicapped person might use to help them walk.

wall
walls *noun*
a vertical surface made of stone, brick, or another material. Walls are used to enclose a space or to form the outside structure and inside divisions of a building.

*There was a high **wall** around the garden.*

wallaby
wallabies *noun*
a plant-eating marsupial from Australia that looks like a small kangaroo.
■ say **wol**-UH-bee

wallet
wallets *noun*
a small, soft case for carrying money.

■ say **wol**-it

walrus
walruses *noun*
a very large sea mammal that lives on the ice in the Arctic and hunts for its food in the icy waters. Walruses have very tough skin and whiskers. They have a thick layer of fat called blubber to keep them warm instead of fur.

wand
wands *noun*
a long, slender stick used for performing magic tricks. In fairy tales, wands are used for casting magic spells.

■ say **wond**

wander
wanders wandering wandered *verb*
to go from place to place without any real purpose or destination.
*My friends love to **wander** around the mall.*
■ say **won**-der

want
wants wanting wanted *verb*
1 to wish to have or do something.
*I **want** a puppy for my birthday.*
2 to need or require something.
*Do you **want** any help?*

war
wars *noun*
a period of fighting between countries or groups of people.
■ say **wore**

wardrobe
wardrobes *noun*
1 a cupboard for clothing.
2 a collection of clothes.
*A winter **wardrobe**.*
■ say **wore**-drobe

warehouse
warehouses *noun*
a large building used for storing goods.

warm
adjective
1 having a temperature that is between cool and hot.

*The hot water bottle felt nice and **warm**.*
2 friendly and kind.
*She gave us a **warm** welcome.*
■ comparisons **warmer warmest**
■ opposite **cool**
warmth *noun*

warn
warns warning warned *verb*
to tell or signal to someone that there may be a problem or danger ahead.

*The sign on the fence **warned** of radioactivity in the area.*
■ say **worn**
warning *noun*

warship
warships *noun*
a ship armed with weapons that is used during a war.

wash
washes washing washed *verb*
to clean yourself or something else with water and soap.
wash *noun*

wasp
wasps *noun*
a type of flying insect that can sting. A wasp uses its sting to defend itself and to catch other insects for food.
■ say **wosp**

waste
wastes wasting wasted *verb*
1 to use more of something than you really need or want.
*Don't **waste** electricity!*
2 to fail to use something.
*He **wasted** the sunny day by staying in bed all day.*
waste *noun*

watch
watches watching watched *verb*
to look at and pay attention to someone or something for a time.

***Watching** birds.*

watch
watches *noun*
a small instrument for telling the time, usually worn on the wrist (see **time** on page 216).

water
noun
a clear liquid that falls as rain and forms streams, rivers, lakes, and oceans.
■ say **waw**-tur

water
waters watering watered *verb*
to supply with water.
*Will you **water** my plants while I'm away?*

water cycle
noun
the process by which water travels around the Earth and its atmosphere. Water from rivers and oceans evaporates into the air, where it gathers to form clouds. The water then falls as rain to fill the rivers and oceans.

waterfall
waterfalls *noun*
a place where a river falls over a steep cliff.

watermelon
watermelons *noun*
a large, juicy type of melon with green skin. The flesh is red and contains black seeds.

waterproof
adjective
not allowing water to pass through it.

*A **waterproof** coat.*

watt
watts *noun*
a unit for measuring electrical power.
*A 100-**watt** lightbulb.*
■ say **wot**

wave
waves *noun*
1 a moving ridge on the surface of a liquid.

2 a vibration of sound or light that travels through the air and moves in a similar way to a wave in liquid.

wave
waves waving waved *verb*
1 to signal to someone by moving your hand or an object from side to side.

*She **waved** good-bye as the ship sailed away.*
wave *noun*
2 to move backward and forward.
*The branches **waved** in the strong wind.*

wax
waxes *noun*
a solid, oily substance that melts when it is heated. Wax is used to make many things, including furniture polish and candles.

way
ways *noun*
1 a direction or route.

*The sign showed the **way** to the village.*
2 a method.
*What is the right **way** to use a video camera?*
3 a manner of behaving.
*She stared at him in a very rude **way**.*

weak
adjective
having little strength or power.

*Baby birds are very **weak** when they are born.*
■ comparisons **weaker weakest**
■ opposite **strong**
weakness *noun*

wealthy
adjective
having a lot of money or possessions.
*The inventor sold his idea and became very **wealthy**.*
■ say **wel**-thee
■ comparisons **wealthier wealthiest**
wealth *noun*

weapon
weapons *noun*
a tool that can be used to hurt someone.

*In the past, spears and swords were used as **weapons**.*
■ say **wep**-un

wear
wears wearing wore worn *verb*
to have on or covering your body.

*He is **wearing** a South American cowboy outfit.*
■ say **ware**

weary
adjective
very tired.

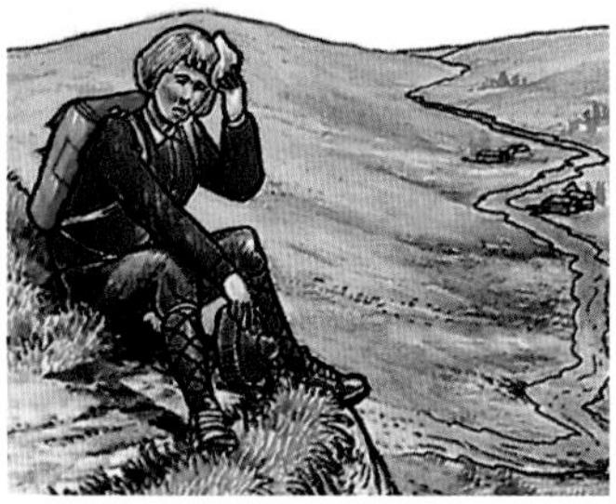

*She felt **weary** after her long walk.*
■ say **weer**-ee
■ comparisons **wearier weariest**
weariness *noun*

weather
noun
the condition of the atmosphere at a certain place and time, such as the air temperature and whether or not it is raining.

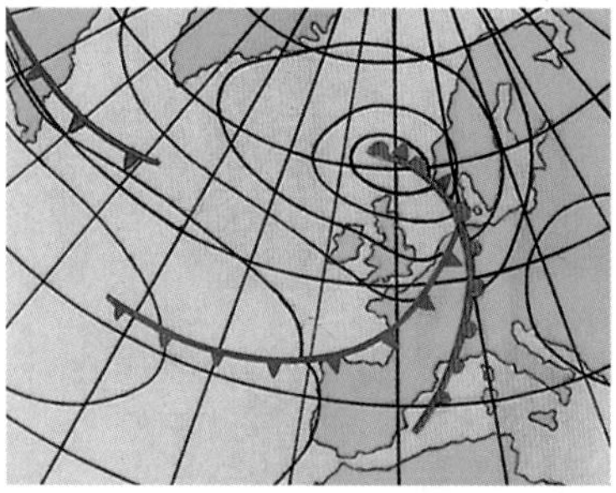

*a **weather** map*
■ say **weth**-ur

weathered
adjective
having changed shape or color due to the effects of the Sun, wind, or rain.
***Weathered** rock.*

weave
weaves weaving wove woven *verb*
1 to pass threads over and under one another to make cloth.

*He is **weaving** a mat out of wool.*
woven *adjective*
2 to move in and out between objects.
*The river **weaves** its way around the hills and down to the sea.*

web
webs *noun*
1 a fine net of sticky threads made by a spider to trap flies.
2 a collection of pages linked electronically via the internet.

wedding
weddings *noun*
an occasion when two people get married.

weed
weeds *noun*
a wild plant that grows where it is not wanted.

*Burdock is a common **weed**.*

week
weeks *noun*
a period of seven days.

weekend
weekends *noun*
Saturday and Sunday, the days when many people do not go to school or work.

weep
weeps weeping wept *verb*
to show you are unhappy by crying.

weigh
weighs weighing weighed *verb*
1 to measure how heavy something is.

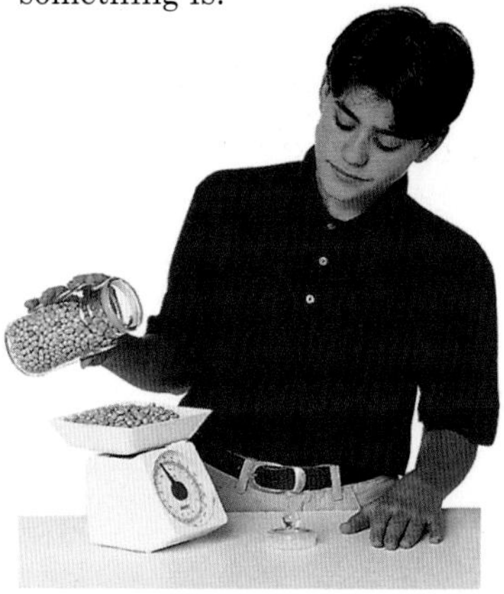

*He **weighed** some beans.*
2 to have a certain weight.
*The package **weighed** half a pound.*
■ say **way**

weight
weights *noun*
1 the measurement of how heavy something is.
2 a piece of metal with a known heaviness, used with weighing scales to determine how much something weighs.
■ say **wayt**

weird
adjective
strange and mysterious.

*The tree had a **weird** shape.*
■ say **weerd**
■ comparisons **weirder weirdest**

welcome
welcomes welcoming welcomed *verb*
to show someone that you are glad they have come.
*He went to the door to **welcome** his guests.*
welcoming *adjective*

welfare
noun
a person's health, happiness, and comfort.
*A principal has to consider the **welfare** of the pupils.*

well
wells *noun*
a deep hole made in the ground to obtain water, gas, or oil.

well
adjective
in good health.
*Are you **well** today?*

well
adverb
1 in a good or suitable way.
*He behaved very **well**.*
2 thoroughly.
*Water the plants **well**.*

went
*from the verb **to go***
*I **went** to the grocery store to buy some bread.*

wept
*from the verb **to weep***
*He **wept** when his dog died.*

west
noun
one of the four main compass directions. West is the direction in which the Sun sets.

western *adjective*

western
westerns *noun*
a film about cowboys and other people living in the western US, usually during the 19th century.

wet
adjective
1 covered or soaked with water.

2 rainy.
***Wet** weather.*
3 not yet dry.
***Wet** paint.*
■ comparisons **wetter wettest**
■ opposite **dry**

whale
whales *noun*
a very large sea mammal with a breathing hole in the top of its head. Whales eat fish or tiny water animals (see **mammal** on page 124).

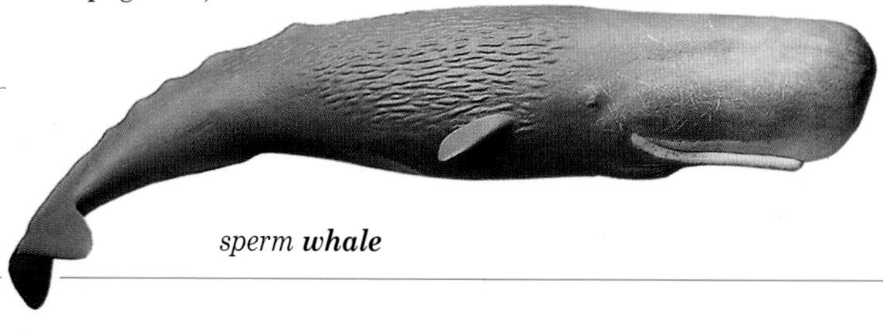

*sperm **whale***

what
adjective
which thing or which kind.
***What** is your favorite color?*
■ say **hwot**

wheat
noun
a type of cereal that is grown on farms. The grains from wheat are used for making flour.

*durum **wheat***

■ say **wheet**

wheel
wheels *noun*
a disk that turns around a fixed, central point. Most land vehicles move on wheels (see **car** on page 39 and **transportation** on page 221).

wheelbarrow
wheelbarrows *noun*
a small cart with one wheel at the front, used for pushing heavy loads by hand.

wheelchair
wheelchairs *noun*
a chair with wheels. People use wheelchairs to move from place to place if they have difficulty in walking.

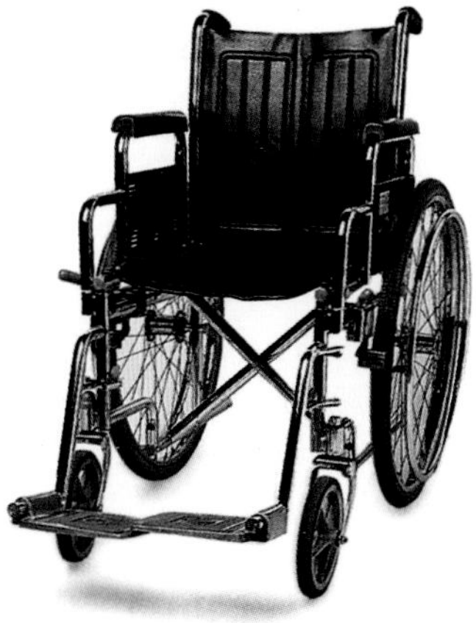

when
adverb
at what time.
***When** did you arrive?*

where
adverb
at, in, or to what place.
***Where** are you going?*

which
adjective
what particular thing or things out of a selection.
***Which** car is yours?*

whine
whines whining whined *verb*
1 to make a long, high cry.
*Dogs **whine**.*
2 to complain unnecessarily.
*The toddler **whined** about going to bed.*

whip
whips *noun*
a rope or strip of leather that is attached to a handle and is used for urging animals to do something.

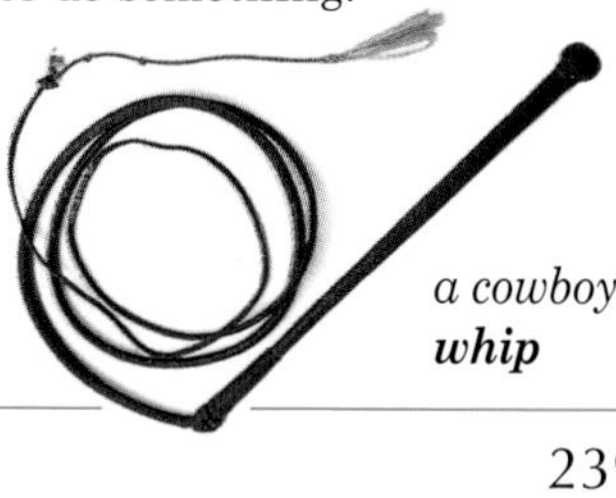

*a cowboy's **whip***

whirl
whirls whirling whirled *verb*
to turn yourself or an object around quickly.

*He **whirled** the lasso around his head.*

whirlwind
whirlwinds *noun*
a very strong wind that blows in spirals, causing great damage.

whisk
whisks whisking whisked *verb*
1 to move quickly and lightly.
*She **whisked** the child out of the way of the bike.*
2 to beat a mixture lightly and quickly.

***Whisk** the egg whites until they are stiff.*

whisker
whiskers *noun*
one of the stiff hairs that grows near the mouth of certain animals (see **mammal** on page 124 and **pet** on page 148).

whisper
whispers whispering whispered *verb*
to speak in a very quiet voice.

*She **whispered** her secret into his ear.*
whisper *noun*

whistle
whistles whistling whistled *verb*
to make a high, shrill sound by blowing air through your lips.

■ say **hwis-ul**

whistle
whistles *noun*
a device that you blow into to make high, shrill sounds.

white
noun
a color.

whizz
whizzes whizzing whizzed *verb*
to move along very fast.

whole
adjective
complete, or with nothing missing.

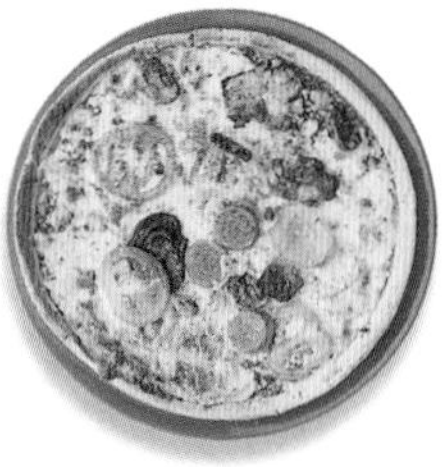

*They bought a **whole** quiche for the party.*
■ say **hole**
whole *noun*

why
adverb
for what reason.
Why did you go?

wicked
adjective
behaving in a bad way on purpose.
*A **wicked** person.*
wickedness *noun*

wide
adjective
1 being a large size, or long distance, from one side to the other.

*A **wide** river.*
■ comparisons **wider widest**
■ opposite **narrow**
2 having a certain measurement from one side to the other.
*The carpet is ten feet **wide**.*
wide *adverb*
width *noun*

widow / widower
widows / widowers *noun*
a person whose husband or wife has died.
■ **widow** is female and **widower** is male.

wife
wives *noun*
a married woman.

wig
wigs *noun*
a false covering of hair for the head (see **costume** on page 51).

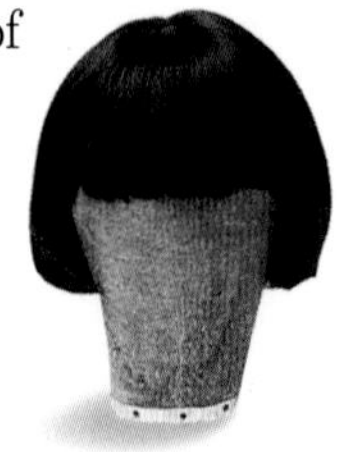

wild
adjective
1 in a natural environment, or not controlled by people.

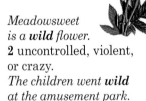

*Meadowsweet is a **wild** flower.*
2 uncontrolled, violent, or crazy.
*The children went **wild** at the amusement park.*
■ rhymes with **child**
■ comparisons **wilder wildest**

wilderness
wildernesses *noun*
a wild area of land where no one lives.
■ say **wil-der-ness**

will
verb
a word used to show that the action of a verb is happening in the future.
*I **will** go out this afternoon.*
■ opposite **will not** or **won't**
■ always used with another verb

will
wills *noun*
1 the power to choose and control your own actions.
She forced me to do it against my ***will.***
2 a document containing instructions about what should happen to a person's possessions after his or her death.

3 determination.
She had the ***will*** *to win.*

willing
adjective
in agreement with something that you are asked to do.
Are you ***willing*** *to help in the garden?*

win
wins winning won *verb*
to come first in a game or competition.

She was very pleased when she ***won*** *the game.*
■ opposite **lose**

wind
winds *noun*
a current of air.

The ***wind*** *blew his umbrella inside out.*
■ rhymes with **grinned**
windy *adjective*

wind
winds winding wound *verb*
1 to twist or coil something up.

He ***wound*** *the clock.*
2 to turn in a curving way.
They could see the car ***winding*** *its way up the hill.*
■ rhymes with **find**

windmill
windmills *noun*
a building with large sails that uses wind power to turn a machine that grinds grain, pumps water, or makes electricity.

window
windows *noun*
an opening in a building or vehicle that lets in light and air, often covered with glass.

wine
noun
an alcoholic drink made from the juice of grapes.

wing
wings *noun*
1 one of the parts of a bird, insect, or bat that is used for flying (see **bird** on page 28, **insect** on page 108, and **mammal** on page 124).
2 one of the large, flat parts on each side of an airplane that acts in a similar way to a bird's wings (see **transportation** on page 221).

wink
winks winking winked *verb*
to open and close one eye briefly as a signal to another person.

winter
noun
the coldest season of the year. Winter comes between the fall and spring.

wipe
wipes wiping wiped *verb*
to clean or dry something by rubbing.

He ***wiped*** *the mirror's surface with a cloth.*

wire
wires *noun*
a long, thin, metal thread that can be bent. Wires can be used to carry electrical power.

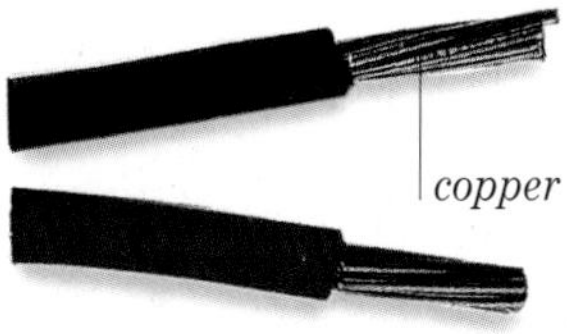

copper ***wire***

wise
adjective
having a lot of knowledge and experience.
The ***wise*** *old lady gave me good advice.*
■ say **wize**
■ comparisons **wiser wisest**
■ opposite **foolish**

wish
wishes wishing wished *verb*
to feel or say that you want something.
I ***wish*** *I owned a car.*
wish *noun*

witch
witches *noun*
a woman who practices magic.

wither
withers withering withered *verb*
to dry up.

Their plant ***withered*** *while they were away on vacation.*

without
preposition
not having or not using.

He went outside ***without*** *his shoes.*

witness
witnesses *noun*
a person who sees an event happen.
Three ***witnesses*** *saw him stealing the car.*
witness *verb*

wizard
wizards *noun*
a man who practices magic.

a b c d e f g h i j k l m n o p q r s t u v w x y z

wobble
wobbles wobbling wobbled *verb*
to move unsteadily.

*He **wobbled** on his ice skates.*

woke
*from the verb **to wake***
*He **woke** her very early.*

wolf
wolves *noun*
a wild mammal that is part of the dog family and lives in cold regions. Wolves live in packs and hunt other animals for food.

woman
women *noun*
an adult human female.
■ say **wum**-an

wombat
wombats *noun*
a marsupial that lives in Australia. A wombat looks like a small bear and lives underground, eating leaves, roots, and bark.

won
*from the verb **to win***
*We **won** the match.*
■ say **wun**

wonder
noun
a feeling caused by an extraordinary or amazing thing.
*They looked in **wonder** at the bright lights in the sky.*
■ say **wun**-der

wonder
wonders wondering wondered *verb*
to question or think about something in a curious or doubtful way.
*I **wonder** how she managed to arrive first?*

wonderful
adjective
amazing or extraordinary.
*A **wonderful** idea.*
■ say **wun**-dur-ful

wood
noun
1 the hard material from a tree's trunk or branches used to make furniture and objects or to burn for fuel.

*The train is made of **wood**.*
wooden *adjective*

2 a group of trees growing together.

woodwind instrument
woodwind instruments *noun*
one of a group of musical instruments that is played by blowing. Some, such as the clarinet, are made from wood while others, such as the flute, are made from metal.

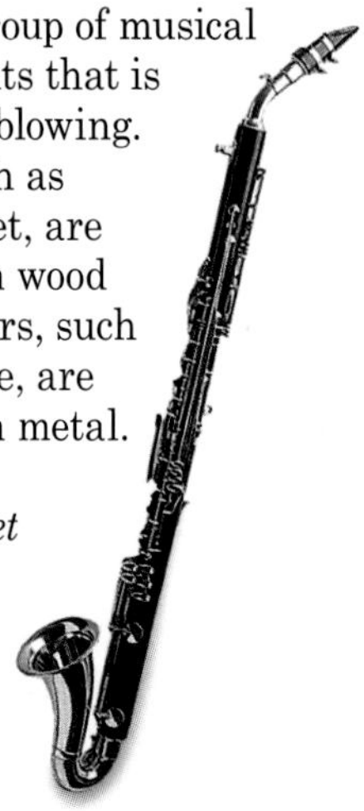

alto clarinet

wool
noun
the soft hair of sheep and some other animals that can be used to make cloth, clothes, carpets, and blankets.

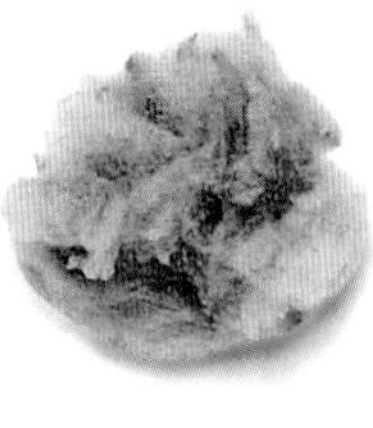

*sheep's **wool***

***wool** yarn*

woolen
adjective
made from wool.

***woolen** hat*

word
words *noun*
1 a sound or group of sounds that stands for an idea, an object, or an action.
2 the group of letters you use to write down these sounds.

word processing
verb
writing, correcting, and storing documents electronically.

wore
*from the verb **to wear***
*He **wore** a yellow T-shirt.*

work
works working worked *verb*
1 to use effort to do something.
*I **worked** hard when I painted the house.*
2 to do a job or task.
*My father **works** in a factory.*
work *noun*
3 to operate efficiently.

*This washing machine is not **working** properly.*

world
noun
the planet Earth and all the people and things on it.

worm
worms *noun*
a small animal with a soft body and no legs or backbone.

*earth**worm***

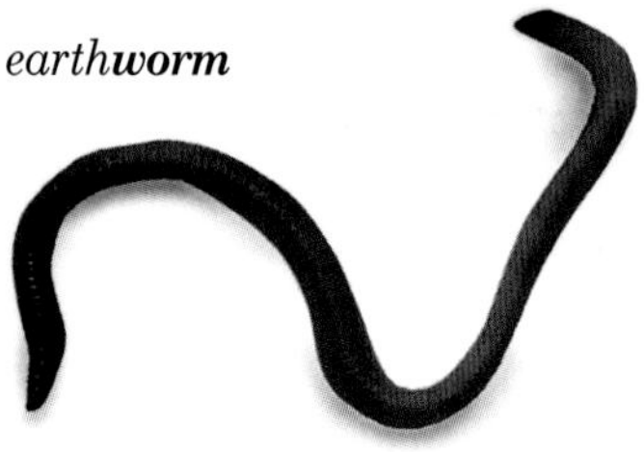

worry
worries worrying worried *verb*
to feel anxious.
*I am **worried** about my exams.*
■ say **wur**-ee
worry *noun*

worse
*from the adjective **bad***
very bad.
*Last week's weather was bad, but today, it is **worse**.*

worship
worships worshiping worshiped *verb*
to respect and love, usually in a religious way.

*The ancient Egyptians **worshiped** many gods.*

worst
*from the adjective **bad***
extremely bad.
*This is the **worst** storm I've ever seen.*

worth
adjective
having a value.

*The crown was **worth** a lot of money.*

worthless
adjective
having little or no value.
*He found an old vase, but it turned out to be **worthless**.*

would
verb
1 a word used to talk about an action that depends on something else.
*I **would** go to the park, but I have to wait here.*
2 a word used to ask for something.
***Would** you like some tea?*
■ rhymes with **good**
■ opposite **would not** or **wouldn't**
■ always used with another verb

wound
wounds *noun*
an injury to the body where the skin is torn or cut in some way.

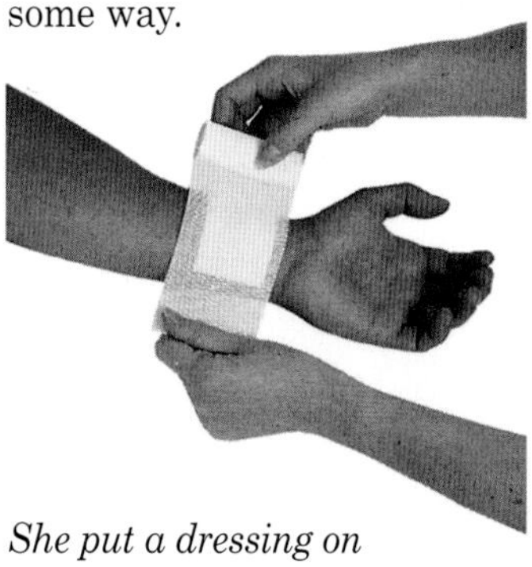

*She put a dressing on the **wound**.*
■ say **woond**
wound *verb*

wound
*from the verb **to wind***
*He **wound** the string around the package.*
■ rhymes with **sound**

wove
*from the verb **to weave***
*She **wove** the wool into cloth.*
■ rhymes with **stove**

wrap
wraps wrapping wrapped *verb*
to fold paper or fabric around something.

*He **wrapped** the present in colorful paper.*
■ say **rap**

wrapper
wrappers *noun*
a piece of paper, plastic, or foil that is used to cover something you buy.

*candies in their **wrappers***

■ say **rap**-ur

wreath
wreaths *noun*
a decoration made from flowers, leaves, or branches tied together in a circle.

■ say **reeth**

wreck
wrecks wrecking wrecked *verb*
to destroy or ruin.

*He crashed into the stone post, **wrecking** the car.*
■ say **rek**

wrestle
wrestles wrestling wrestled *verb*
to struggle with someone and try to force him or her to the ground.
■ say **res**-ul

wriggle
wriggles wriggling wriggled *verb*
to twist and turn from side to side.
■ say **rig**-ul

wring
wrings wringing wrung *verb*
to twist something hard using both hands.
■ say **ring**

*He **wrung** the water out of the cloth.*

wrinkle
wrinkles *noun*
a small crease or fold in skin or fabric.
■ say **ring**-kul

wrist
wrists *noun*
the joint between your hand and your arm.

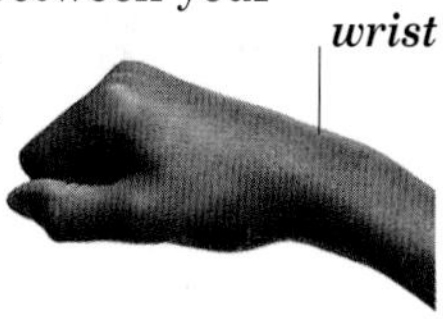

■ say **rist**

write
writes writing wrote written *verb*
1 to form letters and words on a surface.
2 to create something, such as a letter, by using words.
*I **wrote** to my sister last week.*
■ say **rite**

wrong
adjective
1 not correct.
*The **wrong** answer.*
2 bad.
*It's **wrong** to steal.*
■ say **rong**
■ opposite **right**

Xx

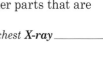

X-ray
X-rays *noun*
a special photograph that shows your bones and other parts that are inside your body.

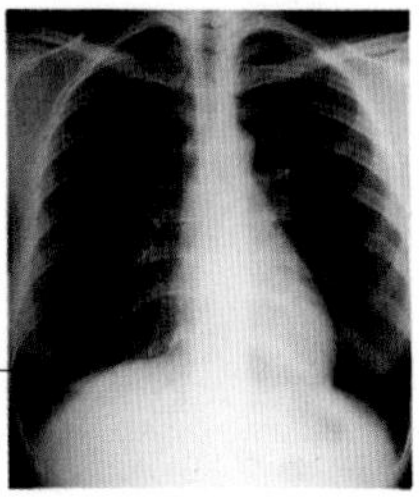
chest ***X-ray***

X-ray *verb*

xylophone
xylophones *noun*
a musical instrument with wooden bars on a frame. Each bar produces a different note when it is struck.

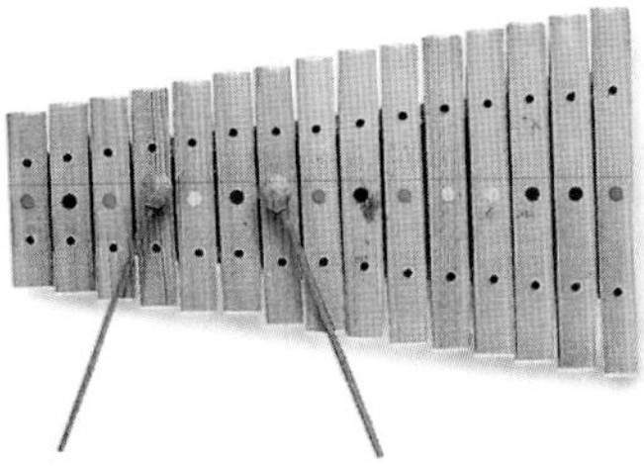

■ say **zy**-luh-fone

Yy

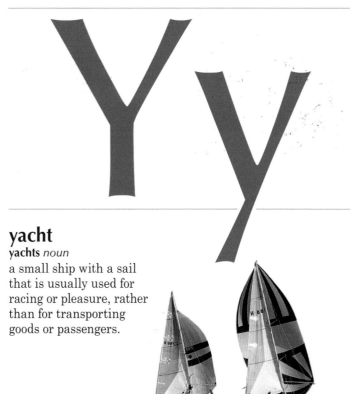

yacht
yachts *noun*
a small ship with a sail that is usually used for racing or pleasure, rather than for transporting goods or passengers.

■ say **yot**

yak
yaks *noun*
a wild ox with long hair and horns that lives in the mountains of central Asia. Yaks eat grass and are often used by people as a source of food or for carrying loads.

yap
yaps yapping yapped *verb*
to bark in a shrill way.

yard
yards *noun*
an outdoor area around a house or building
*Our **yard** is nice and grassy.*

yarn
yarns *noun*
wool, cotton, or another material spun into a thread for knitting or weaving.

yawn
yawns yawning yawned *verb*
to open your mouth and breathe in deeply, usually because you are tired or bored.

■ rhymes with **dawn**
yawn *noun*

year
years *noun*
a period of 12 months. A year is the time that it takes Earth to travel once around the Sun.
yearly *adverb*

yeast
noun
a yellow-brown substance made up of tiny fungi. Yeast is used in bread and cakes to help them rise with air.

*dried **yeast***   *fresh **yeast***

yell
yells yelling yelled *verb*
to shout or scream loudly.

*He **yelled** at the neighbor's cats that were fighting outside the window.*
yell *noun*

yellow
noun
a color.

yesterday
adverb
on the day before today.
*I went to the zoo **yesterday**.*
yesterday *noun*

yet
adverb
up to the present time.
*The letter hasn't arrived **yet**.*

yoga
noun
a system of exercises and deep breathing aimed at making a person healthy and relaxed in mind and body.
■ say **yo**-gah

yogurt
yogurts *noun*
a sour food made by adding bacteria to milk.
■ say **yo**-gurt

yoke
yokes *noun*
a wooden frame that fits over the shoulders of two oxen or other work animals so that they can pull a load. The yoke keeps the animals together.

yolk
yolks *noun*
the yellow part of an egg.

■ say **yoke**

young
adjective
in the early part of life.

*The grandmother held the **young** child in her arms.*
■ say **yung**
■ comparisons **younger youngest**
■ opposite **old**

youth
noun
1 the state of being young.
*In my **youth**, I had dark hair but now it is white.*
2 young people in general.
*A place for the **youth** of the town to meet.*
■ say **yooth**

yo-yo
yo-yos *noun*
a toy that spins up and down on a string.

Zz

zebra
zebras *noun*
a striped African mammal that is part of the horse family. Zebras live in herds on open plains and eat grass and shrubs.

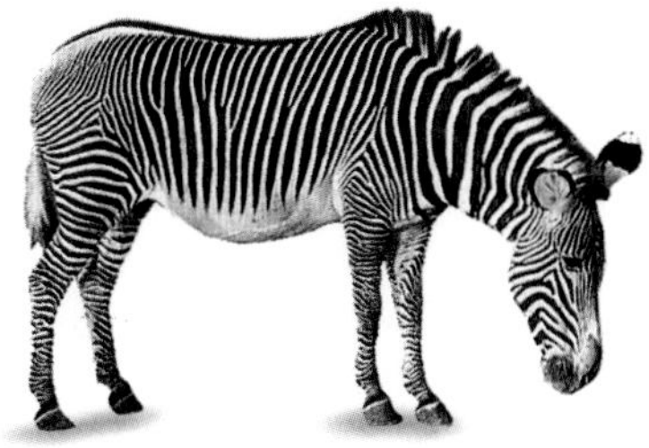

zero
zeros *noun*
nothing or none.

zigzag
zigzags *noun*
a line with a series of sharp turns and angles in it.
zigzag *adjective*

zigzag *verb*

zinc
noun
a blue-white, brittle metal.

zipper
zippers *noun*
a device with two rows of teeth that can be opened and closed. Zippers are used to fasten clothing or bags.

zip *verb*

zodiac
noun
the 12 sections into which astrologers divide the sky. Each part is represented by a sign.
■ say **zoe**-dee-ak

zone
zones *noun*
an area that is divided off for a particular purpose.
*A no-parking **zone**.*

zoo
zoos *noun*
a place where people can observe and learn about animals.

zoom
zooms zooming zoomed *verb*
to move very fast.

*The four motorcycles **zoomed** past me.*

Abbreviations

An abbreviation is a short form of a word or phrase. Some abbreviations are made by just shortening a word. For example, **ad** is short for **advertisement**, and **max** is short for **maximum**. Other abbreviations, such as **CD** for **compact disc**, are made from the first letters of the words that they stand for. On this double page you will find a useful alphabetical list of common abbreviations.

AC air-conditioning, or alternating current
(An electrical current that travels first in one direction, then in another.)

ad advertisement

AD in the year of our Lord
(Used in dates to count the year after the birth of Jesus Christ, e.g., AD 400. From the Latin *anno Domini.*)

AIDS Acquired Immune Deficiency Syndrome
(A disease that makes a person unable to fight illnesses.)

a.m. before noon
(Used with times, e.g., 9 a.m. From the Latin *ante meridiem.*)

anon anonymous

approx. approximately

Apr. April

A.S.A.P. as soon as possible

AST Alaska standard time

Atl Atlantic

Aug. August

Ave. avenue

b born

BA Bachelor of Arts
(A title given to someone who has a liberal arts degree.)

BC Before Christ
(Used in dates to count the years before the birth of Jesus Christ, e.g., 30 BC.)

BS Bachelor of Science
(A title given to someone who has a science degree from a college or university.)

C Celsius or Centigrade

c. about
(Used with historical dates that are not certain. From the Latin *circa.*)

CD compact disc

CIA Central Intelligence Agency
(The US government department that deals with spies and state secrets.)

cm centimeter

Co. Company
(Used after the names of some companies.)

c/o care of

cont'd continued

CST central standard time

d died

DC District of Columbia or direct current
(An electrical current that travels in only one direction.)

Dec. December

dept. department

DIY do-it-yourself
(Used to describe repairs and decorating that people do to their own homes.)

DJ disc jockey

Dr. doctor

DVD digital versatile/video disc

dz dozen

E east

EAL English as an additional language.

e.g. for example
(From the Latin *exempli gratia.*)

Email electronic mail

ESP extrasensory perception
(A sense that some people are said to have that makes them aware of ghosts and other things that most people are unable to see or feel.)

EST eastern standard time

etc. and all the rest
(From the Latin *et cetera.*)

F Fahrenheit

FBI Federal Bureau of Investigation
(An agency of the American Department of Justice.)

Feb. February

flu influenza

Fri. Friday

ft foot

g gram

GMT Greenwich Mean Time
(The time used in the UK during the winter, and from which time all around the world is measured.)

GP general practitioner
(The title given to an all-purpose medical doctor.)

HIV Human Immunodeficiency Virus
(The virus that causes AIDS.)

HMO health maintenance organizaiton

hp horse power

HQ headquarters

HST Hawaiian standard time

hwy highway

ICT Information and Communication Technology

ID identification

i.e. that is
(From the Latin *id est.*)

in inch

Inc. Incorporated
(Used in the names of most US companies.)

Inst. Institute

IOU I owe you

IQ intelligence quotient
(A test score that claims to measure a person's intelligence.)

IVF in vitro fertilization
(a medical technique where a woman's eggs are fertilized outside the womb.)

Jan. January

Jr. junior

kg kilogram

km kilometer

kph kilometers per hour

l liter

lab laboratory

lb pound (in weight) (From the Latin *libra*.)

LCD liquid crystal display

LED light-emitting diode

LP long-playing record

Ltd. Limited (Used after the names of some British companies.)

m meter or mile

MA Master of Arts (A title given to someone who has an arts degree from a university higher than a BA.)

Mar. March

max maximum

MD Doctor of Medicine (From the Latin *Medicinae Doctor*.)

memo memorandum (A message to remind someone about something.)

min minimum

misc. miscellaneous

Miss Mistress (A title that goes before an unmarried woman's name.)

mm millimeter

Mon. Monday

mpg miles per gallon

mph miles per hour

mp3 MPEG (Moving Pictures Expert Group) 1 audio layer 3 (A type of digital computer file used to store music.)

Mr. Mister (A title that goes before a man's name.)

Mrs. Mistress (A title that goes before a married woman's name.)

Ms. (A title for a married or an unmarried woman.)

MS Master of Sciences (A title given to someone who has a science degree from a university higher than a BS.)

MST mountain standard time

Mt. mount or mountain

N north

NASA National Aeronautics and Space Administration

NATO North Atlantic Treaty Organization

NE northeast

no. number (From the Italian *numero*.)

Nov. November

NW northwest

Oct. October

OK all correct

oz ounce

p. page

Pac Pacific

PC personal computer, or politically correct

PE physical education

Ph.D. Doctor of Philosophy (A title given to someone who has studied a subject to an advanced level at university.)

p.m. after noon (Used with times, e.g., 3 p.m. From the Latin *post meridiem*.)

PO Post Office

POW prisoner of war

PR public relations

pro professional

Prof. professor

P.S. postscript (An extra note written at the end of something, such as a letter. From the Latin *post scriptem*.)

PST Pacific standard time

PTA Parent Teacher Association

RAM random-access memory (The part of memory in a computer that you use to work on.)

Rd. road

ref referee

Rev. Reverend

RIP rest in peace (Often written on a grave. From the Latin *requiescat in pace*.)

ROM read-only memory (The part of the memory in a computer that stores permanent information that cannot be altered.)

r.p.m. revolutions per minute (The measurement of how fast records and other things turn.)

RSVP please reply (Used on invitations. From the French *répondez s'il vous plaît*.)

rte. route

S south

Sat. Saturday

sci-fi science fiction

SE southeast

Sept. September

Soc. Society

sq. square

Sr. senior

SS Steamship

St. Saint or street

Sun. Sunday

SW southwest

tel. telephone

temp. temporary

3-D three-dimensional (Having height, width, and depth.)

Thurs. Thursday

Tues. Tuesday

TV television

UFO unidentified flying object

UK United Kingdom

UN United Nations

Unesco United Nations Educational, Scientific, and Cultural Organization

Unicef United Nations Children's Fund

US or **USA** United States of America

UV ultraviolet

v. against (From the Latin *versus*.)

VDU visual display unit

VIP very important person

W west

Wed. Wednesday

www world wide web

yd. yard

Spelling guide

If you are having trouble finding a word in the dictionary, it may be because you are looking under the wrong spelling. There can be many different ways of spelling the same sound. Letters sometimes make a different sound than usual. They may even be completely silent, like the **k** in **kneel**, or the **g** in **gnat**. The spelling guide below will help you to figure out the correct spelling for some tricky words.

Sound	As in	Other ways to spell this sound
a (say **air**)	hair	care, wear, there, their, prayer
a (say **ay**)	cake	rain, straight, break, veil, bouquet, obey, hay
a	rat	laugh
ch	chin	catch, question
d	did	butter
e	ten	any, said, friend, bury, head, leopard
e (say **ee**)	me	meet, seat, key, quay, machine, field, city
f	fall	laugh, telephone
g	get	ghost, guess
h	help	whole
i	fit	damage, pretty, women, busy, build, myth
i	I	eye, sigh, buy, fly, dye
j	jump	trudge, soldier, adjective, magic
k	kiss	come, anchor, sack, biscuit, walk, unique
l	leg	island
m	miss	comb
n	nose	gnat, kneel, pneumonia
o	not	swan, cauliflower, knowledge
o (say **oh**)	go	sew, though, boat, slow
o (say **oo**)	move	threw, zoom, shoe, soup, through, blue, fruit
o (say **aw**)	gone	autumn, awful, broad, ought
o (say **ow**)	now	out, bough
o (say **oy**)	boy	boil
oo	zoom	threw, move, shoe, soup, through, blue, fruit, queue
qu (say **kw**)	quite	choir
r	red	rhyme, wrong
s	saw	cell, psychology, science
s (say **zh**)	pleasure	mirage, confusion
sh	she	ocean, machine, special, sure, conscience, expansion, nation
t	top	debt, bought
u	up	son, does, flood, double
u	pull	woman, wool, would
u (say **ur**)	fur	germ, heard, bird, worm, journey
v	very	of
w	wish	what
y	yard	use, onion
z	zebra	busy, scissors, xylophone

Word building

The charts on this page show how you can take one word and build a new one from it by adding a group of letters called a prefix or a suffix. Prefixes, such as **dis-**, **un-**, or **mis-**, are joined to the front of a word. They are often used to change a word to its opposite. For example, adding the prefix **in-** turns **visible** into **invisible**. Suffixes, such as **-ful**, **-ism**, or **-ment**, are joined to the end of a word. They are often used to change a word from one part of speech to another. For example, adding the suffix **-er** turns the verb **teach** into the noun **teacher**. These charts show some common prefixes and suffixes.

Prefixes

Prefix	Meaning	Example	Prefix	Meaning	Example
anti-	against	antiseptic	non-	makes the opposite	nonfiction
dis-	makes the opposite	disagree	post-	after	postwar
ex-	out of, or from	export	pre-	before	prehistoric
ex-	former	exwife	re-	again	replace
in-	makes the opposite	independent	sub-	under	submarine
inter-	between	international	super-	above, or more than	superhuman
mis-	makes the opposite	misfortune	trans-	across	transplant
multi-	many	multicolored	un-	makes the opposite	unpleasant

Suffixes

Suffixes that make nouns

Suffix	Meaning	Example
-age	a result	wreckage
-ance	an action or state	importance
-ant	a person	assistant
-ee	a person	referee
-ence	an action or state	difference
-er/-or	a person	teacher
-ery	a type or place of work	bakery
-ess	makes a feminine form	waitress
-ful	as much as will fill	spoonful
-ing	an action or result	painting
-ion	a process, state, or result	decoration
-ism	a belief or condition	Judaism
-ist	a person	florist
-ment	an action or state	measurement
-ness	a quality or state	happiness

Suffixes that make adjectives

Suffix	Meaning	Example
-able	able to be	inflatable
-en	made of	woolen
-ful	full of	beautiful
-ible	ability	flexible
-ish	a little	greenish
-less	without	careless
-like	similar to, like	lifelike
-ous	full of	joyous
-some	a tendency to	quarrelsome

Suffixes that make adverbs

Suffix	Meaning	Example
-ly	in a manner	quickly
-ward	shows direction	forward
-ways	shows direction	sideways

Facts and figures

Metric measures

Length
10 millimeters = 1 centimeter
100 centimeters = 1 meter
1,000 meters = 1 kilometer

Area
10,000 square centimeters = 1 square meter
1,000,000 square meters = 1 square kilometer

Weight
1,000 grams = 1 kilogram
1,000 kilograms = 1 metric ton

Volume
10 milliliters = 1 centiliter
10 centiliters = 1 deciliter
10 deciliters = 1 liter

Imperial measures

Length
12 inches = 1 foot
3 feet = 1 yard
1,760 yards = 1 mile

Area
144 square inches = 1 square foot
9 square feet = 1 square yard
4,840 square yards = 1 acre
640 acres = 1 square mile

Weight
16 ounces = 1 pound
2,000 pounds = 1 short ton

Volume
8 fluid ounces = 1 cup
2 cups = 1 pint
2 pints = 1 quart
4 quarts = 1 gallon

Temperatures

Degrees Centigrade / Celsius

Boiling point of water	100°C
Freezing point of water	0°C
Normal body temperature	37°C

Degrees Fahrenheit

Boiling point of water	212°F
Freezing point of water	32°F
Normal body temperature	98.6°F

To convert Centigrade to Fahrenheit: multiply by 9, divide by 5, and add 32. (e.g.: **20°C** x 9 = 180; 180 ÷ 5 = 36; 36 + 32 = **68°F**)

To convert Fahrenheit to Centigrade: subtract 32, multiply by 5, and divide by 9.

The 50 states and their capital cities

State	Abbr.	Capital City
Alabama	AL	Montgomery
Alaska	AK	Juneau
Arizona	AZ	Phoenix
Arkansas	AR	Little Rock
California	CA	Sacramento
Colorado	CO	Denver
Connecticut	CT	Hartford
Delaware	DE	Dover
Florida	FL	Tallahassee
Georgia	GA	Atlanta
Hawaii	HI	Honolulu
Idaho	ID	Boise
Illinois	IL	Springfield
Indiana	IN	Indianapolis
Iowa	IA	Des Moines
Kansas	KS	Topeka
Kentucky	KY	Frankfort
Louisiana	LA	Baton Rouge
Maine	ME	Augusta
Maryland	MD	Annapolis
Massachusetts	MA	Boston
Michigan	MI	Lansing
Minnesota	MN	St. Paul
Mississippi	MS	Jackson
Missouri	MO	Jefferson City
Montana	MT	Helena
Nebraska	NE	Lincoln
Nevada	NV	Carson City
New Hampshire	NH	Concord
New Jersey	NJ	Trenton
New Mexico	NM	Santa Fe
New York	NY	Albany
North Carolina	NC	Raleigh
North Dakota	ND	Bismark
Ohio	OH	Columbus
Oklahoma	OK	Oklahoma City
Oregon	OR	Salem
Pennsylvania	PA	Harrisburg
Rhode Island	RI	Providence
South Carolina	SC	Columbia
South Dakota	SD	Pierre
Tennessee	TN	Nashville
Texas	TX	Austin
Utah	UT	Salt Lake City
Vermont	VT	Montpelier
Virginia	VA	Richmond
Washington	WA	Olympia
West Virginia	WV	Charleston
Wisconsin	WI	Madison
Wyoming	WY	Cheyenne

Cardinal numbers		Ordinal numbers		Roman numerals	
1	one	1st	first	1	I
2	two	2nd	second	2	II
3	three	3rd	third	3	III
4	four	4th	fourth	4	IV
5	five	5th	fifth	5	V
6	six	6th	sixth	6	VI
7	seven	7th	seventh	7	VII
8	eight	8th	eighth	8	VIII
9	nine	9th	ninth	9	IX
10	ten	10th	tenth	10	X
11	eleven	11th	eleventh	11	XI
12	twelve	12th	twelfth	12	XII
13	thirteen	13th	thirteenth	13	XIII
14	fourteen	14th	fourteenth	14	XIV
15	fifteen	15th	fifteenth	15	XV
16	sixteen	16th	sixteenth	16	XVI
17	seventeen	17th	seventeenth	17	XVII
18	eighteen	18th	eighteenth	18	XVIII
19	nineteen	19th	nineteenth	19	XIX
20	twenty	20th	twentieth	20	XX
21	twenty-one	21st	twenty-first	21	XXI
30	thirty	30th	thirtieth	30	XXX
40	forty	40th	fortieth	40	XL
50	fifty	50th	fiftieth	50	L
60	sixty	60th	sixtieth	60	LX
70	seventy	70th	seventieth	70	LXX
80	eighty	80th	eightieth	80	LXXX
90	ninety	90th	ninetieth	90	XC
100	one hundred	100th	one hundredth	100	C
500	five hundred	500th	five hundredth	500	D
1,000	one thousand	1,000th	one thousandth	1,000	M

Symbols and punctuation marks

+	plus	%	percent	&	and	?	question mark
–	minus	°	degree	@	at	!	exclamation mark
×	multiplied by	√	square root	©	copyright	–	dash
÷	divided by	π	pi	.	full stop	*	asterisk
=	equals	≈	is similar to	,	comma	( )	parentheses
>	greater than	$	dollar	;	semicolon	“ ”	quotation marks
<	less than	¢	cent	:	colon	’	apostrophe

Countries of the world

On the next four pages is a list of the world's countries, arranged in alphabetical order. Under each country's name are its capital city, the name of the people who live there, and its currency. When a country has two capital cities, they are both listed. If there is a common abbreviation or symbol for the currency, such as $ for **dollar**, this is shown in parentheses after the name of the currency.

Afghanistan
Capital city: Kabul
People: Afghans
Currency: Afghani (AF)

Albania
Capital city: Tirana
People: Albanians
Currency: Lek

Algeria
Capital city: Algiers
People: Algerians
Currency: Algerian Dinar (DA)

Andorra
Capital city: Andorra la Vella
People: Andorrans
Currency: Euro (€)

Angola
Capital city: Luanda
People: Angolans
Currency: Readjusted Kwanza (Kz)

Antigua & Barbuda
Capital city: St. John's
People: Antiguans
Currency: Eastern Caribbean Dollar

Argentina
Capital city: Buenos Aires
People: Argentinians
Currency: New Argentine Peso

Armenia
Capital city: Yerevan
People: Armenians
Currency: Dram

Australia
Capital city: Canberra
People: Australians
Currency: Australian Dollar (AU$)

Austria
Capital city: Vienna
People: Austrians
Currency: Euro (€)

Azerbaijan
Capital city: Baku
People: Azerbaijanis
Currency: New Manat

Bahamas
Capital city: Nassau
People: Bahamians
Currency: Bahamian Dollar

Bahrain
Capital city: Manama
People: Bahrainis
Currency: Bahraini Dinar

Bangladesh
Capital city: Dhaka
People: Bangladeshis
Currency: Taka (Tk)

Barbados
Capital city: Bridgetown
People: Barbadians
Currency: Barbados Dollar

Belarus
Capital city: Minsk
People: Belarusians
Currency: Belarussian Rouble

Belgium
Capital city: Brussels
People: Belgians
Currency: Euro (€)

Belize
Capital city: Belmopan
People: Belizeans
Currency: Belizean Dollar

Benin
Capital city: Porto-Novo
People: Beninese
Currency: CFA Franc*

Bhutan
Capital city: Thimphu
People: Bhutanese
Currency: Ngultrum (Nu)

Bolivia
Capital city: La Paz, Sucre
People: Bolivians
Currency: Boliviano (B)

Bosnia & Herzegovina
Capital city: Sarajevo
People: Bosnians
Currency: Marka

Botswana
Capital city: Gaborone
People: Batswana (singular Motswana)
Currency: Pula (P)

Brazil
Capital city: Brasília
People: Brazilians
Currency: Real

Brunei
Capital city: Bandar Seri Begawan
People: Bruneians
Currency: Brunei Dollar

Bulgaria
Capital city: Sofia
People: Bulgarians
Currency: Lev

Burkina Faso
Capital city: Ouagadougou
People: Burkinabé
Currency: CFA Franc*

Myanmar (Burma)
Capital city: Nay Pyi Taw
People: Burmese
Currency: Kyat (K)

Burundi
Capital city: Bujumbura
People: Burundians
Currency: Burundi Franc

Cambodia
Capital city: Phnom Penh
People: Cambodians
Currency: Riel

Cameroon
Capital city: Yaoundé
People: Cameroonians
Currency: CFA Franc*

Canada
Capital city: Ottawa
People: Canadians
Currency: Canadian Dollar (C$)

Cape Verde
Capital city: Praia
People: Cape Verdeans
Currency: Cape Verde Escudo

Central African Republic
Capital city: Bangui
People: Central Africans
Currency: CFA Franc*

Chad
Capital city: N'Djamena
People: Chadians
Currency: CFA Franc*

Chile
Capital city: Santiago
People: Chileans
Currency: Chilean Peso

China
Capital city: Beijing
People: Chinese
Currency: Renminbi (known as Yuan)

Colombia
Capital city: Bogotá
People: Colombians
Currency: Colombian Peso

Comoros
Capital city: Moroni
People: Comorans
Currency: Comoros Franc

Congo
Capital city: Brazzaville
People: Congolese
Currency: CFA Franc*

Congo, Democratic Republic
Capital city: Kinshasa
People: Congolese
Currency: Congolese Franc

Costa Rica
Capital city: San José
People: Costa Ricans
Currency: Costa Rican Colón (¢)

Croatia
Capital city: Zagreb
People: Croatians
Currency: Kuna

Cuba
Capital city: Havana
People: Cubans
Currency: Cuban Peso

Cyprus
Capital city: Nicosia
People: Cypriots
Currency: Euro (€) (Turkish Lira in Northen Cyprus)

Czech Republic
Capital city: Prague
People: Czechs
Currency: Czech Koruna

Denmark
Capital city: Copenhagen
People: Danes
Currency: Danish Krone

Djibouti
Capital city: Djibouti
People: Djiboutians
Currency: Djibouti Franc

Dominica
Capital city: Roseau
People: Dominicans
Currency: Eastern Caribbean Dollar

Dominican Republic
Capital city: Santo Domingo
People: Dominicans
Currency: Dominican Republic Peso

East Timor
Capital city: Dili
People: East Timorese
Currency: US Dollar ($)

Ecuador
Capital city: Quito
People: Ecuadoreans
Currency: US Dollar ($)

Egypt
Capital city: Cairo
People: Egyptians
Currency: Egyptian Pound

El Salvador
Capital city: San Salvador
People: Salvadorans
Currency: Salvadorean Colón (¢), US dollar ($)

Equatorial Guinea
Capital city: Malabo
People: Equatorial Guineans or Equatoguineans
Currency: CFA Franc*

Eritrea
Capital city: Asmara
People: Eritreans
Currency: Nakfa

Estonia
Capital city: Tallinn
People: Estonians
Currency: Kroon

Ethiopia
Capital city: Addis Ababa
People: Ethiopians
Currency: Ethiopian Birr (Br)

Fiji
Capital city: Suva
People: Fijians
Currency: Fiji Dollar

Finland
Capital city: Helsinki
People: Finns
Currency: Euro (€)

France
Capital city: Paris
People: French
Currency: Euro (€)

Gabon
Capital city: Libreville
People: Gabonese
Currency: CFA Franc*

Gambia
Capital city: Banjul
People: Gambians
Currency: Dalasi (D)

Georgia
Capital city: Tbilisi
People: Georgians
Currency: Lari

Germany
Capital city: Berlin
People: Germans
Currency: Euro (€)

Ghana
Capital city: Accra
People: Ghanaians
Currency: Cedi

Greece
Capital city: Athens
People: Greeks
Currency: Euro (€)

Grenada
Capital city: St. George's
People: Grenadians
Currency: Eastern Caribbean Dollar

Guatemala
Capital city: Guatemala City
People: Guatemalans
Currency: Quetzal (Q)

Guinea
Capital city: Conakry
People: Guineans
Currency: Guinea Franc

Guinea-Bissau
Capital city: Bissau
People: Guinea-Bissauans
Currency: CFA Franc*

Guyana
Capital city: Georgetown
People: Guyanese
Currency: Guyanese Dollar

Haiti
Capital city: Port-au-Prince
People: Haitians
Currency: Gourde (G)

Honduras
Capital city: Tegucigalpa
People: Hondurans
Currency: Lempira (L)

Hungary
Capital city: Budapest
People: Hungarians
Currency: Forint (Ft)

Iceland
Capital city: Reykjavik
People: Icelanders
Currency: Icelandic Krona

India
Capital city: New Delhi
People: Indians
Currency: Indian Rupee

Indonesia
Capital city: Jakarta
People: Indonesians
Currency: Rupiah (Rp)

Iran
Capital city: Tehran
People: Iranians
Currency: Iranian Rial

Iraq
Capital city: Baghdad
People: Iraqis
Currency: New Iraqi Dinar (ID)

Ireland
Capital city: Dublin
People: Irish
Currency: Euro (€)

Israel
Capital city: Jerusalem
People: Israelis
Currency: Shekel

Italy
Capital city: Rome
People: Italians
Currency: Euro (€)

Ivory Coast
Capital city: Yamoussoukro
People: Ivorians
Currency: CFA Franc*

Jamaica
Capital city: Kingston
People: Jamaicans
Currency: Jamaican Dollar

Japan
Capital city: Tokyo
People: Japanese
Currency: Yen (Y)

Jordan
Capital city: Amman
People: Jordanians
Currency: Jordanian Dinar

Kazakhstan
Capital city: Astana
People: Kazakhstanis
Currency: Tenge

Kenya
Capital city: Nairobi
People: Kenyans
Currency: Kenya Shilling

Kiribati
Capital city: Tarawa Atoll
People: I-Kiribatis
Currency: Australian Dollar (AU$)

Kosovo (disputed)
Capital city: Pristina
People: Kosovars or Kosovacs
Currency: Euro (€)

Kuwait
Capital city: Kuwait City
People: Kuwaitis
Currency: Kuwaiti Dinar

Kyrgyzstan
Capital city: Bishkek
People: Kyrgyz
Currency: Som

Laos
Capital city: Vientiane
People: Laotians or Laos
Currency: New Kip (KN)

Latvia
Capital city: Riga
People: Latvians
Currency: Lats

Lebanon
Capital city: Beirut
People: Lebanese
Currency: Lebanese Pound (£L)

Lesotho
Capital city: Maseru
People: Basotho (singular Mosotho)
Currency: Loti (M)

Liberia
Capital city: Monrovia
People: Liberians
Currency: Liberian Dollar

Libya
Capital city: Tripoli
People: Libyans
Currency: Libyan Dinar

Liechtenstein
Capital city: Vaduz
People: Liechtensteiners
Currency: Swiss Franc

Lithuania
Capital city: Vilnius
People: Lithuanians
Currency: Litas

Luxembourg
Capital city: Luxembourg-Ville
People: Luxembourgers
Currency: Euro (€)

Macedonia
Capital city: Skopje
People: Macedonians
Currency: Macedonian Denar

Madagascar
Capital city: Antananarivo
People: Malagasy
Currency: Ariary

Malawi
Capital city: Lilongwe
People: Malawians
Currency: Malawi Kwacha

Malaysia
Capital city: Kuala Lumpur, Putrajaya
People: Malaysians
Currency: Ringgit

Maldives
Capital city: Male
People: Maldivians
Currency: Rufiyaa

Mali
Capital city: Bamako
People: Malians
Currency: CFA Franc*

Malta
Capital city: Valletta
People: Maltese
Currency: Euro (€)

Marshall Islands
Capital city: Majuro
People: Marshallese
Currency: US Dollar ($)

Mauritania
Capital city: Nouakchott
People: Mauritanians
Currency: Ouguiya (UM)

Mauritius
Capital city: Port Louis
People: Mauritians
Currency: Mauritian Rupee (Mau Rs)

Mexico
Capital city: Mexico City
People: Mexicans
Currency: Mexican Peso

Micronesia
Capital city: Palikir (Pohnpei Island)
People: Micronesians
Currency: US Dollar ($)

Moldova
Capital city: Chisinau
People: Moldovans
Currency: Moldovan Leu

Monaco
Capital city: Monaco-Ville
People: Monégasques or Monacans
Currency: Euro (€)

Mongolia
Capital city: Ulan Bator
People: Mongolians
Currency: Tugrik

Montenegro
Capital city: Podgorica
People: Montenegrins
Currency: Euro (€)

Morocco
Capital city: Rabat
People: Moroccans
Currency: Moroccan Dirham (DH)

Mozambique
Capital city: Maputo
People: Mozambicans
Currency: New Metical (Mt.)

Namibia
Capital city: Windhoek
People: Namibians
Currency: Namibian Dollar

Nauru
Capital city: None
People: Nauruans
Currency: Australian Dollar (AU$)

Nepal
Capital city: Kathmandu
People: Nepalese
Currency: Nepalese Rupee

Netherlands
Capital city: Amsterdam
Seat of government: The Hague
People: Dutch
Currency: Euro (€)

New Zealand
Capital city: Wellington
People: New Zealanders
Currency: New Zealand Dollar (NZ$)

Nicaragua
Capital city: Managua
People: Nicaraguans
Currency: New Córdoba

Niger
Capital city: Niamey
People: Nigeriens
Currency: CFA Franc*

Nigeria
Capital city: Abuja
People: Nigerians
Currency: Naira (N)

North Korea
Capital city: Pyongyang
People: North Koreans
Currency: North Korean Won

Norway
Capital city: Oslo
People: Norwegians
Currency: Norwegian Krone

Oman
Capital city: Muscat
People: Omanis
Currency: Omani Rial

Pakistan
Capital city: Islamabad
People: Pakistanis
Currency: Pakistani Rupee

Palau
Capital city: Melekeok
People: Palauans
Currency: US Dollar ($)

Panama
Capital city: Panama City
People: Panamanians
Currency: Balboa (B)

Papua New Guinea
Capital city: Port Moresby
People: Papua New Guineans
Currency: Kina (K)

Paraguay
Capital city: Asunción
People: Paraguayans
Currency: Guaraní (G)

Peru
Capital city: Lima
People: Peruvians
Currency: New Sol (NS)

Philippines
Capital city: Manila
People: Filipinos
Currency: Philippine Peso

Poland
Capital city: Warsaw
People: Poles
Currency: Zloty (Zl)

Portugal
Capital city: Lisbon
People: Portuguese
Currency: Euro (€)

Qatar
Capital city: Doha
People: Qataris
Currency: Qatar Riyal

Romania
Capital city: Bucharest
People: Romanians
Currency: New Romanian Leu (lei)

Russian Federation
Capital city: Moscow
People: Russians
Currency: Russian Rouble

Rwanda
Capital city: Kigali
People: Rwandans
Currency: Rwanda Franc

Saint Kitts & Nevis
Capital city: Basseterre
People: Kittitians, Nevisians
Currency: Eastern Caribbean Dollar

Saint Lucia
Capital city: Castries
People: St. Lucians
Currency: Eastern Caribbean Dollar

Saint Vincent & the Grenadines
Capital city: Kingstown
People: St. Vincentians
Currency: Eastern Caribbean Dollar

Samoa
Capital city: Apia
People: Samoans
Currency: Tala

San Marino
Capital city: San Marino
People: Sammarinese
Currency: Euro (€)

São Tomé & Príncipe
Capital city: São Tomé
People: São Tomeans
Currency: Dobra

Saudi Arabia
Capital city: Riyadh, Jiddah
People: Saudi Arabians
Currency: Saudi Riyal

Senegal
Capital city: Dakar
People: Senegalese
Currency: CFA Franc*

Serbia
Capital city: Belgrade
People: Serbs
Currency: Dinar

Seychelles
Capital city: Victoria
People: Seychellois
Currency: Seychelles Rupee

Sierra Leone
Capital city: Freetown
People: Sierra Leoneans
Currency: Leone (Le)

Singapore
Capital city: Singapore
People: Singaporeans
Currency: Singapore Dollar (S$)

Slovakia
Capital city: Bratislava
People: Slovakians
Currency: Slovak Koruna

Slovenia
Capital city: Ljubljana
People: Slovenians
Currency: Euro (€)

Solomon Island
Capital city: Honiara
People: Solomon Islanders
Currency: Solomon Islands Dollar

Somalia
Capital city: Mogadishu
People: Somalis
Currency: Somali Shilin

South Africa
Capital city: Pretoria, Cape Town, Bloemfontein
People: South Africans
Currency: Rand (R)

South Korea
Capital city: Seoul
People: South Koreans
Currency: South Korean Won

Spain
Capital city: Madrid
People: Spaniards
Currency: Euro (€)

Sri Lanka
Capital city: Colombo
People: Sri Lankans
Currency: Sri Lanka Rupee (SL Rs)

Sudan
Capital city: Khartoum
People: Sudanese
Currency: New Sudanese Pound or Dinar

Suriname
Capital city: Paramaribo
People: Surinamers
Currency: Surinamese Dollar

Swaziland
Capital city: Mbabane
People: Swazis
Currency: Lilangeni (E)

Sweden
Capital city: Stockholm
People: Swedes
Currency: Swedish Krona

Switzerland
Capital city: Bern
People: Swiss
Currency: Swiss Franc

Syria
Capital city: Damascus
People: Syrians
Currency: Syrian Pound

Tajikistan
Capital city: Dushanbe
People: Tajiks
Currency: Somoni

Tanzania
Capital city: Dodoma
People: Tanzanians
Currency: Tanzanian Shilling (T Sh)

Thailand
Capital city: Bangkok
People: Thais
Currency: Baht (B)

Togo
Capital city: Lomé
People: Togolese
Currency: CFA Franc*

Tonga
Capital city: Nuku'alofa
People: Tongans
Currency: Pa'anga (Tongan Dollar)

Trinidad & Tobago
Capital city: Port-of-Spain
People: Trinidadians, Tobagonians
Currency: Trinidad and Tobago Dollar

Tunisia
Capital city: Tunis
People: Tunisians
Currency: Tunisian Dinar

Turkey
Capital city: Ankara
People: Turks
Currency: New Turkish Lira

Turkmenistan
Capital city: Ashgabat
People: Turkmens
Currency: Manat

Tuvalu
Capital city: Fongafale (Funafuti Atoll)
People: Tuvaluans
Currency: Australian Dollar and Tuvaluan Dollar

Uganda
Capital city: Kampala
People: Ugandans
Currency: New Uganda Shilling

Ukraine
Capital city: Kiev
People: Ukrainians
Currency: Hryvna

United Arab Emirates
Capital city: Abu Dhabi
People: Emiratis
Currency: UAE Dirham

United Kingdom
Capital city: London
People: British
Currency: Pound Sterling (£)

United States of America
Capital city: Washington, D.C.
People: Americans
Currency: US Dollar ($)

Uruguay
Capital city: Montevideo
People: Uruguayans
Currency: Uruguayan Peso

Uzbekistan
Capital city: Tashkent
People: Uzbekistanis
Currency: Som

Vanuatu
Capital city: Port Vila
People: Ni-Vanuatu
Currency: Vatu

Vatican City
Capital city: Vatican City
People: Citizens of the Vatican
Currency: Euro (€)

Venezuela
Capital city: Caracas
People: Venezuelans
Currency: Bolívar (Bs)

Vietnam
Capital city: Hanoi
People: Vietnamese
Currency: Dông (D)

Yemen
Capital city: Sana
People: Yemenis
Currency: Yemeni Rial

Zambia
Capital city: Lusaka
People: Zambians
Currency: Zambian Kwacha (K)

Zimbabwe
Capital city: Harare
People: Zimbabweans
Currency: Zimbabwe Dollar (Z$)

* **The CFA Franc** is used in a number of French-speaking African countries. CFA stands for "Communauté Financiere Africaine".

Acknowledgments

Dorling Kindersley would like to thank the following people for their help in the production of this book:

Additional design assistance

Bronwen Davies, Susan Downing, Karen Fielding, David Gillingwater, Tim Lewis, Sharon Peters, Peter Radcliffe, Sarah Scrutton, Hans Verkroost, Martin Wilson

Additional editorial assistance

Monica Byles, Helen Drew, Stella Love

Picture research

Kathleen Collier, Catherine O'Rourke, Lucy Pringle, Jenny Rayner, Joanna Thomas

Additional illustrations

Janos Marffy, Liz Roberts

Additional photography

Simon Battensby, Paul Bricknell, Geoff Brightling, Jane Burton, Peter Chadwick, Matthew Chattle, Gordon Clayton, M. Crockett, Geoff Dann, Tom Dobbie, Philip Dowell, Michael Dunning, Andreas von Einsiedel, Jo Foord, Philip Gatward, Mike Good, Christi Graham, Frank Greenaway, Peter Hayman, Stephen Hayward, Alan Hills, Jacqui Hurst, Colin Keates, Gary Kevin, Dave King, Bob Langrish, Cyril Laubscher, Bill Ling, Liz McAulay, Andrew McRobb, Diana Miller, Graham Miller, Ray Moller, David Murray, Jack Nicholls, Martin Norris, Ian O'Leary, Stephen Oliver, Daniel Pangbourne, Roger Phillips, Martin Plomer, Laurence Pordes, Susanna Price, Dave Rudkin, Karl Shone, Steve Shott, James Stevenson, Clive Streeter, Harry Taylor, Kim Taylor, David Ward, Matthew Ward. Philip Dowell © 1990 and 1991 page 90 goat and kid; page 111 jaguar; page 118 leopard; page 183 sheep. Jerry Young © 1990 and 1991 page 168 rattlesnake, flying gecko, milkshake, today lizard, starred tortoise, and leopard gecko; page 217 green toad; page 242 wolf.

Models

Shiran Abay, Di Anguige, Sarah Ashun, Oliver Barber, Lindsey Bender, Marvin Campbell, Louis Chan, Puishan Chan, Danny Cole, Andy Crawford, Ebu Djemal, Helen Drew, Andrea East, Josey Edwards, David Gillingwater, Emily Gorton, Julia Gorton, Kashi Gorton, Steve Gorton, Sheena Haria, Laura Hobbs, Paul Holden, Marcus James, Stella Love, Naomi McLean, Rachael Malicki, Jamie May, Ryan Munroe, Emily Parsons, Jade Reading, Jonathon Reed, Tim Ridley, Matthew Saunders, Sarah Scrutton, Silpa Shah, Lee Simmons, Cheryl Telfer, Nicola Tuxworth, Aubrey Weiner, Martin Wilson, David York.

Additional acknowledgments

Anatomical models on pages 20, 98, 114, 120, 122, 202 and 232 supplied by Somso Modelle, Coburg, Germany.

Chest page 43, chest of drawers page 65, and fan page 75 loaned by Gore Booker, Covent Garden, London; drum page 67 loaned by Foote's Musical Instruments, London; leotard page 118 loaned by Porselli, Covent Garden, London; cup page 55 loaned by Whittard, Covent Garden, London; chess set page 43 loaned by the British Museum Shop, London.

Thanks to Clark Denmark at the Centre for Deaf Studies, Bristol University for advice.

Thanks also to the BCP contributors: Gemma Casajuana (Conversion manager), Miguel Cunha (Conversion coordinator), Colleen Dixon (Conversion DTP), Marc Staples (Conversion DTP)

Picture agency credits

KEY: a-above; b-below/bottom; c-center; f-far; l-left; r-right; t-top.

The publisher would like to thank the following for their kind permission to reproduce their photographs:

Action Plus/Tony Henshaw 198cr. **Ayrton Metals Ltd. and The Platinum Advisory Centre** 112car, 112cbfr. **Beaulieu Motor Museum** 39cl, 222tr. **The Bridgeman Art Library/Bonhams, London** 112cb. **Kremlin Museums, Moscow** 54tl. **British Museum** 17cfr, 35tfl, 99bfr, 112ca. **British Museum/Museum of Mankind** 221cafl. **John Bulmer** 224tr. **Christies's Images** 9cbl, 131cbr. **The Coleman Company** 38tfr.Bruce Coleman Limited/Erwin and Peggy Bauer 226bfl; John Cancalosi 179tfl; Peter Davey 42cafr, 211tfr; P. Evans 18cr; Christer Fredriksson 22car; Frans Lanting 70tl; Luiz Claudio Marigo 124tc; William S. Paton 104bfl; Eckart Pott 166br; Andy Purcell 8bfl, 142car; Hans Reinhard 6c, 7tl, 25bfr, 58cfl, 70tfl, 163cbl; Dr Frjeder Sauer 147bfr; Konrad Wothe 97tr. **Compix/A and J Somaya** 56tr. **Corbis** Theo Allofs 66ftr; Andrea Rugg Photography/Beateworks 115cl; Atlantide Phototravel 25cl, 103tl, 169crb; Bilderbuch/Design Pics 169bl; B. Bird/Zefa 211fcrb; Christophe Boisvieux 22ftl; Ron Chapple 171crb; Mike Chew 20cra; Philip Coblentz/Brand X 176clb; Chris Collins 242br; CS Productions/Brand X 200tr; Wolfgang Deuter/Zefa 153br; Dex Image 199fcr; ER Productions 174clb; Fancy/Veer 208fcrb; First/Zefa 45fcra; Bertrand Gardel/Hemis 130br; Uden Graham/Redlink 162fcrb; Mike Grandmaison 176cr; John Harper 46fbl; Ian Hodgson/Reuters 203fbr; Jose Luis Pelaez, Inc. 186cra; Sean Justice 63bl; Jutta Klee 57fbr; Kulka/zefa 192crb; Frans Lanting 163fbl; Klaus Leidorf/Zefa 15fbl; Robert Llewellyn 141cla; John Lund 222bl; Mango Productions 120fcrb; Lawrence Manning 232fbl; Robert Marien 226fcla; Kevin Mason/Loop Images 91ftr; MM Productions 150cr; Moodboard 132fclb, 169fcla, 185cla, 212fcl; David Muench 91tr; Ron Nickel/Design Pics 24tl; Richard T. Nowitz 220fclb; Owaki - Kulla 130tr; Carl Purcell 171fcla; Radius Images 227fbl; Jose Fuste Raga 162br; Eddy Risch/EPA 73ftl; Bill Ross/Corbis Outline 139tr; Charles E. Rotkin 165fbr; Galen Rowell 119fcrb; Kevin Schafer 235tr; Ted Spiegel 77fbl; Thinkstock 190ftl, 196crb; Stefano Torrione/Hemis 139fclb; Visuals Unlimited 228fcrb; R. Wallace/Stock Photos/zefa 71ftr; Weatherstock 215tl; P. Wilson/Zefa 237fcra; Jim Zuckerman 241cr. **DK Images** Jerry Young 15ftr, 171br; NASA 68fcra, 172ftl; Philips Domestic Applicances and Personal Care 69tr; Rough Guides 192bl, 208fclb; The Science Museum, London 43br. **Massey Ferguson** 152bfr. **Ermine Street Guard** 195cbl. **Getty Images** 192cr; Altrendo Travel 235ftl; Image Bank/Tim Graham 160fcrb; Daryl Benson 215bl; Alistair Berg 181fclb; Philippe Bourseiller 232bl; C Squared Studios 219clb; Rosemary Calvert 218fcla; Gabriel M. Covian 227crb; Andy Crawford 113cra; Creative Crop 162tr; CSA Plastock 171fcr; Dex Image/Luxe Party 125fbl; Digital Vision/Erik Von Weber 114cra; Digital Vision/Robert Glusic 116cra; Digital Vision/Steve Wisbauer 118cr; Digital Vision/VisionsofAmerica/Joe Sohm 45tl; Sergio Dionisio 34bl; Dorling Kindersley 105fclb; EschCollection 234fbr; David Evans 240crb; Don Farrall 218fcra; Stephen Ferry/Liaison 62tr; James Forte 198bl; Jill Fromer 200cla; fStop/Stephan Zirwes 116br; Yasuhide Fumoto 212clb; Gallo Images/Travel Ink 125fbr; Glowimages 20ftl; Gorilla Creative Images/Harri Tahvanainen 136clb; Gavin Gough 200ftr; Frank Greenaway 171tr; Iconica/2008 ML Harris Photography 41cla; Iconica/Caroline von Tuempling 95fcr; Image Bank/PM Images 49fbl; Image Bank/Sasha Weleber 101crb; Mathew Imaging/WireImage 21fbr; Seth Joel 195crb; Johner 222tl; Taylor S. Kennedy 206fcra; Pornchai Kittiwongsakul/AFP 14br; Darryl Leniuk 165fcra; Lonely Planet Images/Lee Foster 23br; Lonely Planet Images/Peter Hendrie 110fcra; David Madison 174cla; Simon McComb 237crb; Ethan Miller 38fcra; Mr. Sunshine 202clb; National Geographic/David Evans 59fclb; National Geographic/Paul Nicklen 107fcr; Mark Nolan 42ftl; Thomas Northcut 224tr; Per-Anders Pettersson 113fcr; PhotoAlto/Matthieu Spohn 127bl; Photodisc 88bc, 111bl, 193fcrb; Photodisc/Don Farrall 154ftr; Photodisc/Jack Hollingsworth 50cla; Photodisc/Jeff Maloney 114fbl; Photodisc/Kim Carson 25fcrb; Photodisc/Paul Burns 103fcla; Photographer's Choice/Michael Rosenfeld 37clb; Photographer's Choice/Simeone Huber/Slow Images 40ftl; Photographer's Choice/Tom Walker 144bl; Photographer's Choice/Travelpix Ltd. 60br; Photographer's Choice RF/George Diebold 12tr; Photographer's Choice RR/Fry Design Ltd. 146tr; Photographer's Choice RR/Geoff Du Feu 50fcr; Photonica/Sabine Scheckel 84tl; Photonica/Silvia Otte 62fclb; Andrea Pistolesi 212crb; Plush Studios 165bl; Poncho 167cra; Pool Photo 59ftl; Mike Powell 203crb; Rich Reid 206br; Robert Harding World Imagery/Christian Kober 169cla; Lew Robertson 150cra; Rubberball Productions 88bl; Rubberball Productions/Mike Kemp 111cla; Pete Ryan 163cr; David Sanger 242clb; Science Faction/Jim Reed 96fbl; Zack Seckler 203fcrb; Erik Simonsen 175br; Check Six 211ftl; John Slater 196cra; Luke Stettner 63bc; Stockbyte 12ftr; Stone/Jeff Hunter 117bl; Stone/Kevin Cooley 34tr; Stone/Oliver Benn/Royal Philharmonic Orchestra 142tl; Stone/Rex Butcher 157br; Stone/Roger Tully 64fcla; Stone/Walter Hodges 109fbr; Taxi/Francesco Bittichesu 154fclb; Taxi/Jasper White/jasper@jasperwhite.co.uk 88fbl; Taxi/Kevin Cooley 47fcra; Alan Thornton 166fcrb; Travel Ink 166cl; UpperCut Images/John Churchman 129fbl; Slaven Vlasic 130fcrb; Gary Wade 201cla; Gordon Wiltsie 196clb, 206clb; Yashoda 43fcra. **Greenwich Maritime Museum** 31tr, 31tl, 31cr, 31car, 109cl. **Robert Harding Picture Library/**G and P Corrigan 131tl. **Michael Holford** 112cal. **The Image Bank/**Charles S. Allen 5cl, 6bfr, 39b; Gary Cralle 24cbr; Gary Gay 103tr; Alvis Upitis 23tfr. **NASA** 21fcla, 68tr, 68 cafr, 172 tfl. **National Museum of Denmark, Copenhagen** 112tl. **Natural History Photographic Agency/**Peter Johnson 100cl; David Woodfall 17bfr; Norbert Wu 111tfr. **Nature Photographers Ltd./**David Hutton 115bfr. **Oxford Scientific Films** 76bfr, 99cafr, 131cfl. **The Pitt Rivers Museum** 183cbfr. **Planet Earth Pictures/**Robert Canis 131cafr. **Quadrant** 220br. **Rough Guides** 192 bl. **Rough Guides/** Alex Robinson 208 bfl. **Science Photo Library** 224cal/John Burbridge 80cbfr; CNRI 83cbfr; Peter Menzel 162cbr; Astrid and Hanns-Frieder Michler 245br; Claude Nuridsany and Marie Perennou 192cbr; Jim Selby 232cfl; US Department of Energy 231tr. **Tony Stone Images** 120cbfl, 244bfl/Tim Beddow 226cfl; Dave Bjorn 207tr. **Thistle Quilters/The Quilter's Guild** 161cafr. **Warwick Castle** 95br. **The Worshipful Company of Goldsmiths/**Andrew Grima 112bfl.

Jacket images: Front: Corbis: Corbis: Matthias Kulka/Zefa cb; © 2008 The LEGO Group: MINDSTORMS is a trademark of the LEGO Group clb; Science Photo Library: Mehau Kulyk cr. Back: Alamy Images: Trip tr; Corbis: Tim Davis/Davis Lynn Wildlife clb; Kulka/zefa tc.

Every effort has been made to trace the copyright holders. Dorling Kindersley apologizes for any unintentional omissions and would be pleased, in such cases, to add an acknowledgment in future editions.